A HISTORY OF
EAST AFRICA,
1592–1902

International Library of African Studies

A HISTORY OF
EAST AFRICA,
1592–1902

R.W. Beachey

Tauris Academic Studies
I.B. Tauris Publishers
LONDON • NEW YORK

Published in 1996 by
Tauris Academic Studies
An imprint of I.B.Tauris & Co Ltd
45 Bloomsbury Square
London WC1A 2HY

175 Fifth Avenue
New York
NY 10010

In the United States of America
and Canada distributed by
St Martin's Press
175 Fifth Avenue
New York
NY10010

A full CIP record for this book is available from the
British Library

A full CIP record for this book is available from the
Library of Congress

ISBN 1 85043 994 X

Library of Congress catalog card number: 95 – 060221

Typeset by The Harrington Consultancy
Printed and bound in Great Britain by WBC Ltd,
Bridgend, Mid Glamorgan

Contents

Preface

In this the last decade of the twentieth century it is difficult to grasp what the British Empire meant to those who served it in the field at its fullest efflorescence at the end of the last century. Major Delmé-Radcliffe, on duty in northern Uganda and pressed by his superior, Sir Harry Johnston, to take long overdue leave (which he had twice forgone), cheerfully replied,

> It is no great hardship for me to stay here, or any great act of abnegation beyond the postponement of getting back home. In any case, of course, for the Empire I'd stay till I dropped.

Today, imperialism has become a term of opprobrium, and Delmé-Radcliffe's ardent zeal for empire seems affected in the extreme. There is no doubting however the sincerity of Delmé-Radcliffe and many Englishmen of his time. They saw themselves as serving a noble cause – one much higher than mere career. They were the chosen representatives of a people destined to rule and who conferred on the ruled a beneficent moral order. This was the overriding spirit of their time and class. As English gentlemen, imbued with a Christian sense of purpose and duty, their role was one of service, not exploitation. Zeal for serving the empire even extended into the realm of physical fitness: Delmé-Radcliffe's recipe for such in the tropics was '5 grams of quinine every evening, and half an hour of hard dumb-bell exercise every morning', as a result of which 'I am as fit as in the middle of a stalking season in Scotland'.[1] Délme-Radcliffe's outlook was not necessarily all-pervading among those who served the empire. No doubt for some the main attractions were career advancement and early retirement – in the Indian Army, Indian Civil Service and Medical Service, retirement was as early as 50 years of age; and always in the offing there were coveted honours and titles to look forward to.

Lord Cromer was forcibly struck by these young men 'fresh from British military college or university', who were able to identify themselves with the interests of the wild tribes in the Sudan, and govern them by 'sheer weight of character and without the use of force'.[2] This mystic faith in the imperial destiny was well expressed by Sir Herbert Edwardes (1819–68), who, when asking himself the question, 'Why has God given India to England?', gave his own answer:

All His purposes look through time into eternity, and we may rest assured that the East has been given to our country for a mission, not merely to the minds or bodies, but to the souls of men.[3]

Theodore Roosevelt, ex-President of the United States, on his way out to East Africa in 1908, met young Englishmen, 'dashing army officers and capable civilians', journeying out to take up their posts, and commented that they were 'a fine set', and that they were entering on 'a work of worth to the whole world'.[4]

The empire was no short-term affair. It was seen as stretching illimitably into the future, and of a permanent and enduring character. Joseph Chamberlain, speaking at the Guildhall, London, on 19 January 1904, adjured his listeners to 'Learn to think Imperially', and in a speech at Birmingham in May of the same year, declared that, 'The day of small nations has long passed away. The day of Empires has come.' Rarely was there heard in those days, and even up to the Second World War, talk of devolution of responsibility and preparation of indigenous peoples for independence. Such heady wine was only to be served out in the period following the Second World War. Writing in the early 1970s, a former senior colonial officer in the Sudan stated 'I have often been asked in later years whether in 1922 we were made conscious of an intention to lead the Sudan to self-government in the future, and I have always had to say that I do not remember this goal being put before us.'[5] Cromer refers to the Frenchman who, after visiting India at the turn of the century, stated that the question was not whether England had a right to keep India, but rather whether she had a right to leave it.[6] Good government, not self-government, was the ideal of these ardent votaries of empire at its high noon. Theirs was no flush of enthusiasm of the moment, but a God-given task, and a lasting mission, as affirmed in Lord Curzon's clarion call, in his Mansion House speech, of 20 July 1904:

the message is carved in granite, it is hewn out of the rock of doom
– that our work is righteous and it shall endure.

This 'honour' motif and high emphasis on call of duty which is the
theme of the Epilogue in Sir Gerald Portal's *Mission to Uganda* (London,
1894), reads like the living voice of empire, and was sustained up to the
transfer of power itself after the Second World War. Some British
colonial officials worked hard and conscientiously to the end, to ensure
that affairs were in order when that transfer of power took place.

British East Africa was acquired in the last quarter of the nineteenth
century, when the passion for annexation and expansion of empire was
at its highest, and the *élan* of that period runs through the early years of
its founding. Another British India was in the making. How frequently
there recur in the literature on British East Africa at the time references
to, and similitudes and comparisons with, India! Frederick Holmwood,
Vice-Consul at Zanzibar, and V.L. Cameron, African explorer, saw in the
opening up of East Africa, opportunities for 'sons of gentlemen ...
Britishers of the middle class and public school background', at a time
when the rise of the 'Babu' and Indian University class was cutting
opportunities for Englishman in British India.[7] New avenues for their
employment might be found in East Africa. This new and immense
theatre of empire offered an inspiriting challenge: a Pax Britannica must
be established, the raw material of the 'scramble' must be converted into
well-run protectorates; those twin arms of imperialism – tax-collecting
and road-making – would have to be introduced, and native law and
custom cleverly and expertly interlaced with British/India practice.
Christian Missions would inculcate the respective virtues of their creeds
and at the same time provide a cadre of literate Africans for the lower
ranks of the imperial administration. Serving in East Africa meant
joining in a vast collective enterprise of empire. It would mean for some,
in Cecil Rhodes's words, 'exchanging a life of indigent monotony and
pinched respectability in the great City', for a life of adventure,
'gunpowder and glory'. Rhodes directed his call to the young – the lithe
of limb and spirit, especially the young unmarried man, 'unencumbered
by domestic agenda'.

The question often asked, and as often left unanswered – whence
came this imperial pulse and the force which sustained it? – lies beyond
articulate answer. Lord Salisbury, who was at the centre of it, could offer
no explanation: 'I do not know the cause of this sudden revolution. But
there it is!' Scholars writing in the 1960s could only refer to it as 'an old

problem, still awaiting an answer'.[8] It lies in the realms beyond mere theoretic construction or intellectual rationalization. It was a faith state, a dynamogenic urge, carrying men on to death and martyrdom, in the same way that missionaries were carried to the highest pitch of self-sacrifice by religious faith and fervour. To those schooled in the ethic of empire, it was a force by which men could live: implicit trust in one's country and its expansive destinies, and a readiness for great things.

The wells and springs of these elemental and noble qualities of self-sacrifice for a higher cause, however, are not unlimited. Unless recharged with new energy and vision, and spurred on by fresh cantors, they will, in Tolstoy's words, fall prey to 'anhedonia', the withering away of the life-force which formerly carried men to exalted heights. Already in the early years of the twentieth century, there was noted a 'spirit of weariness' among some British officials in India.[9] In our own time, in the second half of the twentieth century, this 'anhedonia', total collapse of the spirit from within, has been accompanied by a sustained attack from without – from a ruthless and well-planned ideology to whom the spirit of empire is anathema. The individualistic and aristocratic temper which imperialism connotes, accords ill with the collectivized mind of the later twentieth century. Socialism challenged it, and two wars, higher taxation and improved working-class conditions undermined the basis of its belief. Fabian writers, social studies rather than classical education at university level, may also have played a part in depreciating the imperial spirit.

East Africa for the purpose of this study comprises that part of the African continent which, on its eastern side, lies between latitudes 4°30'N and 11°30'S, and extends inland to the great lakes and line of the Ruwenzori range. Its distance from north to south at its greatest is over 1000 miles, and from east to west about 1200 miles – in all an area of some 700,000 square miles, about the size of Western Europe. Straddling the Equator, as it does, this part of the continent should more rightly be termed East/Central Africa, but such is usage, that the term East Africa has prevailed, and so it will be in this study. On the south the area is marked by the line of the Ruvuma River, on the north by the Juba and flanks of the Ethiopian massif, on its western side it is separated from the Congo Basin by the line of the Ruwenzori, and on its eastern side the Indian Ocean confers on it a pelagic coastline. Offshore islands, Zanzibar, Pemba and Mafia, are included under the designation 'East Africa'. Culturally and historically, the territory is orientated eastwards to the Indian Ocean world. The presence of a quarter of a million Indians, thousands of Arabs, a populous Swahili community and, for a time in the 1970s, thousands of Chinese workers in Tanzania, testify to this eastward orientation in the twentieth century.

This study treats with a number of topics in more detail than is accorded them in recent works on African history. Lugard's land settlement in Buganda, for example, scarcely receives mention in the standard biographical account of that important proconsular figure,[10] yet land is the be-all and end-all of existence in Uganda – as in most parts of Africa. The demarcation of boundaries and rounding out of frontiers, the role of the Imperial British East Africa Company in determining the same, vitally concern the partition of East Africa and its aftermath, and are essential to an understanding of the cartographic shape of modern East Africa, and thus receive much attention in this study. The foundation of German East Africa, about which the British were intensely curious, receives, I think deservedly, a chapter on its own; and so also the subject of transportation and communication, since the latter was a dominant and recurring theme in the development of East Africa.

Two events of prime importance in the final year covered by this study were the transference of Uganda's Eastern Province to the neighbouring East Africa Protectorate, and the completion of the Uganda Railway to Lake Victoria. They mark the end of an important stage in the history of British East Africa. No longer would a comprehensive view be taken of the whole, as one territory under one British administration. This concept would not emerge again until the 'Closer Union' controversy of the 1930s. There were now two distinct parts: Uganda, and the East Africa Protectorate; each with its own variegated and absorbing panorama of human and natural resources. Uganda would henceforth be administered as a black protectorate under a veneer of trusteeship. The East Africa Protectorate (later Kenya Colony) was to be a permanent home for European settlers, and in this latter territory the establishment of European latifundia on the Equator, and entrenchment of white privilege, was a unique and anomalous development, with manifold consequences for the mid-twentieth century.

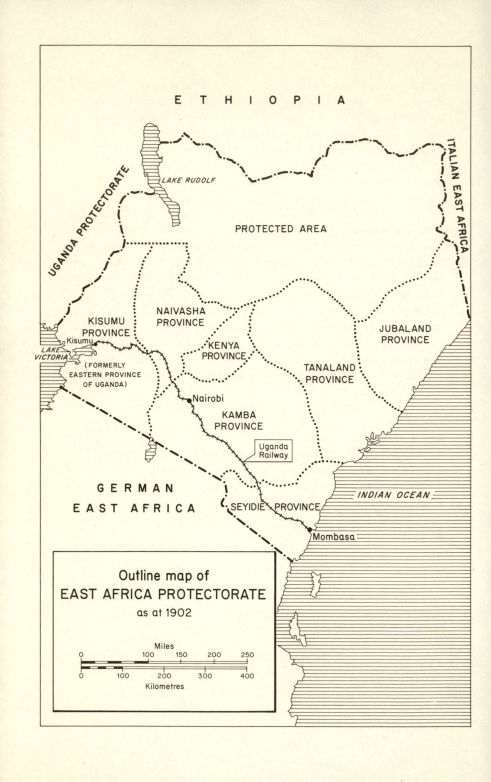

ETHIOPIA

UGANDA PROTECTORATE

LAKE RUDOLF

PROTECTED AREA

ITALIAN EAST AFRICA

KISUMU
PROVINCE

NAIVASHA
PROVINCE

JUBALAND
PROVINCE

Kisumu

KENYA
PROVINCE

*LAKE
VICTORIA*

(FORMERLY
EASTERN PROVINCE
OF UGANDA)

TANALAND
PROVINCE

Nairobi

KAMBA
PROVINCE

Uganda
Railway

GERMAN

INDIAN OCEAN

EAST AFRICA

SEYIDIE PROVINCE

Mombasa

Outline map of
EAST AFRICA PROTECTORATE
as at 1902

Miles
0   100   150   200   250

0   100   200   300   400
Kilometres

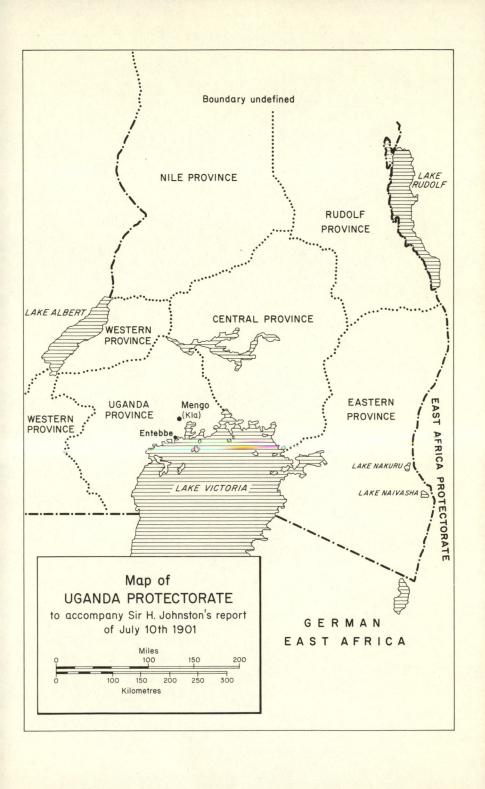

Boundary undefined

NILE PROVINCE

RUDOLF
PROVINCE

LAKE
RUDOLF

LAKE ALBERT

CENTRAL PROVINCE

WESTERN
PROVINCE

UGANDA
PROVINCE

Mengo
(Kịa)

Entebbe

EASTERN
PROVINCE

WESTERN
PROVINCE

EAST AFRICA PROTECTORATE

LAKE NAKURU

LAKE NAIVASHA

LAKE VICTORIA

Map of
UGANDA PROTECTORATE
to accompany Sir H. Johnston's report
of July 10th 1901

Miles
0   100   150   200

0   100   150   200   250   300
Kilometres

GERMAN
EAST AFRICA

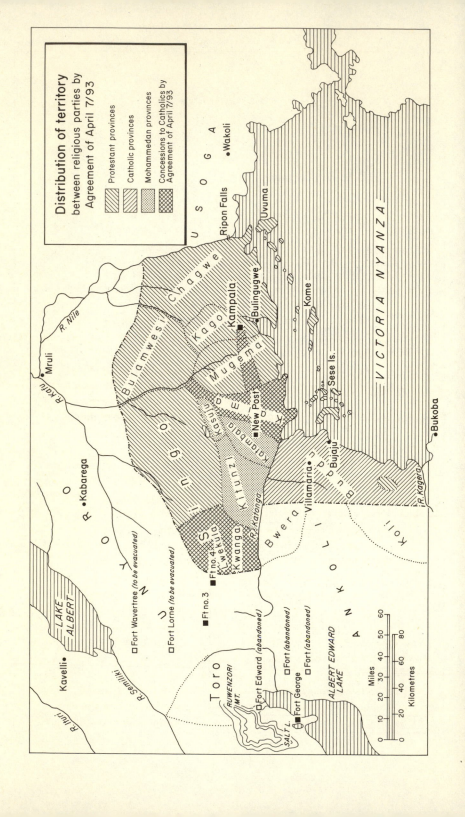

Distribution of territory between religious parties by Agreement of April 7/93

Protestant provinces
Catholic provinces
Mohammedan provinces
Concessions to Catholics by Agreement of April 7/93

USOGA

• Wakoli

VICTORIA NYANZA

Ripon Falls

Uvuma

R. Nile

Chagwe

Bulingugwe

Kampala

Kago

Kome

Mugema

R. Kome

Mruli •

Bulamwesi

Busujju

New Post

Sese Is.

R. Koki

R. Kafu

Singo

Busiro

Kyaggwe

• Bukoba

Kabarega •

R.

Busiro

Izunzi

Kituntu

Bujaju

Villamaria •

R. Katonga

Bwera

R. Kagera

Kwanga

Koki

Ssese

Lwekula

Ft no.4

BUDDU

ANKOLI

R.

Fort Wavertree (to be evacuated)

Ft no.3

Fort Lorne (to be evacuated)

LAKE ALBERT

Kavelli •

Fort Edward (abandoned)

Fort (abandoned)

Fort (abandoned)

R. Semliki

Toro

RUWENZORI MT.

ALBERT EDWARD LAKE

Fort George

Fort Edward (abandoned)

SALT L.

R. Rujru

Miles

0 10 20 30 40 50 60

Kilometres

0 20 40 60 80

Introduction

For the traveller approaching East Africa from the sea a charming and alluring prospect awaits the eye, as though a damask cloth were spread out and thereon was displayed a delightful repast. Pearl-white beaches, breeze-cooled palm groves, the quiet surge of the warm coral sea and hush of the trade winds; all combine to create an enchanting and tranquil scene. This is the Swahili coast – the 'gentle coast' of Vasco da Gama. In this beneficent and paradisaical setting where the senses savour the unmistakable and indefinable tang of the East, thoughts arise as to what further delights lie behind such an inviting threshold. The beauty of the coast lingers in the mind, long after it is left far behind on one's way into the interior.

The bountiful littoral of the coastal stretch, ten to 40 miles in depth, stretching from the Somaliland border to Mozambique, is an area of fairly high rainfall, with the most generous precipitation – 45 to 47 inches annually – being deposited in the central stretch between Mombasa and Dar es Salaam. Within this narrow coastal strip grows a profusion of foodstuffs: Indian corn, millet, sweet potatoes, many varieties of banana, coconut palm and mango trees – the latter probably introduced by the Arabs. This picture of general fertility is interspersed with infertile patches of coral rag, outcrops of the underlying bed and stretches of salt swamp which lie awash during the rains. Along the fertile alluvial river deltas of the Tana, Sabaki and Juba, and on the banks of tidal estuaries, creeks and deep lagoons (as behind the Bajun Islands) grow thick mangrove swamps. Dense tropical rain forests and thick acacia clumps along the river banks contain much useful timber. The natural riches of the coastal strip are still today not fully assessed. Away from the low-lying coastal indentations, interspersed among the copses of bushes, are open glades of tall coarse grasses, and scattered withal are various palm and gum-producing trees, mimosa, silk-cotton tree, miomba, tamarisk and copal – the latter's resinous exudations, deposited as accumulations in the sandy soil over generations, have long been a substantial export of East Africa. The striking 'Baobab', the 'upside-down' tree of African scene, raises its weird arms skyward – belying its role of grand almoner to the weary traveller. Adding to the interest and charm of the coastal strip, with a distinctive character of their own, are the islands of Zanzibar, Pemba and Mafia which, as seen from the air or from out at sea, present an aspect of compact green verdure, the forests of clove trees and graceful palm combining in their fulsome fertility to give a touch of the tropical exotic.

Behind the benign exterior of the coastal strip, and deceptively concealed by its beauty, lies the dreariest and most forbidding region of the whole East African terrain. The Nyika (Swahili for 'wilderness') is at its worst in the patch known as the Taru desert, stretching from the western confines of the coastal strip to about 125 miles inland where the rising ground of the upland interior is met. The Nyika fans out northwards as far as the Tana river and southward to the Umba. This flat and uninteresting terrain is covered with prickly low bush and the mimosa tree with poniard-like thorns; the heat and dryness, and above all the infinite monotony, leave a maddening sense of entrapment. The horizon is unrelieved by any elevation from which a prospect might be gained of more salubrious regions. Lying under a burnished sun and with leached-out soil underfoot, it as though a curse had been laid over the land. The weary traveller foot-slogging across this forlorn wilderness is spurred on only by the desire to run the miserable gauntlet as quickly as possible, before physical endurance collapses. Nature herself appears to have expired under the strain and stern compression of such surroundings; animal and plant life are stunted and listless – quite drained out by the struggle for existence. Even the diminutive antelope, grotesque warthog and lesser rodents find it a forbidding environment.

Immediately after the rains however, and for a brief and sparkling period, the Taru desert comes to life, revivified, and for a brief while it becomes a fairyland, an expanse of green bush interspersed with white and purple convolvulus and other flowers. This flaunting mirage of beauty is short-lived and soon vanishes, only to be followed by months of dryness in which for weeks on end the deeply rooted bushes fight a battle for life under the glazing sun and straining wind. The Nyika is largely uninhabited, being waterless and tsetse-ridden. This region imposed on early travellers the severest strain. It was for Sir Gerald

Portal the most difficult stretch in his whole traverse to Uganda in 1893. Early travellers preferred the longer but easier route through German territory to the south rather than face the Taru desert. It is still today a barrier to civilization. Only water will stir it to life. Unfortunately there is no easy escape from the barrier of the Nyika. There are no natural avenues of access to the interior, no deep coastal indentations nor major rivers tapping the hinterland. The Pangani, Tana and Rufiji are slight in size as African rivers go, and rapids impede navigation on them. Even the great Ruvuma, on which Livingstone had set his hopes of penetrating East Africa, proved unnavigable for much of its length. Tsetse fly and disease debar the use of pack-horse and saddle animal. Early travellers, forced to fall back on foot-slogging, hurried along, forgoing daily rest, intent only on gaining the more salubrious region inland.

The Nyika wilderness persists over a vast distance, embaying into the eastern and northern parts of Kenya where semi-desert conditions prevail, and only shrunken acacia shrubs and bunch grass can survive. It extends into the southern portions of the Rift Valley, across the Maasai plains of north-eastern Tanzania, and down almost to the East African plateau-lands in the south, although presenting in these regions more favourable pastoral conditions than in its bleaker aspect to the north and east.

The interior plateau of central Tanzania is saucer-shaped, and bordered on its eastward side by rim mountains – the so-called Ghats of East Africa which extend in a great arc eastward, from the complex of highlands between the immediate north of Lake Nyasa and the southern tip of Lake Tanganyika, taking in the Iringa, Uluguru, Nguru, Usumbura and Pare highlands, and terminating in the great bulk of Kilimanjaro and Meru in the north. These higher points, isolated bastions as it were, guarding the great interior plateau, are fragments uplifted above the surrounding country. They bring a cooler air and greener environment and have a higher rainfall than the less favoured lower savannah country, although this too is part of the great East African plateau which forms the spine of Africa, from Ethiopia almost to the Cape.

In Kenya, approaching from the eastward and where the plateau rises above the 4000-foot level, a region of vast prairies rises gently to the westward for nearly 100 miles, and thereon is displayed a variety and wealth of antelope life. These plains are intersected by broad and shallow drainage valleys, many of them dry for the greater part of the year. They finally terminate in a long series of embayments running into foothills or more steeply rising country. Here, and onward to the west where the higher parts of the plateau rise in places to 10,000 feet above sea-level, tilted from the horizontal to the eastwards, is a different world. Higher rainfall and volcanic soils support a dense population, the heat is palpably less, evenings are chill and dews frequent. The sterile conditions of the Nyika are now but a memory, and open patches of grassland and glades of turf appear. Mountain ranges or isolated peaks project above a distant and clear-cut horizon. The steep slopes are dissected by a succession of spurs and ravines, deep gullies down which streams tumble to the far-reaching plains below. This is Kikuyu country proper, stretching for some 150 miles over ridges and deep gullies from the Athi plains up to Mount Kenya and Meru, and lying at an altitude of 5000 feet or more. In the coolness of the air, in the streams of running water and the surpassing fertility of its rich red soil, it (and likewise the Mau escarpment to the west) is superior to most parts of Africa. Although much of it is still heavily forested, there is concentrated peasant agriculture in thickly cultivated patches, a profusion of bananas, legumes and cereal crops, the finest coffee; and a temperate climate enabling English vegetables and fruits to thrive with prolixity and ease. The thick uncleared vegetation, a green aromatic bush, provides herbage for innumerable nibbling goats.

To the immediate westward of this abundant world lies the eastern Rift Valley, one of the two great converging troughs of the enormous fissure system – the dominating feature of the hinterland plateau, which scores the surface of eastern Africa from the Red Sea to the Zambezi River. Geologists of the 'faulting and collapse' school and the 'isostatic-tearing apart' school still dispute the evolutionary history of this landscape. But it would appear that back in tertiary times – millions of years ago – the eastern area of Africa was raised up and buckled into a broad flat-topped arch running roughly north to south. This alteration in the earth's crust was associated with the formation of a great depression along the coast of eastern Africa which divided Madagascar from the mainland. Further sinking of this depression and gradual foundering of the ocean floor so weakened the support of the central arch as to cause a falling in of its upper parts as though the keystone had dropped down between its supports. The enormous effects of this cataclysm are most evident in the eastern Rift Valley which traverses the interior plateau from Lake Rudolf to Lake Nyasa, as a great low-lying trough, ten to 60 miles wide, and flanked on either side by spectacular

escarpment walls, rising to 3000 feet or more above the valley floor
which is itself 4000 to 5000 feet above sea-level. This great cleft, easily
visible from the moon and photographed by Apollo 17 when the mission
was 90,000 miles out in space, is shown as a long straggling gash on the
face of Africa, like one of those meandering river beds on Mars.

The Eastern Rift in its eastern branch embraces a host of lesser lakes
– Baringo, Nakuru, Naivasha, Natron and Eyasi. In its western branch
it enfolds Lake Victoria and the drainage system of the Nile. Still farther
west is the Western Rift system, with its floor fractured and divided at
different levels, and aligned in its basins are Lakes George, Edward,
Albert, Kivu, Tanganyika, Rukwa and Malawi (Nyasa) hemmed in by
steep walls, and among the deepest lakes in the world. The fault-lines of
the Eastern and Western Rifts finally converge at Lake Nyasa and thence
follow the Shire River to the Zambezi and the sea. Associated with the
Rift were volcanic disturbances which left outstanding landmarks:
Kilimanjaro – the highest mountain in Africa (19,321 feet), with a crack
in its summit; to the west – some 40 miles – Meru, more striking than
its taller neighbour; Kenya, the severed neck of a volcano, rises to 17,067
feet; Elgon, a close runner-up, with its vast cone of solidified ash and
agglomerate, attains a height of 14,140 feet. The great cauldrons of
Ngorongoro and Menengai were formed and in some cases lava flows
blocked off portions of the Rift Valley, at a time when man himself had
appeared on the East African scene. The more vigorous manifestations
of vulcanism still persist today in the Western Rift and others are hinted
at in tribal legend. Around 10,000 BC, according to radio-carbon dating
at Ishango at the mouth of the Semliki River, the Katwe explosion
craters spread a mantle of ash over an area centred at Katwe, burying
vegetation and mollusca. The noble group of volcanoes, Mfumbiro,
astride the Uganda/Congo border, still give ample evidence of their
youth and power. The greatest mountain massif of all, the Ruwenzori, is
non-volcanic in origin. Rising majestically from the depressed Rift
Valley floor (Mt Margarita, rising to 16,794 feet, is the highest point)
and separating abruptly by only a few miles the basins of the Congo and
Nile, it is one of the great enigmas of the earth's crust – a block of the
ancient land surface left in grand isolation, to allure and beckon.

Rift Valley movements and associated warpings of the plateaux
disrupted ancient drainage patterns, remnants of which still survive in
the Lukuga, the overflow channel whereby the waters of Lake
Tanganyika connect with the Congo drainage system. A new integration
was accomplished by the River Nile and its great reservoirs – Lakes

Victoria and Kioga. Much of the Nile's work is recent, as witnessed by the impressive spectacle of the youthful Murchison Falls. Early man himself may well have inhabited this region during the changes in landscape. With the possible exception of segments of the great Miocene peneplain which survive in innumerable flat-topped hills in Uganda, like great up-raised bowling greens, the landscape of East Africa today is the result of shaping, moulding and building, tilting and submerging, earthquakes and volcanic action, and glacial work, all within human times, and comparatively recent in geological terms. A Maasai legend perpetuates a recollection of early volcanic disturbances in the Lake Naivasha region.

These cataclysmic movements and disturbances which produced the Great Rift system and outstanding landmarks such as Kilimanjaro and Mt Kenya ('never a mountain that made so little of its height', quoth Churchill), do not entirely explain the wide variation in the landscape and vegetation of East Africa: it is to climate that this must also be attributed. Mt Kenya, for example, with its ice and snow-cooled heights, rises above a base from which to the northwards there extend sun-baked wastes up to the highlands of Ethiopia. Here, lying under an exhausted and breathless air, with high evaporation rate and meagre rainfall – less than five inches a year – only hardy nomads like the Samburu and Rendille can survive, eking out a living from the stony soil, their camels subsisting on the coarse tufts of grass. Life for them is an eternal round of raiding and counter-raiding, trekking from water-hole to water-hole. Only Marsabit, rising some 5000 feet above the surrounding sandy wastes, with an ancient crater lake at its summit fringed by tall timbers and dense forests in which roam herds of elephant, provides an agreeable break in the monotonous desert country and stark rocky hills. With its slopes providing good grazing ground for the surrounding nomads, Marsabit is an oasis, a half-way house between Meru and Furoli. The latter place, some 150 miles from Marsabit, and on the Ethiopian border, is a cluster of brackish pools guarded by sentinel-like jagged rocks. East of Furoli, for hundreds of miles, as far as the Somali border, lies barren lava desert of reddish hue, where only thorn scrub and the tooth-brush plant, *mswaki*, survive in the savage heat. To the west of Furoli the prospect is equally unpropitious – waterless desert as far as Rudolf. The latter, a brackish lake, is surrounded by a sepia-coloured vista which, lying under a blazing platinum sun, presents a primeval landscape. As witnessed from the northern spur of the Nyiru range on Rudolf's southern end, it evoked from the explorer, Teleki, the cry: 'Into what a desert had we been betrayed.' The feeder rivers of Rudolf (Turkwel and Kerio) do nothing to relieve the starkness.

Leaving these peregrinations in the north and turning back to the Kikuyu escarpment, descent is made into the plains of the Rift Valley some 2000 feet below, and after crossing these, which extend some 60 miles to the west, there is encountered the steep Mau escarpment, rising to over 10,000 feet. Here well-watered ridges, deep forests, heather and bracken resemble a piece of Scotland or the forest uplands of Malawi. Looking back eastward from the Mau escarpment, over the mighty cleft of the Rift and wide game-dotted plains below, to the blue horizon and peaks of the Aberdares and spurs beyond, the noble dimensions of the Rift can best be appreciated. The Mau, continuing northwards and merging into the Elgeyo escarpment and western Kenya highlands, presents a densely wooded mountain barrier, running in a north and southerly direction, and with its slopes dissected into a constant succession of spurs and ravines. The Mau lies across the route of the present Uganda Railway which rises here to an altitude of over 9000 feet. Northwards from the Mau the plateau continues to the Laikipia escarpment and then flattens out into the low-lying desert trending to the north and Rudolf. The rocky escarpment on the northern edge of Laikipia affords a dramatic glimpse of the eastern Kenya highlands and open wind-swept downs extending to the cedar-forested slopes of the Aberdares. This is a land of wide vistas and clear air. It is excellent sheep country.

The country to the west of the Mau escarpment, between Elburgon and Fort Ternan, consists of enormous forests of fine timber, evergreen pastures and perennial streams. The district of Sotik best represents these attractions. It lies at an elevation of 6000-7000 feet, on the south-west slopes of the Mau plateau, covering an area some 40 miles long by 15 miles wide, and consisting partially of rounded hog-backed ridges, originally covered with dense forest of which only isolated clumps remain; for the rest, it is matted growth, soft-wooded fast-growing bush, rising to 15 feet in height, and almost impenetrable. With a rainfall of 70 to 80 inches annually, vegetation renews itself with perennial fertility. Part of Sotik is also land of rolling downs – fertile, and studded with clumps of trees and bush – although less well-watered than the hill district.

This world of the western highlands drops down gradually westwards to the depression of Lake Victoria and Kavirondo, a land of rich soil and high rainfall. From thence to the west, across Lake Victoria and into

Uganda, the fertility and intense beauty are inspiring. Around the lake shore is luxuriant growth, a profusion of foodstuffs and a dense population. Away from the lake, to the north and west, is drier country, studded with thorn trees and suitable for extensive ranching. Northern Uganda, a country of gentle rolling savannah plains interspersed with rivers and wide swamps, verges on the Nile Valley and here there is an oppressive heat. The salubrious uplands of the plateaux country to the east are now a thing of the past: this is true Sudanic country.

East Africa is a land of striking contrasts where light and shade play fantasies, and dark monotony of landscape confronts sinister green foliage. The limitation of ground and surface water, a high evaporation rate and porous soils, constantly remind of a hard reality. The presence of tsetse fly over enormous tracts of country has a devastating effect on ecology. There are few permanent rivers. The interior lakes – vast areas of water, tending to concentrate population narrowingly on their shores, and interconnecting lines of communication, scattered and tenuous – do not add to the sum total of prosperity. Salubrious conditions exist only in isolated areas. The Kilimanjaro mass is separated from the southern highlands of Tanzania by hundreds of miles of the poorest savannah country. The fertile Kigezi highlands, on the Congo and Ruanda borders, are hundreds of miles from Kampala in fertile Buganda country and separated from the latter by the poorest land in western Uganda. Only the midway portion of the territory between the Indian Ocean and Lake Victoria, the highlands of Kenya with excellent ranching land and higher rainfall, sustains successful arable farming. Most of the eastern Rift Valley is dry infertile grassland with a low and unreliable rainfall, and a soil easily erodible. Rainfall, always the determining factor, varies from ten inches or less in parts of central Tanzania and northern Kenya, up to 100 inches per annum in parts of the highlands. Every variation of physical feature is to be found in East Africa – from the permanent snow of Mt Kenya, Kilimanjaro and Ruwenzori, to the hot coastal belt and arid desert conditions of northern Kenya; from the treeless downs and forests, the lush parklands and perpetual 'English Spring' of the Kenya highlands, to the searing heat of the lower altitudes of Rudolf and the Nile Valley.

There are exotic exceptions. There are the shores of the great central lakes with their rich vegetation. The tall dense forest, bamboo thickets, grass and moorland, giant groundsel and lobelias of the highest slopes of Mt Kenya and Ruwenzori, contrast with the poor grassland and thorn bush country of the drier parts of the Rift Valley, Maasai plains and tableland of central Tanzania. East Africa can both weary and stimulate. It casts a spell over those who have lived there, and they yearn to return: memories of East Africa and its peoples linger in the mind long after years of retirement in far-away abodes, and eyes still light up at the mention of the Mrima and Gilgil.

It was a bonus for East Africa when fossils discovered there in the present century purportedly showed it to be the home of man's earliest progenitors, the anthropoid apes who branched from the primal tree back in the Miocene and Pliocene period some 14-25 million years ago. These fossil finds, coming as they did during the heady period of independence for East African territories, were much acclaimed. Interest in them has since been sustained by further fossil discoveries outlining the evolution of the Hominidae family culminating in *Homo sapiens.* The fossil record is not continuous, and gives no indication as to when that momentous step, the crossing of the threshold from instinct to reflection, might have taken place. The interim nature of archaeology is such that it does not preclude these East African fossil finds being superseded by fossil discoveries elsewhere at some future date. This head start on the path of human evolution has had little impact on human progress in East Africa nor does it have much relevance for an understanding of the peopling of East Africa. This is the result of complex migrations in more recent millennia: encroachment of Hamite from the north-east, Bantu from the west, Nilotic incursions from the Sudanic region and underneath a steadily decreasing stratum of stone age population. The result is a diversity of peoples: Bantu, pure Hamite, half-Hamite, Nilotic, and remnants of click-speaking and indigenous forest dwellers. They range in colour from the honey-tan of the Samburu and Rendille to the sooty black of the Nilotic and make a clear-cut study of East Africa's ethno-history a complicated task. The upshot of it all is reflected in the so-called Bantu line running roughly from Lake Albert on the west, to Mount Kenya and Tana River on the east. It marks the northern line of Bantu advance: to the south of it are outcrops and intrusions of Nilo-Hamite, Hamite and a few aboriginal groups in all territories.

In Tanzania the population is predominantly Bantu; in Uganda to a lesser extent; in Kenya the main Bantu-speaking group is to be found in the central highland and plateaux area. The majority of the Bantu-speaking tribes combine agriculture with the keeping of livestock, and it was only where the presence of tsetse fly excluded domestic animals, or where Bantu-speaking people were deprived of their grazing ground and their stock by tribes of half-Hamitic origin, that they turned solely to a shifting arable agriculture which involved the periodic movement of homesteads or villages. The Bantu-speaking people remain primarily cultivators with individual rights extending only to usufruct, although their shifting cultivation was more difficult to maintain in the face of European encroachment and ideas of landholding in the twentieth century, and with increasing population pressure.

The Nilotic presence is seen along the eastern side of Lake Victoria and extending down into Tanzania, and in Nilo-Hamites (Maasai, Turkana, Pokot (Suk), Nandi, Kipsigis and Samburu) in Kenya. The Nilotics, originally herdsmen, finding themselves in the more favoured environs of East Africa, took to arable agriculture as well as keeping cattle, and in the process gave up many of the social distinctions attached to cattle-keeping and still adhered to by the Nilo-Hamitic pastoralists. Some of the Nilotics, as the Sotik in western Kenya, have maintained their separateness by their fighting prowess, even keeping the Maasai at bay, although turning to agriculture and dependent on the *wembie* seed for food. The Nilo-Hamites – Maasai, Turkana and Samburu, etc. – are predominantly nomadic pastoralists. Within their tribal group, livestock is owned by the individual, but rights in grazing land, water supplies and salt licks are regarded as common to the whole community. The check on the migratory movement of the pastoralists that came with the arrival of Europeans, gave rise to intertribal conflict and competition for grazing land, and increased the importance of social organization – especially the age-group of young men who provided the military of the tribe. In some cases, as with the Kipsigis and Nandi, they were forced to turn to cultivation. The pastoralist shared grazing and water supplies on a community basis, and practised in a very general way an extensive system of pastoral management alternating between wet and dry season grazing.

The true nomads are the Hamitic-speaking groups who roam over the sun-baked plains of northern Kenya: Somali, Gabbra, Orma, Rendille and Boran. They live off their herds, following them in a perennial round from water-hole to water-hole. Their social organization is complex, their life abstemious and difficult, dictated by the harsh environment. They are mostly devotees of Islam – the creed of the desert. The Rendille are recent migrants into Kenya, having taken up their abode at Marsabit in the early twentieth century.

In all tribal groupings, Nilo-Hamite, Nilotic or Bantu-speaking, allegiance is still to the family, clan and local tribe. Security and survival depend on group rather than individual approach, to the physical and human hazards encountered. Bare survival in a harsh physical environment was also assisted by Nature's balancing effects, in the form of epidemics affecting both man and animals, and in periodic famine and intertribal raids and wars. The integrated group making up East African society, while conferring upon the individual certain privileges, subjected him to a series of obligations: the age-group, totemistic family tie, religio-magical controls, cultivation and eating groups, customary systems of land tenure and land use, all forged a closely integrated relationship between members of a traditional group with little scope for individual approach or initiative. For both pastoralist and cultivator life was precarious, sustained at subsistence level.

The peopling of the interior of East Africa took place unknown to the outside world. During the pre-Islamic and medieval period, however, there were a few written references to its coast but these are interspersed by long silences, and 'History cannot proceed by silences'. The first of these references, the *Periplus of the Erythrean Sea*, a sailor's handbook of the late first or early second century AD, by an Alexandrian, throws light on what would otherwise be the preserve of archaeologist and pre-historian. It reveals a world recognizable in our own terms and refers to points on the East African coast identifiable with places today. Ptolemy's *Geography*, a few centuries later, more vague but wider in scope, makes mention of inland lakes and mountains. The sixth century *Christian Topography of Cosmos Indicopleustes* briefly touches on the northern tip of the East African coast. The *Kitab al-Ajaib al-Hind*, an Arab compilation, and a few Chinese writings of the medieval period, based on second-hand information, refer to Arab contact with the coast and its far-flung Indian Ocean trade. These few written references all affirm Arab contact with the coast and that local inhabitants are of a Bantu type.

The rise of Islam would appear to have brought renewed Arab contact with the East African coast. J. de Barros tells us that the Arabs, as a result of absorbing that 'infernal doctrine' which they upheld with arms, became much bolder and journeyed farther afield. Malindi, Mombasa and Mogadishu are now places of permanent Arab residence and trade. There are so-called 'sultanates' with genealogies linking them to the higher world of Arab and Persian culture. The slave-trade is an established feature on the coast. Ibn Battuta, visiting Kilwa in the fourteenth century, refers to the plentitude of slaves there – given as presents and kept as stock-in-trade.

This veneer of Arab civilization and impress of Islam prevailing on the East African coast at the time of the arrival of the Portuguese at the end of the fifteenth century came as a surprise to the latter. It was not to their liking. Captains-General Vasco da Gama, Albuquerque, Almeida and others, coming as they did from a peninsula only recently freed from the Moor, still carried with them something of the spirit of the Reconquista and Crusades. Theirs was keen racial pride and a lofty sense of purpose as to their mission. They were no private adventurers, but sailed under royal commission and in the name of Christ. Their mentor, Henry the Navigator, Prince of Portugal (1394–1460), was Grand Master of the Order of Christ, successor to the Knights Templars of old. The questing spirit of the Renaissance was with them and it received full backing from their king. Henry and his successors encouraged and supported active geographical exploration and navigational study. The results were astonishing: the maritime exploration within one century of a large part of the globe, opening up the south-eastern sea route to the Indies, penetration of Africa and a mission to 'Prester John'. The celebrated Torre de Belem in Lisbon is a fitting tribute to the high navigational achievements of the Portuguese in this era.

Bartholomeu Diaz led the way in 1487 when he rounded the Cape without his knowing and made his way up the eastern coast of Africa as far as what is now Natal. On his return he discovered that he had 'doubled' the Cape. Pedro de Covilhao's peregrinations during the years 1487–90 outrival those of modern-day travellers: to and from Cairo, to India and back, visiting Cannanore, Calicut and Goa, an excursion to Zeila and down the East African coast to Sofala, probably the first European to visit the 'golden port', and thence back to Cairo. Directed by his king (to whom he was sending back accounts of his travels), he continued his explorations, to the Persian Gulf, Hormuz, Aden and Jeddah. In 1490 he reached the court of the Negus, in Abyssinia, where he was still in honourable captivity when other Portuguese arrived there in 1520.

The Treaty of Tordesillas in 1494, between Spain and Portugal, which assigned to the Portuguese the route to the Indies by way of the Cape, encouraged their adventurism in the East. In 1497, the year of Columbus's discovery of America, Vasco da Gama set out on his great voyage of discovery. After rounding the Cape he proceeded up the east coast of Africa. At Mombasa he narrowly escaped a conspiracy to entrap him (for which Mombasa was to pay dearly later); at Malindi, farthest point north on the coast reached by him, he set up the cross of his padrao, of Lisbon limestone, which still stands today; and thence, taking on a pilot provided by the Indian merchants at Malindi, he made his way to India where he dropped anchor at Calicut on the Malabar coast, on 20 May 1498. Here too a marble pillar was set up – a mark of conquest and proof of discovery. Vasco da Gama had come, in the words of one of his sailors, 'to seek Christians and spices'. After visiting Cochin and Cannanor in India, and bearing a friendly letter from the *zamorin* of Calicut – promising a rich trade in spices and precious gems – he left for home, calling at Mogadishu on the Somali coast, in January 1499, and by way of salutation bombarded it. By early September 1499 he was back at Lisbon. He had lost one-third of his men on the voyage, but he could now lay at the feet of his master half the empire of the east. His great journey earned for his master, Manuel I, the title of 'the Great', 'the Fortunate', and a declaration from the Pope that he was 'Lord of Navigation, conquest, and trade of Ethiopia, Arabia, Persia and India'. On Vasco da Gama in turn there was conferred the coveted prefix of 'Dom' and pensions and property. The wheel of fortune had spun in truly marvellous fashion.

Vasco da Gama's discoveries heralded a hundred years of Portuguese activity on the eastern side of Africa, in the Red Sea, Persian Gulf, Indian Ocean world, the Far East and South China seas. In extent and speed of expansion it rivalled the wildfire spread of Islam from the Atlantic coasts of Africa to the Far East, in an earlier era. In the course of far-ranging Portuguese expeditions, Madagascar (named St Lawrence from the feast day on which it was sighted), and the Mascarhenas (Réunion and Mauritius) were discovered; factories were established in India, the Straits of Malacca secured and Macao, on the south coast of China, acquired as a Portuguese trading and missionary post. Goa in India became a dazzling centre of Portuguese culture and missionary fervour: 'He who has seen Goa need not see Lisbon', it was 'a Rome in India'. Terrible chastisement fell on those communities displaying resistance or treachery: Vasco da Gama treated the inhabitants of Calicut with rough savagery for wiping out a Portuguese holding force there, and he thence proceeded on a voyage of correction to Cochin 'doing all the harm he could on the way to all that he found at sea'.

The role of the East African coast in all this was as a lifeline to the East. To guard it, fortresses were constructed at key points on the coast. The Portuguese showed little interest in the hinterland where the repellent nature of the Nyika, presence of savage tribes and absence of navigable rivers deterred entry. At Malindi, however, where a factory was sited, there was an imaginative project to penetrate overland to

Ethiopia; and on the north Somaliland coast a canal was planned to pierce the Ras Hafun peninsula. If accomplished these projects would have outshone all other Portuguese achievements in East Africa. They were frustrated by tribal disturbances inland and diversions elsewhere. The running war with the Muslims dominated Portuguese attention, and in the long run was to weaken them severely.

On their first contact with the wondrous East, the Portuguese at first mistook the Hindus for Christians 'not yet confirmed in the faith'. No such soft feelings were held as regards the Muslims. Against them 'the sharp determination of the sword' was to be used. The conquest of Egypt in 1517 by Selim I, the Ottoman sultan, brought a confrontation of Portuguese and Muslim in the Red Sea. The Muslims had the backing of Venetian traders resentful of Portuguese diversion of trade by the Cape route. Portuguese grand strategy in meeting the Muslim challenge was to occupy Hormuz, Aden and Socotra so as to control the Straits of Hormuz and Bab el Mandeb. At one stage Albuquerque – 'The Portuguese Mars' – considered a plan to divert the Nile waters so as to ruin Egypt, and to attack the holy cities of Mecca and Medina, so as to bring home to the Muslim world the measure of Portuguese might. Neither objective was achieved, although Vasco da Gama was recalled from retirement to display his still formidable talents. Before he could do so, death overtook him on Christmas Eve 1524. A Portuguese expedition against the Turks at Suez in 1541 was unsuccessful, owing to the Portuguese fleet failing to muster in time. Portuguese involvement with Christian Ethiopia (an Ethiopian ambassador had arrived at Lisbon as early as 1509) led to supporting her against the Muslims. This brought little profit for the Portuguese who were faced with troubles of their own on the East African coast: Galla expansion south and westwards, a Zimba siege of Malindi, so-called 'Kafirs' invading Zanzibar and Turkish raids as far south as Mombasa. Communication with Ethiopia was increasingly difficult to maintain, and Portuguese contact there ended with the expulsion of the Jesuits in 1633. On the East African coast there was retrenchment. Fort Jesus, constructed at Mombasa in 1593-96, was to remain as the main symbol of Portuguese pride and strength. Restored in 1635, it still bears today, cut in stone, the Christian symbol 'IHS' together with the eagles of the Austrian/Spanish dynasty which governed Portugal at that date.

In retrospect it is worth noting that, although Portuguese main interest lay in India and the East, still the extent of their reconnaissance and fortifications along the East African and Arabian coasts was remarkable in scope and detail. Captain Owen, no lover of the Portuguese, was nevertheless stirred to admiration by evidence of their wide-ranging empire on the East African and Arabian littoral. The mysterious ruins at Gedi, near Malindi, are more likely the result of a Portuguese onslaught than devastation at the hands of the Galla.

With retrenchment on the northern strip of the East African coast came increasing shift of emphasis to the south, to Sofala, main outlet for the gold trade of the kingdom of Monomotapa, and to the Zambezi valley. Increasingly in these later years of the sixteenth century the strain in holding her vast empire in the East was telling on the Portuguese. Linschoten estimated that not one in ten returned of those who went to the East. Already in 1538 a royal pardon was conferred on criminals who offered to serve in India, saving those convicted of treason and canonical offences. After a bare century of ascendancy in the Indian Ocean, Portugal collapsed under the manifold pressures that bore in on her.

To ruminate on the various causes that brought about this collapse is like peering into a darkling glass. Overextension weakened the heart at the centre; decline in Portuguese sea power – according to the Chinese the Portuguese were like fish, 'remove them from the water and they straightway die'; want of organization in management of her overseas empire; depopulation of Portugal; intermixture with slaves and subject peoples diluted and modified the national character, destroying keen racial pride, lofty sense of purpose, sense of mission and moral poise (it has been said that the Portuguese of the time of the great Captains-General – Vasco da Gama, Almeida and Albuquerque – and the Portuguese of the seventeenth century were two different peoples). Other reasons assigned are the expulsion of the Jews and loss of their acumen; overdominance of ecclesiastical influence in secular affairs; decadence of the monarchy; being tied to the expiring power of Spain as a result of the union of 1580, which dragged her into troubles and wars with the English and Dutch. There was the mounting challenge of the English, Dutch and French as trade rivals – who sought to oust the Portuguese from their lucrative holdings in the East. Spice ships of Portugal might sail under the royal banner and with great aplomb, but those of her rivals were under keen private enterprise, chartered companies accountable to hard-headed shareholders. Unlike Portugal, her rivals had no personal or religious quarrel with Arab and Islam, and English trading interests and those of the Dutch tended to be based farther East.

Augurs of this new European challenge came as early as 1528 when a

French vessel on a snooping expedition visited Kilwa. Sir Francis Drake's voyage round the world (1577-80) marked the entry of the English into the Indian Ocean, as did the arrival of four English merchants in India at about the same time. There were the extensive voyages to the Far East in 1586-91 of the Dutchman, J.H. van Linschoten, and Thomas Cavendish – 'third circumnavigator of the globe' – in 1588. The voyage of James (later Sir James) Lancaster in 1591-94 was the forerunner of the East India Company's arrival in the East: its first expedition there in 1601 was under Lancaster's command. Dutch and French East India Companies were soon to follow. There were Dutch attacks on Mozambique in 1607 and 1608, severe defeats of Portuguese fleets by British naval forces in the Swally roads in 1612 and 1615. In 1618 the British forced open the trade between Surat and Jask, in the Persian Gulf, where a Portuguese fleet was defeated in 1620. Her expulsion from Hormuz in 1622 by a combined English/Persian force, marks the end of Portugal's importance in Arabian affairs, although she still shared in the Mocha coffee trade for years to come. Henceforward the trade of India and the Persian Gulf was in English hands; and by the time Portugal had loosened herself from the fatal union with Spain, in 1640, her power and position in the eastern seas was gone. Ejected from Muscat and the Arabian seaboard in 1650 she bowed to the inevitable. Henceforth all her Eastern possessions lay open to English trade.

Turk and Arab watched with silent satisfaction the unfolding of this drama wherein their long-time enemy was worsted. From the mid-seventeenth century onwards the Portuguese were subjected to unremitting attack and harassment by the Omani Arabs. Loyal Swahili and Arab were ill-served by incompetent Portuguese captains, for there had been a great falling off in the quality of Portuguese officers since the days of the great Vasco da Gama and Albuquerque. Under these unrelenting pressures the Portuguese gave way. The Omani Arabs finally captured Mombasa in 1698 and in 1699 drove the Portuguese out of Kilwa and Pemba. A see-saw struggle for control of Fort Jesus ensued in which it exchanged hands a number of times, and finally ended when the Portuguese force from Goa, after holding it for a year and a half, was finally driven out in 1729. By the early eighteenth century the Portuguese had withdrawn from the Arabian seas and the East African coast north of the Ruvuma River. In the wake of their withdrawal came the Omani Arabs, revival of Islam and the slave-trade. The old political and commercial domain of the Arab was reasserted but with a decided Omani flavour. Little is known of the conditions on the East African coast at this time, but that its peoples were restive under Omani rule is evident in their exodus to the island of Mafia, and in appeals to Goa for the return of the Portuguese. Alas, the latter were in no position to answer the call. Gradually Swahili and coast peoples settled down under the new order, and there was increasing assimilation and the introduction of the coastal peoples into positions of authority. Trade became Omani-orientated; towns, like Pate and Kilwa, retained their former importance; others, like Mombasa and Malindi – key points under the Portuguese – sank into relative obscurity. Following the withdrawal of the Portuguese, there were few continental shorelines so untouched by European influence as the East African coast. Colonial rivalry of the European powers passed it by, for it offered few physical or commercial attractions to lure colonial adventurers off the well-known and lucrative routes to the East. That some British sailors and adventurers, however, were not unfamiliar with the East African coast during this period, will emerge in the next chapter.

1· Early English Contacts with East Africa

The first English attempts to reach the Far East by sailing westwards came in the early sixteenth century. They were unsuccessful. There had to be continued reliance on the eastern Mediterranean route and the Levant for the luxury items of the East, the appetite for which grew with the tasting. The rise of the great Ottoman sultan, Selim I, and his conquest of Egypt in 1517, however, placed a restrictive hold on this near-Eastern trade and caused increasing resort to the Lisbon market for the riches of the East brought home by the Portuguese by way of the Cape route. Lisbon too proved to be a capricious market, following the union of Portugal and Spain in 1580. To break this dependence on others for the luxury goods of the East the English must make direct contact with that source themselves by way of the Cape route. The first English reference to the hazards of this route is by Thomas Stephens (Stevens), later rector of the Jesuit college in Goa. Writing to his father, Master Thomas Stevens, in England in 1579, he states that after rounding the Cape 'so famous and feared of all men':

> there be two ways to India; one within the Isle of S. Lawrence (Madagascar) which they take willingly because they refresh themselves at Mozambique a fortnight or a month, not without great need, and thence in a month more land at Goa. The other is without the Isle of S. Lawrence, which they take when they set forth so late, and come so late to the point that they have no time to take the aforesaid Mozambique, and then they go heavily because in this way they take no port. And by reason of the long navigation, and want of food and water, they fall into sundry diseases, their gums wax great and swell and they are fain to cut them away; their legs swell, and all the body becometh sore and so benumbed that they cannot stir hand nor foot, and so they die for

weakness. Others fall into fluxes and agues and die thereby. And this way it was our chance to make. Yet, though we had more than one hundred and fifty sick there died not past seven and twenty: which loss they esteemed not much in respect of other times.[1]

Stephens's letters to his father roused interest among a few merchants in England, for trade with India. Four of them, Fitch, Newberry, Leedes and Story, set out in 1583 for India where on arrival they were cast into prison by the jealous Portuguese. Following their release, Story settled down as shopkeeper in Goa, Leedes entered the service of the Great Mogul, Newberry died on his way home overland and Fitch finally reached England. These four merchants appear to have made little impact in stimulating further early English trade with India or increasing English knowledge of the eastern seas.

It was Sir Francis Drake's voyage round the world (1577-80), which marks the entry of the English into the Indian Ocean. Coming to the Cape from the East, Drake refers to his rounding that 'most stately thing, and the fairest cape we saw in the whole circumference of the earth', but he makes no mention of the East African coast lying to the north-east of it. It was still *terra incognita* as far as the English were concerned. Even the hazards of the Cape route seem to have come as a surprise to them, more so than to the Dutch: the latter appear to have been familiar with accounts of the Portuguese who had been plying those waters for nearly a century prior to the advent of the English and Dutch. Linschoten, who voyaged to Goa in a Portuguese carrack in 1583, states that

It is as the ships leave the Cape, that it is or is not good to make toward Mozambique: because they cannot come in time to Goa by reason of the great calms that are within the island of Madagascar. It was when against 'the high land of Natal' that counsel was usually taken of the ship's officers whether to sail within, or without, the island of Madagascar. For within that land, they sail to Mozambique, and thence to Goa, and sailing without it they cannot come at Goa by reason they fall down [drift] by means of the stream [current] and so must sail unto Cochin 100 miles south of Goa but they that pass the Cape in July may well go to Mozambique, because they have time enough to refresh themselves there and revictual etc and water, and lie at anchor 10 to 12 days; such as pass the Cape in August come too late and must sail towards Cochin to lose no time yet it is dangerous and much more cumbersome.[2]

The season of the year had to be taken into account. Sailing by the 'Inner Passage', that is the Mozambique Channel, to India was only possible in the south-west monsoon, but the 'Middle Passage' – that is to the south of Madagascar and thence to Bombay – must usually be taken during the north-east monsoon. There were other hazards in taking the Inner Passage – the 'India' shoals – lying between Madagascar and the mainland at about 22°30'S, and about 90 miles from Mozambique; they were 'mostly clear coral of black, white and green colours, which is very dangerous and Pilots ought to have great care'. The usual route to the Bay of Bengal and the farther east was the 'Outer Passage', that is to the south-east, and keeping wide of Mauritius – far enough east to get into the path of the south-east trade winds which would carry one towards Sumatra and the Bay of Bengal.[3] Here also were hazards to keep in mind. For, passing the isles of France and Bourbon and with course set for India, there was the 'archipelago of shoals' to their north; and there were frequent hurricanes in the region between those islands and the Seychelles – the disastrous effects of these hurricanes were demonstrated in February 1771 and April 1773.[4]

The homeward journey from the East by way of the Cape route was as risky as the outward. The Agulhas Bank and Cape Agulhas were often mistaken for the Cape proper and here, with the strong current setting to the west, a grave threat was posed to navigation for it was frequently thought by navigators that at this point they had rounded the Cape, and they then turned north too soon and were wrecked on the south-east coast of Africa or were carried further north along the coast of Natal. And at the Cape itself, where a perennial current sets into the Atlantic, ships were carried round there in the face of a strong north-west gale; and the double strain thus imposed on vessels, especially if overladen, was such that they were frequently brought to disaster. To avoid these hazards there were two courses open: push boldly into land where the wind was less and the sea comparatively smooth, or make boldly out to sea – to the southward and beyond the influence of the currents – this latter course however meant much loss of time; hence the first procedure was usually recommended.

Linschoten states that the Portuguese feared the land of Natal more than the Cape:

for there is commonly stormy and foul weather; and many ships …

have been spoiled and cast away there ... they never pass Natal without great fear; having a good watch and great foresight. All their ropes being stiff, and well looked unto, and danger was increased by their over-loading their ships. Sometimes the ships are so ladened that the cables touch the water, and besides that, the hatches are covered with divers chests, seven or eight one above another ... the East India ships, which are very heavily ladened and so full that they are almost ready to sink; so that they can hardly be steered.[5]

On his way to the East, Linschoten, who sailed from Holland in December 1586, took the Inner Passage, with one eye cocked for the dangerous 'India' shoals. However, he arrived safely at Mozambique in August 1587 and after a stopover at the Comoros, was at Goa by 21 September 1587. On his return journey he kept to the east of Madagascar but, approaching the Cape, was caught up in the great current running there towards the west. He entertained thought at this stage of running up to Mozambique but this involved such a fine calculation, for 'otherwise they cannot come to it again', that the idea was given up. Once past those dangerous waters, Linschoten 'got before the wind' which took him speedily to St Helena.

Thomas Cavendish, third circumnavigator of the globe, rounded the Cape from the East, in the *Desire*, in 1588.[6] He makes no mention of East Africa although he probably had acquaintance with Gastaldi's map of 1564 which shows the East African coast reasonably accurately and was undoubtedly drawn from Portuguese charts, which were in turn based on nearly one hundred years of experience in sailing along those coasts. English contact with East Africa dates from the voyage of Captain James (later Sir James) Lancaster (1591–94) who, in company with two other ships, left England in April 1591 on the first English overseas voyage to India. Lancaster lost one of his vessels at the Cape, overshot his mark at Mozambique, was carried on to the Comoros where he fell foul of the Arabs and lost his master and 30 of his crew, and thence proceeded 'with heavy hearts' to Zanzibar. Here on his arrival at the end of November 1591 he met a hostile reception from the Portuguese. They were most guarded and watchful towards the English, and spread a tale among the local populace that they were a cruel people and also man-eaters. Despite his cold welcome at Zanzibar, Lancaster's relations with the Arabs there were relatively friendly, considering he had sequestered one of their 'shereefs' who had come on board ship, and held him hostage for good

EARLY ENGLISH CONTACTS WITH EAST AFRICA

behaviour and for supply of provisions. After resting at Zanzibar for some three months while refitting and reprovisioning, Lancaster sailed from that place with which he was much taken and

> for the goodnesse of the harborough and watering, and plentifull refreshing with fish, whereof we tooke great store with our nets, and for sundry sorts of fruits of the countrey, as Cocos and others, which were brought to us by the Moores, as also for oxen and hennes, is carefully to be sought for by such of our ships, as shall hereafter passe that way.[7]

Zanzibar, Lancaster noted, was a busy centre for boat-building: 'divers pangias or boates, pinned with wooden pins, and sowed together with Palmito cordes, and calked with the huskes of Cocos shels beaten, whereof they make Occam [Oakum]'. Lancaster carried away with him from Zanzibar some thousand weight of pitch which he mixed with 300 jars of oil taken from a vessel he had seized near Guinea on his way out from England. Despite his three months' stopover at Zanzibar, Lancaster tells us little about the nature of Portuguese rule there, or on the coast. His observations in this respect, coming from the first Englishman to visit East Africa, and at a time when Portuguese power there had reached its height, would have been most revealing. Lancaster was too much caught up in the day-to-day business of bargaining for supplies, negotiating with the local Arabs and attending to the refitting of his ship prior to his departure from Zanzibar, to take a larger view of the East African world. On leaving Zanzibar he took with him a negro guide who 'knew something of the countrey' – the East Indies – since 'wheresoever we came our care was to get into our hands some one or two of the countries, to learn the languages and states of those parts where we touched'. Despite his guide, Lancaster's subsequent sailing course was erratic. Departing Zanzibar on 15 February 1592, and 'deceived by the currents that set into the Gulf of the Red Sea along the coast of Melinde, and by winds shortening upon us to the northeast and easterly, and a westward current', he was driven within 'four score leagues of the Isle of Socotra', and thence bypassed the southern tip of India and arrived at the Malay Peninsula in June 1592. Here he carried out privateering against the Portuguese 'with much success'. On his return journey he kept to the east of Madagascar, but nearing the Cape was so bedevilled by winds that it took him a month to pass that point. A safe journey from there to St Helena was, however, followed by a year of mishaps which took him to the Caribbean, and it was not until 24 May 1594 that he arrived back at Rye, in England, after an absence of '3 years, 6 weeks and 2 days'.[8]

Lancaster's voyage anticipated the founding of the East India Company – the 'Governor and Company of Merchants of London trading into the East Indies' – constituted on 31 December 1600, which sent out its first expedition of four ships under Lancaster in April 1601. On his second voyage Lancaster sailed for Sumatra, arriving at Achin on 5 June 1602, and thence passing on to Bantam, Java, where a factory was established. The return journey to England in 1603 with a cargo of spices was speedy and propitious, and Lancaster was knighted for his services in October of the same year.

This voyage was quickly followed up by other English expeditions. At first the Company sought mainly to trade with the East Indies, but soon its ships were resorting to the Indian mainland. Captain Hawkins in 1608 visited Jahangir at Agra and obtained permission to build a factory at Surat, but an attempt to do so in 1609 was unsuccessful. Everywhere on the Indian seaboard the British met Portuguese hostility. The issue was finally decided at the battle of Swally – off the mouth of the Tapti River, where, on 29 November 1612, a Portuguese fleet under a Portuguese admiral was soundly defeated by an English squadron under Captain Best. In the words of Purchas:

> One English ship, the *Dragon,* commanded by Captain Best assisted only by the *Osiander,* a little ship (scarcely a ship, I had almost called her a little Pinnasse), successfully fought a Portuguese fleet comprising four huge galleons, with five-or-six-and-twenty frigates. The great Mogul – before thought none comparable to the Portugall at Sea, much wondered at the English resolution, related to him by Sardar Chan.[9]

British maritime supremacy in the Indian seas dates from the battle of Swally. There quickly followed the establishment of a factory at Surat, and others at places round the Gulf of Cambay and in the nearby interior. The imperial firman of the Great Mogul of December 1612 signified the acceptance of the presence of British settlement in India. During the first years of its founding the East Indies Company sought slaves from the East African coast for its own use and for sale to the Dutch in Batavia, and in 1614 it directed its ships to Madagascar and the East African coast for slaves – the *Middleborough* and another vessel, name unknown, were at Madagascar and 'Melinde' in February 1616 seeking slaves, but both ships were cast away 'on the coast of Arabia or Sindu'. In 1623 the Company directed that a 'ship or two' should go to the coast of Madagascar and Africa for slaves. Andrew Shilling and Humphrey Fitzherbert tried unsuccessfully to found a settlement at Saldanha Bay, Madagascar, so as to secure a regular supply of slaves but it was much easier to pick up slaves at various points in the Mozambique Channel rather than hold an isolated point on Madagascar that might be subject to enemy attack. The *Hart* in 1628, and the *Blessing* in 1638, took on slaves in the Mozambique Channel and at the Comoros,[10] and the *Advice* at the Comoros in July 1643 was directed to secure 'lustie' blacks from there, but found them too expensive at '20 rials of eight apiece' and few were purchased. It was easier to seize them from the Portuguese – as Captain Benjamin Joseph attempted in 1616, and lost his life in the process: there is record of a Portuguese junk hijacked wholesale with its cargo of slaves off the Comoros in 1622. Poaching slaves from the Portuguese, however, was neither legitimate nor a reliable source of slaves; and when, in the mid-1640s, it was noted that the Company's slaves were 'almost worn out', 'masters and pursers' were again directed to seek slaves from Madagascar and the Comoros, failing which they were to seek slaves from West Africa. In January 1663 Captain Mitchell was instructed to procure from Guinea 'twenty blacks for the Company's service in India'. It is essential not to overemphasize this aspect of the Company's affairs; slave-trading did not rank high in its priorities. Admittedly there are references to English ships carrying slaves from East Africa to the Americas: the *Greyhound* and the *Coroner,* which sailed to Madagascar to carry slaves 'from thence to the Plantations'; an English ship under William Alley seeking slaves for the same purpose in 1667; the *London,* wrecked on the Mozambique bar in 1682, just failed to pick up her cargo of slaves; the *Good Hope* carrying slaves to Virginia in 1686 and the *Mercury* licensed as a slaver but taken over by pirates in 1719.

In addition to the desultory slaving of East Indiamen in East African waters in the seventeenth century there was a short-lived and bizarre period of piratical activity by English seamen at Madagascar and in neighbouring waters, in the 1690s and early years of the eighteenth century. Confused in detail and with much fiction interwoven with fact – largely the result of Daniel Defoe's writings – nevertheless, accounts of this piratical activity suggest greater familiarity with East African waters on the part of English seamen than hitherto supposed. The onset of these English pirates in the western Indian Ocean at this time was largely the result of increasing awareness of the riches to be obtained there following the establishment of the East India Company, a greater knowledge of the movement of trade between Mocha and India and the rich prizes awaiting in the capture of pilgrim ships coming or going to Jeddah, the port for Mecca. As Lord Bellomont, Governor of New York, wrote to the Admiralty in 1699: 'The vast riches of the Red Sea and Madagascar are such a lure to seamen that there's almost no withholding them from turning pirates.' In May 1696 the *Adventure* under Captain Kidd, fitted out and sailing from Plymouth, Massachusetts, proceeded to Madagascar where she arrived in February 1697. In the same year the *Pelican*, from Rhodes Island, although commissioned to go against the Spaniards, proceeded to Madagascar – she is usually referred to as the first British privateer in those waters. The *Adventure*, under Captain Kidd, operated between Madagascar, the Comoros and Babs Key (Perim Island) in the Straits of Bab el Mandeb (where she preyed on the Mocha fleet), and off the Malabar coast. It was off the latter coast that Kidd seized the *Quedah Merchant*, and joined with Captain Culliford of the *Mocha* in piratical ventures. During the course of 1698-99 complaints reached the home government that Kidd, instead of apprehending pirates, had joined their ilk, and had associated himself with the notorious Culliford in capturing native vessels under the pretence that they sailed under French passes. He plundered as far afield as Malabar to the East, and the Red Sea to the West. Kidd eventually returned to America where Lord Bellomont of New York, acting almost as his patron, received booty from him. This was too blatant. Kidd was ultimately arrested and sent to England where he was tried and hanged at Execution Dock, London, in May 1701.

Contemporary with Kidd was Captain Henry Every (Defoe's John Avery) who inspired Defoe's *Life, Adventures and Piracies of Captain Singleton* (1720). Every was the first mate on the *Charles II* (later renamed the *Fancy*), and in 1694 incited its crew to mutiny, took over the vessel at Corunna, set its captain adrift and sailed for Madagascar, from whence he operated in the Straits of Bab el Mandeb preying on the Indiamen who traded at Mocha. His richest prize was the *Gunj Suwai*, belonging to the Great Mogul. Among her passengers was an Indian princess, and she carried great riches in rupees, gold and silver, for she was returning from carrying rich pilgrims to Mecca. The *Gunj Suwai* was taken off Surat, and Every and crew hastened to New England with their great booty.

Every was only one of a score or more of English pirates resorting to Madagascar and the western Indian Ocean at this period. There is reference to the *Speedy Return*, an East Indiaman, carrying slaves from Madagascar to the French islands about 1701-2, and mixing slaving with piracy;[11] the *Bedford* (or *Beckford*), a galley, which sailed from the Thames in June 1698 and was taken over by her crew off Madagascar in early 1699 and converted to a pirate ship. Names recurring in this saga of the pirates of Madagascar are those of Captains Tew, White and North of Bermuda, Captains Wake, Farrel and May of New England – to name a few. Incidents are many. There was frequent and quick metamorphosis, with a mutinous crew member becoming captain within the hour. There was much violence – as in the case of Captain Booth and 20 of his crew killed in a fracas with the Arabs at Zanzibar about 1700, and his vessel, the *Speaker*, under Captain Bowen, continuing her pirating in the Red Sea, off Malabar and in Madagascar waters until she was lost in 1701. There was Captain White who captured the *Dorothy* and *Forgiveness* in the Red Sea about 1704-5, and after a further hectic career of piracy, died in 1708, 'from excessive drinking and other irregularities'. It was a fine life, the best of Cape wines, tropical fruits, rice, spices, dates from Basra, the mysterious Durian fruit from Malaysia, and beautiful womenfolk – ranging from the swart to the lighter and divine: here was passion and life to the full – away from all the restraints of home morality.

This 'loosely knit fraternity of Madagascar' operated mainly from St Augustine Bay on its south-western side, or from St Mary's Island on its north-eastern side. They appeared to circle round Madagascar 'like moths round a candle'. Their activities, however, did not go unnoticed by the English navy, and when, following the advice of the Admiralty, a royal pardon was offered for piratical acts committed prior to 30 April 1699, east of the longitude of the Cape of Good Hope and as far as the meridian of Socotra and Cape Comorin, 20 of the St Mary's Island pirates accepted the King's Pardon from Commodore Littleton. A squadron under Commodore Richard, however, continued to operate against the pirates in the Comoros region until 1703. Following a royal pardon some of these pirates, as with Captain Burgess – pardoned in 1702 – turned to slaving. Captain Halsey, of Boston, in the privateer *Dorothy*, appeared in Madagascar waters in 1706 and, prior to his death in 1709, operated with Captain North from Ambonavoula in Madagascar. They made a resounding prize in the capture in 1707 of the *Rising Eagle* and the *Essex*, two large merchantmen out of a fleet of four

trading from Mocha. £40,000 was taken from the *Essex* but she was
allowed to go free; the *Rising Eagle's* captain, Chamberlain, was killed,
£10,000 taken from her and she was converted to a pirate. The *Neptune*
– under Captain Williams – seems to have been the last of these pirate
ships. Originally a slaver operating off the Masselage River in
Madagascar, she was taken over by her mutinous crew in 1707 and
converted to a pirate vessel; we hear of her and of the *Greyhound* in the
Red Sea in 1708, but shortly after she was lost in a hurricane, 'the last
Ship that Gang of Pyrates ever got possession of'.

Woodes Rogers, who was sent against the pirate capital at Providence
in the Bahamas, in 1718, on completing his work there, did a similar
service on the coast of Madagascar. By this date the era of the pirates was
nearly over; those remaining at Madagascar had turned to occasional
slaving, as had Captain Mackett, owner of the *Drake, Sarah* and *Mercury*
– all slaving ships. Some of the pirates who had joined in the attack on
the *Rising Eagle* in 1707 were still living in Madagascar years later. Apart
from Defoe's *General History of the Pyrates,* the best-known work on this
subject is *Madagascar; or Robert Drury's Journal (1729).* Drury,
apprentice on the East Indiaman *Degrave,* which was shipwrecked off
Madagascar, was one of the survivors and spent almost 14 years in easy
captivity on that island. He and the *Degrave* figure largely in Defoe's
History. Other survivors of the *Degrave's* crew wandered throughout
Madagascar until recruited by the pirate captains, Halsey and White,
and joined in expeditions to the Red Sea. Drury himself returned to
England in 1716.

Apart from two instances there is no record of the Madagascar pirates
visiting the East African coast, although pirate folk from the very nature
of their calling would be little inclined to record their comings and
goings. Their wide-ranging activity in the western Indian Ocean at this
time would, however, suggest a familiarity with the East African coast.
Captain White, in the *Speaker,* stopped over at Zanzibar about 1700 for
provisioning, and in much skimped reference to that island tells us only
that it was the place 'where the Portuguese had once a Settlement, but
now inhabited by the Arabians'. White and his men were set upon by the
Arabs at Zanzibar and in the attack 21 men were slain, the survivors
narrowly escaping by boat. Captain Beavis (or Beawes), commander of
the *Albemarle,* in the service of the East India Company, sailed from
England to Surat in the spring of 1700 with a commission 'to fight with
and secure all pirates in the seas of India', but was caught in the south-
west monsoon and forced on to the 'Coast of Zanguebar in the higher

Ethiopia, on the Continent of Africa'. Endeavouring to 'find out some Place of Safety, that the Ship might ride secure', he cast anchor on 4 December 1700, at Magadoxa (Mogadishu it would seem from the latitude given by Beavis – 1°51'). Beavis found the inhabitants at Magadoxa still able to speak a little Portuguese, but holding a bitter memory of that people – so much so that they were taught from childhood to have aversion to white men. Beavis, fearful of treachery at Magadoxa, did not tarry there and made his way back to the Comoros. One of his crew, a mulatto seaman, was taken captive at Magadoxa and kept prisoner there for 16 years until he escaped on a Dutch ship trading on the coast in 1716, and finally returned to England in 1724. The manuscript account of his experiences fell into the possession of Sir Hans Sloane, and this is likely to be the source from which Defoe drew his story. Lord Keith, who, on his way to the East Indies in 1791, refreshed his fleet at St Augustine Bay, found it scarcely frequented by men-of-war or seeking vessels, and at the time of Owen's visit in the 1820s only an occasional slaver or whaler called there 'either for refreshment or an addition to her cargo'.

Almost from the date of its charter in 1600 the East India Company attempted to establish trading connections with Aden, the Red Sea and Persian Gulf areas. A factory was established at Gombroon (Bandar Abbas) in the Persian Gulf in 1616, and the head of the Gulf had been penetrated by 1640 and a factory established at Basra. At Aden the Company had less success. Its agents, Keeling and Sharpey, failed to open a factory there in 1608-9, and their attempts to foist a cargo of typical English trade goods – iron, tin, lead and cloth – on to the local merchants at Aden were unsuccessful. The Turks were in control there, had garrisoned its fort, stone walls and the outpost on Sira Island; they kept the local population in a state of sullen acquiescence, and posed a continued obstacle to any English attempt to gain a foothold at Aden. Greater awareness of trade possibilities in the Red Sea came from these first English attempts at Aden: Sharpey's factor, John Jourdain, visited Sa'na, Ta'izz and Mocha, the first Englishman to traverse the Yemen,[12] and the Company's ships had passed through the Straits of Bab el Mandeb, and had made contact with the coffee port of Mocha.

Wild coffee plants, probably from Ethiopia, had been introduced into southern Arabia and placed under cultivation there in about the fifteenth century. For the next two hundred years Mocha was the main port for the world's supply of coffee, until the propagation of the coffee plant in other parts of the world led to its decline. Mocha, a port of the

Yemen, lying some 40 miles north of, and inside, the southern entrance to the Red Sea, faces onto an arid stretch of coast, with blowing sand and an inadequate water supply. Amidst evidence of former fine public buildings, residences and mosques, there was also much ruin and decay, and from the sea it presented a picture of sun-baked mud buildings, reared high, and crazy in topsy-turvy fashion; latticed windows and screened balconies look down on a labyrinth of narrow streets far below. Such was the coffee port of the world for nearly two centuries.

English navigators soon found that to sail to Mocha was no daring enterprise if carried out at the right time of year and with a knowledge of the intricacies of the winds and currents of the Red Sea and Gulf of Aden, and knowing when these dovetailed in with the monsoon system of the western Indian Ocean. If made at the right time of year a trading voyage could be carried out with despatch and safety, despite the prevailing view that it was nigh impossible to beat into the Gulf of Aden against headwinds. Aden's place in the trading world of the Red Sea arose from its fine harbour and strategic position. Its hinterland did not produce products for export; Aden was rather an entrepôt, a place of exchange for goods, in the same way as Muscat in Oman, despite bleak and infertile surroundings, and it is this which explains early English attempts to get a foothold at Aden.

In November 1610, Sir Henry Middleton of the East India Company, with three ships under his command and with Sharpey's report in hand, arrived at Mocha,[13] only to be treacherously thrown into prison and an attempt made to seize his ship, the *Darling*. Middleton and companions were taken to the Pasha of Sa'na in March 1611, but escaping from there made their way back to Mocha where they turned the tables on their tormentors, and holding that place in ransom under blockade, extracted compensation of 18,000 dollars. Middleton was single-minded in his desire to trade – in 'silks, spices, coffee and finer wares', and always the competition of the 'Hollanders' loomed large in his mind. He failed to see the superior merits of 'Damascus steel', and when he could not unload his heavy English hardware on Gujerati trading vessels in the Red Sea, he and Captain John Saris took to 'romaging the Indian ships'. They signed a compact 'sealed in writing interchangeable' as to the sharing of booty. The Company's agents tended to avoid Aden over the next few years and concentrated on the Mocha trade. Sir Thomas Roe, English ambassador at the Great Mogul's court from 1615 to 1619, and in a good position to observe the wealth that accrued from the Mocha trade, extolled it to his countrymen. In 1618, Andrew Shilling in the

Lion and Joseph Salbank, 'chief merchant' of the Company, along with Baffin, the Arctic explorer, visited Sa'na and drew up navigational charts and reported on trading prospects in the Red Sea.

The English did not have the Mocha trade to themselves; they were faced with the Dutch as trade rivals from the early years of the seventeenth century. In 1618 the Dutch, after earlier unsuccessful attempts by Pieter Van de Broecke to establish factories at Aden and al-Shihr in the face of the high-handed tactics of Turkish officials, managed to gain a foothold at Mocha in 1618, and henceforth until the introduction of coffee-growing into Java, in the early eighteenth century, they were the main rivals of the British in the Mocha coffee trade. However, with the prospering of the Java coffee industry they closed their factory at Mocha in 1738.[14] The French played a lesser part in the Mocha trade, although a French ship had visited East African waters as early as 1528-29, and in 1619-20 Captain Beaulieu sailed along the coast of southern Arabia. Colbert, Louis XIV's reforming minister, had visions of an extended Red Sea trade and the posting of French consuls at its ports; it was not until 1708 that French ships under M. de Merveille visited Aden and Mocha and a factory was established at the latter. The French trade at Mocha remained on a small scale, for in 1718 coffee was introduced into their Indian Ocean island colony of Bourbon where, like sugar, it flourished and became 'a very important article of trade'. A minor French interest, however, continued in the Mocha trade sufficient to cause them to bombard that place in 1737 when the local Imam endeavoured to impose a trade ban.

Exclusive of the logs of the East India Company's ships visiting the Red Sea, the earliest British works – *Navigation and Voyages to the Red Sea* (1750), *Instructions for Sailing From Cape Guardafui to Babelmandeb, and Through the Straits* (1753), *Journal of the Latham to Jeddah* (1758) – were general and discursive, rule-of-thumb guides. An expedition organized by King Frederick V of Denmark in 1762, under the learned M. Neilbuhr, primarily meant to advance Danish commercial interests at Mocha, made little cartographical contribution, nor did Eyles Irwin's *Series of Adventures in the Course of a Voyage up the Red Sea, on the Coasts of Nubia and Egypt in the Year 1777*. Navigation still remained hazardous owing to the lack of knowledge of the great irregularity and complexity of the movement of Red Sea waters and their interchange with the currents and winds of the Gulf of Aden and the Indian Ocean. Surface current flows inwards to the Red Sea in the eastern channel of the Straits of Bab el Mandeb, while there is an outward current to the Indian Ocean through the western channel of those straits. Tidal streams in the northern part of the Red Sea and Gulf of Suez during the north and north-west winds depress the surface level of those waters by as much as two feet.

The East India Company tended to be secretive about the matter of navigation in the Red Sea, to discourage potential trade rivals, nor was knowledge of the East African coast much more advanced than that for the Red Sea. British vessels after rounding the Cape and sailing for India, still used the Inner Passage – striking north-east for India at about the latitude of the Comoro Islands, or sailed by the Middle or Outer Passage to the east of Madagascar. In either case there was little inducement to run up to Zanzibar in the face of adverse wind or current; and apart from copra, copal and ivory there was little trade prospect at Zanzibar. The East African coast was probably better known to English sailors during the short-lived period of pirate activity at the end of the seventeenth century than in the next hundred years. Alexander Dalrymple (cartographer to the East India Company) in his *General Collection of Nautical Publications* (1772), summed up information to date, and so also did M. Saulnier de Mondevit in *Observations sur la côte du Zanzibar* (1786). These are about the sole additions to knowledge of the East African coast in the later eighteenth century.[15]

The Napoleonic wars made it essential to have up-to-date and accurate sailing directions for the Red Sea and East African coast. In 1795 Lieutenant Robert White of the Bombay Marine, in the *Panther,* made a preliminary reconnaissance of the Red Sea, and when Nelson communicated the intelligence of his victory of the Nile to the Bombay government by way of the land route, through Baghdad, it was soon realized how much more expeditious this would have been if sent by the Red Sea route. The threat posed for India by the French occupation of Egypt made it essential to look more closely at the Red Sea route. Thus Commodore Blankett's voyage to the Red Sea in 1798-99 was to make good this deficiency.[16] Blankett's fleet, despite having 'some of the best ships of our navy', was beaten back by the monsoon. Leaving Johanna in the Comoros on 11 November 1798, and sailing at the wrong time of year, it did not reach Cape Guardafui until 8 April 1799. In its first attempt to force the monsoon it got no farther than the Juba River, and suffered a series of mishaps: the *Leopard's* crew and their leader, Lieutenant Mears, were slain in an attack by the natives near Merka, and the frigate *Daedalus* narrowly escaped shipwreck on the coral bank outside the string of islands between Port Durnford and Kismayu. A thankful Captain Bissell later declared – 'It is hoped that nobody will ever attempt it again; we were forty weeks on this voyage, and ran 18,029 miles.' Information gained from Blankett's voyage was incorporated in the *India Directory* of 1809, thus supplementing Dalrymple's work. Two of Blankett's ships, the *Leopard* and *Orestes,* had stopped over at Zanzibar, and information gained from their visit throws some light on the state of affairs there. Bissell noted that 'There had not been an English ship in Zanzibar within the memory of the oldest inhabitant', the French, however, were actively engaged in the slave-trade at Zanzibar, where many persons spoke French. Following Blankett's voyage, the island of Perim in the Straits of Bab el Mandeb was occupied for a few months in 1799 by troops from Bombay under Lieutenant Colonel Murray, designated 'Political Commissioner for the Red Sea'. However, since Perim proved to be waterless, and guns placed there could not command the straits, the troops were shortly withdrawn to Aden where hospitality was accorded the British by the Abdali Sultan of Lakjeh, who exercised suzerainty there. More important for British interests in the Red Sea was the expedition under Sir Home R. Popham (1800-2) sent to convey troops from the Cape and India by way of the Red Sea to support the army in Egypt under Sir Ralph Abercromby, and to conclude commercial treaties with the Arabs and seek their support against the French. Popham, with the resounding honorific of 'Ambassador to the States of Arabia', set about his task with great energy. He made a commercial treaty with the Abdali Sultan of Lajeh, in 1802; several members of his 'embassy' visited Sa'ana, and Popham travelled in the Yemen, despite great indignities to which he was subjected by local chiefs. As a result of Popham's expedition a chart of the Red Sea was drawn up, and its longitudes determined by chronometer. In 1802-6, Viscount Valentia carried out his *Voyage and Travels to India, Ceylon, the Red Sea, Abyssinia and Egypt,* in the course of which he covered 'A large space of coastline and many islands' – thus reinforcing and supplementing Popham's work.

In January 1809 Henry Salt, who had accompanied Viscount Valentia during the latters's travels in 1802-6, and had visited Abyssinia in 1805, was sent by the British government to Abyssinia to carry presents to its ruler and to report on the state of the country and to cultivate friendly relations with the tribes on the Red Sea coast, all in furtherance of strengthening the British position in the Red Sea in the face of a French threat to India. In pursuance of these instructions, Salt rounded the Cape of Good Hope and proceeded north to Aden.[17] Unfortunately, 'the season being so far advanced', and fearing the onset of the north-east monsoon (Blankett's experience was much on his mind), Salt bypassed Zanzibar and Pemba, and hence we are denied what would have been his valuable comments on those places, for he was a percipient observer. Captains Tomkinson and Fisher, of the *Caledon* and *Racehorse* respectively, had earlier in the same year visited Zanzibar and Pemba, and they commented on the extensive trade there in slaves, gums, ivory antimony, blue vitriol and senna, much of it in the hands of the French, who in turn supplied arms, gunpowder, cutlery, coarse Indian cloths and Spanish dollars. Captain Fisher spoke in 'terms of rapture' of Zanzibar's verdure and beauty: he also noted 'great numbers of slaves, which are generally kept ready for exportation on that island'.

Salt, on completing his mission to Ethiopia and venturing out of the Gulf of Aden in June 1810, was caught at the height of the south-west monsoon. His vessel was whirled round the island of Socotra 'shipping seas, renting her sails and using pumps continuously'. Extricating himself from this ordeal, he managed to bring his ship to Bombay for repairs and the recuperation of his crew. He finally proceeded on his homeward journey round the Cape in 1811. Despite the lack of British contact with the East African coast, the maps Salt had available to him are surprisingly accurate in detail, scale and place-names. His difficulties arose more from lack of hydrographical knowledge and ignorance of winds and currents. With their centuries-old skills in seamanship, Arab sailors would not have attempted to sail southwards at the wrong time of year.

In the same year that Salt returned to England, Captain Thomas Smee and Lieutenant Hardy of the Bombay Marine (the East India Company's navy) carried out a voyage of research on the East African coast.[18] Smee's account of the Zanzibar slave market, probably the first by an Englishman, is expressive of the deep distaste felt by most observers on witnessing the sale of slaves there. The Sultan's governor at Zanzibar, Yacout, was an able and rapacious eunuch with a 'ruling passion for power', who received ten dollars for every slave he sold to the French. The revenue of Zanzibar, 60,000 dollars annually, was largely derived from the slave-trade. Out of the island's total population of some 200,000, three-fourths were slaves. Between six and ten thousand slaves were annually shipped to the Middle East countries. The slave market was the centre of the town's activity.[19] Smee deplored the lack of British influence at Zanzibar, while that of the French was predominant there – their corsairs based on Réunion and Mauritius visited it regularly, and the French were active in trade there.

Smee was unduly pessimistic over the lack of British influence on the East African coast. A change was soon to come. Britain's victories over France in the Napoleonic wars brought her important possessions – the Cape of Good Hope, Mauritius, the Seychelles and Amirante Islands – making her the greatest imperial power in the Indian Ocean. This brought increasing awareness of East Africa. The African Institution drew attention to the East African slave-trade when Mauritius was taken over by the British, and Smee, as we have seen, drew attention to the slave mart at Zanzibar. The slave-trade of East Africa was largely in the hands of Omani Arabs who also supplied slaves – albeit in small numbers – to British India. Correspondence took place between the Bombay government and Said of Muscat in 1812 and 1815, over the matter of his subjects carrying slaves to British India and the depredations of pirates and slavers in the Persian Gulf. In 1820, in an attempt to check the latter, treaties were made with the principal sheikhs of the 'Pirate Coast'.[20] However, the naval squadron of the Bombay Marine to which was assigned the task of implementing these treaties, noted that the main culprits in bringing slaves into the Gulf were the Omani Arabs, who were not covered by the treaties, and who, in Zanzibar, were selling slaves to the Portuguese and French, and feeding the illicit slave-trade in Mauritius.

The African Institution drew attention to this in March 1821, when it requested the East India Company 'to interpose their powerful mediation with the Imam of Muscat for the entire abolition of the slave-trade at Zanzibar'. The Company, in reply, affirmed its 'most cordial concurrence in the benevolent views entertained by the members of the Institution'. In the same year the Governor-General of India, Lord Hastings, consulted with Governor Farquhar of Mauritius in the matter. The connection between the slave-trade at Mauritius and the role of the Omani Arabs in Zanzibar was now clear. Rumours reached Farquhar in early 1821 that the French had recently deployed 24 slave vessels fully fitted out by a Nantes firm for slaving in East African waters, and plans were under way to set up a slave depot on the small island of Providence, between Madagascar and the Seychelles. To check these rumours Farquhar deputed Captain Fairfax Moresby, of HMS *Menai,* to cruise between Madagascar and Zanzibar in 1821. Moresby reported that the proposed base at Providence had not materialized, but there was ample evidence of a brisk slave-trade by the French at Zanzibar. Eight ships under French or Arab colours had sailed from there within a three-week period, each carrying from 200 to 400 slaves. The French brig, *Le Succès*, captured by Moresby, had 340 slaves on board, and there were reputedly 20,000 more awaiting sale in Zanzibar.[21] There was also British concern over the northern Arab slave-trade with British India. The origins of this trade were ancient, for the same monsoon which carried East African slaves to the Middle East also took them to India. The trade was small, and references to it scattered, such as that 430 black boys were reported to be in Bombay at the end of the eighteenth century;[22] that the Third Ceylon Regiment, in 1811, had 800 Africans in its ranks (they had been purchased at Goa at 30 dollars apiece, and then inducted into the regiment); and an official report in 1812 that Arab slavers brought in about 100 slaves annually to Calcutta. A statement in the *Calcutta Journal* in 1823 claimed that Calcutta was a mart where Africans were sold to the highest bidder, and 150 eunuchs had been brought there in the current season by Arab slavers.[23] In Bombay African slaves had long been a familiar sight, for it was the practice from the early nineteenth century to land them there from captured slavers, and they were subsequently cared for by the Church Missionary Society at Nassick near Bombay. Slaves continued to be imported into Karachi as late as 1842. The slave-trade to India was an irritant to humanitarians and they sought to end it.

Legislation against the slave-trade in India had been enacted in Bombay and Bengal in 1805, 1807, 1811 and 1813, but despite this, smuggling of slaves into India continued. The great Act of 1833 which ended slavery elsewhere in British possessions was unfortunately not extended 'to any of the territories in the possession of the East India Company, or the island of Ceylon or the island of St. Helena'. Thus so long as the institution of slavery was permitted in India, efforts would be made to supply that market. It was not until the decree of 1836, forbidding the import of slaves into Sind, Kutch and Kathiawar, and the abolition of the legal status of slavery by the Act of 1843, that the slave-trade to India ceased.

To end the Arab slave-trade effectively, with the French and with British India, there was the need to strike it at its most vital points — Zanzibar and Muscat. This joint goal might be attained by an approach to Said, ruler of Muscat in Oman. Omani commerce had expanded during the Napoleonic wars when the Omani, being neutral, took over much of the carrying trade of the western Indian Ocean; even Indian merchants found it advantageous to ship their goods on Omani vessels to escape the depredations of pirates in the Straits of Mussandam and the

Persian Gulf. By 1802 Omani shipping had expanded so much that Bombay shipyards were busy filling Omani orders for ships. Muscat (literally, 'the place to let down the anchor'), from its commanding and convenient position, was a main emporium on the highway of ocean commerce between the East and West. Its secure harbour, inaccessibility by land and its natural strength made it a place of high value and importance. It was the 'Key to the Persian Gulf' – a central place of trade for Persia, India, East Africa and Mesopotamia. It was to the ruler of Muscat that the British now turned. The time was propitious for such an approach, for Said was now aware of the dominant role of Britain in the western Indian Ocean. The establishment of a British military base at Perim in 1799, a British treaty with the Shah of Persia in 1800, a British treaty of amity and commerce with the Sultan of Aden in 1802 and the capture by the British of widespread French possessions in the Indian Ocean in 1810, left no doubt as to where primacy of naval power in those waters now lay.

It was no easy matter for the British to win over Said from the French. The latter were well entrenched in the Persian Gulf – their influence there extended back to the early eighteenth century – and when it was threatened following the outbreak of war with England in 1793, France stepped in to secure it more firmly, and sent various missions to the Middle East. In 1795 a French consulate was established at Muscat, and soon there was a French physician, supposedly medical adviser to the Sultan, but increasingly active as his confidential political counsellor as well. In the face of what was seen by the British as this close and pernicious French influence at the Sultan's court, the East India Company secured from the Sultan a treaty in the form of a maritime alliance which was directed against the French. It provided that 'a person of the French nation' (either the French physician or a suspect French officer on one of the Sultan's vessels) at this court should be dismissed, and it was agreed that the port of Gombroon (Bandar Abbas) should be occupied by a force of 700 to 800 hundred sepoys of the East India Company. By January 1800 a British physician had replaced the French confidential medical adviser; and in the same month, the treaty of 1798 was renewed with added provision that an agent of the East India Company be appointed at Muscat, and the latter duly took up his post there in 1802.

The French were not quiescent in the face of these British diplomatic gains, but had limited success in offsetting them. A French official mission under M. de Cavaignac, in 1803, failed to wean the Sultan from the British connection, as also did attempts to renew the French friendship with the Sultan in 1804, for continued French privateering had not only been directed against British shipping, but Muscat shipping had suffered as well, and had strained relations with the Sultan. The Sultan's treaty with the French in June 1807, extending 'most favoured nation privileges' in matters of commerce and navigation, and providing for the appointment of French commercial agents in Said's dominions, was soon found to be restrictive on Omani commerce in British ports, and was resented and ignored by Said's subjects. Then, when the threatened French invasion of India failed to take place following Napoleon's costly Spanish diversion, the scales were tipped firmly in Britain's favour. The arrival of a British mission at Muscat in January 1810 was well received.

Said was soon made aware of British wishes in the matter of ending the slave-trade. In early 1812, the Bombay government informed him of the prohibition of the slave-trade in British India, furnished him with a copy of the Bengal regulations of 1811 and requested that he give it publicity throughout his dominions, so that his subjects, 'so much in the habit of frequenting the port of Calcutta', might not incur its penalties.[24] His attention was also drawn to the Arab slave-trade in the matter of the Jawasmi pirates in the Persian Gulf. The Jawasmi, the tribes on the southern 'Pirate Coast' of the Persian Gulf (better known today as Trucial Oman), strung out in a series of scraggy villages on the salt water inlets of the Gulf, unapproachable by British cruisers owing to shallow waters, had long preyed on Omani and British shipping. Their depredations took on new import when, in 1815, a vessel 'with a vast number of slaves on board from Zanzibar to Muscat' was taken by the Jawasmi and every soul on board 'barbarously put to death'. Sir Evan Nepean, Governor of Bombay, sent a personal letter to Said, urging him to take steps against the Jawasmi, and to align himself with civilized opinion in the world by interdicting the slave-trade carried on by his subjects. This pious exhortation against the slave-trade brought no response from Said; he was, however, interested in pursuing joint cause with the British against the Jawasmi.

An effective drive was launched against them in 1819 and by the end of that year their power was broken. By a General Treaty of 1820, they pledged themselves to abstain from the slave-trade.

The carrying off of slaves, men, women or children, from the coasts of Africa or elsewhere and the transporting them in vessels is plunder and piracy; and the Arabs who accept the Peace shall do nothing of this nature.[25]

Even so the treaty with the Jawasmi did not affect the Omani Arabs, Said's own subjects, who were the main culprits in carrying on the external slave-trade from Said's dominions in East Africa. To end this trade Farquhar sought a treaty with Muscat similar to that with Radama of Madagascar, but since the ruler of Oman was 'closely allied in commercial and territorial interests with the English East India Company', Farquhar requested Lord Hastings, Governor-General of India, to approach Said to end the slave-trade from his 'ports and subordinate dependencies of Zanzibar, Kilwa and other petty factories on the East Coast of Africa' so that 'this hemisphere would for the future be cleared entirely of that pollution which has stained it from the earliest times'. Hastings was sympathetic. The Governor of Bombay would make strong representations to end 'this criminal and disgraceful traffic'.

In the autumn of 1821 following further correspondence as to the form of a draft treaty, a joint request was made by Mauritius and Bombay to Said for his 'immediate interference' in the operation of the 'external trade', and for the issue of 'peremptory orders' to prevent all dealings in slaves from being carried on by European agents. This communication caused Said to ponder gravely. He would lose a substantial portion of his revenue if the external slave-trade from his dominions were ended; but the 'legitimate' slave-trade might be increased, and he needed British support in his struggle against the Wahabi and Jawasmi. He was aware that he was principally indebted to Britain for his political security. There were solid advantages for himself and his subjects in their commerce with British possessions in the East. In December 1821 he sent a letter to Farquhar requesting that the vessels of his subjects be placed on the same footing in Mauritius as in other British ports to the eastward, and intimated his desire to meet Farquhar as far as possible in abolishing the external slave-trade.

Farquhar and Elphinstone congratulated Said on his enlightened attitude. His fame, humanity and generosity would be widely spread among the nations of Europe, and his nation would thus 'yield to none in the early adoption of those principles of honour, justice and humanity which have been recognized by the Sovereigns of Europe as the grounds of the annihilation of the slave-trade'. Captain William Bruce, British Resident in the Persian Gulf, who visited Said, found him most anxious to meet British wishes in the matter, although he could not do so as freely as he wished, as it 'affected his subjects in a religious point of view'. However, he had issued the 'most positive instructions to his lieutenants at Zanzibar and the other ports on the African coast hereafter not to allow slaves to be sold to French, Portuguese and American vessels or to any Christian people whatever'. This prohibition cost him an annual loss in duty on slaves of 40 to 50 thousand dollars.

These *pourparlers* and tentative agreements with Said were confirmed in the early summer of 1822, when Farquhar directed Captain Moresby to Muscat to conclude a convention with the Imam. The latter was to be reassured that the British government would not innovate on the religious practices and observances relative to slavery as recognized by Islam, nor would it interfere with the practice of holding and disposing of slaves in Said's dominions. It was solely the export trade in slaves from those dominions which the British government wished to annihilate.[26] Although aware that such annihilation would involve a considerable shortfall in the Sultan's revenues, and that the East India Company had signalled its readiness to find a mode of remuneration for the Sultan for such loss, Moresby was cautioned by Farquhar that on no account must he commit the government of Mauritius to any expenditure not previously sanctioned by the home government.

Moresby was an enthusiastic emissary. His generous and indefatigable exertions for the suppression of the slave-trade on the eastern side of Africa was to win for him an encomium from the great liberator, Wilberforce, himself. The latter looked forward with pleasure to meeting this redoubtable warrior against the slave-trade and of 'paying my personal respects to you'. Just as the treaty with Radama of Madagascar had been the best preventive in that hitherto great mart for slaves, so also, if Moresby could succeed in his mission to Muscat, more would be effected, in his words, 'than has been done since the existence of the Abolition Acts'.

The treaty to which Said assented on 8 September 1822, along with supplementary articles a few days later, prohibited 'all external traffic in slaves' from his dominions and dependencies, and the sale of slaves by any of his subjects 'to Christians of every description'. Violation of these engagements by Omani Arabs would result in seizure and confiscation of their ships, and punishment of their owners and officers as pirates. Such ships might also be seized by British cruisers, if found south of Cape Delgado, 'His Highness's most southern possession in Africa', or to the east of a line drawn therefrom to a point 60 miles east of Socotra, and from thence to Diu Head at the western end of the Gulf of Cambay on the west coast of India, 'even though bound for Madagascar', unless driven east of that line by stress of weather, or carrying satisfactory papers certifying point of departure and destination. Provision was made in the treaty for appointment of a British agent in Said's dominions 'to have intelligence of sale of slaves to Christians'.

The Moresby treaty fell far short of complete abolition, but it was a surprising achievement in the light of slow progress made later in the nineteenth century to end the East African slave-trade, and in that it was a direct blow to Said's revenue, diminishing it, according to Hamerton, British consul at Zanzibar, by 100,000 crowns (about £11,250).[27] Said gained, however, in that his territorial claims to the East African coast were indirectly recognized by the treaty. It referred to his 'overlordship' in East Africa, his 'dependencies' as far south as Cape Delgado, and his governors there. Omani merchant ships were now treated in the ports of British India on the same footing as British ships.

The Moresby treaty by cutting off the slave-trade with Christians and British India left the main slave-trade with the Middle East renewed and invigorated, and gave its main nodal points, Zanzibar to the south, and Muscat to the north, a new significance. As to whether Said was sincere in his intentions to uphold the Moresby treaty, Commodore Nourse, commander at the Cape Station, who visited Zanzibar in HMS *Andromache* in January 1822, noted that

> the Imam of Muscat had issued the most positive orders forbidding the traffic in slaves with any Christian whatsoever; and from all the intelligence I could obtain those orders had been most strictly attended to by the Governor of Zanzibar.[28]

Captain Owen arriving at Pate in January 1824 found that its inhabitants were relying on the protection of the Imam of Muscat under the Moresby treaty, and that the Governor of Lamu had published the Imam's orders authorizing seizure of vessels carrying slaves southward of Kilwa and Cape Delgado.[29] These were auspicious tokens of the Sultan's good intentions, but Owen was not optimistic. Had not the Sultan exclaimed to him when Owen visited Muscat in December 1823, that 'to put down the slave-trade with Mahometans ... was a stone too heavy for him to lift without some strong hand to help him.' According to Owen, the Sultan's power and purse were upheld by this infamous commerce:

His soldiers and his servants are supplied by it, and Persia and
some parts of North India pay him immense sums annually for
slaves to be cut for the seraglios and other faithful services for
which those from the East Coast are held in the highest esteem.[30]

Owen was perhaps in the best position to comment on the efficacy of the
Moresby treaty and probity of the Sultan's intentions. Owen was in the
midst of a great undertaking – a complete hydrographical survey of the
shores and waters of Eastern Africa. It was a task which occupied him
throughout the years 1822-25 and which gave him an intimate
knowledge of, and familiarity with, the East African coast not
commanded hitherto by any other Englishman.

Captain W.F. Owen's *Narrative* is an early nineteenth-century
account of the first great hydrographical survey of the eastern coast of
Africa. It is a maddening, but fascinating book, a compilation by various
contributors – Captains Owen and Vidal, and Lieutenant Boteler – and
running through it all is the capricious hand (nay fist) of an erratic
editor. Events are so decanted back and forth, chronologically, in the
Narrative as to make its time sequence confusing in the extreme. The
exploits of the brig *Barracouta* and frigate *Leven* are presented in such
muddled fashion as to make it most difficult to follow their respective
courses. Captain Owen, at an important juncture in the expedition, slips
off to Bombay quite unannounced and so unobtrusively that the incident
goes almost unnoticed in the *Narrative*. The various contributors to this
compilation say their piece without introduction and take their leave
without notice or permission. These sailormen, in their toings and
froings, provide a whirligig experience for the reader who would follow
them on their travels in the western Indian Ocean, through the pages of
the *Narrative*. The latter is without index, itinerary, or an overall map
showing routes traversed during the course of the survey. However,
despite these limitations, the *Narrative* remains a veritable cornucopia of
information on the history of the East African coast for the early
nineteenth century.

Owen was instructed by the Admiralty 'to proceed with all convenient
expedition to the Cape of Good Hope', and to survey the coast from the
Keiskamma River (northern boundary of Cape Colony) up to, and
inclusive of, Delagoa Bay and the rivers debouching into that bay. He
was then to survey the coast from the northern point of the Portuguese
sphere up to Cape Guardafui, where the survey was to terminate. If the
condition of his ships permitted, Owen was also to survey the numerous

shoals and islands between Madagascar and the mainland. A second set of instructions however, dated 20 May 1823 and received while embarked on his survey, directed Owen to include within it the shores of 'Arabia Felix, where grave discrepancies' in existing charts made navigation exceedingly hazardous, and he was also to complete the survey of the West Coast of Africa on his way home to England. He was given considerable latitude to vary his plans as necessary, but the Admiralty left him in no doubt that the main object of his expedition was to complete successfully an up-to-date hydrographical survey of the eastern coast of Africa and its adjacent waters.

Owen beat into Simon's Bay, at the Cape, on 8 July 1822, with the *Leven, Barracouta* and *Cockburn,* having survived the 'doubling' of the Cape and narrowly escaping the tail of Bellows Rock (a lesson for him on the inadequacy of existing charts) and with the *Cockburn's* coppers burst from the boisterous gales of the south Atlantic. At the Cape, Owen set his chronometers, but even here, at 'the most frequented and prominent cape in the world, considerable discrepancies were found to exist in its reputed situation'. The dangerous waters of the Cape were soon demonstrated to Owen, when, within two weeks of his arrival, ten vessels were driven ashore there, largely the result of their being anchored by the chain cable which caused the 'sudden and violent shocks from the strokes of the sea, which either breaks over her, or causes her to plunge through the waves, instead of riding over them'. The chain cable was the cause of many shipwrecks at Table Bay, and Owen recommended the use of the hempen chain with a few links of cable at the anchor end, so as to enable the vessel to ride the sea with buoyancy and ease.

After completing his survey of the Cape waters, Owen commenced that of the coast between the Keiskamma River and Delagoa Bay. While sailing along the shores of Cape Colony, 'Perhaps the most diversified and fertile in the world, with a climate unequalled, abundantly watered by extensive rivers, and the soil already fit for the plough', he could not but wonder that the people of Great Britain 'should prefer emigrating to the almost barren sands of Swan river (Western Australia) to resting at one half distance upon such a land of promise as this'. It was at this juncture that there commenced the practice of separating the vessels throughout the survey, often for long periods, which makes the task of delineating the course of the expedition so difficult. The *Barracouta* on leaving the Cape proceeded to survey the coastline, newly acquired by the British, from Port Elizabeth to the Keiskamma, while the *Leven* and *Cockburn* commenced a survey of the Delagoa Bay area and the rivers debouching into it. The account of the *Barracouta's* journey along the coast between Keiskamma and Delagoa Bay describes that coast as 'one of the most varied and interesting that can possibly be imagined, presenting every diversity that rich hills and fertile meadows can produce'. The entrance to the River Kye, at St John's, was one of the most 'extraordinary and picturesque entrances in the world', forming by its abrupt and perpendicular heights 'a natural lock, wanting only a flood-gate to make it a perfect wet-dock', but the work of depopulation carried on with savage rapidity by the merciless and destructive conquests of that 'tyrannical monster named Chaka', and his bloody proceedings, promised soon to leave the whole beautiful country, from the River St John to Inhamban, 'totally desolate'. Owen reflected

> The state of these countries, which have scarcely intercourse with civilized nations, is a direct proof in refutation of the theories of poets and philosophers who represent the ignorance of the savage as frugality and temperance and his stupid indolence as a laudable contempt for wealth. How different are the facts! We ever found uncultivated man a composition of cunning, treachery, drunkenness, and gluttony.[31]

Owen was much impressed by Delagoa Bay, as it might offer an effective base to counter French activities in the Mozambique Channel and their influence at the Comoro Islands, Madagascar and Zanzibar. While preparing an excellent and finely delineated map of the Delagoa Bay area, the dreaded fever carried off almost two-thirds of Owen's crew. The other two vessels, *Leven* and *Cockburn,* after returning to the Cape for revictualling, sailed for Madagascar and the Comoros. The latter cluster of islands, Johanna especially, impressed Owen. The scenery was on a grand scale, with mountains capped with verdure, the deep glens and luxuriant vales, and the inhabitants 'delicate, yet well-formed, with complexion lighter than mulatto, and their carriage exhibiting more of the courtier's grace than the manly firmness of independence'. One of their chiefs paraded under the name of 'Lord Rodney', indicative of earlier British contact – a beneficent one it would appear, for according to Owen, 'when British vessels have been wrecked on these islands they have shown the crews every kindness and attention'.

In January and February 1823, the *Leven* and *Barracouta* rendezvoused in Mozambique harbour, a deep inlet of the sea, with anchorage perfectly safe in the worst weather ... the city is formed of coral, very low and narrow, and scarcely one mile and half length. It is situated nearly in the centre of the inlet ... its fort of St. Sebastion ... yet remains a proud monument of ancient Portuguese enterprise. It is of a quadrangular form, and mounts upwards of eighty cannon of various calibre, ages, and nations ... The garrison consisted of about two hundred black soldiers, habited in the Sepoy costume ... the governor's palace is an extensive stone building apparently of great age, with a flat leaden rock and large square court in the centre. The streets in the city are narrow, although the houses are generally lofty and well constructed, but as the place itself is fast sinking into insignificance, so the finest of its buildings are falling rapidly into decay.[32]

Mozambique was now reduced from its ancient wealth and viceregal splendour 'to the almost forgotten seat of desolation and poverty'. Its population of about six thousand was made up of native Portuguese, Creole Portuguese from Goa, Banyans from India, free coloured people and, most numerous of all, resident slaves:

there are no beasts of burden at Mozambique, all the work is done by slaves who, however, lead a very idle life on account of the general stagnation of trade. During the heat of the day, the higher classes, and some even at other times, never appear out of doors except in their hammocks, wherein, stretched at full length, they may be seen lolling in all the listless languor of tropical indolence.[33]

In the spring of 1823, the *Leven* and *Barracouta* returned to their survey work at Delagoa Bay, to find a number of other English vessels there – mostly whalers, but also including the vessel of an English merchant, Henry Nourse (brother of Commander Nourse of the Cape command), seeking openings for trade. It was at this stage that Owen arranged with the Portuguese at Quelimane for a joint expedition up the Zambezi to Senna in the following July (a venture probably suggested by Lord Charles Somerset, Governor of Cape Colony, in 1822). The expedition then adjourned to the Cape for further provisioning. In the summer of 1823, work was resumed at Delagoa Bay, and also commenced at Sofala; Captain Vidal, of the *Barracouta*, noted that at Quelimane, a town with population of about 2800 persons, built on an unhealthy marsh, there was the 'greatest mart for slaves on the east coast' and that

> from eleven to fourteen slave-vessels come annually from Rio Janeiro to this place, and return with from four to five hundred slaves each on an average ... To contain the slaves collected for sale, every Portuguese house has an extensive yard, or enclosure called a Barracon, generally surrounded by a lofty brick-wall, on the inside of which a shed is erected for their accommodation.[34]

At Sofala, famed of old as the outlet for the gold trade from the interior, there was much disappointment – the 'total failure of our expectation' – for the town consisted of only 'a paltry fort very small, in the true Moorish style, and surmounted by thirteen honey-combed guns of different calibres, the largest not being more than a six-pounder, and a few miserable mud-huts, the almost deserted abode of poverty and vice'. Vidal was stirred to remark 'But not only here, every place in Africa and India subject to the Portuguese has withered beneath the iron hand of oppression. Lust and avarice were their idols, and never gods had more devoted worshippers.'

In October 1823, all three vessels rendezvoused at Mozambique where 'Seven or eight vessels, were in this port to take cargoes of slaves to Brazil; one of about 600 tons being fitted for 1200 of these miserable wretches.' It was at this stage that the *Barracouta* and the sloop *Albatross* (brought up from the Cape as replacement for the *Cockburn*) commenced a survey of the coast from Pate to Mozambique, while Owen proceeded to Bombay in accordance with further Admiralty instructions of 20 May 1823, which directed him there to obtain particulars of Smee's voyage of 1812, and that in order to survey the southern coast of Arabia, he should obtain letters of introduction to Said, ruler of Oman, from the government of Bombay, so 'that we might procure such passports from him (and interpreters) as would enable us to proceed peaceably and without risk along the shores of Arabia and Eastern Africa'. It was while refitting and provisioning at Bombay that Owen was inducted into the politics of the Swahili coast. A delegation from the Mazrui (ruling clan at Mombasa) was then at Bombay, seeking British protection and support in their resistance to the claims of Sultan Said of Muscat, their nominal overlord. Although the delegation returned to Mombasa, their appeal for help unrequited, Owen remained mindful of it, and this would have weighty consequences later, when he visited Mombasa.

Owen entered the harbour of Muscat on Christmas Day 1823. The small cove was filled with a forest of dhows, and presented a most interesting and animated scene; every height was surmounted by a fortification, a powerful reminder of former Portuguese prowess when they held this strongpoint.

> The town is situated on the beach, at the foot of a high hill, which completely encircles it, leaving but one pass into the country by the Sudoaf Road: in this gap, and round a noxious muddy pool, numerous miserable mat-hovels are erected by the native Arabs, as they are not allowed to build anything more substantial for fear they should cover the advance of an enemy.[35]

Following a felicitous exchange of gifts, an Arabic copy of the Scriptures from Owen, with which the Sultan appeared to be much gratified, 'not from any thoughts of conversion, but because they are declared by the Koran to be holy books containing God's word'; and from the Sultan, a truly munificent gift, a superb sword, 'an emblematic offering of his creed – its blade of Damascus steel and its handle richly mounted with gold', there then took place further ceremonies. The Sultan made a ceremonial visit to Owen's ship, during which the pigs on board, removed to avoid giving offence to Muslims, made such a noise that

> It was enough to alarm every Mussalman on shore or afloat, for the morning was still, and echoes reverberated from the surrounding hills as if animated with the vulgar desire of offending the religious prejudices of the natives, but bigotry is not amongst the vices of Muskat, and the scene afforded as much amusement to the Mahometans as to ourselves.[36]

Provided with pilot and interpreter by the Sultan, Owen weighed anchor from Muscat on 1 January 1824, and beat down along the barren and verdureless coast of Arabia, past rugged mountains edging the shoreline, ragged villages 'whose tents had a wild and wretched appearance'. Sometimes there was passed the tomb of a sheikh – a holy man revered in the neighbourhood, sometimes the forlorn ruins of a Portuguese fort – a landmark for sailors at sea. Survey work was hampered by the failing of the inshore wind or by difficult approaches. Off Cape Marbat, Owen was taken extremely ill from a stroke of the 'blat', the pernicious land wind peculiar to this coast, which produces rheumatic fever and 'affections of the bones', and drew from Owen the comment, 'Arabia Felix was the most unhappy looking coast we had visited'. By January 1824, Owen was at Socotra and again found sailing directions very faulty; much correction of course was needed. Taking his bearings at Cape Guardafui, 'noble sentinel of the northern tip of the Horn of Africa', he proceeded down the Somali coast, noting the work of the Portuguese in the times of their greatness – their attempt to cut a channel across the peninsula of Hafoon, a task never completed owing to the return of the Arabs to this coastline.

Mogadishu, the only town of importance on the coast, at a distance was rather imposing, but less so on a nearer approach. Its inhabitants appeared 'extremely jealous of strangers'. Nor was Owen much taken with Lamu, a town

> built in the pure Arabic style, that is crammed together as close as space will allow, so as to admit of a narrow and always dirty alley intervening. It has much commerce, and is populous, being decidedly one of the best stations upon the coast. In the centre is a large fortress, about one hundred yards square, and surrounded by walls from forty to fifty high.[37]

On 7 February 1824 Owen arrived at Mombasa to be greeted by the sight of a British flag – 'a home-made jack' – hoisted over its fort, and Said's fleet riding at anchor in a blockade of the port. To understand how this came about, it is necessary to retrace the events consequent on the arrival of the *Barracouta* at Mombasa on 3 December 1823. Lieutenant Boteler records of this visit that there were no bounds to the curiosity of the inhabitants of Mombasa as to his own person, nor to the intensity of their plea to be taken under the 'protecting shade' of the British flag. While waiting the official ceremony of introduction to the leaders of Mombasa, Boteler's 'sword, hat, and every article of apparel, underwent as strict an examination as the short time I had to wait for the Sheikh's nephew would admit'. The two main leaders who met Boteler were the Sheikh – a venerable-looking man – who, however, would not, or could not, do anything without the sanction of the other leader, a Swahili chief who was apparently the main power at Mombasa. The latter was a striking personality, who spoke broken Portuguese and held the title of 'hereditary Prince of Maleenda and Portuguese Consul'. 'His silvery white moustaches afforded a strange contrast to the darkness of his complexion, which differed but little from that of the negro.' During these next few days these two personages and their followers passionately pleaded with Boteler and Captain Vidal to take Mombasa under British protection, and for this purpose the Sheikh had already produced an English ensign, the flag witnessed by Owen on arrival at Mombasa. Boteler could not but admire the audacity of their plea, and marvel at this 'ragged set' at Mombasa, who, although immured in poverty and wretchedness, were yet making ostentatious show of arms. These were the same people who had successfully challenged the Portuguese when the latter were in the plenitude of their power; they had firmly resisted the whole force of the Imam of Muscat, and were still regarded with 'fear and admiration by the inhabitants of the whole coast'. Boteler was also extravagant in his admiration of Mombasa itself. As a strong point, Fort Jesus was unparalleled on the whole East African coast:

> A massive portion of rock elevated some feet above that which forms the surface of the island, serves as an excellent foundation for the substantial castle that the Portuguese erected for its defence. It is cut down so as to form a deep and broad moat, while the masonry above rises as a continuance of the rock, from which, until you are very near, it cannot be distinguished. The whole exhibits the firm union of natural strength, cemented by the ingenuity of man.[38]

The Arabs had allowed this fine fortification to sink into dilapidation, 'so wretched is their masonry, that their attempts to repair the Portuguese work have in general taken away from its strength ... The fine tank, which once contained enough water for two or three years, cannot now be traced without great difficulty.' As to Mombasa's strategic importance as a great port, Boteler's eulogies anticipate those of Lord Kitchener, at the end of the century:

> Perhaps there is not a more perfect harbour in the world than Mombas. It possesses good riding-ground at the entrance, sheltered by an extensive reef on either side; an anchorage, which, from its vicinity to the coast, constantly enjoys the sea breeze; and a steep rocky shore, in many places rendering wharfs unnecessary, and in other forming a shelving sandy strand, where vessels can be hauled up and careened, favoured by a tide rising twelve or fourteen feet ... nature having formed it like a huge castle,

encircled by a moat ... Facility of navigation constitutes one of its greatest recommendations; as, by a proper attention to the monsoons and currents, voyages both to and from Mombas may be effected with safety and certainty at all seasons ... our holding Mombas as a military station would be one of the most effectual steps towards the entire civilization of Eastern Africa and the suppression of the slave-trade.[29]

These were powerful arguments for acquiring Mombasa, but Vidal withstood them and also the blandishment and entreaties of its chiefs for British protection, and he departed Mombasa for Zanzibar on 7 December 1823, leaving them to await 'the expected arrival of Captain Owen as their last resort'. Before he arrived Said's fleet appeared off Mombasa and blockaded it. However, further attempts to subjugate Mombasa were stayed by Owen's arrival there on 7 February 1824. Owen was plied with the same urgent entreaties for British protection, as had been Captain Vidal. Sheikh Suliman ('an old dotard who had out-lived every passion except avarice') and the notables of the town offered tempting prizes to Owen in return for British protection: the formal cession of Mombasa and the neighbouring coastline as far south as Pangani, and the islands of Lamu, Pate and Pemba (which the Mazrui sought to recover with Owen's help). A convention between Owen and Suliman and the council of chiefs confirmed this cession, and in return the Mazrui were confirmed in their hereditary claims as rulers of Mombasa, and there were clauses as to control of revenue, and permission for British subjects to trade at Mombasa and in the interior, and, finally, the slave-trade at Mombasa was to be abolished. A further gain for Owen was that orders arrived from the Imam of Muscat placing his fleet at Mombasa under Owen's direction. With all this accomplished, Owen departed Mombasa on 14 February 1824, leaving Lieutenant Reitz in charge, and taking with him Prince Mombarrok (Mbaruk) and followers, and with the Imam's fleet of five ships accompanying him to Pemba (Owen neatly disposed of Said's fleet by directing it in an anti-slave-trade campaign on the coast). Pleasant stopovers at Pemba and Zanzibar were marred only by reports from Reitz at Mombasa, that the inhabitants there were a fickle lot, forgetful of promises so lately made to end the slave-trade, and were also placing restrictions on British movement at Mombasa.

Owen was now rounding out his work on the East African coast. He says little about Zanzibar. Vidal, who visited there in December 1823, had been much impressed with it:

> A most valuable possession of the Imaum of Muskat's on account
> of its abundant produce of grain and sugar ... In no place were we
> furnished with refreshments so cheap, and of such excellent
> quality, as at Zanzibar ... a dollar upwards of two dozen fowls ...
> sugar of an excellent quality at two pence a pound, very superior
> rice at a penny, and a great variety of fruits in proportion. Bullocks
> of the humped breed, of a moderate size, ... at five dollars a head,
> and sheep of the Tartar kind very cheap.[40]

Owen left Zanzibar on 23 February 1824, with Prince Mombarrok still on
board, and proceeded southwards. Off 'Broken Hills' (Picos Fragos) on
the Mozambique coast, the *Leven* rejoined the *Barracouta* on 2 March
1824, and thence they proceeded to the port of Mozambique where the
two vessels remained until 4 April 1824. There followed a further
examination of the coasts of Madagascar and Delagoa Bay by the *Leven*
prior to visiting Mauritius, where the *Andromache* under Commander
Nourse also arrived. At Mauritius, Prince Mombarrok was presented to
the governor, Sir G. Lowry Cole, and then conveyed back to Mombasa in
the *Wizard*. From Mauritius, Owen sent off 29 sheets of charts to the
Admiralty, before proceeding to survey the eastern side of Madagascar.
He then returned to Mombasa (stopping over at Mozambique from 3 to
11 October 1824), where he arrived on 23 November 1824, rejoining the
Barracouta which had arrived there on 23 October. Owen was greeted
with the sad news that Reitz had died of fever on 29 May that year. He
had been replaced by Midshipman Phillips, who in turn was succeeded
three months later by another midshipman, James Barker Emery. In the
interval between Reitz's death and the arrival of the *Barracouta*,
Commodore Nourse had also been at Mombasa and had promoted two
midshipmen, Emery and Wilson, to the rank of Lieutenant; Emery to
replace Reitz, and Wilson to fill the vacancy created by Emery's
promotion. Events at Mombasa during the summer of 1824 are obscure.
It would appear that measures taken by Phillips against slavers, and the
seizure of a slave dhow, caused great apprehension among the Arabs. On
Owen's arrival at Mombasa, further measures were taken against slavers
– the shipping and banishment to the Seychelles of an African involved
in slaving, and the punishment of a slave-master for re-enslaving freed
slaves. This high-handed action on the part of Owen is in contrast to what
he concedes in the *Narrative* as mild treatment of slaves by Arab masters:

The condition of the slaves belonging to the Arabs at Mombas is highly creditable to their humanity; they cannot always be distinguished from their masters, as they are allowed to imitate them in dress and other particulars.[41]

By December 1824, Owen was on the last lap of his survey. The *Barracouta,* proceeding to the Somali coast to survey the labyrinth of rocks and islands between the Juba River and Kwyhoo Bay, was joined there by the *Leven* from the Seychelles, in early January 1825. At Brava, Owen acceded to the request of a leading chief for British protection in return for his promise to work for the abolition of the slave-trade. The *Leven* then rejoined the *Barracouta* and *Albatross* at Mombasa, this being Owen's third visit there. He, now in council with local notables, formed 'many salutary laws for the government of the natives'. He promised the people of Mombasa that he would request the Imam of Muscat to return to them the island of Pemba; and later when at Zanzibar from 2 to 10 February 1825, with added authority owing to the recent death of Commodore Nourse, he

made necessary arrangements with Said Mahommed, of Muskat, for preserving the peace of north-east Africa until the British Government should have come to a determination respecting the acceptance of the territory, and until then no force or illegal interference should be attempted by the Imaum's officers.[42]

After surveying the Seychelles and sending off to England some 42 sheets of charts, the expedition moved southwards in early April, and from then to early June 1825 there were further visits to Madagascar and Mozambique. At the latter place Owen attended a grand levee and ball in celebration of the King of Portugal's birthday, and the ceremony and scenes witnessed on the occasion stirred Owen into sundry and adverse comments on the effects of miscegenation of the Portuguese with other races. During his final visit to Mauritius, 15 June to 19 July 1825, Owen received news that his protectorate over Mombasa had been set aside by the British government. Lord Bathurst directed that no further steps be taken to extend a British protectorate there. At Mauritius, at Governor Cole's bidding, Owen drew up his account of 'the Slave Trade, Portuguese, French, and Arab, all up the coast as he himself had observed it'. In view of Owen's passionate concern to end the slave-trade and his deep interest in the subject, the account is disappointing: it is meagre and slight, perhaps compiled under hasty last minute pressure, prior to his departure from Mauritius.

There followed further examination and survey of Madagascar coasts, especially the 'dangerous assemblage of reefs' near St Mary's, and this was interspersed with much social life at main ports. The *Leven*, *Barracouta* and *Albatross* rendezvoused at Delagoa Bay on 28 August 1825. Here, under threat of armed action, Owen obtained the release of a British trading vessel, the *Eleanor*, which the Portuguese had seized. The ravages of the Hottentots in the area, and the starvation and slavery consequent on this, were noted and also the activities of French slavers from Bourbon at Delagoa Bay. The three vessels proceeded to the Cape. During their sojourn there, 28 September to 9 November 1825, the great series of charts on the East African coast was completed, and with this in hand and their vessels refitted, they quitted the Cape. In the course of their return journey to England, and prior to their arrival at Spithead, on 23 August 1826, the expedition surveyed the west coast of Africa, in pursuance of the instructions received while at the Seychelles in December 1824.

Owen's expedition had been absent from England five years, during which it had traced

> about thirty thousand miles of coast line, which was transferred by measure paper, occupying nearly three hundred large sheets ... In the course of our service, we were called upon in numerous instances to correct the errors of former navigators, and fix the latitudes and longitudes of places that had not before been determined.[43]

This great and strenuous work had been achieved at a high cost in human lives. The many victims who had fallen to the 'melancholy effects of the Delagoa Bay fever' were a heavy toll to pay for the achievement of Owen's great hydrographical survey. As a result of the latter however, the East African coast was now charted. The elephantine sheets forwarded to the Admiralty encompassed cartographical reality, where hitherto speculation and rule-of-thumb had served as guides. There was nothing in the way of a hydrographical survey, or such a mine of information on the East African coast, produced during the remainder of the nineteenth century, comparable to Owen's work, except perhaps, that of Captain C. Guillain's *Documents sur l'Histoire, la Géographie, et le Commerce de la Côte Orientale d'Afrique* (Paris, 1956), and this is but a pale shadow of what Owen had achieved. Owen, however, as also Henry Salt, did not start from a *tabula rasa*. He had available to him an accumulated body of information on the East African coast: Portuguese maps, the *Indian Directory*, Dalrymple and Blankett's works, Salt's *Voyage*, the practical knowledge and experience of previous seamanship and the log-books of East Indiamen – a record going back to the time of Captains Every and Kidd at the end of the seventeenth century.

That the *Leven, Barracouta* and *Albatross* were able to rendezvous, to arrange their meetings and conjunctures over a vast area of waters and coastlines, as far afield as Muscat and the Cape, and Madagascar, Mauritius and the Seychelles, with such surprising accuracy and timing, bespeaks a familiarity with previous knowledge of those waters, not fully intimated in the *Narrative*. Nevertheless, in its precise detail of inshore waters, rivers and inlets, sightings of headlands and coasts, the sounding of waters, warning of reefs and shoals, Owen's hydrographical survey is an astonishing exhibition of dedicated labour and skill. There are some imbalances. Delagoa Bay, Mozambique and Mombasa are charted in detail, but Zanzibar less so, perhaps because it was already a well-known port and entrepôt off the East African coast – the possession of Said of Muscat, whose emissary there gave a less welcoming reception to Owen than he received at other points in his East African survey.

Sundry errors have been pointed out in Owen's work: confusion as to the designation of 'Kilwa' – was it one, two, or half a dozen places? Also Zanzibar was placed five miles west of its true position, and his chart of its waters failed to indicate the coral reefs lying between it and Tumbatu Island – an error which nearly brought the American vessel, the *Peacock*, to disaster, a few years later.

Turning from Owen's hydrographical survey to his *Narrative*, we find a work of equally fine high art, despite its confused organization and capricious editor. Its vivid and variegated presentation of life on the East African coast at the time of Owen's visit, with many facets of geography and ethnography, are portrayed in pithy language and form. There is much historical lore, from the bygone times of the Portuguese, from the legacy of their occupation of the East African coast over several centuries, and that of the Arabs, before and after it; the sketches of towns and ports, trade and peoples – African, Arab, Portuguese and Swahili – are all so set out in graphic detail and with anecdotal charm, as to provide an admirable introduction for the reader who would cross its threshold and enter the East African scene of the early nineteenth century.

Owen was severe in his denunciation of the 'slipshod and tenuous nature' of Portuguese rule, as witnessed at Delagoa Bay and other points on their East African coast. The Portuguese, when they took possession of that coast, were perhaps as civilized a people as any in the world, yet in every instance they had destroyed what little civilization they found, and had introduced their own 'vices and follies'. The effect was seen in the dishonesty and petty cunning of natives in the neighbourhood of Portuguese settlements. Many natives had also quitted the coast, goaded to desperation by the cruelty and arbitrary exactions of the Portuguese: 'it is probable that the Galla and many other savage tribes were thus driven from the sea-coast, with an unconquerable aversion to white men, or ... to any other people with straight hair'. The Portuguese had also persecuted the Arabs for their faith, but this was too strongly rooted to be driven out by 'violence or persuasion'. The Portuguese in East Africa had one objective, 'to enrich themselves in as short a time as possible'. There was constant reminder of their decadence in the crumbling remains of the grandeur and power of their ancestors. They were always deploring their present decline, but when any proposal was made by which they might improve their condition, 'one answer only is ever returned, "Non pode" – and a shrug of the shoulders settles the point at once'.

Indolence may be taken as the motto of all the Portuguese in Africa, they ... spin out their days in listless apathy, and die in early age, unmourned and unregretted ... the Arabs, who were the contempt of their forefathers, take every opportunity of repaying it to the present generation.[44]

Owen's strictures on the Portuguese should be taken with reservation. It was fashionable for many Englishmen of his time to decry Portuguese administration overseas as of a decadent nature, although mixing this at times with grudging encomiums. Despite his strictures, Owen sapiently remarked that it was doubtful 'whether civilization can be imported, whether it is not a spontaneous growth which must first be planted by the hand of an all-just and wise Creator ... to try at once to introduce civilization ... is like breaking the shell of the chrysalis in order to extract the dormant moth. It is one of the operations of nature which time alone can accomplish, and which any hasty or premature attempt serves only to destroy.'

2· The French, Zanzibar and Muscat

French involvement in the East African world dates from their occupation of the islands of Bourbon and Île de France in 1664 and 1715, respectively. Under an able governor, La Bourdonnais, appointed in 1735, sugar cultivation was encouraged, and the islands became one of the main sugar-producing areas of the world, comparable to the British West Indies and, like the latter, drawing their labour from Africa. The Seychelles, a group of islands farther north annexed by France in 1744, also depended on the same source for labour for its prosperous spice plantations.

Following the withdrawal of the Portuguese to the south of the Ruvuma River by the early eighteenth century, the French roamed unhindered along the northern strip of the East African coast, and for the remainder of the century were the main European traders on that littoral. In their search for slaves they ranged as far north as the Juba River.[1] A French trader, Morice, conceived a plan in 1776 of placing the slave-trade on a regular basis by acquiring from the Sultan of Kilwa the exclusive right to purchase 1000 slaves annually from there at a price of 20 piastres apiece, and a promise that 'No other but he shall be allowed to trade for slaves, whether French, Dutch, Portuguese, etc … until he shall have received his slaves and has no wish for more.' Under Morice's scheme the export of slaves from Kilwa would ultimately rise to many thousands a year, and at a stabilized price would play an important part in French commerce in the western Indian Ocean.

Morice's scheme never got under way. It smacked too much of restriction and monopoly, and French authorities at Port Louis were averse to alienating the Sultan of Oman who claimed sovereignty over the East African coast. Negotiations were already under way with him to recruit labourers from his East African ports. Morice's scheme seemed unnecessary. An attempt to revive it by Joseph Crassons de Medeuil in

1784–85 and by another French trader, Dallons, in 1799, came to nothing. The French revolutionary wars had now intervened, and the law of 1794 which decreed freedom for slaves in French possessions overseas voided any arrangements that Crassons and Dallons might make.

The law of 1794 was fiercely opposed by local authorities at Bourbon and Île de France, and the slave-trade continued to flourish there. Compensation, which might have reconciled planters to the loss of their slaves, was contrary to the spirit of the 'Declaration of Rights of Man and the Citizen' for men were 'naturally free', and slaves must enter into their inheritance at once, without question of payment of compensation to erstwhile owners. An attempt in 1796 to enforce abolition on the islanders was successfully resisted, and the French government, engrossed in the struggle in Europe, tamely acquiesced in this non-compliance. The slave-trade with the two islands continued practically uninterrupted. At the end of the eighteenth century their slave population stood at over 100,000, as against a white and coloured population of 20,000. When in 1807 the French concluded a treaty of 'Amity and Commerce' with the Sultan of Oman according them favoured nation privileges in his dominions, a further boost was given to French trade – including the slave-trade (for Napoleon in 1802 had reversed the law of 1794) – on the East African coast, and French slavers for the next few years roamed freely there, seeking slaves. At Kilwa and Zanzibar French influence was strong, and Austin Bissel, first lieutenant on the *Daedalus* in Commodore Blankett's voyage of 1798–99, observed that many inhabitants at Zanzibar spoke French; and James Prior in 1811 noted the same of the inhabitants of Kilwa and Zanzibar. The French maintained a 'constant intercourse in slaves, ivory and gold dust'. An English presence on the East African coast was scarcely discernible at the time.

The situation began to change following the British occupation of the Seychelles and Île de France in 1810; and when by the Treaty of Paris (1814) Britain gained Île de France (Mauritius) and its dependencies – the Seychelles and former French ports in Madagascar – she was faced with the task of wrestling with the slave-trade that flourished in these new possessions. The slave population in Île de France stood at 60,000, and in the Seychelles at 2500. Although Mauritius was now a British colony with penalties against the slave-trade, up to 4000 slaves were still landed there yearly by 1820 and, it was claimed, with the acquiescence of the governor, Sir Robert Farquhar.

Farquhar did not see eye to eye with humanitarians and abolitionists at home in their enthusiasm for an anti-slave-trade campaign. He was much absorbed at the time in gaining Madagascar as a British possession and in inducing planters from Mauritius to settle there: an altogether more important task than attacking the slave-trade which provided planters with necessary labour. When the French stalwartly and successfully sustained their claim to their possessions in Madagascar on the ground that these had not been specifically referred to in the Treaty of Paris, Farquhar perforce had to confine his attention to Mauritius and the slave-trade there which was under continued attack from abolitionists at home. He was in an anomalous position: sympathetic to the needs of the Mauritius planters for a stable labour force and, like many British officials with long experience in the East, unable to get excited over an anti-slavery campaign, he was nevertheless forced by government and public pressure from home to take stringent measures against the slave-trade. Thus he obtained a treaty from Radama of Madagascar, whereby that ruler was to end the 'sale or transfer' of slaves throughout all his dominions. Even this, and further concessions from Radama, and an understanding with the French at Bourbon to co-operate in ending the slave-trade, failed to save Farquhar from zealots at home who were successful, after a prolonged debate in the House of Commons in 1826, in obtaining the appointment of a body – the *Eastern Inquiry* – under Major Colebrooke, to report on the slave-trade at Mauritius. Its recommendations – especially that of immediate abolition of slavery, and its scathing denunciation of the treatment of slaves in Mauritius – raised a storm of protest from the planters there. Despite their challenge of the Inquiry's claims of mistreatment of slaves, and Farquhar's defence of their interests (he was now retired to England and was a Member of Parliament) they were unable to stave off abolition. The bitterness over this and the loss of their 70,000 slaves, was sweetened by compensation to the amount of two million pounds. An alternative source of labour was found by the planters of Mauritius in India, whence indentured labourers were obtained from the early 1840s onwards. Réunion, unhappily, following the abolition of slavery there in 1849, turned to an alternative form of labour which was little more than the slave-trade in disguise: the so-called *engagé* trade under which Africans from the mainland, Madagascar and Zanzibar were taken on board French, Arab and sometimes American vessels, under the ruse that they had signed on as labourers to serve in Réunion or the Comoros for a number of years. The French were meticulous in observing certain formalities and in seeing that a French official presided over the transaction of taking on board *engagés* – but this was merely a sop to the critics of the system. It was still the slave-trade despite this dressing up. There is little evidence that so-called *engagés* ever returned to their homeland. Rigby, British consul at Zanzibar, attempted to end the engagé system there, but his efforts brought bitter recrimination from the French. The Portuguese connived at the *engagé* trade which perpetrated some of the worst horrors of the more orthodox form of the slave-trade. It was not until the French obtained labourers from India, and the Portuguese were finally weaned from supporting the *engagé* system, that it ended.

The slave-trade at Mauritius and the *engagé* trade at Réunion forced British attention to the East African coast whence these slaves, or *engagés*, were obtained. The main culprits in the carrying trade, as in the earlier phase of the slave-trade, were the Omani Arabs. The trade in *engagés* was a useful adjunct to their main trade between Oman and Zanzibar. It would seem fair to say that, apart from the Napoleonic wars which first brought British seapower into the western Indian Ocean world, it was the slave-trade there which compelled the British to turn their attention to the East African coast.

Oman, on the extreme south-eastern corner of the Arabian peninsula, had fallen to the Portuguese when the great Albuquerque captured the ports of Muscat, Sohar and Karyat in 1508. Portuguese domination was a great blow to the Omani, a seafaring folk of the Ibadhi sect of Islam, fiercely independent under their elected ruler, the Imam. They chafed exceedingly under Portuguese control, and in the mid-seventeenth century, when Portuguese hold on the East was weakening, the Imam of Oman, Sultan bin Seif, roused his people to fight the hated unbeliever. In 1651, the Portuguese were driven out of Muscat, and soon from the whole Omani seaboard. By 1700 the Omani Arabs had gained control of the East African coast as far south as Kilwa. Despite their temporary recovery of Mombasa and other towns in 1727, the Portuguese were finally driven out by 1729. Thus by the early eighteenth century the coast from Mogadishu to the Ruvuma was under the dominion of the Imam of Oman. Constant civil war and internal dissension in Oman, however, prevented him from exercising control in East Africa, and this state of affairs continued under the Albusaid family who became rulers of Oman in 1744. The government of the various towns on the East African coast was entrusted to 'Walis' (governors) who, left to themselves and thrown back on their own resources, became almost independent rulers. East Africa throughout the eighteenth century remained a backwater – scarcely known to the outside world.

In Oman, at Muscat, in 1796, a parvenu line of rulers emerged who, while not carrying the exalted title of Imam, adopted the lesser one of 'Sayyid' (Prince). The first of these Sayyids of Muscat was by name Sultan ibn Ahmad, and soon there was added to the title of 'Sayyid' a further one of 'Sultan'; and when the British unwittingly continued to use the high honorific of 'Imam' (Hamerton, British consul at Zanzibar, used it throughout his career, 1841–57), the ruler of Oman sported three titles, although more usually addressed as 'Sultan' by the British and inhabitants of Muscat and Zanzibar. The first Sayyids of Muscat, commencing with Sultan ibn Ahmad (1796–1803), were faced with a long-drawn-out struggle with the Wahabi of Arabia. The latter, a branch of Sunni Islam, emerged in the eighteenth century from an alliance of Muhammad Abdel-Wahab, a religious reformer, and the al-Saud family. The Wahabi were fundamentalists of the strictest kind – desert Puritans – calling for a return to the word of the Koran as absolute, and for a purified form of Islam. Prayers were compulsory and during prayer time all other activity must cease; religious law must be rigorously applied, even to the amputation of limbs as punishment. Although the murder of their leader Abdul Aziz in 1803 temporarily abated their zeal, the Wahabi gave Mohammad Ali of Egypt and Sayyid Said of Muscat a difficult time.

Sayyid Said (1791–1856) succeeded to the throne jointly with his brother Salim in 1804, but when in 1806 a cousin, Badr, attempted to usurp the throne, Said assassinated him, thereby becoming virtual sole ruler, for Salim was a nonentity – a merely titular figure until his death in 1821. Said used the title 'Sayyid', for he was never elected to the purely religious office of Imam nor that of 'Sherif': not even a pilgrimage to Mecca in 1825 and his laying there 'the richest offering that had been made at the shrine of the Prophet for many years', could win for him those coveted warrants, nor was his title 'Sultan' strictly valid. There was no gainsaying Said's piety; he was punctilious in religious observances, the five daily washings and prayers, and holding the fast of Ramadan. With grave learning he held court twice daily and, in the manner of the East, listened attentively to the grievances of his subjects, dispensing even-handed justice. Said is described as courteous, of dignified bearing and benign countenance; according to Hart, he was tall, strong, noble-looking and greatly attached to the English. His interpreter, Captain Hassan, an Arab, was English educated and pro-

English. Behind Said's velvety exterior and oriental suavity lay an inner cruelty – 'the dagger neath the cloak'. As a mere lad of sixteen, on the instigation of his aunt, the Bintne Imam, he had stabbed to death his uncle, co-regent with her.[2] Said had an unerring instinct for self-preservation.

When he became ruler of Oman in 1806 the country was rent by internal strife, menaced on its landward side by the Wahabi, while at sea the Jawasmi pirates from the south-western side of the Persian Gulf made constant attacks on Omani shipping. Faced with these perils Said needed a powerful ally. His predecessor, Sultan ibn Ahmad, had made treaties with France and Britain during the Napoleonic wars when Muscat, from its strategic situation, had become of great importance, with both France and Britain seeking access to its harbour for sheltering and watering their ships. At first the balance seemed to tip in favour of the French, for a treaty of alliance of May 1807 between France and Persia provided for the cession to France of Bandar Abbas and Kharaq in the Persian Gulf, and this at a time when Britain was intent on keeping the French out of the Gulf – a vital communication link with India: had not the news of Nelson's victory been transmitted to India by way of Baghdad and the Gulf? The French treaty of alliance with Persia brought swift reaction from the British. Their agent at Muscat was ordered to persuade Said to dismiss Frenchmen there, and *pourparlers* were opened with him. Said tried to pursue a middle course, but it was increasingly apparent that mastery of the seas lay with the British. Said also had joint cause with the British in that the Jawasmi pirates were harrying British as well as Omani shipping. The Bombay government, intent on a punitive expedition against these predators, invited Said's co-operation in the venture. Said would supply pilots experienced in the Jawasmi cunning, and with knowledge of the geography of the Persian Gulf. The British would supply various ships and firepower. A joint British/Omani attack launched in early 1810 inflicted punishment on the wily Jawasmi, but further chastisement was necessary in 1819 before they were discouraged from their wonted pillaging and piratical habits.

Said was also soon freed from the Wahabi menace, for Mohammad Ali of Egypt had drawn off their sting. With his trouble in Oman now behind him, and friendship cemented with the British, Said could turn his attention to his claims to overlordship in East Africa. At Mombasa, the powerful ruling clan, the Mazrui, had renounced allegiance to him, and other East African towns soon followed this example of contumacy. At this important juncture Captain Owen's hydrographical survey expedition made its appearance in East African waters. The story of the establishment of Owen's protectorate over Mombasa is told elsewhere in this study. The protectorate had been an affront to the Imam of Muscat, Britain's 'faithful and cordial ally'. At the Cape, on his way home, Owen received further intimation of the disapproval with which his protectorate over Mombasa had been greeted by home authorities. The Admiralty regretted that he had devoted so much time and attention 'to matters foreign to the objects on which you were specially employed'. Nevertheless, Lieutenant Emery remained in charge at Mombasa for almost another two years, without any clear directive being given him for evacuation of that place by the British. Commodore Christian, Nourse's successor to the Cape command, cautioned the Admiralty as to the adverse effects of a British withdrawal: a fine base for action against the slave-trade would be lost, and the French would not be slow to move in and take possession of Mombasa if the British withdrew.

Emery was meanwhile faced with the ill-humour and chafing of the Mazrui chiefs, who felt that the arrangements made with Owen had not been fulfilled. These arrangements as they saw them were simple in the extreme; the British flag was to be run up 'in consideration of the half of the duties being paid to one Englishman who was to remain here, for no other purpose than to receive the money', and the island of Pemba should be restored to their territories. The Mazrui now repudiated Owen's treaty, for the island of Pemba had not been restored, and there was British interference in Arab local government, that is in the system of slavery as it prevailed at Mombasa. With no Admiralty backing to the contrary, the Cape command had no recourse but to order the evacuation of Mombasa, and on 25 July 1826, Captain Acland of the *Helicon* ordered the lowering of the British flag and the withdrawal of the British garrison from there.

Following the disavowal of a British protectorate over Mombasa by the British government and withdrawal of the British garrison, Said set about reasserting his control over that place. In 1826, now in possession of a fleet of seven ships, including the *Liverpool* (a monster, a ship-of-the-line of 1800 tons and of 74 guns), Said sent an ultimatum to the Mazrui demanding their submission. In the face of their refusal and recalcitrance, he moved in to the attack, and the red flag of Oman was again raised over the old fort at Mombasa on 7 January 1828. Several more expeditions against the Mazrui were necessary before their power was broken, and it was not until 1837 that Said had brought them finally to heel.

The affair with the Mazrui at Mombasa had brought Said into contact with Zanzibar. In 1828 he made a short visit there, followed up by one of longer duration in 1829. Like most visitors to that island he succumbed to its charms. Its lush tropical beauty, alluring verdure and abundance of 'all good things to eat' was in complete contrast to the stark dessication of Oman – it was a veritable Garden of Eden. An island, some 640 square miles in area, 25 miles off the African mainland, and with a deep protected harbour on its western and leeward side, it was eminently placed for trade and ease of access to the mainland. Zanzibar was ideally sited to be the capital of an East African empire. Lying in the path of the monsoons, with easy and regular communication with the widest points of the Indian Ocean world, it was a gathering place for many peoples. Contemporary accounts by European visitors to Zanzibar attest to Said's discernment in choosing it as his capital. Horace P. Putnam, visiting there in July 1847, and approaching it from the sea, was eloquent in his praise (apart from the city itself, which on closer view was less attractive. It was dirty, crowded and overrun with slaves):

> I never beheld a more beautiful sight than this island presented to the eye. As we sailed along the shores for miles we beheld nought but was the most grand to gaze upon; fruits of the most delicious kinds we saw in abundance. The cocoa nut and the orange tree were laden with their rich treasure, and almost sunk beneath their burden. The air was fresh and cool; which being scented with the rich perfumes of the shore or land breezes made it truly an acceptable treat to the mariner who had not seen the least particle of vegetable life for 70 days.[3]

With its soft sea breezes, palm-studded beaches, fresh water, green foliage, its tropical fruits and spices, its exceedingly fertile soil, Zanzibar was truly a virtual Shangri-La; and Pemba, its sister island – some 25 miles to the north-east, half its size and less well-known – was scarcely less attractive, as its Arab name *al-Hadhra* (Green Isle) would suggest.

Apart from its physical beauty and commercial advantages, Zanzibar was free from the fierce internecine squabbles which racked dynastic families in Oman and usually ended in the rule of the dagger; it was mercifully free from that stultifying atmosphere which closed in on the crater hell-hole that was Muscat. By 1832 Said began to build a palace at Zanzibar and to lay out clove and rice plantations there. In 1833 he appears to have moved part of his court to Zanzibar. However, according to Captain Hart at Zanzibar in early 1834, Said had not as yet fixed Zanzibar as his permanent place of residence, although 'it has been supposed that His Highness will some day make this his chief residence in preference to Muskat'. The idea of making Zanzibar his permanent home in preference to Muskat seems to have come in the late 1830s, and was a direct result of Said's concern over French encroachment on his East African empire. It was the reputed French activity on the northern line of the coast that caused Said to put in at Pate, in 1840, on his way back to Zanzibar from Muskat. It is more likely that 1840 rather than an earlier date should be fixed as the year when Said decided on Zanzibar as his permanent place of residence, although he continued to make visits to Muscat. These were, however, most trying for his health. According to Hamerton, writing in 1844,

> The Imam is at present 56 years old; and within the last three years he has been much broken and altered in every way from the effects of stimulating condiments which he is constantly taking in order to qualify him for the joys of the harem.[4]

These visits back to Muscat, if taken in one of the light swift dhows of his subjects, would have been speedy and less trying, but for prestige and reasons of state, and to carry his large retinue, Said used one of the large cumbersome ships of his private fleet. That he found these journeys increasingly an ordeal is evident in their increasing infrequency in the latter years of his reign. His death came during a journey back to Zanzibar from Muscat in 1857. He seems to have anticipated his end, for he had a coffin placed on board prior to departure.

Said's increasing attention to Zanzibar came when Omani commercial power in the western Indian Ocean was at its height, when American traders were resorting to Zanzibar in increasing numbers, and so also Indians – the latter bringing with them business acumen and trading links which Said could use. Arrived at Zanzibar, Said endeavoured to strengthen his position there by dynastic marriages; an offer of his hand to Queen Ranavolana of the Hovas in Madagascar in 1834 was unrequited. Her request for a $1000 coral necklace; her pothering a good deal before giving a firm answer – a refusal; her love letters written in English and read to Said by a scribe at his court, that were particularly lacking in endearments and passion (not surprising since she was expected to marry a ruler who was a spouse six dozen times over), all soured Said in the matter and instead he maintained agents at the

Comoros to report on diplomatic and commercial affairs there. Captain Hart in HMS *Imogene*, visiting Zanzibar in January 1834, commented on the brisk development consequent on Said's move to that place. The Frenchman, C. Guillain, at Zanzibar in 1838, described it as the commercial entrepôt of the coast. Said extended a warm welcome to foreign traders and gave them most favourable trading terms – the Americans were the first to enjoy the fruits of this.[5]

American contact with the East African coast goes back to the time when Captains Halsey, Wake, Farrel and May of New England joined the pirate fraternity based on Madagascar at the end of the seventeenth century. American whalers had been calling at Zanzibar since the early years of the nineteenth century; according to Hart, 'it is very common for the South Sea Whalers to come for refreshments.' American commercial dealings at Zanzibar, however, may be said to date from the visit there of Captain Forbes in the *Titus* in 1818, and that of his brother who disposed of a cargo of trade goods at Zanzibar three years later. Taking advantage of the presence of Said at Zanzibar in 1828, an American trader, Edmund Roberts, negotiated favourable trade terms with him, and in September 1833 a treaty was signed between Said and the Americans whereby the latter were granted terms including the privilege of trading for copal and ivory on the mainland – a monopoly otherwise held by Said, and not granted subsequently to other nations who entered into commercial treaties with him. The only tax imposed by Said on foreigners was a 5 per cent duty on cargo landed, or trans-shipped from one vessel to another, at any port in his dominions. There were no harbour or pilot dues.

By the mid-1830s some 33 American vessels were visiting Zanzibar annually, bringing with them American cottons for which there was soon a great demand, and in turn purchasing gum copal and cloves. In 1837 the Americans were allowed to open a consulate at Zanzibar, and in February 1838 the American president himself referred to the importance of diplomatic links with the Sultan. When an American trader, R.P. Waters, was appointed American consul at Zanzibar and entered into partnership with the Chief Customs Master Jairam Sewjee, a Hindu of the Battish sect, a formidable combination was set up. Jairam was all-powerful and directed business in the way of the Americans. American consuls at Zanzibar, unlike the British, tended to be traders, hard-headed businessmen with a vested interest in furthering their own commercial interests. They showed scant respect for oriental ways. Waters, a pious fundamentalist, could only regret that the Sultan was a non-Christian, and Ward, his successor as American consul, thought the Sultan 'crafty, deceitful, faithless, and only operated on by the display of physical powers'. By the mid-century the three main American firms at Zanzibar – Pingree and West (with Waters, ex-consul, as their agent), Shepard and Bertram, and Rufus Greene and Company – were altering their practice of having cargoes unloaded at Zanzibar and placing advance orders there before proceeding northwards to the Red Sea, Muscat and Bombay for further business, prior to return and collecting at Zanzibar. It was increasingly found more expedient to do all business at Zanzibar – leaving to Arab and Indian the bringing down of trade goods from the north, such as Mocha coffee and dates from Arabia and spices and silks from India.

The Americans were particularly successful in the sale of their cotton goods in East Africa, having quickly divined the tastes of these regions. There was a wide demand for 'mericani' – a white cotton cloth of simple loom, manufactured in Massachusetts's mills. Hamerton noted in 1848, that 'this coarse unbleached cotton cloth has come into universal use in Arabia and the coast of Africa, and is fast driving the British and Indian manufacturing articles of this kind out of the market.' Burton made the grave mistake when, outfitting for his journey inland in 1857, of failing to lay in a sufficient supply of this 'silver of the country' and instead relied upon beads, 'the small change'. Imports of American cottons into Zanzibar rose in value from $70,000 in 1841 to $529,788 in 1856 – at the latter date representing an import of over 150,000 yards annually. Other imports from America were guns, powder, crockery, glassware, soaps, white sugar, biscuits, spirits, pine turpentine (the pitch from the latter was especially esteemed), iron hoops, cordage, tobacco and much coinage – mainly in small denominations of the Spanish piastre (on a par with the Maria Theresa dollar until 1847). American purchases at Zanzibar, in the amount of $534,000 by 1859, were ivory, copal, cloves, coconut oil, beeswax, camphor, senna, sesame, mother of-pearl, hides, tortoiseshell and red pepper. Following a cue from the English they also purchased ivory. The Americans were forthright in their business dealings, prompt in delivery and collection of goods, and were popular with Indian middlemen.

American success in trading at Zanzibar was not lost on the English, and Captain Hart, visiting Zanzibar in 1834 to report on the American treaty of 1833, obtained from the Sultan a promise that he would not enter into any treaty with a foreign power without British cognizance, and the Sultan, already subject to French overtures for a treaty, had asked Hart 'if he could have an English person always with him to guide him'. The year of Captain Hart's visit to Zanzibar, 1834, saw the presentation to King William IV of the *Liverpool* – a 'magnificent encumbrance', a ship built for Said at the Bombay shipyards in 1826, and designed for war rather than commercial pursuits. So clumsily built and ill-designed for commerce was she that Said soon sought to get rid of her, and failing to sell her, presented her to the British, hoping for a steamship in return, and as placation for his signing the treaty with the Americans and his flirtation with the French. Taken to England by Captain Cogan, she was renamed the *Imaum*, in honour of Said; and, as a reciprocal gift from William IV, Cogan brought back the yacht *Prince Regent* for Said. His Highness's religion, however, prevented him from using her because of her interior decor, 'The Byayee tribe of which the Imaum is the head hold it to be haram (unlawful) for a Mussulman to say his prayers in any place containing carved images of men or animals, gilding or any ornaments whatsoever, even to repeat the Kalma in such a place is considered as non-orthodox,'[6] so he sought to get rid of her. He presented her to an Indian Prince – a Hindu!

Although the English had had desultory contact with East Africa since the time of Lancaster's stopover at zanzibar in 1591/92, there was no attempt to establish trading contact until the early nineteenth century. Nathaniel Isaacs who visited East Africa in the brig *Mary* in 1831-32, reported that it 'ought not to be neglected by so extensive a commercial and manufacturing nation as Great Britain. In 1833 there appeared in the *Journal of the Royal Geographical Society* an account of commercial prospects at Mombasa by Lieutenant Emery who had been left in charge there at the time of Owen's protectorate. Following the appearance of Emery's account, a British firm, Newman Hunt and Christopher, made an auspicious attempt at trade, sending an agent, R.B. Norsworthy, to Zanzibar in the brig *Sandwich* and with three other small ships directed to Lamu to trade in hides. The firm soon ran into difficulties and the leading partner, Hunt, had to visit Zanzibar to sort out the troubles. The result was the replacement of Norsworthy by another agent, a Mr Thorn, a change which did not improve the fortunes of the Company in the face of the formidable combination of Jairam and Waters. With no English consul to turn to for protection and advice, Norsworthy (now in business on his own) complained of lack of British protection. This gave added weight to the argument for appointment of a British consul at Zanzibar.

Even after Hamerton took up his post as consul in May 1841, matters did not improve for British trade. The Americans tried to undermine Hamerton's authority by stating that he was not properly accredited and that the East India Company was on the wane. Hamerton showed little interest in furthering British trade interests, and Newman Hunt and Christopher ceased operations in the early 1840s. The other English merchant firm with an agent in Zanzibar at this time was George Cram of Liverpool, whose agent in Zanzibar (1846–47), a Mr E. Parker, was an unfortunate choice. The firm of Cram sent out three vessels to Zanzibar, but Parker so mismanaged their business that he was forced to abscond to Aden, and a Mr Nelson succeeded him. Parker, as it turned out, was a rogue; he was well known at the Cape of Good Hope where there were 'strange reports about him'. On the other hand, on the eve of his departure from East Africa, in a most prescient summing up of the state of British interests there, he set out the need for more British consular representation and commercial activity. The arrival of Mr J. Napier as British consul at the Comoro Islands on 4 November 1848 was probably a direct result of Parker's report. However, poor Napier had a short career; by September 1850 he had gone to Zanzibar 'to lay down his bones' – a fatal illness had overtaken him while at Johanna. He was succeeded by William Sunley who took up his post in the Comoros in May 1852.

Two small independent British merchants, Wilson and Pollock, seem to have made little impact at Zanzibar. It was Captain Robert Cogan, of varied career, and backed by the Bombay branch of W. Henderson and Company of Aberdeen, who included farming the guano deposits of Latham Island (near Zanzibar) in his agenda, and who entered into a partnership with Said in developing a sugar manufactory at Zanzibar, with Said supplying slave-labour for the enterprise. Sugar-cane in its raw state had long been a delicacy, but attempts to refine sugar at Zanzibar date from 1819, and in the 1830s, Said had attempted to draw on French expertise from Bourbon – that home of sugar manufacture – but he grew increasingly suspicious of French intentions when they displayed inordinate interest in setting up estates for themselves on Zanzibar island. Thus he approached Cogan, who attempted to introduce steam-driven mills into the sugar industry at Zanzibar; but Cogan soon wearied of the business and quit Zanzibar for Aden in 1847, leaving a Mr Francis Peters to carry on the enterprise. Following Peters's death in 1842, the business was wound up, and by 1848 the Sultan was importing refined sugar from England. Hamerton dolefully informed the Foreign Office in July 1849 that 'The firm of Cogan & Co. was established at Zanzibar from 1841 to 1847 but all persons belonging to the house having died here, the business ceased,' and thus there were no British merchants at Zanzibar.[7]

Thus the British, lacking forceful merchants at Zanzibar, and faced with American competitiveness, failed to achieve the success of the Americans. British cotton goods imported into Zanzibar were scarcely over 10,000 yards annually by 1841, and although there was considerable trade in guns and powder – about 1000 guns and 2000 barrels of powder annually – the total value did not rise to more than $214,000 by 1846/47. The British, however, gave the lead to the Americans in the purchase of ivory; from their experience in India they had a greater realization of the value of that commodity, but even here they were soon overtaken by the Americans who quickly caught on to the advantages of trading in ivory.

In the later 1830s and early 1840s there was a spate of French activity along the East African coast, a recuperation from the eclipse suffered in the Napoleonic wars – a seeking of new imperial pastures. The French could draw on a long acquaintance with the coast, going back to French slave-trading activities in the eighteenth century. Unlike the British naval force in the western Indian Ocean, mainly concerned with the anti-slave-trade patrol at sea, the French naval force, usually five to ten vessels based on Réunion, where the governor was normally a high-ranking naval officer (as in the case of Admiral de Hell), was maintained as a prestige presence; French naval activity against the slave-trade was practically non-existent. Captain Hart, during his visit to Zanzibar in 1834, noted French activity there, and that Said had called on French expertise from Bourbon to develop the sugar industry in Zanzibar. Hart learned that the French were interested in a commercial treaty with Said similar to that of the American treaty of 1833. In 1834 Captain Vailhen in *Le Madagascar* proceeded to Zanzibar to negotiate such a treaty of commerce, and to arrange experimental plots for sugar cultivation, but it was soon suspected that the latter were a guise for agricultural establishments to give the French a toe-hold in Zanzibar. The French had also long been eyeing the guano deposit on nearby islands. The Vailhen mission was inconclusive. Said, with his promise to Hart in mind, was wary about signing a treaty with the French, and matters proceeded slowly. Finally, Vailhen, on his return to Bourbon from Zanzibar, was struck down by fever and in a fit of madness tossed overboard all documents and correspondence relevant to the negotiations. Thus were incontinently destroyed the fruits of work so recently and ardently pursued. Following this unhappy episode, there took place a French reconnaissance of the Red Sea and East African coast in 1838, by Commander Guillain in *La Favorite;* and in 1839, alerted by the recent British occupation of Aden, the French Ministry of Marine directed an expedition to Abyssinia, the Red Sea and Muscat, and sent a French agent to Zaila, and a mission to the Amir of Sind to further commercial relations. From 1840 onwards there was a French agent at Muscat, and Said acceded to a request by Guillain in 1838 for the appointment of a French consul at Zanzibar.

During these years the French were the main trade competitors of the Americans, and far ahead of the English. Commercial treaties between Zanzibar and Réunion in 1822 and 1827 were followed up by the commercial treaty of 1844. French activity continued, and gave rise to Hamerton's observation in March 1847 as to the surprising attention that French traders were giving to East Africa. The Gullain expedition of 1846/47, backed by the French government and various Chambers of Commerce, including the powerful one of Nantes whose representative, Loarer, personally accompanied the expedition and was a prolific advocate of French commerce with East Africa, was seen by Hamerton as a French bid for control of East Africa. The tampering with chiefs at Lamu and Barawa by the French – trying to get them to cede territory – was evidence of this. By the 1850s French commercial houses such as Vidal Bros. and Messieurs Ribaud of Marseilles were sending out annually up to 22 vessels to East Africa, and developing a lucrative trade in semsem oil – a substitute for olive oil. The French brought to East Africa a wide range of exports – specie, cloth, spirits, wine, household goods, clocks of many kinds – and had a monopoly of sale of these, along with mirrors and bureaux; exports amounted to $503,469 and imports to $247,500 in 1856.

The Germans appeared first on the East African scene as traders in cowrie shells. These, used as currency over wide parts of Africa, especially in West Africa, were principally obtained from the Maldive and Laccadive Islands in the Indian Ocean. The Hamburg house of Herz, in 1844, finding that East African cowries, although bigger than those from the Maldives and Laccadives, were acceptable in West Africa, commenced a regular trade in them. Shortly after this, another Hamburg firm, Wm. Oswald and Sons, entered the field – sending out a vessel to Zanzibar in 1847 and opening a factory in Zanzibar in 1849 under its agent, Herr Schmeisser. Oswald also exported cowries to West Africa, varying this with carrying pilgrims to Mecca. In 1854, a third Hamburg house, Hansing and Company, entered the Zanzibar trade. By

1856 some 20 German vessels annually were resorting to Zanzibar for trade and German exports to the Swahili coast amounted to $455,701, and comprised a list ranging from Venetian glass beads to wax candles and brass wire. The $245,000 worth of cowries exported in 1856 were handled by German firms who had found that Pate cowries also sold exceedingly well. German purchases at Zanzibar in 1856 amounted to $391,000. Finally, in 1859, a treaty of amity and commerce and navigation was concluded between the Hanseatic Republic and Majid, who had succeeded Said as Sultan at Zanzibar. This treaty recognized the Sultan's monopoly of the ivory and gum copal trade on the coast from the port of Tanga at 5°S, to Kilwa at 9°S.

The most important and pervading element in the commercial life of East Africa was the presence of a large Indian community. It was of ancient origin and most tenacious in its adherence to trade at Zanzibar and various towns along the coast. These Indians – mainly from Kutch, Kathiawar and Gujerat – strongly linked in business transactions, were a hardy and impenetrable trading body. They retained their ties with home and family in India. According to Hamerton:

> There is not a Banian or an Indian Mussulman who has resided for any length of time in any part of the Imaum's dominions who has not purchased African females with whom they cohabit during their stay in the Imaum's countries, and if they leave they generally make them over or sell them clandestinely to friends. The Banian never bring their wives with them to the Imaum's dominions in Arabia or Africa nor do they take their women away with them when they leave for their own country, but the Indian Mohammedans frequently do.[8]

The Indians were the bankers and moneylenders of the country, holding a virtual monopoly of business on the coast. The Indian traders were avaricious, and noted for exaction of high interest rates – as much as 40 per cent on loans made to Arabs. Said's Arab subjects might complain of Indian avarice and were jealous of their prosperity, but Said welcomed them to his capital, employed them in his service, and his Chief Customs Master was usually a Hindu. Indian trade between Bombay and East Africa flourished under the umbrella of British protection. By 1859 Indian cotton imports into Zanzibar topped American cottons in value – $444, 851 as compared to the latter at $381,850. India was also the great market for ivory, especially the best quality – 'bab Kutch'. In 1848

315,000 lb of ivory worth $315,000 were shipped to India from Zanzibar. Copal exports to India ran a good second. British India in turn exported goods to Zanzibar in 1859, worth $780,000 as compared to $1,000,000 for all other countries. Imports in the same year from India were $708,654 in value, compared to $1,600,000 from all other countries. By 1856, about 300 vessels – Arabian and Indian – were visiting Zanzibar annually.

Imports from Arabia were of an exotic nature. In addition to large amounts of Mocha coffee, there were water jugs, rose-water, gold and silver thread and finer cloths – especially for turbans. Arab imports, for a specimen year (1859), were 200,000 coconuts, 12,000 rafters (mango poles) and 350,000 lb of cloves. Much of the increasing volume of trade at Zanzibar arose from increasing penetration of the East African interior by Arab traders backed by Indian money, or opened up by Indian traders themselves. In Unyamwezi in 1824 there arrived two Khojas from Surat, Saihan and Musa Mzuri, who were backed in their enterprise by the governor of Zanzibar, Said al-Akbhari. In 1831 Lief bin Said reached Lake Tanganyika, and in 1841/42 an Arab caravan reached Kazembe on the west side of Lake Tanganyika. In 1851/52 an Arab trader travelled from the east to the west coast of Africa and back. From this increasing trade in the interior – with profits garnered from slaves and ivory – Arab traders did not amass large fortunes. According to Burton, 'Arab merchants gain little beyond a livelihood in plenty and dignity by their expeditions to the interior.' As to who were the main beneficiaries it is not easy to say, but if one were able to penetrate the labyrinth of trade negotiations that backed each foray into the interior, it would be the Indian financier who would come off best. There were exceptions, however. Snay ibn Amir, former confectioner in Muscat, in sixteen years became one of the wealthiest ivory and slave-dealers in East Africa; he showed 'supreme kindness' to Burton, who spoke of him most generously. Profits from trading ventures in the interior often meant for the Arab the foundation a clove estate in Zanzibar – a life of *otium cum dignate* – the goal of every true Arab. According to Hamerton, 'the Arabs as long as they get sufficient cloves from the plantations to hand over to the Banians to enable them to sleep away their lives and procure women for their harems appear to care little how matters are carried on.' By 1856 there were Arab merchants who owned 80,000 clove trees in Zanzibar or Pemba – representing capital investment of $100,000 along with ownership of a ship or two, and from 1000 to 2000 slaves.

The import of firearms was a main branch of commerce in East

Africa. In the earlier years of the nineteenth century, firearms of the flintlock and muzzleloader type, nigh useless and of greater danger to the user than to the target, were introduced and continued to be in great demand in the interior well on into the latter part of the century. Vast numbers of more sophisticated and dangerous weapons were unloaded in East Africa each time the great powers adopted new weapons and restocked their arsenals. Zanzibar, the nodal point of commerce and trade on the East African coast, was an ideal centre for the dispersal of these large quantities of arms. It was a trade most lucrative to Arab caravan leader and to Indian merchant.

Copal was also an increasingly profitable trade item. Zanzibar, or East African, copal was a form of resin – whether of the 'sandarusiza miti' – true copal type – or 'chakazi (corrupted to 'jackass') type; the latter, obtained direct from the tree, or near its roots or on the surface of the ground, was of lesser value and shipped mostly to India and China for the making of a coarse kind of varnish. The true, or fossil copal, was found embedded in the earth to a depth of four feet, distributed over a wide belt of the mainland coast on tracts where trees were scarcely visible, and pieces varied from small pebble size up to lumps of several ounces and even 4 to 5 lb in weight. The resin had to be cleared of its foreign matter and its 'goose skin', a peculiar pitted surface resulting from oxidation and intermolecular change, removed. Copal of the better variety was in great demand in Europe and America during the Victorian Age for the making of the best sort of coach and furniture varnish, and proved a most lucrative export: 1,872,500 lb of copal worth $322,000 were exported in 1848/49, cloves being next in value,[9] followed by copra and coconuts.

The mixed and exotic nature of the trade based on Zanzibar was reflected in the cargo of the Sultan's vessel, *Sultana,* which arrived at New York in 1839. She carried 300 Persian carpets, 1035 hides, 1287 sacks of dates, 100 bags of coffee, 108 tusks of ivory, 138 bags of cloves and 71 boxes of gum copal; her return cargo consisted of guns, gunpowder, cloth, beads and gold leaf. The Sultan's essay into international trading – his ship *Caroline* in July 1845 carried to London cloves, coffee, dates and coconut oil to the value of $100,000 – was not entirely successful, for Said found to his surprise that, great potentate though he was, his ships were subject to port dues and expenses, the same as an ordinary vessel. He gave up the enterprise owing to reduced profits and pressure from the Americans who discouraged Said from competing with them.

Within a decade of Said's move to Zanzibar the vigour he gave to commercial development there was felt on the mainland. Arab trading caravans were at Tabora – some 600 miles from the coast – on the line of march to Lake Tanganyika by 1840. By the mid-1840s they were at the lake itself, and about the same time an Arab trader arrived at the court of Suna, ruler of Buganda, to the immediate north-west of Lake Victoria. Burton, on his expedition to the interior from 1857 to 59, was surprised to find that Arab traders were already on the western side of Lake Tanganyika, and had set themselves up in comfortable fashion, with permanent homes, slaves and household establishments, a profusion of foodstuffs, and were growing rice. It was like a bit of the Swahili coast transmitted to the interior. These Arab trading forays into the interior brought slaves and ivory to Zanzibar. Said, owner of 46 clove plantations and 25 merchant ships, and generating much of Zanzibar's revenue himself, invested this in turn, in these trading ventures in the interior, the profits from which increasingly affirmed the desirability of Zanzibar as the seat of his authority, rather than Muscat.

Although he never set a northward limit to it, Said appears to have considered his writ to run as far northward as Mogadishu on the Somali coast and as far southward as the Ruvuma River, but in later years he was wont to press his claims still farther north to Berbera itself, and in the interior as far as the great lakes. His claim to sovereignty over this vast coastline was exercised in slim and inexpensive fashion – through 'Walis' (governors) who were sometimes a local sheikh, or a man from Zanzibar or Muscat. They collected his customs dues in rough and ready manner, took their own portion and administered authority in the Sultan's name, reporting on their stewardship in the leisurely fashion of the East. They were self-styled 'sultans', acting with impunity in administering their areas, for Said rarely visited the mainland dominions over which he claimed sway, and he had but a small force to exercise authority even if he had wished to do so.

Apart from the Arabs who formed the ruling caste, the majority of Said's subjects on the coast were the Swahili – a people of mixed African and Arabian descent – the result of intermarriage between African and Arab over many centuries. The Swahili, though Muslim in religion, and modified by a strain of Asiatic blood, were basically African in stock. In religion, dress and social life they reflected the Arab and the East, but their language, Swahili, despite generous imports of Arabic, was Bantu in structure. It had become a kind of lingua franca – carried inland as far as the great lakes by Arab traders from the coast who acted as channels of influence for transmitting the Swahili language, and the religion of Islam.

In July 1834, Newman Hunt and Christopher's ship carried back to England the Swahili adventurer, Khamis bin Uthman, one-time head drummer at Zanzibar; erstwhile slaver, consummate linguist, a man of many parts (including that of rogue, for he had swindled Said out of many thousands of dollars and was thus forced to depart hastily for England on Newman Hunt's ship). In England Uthman met W.D. Cooley of the Royal Geographical Society and purveyed to that eager ear much geographical information on East Africa. Uthman, portraying himself as a personage of importance, sought royal audience, failing which he managed an interview with Palmerston. While in England he was also in touch with his old master Owen, and the latter, reanimated by this contact with old times and with events of East African days relived, pressed Palmerston for greater British trade contact with eastern Africa – 'which aforetime furnished even to Solomon his Ivory, his Pearls, and his Gold'. In furthering such good work, Owen offered his services as British consular agent in East Africa.

The august India Board, and Secret Committee of the East India Company, were jealous and watchful of any such invasion of their prerogative in the East. Hart's mission to Zanzibar in 1834, under Admiralty aegis, had not been to their liking, nor also that of Captain Owen – he was looked upon as an interloper in their domain when he sought to establish a protectorate over Mombasa in 1827. And he was now to reappear in East Africa as consular agent! This was too much! Thus did they fall back on the resounding declaration, an Act of Parliament which pronounced as regards countries in the Indian Ocean world, that

> No communication on general subjects of government shall be held with those states except through the Governor-General in Council.[10]

Although the matter of Owen's appointment was dropped, the need for British consular representation at Zanzibar remained, and received added emphasis when Norsworthy pressed for British protection and help in the matter of British legal backing for business transactions and collection of debts. He appealed in this sense to the Bombay government in December 1837. In the face of competition from the Americans and the support they had from the formidable Customs Master, Jairam, and soon also with an American consul at Zanzibar to protect their interests, the firm of Newman Hunt, despite having replaced Norsworthy by another agent, were still unable to make headway. Norsworthy, as an independent trader on his own, soon found it necessary to appeal to Bombay for assistance. He urged the appointment of a British consul at Zanzibar, and in this was supported by Captain Cogan of the Indian Navy who favoured such a move and also the signing of a commercial treaty with Said. Under this impulse there followed the treaty of May 1839, whereby Britain was granted the same terms as the Americans in their treaty of 1833, in the matter of 5 per cent duty on imports and exports and on goods transshipped at Zanzibar, and with similar clauses regarding commerce, bankruptcy proceedings, collection of debts and other trade matters. There was to be reciprocal appointment of consuls, and reference was made as to the need to check the slave-trade. The favoured American position as regards access to the ivory and copal trade on the mainland, however, was denied the British in this treaty with Said.

The matter of appointment of a consul to Said's court received added importance at this juncture owing to events in the Middle East. Mehemmet Ali at the end of the 1830s, supported by the French, was threatening the Ottoman Empire which Britain was committed to uphold, and when an attempt was made to weaken Turkey and take the island of Bahrain in the Persian Gulf Said, long covetous of that island, turned to Britain for support. Britain was already preoccupied with Afghanistan, and was also more concerned in occupying Buraimi, the important citadel in the Omani interior threatened by an advance of Mehemmet Ali. Meanwhile the Foreign Office decision to appoint a consul at Zanzibar had been interpreted by the Bombay Residency as referring to troubles in the Persian Gulf area, and instead of a consul being sent to Zanzibar, Captain Atkins Hamerton, interpreter with a Field detachment on service in the Persian Gulf, was directed to Muscat as consular agent for the East India Company to report on the feasibility of fortifying Buraimi.

French activity, commencing in 1839, had resulted in the occupation of Nossi Bé off the north-west coast of Madagascar and the reconnaissance by Captain Guillain of the shores of Somaliland in the region of Mogadishu and Brava in 1840, apparently with the purpose of obtaining sites for French factories; this caused a shift of diplomatic activity from Muscat to Zanzibar. Said, much perturbed over the French occupation of Nossi Bé where he exercised nebulous claims, and alerted over Guillain's probing activity near Mogadishu and Brava, was in a state of high tension. These pressures on him came while he was at Muscat, during a visit there from September 1839 to late 1840. He wrote to Palmerston in May 1840 complaining of the French action at Nossi Bé, and looked to Britain for sympathy and help in the matter. When news came of Guillain's activities along the northern strip of coast he could contain himself no longer and sailed for Zanzibar. Leaving Muscat on 10 November 1840, he put in at Merka on the way south, to check on the interference of the French at that place. He lost no time on arrival at Zanzibar in running up his flag at various points in his dominions to anticipate any French action similar to that at Nossi Bé and on the Somali coast. There soon followed in Said's wake at Zanzibar, the recently appointed British agent at Muscat, Hamerton. He had been directed in December 1840, by the government of India, to proceed to Zanzibar 'with as little delay as possible for the purpose of ascertaining all the particulars of the aggressions attributed to the French'.

Arrived at Zanzibar in May 1841, Hamerton observed the dreadful spectacle of the slave-trade as carried on there, with dead and dying slaves on the waterfront – their owners refused to pay duty on merchandise which would soon perish. Hamerton's subsequent correspondence is much dominated by the subject of the slave-trade, and Said informed him that his subjects feared that he had come to Zanzibar to free slaves. There was more to depress Hamerton on arrival. British influence at Zanzibar was at a low ebb, and that of the French and Americans was high. He complained of the Americans who, in most incontinent fashion, ran up their flags all over the place on ships and houses to celebrate Independence Day. As to the Sultan's grandiose claims of sovereign rights, as at Nossi Bé, these were groundless. Although Hamerton soon established himself at Zanzibar, as a typical British 'type', socially conscious and upholding the proprieties of diplomatic usage, there was another side to him. The French claimed that he was an 'ivrogne' – a drunkard; and that Hamerton had taken more than literally Burton's recipes for survival in the tropics: 'avoid noxious mists', 'flannels must always be worn'; that Bacchus was the ascribed healer – thus 'an abnormal amount of stimulants' was recommended for 'in these lands a drunkard outlives a water-drinker'. The French, perhaps egged on by Cogan who was soured over his failure to get the consulship, were prone to exaggerate Hamerton's crapulous state: they retailed a story how, in a drunken stupor, he clambered on board a French vessel in Zanzibar harbour, mistaking it for an English vessel. That Hamerton at times was less than correct in his relationship to the Sultan, that he was irritable, haughty and at times downright rude, is undeniable; the Sultan's complaint to the Foreign Office led to a rebuke to Hamerton in November 1844, directing him to be 'more respectful and guarded in his manner to the Sultan who has complained of it', and to 'remove the coldness that exists between the Imaum and himself'. Following the painful extraction from Said of the Hamerton treaty to check the slave-trade, a complete break between Sultan and Hamerton seemed imminent, and also an end to Hamerton's career at Zanzibar. In 1846, Aberdeen ordered his removal following a complaint from Said that 'The trouble that I have had is more than I can well bear'. Bombay was unwilling, or unable, to find a successor – Hamerton was an able Arabist and fluent in Hindustani, high qualifications which had initially recommended him for the post. Luckily, relations between Said and Hamerton subsequently improved. Said was not overimpressed with the Americans, and he suspected the French of having designs on his territory; on the other hand he was grateful for Lord Palmerston's warning to the French that Britain 'was concerned' to maintain the integrity of Said's dominions, and also for the opening of British India ports to Omani shipping, a concession to Said for the Hamerton treaty against the slave-trade.

Hamerton was in an increasingly strong position at Said's court. He held the consulship from 1841 to 1857 and, it would appear, rarely went on leave. In the latter years of his consulship he was almost continually ill – so ill in fact (and this was a sign of its gravity to those experienced in such matters) that he refused to go home. Burton stated as regards Hamerton, that although only 50 years of age, 'his head already bears the blossoms of the grave'. Yet Hamerton weathered the climate and strain of Zanzibar, while French consuls came and went.

The Americans with their 'know-how and push' made great strides commercially at Zanzibar, but Hamerton, as befitted the representative of the greatest naval power of the time, had diplomatic ascendancy. This was acknowledged by Ephraim A. Emmerton (an American) visiting Zanzibar in 1848, when he observed that Hamerton was 'virtually King at Zanzibar ... the Sultan actually trembles for fear of displeasing him'. And according to Burton Englishmen were 'better received at Zanzibar than any of our Presidencies', wholly as the result of Hamerton's influence. Hamerton was busy keeping an eye on the French and American trading activities, for the latter, with their favourable trade terms and strong link with Jairam, Chief Customs Master, outpaced both French and British in the volume of their commerce. But it was the slave-trade which increasingly absorbed Hamerton's attention and which was increasingly a cause of his despondency and cynical resignation, so discernible in his later despatches.

With its insular position and accessibility to the mainland, Zanzibar was an ideal holding depot for slaves. They had no avenue of escape here, and their maintenance was cheap. There was a continuing demand for slave labour in the island as well as for overseas export. Said's move there had made Zanzibar the 'Lagos of the East'. He and his family and most of the leading Arabs were soon involved in the slave-trade. Their business dealings in it and the support for slavers had caused the latter to extend their transactions ever further inland, so that they were established at Tabora some 600 miles from the coast by 1840, and were at Lake Tanganyika by the late 1840s. An Arab trader at the court of Suna, ruler of Buganda, by 1843 was generously supplied with slaves by that potentate. As the slave-trade from the interior developed, Bagamoyo on the coast opposite Zanzibar became an outlet for it, thus augmenting the long-standing slave export from the Nyasa area through Kilwa.

The Moresby treaty of 1822, and the Hamerton treaty of 1845 and its various supplementary clauses, brought small relief. For so long as a market for slaves existed a slave-trade would supply it. Hamerton's treaty was riddled with loopholes, and Arabs were adept at circumventing anti-slave-trade legislation. The task of suppressing the slave-trade seemed almost insuperable. Hamerton in worsening health, emotionally tired and exhausted, disillusioned and prematurely aged, sick to death of it all, lived only for the evenings – 'the ungirt hour', when on the long low verandah of the consulate, looking out over the Indian Ocean and deep in his cups, he could forget it all. The soft sussuration of the trade winds and lapping of the waters of the nearby Indian Ocean were balm to his taxed mind. In this outpost of empire far from home, he was, in the words of his colleague the American consul, Waters, 'willing to work hard for a few years, and be separated from dear friends ... to acquire a necessary portion of riches'.

Said's death in October 1856, followed by that of Hamerton in July 1857, marked the end of an era, one in which British diplomatic influence was firmly established at Zanzibar. Said's will, made in 1844, provided for his succession in Zanzibar and his East African dominions to go to his second surviving son, Seyyid Majid; and in Oman, to his eldest surviving son, Seyyid Thwain. On Said's death, Thwain disputed his brother's succession to the Zanzibar and East African dominions, and threatened to send an expedition against him in 1861. It was at this juncture that Lord Canning, Governor-General of India, by his 'Canning Award' of April 1861 confirmed Majid as Sultan of Zanzibar and the East African possessions, and Thwain as ruler of Oman. Thus was severed an ancient connection between Zanzibar and Oman. It was further sealed by an understanding between France and Britain in 1862. France, desirous for control of Madagascar and the Comoro Islands, was ready for an agreement 'on the basis of mutual self-denial'. By the Anglo-French Declaration, signed at Paris in March 1862, 'taking into consideration the importance of maintaining the independence' of the Sultan of Oman and the Sultan of Zanzibar, the two powers engaged to respect the independence of both rulers.

The agreement brought an accession of British strength at Zanzibar and the Sultan became increasingly dependent on British support and goodwill. Hamerton's reports had provided much information on Zanzibar and the neighbouring coastline and brought that part of the world increasingly before British attention. Thousands of British settlers were making their home in what was later to become Natal and the eastern Cape Province. British possessions in the western Indian Ocean included Mauritius, the Seychelles, Socotra, Aden and Perim, and Britain exercised a watching brief over the Persian Gulf. All that was needed was to close the gap between the Horn and the Ruvuma River, and a vast world would be brought under British control. Yet the prevailing economic theory of the 1860s was that colonies were unprofitable, encumbrances, incurring charges unrecoverable in trade profits. The ideal was *laissez-faire*. What need was there for acquiring more colonies when trade could be carried on freely anywhere and to the best economic advantage? The abolition of the slave-trade, however, was a different matter; there was a moral imperative here which no Christian conscience could shirk. Burton, writing in the late 1850s, saw little hope of ending it so long as the Sultan was in control at Zanzibar, and he claimed that Britain should establish commerce and control in East Africa which would rival 'Western India', and thus help to oust the slave-trade.

During the 1850s and 1860s, Britain was unable to effect any lessening of it at Zanzibar. The slave market there operated daily – one of the sights of the town for visitors. The slave-trade based on Zanzibar and with imports mostly from Kilwa, amounted to 20,000 slaves annually. Britain seemed the only European power concerned in the matter. The thankless and daunting task of suppressing the slave-trade at sea was cast almost entirely on the small British naval patrol operating off the East African coast. Anti-slave-trade legislation – wheedled out of the Sultan piecemeal for he was deeply averse to going against the wishes of his subjects in a matter touching on their nearest and dearest concern – seemed to avail little. The Sultan, too, had a vested interest in maintaining the slave-trade. From it he derived much of his revenue; and he was the largest slave-owner in Zanzibar. Concessions were wrung from him with extreme difficulty, and anti-slave-trade legislation was easily circumvented by his Arab subjects – who were adept in such matters. The suppression of the slave-trade at Zanzibar became the dominant consideration for the British. A separate department in the consulate was set up to deal with it.

Hamerton's four immediate successors as consuls held office for periods of short duration. Colonel Rigby, consul 1858–61, was the most able of these four. A long report on Zanzibar and the mainland coast which he submitted to the Foreign Office in May 1860 provides a most valuable source of information as to commerce, trade and the extent of the slave-trade. Of the other three consuls, there is little to be noted; they took no strong action against the slave-trade, in fact two of them reversed anti-slave-trade legislation introduced as a result of efforts by their predecessors.

British interests were more ably represented at Zanzibar during the period following the appointment of Dr (later Sir John) Kirk as consul in 1870, a post he held until 1886. Kirk had come to the Sultanate as surgeon to the British Agency in 1866. Soon afterwards he became acting Political Agent and Consul owing to the illness of that officer, and later he was appointed Consul-General. Kirk, like Hamerton, attained a unique position as British representative at Zanzibar, taking the lead among all the European consuls there, and acquiring a profound knowledge of East African affairs. He became almost mentor to the Sultan, obtaining from him a promise that no concession would be granted any other nation without British cognizance. During Kirk's consulship there was the all-important development of communications – the opening of the Suez Canal in 1869, the inauguration of monthly mail services between Aden and Zanzibar in 1872 and the laying down of a telegraph cable from Aden to Zanzibar in 1879. Zanibar was thus brought into closer touch with the outside world and British connection with that island was especially enhanced. By the time this had come about, momentous happenings were taking place in the interior of East Africa. David Livingstone's cry 'I go back to Africa to make an open path for commerce and Christianity', in the year of Hamerton's death, marked the commencement of a remarkable period of exploration in which the frontiers of East Africa, as understood by Western geographers, were pushed back to the great lakes, and were finally removed by the time of Livingstone's death in 1873, in the early years of Kirk's consulship.

3· European Exploration of East Africa

By the first half of the nineteenth century the geography of the north-western part of Africa had been opened up to European knowledge by the discovery of the course of the Niger River and its debouchment into the Bight of Benin, and by the great Saharan journeys of Heinrich Barth in the 1840s in the vast region between the Gulf of Gabes on the Mediterranean and Timbuktu. In the southern part of the African continent, European settlement at the Cape was centuries old, and a movement of settlers inland and along the eastern seaboard of the Cape and as far north as Natal had taken place in the early nineteenth century. The Portuguese, from their colony of Angola on the west, had penetrated inland as far as the upper reaches of the Zambezi and to Barotseland; while from Mozambique on the eastern side of the continent they had penetrated up the Zambezi to Tete (founded in 1531) and beyond to Zumbo some four to five hundred miles from the coast. Thus the Portuguese had practically linked arms between their possessions on the eastern and western sides of the continent; and they averred that they had crossed the continent and had discovered Lake Nyasa, before Livingstone's journeyings of 1854–56.

Between these northern and southern parts of the continent opened up to European eyes lay the vast heart of Africa, between latitudes 10° to 20°N and 10° to 20°S, the broad torso of its middle part, and comprising its most tropical portion. It lay still unexplored, enfolding in its centre the mystery of the great lakes and sources of the Nile. Attempts to solve this mystery came from the east and the north. By the mid-century these attempts were firm and decisive, but it was the final penetration from the east coast which solved the mystery.

The African Association, founded in 1788 'for promoting the discovery of interior parts of Africa', was at first concerned more with West Africa and determining the course and termination of the Niger River, but it had evinced interest in East Africa as early as 1809 when

Henry Salt, at its prompting, visited Mozambique, during the course of his journey up the East African coast in 1809.[1] With the information from Owen's great hydrographical survey (1824–26) available by the early 1830s, the exploration of the Niger now virtually rounded out and the founding of the Royal Geographical Society in 1830, with which the African Association merged shortly after, and the latter in turn linked with the Bombay Geographical Society as a branch in India, there was a strengthening of interest in Africa on its Indian Ocean side. In its support for exploratory journeys, the RGS played an important role in opening up the eastern half of the African continent in the nineteenth century. The RGS was a highly respected institution – the centre and bureau for sharing and diffusing of geographical knowledge. Its gold medals, awarded for outstanding achievement in the field of geography and exploration, were much sought after and were prized accolades. Its support for a venture was usually sufficient warrant for financial support from the British government (and Indian government, too). It promoted practically all the major exploratory journeys of the century – by Burton, Speke, Livingstone and Cameron. Sir Roger Murchison, its President for some 15 years, between 1843 and 1871, did much to popularize the RGS among the influential and rich, public figures and littérateurs of the day; and by means of soirées and debates stirred up a lively interest in its work in a wider public. Its numbers rose from about 600 to almost 3500 during the period 1847 to 1877, with many of these members having a background in the Services – Military and Naval, and Indian Civil Service. The headquarters of the Society, centred in the great imperial city of London, was fittingly placed. Its Victorian Palladian style, rooms betokening high solemnity, with their great atlases, meridian globes and bookcases, handcrafted in the best mahogany, and against a background of leather-bound gazetteers, lent an air of opulence and high purpose to the RGS.

It was Livingstone who caught the imagination of the English Victorian public and awakened the interest of the RGS in supporting him. After discovering Lake Ngami in 1849, for which he received the RGS gold medal (it has recently been argued that this honour should have been shared with others),[2] he directed his exploratory endeavours northwards to the territory of the Makololo chief, Sebebwane, which was reached in 1852; and from thence he worked his way westward to Loanda on the west coast, where he arrived in June 1854. Leaving Loanda on 20 September 1854 on his return trip, he retraced the course of the Zambezi eastwards – arriving at Quelimane on the east coast, on

20 May 1856. During this return trip from Loanda he witnessed the full extent of the slave-trade as carried on by Portuguese slavers, at first from the west coast, and then from the east coast. The attitude of the Portuguese to the slave-trade was to Livingstone quite inexplicable, for they were not 'at all bigoted in their attachment to slavery, nor in their attitude towards colour'; and the Portuguese government seemed well-intentioned, but it was ill-served by men on the spot, and these in turn were ill-served by men in the interior – many of them half-caste Portuguese – for the latter Livingstone expressed a withering contempt.

This first great journey of Livingstone into the interior of East/Central Africa brought him the highest laurels – he was the great medical missionary explorer, unparalleled in African history. It also, however, introduced him to the misery of the slave-trade, concern for which became for him his heart's great burthen for the remainder of his life-work in Africa. When he arrived back in England in December 1856 (Speke and Burton had already left on their momentous journey to East Africa) he received a joyous welcome, hailed as one upon whom the mantle of saviour and hope of Africa had descended. His heart-awakening appeal to all right-minded men to turn their thoughts and give help to the suffering African people made a deep impression; especially his dramatic leave-taking at Cambridge: 'I go back to Africa to try to make an open path for commerce and Christianity.' The right note of appeal to a Victorian audience!

Having severed his connection with the London Missionary Society, thus freeing himself from the restraints of missionary directives, he placed himself under the equally restrictive control of government. With a grant of £5000 to equip his expedition to explore the Zambezi and with the title of British consul, he returned to Africa in May 1858 accompanied by his wife and six assistants, among whom was Dr John Kirk, destined to have a later influential career in East Africa. The years 1858 to 1864 were devoted to various journeys on the Zambezi and in the discovery of Lakes Nyasa and Shirwa (this discovery is also disputed: it is claimed that the Portuguese were there first).[3] The ascent of the Zambezi, which it was hoped would take him near highlands where a 'central station' for missionaries and traders might be established, was blocked by the Kebrabasa Rapids, and his little river steamer *Ma-Robert* also gave much trouble – it was abandoned and replaced by a larger vessel, the *Pioneer*. Proceeding up the River Shire and leaving the *Pioneer*, and passing the Murchison cataracts, the Shire highlands were explored, and then Livingstone sailed into the hitherto undiscovered

Lake Nyasa. Marching along its western shore, while his boat sailed up
its west side, he was in upland terrain suitable for a European colony in
Africa; not one where the English races would compete in manual labour
with the natives but where they

> can take a leading part in managing the land, improving the
> quality, creating the quantity and extending the varieties of the
> production of the soil; and by taking a lead too in trade and in all
> public matters the Englishman would be an unmixed advantage to
> everyone below and around him; for he would fill a place which is
> now practically vacant.[4]

This ideal colony of Livingstone's never got off the ground in
Nyasaland; the nearest semblance to it was to come almost a century
later, in Kenya Colony. His central mission station fared badly, for
following the founding of its first station at Mogomero above the Shire
in 1861, it suffered severely from the effects of malarial fever, the bane
of the tropics – which had also struck down members of Livingstone's
expedition.

Livingstone, meanwhile, in the period 1860 to 1862, had seen the
slave-trade in its varied aspects. He had witnessed the escape of a 'free'
labourer from a French vessel, the *Mazurka*, at Johanna, and was thus
introduced to the *engagé* system, whereby Africans under the guise of
contract labour were hauled off to Réunion and other French islands to
work on sugar estates. On the Shire in 1858 and 1859, he had witnessed
the work of the slave-dealers from Tete, and again when in 1860 he
revisited Victoria Falls and Linyanti. In 1861, during his journey up the
western shore of Lake Nyasa, he had run into Arab slavers ravaging both
sides of the lake. It was this second journey to Africa which set him
against slavers, Portuguese and Arab alike, for the rest of his life.

Livingstone returned from this journey up the lake resolved to stir up
civilized opinion against the slave-trade. The Portuguese were the main
culprits, and because of them 'our labours will be in vain'; and the most
effective way to undercut them was for Britain to annex the Shire
country, as he suggested to Lord John Russell, Foreign Secretary, in
November 1861. The Portuguese, for their part, were disquieted by the
irruption of a wandering British missionary in their sphere, and his
sending out reports therefrom to Portuguese disadvantage. They thus
tried to prevent Livingstone from ascending the Ruvuma River in the
Pioneer in early 1861 and it was Portuguese pressure that influenced the

Foreign Office to recall his expedition before he had carried out his plans to place a steamer on Lake Nyasa.

Malaria fever was a constant affliction. It sorely weakened Livingstone and his companions, three of whom died between 1861 and 1863, and also his wife, Mary, who had come out to join him and had died at Sharpanga at the mouth of the Zambezi in April 1862. Despite these heavy burdens on his heart, Livingstone was soon busy with future plans. An attempt to find an alternative waterway to Lake Nyasa by the Ruvuma River in the autumn of 1862 was frustrated by the rocks and rapids about a hundred miles from its mouth. In 1863 Russell ordered the expedition to be withdrawn. The Universities Mission also, about the same time, withdrew from its mission station above the Shire, and under Bishop Tozer established itself at Zanzibar. Livingstone took the small steamer *Lady Nyasa* to Bombay where she was sold; by 1864 he was back in England and soon ready to embark on his last great enterprise.

By the time Livingstone had completed his first journey of exploration on the Zambezi in the early 1850s, missionary explorers farther north, on the East African coast, were also making a contribution to the opening up of the interior. The Church Missionary Society in 1829 had unwisely chosen Abyssinia as its field of evangelization in eastern Africa, but in this theocratic country where a zealous Coptic priesthood held sway there was small chance of winning converts – had not those tenacious Portuguese Jesuits of two centuries previously, and after a hundred years of labour there, been forced to leave this 'Afghanistan of Africa'? Thus the CMS and its stolid missionary-minded German colleagues, Samuel Gobat, Christian Kugler, C.W. Isenberger and J.L. Krapf, were expelled in 1842. Still intent on pursuing their work in eastern Africa, they found a more propitious field in the dominions of the sultanate of Zanzibar, to where Krapf proceeded and had audience with Sayyid Majid, from whom permission was obtained to establish a mission station at Rabai, near Mombasa. Krapf was soon joined by a fellow Württemberger, John Rebmann, and their arduous missionary labours were soon interspersed with acquiring a knowledge of Arabic and African languages, and a Swahili grammar and dictionary were produced. Their zealous attempt to plant the Christian Gospel was however quite outshone by their endeavours in the field of exploration. At a time when it was scarcely realized in Europe that East Africa existed, these intrepid missionaries with small resources had made notable achievements in exploring East Africa.

Soon after their arrival at Rabai, there had come to their ears stories of the interior, retailed by Arab traders who had reached Lake Tanganyika, and who had brought back rumours of another great lake to its north (Lake Victoria Nyanza); and there were also stories of a 'Mount Olympus', 'exceedingly high' (referred to in a Portuguese work of 1530), and beyond it were the Mountains of the Moon – the sources of the Nile. Krapf and Rebmann made several journeys inland: Rebmann into the Chagga country, Krapf into Usambara and through the Nyika to the upper reaches of the Tana River. In 1848 Rebmann sighted Mount Kilimanjaro, and in 1849 Krapf not only confirmed Rebmann's discovery of Kilimanjaro but, pushing his way far enough inland, caught a glimpse of Mount Kenya, and heard of a salt lake (Baringo) to its north-west. Thus by 1850, through the agency of the CMS, Rebmann and Krapf were able to report from their own observations the existence of snow mountains nearly under the Equator. They also sent to Europe about this time stories gathered from reports of native and Arab traders, which tended to show the existence of one large body of water in the interior – the so-called 'slug' lake shown in the map published by Erhardt and Rebmann in 1855. Although this view of one large lake – shaped like the Caspian Sea – was soon dispelled by further exploration, nevertheless by the time Krapf returned to Europe, broken in health, in 1853, to be followed by Erhardt in 1855 (leaving only Rebmann to carry on the missionary work at Rabai for another 20 years), their achievements were noteworthy: the great mountains of Kilimanjaro and Kenya were now known to the outside world. These German missionaries in their exploratory work were an exception to East African missionaries on the whole who, considering their number on the ground (Livingstone excepted, and he, apart from his early years in southern Africa, can hardly be called a missionary), made little contribution to geographical exploration. Even the pragmatic MacKay of the Church Missionary Society in Uganda, was singularly incurious as to the geography of the country, and for over a period of ten years was apparently unaware that to the westward, some 150 miles as the crow flies, lay the great and striking range of snow mountains, Ruwenzori. Even with the mist and haze of the Semliki valley, Ruwenzori is visible at a distance of 75 miles (Mt Kilimanjaro has been sighted from the Indian Ocean, at a distance of 150 miles, from the high rigging of a ship).

'Aut Nilus, aut nihil.' From time immemorial the great river has cast its spell – almost one of mystical reverence – over those who have sought its source and gazed on its life-giving waters. What mighty pulse is necessary to send those waters on their way to Egypt, and to sustain their force through the appalling wastes of the Sudan and Upper Egypt, where parched sands drink thirstily of its overspill yet leave sufficient to revitalize the delta of Lower Egypt after this four-thousand-mile journey! The gift is truly prodigious. No wonder the ancient Egyptians worshipped the Nile, and 'prince, priest, and peasant' looked southwards 'with anxious attention for the fluctuating yet certain rise'.

Every year when the rains fall and the mountain snows of Central Africa begin to melt, the headstreams become torrents and the great lakes are filled to the brim, then the Bahr-al-Ghazal becomes a broad and navigable stream and the Sobat and Atbara, from dry watercourses with occasional pools in which fish and crocodiles are crowded, turn to gushing rivers. Sir Samuel Baker gives a dramatic account of the Nile flood. On 24 June 1861, Baker, lying half asleep on his bed by the margin of the River Atbara, fancied he heard a rumbling sound like distant thunder:

> We were up in an instant, and my interpreter in a state of intense confusion exclaimed that the river was coming down, and that the supposed distant thunder was the roar of approaching water ... Many of the people were sleeping on the clean sand of the river's bed, and were only just in time to reach the top of the steep bank before the water was on them in the darkness ... The river had arrived 'like a thief in the night'. When morning broke I stood upon the banks of a noble river, the wonder of the desert! Yesterday there was a barren sheet of glaring sand with a fringe of withered bush and trees upon its borders ... No bush could boast of a leaf, no tree could throw a shade: crisp gum crackled upon the stems of the mimosas ... In one night there was a mysterious change ... An army of water was hastening to the wasted river, which had become a magnificent stream some five hundred yards in width and fifteen to twenty feet in depth. Bamboos and reeds with trash of all kinds were hurried along the muddy waters ... I realised what had occurred: the rains were falling and the snows were melting in Abyssinia.[5]

The classical tradition of the Nile issuing from vast lakes, fed by snowy mountains, was tenaciously preserved from the earliest times. In about 457 BC Herodotus visited Egypt and collected information as to the regions beyond, ascertaining that beyond the great bend of the Nile at Merowe (Merawi of today) nothing certain was known; yet the verse of Aeschylus (525–456 BC) speaks of Egypt 'nurtured by the snows' and Aristotle, more than a century later, refers to the 'Mountains of Silver' and recorded that south-west of the Nile were Pygmy races who frequently warred against the cranes. About 200 BC, Eratosthenes, Greek geographer and sometime librarian at Alexandria, sketched with fair accuracy the course of the Nile and its great Abyssinian affluents as far south as Khartoum, and hinted at its lake sources, and mentioned the Nubians. It was Strabo, geographer of the Roman world born about 50 BC, who journeyed up the Nile as far as Philae beyond the First Cataract, who brought some credence to these classical legends. Two centurions in the reign of the Emperor Nero, who supposedly got as far as the Great Marsh – the sudd, where they were stopped – had reached 'the land of the naked Nile Negroes'. This was likely the farthest thrust southward from the north during the classical period.

Following the classical period there appears to have come about a severance of relations between Egypt and the Upper Nile, although an overland route to the Land of Punt (Somaliland), either through Abyssinia or to the east of it by way of the Red Sea, continued. The ancient Egyptians, even in the pre-Dynastic period, regularly carried out long-distance trading down the Red Sea and to Somaliland, and must have been familiar with the mountainous interior of Abyssinia, wherein lay Lake Tana and the source of the Blue Nile; and since the Nile came from the same direction as these mountains, it could probably be assumed that the source of the White Nile lay in the extension of these mountains south-westward.

On the eastern side of Africa, classical references to the sources of the Nile stem from the report of the Greek merchant, Diogenes, who, returning from a voyage to India in about AD 50, landed on the East African coast at Rhaptum (Pangani or near the mouth of the River Rufu) and claimed to have travelled inland on 'a 25-day' journey, and arrived in the vicinity of two great lakes and a snowy range of mountains whence the Nile draws its 'twin sources'. The inadequacy of a '25-day' journey to reach the great lakes of the interior and the absence of any mention of Diogenes' return therefrom, cast doubt on his story; and it may well be that it represents information gained from Arab traders with whom he had contact. The story was retailed by Diogenes to the Syrian geographer, Marinus of Tyre, and picked up by Claudius Ptolemy, Greek/Egyptian geographer of the second century AD, from whom is usually dated the theory of the origin of the White Nile from the twin lakes and 'Mountains of the Moon'. Ptolemy states that the Nile derived its waters from two streams which rise in two lakes a little south of the Equator, and he introduced a range of mountains running from east to west which he calls the Mountains of the Moon – this might represent the Alpine highlands in the neighbourhood of the Nyanzas and Ruwenzori, or Mounts Kenya and Kilimanjaro. Ptolemy was careful to discriminate between the lake sources of the White Nile and the lake (Tana) from which the Blue Nile issues in the highlands of Abyssinia. In his *Regio Cinnamonifera* (1849) and *Claudius Ptolemy and the Nile* (1854), Cooley dealt with Ptolemy's distortion of Marinus of Tyre's information on the interior. Ptolemy had given two separate accounts of the Nile. One spoke of the sources being found in two lakes in about latitude 6°S and 57° and 65°E longitude. The other mentioned that west of the land of the cannibals in about 12½°S latitude lay a range of snow-covered mountains – the Mountains of the Moon, whose melt-waters fed the two lakes. Opinion has remained divided about the validity of Ptolemy's Nile passages. The majority of scholars seems agreed that Cooley was right to criticize Ptolemy's positions and his general air of scientific accuracy, but there is no reason to doubt that Ptolemy had authentic if vague reports of great lakes and mountains in the East African interior. Ptolemy was simply extending Ethiopian features too far south. This ancient legend of the Nile sources persisted throughout the Middle Ages, in the works of Prior of Neuville les Damos, and Alphonse de Sainturge.

The inscriptions on the monument that the inveterate traveller, Cosmos Indicopleustes, saw at the port of Adulis (near Massawa) in AD 520, recorded that in the reign of Ptolemy III of Egypt (285–247 BC), Egyptian expeditions had partially conquered the coast regions of northern Abyssinia, and also recorded the victories and territories of the Abyssinian ruler (probably Ela-Auda) in about AD 127. Christianity was carried from Abyssinia from the fourth century AD onwards, far afield – as far south as modern Kaffa and as far west as Khartoum. Abyssinian penetration may have reached to the northern tip of Lake Rudolf. From these points it is not too distant from the sources of the Nile. Reports of the great lakes to the south and west probably filtered through to Egypt and Abyssinia by the Middle Ages.

The belief in snow-clad mountains and great lakes in the interior as sources of the Nile persisted with peculiar tenacity among the natives of the East Coast of Africa, and gathered fresh strength in the nineteenth century with news coming in from trading caravans returning from the interior. Burton, Speke and Baker heard it again and again with positive affirmation both from the Arabs and the Africans.

The translation of the works of Jesuit missionaries on Abyssinia, coming at a time of the great revival of learning in the reign of Charles II, stirred British interest in the Nile sources. Richard Pococke, who visited Egypt in the early part of the eighteenth century, was intrigued by its mystery, and so also were other English scholars, philosophers and statesmen. It was the first Lord Halifax who stirred James Bruce, the Scottish traveller, to undertake his dramatic journey to Abyssinia. After a circuitous journey by way of Arabia and a landing at Massawa, port of Abyssinia, Bruce made his way to the capital of the emperor, who so cherished Bruce that he was loath to let him go; Bruce managed, however, to reach the source of the Blue Nile, Lake Tana in 1870. Like the Portuguese missionaries of olden times, he was convinced that the headstream of the Nile was the Blue Nile of Abyssinia, rising in Lake Tana. He followed the Blue Nile downstream to its confluence with the White Nile at the site of Khartoum, but Bruce, great traveller that he was, accurate observer and far-sighted 'Imperialist', could not brook the idea of any river but the Blue Nile being the main stream. According to Schweinfurth

> It is absolutely impossible that Bruce could have returned from Sennar to Berber, along the left bank of the Blue Nile, and could have crossed at its mouth from the very spot where Khartoum now stands, without being aware that close behind him there was rolling its waters a stream as broad again as the Blue Nile. The record of his travels does not contain one word about the White Nile. The plain truth is that the White Nile was overlooked and disparaged because it would have thrown his Blue Nile into the shade.[6]

Bruce's perambulations in the Red Sea and Abyssian world made deep impress on his mind. Not long after his return to England in 1775 he urged the establishment of British control in Egypt to secure communications with the East India Company's possessions in India. It is also averred that Bruce obtained from Turkish authorities in Egypt an English concession on the shores of the Red Sea. Any idea that the British government might follow up this opportunity was interrupted by Napoleon Bonaparte's invasion of Egypt in 1798.

From the time of Louis XIV it had long been held that Egypt, loosely controlled by Turkey, would be an admirable base for a French conquest of India, and the idea was taken up by Napoleon Bonaparte. Although British forces obliged the French to evacuate Egypt, the scientific results of Napoleon's venture roused much European interest in the valley of the Nile, and when Egypt settled down under that remarkable soldier of fortune, Mohammad Ali Pasha, Nile exploration caught the European imagination. A Frenchman, Frederic Caillaud, accompanied the military expedition under Mohammad Ali's son, Ibrahim Pasha, which founded Khartoum in 1823, and explored the Blue Nile as far as Fazokl. A young Swiss, Johann Ludwig Burckhardt (1784–1817), an earlier nineteenth-century version of Richard Burton, after a grounding in Arabic and the niceties of Islam, made a great circuitous journey – down the Nile to Korosko, east across the Nubian desert to Berber, Shendi, Suakin, and thence across the Red Sea to Jeddah, where he made the pilgrimage (the first European to do so) to Mecca. Burckhardt's death in 1817, at Cairo, while preparing an expedition to Fezzan and the Niger, was a great loss to African exploration. A profound orientalist, his great collection was deposited at Cambridge University. Another protégé of the British African Association was the Belgian, Adolphe Linant Bey (later known as Linant de Bellefonds), who in 1827 ascended the White Nile to a point nearly 150 miles south of Khartoum.

Mohammad Ali himself, recruiting in the Sudan in his restless quest for troops, did much to further Nile exploration. The last of three expeditions he despatched southwards between 1839 and 1842, which were accompanied by French officers, reached Logwek, on the west bank of the Nile a short distance beyond Gondokoro in latitude 4°32'N (near what was later the site of the Belgian station of Rejaf), the first high and stony land met with in ascending the White Nile after hundreds of miles' journey through marshes. Here the White Nile is unnavigable to the southward owing to 70 miles of rapids which cut off navigation of the river beyond Nimule to the south, and Gondokoro on the north, and which result from the thousand-foot fall between Dufile and Gondokoro. Dr Ignatz, an Austrian missionary, who reached Logwek in 1848, heard from the Bari that far to the south the Nile issued from a lake. Austrians were early in the missionary field in the Sudan. The Pope created a Bishop of Khartoum in 1849, and by 1851 a mission station had been founded at Gondokoro by Knoblecher and Vinci of the Austrian Mission.

The rapids on the Nile, southwards from Gondokoro, tended to divert exploring enterprise in the period from 1840 to 1860 to the great western tributaries which form the Bahr-al-Ghazal. Here John Petherick, an

Englishman and ivory trader, had explored as far as the Nyam-nyam country in the years 1853–59, and a Frenchman, Dr Peney, during the years 1856–61 explored the Yei – to the west of the Bahr-al-Jebel, and the country east to Latuka.

In addition to the obstacle of the rapids from Gondokoro to Nimule, the Bari – a Nilotic tribe – much harried by slave-traders, had turned on tormentors and others alike, and had become an obstacle to further advance up the Nile. Signor Vaudet, Sardinian pro-consul at Khartoum and ivory trader, was killed by the Bari near Gondokoro about 1859.

Thus, the extent of European knowledge of the Nile basin at about 1858–60 was as follows: there had been a partial mapping of the course of the Blue Nile from its source in Lake Tana; the Sobat had been explored for a hundred miles or so, as far as steamers could penetrate; the White Nile had been surveyed from Khartoum to its junction with the Bahr-al-Ghazal; south of that point, the river and some of its branches such as the Giraffe River (Bahr el Zeraf) – had also been explored; the River of the Mountains, as the upper White Nile was termed by the Arabs, had been ascended to a distance a little south of Gondokoro; the Bahr-al-Ghazal, the great western feeder of the Nile, and several of its more important affluents, such as the Jur and the Bahr-al-Arab, had been made known; and the existence of the Nyam-nyam cannibal country ascertained; but the ultimate sources of the Nile stream were still undiscovered. This problem was now to be attacked from two very different sources.

Erhardt's and Rebmann's 'slug map' and their accounts of snow mountains near the Equator were scoffed at by theoretic geographers. Even Sir Roger Murchison, dignified President of the RGS, sought witness from Livingstone that the existence of snow mountains in central Africa was doubtful. German geographers were sceptical; only the French seemed open-minded in the matter, and were ready to concede the missionaries' claims – for were not snow-capped mountains found in other parts of the world in similar latitudes, and might not the 'slug map' represent a confused account of a cluster of several lakes? It was the Paris Geographical Society which awarded the missionaries a medal for their achievements.

A persistent critic was the 'armchair geographer' W. Desborough Cooley (1795?–1883), an avid 'Africa watcher' – one of those 'unclassified waifs' attracted to the RGS in its early years. Cooley was a 'stormy petrel', a pernicious gadfly. Without experience on the ground in Africa, he was surprisingly well-informed about the continent. His esoteric knowledge, gleaned from many sources and collated in the comfortable security of London reading rooms, was used to keep geographers and explorers up to the mark. At times his was an inhibiting rather than an encouraging force for African exploration. He was in contact with Lieutenant J.B. Emery, who had presided over the short-lived Owen protectorate at Mombasa, and during his two years there had acquired a familiarity with the surrounding district. Emery had contacted the Sultan of Ozee, on the Tana River, who had ascended that river for a distance of two months' journey (about 400 miles), and Emery apparently contemplated an expedition inland from Ozee, accompanied by the Sultan's son; and he would 'have crossed Africa from this point', so he claimed, if he had been 'superseded from the government of Mombas', and if it would not have affected his career in the Navy. He had neither of these assurances, and thus the plan came to nought. In 1833 Emery and Cooley were in touch with each other; both published a Paper in the *Journal of the Royal Geographical Society* in that year which indicated their interest in East African exploration. In 1834 Owen was also pressing for renewed British attention to East Africa, and approached the Foreign Office as to the possibility of his being designated Consul-General in East Africa to resume the attack on the slave-trade there.

It would seem that all three, Cooley, Emery and Owen, about this time were in touch with Khamis bin Uthman, former interpreter to Owen's expedition, an adventurer of sorts, who visited England in 1834. Cooley drew much information from him as to the nature of the country behind Pangani and Mount Kilimanjaro, and Khamis stirred the interest of the three with his tale of a great lake in the interior. It was this information, and that which Cooley drew from other sources, which stirred him into supporting a number of vague and poorly matured plans for East African exploration and which had neither RGS nor government support. Australian and Polar exploration were in the air and absorbing RGS and public attention; and Erhardt's 'slug map' had not yet appeared to intrigue the imagination and direct attention to East Africa. Also, it must be admitted, the advocacy of the wearisome Cooley was not helpful in commanding official support for these lesser ventures which included plans to explore inland from the East African coast and with which the names of William Bollaert, Captain Turner, RN, and Lieutenant Ormsby are associated: these proposed ventures failed to materialize. There was also the ill-founded venture of Dr Bialloblotzky, in 1849. A learned divine, who had vague ideas of seeking the Nile sources, he ended up stranded in Zanzibar, dependent on the hospitality of the British consul. In contrast to all this was the work of Lieutenant W. Christopher, of the brig of war, *Tigris*, in early 1843. He traced the course of the mysterious river which ran southwards inland a few miles from, and parallel to the Somaliland coast, and which he named after his superior, Captain Haines, at Aden. His comments on the extent and cruelty of the slave-trade in the area were eagerly picked up by anti-slave-trade campaigners, for example, with regard to the severity with which runaway slaves were treated. One who had thus offended was fettered with shackles on his legs, and had been so for three years. He could advance only 10 inches at a time, and was condemned in that state to carry water.

Cooley's positive contribution was his paper 'On the Regio Cinnamonfera of the ancients' outlining trade prospects in Somaliland, which drew the attention of the East India Company to that region, and was probably influential in the launching of the Burton/Speke expedition of 1854/55.[7] Cooley also drew attention to the work of the Hungarian explorer, Laszlo Magyar, in western central Africa, whose achievements tended to be overshadowed by those of Livingstone. Cooley deserves credit for sustaining interest in East African exploration and ultimately stirring the RGS into mounting its great series of expeditions there in the second half of the nineteenth century. His recognition of Rift Valley features antedates the work of Gregory by many years. He set Speke right as to the bogus nature of the 'Hindu map' which the latter included in the first edition of his *Journal* but which, when apprised as to its fraudulent nature, he prudently withdrew from subsequent editions.

In one thing Cooley never relented; he perversely and stubbornly insisted that Lakes Tanganyika and Nyanza were one. Even after Livingstone rounded the southern end of Lake Tanganyika in 1867, and disposed once and for all of Rebann's 'slug lake' and showed that the two lakes were separate, Cooley tenaciously adhered to the view that they were united. Cooley was also an ingrate, for despite the RGS granting him free membership and petitioning for his civil list pension, he continued to snap at the hand that fed him, and persisted in his attacks on the so-called geographical establishment.

As mentioned above, Cooley's paper 'Regio Cinnamonifera' stirred the East India Company's interest in Somaliland, with which there was increasing British contact following the acquisition of Aden, and places in the Red Sea area.

In the early nineteenth century the Indian Navy's presence was increasingly evident in the Gulf of Aden, and treaties were made with the Somali tribes for the protection of East India Company interests and 'for the harbour of their ships without any prohibition whatever'. Captain Moresby, of the Indian Navy, made treaties with the Sultan of Tajurra and the Governor of Zeila to secure British interests. With the development of steamship communication with Suez more permanent acquisitions were needed, and British influence was strengthened by the occupation of Socotra (1834), Aden (1839) and Perim (1857), and by the purchase of a number of smaller islands, Bab, Aubad and Musha (acquired for 'ten bags of rice'). These acquisitions, administered from Bombay, brought added interest in Somaliland.

Harrar, the capital of that territory, lying some 250 miles inland and south-west of Berbera, its main port, was another 'Timbuktu' – an ancient mysterious metropolis, centre of the slave-trade and home of the 'Kat' plant, the mild narcotic widely used in the Yemeni and Aden world. Harrar beckoned to the adventurous, and the same white man, probably the first after Burckhardt to enter Mecca, was the first to enter Harrar. After returning from his pilgrimage to Mecca and Medina in 1853/54, Richard Burton's proposal to the Indian government to explore the interior of Somaliland was accepted, and in 1855, accompanied by Lieutenants Speke and Stroyan, fellow Indian Army officers and in the pay of the East India Company, Burton penetrated Somaliland from the neighbourhood of Berbera. On his own, he reached Harrar, and after an absence of four months reappeared at the coast with strange tales to tell of that forbidden city. He had stayed there ten days, talked to its king, and courted grave peril, and had then re-traversed the desert route running the gauntlet of Somali attack most of the way. Undeterred by this experience, Burton set out again for the interior, but was checked by a skirmish with the Somalis, in which Stroyan was killed, and Burton and Speke both severely wounded. They were lucky to emerge alive from this exploratory attempt in Somaliland.

The results of this rapid and short incursion into Somaliland were not spectacular. Despite his dramatic account of it Burton wasted much time in going to Harrar; all that came of it was the revelation of the volume of the slave-trade at that place, and about which nothing was done! Speke, for his part, had lost money in the venture which was sorely underfinanced; the wonder is that he proffered his services for a further expedition under Burton, to the interior lakes of East Africa! For no sooner was the Somaliland enterprise finished, than substantial preparations were under way to pierce the Nile mystery from the East African coast, farther south.

Here Krapf's and Rebmann's report of 'snow mountains' and 'Sea of Unyamwezi' (Land of the Moon) warranted further investigation. Burton, fresh from his Somaliland venture, was eager to try his hand, and his application to the RGS in 1855 to lead an expedition to East Africa 'primarily for the purpose of ascertaining the limits of the Sea of Ujiji and secondarily to determine the exportable produce of the interior and ethnography of its tribes' arrived about the same time (1855) as Erhardt's 'slug map' reached the RGS, whose President, Murchison, and Colonel W.H. Sykes, Chairman of the Court of Directors of the East India Company, supported the idea of a major expedition (the Society's first) to East Africa. Murchison was influential in obtaining a grant of £1000 from the Treasury, although the East India Company failed to honour its promise of a similar amount, thus leaving the expedition severely underfinanced. Burton was instructed to

> penetrate inland from Kilwa or some other place on the east coast of Africa and make the best of your way to the reputed Lake Nyasa ... Having obtained the information you require in this quarter you are to proceed northward toward the range of mountains marked upon our maps and containing the probable source of (the Nile) which it will be your next great object to discover ... you will then be at liberty to return to England by descending the Nile ... or you may return by the route by which you advanced or otherwise.[8]

Burton, with Speke again as his companion, arrived at Zanzibar at an important juncture in that island's affairs, for in the interval between the planning of their expedition in 1856 and its final departure in the summer of 1857, two important figures on the Zanzibar scene passed away. The Sultan's death in August 1856 was followed by that of Hamerton, the veteran British consul, in the following July. The new Sultan, Majid, had scarcely been installed by the time the two explorers arrived in Zanzibar at the end of 1856 .

Much information on the interior was now available to Burton and Speke for the Arabs' and Said's trading caravans had penetrated inland as far as Lake Tanganyika and there were permanent Arab trading centres *en route* there. While waiting a propitious season to commence their journey inland, the two explorers visited the important Shambaa chief, Kimweri (the same Kimweri visited by Krapf), at his capital,

Vuga, in the Usambara Mountains, and they had tarried sufficiently to get the feel of the Swahili coast. By August 1857 they were on their way, on the well-trodden path to Tabora, where they arrived in November 1857. Here a kindly reception from the Arabs and information as to several lakes in the interior, not one, as indicated by Rebmann's 'slug map', engaged their attention. By February 1858 they had arrived at Ujiji on the shores of Lake Tanganyika, the first Europeans to look out over those waters. Two months were spent in exploring the lake, and evidence was collected which indicated that the river at its northern end was an affluent, not an effluent of the lake.

By June 1858 the two explorers were back at Tabora, and from here, where he left Burton who was too ill to travel, Speke made his 'flying trip' to the north, and in August 1858 gazed out through fever-laden eyes over the expanse of water to which he gave the name of Lake Victoria Nyanza, and which he rightly guessed, 'gave birth to that interesting river, the source of which has been the subject of so much speculation, and the object of so many explorers'.

The need to return to Burton, who appears to have lost much of his old vigour and daring, prevented further exploration, and from Tabora there recommenced the long trek to the coast where they arrived in March 1859. The results of their expedition had been substantial: it had led to the discovery of two lakes – Tanganyika and Victoria Nyanza – and was the incentive for a series of major explorations which followed it by Speke and Grant, Baker, Livingstone and Stanley. Burton's masterly account of the expedition, in the *Journal of the RGS* and his *The Lake Regions of Central Africa* (1860), initiated a spate of literature on African exploration.

No sooner had Speke returned to England than he was promptly commissioned by the RGS, with support of the British and Indian governments, to return to East Africa and confirm that he had found the Nile's source. Burton, with his outlandish proposal to work his way in from the Juba, in disguise, even using walnut-juice to darken his already dark complexion, was passed over in favour of the more practical Speke.

By October 1860 Speke was again on the road to Tabora, with a younger and more congenial companion, also an Indian Army officer, A.J. Grant. Their progress inland was hampered by the unsettled nature of the country, for the Arabs at Tabora had taken sides in tribal wars and rendered whole districts in a state of turmoil with their arms, there was difficulty in procuring porters, and the old scourge of 'hongo' slowly spirited their trade goods away. Speke was also distressed by a persistent lung complaint. It was not until October 1861 that they reached Usui district to the south-west of Lake Victoria, threshold to the attractive upland world of Karagwe. What a joy to enter it!

> wherever you stop a day, the village officers are instructed to supply you with food at the King's expense, for there are no taxes gathered from strangers in the Kingdom of Karagwe ... Leaving the valley of Uthenja, we rose over the spur of Nyamwara, and found we had attained the delightful altitude of five thousand feet. Oh, how we enjoyed it! – every one feeling so happy at the prospect of meeting the good king Rumanika. Rumanika the king and his brother Nyanaji were both of them men of noble appearance and size. They had fine oval faces, large eyes, and high noses, denoting the best blood of Abyssinia. Having shaken hands in true English style, which is the peculiar custom of the men of this country, the ever-smiling Rumanika begged us to be seated on the ground opposite him, and at once wished to know what we thought of Karagwe, for it had struck him his mountains were the finest in the world; and the lake, too, did we not admire it? ... the queens and princesses of this royal family, by means of a milk diet, are kept immoderately fat. One of them ... could not rise; and so large were her arms that between the joints the flesh hung down like large, stuffed puddings. Then in came their children, all models of the Abyssinian type of beauty, and as polite in their manners as thoroughbred gentlemen.[9]

It was from Rumanika's capital that Speke caught a distant glimpse of the noble Mfumbiro volcanic group astride the Uganda/Congo border, which confirmed him in his belief that in this region lay the Mountains of the Moon, but without pursuing the question further he pushed on into Uganda. As in the case of Burton, Grant was an ailing partner, for twice during the journey he had to be left behind while Speke made the further advances. Speke on his own crossed the Kagera River, frontier of Uganda, on 16 January 1862, and arrived at Mtesa's capital near Kampala on 19 February 1862. Grant did not catch up with him until the following May; there then followed a wait of another two months before the capricious Mtesa would permit their departure. During this prolonged and enforced stay in Buganda Speke had ample opportunity to learn something of its people and history. It had been part of the ancient kingdom of Kitara, which it had shared with the district of

Bunyoro to its north-west. The Baganda were a Bantu people with a blend of Hima aristocracy in their upper classes; it was the practice among these to take Bahima as wives. The resulting off-spring was an intelligent and physically attractive people – Speke seems to have been unable to resist their charms, for he fathered a daughter by one of the Kabaka's sisters. Beneath the polished surface of this apparently advanced Bantu kingdom lay dark and sinister deeds. Speke witnessed daily executions for trivial offences, ordered at the whim of the king who wallowed in the luxury of absolute power. There was craven subservience at his court, and his followers were not an inspiring lot, despite their outward show of urbanity and sophistication.

It was with relief that the two explorers got away from Buganda on 8 July 1862. On the twenty-eighth of that month, Speke stood on the banks of the Nile – 'the Holy river, the cradle of Moses' – at its exit from Lake Victoria Nyanza and at the falls which he named after Lord Ripon. Here was the culmination of his whole journey. He had determined what he had set out to do. He had fixed the source of the Nile. The pity is that he did not subsequently trace its course northward in detail. Instead he struck inland to Hoima, capital of Kamrasi, King of Unyoro, lying between the Nile and Kafu Rivers; and after being detained here for two months was finally on his way northwards by early November 1862. Travelling sometimes by river, sometimes overland, in a northerly direction, he reached Faloro on the Nile in February 1863.

It had been arranged before he had left England that at Gondokoro, on the Nile, he would be succoured by John Petherick, unpaid British consul at Khartoum, who received funds for this purpose. The arrangement had an air of indefiniteness about it. Petherick claimed that he was insufficiently financed, that his support was only to be given if strictly necessary, and then only at a point a little south of Gondokoro. He had waited months for news of the expedition, and as none was forthcoming he had sent a military force of 200 Sudanese south to Faloro to await Speke and Grant, while he himself went off to the west on business of his own. Speke seems to have been expecting something in the nature of a 'grand almoner' – like Stanley's relief of Livingstone. Instead there was only a ragamuffin force at Faloro, who, instead of assisting, hindered them almost to the point of making them prisoner. At Gondokoro they were met not by Petherick, but by the burly figure of Samuel Baker, who had independently followed the White Nile southwards in the hope of meeting Speke's expedition. Baker's good work in giving sustenance to the explorers showed Petherick up in a poor light. The latter had been exploring the affluents of the Bahr-al-Ghazal and prosecuting slave-hunters, and had great difficulty getting back to Gondokoro; by the time he arrived Baker had stepped into the breach. Petherick's critics and enemies – and among them slave-dealers whom he had roughly handled – made the most of his predicament. He seems also to have lost the confidence of the Foreign Office, and his consulate was abolished in 1864. It is difficult to escape the conclusion that Petherick was shabbily treated in the whole affair of the provisioning of Speke at Gondokoro.

From Gondokoro where they arrived in February 1863, Speke and Grant had easy going northwards, and from Khartoum a telegram was wired back home: 'The Nile is settled!' By June 1863 Speke was back in England and hailed as one of the greatest African explorers; he had solved the age-old mystery of the Nile's sources which had haunted men's imagination for so long. There was only one flaw in his claim. He had not traced the Nile in detail down its full length, from its exit out of Lake Victoria Nyanza to Gondokoro. Critics were soon to question Speke's assumptions – for they were no more than assumptions – that he had discovered the true source of the Nile, and they were soon challenged by Burton and James M'Queen. Speke was only 37 years of age, when in September 1864, on the eve of a debate with Burton over the momentous discovery of the Nile sources, he accidentally shot himself. Thus was lost in his prime one of the youngest and most able of African explorers. Speke's *Journal* is full of geographical, ethnological and topographical detail, demonstrating his long and arduous training as an accurate observer, and it is a model of simple straightforward style, pithy and clear – a contrast to the harsh, angular and archaic prose of Burton with his tendency to word-coining.

While Livingstone, Burton, Speke and Grant were making their great journeys, a smaller band of explorers – mostly German in the tradition of Krapf and Rebmann – were making solid contributions to opening up the interior, although less well known and oft touched by tragedy.

Albert Roscher was lately from university and completion of his doctoral thesis on Ptolemy and the trade-routes of Central Africa, when, under the patronage of Ludwig, exiled King of Bavaria, and with the good opinions of Lord Clarendon, Rigby and Sultan Majid, he set out in 1859 from Kilwa in search of the inland sea of Erhardt and Rebmann. Attaching himself to an Arab caravan, he reached the eastern shore of Lake Nyasa by October 1859. But unbeknown to him, Livingstone, a few weeks previously, had reached the same lake from the southwards – thus claiming its discovery. Roscher's return journey from the lake in a northerly direction had barely commenced before he was robbed of his possessions and murdered. The retributive punishment that followed this crime supported the Sultan of Zanzibar's claim that his writ ran far inland, for the chief of the district in which the murder was committed sent those suspected as guilty of it to Zanzibar for trial. Grant, at Zanzibar in August 1860, witnessed their public execution.

News of Roscher's death reached Zanzibar just when Baron von der Decken had arrived there and was about to set out to join him. From an old Hanoverian family with considerable influence (the RGS had persuaded the Danes to lift the blockade of the Elbe to permit his boat to pass through on its way to East Africa), he carried seals for his good conduct in the lands through which he wished to pass from Lord John Russell, Rigby, Witt (German consul at Zanzibar) and Majid. Proceeding inland from Kilwa he faced obstruction from the local Arabs fearful of his interference in the slave-trade, and worried that he would stir up trouble in the interior by seeking to revenge Roscher's death. Lack of porters and food soon forced his return to Zanzibar, after getting no farther inland than 160 miles from Kilwa. Arriving back at Zanzibar in early 1861 he learned that Lake Nyasa had been discovered by Livingstone, and that Lake Tanganyika (and possibly to its north the Victoria Nyanza) had been discovered by Burton and Speke. The existence of the 'snow mountains' of Krapf and Rebmann still had to be confirmed.

Taking with him Richard Thornton, geologist, formerly with Livingstone's Zambezi expedition, von der Decken proceeded to Kilimanjaro in June 1861. Here he met the well-known Wachagga chief, Mandara, and ascended the mountain to the 8000-foot level, and thence returned to the coast, arriving back at Zanzibar on 8 November 1861. In August of the following year, accompanied by Dr Otto Kersten, he made a second attempt on the mountain and reached the 14,000-foot level. This accomplished, it was his intention to work his way westwards towards Lake Victoria through the country of the Maasai, but the latter, in that heightened state of marauding remarked on by New in 1871, prevented his advance. He was thus back at Zanzibar by December 1862.

He next conceived the idea of reaching the other snow mountain, Kenya, by way of one of the rivers known to debouch at the coast north of Mombasa. While waiting the arrival of a low-draught steamer from Europe, he made a wide-ranging perambulation of the western Indian Ocean, visiting the Comoros, Madagascar, the Seychelles, Réunion and

Mauritius. By the end of 1864 he was back at Zanzibar, ready to advance on Kenya. Finding the mouth of the Tana blocked by a sand bar; and the Ozi inadequate for his purpose, he decided on the Juba, although he seems to have been unaware that its sources were nowhere near Kenya mountain.

In August/September 1865, he ascended the Juba as far as the rapids 20 miles above Bardera, and about 180 miles from the coast. Here the steam paddle-boat was wrecked and had to be abandoned. Leaving the main party at the site, von der Decken, taking with him a few companions, made his way on foot to Bardera for provisions. Here, in an attack by the Somalis, von der Decken was killed and only a few of his companions survived. The main party waited in vain for their return, and finally made their way back to the coast and Zanzibar. The Sultan of Zanzibar tried to help, and the British directed HMS *Vigilant* to their aid, but little could be done. By now the survivors of the massacre at Bardera had returned to the coast with details of von der Decken's murder. With their leader gone, the steamboat wrecked and their numbers sadly depleted, there was little to do but return to Europe, and the party left East Africa in January 1866 .

There was a sequel to the story. Von der Decken's mother, Princess Adelheid of Pless, refused to believe that her son was dead, and commissioned Theodor Kinzelback and Richard Brenner (a survivor of the Juba expedition) to return to East Africa to seek out news as to whether he might still be alive. Kinzelback failed to reach Bardera overland from Mogadishu, and perished at Geledi, in January 1868: Brenner got no farther than Sorori, one hundred miles up the Juba. Thus ended the saga of the Juba expedition. It had an important result, however, for out of Brenner's attempt to ascertain von der Decken's fate, came the beginnings of German settlement in East Africa. Brenner had visited the town of Witu, some ten miles north of the Tana's mouth, which was the capital of the Bajun chief, Ahmed Fumo Luti, better known as 'Simba' (the Lion). Simba, on succeeding to his father's chiefdom in Pate Island in 1856, had migrated to the mainland and had built up a new sultanate at Witu. He ran up his own standard, and resisted the claim of the Sultan of Zanzibar to suzerainty over Witu. When Brenner visited him he apparently made a request, possibly at Brenner's prompting, that the Prussian government conclude a Treaty of Friendship and take him under its protection. Germany was to advert to this later.

Similarly, von der Decken's attempts on Kilimanjaro were to have a

follow-up, for at Zanzibar in 1863 he met Charles New, missionary, from
the Methodist station at Ribe near Mombasa, and inspired him with the
ambition to reach the snow-line of the mountain. It was not until July
1871 that New was able to make the attempt. With only 15 porters, and
goods and cash to the amount of £32, he arrived in August 1871 at the
town of Moshi where he met the 'monocular' Mandara – 'his right eye
being nearly closed and dark as pitch' – who took a friendly interest in
his plans and provided him with escort. With a few frightened natives,
and mentally and physically fatigued by the great heights and bitter cold,
New finally reached the snow-line on 26 August 1871. By October he
was back at Ribe. His first glimpse of Kilimanjaro had been awe-
inspiring:

> over the tops of the plantains, moved slowly and majestically a
> mass of white pile-cloud. But above and beyond, in beautiful
> circular outline, as round and smooth as the edge of the moon, was
> seen something far whiter, exciting the unconscious exclamation,
> 'as white as snow' ... It was a truly magnificent sight. Behind the
> moving clouds, set up against a sky of purest azure, there it shone
> motionless and sublime ... a beautiful dome of stupendous
> proportions, and as the clouds passed the whole of it became
> exposed ... The aspect presented by this prodigious mountain is
> one of unparalleled grandeur, sublimity, majesty, and glory. It is
> doubtful if there be another such sight in this wide world.[10]

The world of Kilimanjaro fascinated New. He was used to the dull-
witted Wanyika, and the Wachagga were energetic and prosperous, able
smiths. At Taveta he saw 'one of the greatest attempts at fortification I
had yet seen in the interior of Africa'; and the slopes of Kilimanjaro were
'the Canaan of Eastern Africa, for it may be said to flow with milk and
honey'. This African Cyclops, Mandara, for all his eccentric demeanour,
displayed an avidity for mathematics. The nearby Maasai seem to have
kept the Kilimanjaro folk on their mark and to have sharpened their wits.
Yet despite all this the Wachagga had made no attempt to scale
Kilimanjaro. Great was their astonishment at the 'white stone' which
melted before they got their lumps of it home, and which turned to
water when placed in their mouths.
    Livingstone, on his return to England in July 1864, accepted Speke's
grand discovery of the main source of the Nile, unlike some armchair
geographers such as M'Queen who still placed it in the 'snow

mountains' of Ptolemy – wherever these were. Petherick claimed that Speke's Nile was really the Sobat, and Burton, although at first ready to accept Speke's lake as 'one of the feeders of the White Nile', later asserted that its western 'top head' or reservoir, was Lake Tanganyika, and that the Victoria Nyanza was merely a 'lake region'. Speke, on his part, drew attack on himself; he was far too prone to accept as proven what were merely assumptions, even though these ultimately turned out to be true.

Livingstone, persuaded by Sir Roderick Murchison, President of the RGS, to return to Africa to report more extensively on the slave-trade and carry out further explorations as regards the source of the Nile, left England in August 1865, with the official title of British Consul to Central Africa and the assurance of the British government's 'deep and lively interest' in the objects of his expedition. These were to explore that part of Africa lying between 5° of north and south latitude, to encourage lawful trade and discourage the export of slaves. Livingstone, sustained in his views that the Nile sources lay further south than Speke would have them, and with the shock of the Zanzibar slave market still fresh in his mind, set out from the mouth of the Ruvuma on his last great venture in East Africa. Working his way up that river, towards Lake Nyasa, he was again confronted with the predations of the slave raiders – the Arabs and their henchmen, the Yao – and also with the ravages of the Mazitu (Mavitu or Maviti, as variously called).

Rounding the southern end of Lake Nyasa, Livingstone headed northwards, to the southern end of Lake Tanganyika, and here, hearing news of a lake – Mweru – to the westward, he proceeded thencewise, proving once and for all that Rebmann's 'slug map' was fiction, and that Cooley's view that Lakes Nyasa and Tanganyika were connected was arrant nonsense. His wanderings during the next two years were spent almost entirely in the discovery of Lakes Mweru (November 1867) and Bangwelu (July 1868), for which he received the RGS gold medal. Moving northwards, Livingstone, by the time he reached Ujiji on the east side of Lake Tanganyika, in March 1869, was wearied in body – a 'ruckle of bones' – foot-slogging had become a chore, and he was sorely depressed in mind at the extent of the slave-trade he met in the Tanganyika area.

A report had been leaked out in early 1867 by absconding porters from his caravan that Livingstone had died, which resulted in a rescue party reaching the Lake Nyasa region in September 1867 to ascertain the truth of this report. Here it was learned that Livingstone was alive and somewhere to the north. By early 1868, letters from Livingstone himself confirmed this fact.

Arriving at Ujiji in March 1869, Livingstone was keenly disappointed to find expected supplies from Zanzibar had been pilfered and, worst of all, precious medical drugs had disappeared. His own original medical chest had disappeared with an absconding porter, shortly after leaving the Ruvuma mouth in 1866. Drugs were sorely needed. The great choleric epidemic of the late 1860s, which affected most parts of Eastern Africa, had exacted its toll from his party, later to be weakened by malaria and dysentery. A few months' rest at Ujiji enabled Livingstone to continue on his way again. In July 1869 he was to be found to the westward of Lake Tanganyika seeking out the rivers flowing north of Lake Mweru, trying to ascertain their connection, if any, with the Congo or Nile systems. This search took nearly two years and left him sorely wearied in mind and body, without drugs and ridden by fever; to his 'choleraic purging' there was now added ulcered feet. He arrived in Manyuema land, recently penetrated by Arab slavers, to witness at Nyangwe, on the Lualaba, in July 1871, 'the most terrible scene I ever saw' – the onslaught of Arab slavers on the market-place at that town. From thence Livingstone struggled back to Ujiji, arriving there on 23 October 1871 – 'I felt dying on my feet'.

He was determined to break with the Arabs, and eager to follow up his plans to pursue the Lualaba northwards; for he sketched and compared the different species of fish brought to market with those of the lower Nile to see if they were the same kind. The disturbed political situation, largely the result of the depredations of the Arab slavers, prevented him from following the Lualaba downstream, and he returned to Ujiji, where on 9 November 1871 H. M. Stanley 'found' him.

The entry of Stanley on the African scene marked the appearance of a new breed of explorer. With him commences the 'Scramble' proper – the appropriation of African territory by European governments through the instrument of treaty-making – that dubious arrangement whereby non-comprehending African chiefs, under their so-called signatures, were legally deemed to have assigned sovereign rights over vast territories to European powers. With Stanley begins the era of 'spheres of influence', the staking of claims and demarcation of boundaries. It is the dividing line between the humane exploratory instinct – epitomized by Livingstone and Speke – and the expansion of empire of the later nineteenth century. It was above all a period in which Stanley, the supreme journalist, could make his journalistic 'scoops'. His search for Livingstone, kept a secret purportedly, lest the elusive bird might fly at the last moment of approach, was more likely so closely guarded to enhance its news value: the cash value of 'discovery'!

Livingstone was not 'lost' when Stanley set out to 'find' him. He knew his geographical position, had an agreed supply base at Ujiji to which British consular authorities at Zanzibar directed two supply caravans – the first of which, however, was pilfered before reaching there, and the second lingered at the coast long after its expected time of arrival at Ujiji.

Livingstone was thus in dire need of supplies, especially medical, and in this sense Stanley's mission was a godsend. Stanley moved inland with directness and despatch; neither weariness nor sickness delayed him. The sick were left to fend for themselves on the way; and, arriving at Tabora, where he was temporarily involved in the wars between the Arabs and Mirambo at that place, he hastily brushed aside this interruption, and pressed on, arriving at Ujiji in early November 1871, where he met the object of his expedition, the great explorer-missionary, Livingstone.

Along with medical supplies and food Stanley brought the latest news from the outside world. It was gratifying to Livingstone to learn that the RGS sustained its interest in his work and that HMG had provided £1000 for a further expedition to relieve him. Stanley also brought a letter from Murchison asking Livingstone to explore the northern end of Lake Tanganyika to ascertain its connection, if any, with the Nile system. Livingstone, even before leaving England in 1865, was tending to the view that the Nile sources lay to the south-west of Lake Tanganyika and it was with less than enthusiasm that, with Stanley in November and December 1871, he examined the northern portion of the lake. This excursion to the north showed that the Rusizi flowed into, not out of the Lake – thus confirming Livingstone's conviction that Lake Tanganyika had no connection with the Nile system. Thus Speke's case was also strengthened, and that of Burton weakened. Livingstone was now encouraged in his determination to seek out the Nile's sources to the south-westward of Lake Tanganyika.

He accompanied Stanley back to Tabora, parting with him on 14 March 1872. Stanley returned to Zanzibar, taking with him Livingstone's journals, and arriving there on 7 May 1872. Livingstone, despite Stanley's urgings to return to England with him, set his face south-westwards – his last great journey – for the search for the Nile sources, which he thought to lie at about 10°S latitude and to the west of

Lake Tanganyika. He seems to have converted Stanley in the matter, and the latter was surprised to find considerable disbelief among geographers and explorers in England on his arrival there as to Livingstone's thesis concerning the Nile sources. Sir Henry Rawlinson, President of the RGS, had already sent a letter to Livingstone with an expedition organized under Lieutenant V.L. Cameron for his relief, informing him that, despite Stanley's support for his views, it was now generally held in geographical circles in England that the Lualaba was part of the Congo system, not the Nile.

Meanwhile Livingstone, still at Tabora, although well-stocked with food and medicine thanks to the 'grand almoner' Stanley, and with a promise of more on its way up from the coast, was faced with difficulties in getting porters, and it was not until August 1872 that he got away from Tabora, just when the rainy season was about to begin. He soon found that, tough-seasoned walker though he was, he quickly tired in limb; he was an old man, in body at least, if not in age, in his sixtieth year. A long march down the rugged south-eastern side of Lake Tanganyika took him to its southern end, rounding which he struck out to the westward – towards the Katanga region, wherein he sought the uttermost sources of the Nile. Already, in early 1872, he seems to have had a premonition that this was his last chance of success: in January 1872, he recorded 'May the Almighty help me to finish my work this year for Christ's sake!'; in April there was a note of urgency, 'I pray the good Lord of all to favour me so as to allow me to discover the ancient fountains of Herodotus', and by May 1872, and in retrospect – 'I am oppressed with apprehension that after all it may turn out that I have been following the Congo'.

Progress was infinitely slow, through swamps and swollen rivers, floundering in the wastes to the east of Bangwelo. By the time he reached the Chambezi River he was so tired in body and racked by persistent choleraic haemorrhages against which he had no treatment, that those famous legs gave out, and for weeks he was litter-borne. At last merciful death brought release, at Chitambo, some 30 miles to the north of one of the branches of the Luapula, in the early morning hours of about 1 May 1873.

The expedition which HMG had organized, with Lieutenant Dawson, RN, in command, supported by Lieutenant Horn, Charles New, missionary, and Livingstone's son, Oswell, had already assembled at Zanzibar when Stanley returned from his relief of Livingstone. Their work was now unnecessary and the expedition returned to England. A

second 'Relief Expedition' organized by the RGS, and under Lieutenant
V.L. Cameron, accompanied by Dr Dillon, Lieutenant Murphy and
Robert Moffat, nephew of Livingstone, left Bagamoyo in the following
year, on 28 March 1873. During its progress inland, fever struck down
its members – causing the death of Moffat in May 1873, and then Dr
Dillon, in November, who in a state of delirium shot himself.

Meanwhile, on 20 October 1873, Chuma, one of the 'three faithfuls'
who had stuck with Livingstone throughout the trials of his last great
journey, arrived at Tabora with the news of Livingstone's death, and that
his body was being conveyed to the coast, embalmed and packed to avoid
the prying eyes of the 'thieving Wagogo'.

Although the purpose of the relief expedition was now nullified,
Cameron carried on to Ujiji to collect Livingstone's belongings. He
arrived there in February 1874, and found himself at the great slave-
trade centre of western Tanganyika, with Arabs in permanent residence
– one of whom had been there since 1858, when Burton arrived. They
possessed great numbers of domestic slaves – 20 to 100 each – employing
them as watercarriers, bodyguards and boatmen, and placing the females
in the harem. Ujiji was the main trade centre in the interior after Tabora;
slaves, ivory, Katanga copper and Mwili palm cloth were disposed of
there in return for trade goods from the coast; 'everything was priced in
beads' – the currency of the interior.

After mapping the lake and proceeding across it to Nyangwe,
Cameron, wishing to emulate the crossing of the continent by some Arab
merchants from Zanzibar a few years previously, continued south-
westwards, till in November 1875 he emerged on the Atlantic coast near
Benguela. During this crossing Cameron conceived the idea that the
Lukuga River was the outlet of Lake Tanganyika; he ascertained that the
Arabs in the interior knew that the Lualaba was part of the Congo
system, and he himself, by taking the level of the Lualaba at Nyangwe
and finding it lower than that of the Nile at Gondokoro, ruled out any
connection of the Congo with the latter. Cameron's was an epoch-
making journey across the continent – antedating that of Stanley's by
three years – but it has tended to be overlooked, overshadowed by the
great journeyings and death of Livingstone. Cameron was quick to pay
tribute to the latter: he found that to the west of Lake Tanganyika 'the
peaceful and unoffending progress' of Livingstone through the land
tended to make an Englishman respected by the natives.

Livingstone's death marks the end of an era – for the great central
lakes system was now made known, and all else would quickly fall into

place. Livingstone's achievements as an explorer are unsurpassed. During his great journeyings, covering the years 1859 to 1873, he had traversed one-third of the continent, and rounded out the map of eastern Central Africa. He had made his way peacefully, all on foot, and without bombast or crudities. For the Africans he was the 'river searcher', and for the Arabs 'the very great doctor'. His lonely death in the heart of Africa seemed to symbolize the cause for which he had striven – the bringing of Christianity and civilization to that continent, and the anti-slave-trade cause. He worked quietly and thoroughly in his explorations. With wide interests he was yet no mere philomath, for he was an acute scientific observer and one of rare geographical instinct – especially for sensing the lie of the land and for the delineation of watersheds. His great work gained for him the award of the RGS medal, and as to his astronomical observations for latitude and longitude, it has been said 'that there is more sound geography in the sheet of foolscap which contains them, than in many volumes of much more pretension'. Among African explorers only the German, Heinrich Barth, approximates near to him in stature as a great explorer and in rectitude of character. The latter's great traverses in the western Sudan in the years 1849–55, set out in his five-volume account of his travels, merit for him, some would aver, the mantle of Africa's greatest explorer in the nineteenth century. Others, however, would plump for Livingstone. It is more likely that the god of fairness which apportions in such matters, would bestow the mantle of greatness equally on both.

It was while returning to England in April 1874 from the Ashantee War that Stanley received news of Livingstone's death, and that his body was on the way to England. The effect upon Stanley 'after the first shock had passed away' was to fire him with a resolution to complete Livingstone's work. He had also by now sufficient contact with Africa to whet in him a desire to know more about that continent; he had begun to build up a library on it.

It was almost 15 years since Speke and Grant's mission, and many problems of the Upper Nile were still unsolved, and Baker's discovery of Lake Albert had left its southern limits undefined – 'illimitable'; and whether the Lualaba was connected with the Congo or not, had still to be demonstrated, and then the course of the Congo westwards to the Atlantic remained to be settled. No wonder Stanley had little difficulty in persuading the *Daily Telegraph* and *New York Herald* to back jointly his expedition in clearing up these mysteries! The heightened interest in Africa at the time is seen in the many applications to join Stanley's proposed expedition: 'Before I sailed from England, over 1200 letters were received from generals, colonels, captains, lieutenants, mid-shipmen, engineers, commissioners of hotels, mechanics, waiters, cooks, servants, somebodies and nobodies, spiritual mediums, and magetizers, etc.'

Once a decision was taken to send an expedition into the interior, Stanley acted with much firmness and promptitude. By 17 November 1874 he was on his way inland from Bagamoyo; on 27 February 1875 he sighted Speke Gulf – the broad arm of Lake Victoria Nyanza which 'stretched like a silvery plain far to the eastward, and away across to the boundary of dark blue hills and mountains'; and by 7 March 1875, the *Lady Alice* (carried inland in sections) was reassembled and afloat on the waters of Speke Gulf.

Stanley then proceeded to circumnavigate the entire expanse of the lake, and travelled on foot along its northern shores, thus revealing its unity and approximate size. He was thus also brought into contact with the kingdom of Buganda whose 'extraordinary monarch and extraordinary people' made such a deep impression on Stanley's mind: 'What a land they possess! and what an inland sea!' Mtesa, the king, was 'The Foremost Man of Equatorial Africa'; his features reminded Stanley of those of the great stone images at Thebes and of the statues in the museum at Cairo. Stanley's sojourn among the Baganda resulted in his sending a letter to England, a clarion call to missionaries – 'Oh! that some pious, practical missionary would come here! What a field and harvest ripe for the sickle of civilization!' The response was immediate – the first step in a chain of events which was to bring Uganda under British influence.

Leaving Buganda in April 1875 – with most pleasant memories – for it had been a most welcome and reinvigorating respite on his journey, he set out with a large force to explore the countries between Lake Victoria and Lake Edward. He sighted a portion of the latter lake, and camped within a short distance of the Ruwenzori mountains of whose existence he was unaware, although they were towering over him. From thence he struck southwards across the Katonga lagoon and down to the Kagera – principal affluent of Victoria Nyanza – on its western side (which he named Alexandra Nile). On 7 April 1876 he directed his face towards Lake Tanganyika, having completed the 'Exploration of the Southern Sources of the Nile and solution of the problem left unsolved by Speke and Grant – Is the Victoria Nyanza one lake, or does it consist of five lakes, as reported by Livingstone, Burton and others?' It was with relish that Stanley set out for Tanganyika.

The 'bright waters' of Lake Tanganyika broke upon Stanley's view at noon on 27 May 1876 – at Ujiji, where he had met Livingstone some four and a half years previously. Within the next few months he circumnavigated the lake and showed that its outlet, the Lukuga, drained to the westward. Thence, proceeding westwards to Nyangwe, on the Lualaba, the point where Livingstone and Cameron had turned aside, he followed that river north-westwards to Stanley Falls, and proved its connection with the Congo. This demonstrated, he traced the course of the latter westwards to the Atlantic. Thus was encompassed the width of the continent. It was a marvellous achievement, in keeping with the image that Stanley had built up for himself as the man of iron will who would brook no opposition and who could survive amidst appalling hardship. Of the three white men who accompanied him all died during the journey and he himself was prematurely aged, but he had cleared up great geographical problems, and his journey led directly to the founding of the Congo State and the partition of Africa.

Stanley's third great journey into the interior of Africa, like his first, was a mission of relief. It was not directed like his second expedition to seeking out definite geographical information and for exploration. He sought to relieve Emin Pasha, Governor of the Equatoria Province, who had been cut off from the north since April 1883 and who, under pressure from the Mahdi's forces, had been forced ever further southwards until he was now based on Wadelai and Lake Albert. Although he felt himself abandoned by the Egyptian government, Emin was nevertheless determined to hold out, for he had no official release from his post. 'We shall hold out until we obtain such help or until we perish. In a letter to Mackay, missionary in Uganda, of 6 July 1886, he stated:

In the first place believe me that I am in no hurry to break away from here, or to leave those countries in which I have now laboured for ten years ... all my people, but especially the negro troops, entertain a strong objection against a march to the south, and thence to Egypt, and mean to remain here until they can be taken north ... I am ready to stay and to hold these countries as long as I can until help comes, and I beseech you to do what you can to hasten the arrival of such assistance. Assure Mwanga that he has nothing to fear from me or my people, and that as an old friend of Mtesa's I have no intention to trouble him'.[11]

While Emin might be determined to remain at his post and to protect Egyptian interests till relief arrived, plans were shaping up in England for his relief. It suffices at this stage to say that early in October 1886, Sir William Mackinnon and Mr J.F. Hutton, ex-President of the Manchester Chamber of Commerce, had spoken to Stanley respecting a relief expedition to Emin with a view to enable him to hold out on his own.

By 24 December 1886, in response to a call from Mackinnon, Stanley was back in England from his curtailed lecture tour in America, ready to undertake the organization of an expedition to relieve Emin; and he would march under the Egyptian standard. Stanley won his point against the Relief Committee which wanted the expedition to take the Eastern route into the interior. 'I was firmly convinced that the Congo River route was infinitely the best and safest', and did not Stanley know both the route from the east coast and that from the west coast? His arguments along with others marshalled later, prevailed in favour of the Congo route.

It was a powerful expedition that Stanley collected at Zanzibar in January 1887, with great quantities of supplies – especially armaments – and to ensure a supply of porters to carry these, Stanley entered into an agreement with Tippu Tib, doyen of Arab traders in the interior, who was to have carriers available at an agreed staging point on the Congo route to Lake Albert. Leaving Zanzibar on 25 February 1887, and rounding the Cape, the expedition's steamer was launched on the Congo on 30 April: the journey inland had commenced.

Without going into detail of the long journey up the Congo, Aruwimi and Ituri, which are set out in Stanley's account, suffice it to say that Lake Albert was reached on 14 December 1887, But it was not until 29 April 1888 that Emin Pasha was contacted. Stanley described him:

> a small spare figure in a well-kept fez and a clean suit of snowy cotton drilling, well-ironed and of perfect fit. A dark grizzled beard bordered a face of a Magyar cast, though a pair of spectacles lent it somewhat an Italian or Spanish appearance. There was not a trace on it of ill-health or anxiety; it rather indicated good condition of body and peace of mind.[12]

Stanley could scarcely have surmised that it would be a year and a half before he could commence his return journey with Emin to the east coast. There were immeasurable delays. There were long negotiations with Emin as to the terms of his evacuation; Emin's own reluctance to leave was compounded with that of his troops, they showed little desire to return to Egypt by way of the east coast. Emin had to consult his scattered forces at Lake Albert and at Wadelai, a time-consuming affair, and during it Emin and Mr Jephson, one of Stanley's party, were for some months virtually held prisoner by Emin's rebellious forces. In the mean time Stanley had retraced his steps to Yambuya to bring up the rear column, only to find everything had gone wrong at that end of his expedition. Then, after arriving back at the lake in January 1889, further delays ensued before the expedition, now swollen to some 1500 persons, could set out from Kavallis on 9 April 1889. A few miles to westward from here, another month's delay occurred owing to Stanley's illness. By 8 May the expedition at last turned its face southwards to the Semliki Valley, with its great white expanse of ripe grass which probably fooled Baker into his remark as to the illimitable nature of Lake Albert's southern end – it also fooled some of Stanley's men! Stanley now discovered the Semliki River a broad and deep stream, 80 to 100 yards wide and flowing into the lake. Then skirting their flanks to the immediate westwards, he had further glimpses of the unforgettable Ruwenzori, which it had not been his purpose to discover but 'It simply thrust itself direct in our homeward route'. Stanley was stirred into flights of rhetoric by the magnificence of the dominating and unsurpassed heights of Ruwenzori proper, 'a congregation of hoary heads, brilliant in white raiment'. On 24 May, 1888:

> When about five miles from Nsabe camp, while looking to the south-east, and meditating upon the events of the last month, my eyes were directed by a boy to a mountain said to be covered with salt, and I saw a peculiar shaped cloud of a most beautiful silver colour, which assumed the proportions and appearance of a vast mountain covered with snow. Following its form downward, I became struck with the deep blue-black colour of its base, and wondered if it portended another tornado; then as the sight descended to the gap between the eastern and western plateaus, I became for the first time conscious that what I gazed upon was not the image or semblance of a vast mountain, but the solid substance of a real one, with its summit covered with snow.[13]

During their progress along its westward flanks Lieutenant Stairs ascended the Ruwenzori to a height of 11,677 feet; and thence the expedition proceeded round its southern flanks, in the course of which the dimensions of Lake Edward were revealed. From here the expedition set out in a south-easterly direction towards Lake Victoria, picking up Stanley's early tracks from his expedition of 1875/76. His journey to the coast was uneventful, and on 3 December 1889 he heard the evening gun at Zanzibar; by 6 December 1889 he was at the island itself.

This expedition, although not one of exploration, made solid achievements in this field. The Semliki River had been discovered; the true dimensions of Lake Albert at its southern end had been confirmed; and considerable knowledge of the region had been gained. Baker's 'illimitableness' of Lake Albert's southern extension had been ruled out. More important, Stanley 'discovered' the Ruwenzori mountains. In tracing the course of the Semliki southwards he 'discovered' Lake Albert Edward and showed its connection with the Nyanza system; he also showed the existence of a great south-western gulf of Victoria Nyanza.

There still remained the blank space stretching westwards from the Indian Ocean to Lake Victoria, comprising what is today modern Kenya. The major journeys of the European explorers inland and the track of Arab traders had been more to the south – from Bagamoyo inland to Lake Tanganyika by way of Tabora, from which place trade-routes also branched northwards to Uganda.

Access to the highland area of Kenya meant crossing the Maasai steppe country, and here the 'holy terror' of the Maasai made the more cautious weigh carefully any advance by this way. Kamba traders, however, had been pushing down to Mombasa early in the nineteenth century – driving their cattle coastwards and bringing down ivory; they had thus to some extent demolished the legend of the invincibility of the Maasai and their avant-garde marauders, the Maviti. Inland towards Lake Victoria a further threat was posed by the Nandi and Kipsigis. The continued arrival of Arab caravans at Lake Victoria and in Uganda from the mid-century onwards awakened interest in the more direct route from Mombasa through Maasai country; it was more bracing in climate, considerably shorter, and there were reports of abundance of ivory in this region. Krapf's chain of missionary stations projected to spread-eagle the continent from east to west would have started from Mombasa, and so also the unwordly Dr Bialloblotzky's scheme was to be based on Mombasa as the starting-point for an advance into the interior. Keith Johnson's ill-fated attempt to use the Maasai route in 1877 did not deter other travellers intent on exploring the region of what is present-day Kenya. In the course of the 1880s two large, well-armed caravans, one led by the German explorer, G.A. Fischer, and the other by the Hungarian traveller, Count Samuel Teleki, forced their way across Kikuyu country. In addition to the Maasai threat, there was also that from the Kikuyu; Fischer and Teleki found them decidedly hostile; so the Kikuyu too earned for themselves an 'evil reputation among European travellers'. Thus did the caravans led by Bishop Hannington, Joseph Thomson and Frederick Jackson carefully traverse the Kenya highlands on their way inland to the lake.

The work of filling in the details which had commenced with the earlier journeys of Krapf and Rebmann, von der Decken and Roscher, was continued, notably by Joseph Thomson (1883-84) who sought to find a route from Mombasa to Lake Victoria through the Kenya highlands and the Maasai country – so long *terra incognita*. In 1877 a project mounted by the RGS and led by Keith Johnson to enter the Maasai country foundered in tragedy, but it left the RGS much interested in opening up this route. In 1882 it requested Joseph Thomson to report on its feasibility, for no European as yet had penetrated Maasailand. In proceeding inland Thomson's porters were so dispirited at the prospect awaiting them that they deserted wholesale, and Thomson was obliged to return to the coast for further recruits. Thomson then crossed the Njiro desert; explored the eastern Rift Valley and thence passed through Laikipia to Mount Kenya and Lake Baringo. He afterwards traversed the unknown region between Baringo and Victoria Nyanza, which he reached on 10 December 1883. On his way back from the lake he discovered the wonderful caves on Mount Elgon. Thomson's account of the extremities to which he was driven on this return journey from Lake Victoria, for want of water and grain, was extremely unfavourable as regards the use of the route from Mombasa to Lake Victoria, although he did much to bring the country of the Maasai and the Maasai themselves into clearer perspective, demythicizing much of the lore and nonsense that had been built up around that tribe in the nineteenth century.

The filling in of details continued into the 1890s and early twentieth century. In northern Uganda Macdonald's expedition of 1897/98 opened up new country, and in northern Kenya the work of Dr Donaldson in 1893–95 was similarly valuable. In the German sphere to the south Count Pfeil and Lieutenant Schluter explored the country between the Wami River and Lake Nyasa; Langheld, the Bukoba region to the west of Lake Victoria; and Oscar Baumann, who journeyed from Pangani through Maasailand to Ruanda and Urundi in the early 1890s, continued the work of filling in blank spaces.

The nineteenth-century pioneer explorers found around the equatorial lakes a region favoured by a reasonable rainfall and equable climate and a remarkably well-organized system of life; but it was self-contained and cut off from outside influences. The social conditions of the population had not engendered a need, as in ancient Egypt, to evolve a system of writing, architecture, attention to land use and production of surplus to command luxury goods, and the urge was lacking which elsewhere had led peoples untouched by Western civilization, such as the Eskimos and some Pacific Islanders, to provide themselves with primitive charts. Nothing resembling an indigenous map has come to light in East Central Africa. Cameron, when he tried to get the Arabs at Ujiji to draw a map, found that 'north and south, east and west, and all distances were irretrievably lost in a couple of minutes'; and Cameron continued to be struck by the general haziness of people's ideas as to general geography, although their local knowledge might be 'wonderfully good'.

Apart from the representation of geography that might be gathered from the graphic detail in travellers' tales, the earliest topographical maps were built up on itineraries and these, although remarkably good, were neither fully comprehensive nor wholly accurate. The introduction of the scientific surveys of the twentieth century had to happen before full accuracy could be attained. These early maps were perforce constructed upon sketches of routes traversed at first by explorers and later by soldiers and administrators, whose duty led them into this remote region and who were not always supported by astronomical observations. In the case of Speke and Grant's expedition of 1860–62, however, two hundredweights of 'instruments for observing' were carried. Speke's experience in mapping and surveying in India stood him in good stead, for his careful observations greatly enhanced the value of his route map, and some of his latitudes have proved remarkably accurate. The majority of travellers relied on time and compass traverses; Emin, for example, confined himself solely to compass survey. At the end of the nineteenth century when the War Office prepared maps of East Africa, such as that for Uganda, these were nearly all compiled from the thousands of miles of route sketches of these early travellers; and these route sketches continued to multiply with the extension of administration into the farthest corners of the various territories as the European administrators got a grip on their country.

The opening up of East Africa encountered little resistance. Seyyid

Majid may have tried to block the inland path in devious ways, even though all the expeditions except Stanley's were commended to him by the British government and its agent at Zanzibar, and to all of them he gave his 'passport'. Arab and Swahili traders residing on the coast could be obstructive and were not always helpful; but inland the explorers testify to a sympathy and helpfulness on the part of the Arabs that was more than formal. Of those he met at Kazeh, Burton states:

> nothing could be more encouraging than the reaction experienced from the Omani Arabs, striking indeed, was the contrast between the open-handed hospitality and the hearty good-will of this truly noble race, and the niggardness of the savage and selfish African – it was heart of flesh after heart of stone.[14]

Speke was equally appreciative when he was entertained by a lonely Arab trader on an island on Lake Tanganyika: 'These Arab merchants ... are everywhere the same. Their warm and generous hospitality to a stranger equals anything I have ever seen elsewhere'. Cameron complained that some lesser Arab or Swahili traders at Tabora obstructed him and induced his porters to desert, but still had to concede that he was warmly welcomed by the Arabs of Ujiji. Livingstone also, despite the slave-trade in which the Arabs engaged, had to admit their generosity. New, on the other hand, declared 'The Arabs, taken as a whole, are a detestable race, with scarcely a redeeming quality', but New's experience was limited to the coastal Arabs and Swahili.

From the Indian community in East Africa, explorers – especially officers from India – had a warm welcome. The German Dr Roscher, too, spoke well of them; in exploring the Rufiji River for a considerable distance he experienced much hospitality and kindness on the part of the Banians. Speke and Burton 'being Indian Officers' were 'looked upon as their guardians ... as if after a long banishment they were suddenly thrown amongst their old and long-lost friends'; and inland at Tabora, Musa, the leading Indian trader, went out of his way to help them.

African reaction to the European incursion was varied. Burton claimed that 'During thirty years, not an Englishman of the many who had visited it had been molested at Berberah'. Elsewhere, in East Africa 'hongo' was the curse. It predisposed Europeans against Africans like no other harrassment. This exacted tribute – a form of hostage for safe passage through an African chief's territory – was a veritable curse; it revealed the lowly state of African culture, their avidity and rapacity for

European goods – far beyond the wildest expectations of their own attainment and in European eyes revealing their inferiority. Wonder and astonishment attended the appearance of a European apparition and his marvellous goods in an African world. How the explorers cursed this burden of 'hongo'! Africans exacted their pound of flesh at literally a pound (sterling) a mile. The only way in which Thomson could mollify Mandara after all other gifts had failed, was to offer his own 'trusty double-barrelled smooth-bore, a steel box, a suit of thick tweed complete with a pair of shoes'. The view that 'hongo' was more rampant among petty chiefs than the paramount or kingly chiefs was certainly not the case with Mtesa, who was rapacious, and could scarcely conceal his avidity for the goods that Speke carried with him. Only Rumanika of Karagwe, the 'good Rumanika', as Speke termed him, seems to have exhibited dignity and restraint in the matter; he in turn pressed a large quantity of ivory on Speke, about the only commodity a European might desire.

There are varied comments on European reaction when first meeting Africans. Speke spoke of that crisis of the peoples of the interior ... want of a strong protecting government, without which nothing can prosper; and his remedy was simply the imposition of a strong protecting government like that in India. According to Livingstone, 'The great want of the Manyuema is national life, of this they have none, each headman is independent of every other'. But Livingstone added: 'Nothing but the most pitiable puerility would lead any manly heart to make their inferiority a theme for self-exaltation: however, that is often done, as if with the vague idea that we can, by magnifying their deficiencies, demonstrate our immaculate perfections'. Europeans, like gods, might tender cures and placebos to eager outstretched hands. New observed: 'with what readiness and confidence they take our drugs. No suspicion of poisoning ever seems to cross their minds'. New was interested in the cult of 'Moro' and 'Muanza' of the Wanika, the deeper meaning of their recreations and dances; but what a low opinion he had of them! 'Lying is to the Wanika almost as the very breath to their nostrils ... allied to their laziness is their mendacity; all the Wanika are great beggars ... They are altogether without history, and tradition is almost mute'. Another missionary, Roscoe in Uganda, was interested in the religion and customs of the Baganda and the Banyoro; but only settled missionaries had the time and interest for these luxuries of the mind. Not so travellers. Speke was unrestrained in his comments: 'the curse of Noah sticks to these his grandchildren by Ham'. Thomson, more tolerant, seeing humour – even in the spitting of the Maasai as a form of greeting – and in turn using Eno's Fruit Salts to astonish them, observed that the Kavirondo, despite their nakedness, were the most moral of all tribes of this region, 'angels of purity beside the decently dressed Maasai, among whom vice of the most open kind is rampant'.

There seems to have been little if any African interest in knowledge of geography, cosmography or topography. They seemed to be completely beholden to Europeans in this respect. Their contribution to the lifting of the veil from the unknown of East African geography, apart from providing carriers and gunbearers for the Europeans, seems to have been negligible. Instead they obstructed at times by their downright hostility or exaction of hongo. There seems to have been no great curiosity on their part as to the work the Europeans explorers were undertaking, merely a bemused detachment: they were singularly unexcited about the whole business. 'Well-documented cases of African reaction to explorers are hard to find'. For all the vast unknown of East Africa, there is no record of Europeans being 'lost' in East Africa, nor for that matter of Africans either! The latter seemed to have had little idea of the wider world outside their own tribal area, which was often of limited size. As has previously been pointed out, Cameron, moving westwards from Ujiji in 1874, commented on the haziness of peoples' ideas as to general geography, although local geography was wonderfully good. And Lieutenant Christopher, exploring the immediate hinterland of Somaliland in 1843, commented that the Africans were 'very ignorant even of their own neighbourhood, and continually making contrary statements as to distances, numbers, and qualities'; after all it was doubtful whether the African could comprehend any number beyond that of his own digits! Keith Johnson observed: 'It is remarkable that there is not one single name of a district, a people or place, with the exception of the Wamasai – a general name for the people of the whole region west of the Lake'; and New could not understand how Cooley could base his description of the country near the Sabaki on information which was 'a perfect jumble of mistakes' gained from Khamis bin Uthman whose 'opinion goes for nothing against facts'. Among Africans, it was only Rumanika who seems to have had a real desire for a wider geographical knowledge.

As to establishing British colonies in East Africa, there was no formal attempt until the last quarter of the century. Livingstone's Zambezi expedition of 1858–62 sought to establish a commercial enterprise – a settlement of missionaries and traders rather than white farmers – in the upper Shire area, and throughout his peregrinations Livingstone seems to have kept his eyes open as to trade prospects and the growing of commercial crops.

However, the nearest thing to a formal approach to the establishment of British enterprise in East Africa, apart from that of Owen at Mombasa in the 1820s, was the interest shown by the Bombay government in Somaliland (possibly because it was so near Aden), which led Lord Elphinstone to support Burton's expedition of 1859. The British preoccupation with the East African slave-trade precluded other considerations, but not so the Germans. Von der Decken had the idea of establishing a German colony in East Africa much on his mind. In the summer of 1869, while on the Juba, he wrote:

> I am persuaded that in a short time a colony established here would be most successful, and after two or three years would be self-supporting. It would become of special importance after the opening of the Suez Canal. It is unfortunate that we Germans allow such opportunities of acquiring colonies to slip, especially at time when it would be of importance to the navy.[15]

Von der Decken said on many occasions that he would not hesitate, if Seyyid Majid agreed to it, to buy Mombasa from the Sultan in order to found an establishment and place the commerce of the interior in the hands of Europeans and especially of Germans. 'After two or three years' stay at Chagga ... the colonists would obtain more results than emigrants who wander far across the seas. I recommend to my country an enterprise as advantageous as it is glorious for individuals and for the nation'.

Missionary extension into East Africa paralleled that of the explorers and in some instances was in advance of it. The German missionaries, Krapf and Rebmann, were first in the field, both as explorers and missionaries; they had to start *ab initio*, for despite the presence of the Portuguese some centuries before, nothing remained of Christianity in East Africa at the time European missionary activity commenced in the nineteenth century. Krapf and Rebmann made little headway, much less so than the Roman Catholic Holy Ghost Mission established at Zanzibar in 1860, with a branch at Bagamoyo on the mainland by 1868. The practical training at the latter Catholic Mission in carpentry, blacksmithing, building and vanilla-growing was a demonstration of practical Christianity – 'laborare est orare' – and so impressed Sir Bartle

Frere after visiting there in 1873, that he recommended it as a model of its kind – an example for other Christian Missions to follow.

Arab and Islamic resistance to Christian missionary extension in East Africa was surprisingly small, in view of the near monopoly the Arabs had over the coastline and in that they had been in the interior some decades in advance of the missionaries. Apart from Uganda, and a few instances elsewhere such as quarrels with missionaries at Mombasa, there was nothing in the way of a jihad against the Christian; perhaps this was because of the comparatively small number of Arabs in East Africa, and the early presence of British power at Zanzibar, and their influence with the Sultan there which tended to command their respect.

In the interior of East Africa, with the exception of Nyasaland where missionary enterprise was started shortly after Livingstone's visit, the first Christian enterprise was started in the kingdom of Buganda by the CMS in 1877, and by the Roman Catholic White Fathers in 1879. This kingdom was to become the focal point of a British advance on Uganda during the scramble in the last quarter of the century; and it was also to be the scene of a bitter and disastrous religious civil war. Before this was to happen other English missionary societies had established themselves in East Africa. The White Fathers were established at Zanzibar, in the interior as far as Lake Tanganyika; at Tabora, Karema, Mpala and Uvira; at Bukumbi on the southern end of Lake Victoria; and at Rubaga in Uganda; and they had penetrated into the eastern Congo, with a station at Kibanga in the remote Manyuema country. There were CMS stations at Freretown and Rabai near Mombasa; at Mpwapwa on the caravan route to Tabora; at Kamlikenia and Moshi in the Chagga country near Kilimanjaro; at Usambiro on the southern end of Lake Victoria; and at Mengo in Uganda. London Missionary Society stations were sited at Niamkolo to the south of Lake Tanganyika, and at Ujiji and Mtowa on its eastern and western sides. University Mission stations were concentrated to the south – at Masasi and Newala, inland from Lindi on the coast; at Likoma on Lake Nyasa; and at Magila in Usambara district. The United Methodist Free Churches Mission at Ribe near Mombasa was founded in 1862 and had among its first members two outstanding missionaries: Thomas Wakefield and Charles New who both made substantial contributions in the field of East African exploration – approaching the work of Krapf and Rebmann in this respect. The United Free Churches Mission also extended its work into the Tana River district, and before the end of the century had stations at Golbanti and Kulesa. The Neukirchen Evangelical Mission society was also established in the same area, with stations at Golbanti and Ngao on the Tana. The work of the Church of Scotland Mission at Blantyre, and the Free Church of Scotland Mission at Livingstonia and Bandawe (on the west side of Lake Nyasa), lie outside this study.

By the mid-1880s missionary activity, largely British, as represented by dots on a map might seem remarkable in coverage, but in fact was mostly confined to the main caravan routes into the interior, and elsewhere had made little impress. It is doubtful whether there were more than 350 Europeans engaged in missionary activity over the whole vast area of East Africa at this time.

European penetration into the East African interior coincided with tribal movements that had commenced early in the nineteenth century. From the south, forcing their way up through the gateway between Lakes Nyasa and Tanganyika, had come the Ngoni, an offshoot of Chaka's Zulus, who, like the Matabele and Shangaans, to escape Chaka's tyranny had trekked northwards. The Ngoni had almost reached Lake Victoria before their drive was blunted by the Uniamwezi ruler, Mirambo, in the 1860s. Reverberations of the northward drive of the Ngoni were still manifest at the time of Livingstone's entry to the north of Lake Nyasa in the mid-1860s, where he witnessed the chaos consequent on it.

Elsewhere in East Africa there were population movements. Moving southwards into Uganda from the southern Sudan came the Nilotics, impelling into movement previously settled tribes and stirring up long established patterns of habitation; the upset resulting from this was felt by Europeans at the time of the building of the Uganda Railway through the Nandi country at the turn of the century. Farther east, in the Great Rift Valley region and south of Mount Kenya, the Maasai, racked by plague and internecine warfare, had declined in power relative to their neighbours the Kikuyu and Kamba whom they had hitherto terrorized, but who now made the most of Maasai decline and turned on their former tormentors. European explorers, like Joseph Thomson and Lugard, witnessed this remarkable volte-face in which the Maasai were displaced from their traditional grazing ground. In the Horn of Africa the Galla and Somali, following ancient migration patterns, were moving southwards and ousting former occupants and taking over the pastoral land. The turbulence consequent on tribal movements in Somaliland reached its climax with the rise of the Mad Mullah at the end of the century, and commenced an episode which saw no end either for Italians or British, almost until the 1920s, and the vibrations of which were felt in British East Africa.

These tribal movements and countermovements were as old as time itself and were merely accentuated as seen through European eyes in the nineteenth century. Amidst this kaleidoscope of peoples on the East African scene a number of tribes stood out as political entities. The Chagga on the slopes of Mount Kilimanjaro were thrifty agriculturists – an intelligent and industrious people who under able leaders such as Fundikira and Mandara in the mid- and latter years of the nineteenth century, managed to play off both German and British against each other with considerable skill. The Chagga were in contrast to the more backward peoples such as the Giriama and Nyika groups between Kilimanjaro and the coast, and were also a contrast to the Maasai who marauded between Kilimanjaro and the farther interior.

Far inland, arching around the northern and western sides of Lake Victoria, lay the kingdom of Buganda – a country of Bantu agriculturists with a strong Hima strain in their upper classes; a people who exhibited in their governmental and hierarchical structure a high degree of organization. The Baganda had attained such military efficiency that they had laid under tribute surrounding tribes and districts. By the time of British entry in the 1880s the Baganda had reached the height of their power and there were signs of decadence and the waning of this power. The practical result of this decline was seen in the upswing of Bunyoro, the kingdom on the western borders of Buganda, with which a common ancestry was shared in the ancient kingdom of Kitara. Barring European intervention into Uganda, Bunyoro might well have regained her ancient paramountcy over Buganda. Stanley, during his Emin Pasha rescue expedition, observed that Kabarega, ruler of Bunyoro, was a power in the land, remarkably well-informed as to Stanley's movements and widely feared by surrounding lesser tribes. But for the Mahdi uprising in the Sudan which cut off European penetration southward by way of the Nile, and the continued waywardness of Kabarega in the matter of the slave-trade which drew on him British punishment, he might have made the Baganda surrogate to him. But joining with the British, the Baganda entered into an attack on the Banyoro with gusto. In this campaign Kabarega staunchly held out as one of the last rulers in East Africa to defy a European power.

South-west of Buganda, the small kingdom of Ankole and the Tutsi kingdom of neighbouring Ruanda impressed the first European visitors to come in contact with them; they were also political entities with 'kings' and a portfolio of ministers in ascending rank. Similarly, the centre of native power in the Uniamwezi country at Unyanyembe near present-day Tabora in Tanzania was impressive. Under rulers such as Fundikira at the mid-century, and Mirambo in the later nineteenth, a virtual 'empire' had been built up here at the junction of the great trading routes between the coast and Lake Tanganyika and running to the north and south. By 1876 Mirambo had reached such a point in his wars with the Tabora Arabs as practically to exploit connections with Zanzibar: he was a political force to be reckoned with by both European and Arab. Mirambo's power blunted the Ngoni thrust northwards from southern Africa as well as withstanding the incursions of Arab slavers in his territory. In the highlands of southern Tanganyika another Bantu people, the Wahehe, also withstood Ngoni pressure and emerged at the end of the nineteenth century as a formidable challenge to the Germans. Also influential but less well-known and less directly involved with Europeans was a grouping of peoples under Nyunguya Mawe in the district south-east of Tabora: here also was an empire similar to Uniamwezi, controlling the long-distance trade-routes that passed through its territory.[16] This conspectus of peoples in East Africa touches only those on, or near, the great trade-routes running into the interior, and first contacted by European explorers and missionaries; outside these points lay vast areas, the outer margins – northern Kenya, north-eastern Uganda and southern Tanganyika – about which little was known until European administration extended into them in the early twentieth century.

The first European travellers journeying into the East African interior were confronted with a confused welter of tribes, the constant supersession of one over the other, and ensuing enslavement. In wide areas starvation was a predominant threat, and life was maintained at bare subsistence level, with thousands being wiped out in time of famine. Parasitical disease and bodily discomfort were accepted as part of the nature of things, for which there was no antidote. Life expectancy was short. In this attenuated and harsh environment kinship and tribal groupings were necessary for survival. These stark realities often eluded the first European travellers who, marching inland during the exhilarating hours of a fresh African morning and caught up in the *élan* of adventure, and the novelty of constantly changing scenery and African life, tended to see all through roseate spectacles. Joseph Thomson extolled a district through which he had passed as:

a perfect Arcadia, about which idyllic poets have sung, though few have seen it realized. Imagine a magnificent grove of bananas, laden with bunches of fruit, each of which would form a man's load, growing on a perfectly level plain, from which all weeds, garbage, and things unsightly are carefully cleared away. Dotted here and there are a number of immense shady sycamores, with branches each almost as large as a separate tree. At every few paces are charmingly neat circular huts, with conical roofs, and walls hanging out all round with the clay worked prettily into rounded bricks, and daubed symmetrically with spots. The grass thatching is also very neat. The *tout ensemble* renders these huts worthy of a place in any nobleman's garden.[17]

Thomson was young (he was only 22) and a little blasé about it all. Not so Captain Owen who, at the mouth of St John's River, that extraordinarily beautiful and picturesque entrance, could not but reflect as to what was happening in the surrounding district:

At this time the work of depopulation was carried on with savage rapidity by the merciless and destructive conquests of a tyrannical monster named Chaka, whose bloody proceedings promised soon to leave the whole of the beautiful country, from the River St John to Inhamban, totally desolate.[18]

Burton, with crude contemptuousness, remarked:

After eating the East African invariably indulges in a long fit of torpidity – from which he awakes to pass the afternoon, as he did the forenoon, chatting, playing, smoking and chewing 'sweet earth' ... In intellect the East African is sterile and incult, apparently unprogressive and unfit for change.[19]

Similar contempt is tossed out by Winston Churchill regarding the folk on the upper Nile: 'The qualities of mongrels are rarely admirable, and the mixture of the Arab and negro types has produced a debased and cruel breed, more shocking because they are more intelligent than the primitive savages.

Speke's description of events at Mtesa's court indicated anything but an idyllic classless society so often attributed to African traditional life. Here were serfs, slaves and lords; and unparalleled cruelty on the part of Mtesa towards his subjects – especially the women at his court. Sir

Bartle Frere, well-travelled and seasoned administrator in the East, saw little or nothing in the African tribal system to admire; it was bound together by social ties no higher than those 'which keep together a herd of bison ... an effectual obstacle to anything like permanent civilization'. Similar to Frere's view was that of Sir Philip Mitchell, writing in the mid-twentieth century and with long years of administrative responsibility in Africa behind him:

> They had no wheeled transport and, apart from the camels and donkeys of the pastoral nomads, no animal transport either; they had no roads nor towns; no tools except small hand hoes, axes, wooden digging sticks and the like, no manufacturers and no industrial products except the simplest domestic handiwork, no commerce as we understand it and no currency, although in some places barter of produce was facilitated by the use of small shells; they had never heard of working for wages. They went stark naked or clad in the bark of trees or the skins of animals, and they had no means of writing, even by hieroglyphics, nor of numbering except by their figures or making notches on a stick or knots in a piece of grass or fibre; they had no weights and measures of general use. There was a great variety of language or dialect, largely within the great linguistic group now called the 'Bantu' by European scholars, and it was common, as it is today, for an area the size of an English county to contain several groups speaking different languages. They were pagan spirit or ancestor propitiators in the grip of magic and witchcraft, their minds cribbed and confined by superstition.[20]

Schweinfurth states apropos the Madi: 'Like most other people of Africa, the Madi can only count up to ten, everything above that number having to be denominated by gestures.'[21] Certainly Africans south of the Sahara could pose nothing like that wonderful art of Islam in which are seen higher influences of the aesthetic force derived from above. One marvels at the zealous attempts and relish with which many scholars try to play safe by overeulogizing African art and culture. This is a reaction from the earlier period when these were depreciated. After the Second World War, when African studies came into its own as a respectable academic discipline with its own crops of specialists, and when a more stringent intellectual inquiry brought a new and deeper understanding of the psychological and sociological content in African society, there was increasing recognition and respect for the high degree of sophistication and sensibility necessary for the working of the complex system of rights and duties which accompanied the African from the cradle to the grave; and an increasing realization of European impact on the African way of life. Long before these glimmerings of the mid-twentieth century had been apprehended, British interests were well on their way to a permanent establishment in East Africa.

Although England had been virtually protector of Zanzibar since 1841, she had not as yet acquired a foothold in East Africa. While King Leopold had obtained his Independent State of the Congo, and Portugal, that 'chronic grumbler', had obtained European approval for her possessions in Southern/Central Africa, England, whose explorers – Livingstone, Burton, Speke, Grant, Baker, Keith Johnston, Thomson, Elton, etc – were first in the field, and whose cruisers for near half a century had policed the Indian Ocean in the task of suppressing slave-catchers, had no concrete possessions there. It was only with Mackinnon that there commenced an endeavour to acquire a portion of East Africa as part of the 'Third British Empire' in the last quarter of the nineteenth century. For eight years the matter of a concession from the Sultan lay before His Highness – awaiting his signature. Events were soon to spur him into action.

4· The First Partition of East Africa and Establishment of the IBEAC (Imperial British East Africa Company)

British interest in acquiring a foothold on the East African coast in the earlier nineteenth century stemmed from a desire for a base from which more effectively to pursue an anti-slave-trade campaign. This had been the aim of Owen in his brief attempt to establish a British protectorate at Mombasa (1824–26), and also that of Thomas Fowell Buxton in his plan for a British commercial settlement at Mombasa in 1838; likewise the proposal put before the Select Committee, 1870–71, that Britain buy out Zanzibar. All these projects were turned down by the British government as being unrealistic. In Palmerston's words, it would be necessary to 'begird' the continent of Africa with naval bases, if the slave-trade there was to be extirpated.

A more realistic approach to establishing the interests of an external power in East Africa came in the second half of the nineteenth century, when Gordon was directed by Khedive Ismail to conquer Uganda 'up to the shores of the lake and Ripon Falls', and to incorporate it within the Egyptian Sudan. In pursuance of this object, Gordon despatched Chaillé-Long, an American officer in Egyptian employ, on a mission to Mtesa of Uganda in April 1874, as a result of which Chaillé-Long obtained a treaty from Mtesa whereby the latter recognized an Egyptian protectorate as far south as, and including Uganda. Gordon, however, was concerned over the difficulty of communication by way of the Nile with the equatorial region, owing to the obstacles posed by the sudd, cataracts and rapids of the Upper Nile, and he advised the Khedive that Uganda could not be developed nor held from the north, but only from the east – from Mombasa, whose distance, however, from advanced

Egyptian posts in Equatoria Gordon underestimated by some 400 miles. Once this route was opened 'a firm hold would be established on the rich and promising lands south of Gondokoro'. The Khedive was intrigued with this suggestion, for he had already taken possession of the African side of the Red Sea coast and had conquered the Abyssinian province of Harrar, and thus when in January 1875 (after the return of Chaillé-Long from Uganda) Gordon proposed to the Khedive that he seize Mombasa, the latter fell in with the plan.

Command of the Juba River expedition was given to a Scotsman, McKillop Pasha, who was accompanied by Colonels Ward and Chaillé-Long. Secret instructions, which Chaillé-Long opened when 500 miles south of Suez, fixed the Juba River as the objective of the expedition. Anchorage at the mouth of the Juba, however, proved impracticable, so bad in fact that the expedition proceeded farther south to Port Durnfurd, and then to the harbour of Kismayu. The latter town was occupied in October 1875. This encroachment on the Sultan of Zanzibar's territory elicited from that potentate an alarmed response, and the sending of a hurried cable to the British Foreign Office, claiming that 'Egyptian pirates have seized my army and country and massacred my people. Come to my aid.' The British representative at the Sultan's court, Sir John Kirk, was much disturbed over this Egyptian action, and pressed the British Foreign Office, in line with its policy of supporting the Sultan's authority on the East African coast, to respond favourably to the Sultan's appeal. There followed a British behest to the Egyptian force to withdraw.

On Christmas Day 1875, when poised for a further thrust southwards, Chaillé-Long received a letter from the Khedive ordering his withdrawal. Before evacuating the ports of Barawa and Kismayu, McKillop Pasha reported that Mombasa was the true entrance to the Upper Nile Valley. The episode, however, had the result of stirring the Sultan into asserting his authority more firmly along the coastline. He now heeded British advice to establish an armed presence there, and to agree to the appointment of a British vice-consul at Mombasa. The advice, timely though it was, did not prevent another challenge to the Sultan's authority.

As a result of the conference of geographical experts convened by Leopold II at Brussels in September 1876, which led to the founding of the International African Association with its professed object of exploring and civilizing Africa, plans were drawn up for an expedition into the Congo Basin by way of Zanzibar, and this caused its Sultan to look again to Britain for the security of his territory against possible foreign aggression. In December 1876 the Sultan intimated to Sir John Kirk (possibly at the latter's behest) that he was willing to accept a British occupation of his mainland dominions. This intelligence came to the notice of William Mackinnon, a Scottish shipping and commercial magnate, who had already embarked on a project of road-building in East Africa with Sir Thomas Fowell Buxton. Their aim was to strike a blow at the slave-trade by the construction of a road from Dar es Salaam to Lake Nyasa, thus opening up the country to alternative commerce. Mackinnon was a self-made man whose early career and fortune were made in India. He had founded the Calcutta and Burmah Steam Navigation Company, and also the British India Steamship Line, and had waxed well in the wake of the termination of the East India Company's monopoly of trade. Mackinnon now found in East Africa a field especially congenial to one of his business talents and religious proclivities. In one of his 'nippiest deals' he acquired the mail contract from Aden to Zanzibar in 1872, which brought with it substantial merchant business. In the same year the British India Steam Navigation Company Limited inaugurated a steamer service between Bombay, Aden, Zanzibar and Portuguese East Africa. Captain H.A. Fraser was appointed the company's first agent at Zanzibar, and on his death in 1874 was succeeded by Messrs Archibald Smith and E.N. Mackenzie. In 1877 a new firm, Smith, Mackenzie and Company, was formed and took over the agency at Zanzibar.

Multifarious business fell to the agency from its inception in 1872 and it expanded under Smith, Mackenzie and Company. Among its first transactions are recorded the sale of a double-barrelled gun to Mtesa of Uganda, and trade goods to a ruler in Madagascar. Indents for 1879 show import into Zanzibar of 30 copies of the Koran, 3000 Tower muskets and 30 cases of dates from Basra. The agency arranged the conveyance of Livingstone's body from Zanzibar to England in 1874, and for burial in Westminister Abbey. It acted as Reuter's representative and agent for Lloyd's Insurance. The Sultan increasingly resorted to it and in 1887, in recognition of its services, presented it with a very fine 'Arab' chest and a handsome Persian carpet. It was now an established institution in East Africa. Along with his pleasure at this increasing business, Mackinnon was under the spell of Africa. He was fired by Livingstone's cry of 'Commerce and Christianity' as going hand-in-hand in Africa: a most attractive vade-mecum for one of Mackinnon's shrewd business acumen. He had attended the international conference at Brussels; had been captivated by its appeal for the conversion of African peoples to Christianity; and he now wore the mantle of a Victorian evangelical. An ardent votary of missionary work and a believer in the moral enlargement of Christianity when combined with practical business sense, philanthropy and commercial acumen struggled for place of primacy in Mackinnon's shrewd Scottish mind. Prospects for trade in East Africa, apart from the entrepreneur trade based on Zanzibar were not bright. There was no palm oil, tea, cocoa or coffee. The trade in slaves and ivory, copal and a little rubber, the main exports, was drummed up mainly by Arabs and Indians and was in their hands. Yet great opportunities awaited an entrepreneur, especially one with Indian experience, to develop the country, for conditions in East Africa were not unlike those in India, and there was also a British presence here. And was not East Africa the field wherein the great missionary, David Livingstone, a Scotsman like himself, had laboured and died? Livingstone's appeal to others, to follow him in the work of Christianizing and civilizing Africa, could not be ignored. Mackinnon would not be found wanting in this respect. The Sultan's offer, which came to his notice in January 1877, was thus of special interest to him. It was a generous concession – a 70-year lease of the customs and administration of the Sultan's mainland dominions – 1150 miles of coastline, from Tunghi Bay in the south, to Warsheikh in the north, and stretching inland as far as the great central lakes. Kirk, British consul at Zanzibar, at first seemed to favour this concession – for it would serve the Sultan's interests, relieving him of the trouble and expense of administration and assuring him of a portion of the duties collected by the concessionaire. It seemed an attractive arrangement.

A year later, however, in April 1878, when Mackinnon's agents (George Waller and Dr G.P. Badger) arrived in Zanzibar to finalize negotiations, they found a decided change of atmosphere. Badger, an Arabist, was testy, bad-tempered and ambivalent (he was under private instructions from Lord Salisbury not to commit the Foreign Office to guarantees), and his manner smacked too much of that of Sir Bartle Frere's – the British emissary who had wrecked negotiations with the Sultan in 1873. Also, in the interval since January 1877, the Sultan had been subjected to influences averse to a concession, that of the leading Arabs at Zanzibar, and of Henry Stanley who had stopped over at Zanzibar in December 1877, and who did his best to influence the Sultan and Kirk against the concession. Stanley was now the pacemaker in African events, participating in Leopold's grandiose plans (when he sailed from Zanzibar on 13 December 1877, he had a stateroom especially ordered for him by the unwitting Sir William Mackinnon). Kirk, too, was now less favourably disposed towards a surrender of the Sultan's authority on the mainland for it would mean a diminution of his, Kirk's, authority and importance: a truncated sultanate was not to his liking. At the Foreign Office, too, second thoughts had been raised in the matter. The backsliding and timorous attitude of Mackinnon and associates did not comport with Salisbury's view of British imperial vigour. British imperial interests could best be advanced by obtaining 'unrestricted right of access' and in a few years, the English would govern 'without ever drawing a sword'.

> When you bring the English in contact with inferior races, they
> will rule, whatever the ostensible ground of their presence. They
> assert the English domination, not by any political privilege or
> military power, but right of the strongest mind.[1]

Mackinnon and associates, by soliciting Foreign Office financial guarantees to back up their concession and then waxing hot and cold when these were not forthcoming, raised doubts in Salisbury's and Kirk's minds as to their ability to make the enterprise a success. A report from a Lieutenant O'Neill, regarding the road-making activities of Mackinnon and Buxton on the mainland, did not instil confidence. The so-called Nyasa road was no more than a bit of 'dirt-scratching'; and if the two entrepreneurs thought they possessed a highway, they were under a 'complete delusion'. O'Neill's derogatory remarks, and the trouble given to authorities in Zanzibar by the 'drunken set of men' employed on the Nyasa road, weakened Mackinnon's case for support from the Sultan.

Barghash, now aware of Kirk's and Foreign Office reservations in the matter, and possibly to test the sincerity of Mackinnon's intentions, pressed for the concession to be taken up by 1 January 1879. But Mackinnon hesitated: he still hoped for Foreign Office guarantees, and when these were not forthcoming, negotiations were broken off in May 1878. Mackinnon's friends, however, were relieved for they had always looked upon the whole affair as somewhat wild and impractical.

The Sultan's offer of 1877 was never formally withdrawn, and remained at the disposal of Mackinnon and associates if they chose to take it up. Mackinnon continued to toy with the idea of doing so. In March 1879 he approached the Sultan for an outright lease of Dar es

Salaam and a strip of land along the coast. The French and American consuls at Zanzibar complained that this infringed the Sultan's sovereignty, and hinted that they too might seek similar concessions if the Sultan complied with Mackinnon's request. The Sultan was of two minds in the matter, and pleaded that such a concession would lead to the economic ruin of the small port of Bagamoyo, to the north of Dar es Salaam, and the ivory and slave-trade based there. Mackinnon bided his time until the Sultan's original offer was to revive again in a few years' time. The first endeavours of the International Association to acquire the Congo Basin was by sending expeditions from the East. After the failure in 1884 of the fifth of these expeditions, in which the use of elephants was a novel feature, Leopold decided that an approach from the west was more feasible. The achievements of the Belgians awakened German interest, and it was largely as a result of German action in East Africa that Britain was forced to declare her intentions there.

The German colonial movement is comparatively modern in origin. Tentative efforts by the Great Elector of Brandenburg (1640–88) to establish settlements in West Africa in the seventeenth century, and attempts by the outward-looking Hanseatic Free Cities to establish commercial interests overseas, could not be described as concerted colonial enterprise. The maxim of Frederic the Great (1740–86) that 'All distant possessions are a burden to the state' seems to have been the prevailing view in the German world prior to the nineteenth century. In the early nineteenth century large-scale German emigration overseas, and letters from Germans abroad, tended to make Germans more outward-looking. An interest in colonial enterprise was also stirred up in the early nineteenth century by Germany intellectuals such as Frederich List, who argued that colonial enterprise was necessary for German economic and political well-being, and Wilhelm Roscher, who warned Germans against idly sitting back and leaving to other nations the acquisition of prized possessions overseas.

The unification of Germany following the Franco-Prussian War of 1870–71 gave the necessary fillip to a colonial movement. A surge of pride and energy emanated from this new-found, self-conscious power. A Central Association for Commercial Geography and Promotion of German Interests Abroad, formed in Berlin in 1868, pressed for 'furtherance of trade and navigation and the acquisition of colonies'. The imperial constitution of 1871 appears to have anticipated overseas possessions with its clause stating that 'The Law of the kingdom shall be extended over the colonies and settlements in the lands overseas'.

They were first to be attained in Africa. Hamburg trading interests were well established at Zanzibar, with O'Swald and Company's agency there, by 1849. In 1859 the Sultan of Zanzibar concluded a treaty of commerce and amity with the Hanseatic Republics of Hamburg, Bremen and Lübeck.[2] Shipping returns at Zanzibar by the mid-century show Germany well to the fore. In the field of missionary endeavour and exploration the Germans were also in the vanguard in East Africa. German explorers, Roscher, von der Decken and Kerstein, and missionaries such as Krapf and Rebmann, had made solid achievements in East Africa by the early 1860s. The German Society for the Scientific Exploration of Equatorial Africa, founded in 1873, and the German Africa Society (a branch of Leopold's International Association) founded in 1876, merged in 1878 into the German African Society of Berlin, signifying a growing German interest in Africa. In 1880–81 an expedition under Count Schoeler, backed by the German African Society of Berlin, attempted to occupy the region between Mpwapwa and Karema and establish a station near Tabora. A site was selected at Kakoma, but because of its unhealthy situation the members crossed over to the Congo and eventually returned to Europe. This first attempt at German settlement in East Africa was not too successful. The German government was still apparently disinclined and uninterested in furthering colonial development.

Bismarck, in earlier years, if his feelings can be deduced correctly from his utterances on the subject, was a decided opponent of overseas expansion:

The advantages expected from colonies for the trade and industry of the mother country rest for the most part on illusions. For the costs entailed by the establishment, support, and particularly by the retention of the colonies, very often exceed – as the experience of the colonial policy of England and France proves – the benefit derived by the motherland, apart from the fact that it is difficult to justify the imposition of heavy taxation upon the whole nation for the benefit of a few branches of trade and industry.[3]

Bismarck held that colonies were expensive and unnecessary excrescences, which drained the mother country of energy and capital and imposed a costly burden of defence. In 1867 when Sultan Simba (the Lion) of Witu was visited by Richard Brenner, that ruler expressed a wish to place himself under German protection, but the Germans declined the offer with thanks. When in 1870 the German consul at Zanzibar informed his government that Seyyid Barghash had asked to be placed under German protection, no answer was forthcoming. Bismarck also resisted pressure to seize part of France's colonial empire as a 'prize of war' at the end of the Franco-Prussian War of 1870–71, that great convulsion which brought a dramatic shift in the balance of power in Europe. He also turned down an opportunity to extend German protection over the Fiji Islands in 1872. 'No colonies,' Prince Bismarck had emphatically said in 1873; and he told Lord Odo Russell 'that he desired neither them nor fleets'.

A change in Bismarck's attitude is discernible by the late 1870s. He was annoyed when German interests were lightly treated by Britain and that power annexed the Fiji Islands to herself in 1874. The acquisition of a colonial empire increasingly connoted well with Bismarck's protective policy, and his rejection of the Liberal party view that Germans already had access to the tropical markets in British colonies. When rapid steam communication hurried up commerce, bringing tropical fruits and produce more quickly to Germany where the industrial revolution had brought affluence, there was a desire to control the source of the exotic products of the tropics which hitherto were imported from French and British tropical possessions.

The key years marking a change in Bismarck's colonial policy are 1879–83. In 1879 the failure of a Hamburg firm, the house of Godefroy, with extensive interests in the South Seas especially Samoa, was a reflection of the Reichstag's failure to underwrite it, despite an impassioned appeal by the protectionist party. The resignation from office of a number of political figures long known for their anti-colonial views, notably that of the Prussian Minister, Martin Delbruk (1817–1903) in 1879 (following the failure of his efforts in the Reichstag to oppose the new protection tariff), and at the same time the appointment of Baron von Kusserow, a colonial enthusiast, to the Foreign Ministry, all denoted a change of policy. The Liberals were much weakened when Ludwig Bamberger (1823–99), economist and politician, member of the National Liberal Party and prominent leader of the free traders and opponent of bimetallism, refused to follow Bismarck in his new policy of protection, state socialism and colonial development, and left the National Liberal Party and formed the so-called 'Secession' group in 1880.

The Franco-Prussian War had wrought a profound change. It had deposed France from her leading position and led to the establishment of a German gold currency with a different unit from the franc, accompanied by the demonetization of the silver currencies previously in use in the German states. No doubt France's involvement in Africa would distract her from brooding over her decline in Europe and the tremendous shock of defeat by Germany; but France's involvement in Africa was only part of the general European scramble in that continent which had heightened in the early 1880s, and which caused apprehension in Germany lest her interests as a great power might be minimized and disregarded unless she too entered into the general partitioning of Africa.

In 1880 Bismarck expressed his disappointment at the Diet's failure to support an imperial guarantee for the bankrupt house of Godefroy, and pointed out that private enterprise, however, had gone ahead and seized the opportunity which government had failed to grasp. The German Colonial Society, founded in December 1882 at Frankfurt under the presidency of the Prince of Hohenlohe-Langenburg, urged government action in acquiring colonies. The Society's publication *Colonialzeitung* had a wide circulation and stimulated public interest in overseas enterprise, and the Society's membership expanded by 400 per cent by 1885. Similarly the German African Society, founded in 1878 to encourage African exploration, pressed government to encourage German enterprise in Africa.

The pressures on the German government wrought a change in its attitude. In 1881 it submitted a proposal for subventions to German shipping on the high seas, although energetically opposed in this by the 'free traders' led by Bamberger. In 1884 the Bill was introduced again but abandoned in the face of free-trade opposition, but in the same year a bill doubling the bounties on beet sugar exports was passed and was eminently successful in inducing great yields of beet sugar, thus confounding the arguments of the free traders. Bismarck courted the protectionists in the elections of 1883 and 1884, by averring an interest in colonies. This was also the year of the Hicks Pasha disaster, the French attack on Madagascar and the outrage offered the British flag there. The *schadenfreude* of certain elements in Germany over these British set-backs was quietly concealed, and when the Prince of Wales visited Berlin in 1883 he charmed Bismarck. A memorandum to the imperial government in July 1883 from the Hanseatic Chamber of Commerce urging support for German enterprise in West Africa was preliminary to that wonderful burst of energy that Germany was to display within the year in acquiring vast areas of Africa. The non-ratification of the Anglo-Portuguese treaty of February 1884 which would have secured for Portugal her interests in the Congo was primarily the result of German protests, although there was opposition to it from France, Belgium and also in Britain itself. Then the favourable reaction to the activity of the Bremen trader, F.A.E. Luderitz, on the south-west African coast, and treaty rights acquired by him in the face of British backsliding, resulted in the declaration of a German protectorate there on 8 September 1884. In April of the same year the efforts of the imperial consul-general, Dr Nachtigal, in the gunboat, *Mowe*, in outwitting the French and British, resulted in the declaration of a German protectorate over Togoland and Cameroon districts in July 1884, pre-empting an attempt by Edward Hyde Hewett to do the same for Britain. German pride was running high!

A parallel to these gains on the west coast of Africa was also to take place on the east coast, where Carl Peters stole a march on the British and forced the hand of his own government in participating in the partition of East Africa. In March 1884 Peters, an energetic and resourceful adventurer and sometime student of British colonization, along with like-minded friends, founded the 'Society for German Colonization'.[4] Its object was to acquire land overseas and foster colonization; and throughout the summer of 1884 much thought was given to where a colonial venture might commence. Public subscriptions were raised to support its objects and wide interest awakened in its aspirations. At first attention was directed to Brazil; then southern Africa – to St Lucia Bay, north of Durban; to Mashonaland; and then Angola. All were possible locations for the ideal colony, but the Society was informed in July 1884 by the German Government that it considered the southern part of Africa to be within the British sphere of influence. Following government's negative reaction to the Angola scheme, Peters fixed his eyes on Usagara in East Africa, and with the support of Count Otto Pfeil swung the balance of opinion in favour of starting there. At a meeting of 16 September 1884 the Society decided to send its first expedition to Usagara with Peters as its leader.

The selection of East Africa as the site of a German colony was not unexpected. Baron von der Decken had made a survey of the Mount Kilimanjaro area in 1861-62 and had advocated a German colony there. Dr Fischer, also a German, had journeyed in the Kilimanjaro area in 1882 and had spoken highly of its possibilities for European colonization. Stanley's published accounts, read with interest in Germany, had referred to the Usagara region as the 'paradise of Africa'.

Germany was not tied to the self-denying ordinance of 1862 which bound Britain and France to respect the sovereignty of the Sultan of Zanzibar's dominions. The German consulate at Zanzibar was aware of the *pourparlers* between Mackinnon and associates, and the Sultan in 1877–78, and also Kirk's contact with Mandara on Kilimanjaro. The mooting by the British Association and Royal Society, with Kirk's approval, of a plan for a collector's mission to study flora and fauna on Kilimanjaro was known in Germany, and stirred her to act. The time was favourable. Gladstone, now in office (1880–85), was averse to British expansion in Africa, and his foreign minister, Lord Granville, leaned over backwards to meet German wishes. Peters had chosen his time and place well.

Peters and his associates, Dr Karl Jühlke, Count Pfeil and August Otto, reported their plans to the German Foreign Ministry in a letter of 20 September 1884, and assuming that government protection would be accorded to any acquisitions they might make, in October 1884 boarded the steamer *Titania* from Trieste to Aden, whence they sailed for Zanzibar in the steamer *Baghdad*, not denying a rumour that they were bound for the Transvaal. On 4 November they disembarked at Zanzibar. The German consulate there had already been informed that the home government disclaimed any responsibility for their protection and would not recognize any territorial claims they might make in East Africa, although leaving some margin of doubt in the matter of territory they might claim outside the domains of the Sultan of Zanzibar. All this did not escape the sharp ears of Kirk, the British consul.

Six days after landing in Zanzibar the party, with 36 porters, left Sadaani for the interior – following the Wami River route – and thence to the Usagara country where Peters concluded agreements on behalf of his Society, acquiring the districts of Usagara, Uzigua, Ukami and Nguru. Count Pfeil, the only member of the party who sustained good health, was left in Kiroa to establish the first station; the others returned to Zanzibar on 17 December 1884, whence the news of their acquisitions was wired home to the Society. It now requested government protection for these territories, and spoke in terms of a vision of an East African empire extending inland to the great lakes, an extension inland which would not be thwarted as was the case with the Cameroons and Togoland on the western side of the continent. An area of 60,000 square miles to the north-west of Bagamoyo had been acquired at practically no cost. The 12 treaties obtained from African chiefs signified the surrender of their sovereignty; they disclaimed allegiance to the Sultan of Zanzibar; nay, even claimed ignorance of his existence. Peters, in a letter to the Foreign Ministry, 8 January 1885, spoke of these territories providing 'the nucleus for a German India' in East Africa. By mid-February 1885 Bismarck was converted to the annexation and instructed Rohlfs, who had arrived to take up his post as German consul at Zanzibar in January 1885, to secure free transit through the Sultan's territories for these new German acquisitions; following a powerful plea from Peters for German protection on 23 February 1885, Bismarck supported a draft for an imperial *Schutzbrief* which the Kaiser signed on 27 February 1885, the day after the momentous Berlin West African Conference had adjourned. That conference, convened in mid-November 1884 and attended by representatives of 14 powers including the United States, had declared a free-trade zone across the breadth of central Africa, but respected the sovereign rights of the Sultan of Zanzibar as a non-signatory power. His sovereign rights were not defined at the Conference, but it was placed on record there, without affirming or denying their validity, that the Sultan claimed sovereign rights on the mainland of East Africa as far west as Lake Tanganyika. The Berlin Conference had been convened to deal with West Africa, but found itself directing attention to the eastern side of the continent, and the vast free-trade area now declared there provided a field within which German traders could operate unhindered. By Article VI of the Conference's General Declaration the existence of a 'sphere of influence', as distinct from territorial acquisition, was for the first time formally enunciated. This accorded well with Bismarck's idea of 'informal empire'.

Peters's achievements were deprecated in some quarters in Germany. The *National Zeitung,* referring to the ill-health experienced by members of the expedition, cited this as proof that Europeans could not survive in this part of Africa. It also asked why Peters and friends had not looked to the Upper Congo, where the Congo Association was building a railway to bypass the Congo cataracts, and which was an area not too distant from the Cameroons recently acquired as a protectorate by Germany. Peters's action had also disturbed the amicable relations with the Sultan and Arabs and would threaten Germany's important East African trade. As to the question of the validity of Peters's treaties, made with chiefs not entitled to sign away land nor perhaps aware of the import of their actions, Peters did no more nor less than many other European adventurers in Africa – Stanley for example; and when he sought recognition from his government, his achievements could not be ignored. Emperor William's Charter of Protection declared the annexed territories to be 'west of the empire of the Sultan of Zanzibar, outside the suzerainty of other Powers'; and the Society was granted 'authority to exercise all rights arising from the treaties submitted to us, including that of jurisdiction ... subject to other regulations to be issued by us, and supplementary additions to this our Charter of Protection'. The *Schutzbrief* was made public on 3 March 1885, and the treaties notified to the British government and Sultan of Zanzibar on 6 March.

Although not quite an 'accidental by-product of an abortive Franco-German entente' as has been averred, nevertheless Germany had politically timed her action well: it coincided with Britain's embarrassment over the Mahdi rising and Gordon affair in the Sudan. German activity in East Africa did not go unnoticed in Britain. A pamphlet in the autumn of 1884 by Vice-Admiral Livonius, recently retired from the German Navy, urged German colonial enterprise in the Zanzibar dominions to forestall Britain there. According to Livonius the British were anxious to hold East Africa in reserve against the day when the Russians would finally succeed in expelling them from India. In November 1884 the Berlin correspondent of *The Times* raised the possibility of whether Rohlfs had been commissioned to engineer a German protectorate over Zanzibar, thus paralleling the work of Nachtigal and Luderitz on the western side of Africa. In the light of these rumours, Bismarck felt it necessary at the end of November 1884 to assure the British ambassador at Berlin that Germany had no designs on Zanzibar. He would recognize Britain's special position there and he acknowledged her great work in suppressing the slave-trade, but he pointed out that Britain herself had recognized the independence of Zanzibar and with it the implication that the Sultan was free to make agreements with whomsoever he pleased. It seemed to Germany that Britain intended to monopolize the resources of East Africa through the agency of the Sultan of Zanzibar, and encourage the extension of the territorial claims of the latter to the disadvantage of the Germans. In this momentous year of German eruption in Africa, Henry Hamilton Johnston led an expedition organized by the Royal Society and British Association to study the flora and fauna on Kilimanjaro – largely in response to Sir John Kirk's urgings that British scientists should not let those of other countries take the lead in East Africa. The Foreign Office assumed before Johnston's departure that his expedition might be 'deflected to political purposes', and when Johnston arrived at Moshi on the southern side of Kilimanjaro, in June 1884, he set about obtaining a treaty from Mandara for a tract of land as a site for a settlement. The watchful one-eyed Mandara sought only aid against his rivals, and viewed the British in no more favourable light than he did the Germans. In a letter to Lord Edmond Fitzmaurice, 10 July 1884, Johnston extolled the attractions of Kilimanjaro, a choice area in East Africa 'as completely English as Ceylon', with the vast bulk of Kilimanjaro and its twin summits Kibo and Mawenzi rising to 19,340 feet, along with the noble mass of Meru some 25 miles to the west, spreading out cone-like over many hundreds of square miles, their slopes furrowed into deep narrow ravines down which flow clear water streams tumbling into the fertile lands below. On the southern slopes of the massif dwelt the Chagga people and their smaller subtribes – all expert agriculturists. In this rich fertile well-watered world, vegetation shaded up from the more tropical to the alpine zone of tree lobelias and *Senecio* and finally into dwarfed patches and snow at the highest levels.

Lister, at the Foreign Office, impressed by Johnston's accounts of this wonderland, favoured establishing a British protectorate over the Kilimanjaro area at once, but when Kirk at Zanzibar was consulted in the matter he raised doubts as to whether it could be administered without a port at the coast, either Mombasa or Tanga. To acquire these, let alone the Kilimanjaro area, would alter British relations with the Sultan and would be a 'signal for a general scramble and there would be little left of Zanzibar'. Johnston meanwhile dithered. In the face of Mandara's caprices he moved to nearby Taveta and entered into an agreement with chiefs there, obtaining from them a small tract of forest land, before leaving at the end of October 1884. At the same time Carl Peters was about to enter into his historic treaty-making in Usagara. Kirk at Zanzibar, alerted over Peters's and Johnston's enterprise on the mainland, pressed for a venture in the Sultan's name and with Foreign Office backing. Respectable figures – Sir Charles Dilke, Lord Granville, Lord Kimberley and Lord Derby – were drawn into the scheme. A Foreign Office dispatch of 5 December 1884 directed Kirk to support the Sultan's claims to the Kilimanjaro area and to make treaties with local chiefs, and in the name of HMG if necessary to gain these ends. When Gladstone got wind of this plan he soon scotched it: he was 'puzzled and perplexed at finding a group of the soberest men among us to have concocted a scheme such as that touching the mountain country behind Zanzibar with an unrememberable name'. The scheme was thus shelved, and so also a plan to press the Sultan into asserting claims to sovereignty over the Kilimanjaro district.

It was only a temporary setback, for the treaties acquired by Johnston were now transferred to James F. Hutton, President of the Manchester Chamber of Commerce, and to Mackinnon and other enthusiasts for an East African enterprise. Kirk and Holmwood, alarmed at German pretensions in the Kilimanjaro area, backed Hutton and colleagues in the formation of a British East African Association, 'on the principles of the old East Indian Company'. Holmwood, with vague ideas of East African geography, waxed lyrical over trade prospects: a vast network of British-controlled communications would link East Africa with the Nile and Egypt; a railway line would run from Tanga to Kilimanjaro; thence to Speke Gulf on Lake Victoria, with another 180 miles by steamer connecting with Uganda whence a connection with Lake Albert and the Nile would link with Khartoum and Egypt. The addition of two short lines of railway and a few steamers would therefore bring Zanzibar in communication with the Nile, and Khartoum could be reached in ten days by rail and steamer. Holmwood quoted copiously from Joseph Thomson's book on the Kenya highlands: a vast upland with soil of unsurpassed fertility and a climate more like that of Europe than the tropics; Kavirondo on the eastern side of Lake Victoria – the terminus of the projected railway – was a 'veritable land of Goshen'. The railway would counter German pretensions in Usagara and would rapidly pay for itself in hauling products from the interior – such as the vast accumulation of 'dead ivory' reputed to exist there. British trade goods would find a ready market in the interior in exchange for these raw staples. Thus there would develop an admirable system of exchange, such as extolled by Adam Smith. The whole enterprise could be built on the old Mackinnon concession of 1877/78 which was still available – it had never been formally withdrawn by the Sultan.

Thus on 22 April 1885 a delegation from the British East Africa Association approached Lord Granville, Foreign Secretary, on the matter, and in Zanzibar Kirk sounded out the Sultan. Anderson, at the Foreign Office, had grave doubts about the whole scheme, and Granville, deeply immersed in other diplomatic problems, was averse to giving Germany umbrage over East Africa. (In June 1884, Count Munster, German ambassador in London, warned Granville that Germany would make matters difficult for England in Egypt, if she continued to thwart German colonial aspirations.) The initiative was passing to Germany. She brushed aside the Sultan's protest over a German protectorate over Usagara, and when the Sultan, prompted by Kirk, sent General Lloyd Mathews to occupy the Usambara–Chagga region, two Germans, Dr Jühlke and Lieutenant Weis, quickly offset this by acquiring eight treaties in the same region and thereby securing the Pangani route. Within a year the Germans were in occupation at Korogwe, some 60 miles up the Pangani, and had erected substantial buildings there and had set out various crops, including cocoa. The British and the Sultan, in a last-minute bid to forestall the Germans had been outwitted. (Mandara himself stated that he had been briefed by Mathews to hoist the Sultan's flag, although in defence of this, Archdeacon Farler, with long residence in Usambara, and one who had persistently urged declaration of a British protectorate there, averred that the Germans were 'a lot of low adventurers … even if they can't get a chief to sign any paper they still proclaim that they have made a treaty with him'. The wily Mandara would accept both the German and Sultan's flag, and 'playing on two strings', ran up whatever flag suited the circumstances, taking down the Sultan's flag on such slight excuses that it 'makes such a noise when it rains'.

This jockeying for position in East Africa was in line with Bismarck's view that colonies were only pawns on the European chessboard: 'My map of Africa lies in Europe.' He saw his opportunity. Granville was a weak opponent: 'Lord Granville did not feel the slightest jealousy of the Germans acquiring colonial possessions.' England had suffered a grave loss in the death of Lord Ampthill (British ambassador to Berlin for 13 years) on 25 August 1884; his personal influence with Bismarck had weighed heavily: according to Herbert Bismarck 'he might have kept our relations free from every sort of uneasiness'. Ampthill had warned his government of Bismarck's hatred of British Blue Books and his conviction that the British were blocking German expansion in Africa. Granville, an early free trader, more interested in domestic affairs than foreign, courteous and suave rather than a man of action, had been forced somewhat ignominiously to yield to Bismarck over the Angra Pequena question and was ultimately to be replaced by Lord Rosebery as Foreign Secretary in Gladstone's Third Cabinet, formed in February 1886. Cromer's comments on Granville's lack of initiative and tendency to drift into a solution, and on there being only one Bismarck in a generation but many Granvilles,[5] bespeaks a general low estimate of Granville's effectiveness. 'His light touches on serious questions were inimitable … it was possible to disagree with him, but it was impossible to be angry with him. It was also impossible to get him to give a definite answer to a difficult question when he wished not to commit himself. His power of eluding the main point at issue was quite extraordinary.' When Bismarck's annoyance over the Sultan's protest (seeing behind it the hand of Kirk) became known, Granville, on the 25 May 1885, placated him thus:

> Her Majesty's Government have no intention of opposing the German scheme of colonization in the neighbourhood of Zanzibar ... Her Majesty's Government on the contrary, view with favour these schemes, the realization of which will entail the civilization of large tracts over which hitherto no European influence has been exercised.[6]

And as for the British East Africa Association, Granville stated that Her Majesty's Government would not accord these 'prominent capitalists' the support they asked

> unless they were fully satisfied that every precaution was taken to ensure that it would in no way conflict with the interests of the territory that has been taken under German protection.[7]

Granville went further and suggested that Britain and Germany enter into delimitation of the Sultan's and their own spheres of interest in East Africa – as had been done in the Gulf of Guinea to avoid a clash between them there.

Bismarck, in his reply of 2 and 3 June 1885, while accepting the principle of a delimitation commission, blamed Kirk's 'vexatious attitude' and the hostility of *The Times* for the Sultan's recalcitrancy; and he reminded Granville that other powers might feel it incumbent to support the Khedive of Egypt and the Boers in South Africa, in the same way as Britain upheld the claims of the Sultan of Zanzibar. So strong did Bismarck feel on the subject, that Malet warned Granville that

> If we cannot or will not work with Germany we shall be in a very awkward position, because German protection will be rendered despite us.[8]

Instructions were immediately sent to Kirk that he should advise the Sultan not to oppose Germany or he would invite conflict fatal to his independence, but that he should co-operate with the Germans and he would thus share in the benefits secured under the Berlin Act for a free-trade zone across central Africa. Kirk was also directed to seek amity with Rohlfs, German consul at Zanzibar. His little world now rudely shaken, Kirk was to learn what many overseas servants of the Crown had to learn at one time or other, namely that in the last resort colonial interests must give way to the exigencies of foreign policy as determined at home.

Lord Salisbury (now back in office as Foreign Secretary as well as Prime Minister) unlike Granville, favoured meeting German claims with solid British claims. He agreed to the appointment of a delimitation commission, but first sought to have a British settlement established in the Kilimanjaro area to pose against German pretensions there. Holmwood and colleagues, however, asked such ridiculous guarantees before committing themselves, that Anderson remarked:

> I am convinced that no money will be embarked without the security of large concessions from the Sultan guaranteed by the British Government, conditions, under present circumstances, incapable of realisation.[9]

The promoters hesitated, quibbled over details, queried the danger posed by the Maasai, and questioned whether a market existed for ivory and hides.

Holmwood's scheme, like the Mackinnon concession of 1877, foundered because a government guarantee and security for investors were not forthcoming. It is doubtful, however, whether the Germans would have permitted encroachment on Kilimanjaro at a time when the Sultan's rights there were *sub judice,* and negotiations were under way between Great Britain, Germany and France for a delimitation of the Sultan's territory on the mainland. The failure to attain a British base on Kilimanjaro caused Anderson to remark ruefully:

> We have told the Germans that we have interests there, but have been puzzled to say what they are, as the British traders have never got beyond talking of going there ... British merchants have had for four years the opportunity which the Germans have now seized of working the interior markets, but have not taken advantage of it: the field is now in the possession of the rivals.[10]

And these rivals were active. During 1885 and early 1886 the Germans sent out a dozen expeditions – half of them to what was to become German East Africa, four to Somaliland and two to the Comoros. The region covered by Carl Peters's treaties was taken over by the German

East Africa Company (which was formed at the end of December 1884 and received its charter on 7 September 1885, with Peters as Director-in-Chief and Prince Hohenlohe-Langenburg Chairman of the German Colonial Society, as President). Stations 'Simaberg' and 'Kiota' were established on the upper Wami River, and with their stone buildings, experimental gardens and tobacco plantations, testified to the energy and zest of the Germans. In August and September 1885 Lieutenant Schmidt and a merchant, Sohnge, concluded 21 treaties near the coast, including Usaramo, the district containing Dar es Salaam. To the southward, during an extensive tour in November 1885, Count Pfeil and Lieutenant Schluter claimed a vast region between the Wami River, Lake Nyasa and the Ruvuma, and in virtue of having merely glimpsed the Ruaha, a tributary stream of the Rufiji, they claimed the whole Rufiji valley and Kuigani country for Germany. Hence the British assertion that if a German got within one hundred miles of a district this was deemed sufficient grounds to claim it for Germany.

The exuberance of the Germans knew no bounds. In September 1885, after purchasing a dhow at Zanzibar and sailing to Kismayu, Lieutenant von Anderten, in a grandiose gesture, annexed the whole Somali coast from the immediate west of Cape Guardafui to as far south as Warsheikh, and in the following year planted a station, 'Tanganiko' (site of modern Takaungu), on the River Kilifi – about 20 miles north of Mombasa. He founded 'Petershofe', near Mbufine, 100 miles up the River Wami, and by the end of 1886 two German officers with a staff of 40 natives were stationed at this point. In mid-1886 Jühlke selected the mouth of the Wabushi River with its large and roomy harbour – known as Port Durnford – and renamed it 'Hohenzollern Harbour'.

These annexations were flaunted in the face of the Sultan, and German pressure on him increased throughout the summer of 1885. The Sultan was physically ill, disturbed by political troubles, deeply embarrassed and his resistance weakened when Madame Reute, his sister (who had married a German) with German encouragement flaunted her presence at Zanzibar, although as one who had married an infidel, she was dead to her family. German action at Witu was especially provocative to the Sultan. The local sultan there, Simba (the Lion), had defied his overlord, the Sultan of Zanzibar, and had made a treaty with the Germans, placing himself under their protection and giving them land and special concessions in his territory. This action stirred the Sultan into sending troops to Witu and telegraphing a direct protest to Bismarck in June 1885, reminding him that the red flag of Zanzibar flew at Ujiji and Unyanyembe in the interior.

The Sultan of Zanzibar's protests and obduracy brought formidable response from Germany. In early August 1885 five German warships under Commodore Paschen dropped anchor off Zanzibar, and on 11 August the Commodore submitted a formal document to Barghash in which the German Emperor's desire for friendly relations and to negotiate certain treaties was expressed. Negotiations could not commence, however, until he received:

> the clear and unevasive declaration of Your Highness that you withdraw your protest against the treaties made with the free and legal Sultans of all the lands of Usagara, Nguru, Useguha and Ukami ... and recall your troops and agents from those regions.[11]

A further note on 16 August demanded the immediate recall of the Sultan's protest over Witu. At the same time the decks of the German warships were cleared for action. It was a daunting moment, and Barghash submitted. He acknowledged the German protectorate over Peters's acquisitions and the independence of the petty sultanate of Witu, and undertook to withdraw his forces from these places.

With this victory secured, Germany next set about obtaining a port for her hinterland possessions. On 19 August Admiral Knorr, Paschen's successor, obtained Dar es Salaam from the Sultan, with the stipulation that the port should not be fortified nor garrisoned by German troops.

No British protest came in the face of these German moves. Plans for the joint commission to

> inquire into the claims of the Sultan of Zanzibar to sovereignty over certain territories on the east coast of Africa, and of ascertaining their precise limits[12]

went ahead. Admittedly the Sultan's claims to sovereignty over the mainland were weak. His argument that holding the coast gave him rights over the immediate interior was untenable. There must be *de facto* occupation. In the Angra–Pequena discussions, Portugal's case had foundered on this very principle. The same test would be applied to the Sultan of Zanzibar's claims. Similarly the claims of British entrepreneurs in the Kilimanjaro area would rest on the same ground of *de facto* occupation.

While arrangements for the Delimitation Commission went ahead, both powers agreed to refrain from sending expeditions into the interior. In view of the spirit of friendly co-operation that now existed between them, Bismarck even suggested that it might be necessary for Britain and Germany to combine to prevent the interior from falling under an Arab domination 'akin to the Mahdi movement'. In April 1886 there also seemed a possibility of a joint Anglo–German enterprise in the Kilimanjaro area. The German East Africa Company, finding difficulty in financing a proposed Tanga–Kilimanjaro railway, suggested that Mackinnon and associates dispose of their Kilimanjaro concession to Peters, and that they should join with Peters in an Anglo-German syndicate, with Mackinnon and Company providing one-third of the capital. Negotiations were already under way for the purchase by Peters of the 70 miles of road at Dar es Salaam, constructed by Buxton and Mackinnon; thus co-operation seemed to be in the air. However, Mackinnon, with his eyes now set on horizons much wider than the Chagga district or Kilimanjaro, commented that 'These proposals do not commend themselves to those interested with me in the Kilimanjaro district'. Mackinnon had undergone a recent change of view as to the desirability of the Chagga area. J.W. Buchanan, whom he sent there to report on the tract acquired by Johnston, found little to justify Johnston's fulsome praise.

> He must be either drawing on his imagination or have eaten up all the good things and caused a famine, … he has a mania for making roads from anywhere to nowhere … he made a road through the Taveta forest … the very thing the Watayeta did not want … it ruined their security.[13]

Mackinnon was disenchanted with the Chagga area, and the possibility of joint Anglo-German enterprise had no appeal for him. Germans and British thus went their own way. The Delimitation Commission affirmed their separateness.

The Commission was faced with the respective claims of the Sultan, Germans and British, in the Kilimanjaro area, in addition to its major task of determining the Sultan's authority at the coast and in the hinterland. The Commission was loaded in Germany's favour. Kitchener, and the British representative, had failed to get a seat on it for General Mathews representing the Sultan of Zanzibar, and had also failed to prevent the attachment to it of one of the Denhardt brothers (with holdings at Witu), as interpreter for the German delegation.

British protestations against Denhardt involvement were brushed aside, and came too late – the Commission had completed its work. Kitchener was thus deeply suspicious of the Germans from the start.

> On my journey out between Aden and Zanzibar, the German Consul-General once or twice spoke to me of the great help Prince Bismarck would give England in Egypt if I acted on the Commission in German interests.[14]

The German Commissioner, Dr Schmidt, worked closely with the German consul at Zanzibar, Dr Arendt, in seeking to limit the Sultan's territorial claims. France was given a seat on the Commission in view of her special treaty rights at Zanzibar under the treaty of 1862, but Portugal, more intimately concerned than France in the matter, was not invited to participate. England favoured her representation on the Commission, but Germany opposed it, arguing that the Portuguese boundary was already well defined by the Ruvuma river. Britain half-heartedly acquiesced in this view.

Starting at Tunghi, to the immediate south of Cape Delgado, the three commissioners commenced their work on 19 January 1886. Proceeding northwards, they visited coastal towns as far as Kisiju, 40 miles south of Dar es Salaam, where they were halted by Mbaruk's rebellion. It was not until late February that they recommenced their task and proceeded to Mombasa. There was great difficulty in defining the extent of the Sultan's authority inland. Throughout the recorded history of the coast invaders had left the hinterland untouched, intercepting trade and exacting toll where it debouched at the coast. The Sultan's occupation of the coastline was resented by the Germans for it blocked communications with their possessions in Usagara; and they denied the Sultan any rights under the so-called 'hinterland doctrine', even though this was a German interpretation. The British approach, that the work of explorers, traders and missionaries should be followed up by proclamation of a British colony or protectorate, was the obverse of the German view that government should pioneer the venture – appropriating territory and then encouraging settlement by model plantations, sponsored with government backing and proved to be going concerns. The long-term result might be the same but the intermediate steps were vastly different, British probing tactics versus German bludgeoning methods.

The Germans had little difficulty proving the weakness of the

Sultan's claim to the mainland. Colonel Hamerton stated in the 1840s, 'I assure Government that the Imam's authority on the Coast of Africa, if he has any, is very trifling' and he had spoken of the dread of His Highness's troops of the notorious See Wee. According to Rigby, in the 1850s, the Sultan's authority did not exist in the interior; and Kirk in October 1880 admitted that it did not run even as far as the Chagga district. Sir Bartle Frere, in 1873, referred to it as of an 'extremely superficial character':

> I knew his authority did not extend far inland, but I was not prepared to find it so entirely confined to a few ports on the coast; and that even at some of the more important of these ports, his garrisons are hemmed in by the petty chiefs of neighbouring tribes. At one place, Lindi, which is the principal garrison to the south — we found the town in nightly expectation of a plundering attack from some negro tribes who have never acknowledged the Sultan's authority.[15]

Stanley at the Berlin Conference placed the 'free zone' to within 40 miles of the East African coast. When it was pointed out that such a line would pass through Zanzibar country, he replied that he had never seen any sign of the Sultan's authority more than that distance from the coast. The Reverend J.T. Last, missionary, stated in May 1885 that from his personal knowledge the Sultan had about 40 troops at Mamboia and officers at five other places on the road to Ujiji; but Rohlfs, German consul at Zanzibar, in June 1885, claimed that the Sultan's so-called stations in the interior were simply 'mercantile settlements', established in the interest of caravans: chiefs in the interior levied tribute at will on passing caravans. Salisbury, in August 1886, stated that records of the Foreign Office showed the rights of the Sultan of Zanzibar on the coast to be 'tolerably clear and well-established', and extending inland roughly 80 miles, and there was evidence that the Sultan's military occupation on the road to Lake Tanganyika and his sovereignty there had been acknowledged by chiefs in the Kilimanjaro and Chagga areas. Kitchener also claimed there was ample evidence of the Sultan's control over the coastline:

> There are, I believe, very few coast-lines in the world where there are so many Governors, garrisoned places and customs-houses as are found on the Zanzibar coastline, examined by the

Commissioners up to the present ... the Sultan's government was found everywhere firmly established and the Commission was unable to find any contrary tendency, although it visited some people secretly in their houses so that they might be perfectly free to make any declaration without fear of the consequences.[16]

The Sultan's governor at Tanga had collected debts for his overlord the Sultan from tribesmen three days' (about 45 miles) inland, and the Sultanc had brought to justice the murderers of Albert Roscher in the region of northern Nyasa. The Germans inadvertently admitted the Sultan's sovereignty in the Kilimanjaro region, when they objected to the Commission extending its inquiries there on the ground that the Sultan had sufficient influence in the area to sway evidence in his favour. Unfortunately, despite circumstantial evidence in support of his claims to sovereignty, there was no one to argue the Sultan's case.

As the work of the Delimitation Commission proceeded, it became clear that there was considerable divergence of views between the German delegate and the British and French representatives. Dr Schmidt complained of the 'fixed views' of the British representative when the latter claimed that country contiguous between the Sultan's posts should be deemed as belonging to him; and Schmidt refused to be bound by *procès-verbal* evidence and complained that Kirk was inciting the Sultan against the Germans. In this duel with the German commissioner Kitchener was left isolated; there was a rapid change of French commissioners, and the latter were less vitally interested in the Commission's work than the British and Germans. When pressure from Bismarck forced the British and French governments to agree that only 'unanimous' findings of the commission should be recognized, Kitchener overstated the Sultan's case, to offset German attempts to minimize it. At almost every point the commissioners had found representatives of the Sultan along the coast and mainland, and Kitchener and his French colleague were ready to accept Barghash's contention that his sovereignty covered a strip ten miles in width (Kitchener would have placed it at 40 miles). Dr Schmidt, at one point, contended that it should be confined to three miles. A deadlock followed with Kitchener informing Salisbury

In my opinion the German Delegate's delimitation of the Sultan's territories would lead to the entire disintegration and annihilation of His Highness's dominions on the continent. The French and ourselves are in complete agreement. The German delegate has taken up a position which makes agreement impossible.[17]

In England, however, friction at this time with Russia made it desirable to avoid friction with Germany, and Kitchener was told to give way. On 7 June 1886, in a letter to Salisbury, he expressed his disappointment.

It appears to be generally considered by my colleagues that the work of the Commission is now at an end. I can only say I deeply regret, if such be the case, that the last act of the Commission should have necessarily been the recording of one member's to my mind biased opinion as the unanimous one of the Commission.[18]

Under this 'unanimous' ruling, an entirely false impression was given. Although Kitchener and the French delegate, Raffray, considered that the Sultan should have a strip 40 miles wide, and Schmidt adhered to a ten mile-wide strip, the latter was given in the Report as *'unanime'*. The opinion of two of the three Commissioners that he ought to have a wider strip was unrecorded. The joint Anglo-French award of territory to the Sultan was put out as the unanimous verdict of the commissioners. The final report stated that the Sultan's claims on the mainland extended over a coastal strip extending, at the most, to no more than ten miles inland. Kitchener agreed to this document on instructions from London, but signed under protest, and submitted separately his own version as to the rights of the case. Kitchener's preoccupation with strategy and defence was reflected in a memorandum he drew up on his way out to East Africa. The way he saw it was that France still played a major part in control of Suez; she had recently occupied Diego Suarez at the north end of Madagascar, where a whole fleet could shelter; she was in strong position at Mayotta – one of the Comoros; France was a formidable power in the Indian Ocean; the Germans had recently acquired Dar es Salaam and had eyes on Tanga. And England could only pose against these rivals her base at Aden and a potential one on the island of Socotra. At the Foreign Office, Villiers Lister, in a review of the British strategic position on the East Africa coast, in March 1886, pointed out as regards Zanzibar

It is not impossible that at some future time the Sultanate might be placed under the Protectorate of a European Power, or might fall under influence unfriendly to Great Britain. In such a case, the harbour of Zanzibar might not be as available as it now is for British ships.[19]

and

Our large coaling-station at Zanzibar is at the mercy of any attack, and English ships in these waters have to rely, in case of breakdown or mishap, on the Seychelles, an undeveloped station of doubtful capabilities and at a considerable distance.[20]

Whereas Zanzibar's harbour was wide open and unprotected, Mombasa, on which Kitchener had set his eyes, was a superb harbour and supremely defensible – a fitting complement to British defences and lines of communication in the Indian Ocean and in protecting the vital Cape-to-Cairo telegraph line. Mombasa was also the likely starting-point for a railway line to Uganda. Thus Kitchener pressed for its immediate occupation. The Admiralty was brought round to Kitchener's view.

It is surprising how quickly the Anglo-German Agreement of 1 November 1886 was arrived at, in view of the divergent opinions of the commissioners and mutual suspicions. Anderson at the Foreign Office, objected to the undue haste with which the agreement was concluded – the commissioners' report was made on 9 June 1886 and the agreement was signed on 1 November 1886. He feared that the Sultan's claims if crudely dealt with might adversely affect British relations with dependent Indian princes. Britain should not, for the sake of a European alliance, be wanting in good faith towards them; and 'With Orientals, haste and pressure is the extremity of unfriendliness'. On the German side the press and public were puzzled and dubious about chancellery diplomacy, and sought ulterior motives behind Britain's role in the Agreement. The *Cologne Gazette* remarked in October 1886:

that England would attempt to hamper German interests in East Africa, by secret intrigues is confirmed to us from a reliable source.[21]

German apprehensions were unfounded. The two powers closed their deal amicably, and there were no unwelcome surprises for either. By the Agreement, the extent of the Sultan's East African possessions was clearly defined for the first time. His sovereignty was confirmed over the coastal strip – a stretch of 600 miles from Tunghi Bay in the south to the mouth of the Tana River in the north, and extending inland for a distance of ten miles. His sovereignty was also confirmed over the islands of Zanzibar, Pemba, Mafia and Lamu, and the towns of Kismayu, Barawa, Merka and Mogadishu, with a radius of ten miles around these places, and Warsheikh with a radius of five miles. Sovereignty over the intervening strip between Kipini and Warsheikh – the Bajun coast – was left undetermined, and so also that over Manda and Pate. Kitchener pressed for recognition of the Sultan's authority inland at Tabora and Ujiji, but was overruled. With the Sultan's territory clearly demarcated for the first time, the mainland territory, bounded on the south by the Ruvuma and on the north by the Tana, was divided into two spheres of influence, British and German. The line of demarcation between them ran from the mouth of the Umba River (opposite Pemba) in a north-westerly direction to the point of intersection of 1°S latitude with the eastern shore of Lake Victoria, leaving the Kilimanjaro area in the German sphere. Each power pledged itself not to interfere in the other's sphere of influence. Germany bound herself to recognize the Anglo-French declaration of 1862 which affirmed the Sultan of Zanzibar's independence.

The Sultan did not readily assent to this severe circumscription of his dominions and was subjected to intense diplomatic pressure from Germany. Dr Arendt, German consul at Zanzibar, claimed that the murder of Dr Jühlke by a young Somali at Kismayu was connived at by the Sultan's governor there, and demanded that the *jus talionis* ('the only law within the comprehension of the coloured races') be applied 'with the same vigour and justice as has been done on the West African Coast'. The British also pressed the Sultan, urging him to withdraw his claims to the Kilimanjaro area; and the French warned that they too might demand concessions if he yielded too much to the British and Germans. The poor potentate, empty of power and influence, deserted on all sides, scarcely knew where to turn, and finally gave way. He first sought to guard against further weakening of his sovereignty by adhering on 8 November 1886 to the stipulations of the General Act of the Berlin Conference, whereby the principle of free trade was not to be applied to his territories. Further pressure on the Sultan eased when, on 8 December 1886, the French acquiesced in the Anglo-German Agreement of November 1886, in return for recognition of French claims to the Comoro Islands. This meant disregarding the historic claims of the Sultan of Zanzibar there, but it did prevent Germany from acquiring them: she was already casting covetous eyes in their direction.

The Anglo–German Agreement of November 1886 left much tidying up to be done. The Portuguese, embittered at being debarred from the delimitation proceedings, now pressed for the whole of Tunghi Bay, which Kirk claimed had been 'long and continuously held by Zanzibar'. Failing negotiations, the Portuguese seized the town of Tunghi in February 1887 and captured the Sultan's steamship, forcing him to concede Portuguese claims. The Anglo–German Agreement placed Christian missions in an anomalous position. Some English missions now found themselves in German territory. Bishop Smythies of the University Mission to Central Africa which had four stations in Usambara, had sought to safeguard them against the effects of the Anglo–German Agreement by arguing for a natural boundary following the Pangani River, which would have left the four stations in British territory, and would have given a boundary line following more closely tribal divisions. But Germany had her eyes set on the Usambara and Kilimanjaro region, and Britain was anxious not to give her umbrage: thus the fate of mission stations was disregarded in the delimitation proceedings.

The upshot of the Anglo–German Agreement of 1886 was that Britain and Germany, with thresholds now well established on the mainland, were well placed for further advance into the interior, and this would necessitate another and final demarcation of their interests there in a few years' time.

The Germans were quick to entrench on ground gained by the 1886 Agreement. Peters, in a series of whirlwind tours in Germany, stirred up much interest in the new-found possessions in East Africa. He painted an attractive picture of opportunities awaiting young Germans, and appealed to their sense of adventure: he was indefatigable as a colonial enthusiast. A rumour that the German Emperor, the Chancellor and several German princes had invested in the German East Africa Company was traceable to Peters's smooth tongue. The confidence he radiated was paralleled by the fervour of officers in the field and the vigour with which they brought the rude and vast territory under German rule. In their fresh enthusiasm and no-nonsense approach to subordinate peoples the Germans would excel in colonial administration and teach the British and French how to manage subject races, but behind this appeal to young Germans lay a more sober calculation. Peters, in his address to the Dresden branch of the German Colonial Society in March 1887, stated

the main object of the colonial movement is the transfer to
German hands of the annual profit pocketed by the English and
Dutch salesmen of the tropical products required by Germany.[22]

and Bismarck in a speech to the Reichstag in January 1889, although
claiming that he was not at heart colonial-minded, had to admit there
was something to be said for the acquisition of an East African colony.

For tropical produce we pay about 500,000,000 marks in cash to
other countries. If we could gain a tenth of that for German
proprietors it would be a good start.[23]

Bismarck did not envisage German colonies as offshoots of the mother
country, places where Germans would emigrate as settlers, creating a
wider Germany overseas and incorporated in the German Empire; nor
would they be another British India: a place for upper-middle classes,
bureaucrats and military to find employment. German colonies would
be commercial undertakings protected by the imperial government –
hence their designation as 'protectorates' (*Schutzgebiete*). Bismarck
favoured colonization by chartered companies: the New Guinea
Company formed in 1885 was an example of what he had in mind.

My aim is the governing merchant and not the governing
bureaucrat in those regions. Our privy councillors and expectant
subalterns are excellent enough at home, but in the colonial
territories I expect more from the Hanseatics who have been there
for generations.[24]

The Hamburg firm of O'Swald and Company had been at Zanzibar
since 1849, and generations of O'Swalds had served there as consuls,
alternating this with high civic office in Hamburg.[25] O'Swald and
Company in its founding years carried on a trade in cowrie shells (used
as currency) in East and West Africa, and in the transport of pilgrims to
Mecca. Following the First World War the firm's property was
liquidated but it re-established itself in East Africa during the interwar
years, only to be ousted again as a consequence of the Second World
War. By the mid-twentieth century the firm was back, trading in a range
of goods from 'pins to machinery'.[25] Thus East Africa was not an
unknown world to Germans when they proceeded to establish a colony
there. Within a month of its receiving its charter (7 September 1885) the

chief representative of the German East Africa Company, Alexander Lucas, and a cadre of young men, Ramsey, von Bulow, Pfeil, Reichard and von St Paul Illaire arrived at Zanzibar. They and other young Germans – the Denhardt brothers, Jühlke and von Wissmann – were from the officer corps or universities, zealous, eager and ambitious. Germany's new colonial empire provided outlets from the stifling life of military cantonments at Strasbourg and Metz. This was the first great German adventure since Sedan, and fresh laurels could be won.

The Anglo-German Agreement of 1886 had placed the valuable massif of Kilimanjaro with its fertile slopes in the German sphere, and this region and the cordon of the Usambara and Pare mountains quickly became the favoured site of German enterprise. It was fairly adjacent to the coast and easily accessible, thus German advance into this region was rapid. By the autumn of 1886 a station had been constructed at Arusha as a base against Maasai raids, and by early 1887 another at Mafi on the Pangani, above Korogwe. Farther upriver the station of Deutschenhof was constructed about the same time. Around these stations extensive plantations of cotton and tobacco were set out. At Lewa in Usambara, established in 1887, tobacco cultivation was so successful that labourers were imported from Singapore, in view of the absence of local labour. Kikokwe, founded in 1887, became an important centre for cotton-growing. With the advance up the Pangani continuing, the Germans began to settle on the slopes of Kilimanjaro, and this region tended to outrank all others in importance for the Germans. Other regions proved less attractive than first imagined. In November 1886 the steamer *Neckar* sailed from Bremerhaven with a large cargo of seeds and planting equipment for Hohenzollern Harbour (Port Durnford) on the Somaliland coast, where the German East Africa Company had directed Max Winter to take charge and develop a settlement. The assassination of Dr Jühlke who was actively fostering the settlement, and the early realization of its small possibilities for colonization, ended the experiment. The Germans, as did the English and Italians, at first tended to overrate the potential of Somaliland.

By March 1887 the German East Africa Company had 12 stations in East Africa. There were well-constructed buildings and plantations around them, with an air of permanency and orderliness in contrast to the flimsy structures and the scrub patches of garden around them which were designated as stations in the brochures of the IBEAC in the British sphere to the north of the Germans. In German East Africa the choice of settler was also to be selective: he must be from a class of persons 'which in England was, and still is, the natural mainstay of the British colonies, namely, resolute sons of good families, who were possessed of some means'; there must be no great movement of peasant stock – apart from the few hundred Greeks and Italians who later arrived, as skilled labourers and artisans. Non-Germans were not welcome – as non-imperial citizens they would be in an inferior legal position anyway as compared to German citizens. There must be no mistakes in establishing German East Africa as an ideal colony.

Peters arrived back at Zanzibar in May 1887 with a party of 20 young German assistants and was soon pressing for control of the Sultan's coastal strip and a lease of the customs at Dar es Salaam and Pangani. There was local Arab resistance to this; the Liwali at Dar es Salaam only acquiesced when Captain Hauptmann Leue arrived with a bodyguard of Arab soldiers provided by the Sultan of Zanzibar. Peters was unremitting and unscrupulous in his methods. He was the 'secret influence' referred to by Holmwood as behind the undignified pressure on the Sultan by the Indian firm of Jairam Sewjii which threatened to sue him over financial dealings and thus embarrass him. The German consul-general at Zanzibar and officials at home were no great lovers of Peters, but he was popular in Germany, where his great drive, almost fanatical belief in Germany's role as a colonial power, his pamphlets and speeches and remarkable energy, induced the public to take an interest – and shares – in the *Gesellschaft*. Peters's enthusiasm for colonial enterprise was not to be equalled until Dr Bernhard Dernburg was appointed to the Colonial Directorship in 1906 and in him the same tactics and fine words in whipping up public enthusiasm for colonial enterprise were exhibited.

Peters was a difficult man to manage, and he was increasingly at odds with the President of the German East Africa Company. He was eventually replaced as Director-in-Chief in the spring of 1888 by Herr Ernst Vohsen, a man of 38, formerly commercial consul at Sierre Leone where he had been manager of the French Senegal Company. Vohsen brought with him testimonials from influential Muslims on the West Coast, testifying to his success and conciliatory manner in dealing with Muslims. His assumption of office was marked by the Sultan's granting (with British prodding) on 28 April a 50-year concession to the German East Africa Company for the administration of the coastline strip from the Umba River in the north to the Ruvuma in the south. It was to be administered in the Sultan's name and the customs would be farmed by the Germans experimentally for 12 months before annual payment for the lease would be determined. The Company assumed control over the coastline on 16 August 1888.

With the concession in hand Herr Vohsen undertook what he termed a policy of 'Germanization'. A staff of 60 Germans was soon available and embarked on a course in Swahili at Dar es Salaam. Vohsen had the support of Dr Michahelles, German consul-general at Zanzibar, in a way Peters had never enjoyed, and he shared with him plans for developing the colony. The Germans would surpass the British: they would advance into the interior by rail; and the German East Africa Company would be comparable to the 'late East India Company' of the British and would have the same 'full-blown status and powers' of the latter. The Germans meant business. Euan-Smith, the English consul-general at Zanzibar, reported to Salisbury in June 1888:

> Everything leads to the belief that the Germans out here regard their enterprise in East Africa as likely to lead to permanent results. They have thoroughly surveyed the country for a railway as far as Mwapawa, they are building houses all along the coastline, and the German Consul-General is just leaving on an extended tour of inspection of the various new stations that are to be occupied. This activity has made a marked impression upon the native population who are commencing openly to express doubts as to whether the British Company has ever received or intends to work a similar concession.[26]

The German Speech from the Throne of November 1888 emphasized the duty of the German Empire to 'win the Dark Continent for Christian civilization'.

British grudging admiration for German methods and energy soon changed to one of patronizing amusement, for the Germans in the autumn of 1888 were faced with rebellion in their territory. They had brought it on themselves, according to the British, because of their insensitivity in dealing with orientals. Shootings of natives, and violent ill-thought-out methods of inducing respect and obedience from Arabs and Africans brought the uprising on their own heads. Arabs arriving from the mainland to make their salaams to the new Sultan at Zanzibar, were bitter about the 'Germanization' of the mainland: the Germans had run up their flag in a position of equality with the Sultan's. At Pangani in August 1888, Lieutenant Zelewski had downed the Sultan's flag and run up the German flag instead. German officials openly abused the

Sultan for not spending his income on improving utilities such as harbour installations; the Germans were contemptuous of the Arabs' lack of personal hygiene; there were brutalities and beatings attributed to the Germans, and summary executions for relatively minor crimes. Petty and irksome discipline was enforced: Africans, Indians and Arabs alike had to salute Germans – civilian or military. Violation of mosques, molestation of women by 'low-class' Germans, all were catalogued by the British as causes of the revolt. According to the Reverend H.H. Clarke the Germans had undone all that Livingstone and others had died to accomplish.

It was easy to attribute German mistakes to inexperience; their attempt to apply bureaucratic methods which worked well at home to an unknown and different culture could not but bring trouble. Among the first cadre of officials sent out to East Africa there were misfits – persons prone to cruelty and inflexibility of mind – but many were of the highest quality, men who maintained throughout their careers standards of probity and justice equal to the best in British tradition. Von Wissmann bore himself throughout his career as colonial administrator with what Bismarck would have described as a 'white waistcoat'; Langheld at Bukoba won the highest praise from British officials in Uganda; and Johannes in command of Moshi station for over ten years; Franz Stuhlmann, soldier and scholar, represented the German official at his best. Nevertheless there was danger in German East Africa of arousing a movement among the Arabs akin to that of the Mahdi in the Sudan: an outbreak of 'fanatical stranger-hating feeling' – *Freudenfeindliche* – at a time when there was widespread Arab insurgence in the interior. Resentment felt by Arab leaders, especially Kadis, whose authority had been greatly curtailed by the Germans, and of African chiefs whose practise of levying hongo had been halted by the Germans, was the main cause of the uprising which now took place.

It took the form of attacks on Germans – officials and missionaries alike – and culminated in acts of cannibalism in some outlying districts. Both British and German were subject to hostility; Sir Lloyd Mathews, in the employ of the Sultan, was detained at Bagamoyo and his life threatened – as a Christian and suspected German spy. The uprising commenced almost simultaneously in the Usambara region, at Kilwa and Pangani, and soon the whole coast was aflame. The Germans were forced to evacuate all their stations except Bagamoyo and Dar es Salaam. The main leader of the revolt, an Arab, Abushiri ibn Salim al-Harthi, generally known as 'Bushiri', long a troublesome element on the coast, was supported by an able emulator, Bwana Heri, of the Zigua tribe. Together they gathered round them a host of dissident Arabs and Africans, and waged unremitting war against the Germans, relieved by occasional quixotic acts of chivalry on Bushiri's part. The war brought unexpected Anglo-German co-operation. Pleading that the Sultan's control over the coast was ineffectual and suspecting that he was even encouraging it (when Bushiri was captured letters were found on him implicating the Sultan), the Germans proposed a joint Anglo-German blockade of the coast to cut off arms for the rebels. The blockade could also be portrayed as part of an anti-slave-trade campaign, and thus help to deflect growing criticism of the German Company in Germany (it had attempted to prevent the correspondent of the *Tageblatt* from telegraphing news home).

British officials claimed that 'to blockade such a line of coast, is folly, it is physically impossible'; but owing to the 'exigencies of European politics' Britain joined in, and Italy gave token support to a commendable international venture in halting the arms and slave-trade. The blockade instituted on 19 November 1888 was to extend from the Tana to the Ruvuma, although the British claimed that the strip from Mafia Island to the Ruvuma most needed watching: if confined here it would less seriously affect trade in the British sphere.

By December 1888, Bushiri, well-armed with breechloaders and cannon, his power increased by loot and plunder, and recruits flocking to join him (he cut off the hands of those who refused), was moving against Bagamoyo. The Company's resources were at low ebb, its stations were deserted and its officials confined to Dar es Salaam and Bagamoyo; plantations, formerly promising, were now receding into scrub. The levying of hongo revived. It was thus a subdued Company which appealed to the Reichstag in January 1889 for a grant of 1,000,000 marks to fight the rebels. The German government, concerned over the blow to German prestige, took up the fight. Two million marks were voted for a military expedition to be led by Hermann von Wissmann as Imperial Commissioner. At the age of 39 years, he was destined to be one of the luminaries on the German East African scene. Arriving there in March 1889, having collected a force of 600 Sudanese in Egypt on his way out, and adding to these 50 Somalis and 500 Zulus, he was now cast in the role of knight errant in suppressing the slave-trade and Bushiri's revolt. This would connote well with Bismarck's policy of improving relations with the Catholic Church and signify a humanitarian and Christian mission in German colonization.

With the Imperial Commissioner came the 'Wissmann troupe', 40 German officers, maturer and older than Lucas's recruits and with higher academic qualifications than British colonial officials. Wissmann, seasoned African traveller who had crossed the continent from Angola to the east coast and explored the Kasai area of the Congo, an able and fair administrator, was well liked by the British and his relations with them were always cordial.

His first object was to bring Bushiri to terms. An offer to the latter to enter German service at a salary of 3000 rupees per month was spurned (Bushiri feared it as a trap). Wissmann then moved in on him. Quick and resolute action saved the German station of Mpwapwa – 'the most important caravan junction in Africa'. Achieving a record for African travelling – 25 to 30 miles a day, the result of good commissariat and organization – Wissmann saved Mpwapwa, erected a fort there and then headed off Bushiri from attacking Bagamoyo, Wissmann's headquarters. Meanwhile the blockade at sea was sustained, although imposing a severe strain on German officers and men who, not inured to the tropics, paid dearly with their lives; and the hottest time of year was still to come. The British, with half a century's experience, including the anti-slave-trade patrol on the East African coast and in that worst hell-hole of all, the Persian Gulf, took it calmly!

Disillusionment in Germany over the initial failure to establish the ideal colony is evident in the Emperor's and Chancellor's considering abandonment of the East African venture. Bismarck toyed with the idea suggested to him by Euan-Smith – that the Sultan should reassume authority over the whole coast except Bagamoyo and Dar es Salaam; and Bismarck thought German colonial enterprise might perhaps make another attempt 25 years hence, if the time was favourable; present experience might then still be useful. The British, feeling the strain of sustaining a blockade in which their interests were not vitally concerned, and in which they were becoming identified with 'crude German unbelievers', were ready to withdraw.

Bismarck was also willing to end the blockade if it could be done with a flourish and without loss of German prestige. A suggestion made by Euan-Smith some months previously that the Sultan, in return for the lifting of the blockade so injurious to his revenue, should agree to the abolition of slavery, was now eagerly taken up the the Germans. The German government would thus be shown to be magnanimous, concerned for the Sultan's interests and in the vanguard of the anti-slavery cause. The German government was under fire from the opposition and a general election was pending. Thus military defeat and retirement before a 'barbarian like Bushiri' was inadmissible. That the Sultan had already been brought round to signing an anti-slavery decree was not generally known, nor that the British had helped the Germans to save face.

The blockade ended on 1 October 1889. It had far-reaching effects. It had brought the imperial authorities into firsthand contact with the overseas territory and a realization of the difficulty of administering it through a chartered company. The latter was now discredited. On 22 October 1889 the German government firmly stepped in and wrested control from the latter, and declared the territory to be an imperial protectorate as from 1 January 1890. The Company was left as a purely commercial concern. The imperial government now took up the drive against Bushiri with vigour and stratagem. His end was quickly encompassed, for despite support from thousands of Maviti (synonym for a motley collection of Yao and allied tribes) he failed to capture Bagamoyo, and was soon himself on the run, an isolated refugee. He faced an implacable foe. His capture and execution soon followed. There was nothing *dulce et decorum* about his death at Bagamoyo on 15 December 1889. Under brutal pressure and subjected to great indignities he revealed that the Sultan of Zanzibar had promised to make him governor of the whole coast when he had routed the Germans.

Bushiri's execution took place a few days after the arrival of Henry M. Stanley at Bagamoyo with Emin Pasha in tow, and together these events marked a new era. The stage was now set for another, a second partition of East Africa.

The Anglo-German Agreement of November 1886, which had secured the way open for British and German enterprise on the mainland, also left the Sultan bruised by the recent encounter with Germany and smarting over the diminution of his sovereignty. Isolated and vulnerable, he turned to Britain as the lesser of evils. Kirk, before retiring as consul in July 1886, and Holmwood his successor as acting-consul, both persuaded the Sultan that this was the wiser course. Henry Stanley, at Zanzibar in February 1887, preparing for his expedition to rescue Emin Pasha, also played an influential part in persuading the Sultan. Writing from the Cape of Good Hope, 9 March 1887, after leaving Zanzibar, Stanley stated:

I have settled several little commissions at Zanzibar satisfactorily. One was to get the Sultan to sign the concessions which

Mackinnon tried to obtain a long time ago ... For eight years, to my knowledge, the matter had been placed before His Highness, but the Sultan's signature was difficult to obtain. Arriving at Zanzibar, I saw the Sultan was aging, and that he was not long to live [Barghash died a year later]. Englishmen could not invest money in the reserved 'sphere of influence' until some concessions were signed. 'Please God', said the Sultan, 'we shall agree; there will be no further doubt about the matter'. But his political anxieties were wearing him fast, and unless this matter is soon completed it will be too late.[27]

The Sultan had apparently communicated with Stanley respecting Portuguese aggression, and the indignities he had been subjected to by the Germans. In February 1887 he was prompted by the British consul to wire Mackinnon to 'save him from the Germans', informing him that the 1877/78 concession was still open for him to take up, but Mackinnon was still cautious, and sounded out the Foreign Office as to whether financial support might be forthcoming if the concession were taken up. A letter to the Foreign Office from Stanley gave the desired impetus. The Foreign Office was favourable to the scheme of a renewed concession if it did not excite the Germans, but as to government financial support, the response was not propitious.

Mackinnon was not deterred. Times had changed since the 1877/78 offer of a concession. The British sphere of influence was now more clearly demarcated; much more was known about the East African mainland; the highlands of Kenya had been reported on favourably; British missionaries were now established in Uganda and would support any extension of British influence there; and did not he, Mackinnon, have around him wealthy colleagues, persons of consequence, well-connected, who were in favour of his taking up the Sultan's offer?

Thus was formed the British East African Association which took up the proffered concession on 24 May 1887, under which it was granted, for a term of 50 years, control of the Sultan's mainland coastal strip, from Wanga to Kipini. The Association would administer it in the Sultan's name, under his flag, and subject to his sovereign rights; and the Sultan was to receive a portion of the customs duties and to have a founder's share in the Association. The Foreign Office view that 'It is notorious that the majority of, if not all, the subscribers are actuated more by philanthropic motives than by the expectation of receiving any adequate return for their outlay', needs qualification: the directors were much desirous for government financial help, instancing that given to the North Borneo Company and the Royal Niger Company and the support given to the German East Africa Company by the German government. The directors intimated that they expected the establishment of regular steamship services with East Africa – and not at their expense: not an undue expectation in view of Mombasa's being the major British port there.

With the concession in hand the Association selected Mombasa as the site of its main agency in East Africa, thus sharing in the development of a great port. The whole seafront on the western side of the island and that on the mainland opposite were now acquired. The firm of Smith, Mackenzie and Company, already with a branch agency at Mombasa, became the headquarters of the Association. The latter had its eyes not only on the coastal strip, but on the interior beyond it within the British sphere of influence. It was not encouraged by government to expand into the interior, neither was it discouraged; appetite grew with feeding, and the advance inland was ultimately to lead to Uganda. An advance into the interior meant getting recognition of its claims from native chiefs and the avoiding of the disturbances which marred the German take-over of the mainland. George Mackenzie was sent inland immediately behind Mombasa, and by mid-July 1887 had acquired some 20 treaties – all within 200 miles of the coast – conferring sovereign rights on the Association. In August 1887, after Holmwood had visited Kilimanjaro to examine the feasibility of a railway there, and his favourable report thereon, Taveta was selected as the main station of the IBEAC in the Kilimanjaro area.

The Association then, with treaties in hand covering the country for some 200 miles inland, was converted into the British East Africa Company (with nominal capital of £2,000,000 (100,000 ordinary shares at £20 each)), on 18 April 1888. It next applied to the British government for a charter, which was granted on 3 September 1888, the original Association now becoming the Imperial British East Africa Company (IBEAC). Under the charter a grand opportunity seemed to open up for the Company, apart from the complexity which now entered into British and German expansion into the interior as a result of the so-called 'hinterland agreement' of July 1887 between England and Germany, which provided that neither power would permit extension behind their respective spheres of influence as demarcated by the Agreement of 1 November 1886, an agreement which was more honoured in the breach than the observance. German annexations in the rear of the British sphere would be discouraged, and

England would leave Germany a free hand for the future in the
territories south of the Victoria Nyanza, and, without interfering
with the territories lying to the east of Lakes Tanganyika and
Nyasa at the back of the German Protectorate, would confine
herself to opening up the territories lying to the north of the
agreed line.[28]

The powers granted to the IBEAC under its Charter were truly wide
and can be explained only in terms of Salisbury's recognition at this date
that British occupation of Egypt was a long-term commitment and with
it there must be control of the Upper Nile and Equatoria; and the
IBEAC could help in securing this. Over the East African mainland and
offshore islands the Company was authorized

> to obtain and administer concessions from Native Chiefs, make
> and enforce laws, establish Courts, appoint Judges, levy taxes,
> customs, construct roads, harbours, erect waterworks, establish
> banks, issue notes, coin money and undertake trading operations.[29]

Its obligations were not so clearly spelled out, apart from being directed
to do all in its power to end the slave-trade. Its charter was *carte blanche*
authority to enter into the development of the British sphere of
influence.

Even while directing their interest inland, the directors of the IBEAC
were fearful lest they be weakened at the coast if the Germans might
lease the portion of the Sultan's coastline north of the Umba and thus
effectively choke British expansion on the coast. Thus the Company on
9 October 1888 obtained a supplementary concession from the Sultan,
converting its concession of May 1887 into a lease in perpetuity and with
guarantee of a further grant of his ports north of the Kipini whenever
the Company might wish to take it up. With this secured the Company
still complained of the disabilities under which it operated, such as that
the rent for the coastal strip was too high, being based on the first year's
customs returns which were unduly inflated owing to the blockade of the
German coast and diversion of trade to the British sphere; thus an
arbitrary figure was struck, for the first year only. By its concession the
Company could claim the same rights as the Sultan accorded the
German East Africa Company, and when the latter, in the autumn of
1890, obtained permanent concession of their coastline for a lump sum,
the IBEAC sought to commute its annual rent for payment of a lump

sum, but was reminded by the Foreign Office that the IBEAC had not received permanent cession of territory as had the Germans.

On this sour note the Company turned to the assessment of the coastline it had leased. Mr W.W.A. Fitzgerald, expert in tropical agriculture, was directed to examine and report on its suitability for cultivation of oil seed, groundnuts, rice, etc, and whether Indian cultivators might be settled there. Fitzgerald's recommendations were favourable, but the Company paid no heed to them for it was now dwelling on the injurious effect of the rivalry of the Germans at Witu – the small state on the mainland opposite Lamu island and comprising a 60-mile coastal strip from Kipini to Manda Bay – the last fertile stretch to the immediate south of the desolate Bajun coast. Witu acquired a new importance in 1856, when Ahmed bin Fumo Luti, Simba (the Lion, last of the Nabhan sultans of Pate, whose origins date from the early days of Arab and Persian settlement) and his ally Mohammed bin Malak of the island of Siu, fled from Pate to Witu on being outlawed by the Sultan of Zanzibar for contumacy. In the forest depths of Witu, Fumo set up a petty sultanate, and here, surrounded by malcontents and runaway slaves, he became the centre for potential rebellion during the period 1860–85, a veritable thorn in the side of the Sultan of Zanzibar, and a scourge to the surrounding countryside. The British vice-consul at Lamu, J. Haggard, urged the destruction of the town. And when German attention was turned to Witu in the 1880s with the Denhardt brothers (Sustan and Clement) making a treaty with Simba whereby he surrendered a portion of his territory to them and with it sovereign rights, the Sultan of Zanzibar in May 1885, affronted over Simba's defiance and concessions to the Germans, despatched a force of 600 men against him. This brought German intervention. Bismarck in a despatch of 2 June 1885 warned the Sultan of Zanzibar against attacking Witu: Germans had settled there and their interests must not be threatened. Thus was brought home to Barghash in his declining years the mailed fist of the Germans. He held back his troops at Lamu, and meekly acquiesced in a German protectorate over Simba's territory.

The Denhardts, following the Anglo-German Agreement of 1886, transferred their interests at Witu to the newly-founded German Witu Company under Prince Hohenhlohe-Langenburg. Soon German settlers established themselves at Witu; the Anglo-German Agreement of 1886 had strengthened German claims there by recognizing it as a separate district. The Germans next cast covetous eyes on the commerce of the Tana and Ozi Rivers, which were, however, controlled by Lamu and the nearby port of Kipini at the mouth of the Ozi. But the IBEAC was also aspiring to control these ports claiming that it had

> no option but to take over the northern ports ... Had no attempt been made to obtain these northern possessions of Zanzibar by a foreign power it would not have been in their interest nor was it the desire of the British East Africa Company to extend so far for perhaps several years to come.[30]

Accusations against the Germans were many: they attempted to control postal communications at Witu; spread rumours that the British Company aspired to seize Witu (the British Company had pressed the Germans to sell Witu to it); had demanded the cession of Lamu on the basis of an alleged verbal promise by the Sultan, and challenged his right to cede Lamu to the IBEAC. Charge brought countercharge and became so acrimonious that, by mutual agreement, the dispute was submitted for arbitration to Baron Lambermont, Minister of State to the King of the Belgians. His award, made at Brussels on 17 August 1889, was to the effect that since the Sultan's signature was given to neither Germans nor British, he was free to sign a concession wlth whomsoever he wished. Lambermont also recommended that the delimitation arrangements of 1886 be carried north of the Tana River, so as to eliminate further discord. It is a pity that this recommendation was not taken up.

The Germans accepted the award with ill-grace, and sought elsewhere to make trouble. They contested the claim of the Sultan to the islands of Manda and Pate (sovereignty over which had been left undetermined by the Anglo-German Agreement of 1886), and when the British Company hoisted its flag there in October 1887 the Germans maintained that these islands belonged to the Sultan of Witu; and they then cast covetous eyes on the 'Bajun' Strip, unpropitious territory though it was. This action on the part of the Germans caused the directors of the IBEAC to ponder. Might not the next goal of the Germans be to acquire the coastline north of the Juba River? If they were to succeed in this it would leave the British Company in an intolerable position, squeezed in by the Germans both on the south and the north. The Benadir must not fall into the hands of a powerful competitor like the Germans. The Company was not itself ready to take over the northern strip. The answer was to place it under the control of a friendly European power – sufficiently strong to hold the restless and fanatical Somali in check, yet not to pose a danger to the Company's interests.

France, traditional imperial rival, was out of the question: Germany – *agent provocateur* – was unthinkable; she had hurried the Company into unwonted paths of expansion. There was only one European power in the running, namely Italy. The Italians had been slow to heed Sir Bartle Frere's advice when he stopped over at Rome in early December 1872 on his anti-slave-trade mission to Zanzibar. Frere, as well as being received by the Pope, met high-ranking Italian officials and offered to supply them with a memorandum on the probable growth of Italian trade with East Africa', and suggested that a commission visit there 'on behalf of Italian merchants'. Italy, at the time of Frere's visit, had barely entered on the imperial path in Africa: her efforts were still largely confined to the Red Sea area. A move southward to the East African coast from there, however, was a natural step. In May 1885 Italy negotiated a commercial treaty with the Sultan of Zanzibar which brought her into contact with the Sultan's possessions on the mainland, and she soon sought to control the coast north of Kismayu. In July 1885 Captain Antonio Cecchi in the *Barbarigo* made a landfall at Port Durnford – supposedly an emergency stop for supplies, but in reality a reconnaissance survey of the country. In September of the same year Cecchi made a verbal request to Barghash for cession of the mouth of the Juba River, in return for an equal share in its custom revenue. The Sultan, in reply, 'like a well-bred Oriental', asked that the matter be placed in writing. This scared off the Italians, for they knew that such a document would be immediately referred to the British consul. They pressed the matter no further.

Barghash died on 27 March 1888. His successor, Seyyid Khalifa, of weaker disposition and 'abnormally ignorant' of the ways of the world, was soon subjected to Italian pressure and their claim for Kismayu on the grounds that his predecessor had promised it to them (no documentary evidence of this could be produced). In May 1888, Signor Vincenzo Filonardi, Italian consul at Zanzibar, under the pretext that the Sultan had deliberately affronted the King of Italy by not answering a letter from him (it being the month of Ramadan, the Sultan had transacted no official business), suggested that satisfactory compensation for this terrible transgression might be made by ceding to Italy the district of Kismayu. Ignoring the Sultan's apologies for the oversight, Filonardi, on 5 June 1888, pressed for the unconditional surrender of Kismayu to Italy. On the Sultan's refusal, Filonardi abruptly broke off relations and adopted a truculent attitude.

Within the month Captain Cecchi and two ships of war appeared at

Zanzibar; 'public opinion in Italy waited impatiently for a solution in a sense creditable to the position, and satisfactory to the public sentiment of the country'. In the face of this threat, and prompted by 'his extreme alarm at the violent proceedings of the Germans upon the coast-line', Khalifa turned to the IBEAC. He could put Italy off by pleading that he was already committed to ceding Kismayu to the IBEAC, in fulfilment of a promise made by his late brother to the Company. The move was a godsend to the IBEAC. Negotiations for a concession of the five northern ports, initiated by Mackinnon in the time of Barghash, and renewed in May 1888, were now pressed forward, and at the end of August 1888, Sultan Khalifa offered to Mackinnon the concession of these ports, and all other places on the mainland and islands, which remained in His Highness' undisputed possession, on condition that the IBEAC would never alienate this concession to another party, and that HMG would accord protection to the Sultan in the face of anticipated Italian anger. The date and terms of the concession would be finalized as soon as the 'Italian question' was settled. Signor Cecchi at Zanzibar, in the face of this development, was in a 'very unhappy and dejected state'.

The Italians, too, now turned to the IBEAC to achieve their goals in East Africa. In early September 1888 (the same month as the IBEAC received its Royal Charter), Mackinnon and Signor Catalani, chargé d'affaires, met on board the yacht *Cornelia* and arrived at an understanding whereby Mackinnon would use his friendly offices with the Sultan to obtain his assent to Italian control of the Benadir, and the Italians in return would pay any 'moderate sums' necessary to bring the Sultan around in achieving this and they would also withdraw their naval presence from Zanzibar.

When G. Mackenzie, director of the IBEAC, arrived at Zanzibar on 6 October 1888, to renegotiate the terms of the Company's 50-year lease and convert it into one in perpetuity, in the face of German expansion, he had also before him the Sultan's offer to the Company of his ports north of Kipini, whenever the Company might wish to take it up. To bring the Sultan around to agreeing to the transfer of a lease of these northern ports to the Italians would be no easy matter: any approach to the Sultan would have to be carefully timed and there must be no undue haste. By the time Mackenzie had obtained the supplementary concession on 9 October 1888, the Italian warships had been withdrawn to ease negotiations with the Sultan. Events elsewhere seemed to be strengthening the Italian position in the Horn of Africa. In February 1889 Yusuf Ali, Sultan of Obbia, as the result of a boundary dispute with the Sultan of Zanzibar, placed his sultanate under Italian protection, and on 7 April 1889 his son-in-law, Osman Mahmud, Sultan of Mijjertein (to the immediate north of Obbia), did likewise. On 2 May in the same year, the famous Treaty of Ucciali gave Italy (or so she claimed) a protectorate over the whole of Ethiopia and with it also pre-emption to Abyssinian territorial claims to a 'greater' Ethiopia. Cecchi's dreams of an Italian empire embracing the Horn of Africa seemed near realization. There only remained control of the Benadir to bring this about, and give Italy the natural boundary of the Juba as the southern line of her protectorate. Negotiations in the summer of 1889 between Mackinnon and Catalani culminated in a formal agreement on 3 August 1889, whereby

> the Imperial British East Africa Company agreed to transfer to the Italian Government the lands, territories, and countries lying on the coast north of the mouth of the River Juba, including Brava, Merka, and Mogadisho, with radii landwards of 10 sea miles, and Warsheikh, with a radius of 5 sea miles, to be held by the Italian Government (or their transferees) on the same terms and conditions as those contained in the Concession which the Sultan of Zanzibar was then about to grant to the Imperial British East Africa Company concerning such lands, territories, and countries. The transfer by the Imperial Biritsh East Africa Company to the Italian Government to be effected when the Sultan's concession and consent was obtained.[31]

Kismayu would be jointly occupied by the IBEAC and the Italians, and they would share rights of navigation on the Juba and its tributaries. The Italian sphere of influence, as defined by the agreement, lay to the north of the line of the Juba River – 'the natural boundary' of the Italian sphere – up to its intersection with the 40th meridian of east longitude and 8th parallel of north latitude, and along the 8th parallel to 37°E longitude, and then in a north-westerly direction to the Blue Nile, and following that river to 35°E longitude.

The Lambermont Award of 17 August 1889, which pronounced in the Sultan's favour, encouraged him to grant to the IBEAC on 31 August 1889 a concession of his possessions north of the Juba and islands – Lamu, Manda and Patta – but stipulating that the concession should not be transferred to the Italians. The concession was for five years, with an engagement to renew it for not less than another five years, if agreed upon. The Sultan would hand over all the customs to the IBEAC after five years, when the Company and the Sultan were to divide any increase in net profits.

This concession brought sharp response from the Germans. On 22 October 1889, disregarding the ten treaties the IBEAC had made with chiefs between the Tana and Juba Rivers – including one with Avatula, paramount chief of the Waboni – the Germans made a sweeping claim to the same seaboard, on the basis of treaties purportedly made with 'Sultans and Chiefs' there. It largely comprised the 'Bajun' strip, but on the basis of holding it, and under the 'hinterland' doctrine, the Germans could claim territory as far inland as Uganda. That this was German intention was given credence, in view of Carl Peters's advance on Uganda from Witu.

The British were not slow to act in this game of leap-frog. On 18 November 1889 the IBEAC, by formal deed, transferred to the Italian government, subject to the Sultan's approval, the lease it had obtained over his possessions north of the Juba River – Brava, Merka, Mogadishu, Warsheikh and Mruti. On 19 November, and before the Sultan's approval had been obtained, Italy notified the signatories to the Berlin Act that she had assumed a protectorate over the coast from the Juba mouth to 2½°N latitude. The Filonardi Company (founded by Vincenzo Filonardi, Italian consul at Zanzibar, and influential trader) would administer the protectorate on behalf of the Italian government.

In the face of this move, and frustrated by IBEAC treaties with chiefs in the Bajun strip, the Germans stirred Fumo Bakari, Sultan of Witu, into occupying the Belesoni district and claiming the islands of Pate and Mande. The Sultan of Zanzibar in response, pressed by the IBEAC, sent an armed force against the intruders and issued an ultimatum for their withdrawal. Before the ultimatum expired (31 December 1889) a German man-of-war withdrew the occupying forces. German action was soon explained. On 24 January 1890, HMG informed the IBEAC that the question of Mande, Pate, Witu and the Belesoni district were all part of a larger settlement which was being negotiated between Germany and Britain; and Salisbury advised 'great prudence on anything that might give them (the Germans) umbrage'. On 21 February 1890 the IBEAC was instructed to 'down' its flag on Mande and Pate.

Ratification of the proposed transfer of the IBEAC concession of the Sultan's northern ports to the Italians was delayed by the unexpected death of Sultan Khalifa on 13 February 1890. The Italians took advantage of this delay to seek a modification of the terms of the concession – to extend its duration to 50 years instead of five years, and bring the boundary of the Italian sphere, as agreed under the Mackinnon/Catalani agreement, into line with that of Treaty of Ucciali which gave Italy a much more generous southern boundary, and included Kaffa. They thus proposed a vague wording in the concession whereby the boundary would follow the Juba River to the point 'Where it penetrates into the country belonging to the Ethiopian Empire', leaving the definition of that country undetermined. This the British company would not accept, nor the Italian interpretation of 'joint administration' of the port of Kismayu and surrounding territory, and the sharing of 'navigation rights' on the Juba River − an interpretation which would bring a collision with the Somali at a time when the British were already facing difficulties in reconciling the Somali in the neighbourhood of Kismayu to Italian rule. Even before these differences could be resolved, the Italian government sought to announce to the great powers that the concession had been transferred to Italy. This the IBEAC would not have.

The Company was affrighted by the recent declaration of a German protectorate over the Bajun coast and a rumour, one of many afloat at the time, that HMG was contemplating surrender of the coast north of Kipini to the Germans, in exchange for an extension of the British coastline south to Pangani, including territory around the latter place. This would mean sandwiching the Company in between the Germans. In the face of this threat, the Company obtained a new concession from the Sultan on 4 March 1890, whereby the concession of 31 August 1889 was extended for a period of 50 years, instead of five, and the rent payable for the Benadir ports was raised to 90,000 dollars, plus 50 per cent of any additional net revenue. Italy was rightly annoyed when the IBEAC demanded 'a formal deed of indemnity' against these new liabilities. The question of 'joint occupation of Kismayu and rights of navigation on the Juba' also continued to be a cause of dissension.

The defects in the Mackinnon/Catalani agreement were increasingly revealed. The IBEAC had more than it could manage at Witu without taking on the administration of the vast tract assigned to it under the Mackinnon/Catalani arrangement. The Company could not even police the Juba − although Mackenzie had claimed that river to be next in importance to the proposed railway to Lake Victoria, as an artery into the interior. On 5 March 1890, in a long memorandum to the Company, the Foreign Office suggested that it should curtail its ambitions, and that Italy should relinquish her claims to Kismayu and territory between that port and the mouth of the Juba, in return for a more southerly boundary for her sphere of influence which would give her territories she had long coveted, including Shoa and Kaffa.

The Company was in a weak position, and arguments against relinquishing the Mackinnon/Catalani arrangements were hastily dropped when a few days after the receipt of the Foreign Office memorandum, news was received that a force of upwards of 7000 Abyssinians was moving southwards towards Arussi in the Galla country. The Company quickly began to negotiate for a transfer of its 50-year lease of the Benadir ports to Italy except for Kismayu and territory immediately south of the Juba mouth, and it would agree to an extension of the Italian sphere southwards to 5°N latitude. The IBEAC would be left in control of Kismayu, that coign of vantage, and a hinterland taking in much of the Galla country. But even this truncated empire was too much for the Company and it was soon negotiating with the Italians for help in policing the upper Juba.

These dealings of the IBEAC came at a time when negotiations were under way between Percy Anderson and Dr Krauel in London. Before the Company could complete any further negotiations with Italy, the Anglo-German Agreement of July 1890 intervened and nullified any further arrangements that the IBEAC might make with Italy. The southern boundary of the Italian sphere of influence, as a result of the Anglo-German Agreement of 1 July and Anglo-Italian Agreements of 24 March and 15 April 1891, was defined as the Juba River as far west as its intersection with the 6° parallel of north latitude, and along that parallel to the 35th meridian of east longitude, and thence along that meridian to the Blue Nile, whence it ran in a north-easterly direction to the Red Sea at Kassar, British and French possessions in Somaliland being excluded. This delimitation left the Italian sphere of influence removed from the Nile by some hundred miles to the east, and insulated the Sudan from Italian encroachment. It tacitly admitted British claim to paramountcy in the Nile Valley, despite the assertion of Crispin, the Italian minister, that England had lost all prior claim there when she abandoned the Sudan.

With the delimitation arrangements completed and their protectorate over the Horn secured, the Italians now had the Sultan's Benadir possessions in their pocket. The Mackinnon/Catalani agreement and negotiations with the IBEAC for transfer of the Benadir lease, were now irrelevant. Direct negotiations between the Italians and Sultan were in order. On 11 August 1892, after considerable pressure from Portal, acting consul-general at Zanzibar, the Sultan agreed to lease the Benadir to Italy for 25 years at a rental of 160,000 rupees annually, and a bonus payment of 40,000 rupees to the Sultan when the concession was taken up. Once the lease was in hand the Italian government turned it over to the Filonardi Company for a three-year period, commencing in July 1893. The latter's efforts to administer were as ill-starred as those of the IBEAC: it was unable to cope with the financial demands made on it, the disasters that befell Italian expeditions into the interior and constant native uprisings, and above all – overshadowing everything – there was the approaching disaster of Adowa.

With what slim apparatus the Italians attempted to administer the vast territory they had taken over! A few officials at the four isolated ports of the Benadir, and two little fortresses at Gobwen and Lugh on the Juba River, each garrisoned by a handful of soldiery. Trade revenue was practically non-existent despite timorous attempts to ascend the Juba – usually on the British, the safer side. A few stray caravans were dragooned into paying custom dues. A catena of disasters summed up Italian exploratory attempts in the interior. Prince Raspoli's expedition of 1892 was left stranded; its Somali porters fled, taking with them the guns and property of the expedition. Then followed the massacre of an Italian expedition to relieve Lugh; and, worst of all, the wiping out of the large expedition under Captain Bottego in March 1896, when he attempted to explore the Lake Rudolf region. To these disasters was added the touting about the country of the looted goods of the ill-fated caravan. An expedition in 1896 led by Antonio Cecchi, to explore the Shibeli River area, was ambushed (betrayed, it was claimed, by a former Arab employee of the Filonardi Company), and Cecchi and his companions were killed in 1897. This was followed by an ineffectual attempt to avenge it.

The weakness of the Italians in the face of these reverses can only be explained by the approaching collapse of the Filonardi Company and the shock of the defeat at Adowa in March 1896. The Italians were also hampered by the fact that punitive expeditions against the Somali were exceedingly difficult during the months of December to March when the full fury of the north-east monsoon broke on the Somali coast, making it almost impossible to land forces and war equipment there. The Somali, however, with their intimate knowledge of the coast and lighter dhows, made the most of the opportunity to bring in arms and ammunition, despite bombardment of coastal villages by the Italian warship *Governoto*.

When the Filonardi Company's concession expired in July 1896, the

Italian government moved in. Despite an offensive launched by M. Perducchi, Italian Resident at Gobwen, and the efforts of Commander Giorgio Sorrentino, sporadic massacre of Italians continued. The Italians, like the Germans, were almost brought to the point of abandoning their territory. It was only the cheering news that harbour rights at Kismayu and the moral support of the British were forthcoming, which restored their morale. Hardinge saw the Italians as a necessary buffer against the Somalis, and in seeking permission from his home government to grant them port facilities at Kismayu, stated that he was not

> desirous of acquiring the Benadir for our Protectorate, more especially in view of the complications with Abyssinia which the extension of our administration over the 'Hinterland' might entail. I would far rather see the Italians consolidate their position there, and work in harmony with us in all East African questions, in such a way as to make them feel that they derived a substantial advantage from the cordial understanding existing between us, and lead them to attach value to its maintenance.[32]

Coincident with the acquiring of harbour rights at Kismayu, a group of Milan financiers formed themselves into the Benadir Company, to take over the administration and development of the Benadir coast, with a handsome subsidy from the Italian government, and power to levy customs and with 'free and gratuitous use of the land', in return for a quit rent to the Sultan of Zanzibar of 16,000 rupees annually. The Benadir Company soon foundered on the same shoals as other African trading companies: namely, overreaching defence commitments, inadequate revenue, and constant sniping from critics at home. It relinquished its concession in January 1905, and in the same year the Italian government purchased the Benadir outright from the Sultan for £144,000. Meanwhile the rounding out of the boundaries of Italian Somaliland continued. A convention with the Negus Menelik of Ethiopia in May 1908 demarcated its hinterland, and a treaty with Britain in June 1925 brought the splendid acquisition of the Jubaland Province of what was now the British Colony of Kenya, a reward for Italy having been the ally of Britain in the First World War. This gave Italy permanent possession of Kismayu and its port facilities.

The IBEAC for its part, following the curtailment of its ambitions and designs on the Somali coast north of the Juba, was only left in control of that river and Kismayu. Increasingly its attention was being directed to the African interior, to Uganda and the problem of its own impending liquidation. In retrospect, the Mackinnon/Catalani agreement and the complicated negotiations with the Sultan for the transfer of the Benadir to the Italians had been, in the words of Anderson,

> a bungle, hardly worth fighting for, and it seems ridiculous that the Company which is frightened out of its wits at Witu should talk of ruling the Gallas, more or less tributary to Menelik. And I believe that our sphere is better if confined to good ports on the coast and good communications with the lakes, and Upper Nile than if we meddle with the Galla on the Abyssinian frontier.[33]

These forays and failures of the IBEAC at the coast were far over-shadowed by its grand designs in the interior which revolved around the figure of Emin Pasha, isolated in Equatoria.

5· The Relief of Emin Pasha and the Race for Uganda

The background to the Emin Pasha rescue mission is well known. The resignation of General Gordon from the Khedive's service in 1879, followed by the eruption two years later of the fanatical religious movement of the Mahdi, raised the question whether the extension of British rule over Egypt in 1882, with the Khedive's government subordinate to that in London, also placed on Britain responsibility for recovery of the Sudan. Prime Minister Gladstone believed that it did not, and in 1884 he was determined to abandon the Sudan: he 'would no longer suffer the Egyptian Government to interfere' in its affairs. This decision was coincident with the siege of Khartoum by the Mahdi's forces, with Gordon (now returned to the Sudan) holding out there. Gordon himself seems by now to have come to the view that it was an insuperable task to retain the Sudan, excepting the farthermost provinces to the south – the Bahr el Ghazal and Equatoria – and was in negotiation with Leopold of the Congo to take them over, with him (Gordon) as administrator. But then fate intervened! With the death of Gordon at Khartoum in January 1885 all was rack and ruin in the Sudan. Only Emin Pasha was left, holding out, as Governor of Equatoria, the last remnant of Gordon's old empire until he too was 'rescued' by Stanley in 1889.

In Egypt the loss of the Sudan was acutely felt, not only because of the military defeats and loss of empire, but because it meant loss of control of the Nile. The hydrography of the Nile was coincident with Egypt's prosperity, a fact clearly grasped by the ancients. Any threat to alter the ebb and flow of its waters was a cause of uneasy apprehension in Egypt. In Sir Samuel Baker's words – 'If I were myself the enemy of Egypt I know the place where I should commence the fatal work upon the River Atbara.' The summers of the late 1880s were seasons of severe water shortage, as though Nature itself had conjoined to make the most of Egypt's troubles, and now the Nileometer readings at Khartoum were no longer available to provide advance warning of the time and capricious nature of the Nile flood. The answer lay in the construction of barrages near the Cataracts and the outlets of Lakes Albert and Victoria. The fear that some power, hostile to Egypt, might control the Upper Nile and its sources, in 1892 impelled Baker, Sir Colin Scott-Moncrief (chief of irrigation works in Egypt), Riza Pasha (Egyptian statesman) and Lord Milner into serious deliberations as to what the loss of these would mean for Egypt's continuation as a nation. Yet England was not yet ready to enter into a reconquest of the Sudan: the destruction of Hick's army in 1888/89 had knocked the heart out of English belligerency. For the time being there was resignation to the Mahdist control of the Sudan, but this did not mean there was no British concern lest other powers move in and occupy it.

Baker and Lugard warned of the danger of Britain abandoning the Sudan as other powers were already casting covetous eyes on it. For Lord Salisbury the watch on the Upper Nile became one of the keynotes of British policy, an *idée fixe*, until the Fashoda settlement with France in 1898. The Upper Nile could be threatened from various directions, the most obvious being that from the Red Sea – a distance of only a few hundred miles – and the threat might come from the Italians. Thus the British encouraged the latter to establish themselves at Massawa – with the threefold purpose of diverting the Italians away from the Nile; also the Abyssinians, who were alarmed by the Italian threat to their main outlet on the Red Sea; the French, busily securing their base at Jibuti, who were hurried into delimitation arrangements with Britain by an agreement of February 1888. More important was the Treaty of Ucciali (May 1889), whereby the Italians claimed protectorate rights over Abyssinia and all territory (including Kassala, half-way between Massawa and Khartoum) as far as the Nile. Italy argued that England had forfeited any prior claim she might have had to the Nile Valley when Gladstone abandoned the Sudan. Under the Treaty of Ucciali Italy could claim protectorate rights westwards to the Upper Nile, and this posed a real threat to British pretensions there. Menelik's denunciation of the Ucciali Treaty, however, was the Achilles' heel of Italy's claims, and ultimately led to her downfall in Abyssinia. Before this took place Italy, reading aright where the greater danger lay, curtailed her claims to the Upper Nile by two Anglo-Italian Agreements of 24 March and 15 April 1891, whereby the Italian sphere of influence was defined as east of a line drawn from the mouth of the Juba river, to the point of intersection of the 6th parallel of north latitude and the 35th meridian east longitude, and northwards along that meridian to its point of intersection with the Blue Nile, and thence north-east in a broken line to Ras Kasar on the Red Sea coast. Thus was Italy cordoned off from the Nile, as was Germany by the Anglo-German Agreements of 1886, 1887 and 1890. Behind these delimitation arrangements was the question of the rescue of Emin Pasha: the Egyptian government would have him out of Equatoria, for his presence there implied Egyptian responsibility for him.

The relief of Emin Pasha (Edward Schnitzler), 'the inoffensive and mild Emin', a lone figure making a last stand, isolated in the heart of the continent, the last remnant of Gordon's old empire, and undergoing goodness knows what strains and privations, caught the imagination and interest of Victorian England. As Stanley remarked 'There is at the present time a huge craving after anything and everything relating to Central Africa.' Emin's rescue would be partial reparation for the failure to support Gordon in his last stand at Khartoum but no one ascertained whether Emin wanted to be 'rescued'. Relief, yes! But not 'rescue' or 'evacuation'! In a letter of 14 November 1884, to Mackay, missionary in Uganda, Emin stated that the Sudan had become a theatre of insurrection and that for 19 months he had been without news from Khartoum. In the same year, in a letter to another CMS missionary, R.W. Felkin, he indicated that he did not want to leave Equatoria but needed supplies, especially ammunition to 'bring about a better understanding with the King of Uganda, and open up a safe route to the coast'.

Within a few months of Gordon's death, plans to rescue Emin emanated at a meeting in London at the Mansion House, on 22 July 1885, of prominent humanitarians, among them Cardinal Manning and Baroness Burdett-Coutts. Possible leaders of a relief expedition were discussed; the names of Joseph Thomson and George Schweinfurth were mentioned, but neither were available: the former was in Nigeria, and the latter in ill-health.

The question of Emin's relief became urgent in 1886 when Dr Junker, who had left Wadelai in January of that year, brought down fresh news to the coast of Emin's plight: he was cut off from the outside world, awaiting a merciful mission to relieve him. On 6 July 1886 he had written to Mackay, 'I am ready to stay and to hold these countries as long as I can until help comes.' Deeper forces were already at work to utilize Emin's plight to serve their own ends. In September 1886, Holmwood, British vice-consul at Zanzibar, and Mackay of Uganda, pointed out that the relief of Emin might be combined with a take-over of Uganda and the thwarting of German designs on the interior. Felkin, in England in 1886, lobbied the Scottish and Royal Geographical Societies, the African Lakes Company (making Glasgow for the time the fulcrum of Central African affairs) and the Foreign Office on Emin's behalf, and made a plea to sustain him in Equatoria until the British could extend their influence there. Emin's would be a holding operation. He had written again to Felkin in July 1886, expressing his hope that England would occupy Equatoria. Salisbury stood out against a large-scale expedition which might result in another fiasco à la Gordon; and, as he pointed out, was not Emin a German, and therefore 'Germany's business'? Salisbury's caution was disregarded, and plans went ahead to relieve Emin. They ranged from an expedition from Egypt southwards (for which Schweinfurth was again considered as a leader) to that of a group of Quakers for an expedition from the west by way of the Ubanghi and Wele Rivers, and a suggestion by the Directorate of British Military Intelligence that 'the people of Uganda might go to Emin's assistance on the promise of a reward'. By October 1886 plans were more clearly formulated: Mackinnon and Hutton had raised with Stanley the possibility of a relief expedition to Emin, and 'there is only one route which is safely open for the money, and that is the Congo'.

By November 1886 Mackinnon informed the Foreign Office that a plan had been matured for an Emin Pasha Relief Expedition to be led by Henry M. Stanley. Its estimated cost was £20,000 (the final figure was nearer £30,000). The list of contributors was impressive (it is set out in Stanley, *In Darkest Africa*, i, 35), and included a small clutch of the IBEAC directors. Mackinnon's contribution was £3,000, but along with his 'Clan' (Stanley's term), £11,500 was raised. Lesser contributions were as little as £250. The largest, £14,000, was that of the Egyptian government – acquitting itself of further responsibility for Emin, and also hoping to recoup something from the recovery of Emin's ivory, reputedly 75 tons, worth between £60,000 and £100,000.

Stanley would march under the Egyptian flag – 'whose red colour and white crescent and star are everywhere conspicious'. The British Treasury would provide the coal for the steamer to carry the expedition from Zanzibar to the mouth of the Congo. Leopold, whose hope of securing the southern Sudan ended with Gordon's death in January 1885, was linked with the expedition. He had long been in close communication with Mackinnon (the latter had subscribed to Leopold's *Comité d'Études*) and saw in the rescue of Emin new possibilities for himself. Thus he loaned Stanley's services as leader on condition that the Congo route be used – and thereby could bring his own Congo empire to the threshold of the Nile (that Stanley was paid agent of Leopold as well as leader of the East African Association's Relief Expedition was not notified to the British government until later). The original idea seems to have been that Emin would willingly co-operate in an expedition to relieve him, and would transfer his province to the IBEAC. Once reinforced, his troops and experience could be used to establish a great inland trading empire, the terminus for routes to be opened up from the Congo State on the one hand, and the East African coast on the other. After much debate the Relief Committee yielded to Leopold's insistence that the expedition go through the Congo and return by the East African coast. Apart from serving the interests of the Congo State, there were other arguments for using the Congo route. Stanley was familiar with it; there were supplies of food and water available along it; and it provided ease of transport over long stretches (Stanley traversed 1400 miles in one month). Also it would avoid trouble with tribes such as the Maasai (Thomson warned against any large-scale expedition attempting to breach their country). The Congo route, according to Stanley, would give 'Greater immunity from the desertion of the Zanzibaris who were fickle in the neighbourhood of Arab settlements'. It would disarm German suspicions and not endanger the missionaries in Uganda (already apprehensive of an approach from the east, the murder of Bishop Hannington being still fresh in their minds). When concrete plans were finally drawn up in the autumn of 1888 the wisdom of using the Congo route seemed indisputable.

As the magnitude of the task facing the relief mission began to bear in on them, the ardour of some of its supporters began to wane, but a small inner group led by Mr W. Burdett-Coutts and Baroness Burdett-Coutts sustained the drive and enthusiasm. The commercially minded needed no such spur – prospect of financial gain was sufficient lure.

Stanley arrived at Zanzibar on 22 February 1887 and set about collecting his porters – some 700 in all – Swahili, Somali and Sudanese, and he bundled and packed his supplies. Arrangements were made with Tippu Tib, doyen of caravan leaders, to supply extra carriers en route so that Stanley would have sufficient porters to cover losses and carry his ammunition to Lake Victoria. Tippu was to be well paid for these services and was made 'Governor' of Stanley Falls, on behalf of the Congo State, but enjoined to desist from slave-raiding. The wonder is why Stanley had any truck with Tippu, for the latter had broken a contract with him and deserted him in 1876. He had also played the Austrian traveller, Dr Oscar Lenz, false, when Lenz sought to reach Equatoria by the Congo River in the summer of 1885. Tippu, already aware of Emin's plight, and learning from Lenz of Emin's hoard of ivory, seems to have entertained the idea of leading an expedition of his own to Wadelai. Stanley could have had no illusions about the man with whom he was dealing, but Tippu Tib was 'Chief of the Congo Arabs'.

While at Zanzibar Stanley, as we have seen, attended to the important matter of persuading the Sultan to give Mackinnon a lease of his mainland dominations, and he seems to have established good rapport with the Sultan who gave him a fine sword ('with Shirazi blade ... richly mounted with gold'), a magnificent diamond ring ('which makes Tippu's eyes water') and the 'golden belt of His Highness with clasp bearing his name' – a useful present to influence the Arabs in the interior.

These things done, in the space of three short days, Stanley, with Tippu Tib, porters and a vast arsenal of firearms etc, sailed for the Congo mouth by way of the Cape. By 30 May 1887, the expedition was some one thousand miles up the Congo, at Bangala, and here it divided: Tippu Tib to Stanley Falls, and Stanley up the Aruwimi to Yambuya, '330 geographical miles from Lake Albert', where he arrived on 15 June. Making his base camp here, he left Yambuya on 28 June 1887, and with a party of 388 persons, including four Europeans, he headed into the endless tract of forest and jungle – 'region of horrors' – from which he emerged 160 days later, having lost nearly half his men and with his own hair turned white. The desertions of the 'cowardly Zanzibaris' had been frequent and had cost him a box of ammunition 'per diem', until he resorted to lashing the cases together. By 13 December 1887 he was gazing out over the waters of Albert Nyanza, and it was only here that he caught up with 'happenings' pertinent to his mission. He learned that the Italian, Casati, was at the court of Kabarega, ruler of Bunyoro, not too far away, and that letters he was carrying for Stanley had been lost; people on the lakeshore still had remembrance of Mason's visit in a 'smoke boat' many years before. The weeks and the months then go by. It is not until 29 April 1888 that the object of the rescue expedition, its *raison d'être*, makes his appearance. Emin Pasha, in the steamer *Khedive*, veteran of twenty years' service on the Nile, comes sailing blithely across the lake. It is a slight figure which greets Stanley, and with a face 'like a Professor of Jurisprudence'. From the time of their meeting onwards, the focus of attention switched to Emin. It was 'the Pasha this, and the

Pasha that', and this was not to Stanley's liking.

In early 1888 the 190 Rifles of the First Battalion of the Egyptian forces, which had gone over to the Mahdi, had set out for Wadelai where Emin resided, to capture him in view of a rumour current that an expedition was advancing from the south and west to relieve him; and this was associated in their minds with Emin's intended flight. They were unwilling to accept any other orientation of authority other than from the north: 'We know of only one road, and that leads down the Nile by Khartoum'. Hearing of his intended capture, Emin escaped from Wadelai to Msua station on Lake Albert.

Emin Pasha was neither excited nor enthralled at the prospect of 'rescue' by Stanley. He had neither invited nor welcomed it, and his subsequent relations with the latter were never more than passable. Emin had lived much on his own in his vast Equatorial Province over which he was virtually king. The nature of his rule only came to light in the twentieth century, although details are still obscure. When Baker visited Gondokoro in 1863 it was the centre of a populous region with vast herds of cattle. By the end of the century the Bari, Latuko and Madi – once powerful and warlike – had been almost wiped out, the result of successive regimes, Egyptian, Emin's and the Dervish. During Emin's administration of Equatoria Bari slaves were taken down the Nile in boat-loads, and Bari chiefs who protested were ordered to be brought in dead or alive. Punitive expeditions under native officers worked their will on the unfortunate people, while Emin remained immersed in his academic pursuits – poring over his natural history collections: his love of science, according to Stanley, 'bordered on fanaticism'. Emin would have boiled down the skulls of slain Wanyoro, and the relief expedition would have become 'a travelling museum and cemetery' if Stanley had not protested. There was also a streak of hard calculation in Emin. He imposed a grain tax on the countryside surrounding his headquarters, and recaltricant tax-payers were gathered in, clothed, drilled and drafted into the 12 companies which Emin had set up to discipline the new Province of the Nile. The new recruits were quickly absorbed in Emin's soldiery. They adopted the manner and customs of their captors; acquired a knowledge of Arabic; made themselves comfortable in their new quarters; and, like the Sudanese, gathered round them a following of females: it was the way of the East, the extended family of the 'Third World'. Thus Emin's remark: 'They have led such a free and happy life here, that they would demur at leaving a country where they enjoy luxuries such as they cannot hope for in Egypt ... each soldier has his harem: *de gustibus...!*

Emin's equatorial empire was of a scope and nature little understood by the outside world. He had some eight stations in the Nile district, apart from half a dozen in Latuka, Acholi, Congo and districts further west. Mount Ajaru – east of Obbo – was a sanatorium and place of refreshment for officers wearied by military stress and 'uxoric excesses'. The challenge of the Dervishes spelt the ruin of the Equatorial Province. The natives, much wronged and hurt during Emin's regime, rose up and ousted the Sudanese garrisons. In the face of this *'revolvé d'affaires'*, Emin retired to the south of Wadelai.

Within the year the Dervishes had overrun Emin's former province. With the connivance of Egyptian officers of the old regime they wiped out entire villages, killing men and enslaving women and children. They established posts throughout the country. The remains of their stone zeribas (camps) were still evident in the early twentieth century. The Bari, in the face of this new threat, fled to the hills and mountains to the east and south-west into the Congo. Their cattle were captured, and by 1902 few Bari chiefs could boast of one hundred head. An epidemic of smallpox finished off the tale of woe. It was only by the twentieth century that the Bari began to recover. Of these facts the outside world knew little. The drama of Gordon at Khartoum and Stanley's rescue of Emin dominated interest in that part of Africa.

At Cairo, Stanley had received from the Egyptian government letters making clear that Emin was to come out with his men, and if he insisted on remaining he did so at his own risk. Emin's rejoinder to this was that he would come out if his people were willing, otherwise not. Thereupon Stanley, according to his version, put forth three propositions. First that Emin, continuing to be the obedient soldier he had always been, should return to Egypt, and he and his soldiers would be paid. The second proposition was from His Majesty Leopold, King of the Belgians, which authorized Stanley to inform Emin that in order to prevent the Equatorial Province from relapsing into barbarism and to hold it for the Congo State, Leopold would allow him £1500 sterling as governor, with the grade of general, provided that Emin could secure revenue from the province in the sum of £10,000 to £12,000 to be raised from ivory. Emin would keep open communications between the Nile and Congo and maintain law and order in the province. Stanley states that this offer was conditional on Emin's making the province pay, but there is nothing in Emin's diary to bear this out. In any case the proposition did not appeal to Emin. He had previously expressed doubts as to whether the Congo

State had a future – it was likely to fall into the hands of the French after Leopold's death, and he saw little hope of the Belgians administering this remote region when they were already overstretched in the Congo Free State. Stanley did not unduly press Leopold's offer on him. For he had in abeyance a third and more important offer to make (Stanley claims that he was free to carry offers from any power, 'as I was free to carry that from Belgium').

This third offer was that Emin, if convinced that his soldiers would not follow him back to Egypt, should gather as many as would follow him (estimated at 3000–5000), and accompany Stanley southward and around the southern end of Lake Victoria to Kavirondo on its eastern side, where Emin would make his headquarters after establishing several stations *en route*, and wait for the Company's forces to reach him from the coast. Stanley would establish him in the name of the East African Association (by now the IBEAC), and would aid him to construct a fortress, leave him his boats and other accessories. Stanley would then go down to Mombasa to bring up two portable steamers for use on Lake Victoria. Emin, meanwhile, would conquer Uganda and Unyoro and with these territories would form a new province extending northwards to his old district in the southern Sudan. Emin would be an entirely independent governor of this new province, in the service of the IBEAC, with a salary to be agreed on. This offer was in line with previous correspondence between Emin and Felkin, in which the latter had consistently urged Emin to stay in his province and act as representative of the newly chartered Company and conclude an agreement with it by which the Equatorial Province would be handed over by Emin, who would serve the Company as administrator.[1]

In the face of these offers, 'Emin hesitated,' says Stanley. Emin did, however, incline favourably to the idea of entering the service of the British Company, as their chief administrator over a vast province taking in Buganda, Bunyoro and Equatoria. He saw a natural unity in bringing these territories together in one inland empire – it would be realization of Ismail's old dream of an 'Equatoria' extending to Lake Victoria. But he could not make up his mind at once. To hasten his decision, Stanley showed him a letter Emin had written to Sir John Kirk in July 1886, offering to surrender the Equatorial Province to England or any other interested party.

'Ah,' said the Pasha, 'they should never have published this letter. It was private. What will the Egyptian Government think of my conduct in venturing to treat, of such matters?"[2]

This stirred Emin into returning to Wadelai to consult his men in the matter. He was much perturbed over the revealing of his letter to Kirk and the effect it would have on his master, the Khedive. It was lese-majesty and Stanley would make the most of it. It has also been suggested that Emin was waiting for the price of his treason, selling the Equatorial Province to the highest bidder; in this case the British Company, and their offer, had not come up to his expectations. There was also his hoard of ivory, the whereabouts of which he had not yet revealed to Stanley.

Stanley himself could not press on with the negotiations. His rearguard having failed to come up, he had to leave his camp, Fort Bodo near Lake Albert, on 16 June 1888, and retrace the terrible march to Yambuya, where he arrived in August 1888. Here he learned that Tippu had broken faith, and that of the Europeans only one, William Bonny, was alive. Major Bartlett had been murdered, and Jameson, who had gone to Stanley Falls to seek out Tippu, had died of fever. There was little left for Stanley to do but collect his forces and traverse again, for the third time, the march to Lake Albert. He rejoined Emin there in February 1889. By this time, out of the 647 men with whom he had entered the Congo, only 246 remained. By now he was completely disenchanted with the Congo route; it would be nigh impossible to keep the Pasha supplied from this direction.

During Stanley's absence Emin was sorely weakened by an insurrection of his troops and was temporarily a prisoner of his own officers. His authority over them had noticeably lessened since Stanley's arrival. The troops had become mutinous at the thought of withdrawal – a rumour spread that they would be sold into slavery at Zanzibar; and during the time that Emin and Mounteney Jephson were held as prisoners at Dufile, a letter had come from the Mahdi's general offering Emin a free pardon and stating that Lipton Bey and Slatin Pasha, European officers, had come over to the Mahdi's cause, and that the Khalifa (the Mahdi's successor) wished to take Emin out of the 'land of the infidels to join your brethren the Moslems'. In a long flowery letter, especially meant to appeal to the Pasha – a converted Muslim – and with reference to a letter of Emin's to the Mahdi, intimating his submission, there was only compassion for this prodigal son. Emin's men, too, were unable to resist the lure of the Mahdi's bird call. His followers showed little enthusiasm for a return to Egypt; out of 10,000 people only a handful were willing to do so.

Thus, when Emin and Stanley met again, Emin was in a sorely weakened state; gone was the old self-sufficiency which had stood him so well in his outpost in Equatoria. He was no entirely dependent on Stanley; but Stanley's opinion of Emin had undergone a radical change, there was now much damning with faint praise in his references to the Pasha. Emin, according to Stanley, was entirely unsuited for the role of chief administrator of a projected inland empire of the British Company. Emin lacked administrative gifts, was too unworldly and introspective – wrapped up in 'African Studies'. He lacked practical sense. There was tension between Emin and Stanley. They were incompatible in temperament and interests, the go-getter versus the reflective thinker! In Stanley's words 'Our natures were diametrically opposed'. Stanley already seems to have suspected Emin's pro-German sympathies and was reluctant to leave him in Equatoria, and not without good reason. A German map (from Stieler's *Handatlas*) titled 'Emin Pascha und Stanley in Zentralafrika 1889' shows the partitioning of Uganda with the Victoria Nile as the boundary between the British and German spheres. Stanley was impatient to be on his way to the coast. No longer did he wish to press the choice of offers on Emin, who was still dithering as to with whom he should cast his lot. Stanley was only concerned now to fulfil his role as reliever of Emin, in the same way as he had relieved Livingstone some 17 years before, but this time with a difference – he would produce his prize at the coast.

Emin's reluctance to return with Stanley was overcome by Stanley threatening him with immediate dismissal from the Egyptian army and with cessation of pay for himself and his men; and always over his head Stanley held the damning letter Emin had written to Kirk. Such power of dismissal, Stanley claimed, had been conferred on him by the Egyptian government; and it would be invoked if necessary. Emin, weakened and isolated, could only submit.

In April 1889, the long trek to the coast with Emin commenced, with the travelling museum in tow. In the course of his return journey Stanley, as has been shown, revealed the existence of the Ruwenzori – 'It simply thrust itself direct in our homeward route.' He was not taken in by the so-called lake, a broad valley – a field of ripe grass which resembled an extension of Lake Albert and which fooled some of his companions, as it had Baker. He also traced the course of the Semliki River, discovered Albert Edward Nyanza and the great south-western Gulf of Lake Victoria, and added much information regarding the

pygmies of the eastern Congo. In a long report of his activities on his
return journey to Euan-Smith at Zanzibar, Stanley makes no mention of
his treaty-making in south-western Uganda, although this, planned in
advance with Salisbury's approval in March 1887, was vital to his
expedition. Stanley's treaty-making in Ankole and elsewhere was of a
dubious nature – based on blood-brotherhood ceremonies and oral
affirmations, later put down in writing. Lugard, who arrived in Uganda
in December 1890, was instructed to confirm these by new treaties,
signed and witnessed.

Stanley, on his return to the coast, was in a hurry, brusque and brief
in his description of the ivory and slave-trade in the interior, the rigours
of the march and the necessity of hard discipline – he executed four
members of his party in imposing it. He ignored appeals from Baganda
Christians who sought his aid in the bitter religious struggle then
reigning in Uganda. He continued his trek southwards to the west of
Lake Victoria. He had no time to interfere in the religious affrays in
Buganda. His Egyptian refugees were a more serious problem:

> a people unqualified by nature and habits for an African journey,
> the scratch of briar, the puncture of a thorn, a 10 mile march is
> quite enough to increase my sick list, ... the Egyptians have sought
> every opportunity to rid themselves of the daily fatigues of the
> march. ... These whining people, who were unable to walk empty-
> handed two and a half or three hours per day, were yellow
> Egyptians; a man with a little black pigment in his skin seldom
> complained, the extreme black and the extreme white never.[3]

So many troubles vexed Stanley in his trek to the coast: the rear column's
trouble at Yambuya and Tippu's failure to live up to his contract was still
in mind; the troubles with the rebels, the Mahdists, and petty strife on
the way to the coast; and as he neared it he found 'German-Arab
troubles at hand, 'I am struck with the idea that this is a very unlucky
year in Africa'. But he had relieved Emin, and he had made an
unexpected discovery – Lake Victoria was 1900 square miles greater in
area than previously accepted – and he had concluded agreements with
various chiefs in the lake region in favour of the IBEAC. Emin's future
role in the service of Leopold, the British Company or for that matter
even the Germans, loomed less and less in importance in Stanley's mind;
he sought only to deliver Emin bodily at the coast. Other interests –
those of the CMS pressed on him by Mackay, at Usambiro on 28 August

1889, that Emin should serve the Company – failed to swerve Stanley from his course. He pushed onwards; and on 10 November 1889 the expedition reached the German station of Mpwapwa, commanded by Lieutenant Rochus Schmidt, where Stanley noted the signs of German industry well displayed in the fine stone breastwork round the camp – a miniature centre of civilization. Here he met the Reverend Mr Price, Baron von Gravenreuth and his forces and two correspondents of the press – one from the *New York Herald*. It was all reminiscent of the relief of Livingstone.

Proceeding coastwards, on 3 December the evening gun at Zanzibar was heard, and the next day Stanley looked over 'the softly undulating Indian Sea, one great azure expanse of purified blue'. That night, at dinner at Bagamoyo with von Wissmann and his own countrymen, Emin ignominiously ended his long journey by falling out of an upstairs verandah: Stanley did not pause more than a day, and pressed on to Zanzibar, where he arrived on 6 December 1889.

More was yet to unfold. Stanley claims that he knew on 4 December 1889 that Emin was going over to the Germans, and that he reminded him that it was English money which had relieved and rescued him. Behind the scenes, forces were shaping up which would obviate both Stanley's work in rescuing Emin and any tergiversations that Emin might be up to as to transferring his services to the Germans. The fiasco of the relief expedition – for so it turned out to be – left Equatoria a no man's land. The Mackinnon clan were profoundly disappointed at its abandonment. Felkin, fearing this would happen, wrote to Emin on 1 November 1889 saying he hoped it was not true he was coming out with Stanley – 'it seems to be the universal opinion that you should stop for another year or so before coming home, so that you might leave the province properly organized'. It was now too late: discussions were under way between Germany and Britain for the final division of East Africa between them. Stanley's relief of Emin, no less than Carl Peters's attempt to forestall the British in Uganda, was to no purpose. Euan-Smith, on leave in London in November 1889, in a long interview with Count Hatzfeldt, German ambassador, learnt from him that Germany hoped to play a direct part in the development of East Africa and that they saw little place for the Sultan of Zanzibar in the scheme of things. The Germans had little love for the Sultan. They saw him as behind the recent insurrection and arms trade in their territory. They were exasperated with his inefficient customs organization at Zanzibar – and averred that it would be much better if Germany operated it: these Arabs and their philosophy of 'Inshallah' were *bêtes noires* to the Germans. From the German viewpoint the ultimate partition of the Sultan's dominions or absorption of the sultanate itself by a foreign power – possibly by Germany (this had already been discussed at Berlin) – seemed a foregone conclusion. As for the British, it was the German view that they resented German intrusion in East Africa, as though they, the British, had a prescriptive right there. Had not revealing letters found on Bushiri, the rebel, prior to his execution, incriminated the British? These letters, from Mackinnon and his agent, Nicol, to Stanley, dated between April and November 1889 and handed over to Salisbury by Hatzfeldt on 7 February 1890, showed that the IBEAC aimed at securing territory between Lakes Victoria and Tanganyika so as to join up with Rhodes's Company from the south, and that the work of securing treaties in this territory was to be left to Stanley, who was expected to complete his task before a new Anglo-German Agreement could be signed. Salisbury saw in these letters, and the IBEAC's premature occupation of the islands of Manda and Pate, the cause of the ill-feeling which had crept into Anglo-German relations over Africa – they also explained Emin's volte-face in going over to the Germans and his return to the interior in April 1890.

The origins of the Anglo-German Agreement of July 1890 lie in this meeting between Hatzfeldt and Euan-Smith in London in November 1889. Hatzfeldt suggested a settlement of Anglo-German differences in East Africa before intense rivalry led to a breach of relations between them. A new and dangerous position had already arisen, with expeditions such as Peters's and Jackson's currently under way in East Africa, and the mutual suspicion that existed between the British and German East African Companies. British response was favourable. In December 1889 Hatzfeldt informed Bismarck that Lord Salisbury desired 'a simultaneous understanding' with Germany on outstanding colonial questions. In late January 1890 Count Herbert Bismarck, German foreign minister, on a private visit to London, discussed the matter further with Lord Salisbury.

Meanwhile, in East Africa both powers tried to place themselves in a favourable position to gain advantageous terms before an Anglo-German Agreement was arrived at. The Germans, now recovered from Bushiri's revolt, were busily active (some 250 of them, more than all other European officials in East Africa) and were seen much about the coastline and at Zanzibar, where they had transferred their headquarters during the height of the troubles with Bushiri. The English, however,

were scarcely apparent in Zanzibar, although three British companies
(the IBEAC, Charlesworth and Company, and Smith, Mackenzie and
Company) were established there. Euan-Smith complained that 'The
Imperial British East Africa Company had not the least interest in
Zanzibar', as its directors had eyes only for the interior where Protestant
missionaries in Uganda were urging it to hasten inland. Mackay had
pressed this on Stanley when he was at Usambiro in August 1889, and
again in a letter from there, dated 1 January 1890, stressed its urgency,
for the Christians in Uganda were fighting for their lives against the
Muslims. Finally, when news reached the coast on 15 February 1890 that
the Muslims had been overthrown, Euan-Smith telegraphed to
Mackinnon to dispatch a caravan to Uganda immediately. It would be a
race with the Germans, who were planning an advance on the interior,
with Emin as the likely leader.

The incidents concerning Emin's return to the coast with Stanley and
the accident which he suffered at Bagamoyo, are well known: Emin
inadvertently stepped outside from an upstairs balcony mistaking it for
a ground-level door and suffered a severe fall and fractured skull. In long
convalescence in the German hospital at Bagamoyo he underwent a
decided change of attitude towards the British and especially towards
Stanley. According to the latter he received 'never message nor note'
from Emin after the accident, and his conduct after entering the German
hospital at Bagamoyo was marked by strange ingratitude and 'sudden
and inexplicable cessation of intercourse with any member of our
Expedition', and Stanley bade him farewell for the last time on 6
December 1889. Emin had apparently fallen into the German pocket.
Stanley claims that he suspected this even before he left for Cairo, and
thus it was that on arriving there on 16 January 1890, and remembering
Emin's fears that if he returned to Egypt he would be unemployed,
Stanley, before settling down to write his long account of the Relief
Mission, set about to help Emin, a last-minute effort to wean him over
from the Germans. 'Within half-an-hour of my arrival in Cairo, I took
the liberty of urging upon the Khedive Emin's employment.' The
Khedive consented, but when an advance credit of £400 towards this
was wired out to Emin, the latter wired back his disappointment – 'Since
you cannot treat me better than that, I send you my resignation.'
According to Stanley, Emin had already agreed to serve Germany 'one
month previous to his offer of service to the British Company'. Thus it
was that Stanley had sent Mackinnon a message on 4 February 1890,
urging that the British Company bring Uganda under its control.

After his recovery Emin had an interview with Euan-Smith in Zanzibar on 14 March 1890. The latter had two days previously received a telegram from Mackinnon suggesting Emin's appointment as Acting Administrator-in-Chief for the British Company. Following his interview with Emin, Euan-Smith deprecated any suggestion that Emin be employed in this capacity: he was 'wholly unfitted for such an appointment, which indeed he would not himself desire'. He was possibly suited to lead a caravan to Uganda and initially establish the Company's rule there, but no more than that. For Emin's part he desired to serve under the British, he was familiar with their aims after service under Gordon, and he was grateful to them for his deliverance. He was surprisingly candid in imparting to Euan-Smith 'in the strictest confidence and with much earnestness' the intelligence that the Germans were secretly planning an expedition to Uganda and that he, Emin, should lead it; and that in Uganda the Germans were expecting to be welcomed by the French missionaries, who cherished a bitter hatred of the English. If the British Company was to secure Uganda they must act without delay.

This information chimed with what Euan-Smith already knew of a proposed German advance into the interior, and it can only be surmised that in imparting it to the British, Emin was still open to the highest bidder, and hoping the British would could come forth with a more attractive offer than the Germans. That same evening Euan-Smith telegraphed Lord Salisbury, warning of the proposed German expedition, and urging the IBEAC to act with vigorous promptitude to bring Uganda under its influence. For if the Germans arrived there first, grim indeed would be the future prospects of the IBEAC in East Africa. Emin could still be used to serve British plans; and to avoid wounding German susceptibilities a pretext for employing him might be found in the recovery of his immense hoard of ivory reputably worth £500,000 in the money of the time. A telegraph to Baring in Egypt, on the same day, requested permission from the Egyptian government to employ Emin 'to recover stores of ivory abandoned'.

It came as no great surprise when on 1 April 1890 Euan-Smith learnt that Emin had turned down the offer of employment in the service of the IBEAC and had taken service under von Wissmann at £1000 a year and, despite the rainy season, was to head a large German expedition into the interior; and that he had proclaimed Equatoria his province and would turn it over to the Germans when he regained his position there; for Euan-Smith had heard from Emin himself, from Hatzfeldt in November

1889, and from von Wissmann in January 1890, that the Germans aspired to bring Emin into their service. He was to leave for Uganda on the 20 April 1890, his porters were to receive extra wages and to march at the greatest speed 'to anticipate the English plans in the direction of Uganda'. Von Wissmann had engaged Charles Stokes, late of the CMS, now caravan leader, and whose influence was expected to turn the Arabs of the interior in favour of German rule. To misrepresent the purpose of Emin's expedition and mislead the British, bogus telegrams purporting to show that Emin was heading for Ujiji were to be circulated in Zanzibar. Finally, when news of the expedition leaked out, the German government claimed its purpose was to succour Carl Peters – hence *The Times* caption, 'The Reliever Relieved' – but *The Times* also saw it as a threat to cut the British off from the interior and the Nile.

According to Euan-Smith, Emin's transfer to German employ arose from his fear of loss of his German citizenship if he did otherwise, but it is doubtful whether such a threat would mean much at the time. As has been said of the average Englishman in the years before the First World War, 'He had no official number or identity card ... He could travel abroad or leave his country for ever without a passport or any sort of official permission'; this could equally apply to the German. As for Emin, he had lived a nomadic existence for many years – he was a Bey in the Egyptian army, an avowed Muslim. Such a threat made in the 1890s could not possibly have the effect it would have in the second half of the twentieth century! More likely Emin's reversal of attitude was the result of bitterness apropos Stanley's depreciative remarks regarding his lack of drive and administrative ability. Stanley continued verbally chastising Emin after arrival at the coast. He claimed that much of the delay at Kavalli's could have been avoided if Emin had assisted in his own relief, and that he had had practically to bribe Emin to leave his inland province; and that Emin was an 'unmanageable fanatic'. Months later, when Ernest Gedge met him at the south of Lake Victoria, Emin was still smarting and resentful – 'only too glad to give vent to his bitterness against the English apropos the remark made about his weakness and lack of administrative power by Stanley'.

Euan-Smith shared Stanley's doubts as to whether Emin would be a successful leader, even of a German expedition. He was merely a figure-head to be produced before the Arabs: 'His oriental mode of conducting affairs is entirely at variance with the stress and eagerness of the German method.' Nor is there clear evidence that the IBEAC considered seriously Euan-Smith's suggestion that Emin should lead their expedition to Uganda. They had already in mind Lieutenant Stairs, lately returned from the Emin Pasha expedition, as a 'natural leader', but had turned to Lugard as their definite choice by March 1890. Lugard had arrived in Mombasa on 8 December 1889 from England, on the same boat as George Mackenzie, an active director of the IBEAC, and Euan-Smith. On the voyage out Mackenzie had sounded him out about taking service with the Company and leading an expedition to Uganda to follow up that of Frederick Jackson. Letters to Lugard on 12 and 22 March 1890, when he was busy on the Sabaki River opening up a road to Machakos, reveal that the directors planned to use him to

> secure supremacy for the Company in Uganda and also from the south of Victoria Nyanza to a point on Tanganyika where the 4° parallel intersects it so as to secure access to, and free communication with Nyanza.[4]

There was need for haste. In early April came news that Peters had arrived in Kavirondo and that Jackson, hovering on its borders, was diffident and indecisive – he had not responded positively to the appeal from King Mwanga and the missionaries in Uganda to come there, but was haggling over terms, claiming that his instructions from the Company did not permit him to enter Uganda. Jackson's dithering caused the Foreign Office to question the Company's intention of winning Uganda. They asked – was not its principal object to secure paramount influence there? Was the Company not aware that native envoys from Uganda were on their way to the coast to ascertain the position of their kingdom as regards the German and British spheres of influence? The sense of urgency was underlined by news of Emin's dash for the interior and Peters's entry into Uganda. The British were about to be hemmed in, and what was the IBEAC doing to prevent this?

Foreign Office prodding stirred the IBEAC into announcing on 22 April 1890 that Lugard was to march to Uganda to obtain a treaty from Mwanga, and the directors were so certain of obtaining it that they had requested the Foreign Office to inform other powers that Uganda was already in the British sphere of influence.

For Lugard, busy outfitting and collecting porters for the long trek to Uganda, it came as a shock to learn that his was but a secondary role, no more than that of advance scout, while a major expedition under Major General Sir Francis de Winton, Administrator-General for the Company, was to have the main task. Lugard's assessment of his own abilities was not inconsiderable; and he had been promised the leadership. Thus in disgust he tendered his resignation and made plans to return to England, but when de Winton taunted him for 'turning back when harnessed for the day of battle', Lugard relented. By July 1890 he was once more back on the Sabaki, awaiting the call to advance on Uganda. On the 27 July the directive came: he was to start at once, follow the route to Machakos and thence to the lake – establishing posts *en route* and making treaties with the Kikuyu and Maasai; at Nakuru he was to stay his advance and await the arrival of de Winton who would then take over command.

By mid-October 1890, Lugard was in Kikuyu country where he obtained a treaty from them, and thence planned to proceed westward in 'as straight a line as possible' to Kavirondo Bay on Lake Victoria, whence it was to be a short and easy step across the lake to Uganda. It was all very straightforward. But on 19 October, while at Kikuyu post, came instructions dated Mombasa, 17 September, which announced an important change of plan. The import of the Anglo-German Agreement of 1 July 1890 was now imparted to him. De Winton would not now go to Uganda. Lugard was to do so, and was to proceed at once and with great dispatch. He was to administer the country on behalf of the IBEAC. His instructions were 'to guarantee peace in Uganda'. Precise details were set out as to the caravan he was to lead there: 215 porters, 75 Sudanese soldiers and up to 15,000 rounds of ammunition. Leaving George Wilson, an IBEAC officer, to complete the fort at Dagoretti – a midway strongpoint between the coast and the lake, Lugard set out immediately.

A whole new disposition had taken place as a result of the Anglo-German Agreement of 1 July 1890, but before adverting to this, it is necessary to recount the happenings of the spring and early summer of 1890. Jackson's ditherings in the interior, Lugard's expedition to Uganda, the political activity of the missionary, A.J. Swann, on Lake Tanganyika and the Company's attempt at a grand coup in the interior had all alerted the Germans to what they saw as a violation of the 1887 'hinterland' understanding. Salisbury's and Malet's denial that there had been such an undertaking to maintain the *status quo* 'in such a large place as Africa', was seen by the Germans as cover for a British take-over of the interior to the south-west of Lake Victoria where Stanley had made treaties – treaties now in the possession of the Foreign Office to whom they had been transferred by the IBEAC. Stanley's busybodying especially stirred German ire. While at Cairo on his way home from the

Emin Pasha Relief Expedition, he had urged the directors of the IBEAC to be 'resolute and prepared to spend £50,000', to employ Tippu Tib, Stokes and two other Europeans, in making a three-pronged advance, 'simultaneously and in absolute secrecy', on the vast interior, 'from the River Zambezi right up to the Nile'. This essay at master strategy received short shrift from Euan-Smith at Zanzibar, but the Germans had already heard of it and also of another master plan by Mackinnon and Leopold.

By April 1890 Stanley had returned to Europe. On his way home from Cairo, he had met Mackinnon at Cannes and had long conferences with Leopold at Brussels. Back in England by May 1890, Stanley, in a series of public addresses, pressed that England should claim all territory between Lake Victoria and the Congo State: thus did Salisbury complain to the German Ambassador over the difficulties he faced by this stirring up of public opinion by the insensate Stanley. Letters from Queen Victoria show that Salisbury, Stanley and Mackinnon dined at Windsor on 6 May 1890. At a time when negotiations were under way between Germany and England, preparatory to a settlement of their claims in East Africa, Mackinnon, fearful lest Rhodes's plan for an all-British Cape-to-Cairo route be frustrated, submitted to Salisbury on 18 May 1890 a draft agreement made with Leopold. Under it the Congo State would secure a corridor on the western side of Lake Albert giving it access to the Upper Nile, and giving the British Company its heart's desire – a corridor from the southern end of Lake Albert to the northern end of Lake Tanganyika with free traffic on the latter lake, and a vital link in the Cape-to-Cairo scheme, an admirable quid pro quo for Leopold's Nile outlet. Individual enterprise could arrange quietly and effectively what chancelleries stumbled over.

Salisbury at the time was thinking of the ultimate reconquest of the Sudan and the Uganda problem; and the Mackinnon/Leopold arrangement did not accord ill with this. From his conversations with the German ambassador on 14 May 1890, Salisbury was convinced that the Germans would not permit a British wedge between them and the Congo State – it would have no international validity and the Germans would object to it. In a letter to Leopold on 21 May 1890 he stated that he saw nothing substantial in the draft agreement to which the Foreign Office could object, but that he would like more detail. Before this was given the so-called Mackinnon agreement was signed by Mackinnon and Leopold on 24 May 1890.

This intelligence was not communicated to Salisbury until 7 June, and in the interval, on 2 June, came news that the notorious Peters had signed a treaty with King Mwanga of Uganda. Salisbury at once dropped the plan to secure a connecting strip between Uganda and Lake Tanganyika, and concentrated on the need to save Uganda: hence his tempting offer of Heligoland to the Germans, and the attention he gave to a railway to Uganda. In a letter to Leopold, of 9 June 1890, he reiterated his non-objection to the Mackinnon agreement in principle, although warning that cession of territory by the Congo State to a private company might be challenged by France under her right of pre-emption to the Congo State. A way out might be found if Leopold, while retaining sovereignty, parted only with occupation rights. This judicious compromise was not, however, to the liking of Mackinnon and Company – imbued as they were with Rhodes's grand concept of an all-red route from the Cape to Cairo: they would brook no limitation on the fuller rights granted by Leopold, nor would he, on his part, relish any limitation on his control over his corridor to the Upper Nile. Both parties insisted on the agreement being fully honoured. The question thus remained deadlocked. Germany and England, however, continued to work out their respective bargaining positions prior to an overall agreement. Salisbury never fully accepted the German interpretation of the 'hinterland' principle that, 'where one power occupies the coast, another power may not, without consent, occupy unclaimed regions in its rear', for this would place English missions and stations of the African Lakes Company on the line of the Stevenson Road between Lakes Nyasa and Tanganyika in an anomalous position, for they lay within the same parallels of latitude as Germany territory to the east of them. Similarly, on the basis of her protectorate over Witu, Germany could claim territory to the west of it. As regards the territory between the immediate north of Lake Tanganyika and Uganda, there were no English settlements here – Stanley's treaties only extended some 20 to 30 miles south of 1°S latitude and the German claim that the 1886 boundary line if extended westwards would evenly divide Lake Victoria between Britain and Germany, had validity. England would not contest it if she could gain the line of the Stevenson Road, the region of the Mfumbiro peaks covered by Stanley's treaties of 1889, and freedom of passage along the line of Lakes Nyasa and Tanganyika.

At the coast Germany would surrender her protectorate over Witu, her claim to Manda and Pate and the 200 miles of coast north of this. As for Zanzibar and Pemba, the Sultan on 14 June, 'Powerless to contend against the decrees of fate', accepted 'with joy and gratitude the proposed protectorate of Great Britain, although leaving him a 'mere pensioner' of Britain. The acquiescence of France was necessary, under the Declaration of 1862, and this was obtained by recognizing her protectorate over Madagascar. As for the Sultan's coastline which the Germans were leasing, and which they sought to acquire, an appropriate indemnity and a little persuasion would ease its transference into their hands. Britain promised her support in this.

The surprise makeweight in all these transactions was the island of Heligoland in the North Sea. Lady Cecil writes of the 'touch of unconscious drama' with which Lord Salisbury played his trump card. On the 13 May 1890, when he and Hatzfeldt were in long and wearying discussion over apparently irreconcilable issues, there was a sudden break in the conversation and 'after some hesitation' Salisbury revealed to Hatzfeldt the 'sum of his wishes' regarding East Africa. Hatzfeldt was taken back at the list presented – especially the request that Germany cede Witu and rights over neighbouring districts and recognize an exclusive British protectorate over Zanzibar. 'Then without further preface or any hint of invitation from the wholly unprepared ambassador, the Prime Minister threw down Heligoland on the table.' This Gibraltar of the North Sea had been annexed by England from Denmark in 1807 and was retained in 1814, probably because of its proximity to Hanover the crown of which was united with that of Britain. Heligoland had little defensive or military value in the eyes of the experts – and according to the Admiralty it was a liability in time of war. It was more important to secure British influence and dominion in eastern Africa than to retain Heligoland. Germany, however, viewed the control of Heligoland with an almost increasing mystical attachment, for it lay in German coastal waters and had taken on added significance with the completion of the Kiel Canal – its attainment was necessary for German pride. Thus here was one of those rare occasions where a gain for one power signified no loss to the other but was a useful makeweight in arriving at a settlement.

The Anglo-German Agreement was signed on 1 July 1890. It freed Britain from the pushing tactics of the Germans in East Africa and left her unchallenged as the protector of the Sultan of Zanzibar – thus gaining enhanced prestige in the Muslim world: the Sultan's status was now comparable to that of an Indian prince under the British Raj. The agreement left the IBEAC in a prime position to expand unhindered into the interior. Uganda – the 'pearl of East Africa', embracing the source of the Nile – now came under British control. The Anglo-German

Agreement, while admitting Germany into the proprietorship of a great portion of Eastern Africa, gave Britain the predominant role in that it was an extension of her power in the western Indian Ocean – and comported well with her Indian empire.

As for Germany, the agreement placed her in sight of her main prize – control of the Sultan's coastline without which the possession of the interior would be valueless. The sacrifice of Witu was well worth this inestimable prize, and good relations had been maintained with Britain. According to Bismarck 'to keep Lord Salisbury is of more importance than all Witu'; already the German Emperor in May 1890 had directed that East Africa should have first claim on German resources for colonial purposes. Germany was prepared to pay £500,000 for the coastline, the Sultan asked £600,000. But British support for the Germans in the bargaining was forthcoming; the price paid by the Germans for their coastline would also determine that paid by the British – for the Sultan's northern coastal strip to which they aspired. The upshot was that the Germans got a bargain – the final price was £200,000.

The lesser issues in the agreement proved the most contentious – the boundary line at the mouth of the Umba River, and possession of Wanga. Much fuss was made about these – perhaps as a screen for gains elsewhere. On British maps the River Umba was shown as the Wanga or Yimba. Its course was capricious – it was either in a state of flood or dried up. Similarly there was confusion as to the course of the Osi River and whether it was the real mouth of the Tana. A large sand-bar blocked the entrance to the latter, and navigation on it was by way of a canal leading from the Osi. Thus much surveying and settling of minor details were necessary before all this was sorted out. By contrast larger issues – assumption of a British protectorate over Zanzibar and Pemba, and surrender of Witu by the Germans, proceeded amicably and smoothly. Anderson, who had been sent to Berlin, played an important part in these negotiations and gained a reasonable frontier for Rhodesia and Nyasaland and the line of the Stevenson Road, but he was unable to move the Germans in regard to British claims to the Mfumbiro region as based on Stanley's treaties. Territory covered by these treaties extended some 20 miles southward of the resulting boundary line with Germany. That Stanley's treaties were questionable was recognized by the British themselves. South-west Uganda was vulnerable until these treaties were ratified by more formal instruments. It was Lugard's task to obtain these: thus his journey there in 1891. As in any great settlement, and as in the 1886 Anglo-German Agreement, some interests suffered in the agreement of 1 July 1890. The rights of English missionaries in the German sphere were again ignored. Bishop Smythies's episcopal journey to Berlin in September 1890 was undertaken to plead the cause of his mission – and it resulted in the transference of some English missions to brother missions in Germany.

British public reaction to the agreement was favourable - it was but another settlement in many such of colonial interests overseas – but in Germany and in German East Africa initial public reaction was that 'German Simple Simon had once more been duped by perfidious Albion'. So incensed were officials in German East Africa over the agreement, that von Wissmann and brother officers were reported to be contemplating resignation and Emin Pasha was to be recalled from the interior to take over from von Wissmann; but these were mere rumours. A longer and maturer view showed German gains to be substantial: the hinterland of German East Africa now extended right up to the borders of the Congo State. The Emperor was pleased and so also was the Reichstag.

The grand reshaping of East Africa by the Anglo-German Agreement of 1 July 1890 opened up new vistas for the IBEAC. Its directors were still dazzled by dreams of an inland empire. There was now, however, a change in its plans for an advance on Uganda, for that territory was now safely within the British sphere and had lost its former strategical importance. There was no need for a major-general to go there. The task of obtaining a treaty from Mwanga could be safely left to Captain Lugard. He was already on his way there. Mackinnon and his co-directors were interested not merely in the occupation of a coastline of customs ports, but in the acquisition of the interior, in establishing trading stations and fortified posts, setting up a regular caravan and trade service, and ultimately connecting the coast with the interior by a railway. All this was contingent on their gaining a pear-shaped empire extending inland from the Indian Ocean and fanning out in the interior to embrace Uganda, the Ruwenzori, the Equatorial Province, and linking up with Lake Tanganyika on the south.

Expeditions had already been launched into the interior. One under J.W. Buchanan was directed to the Kilimanjaro area in 1888; there was a series of thrusts up the Tana by J.R. Piggott, and the siting of a small fort at Hameya on the Tana; a traverse of the region between the Tana and Mombasa was carried out, and a sternwheeler, *Kenia*, placed on the Tana – all by 1890. In 1891, C.W. Hobley, geologist, explored the country between the Tana and Machakos; and W. Gilson and R.J. Macallister, the country between the coast and Mount Kenya. The most important expedition sent into the interior by the IBEAC before the Anglo-German Agreement 1890, was that of Frederick Jackson's, consisting of 700 porters – 'to impress the Masai' – which left the coast in November 1888, and was directed to the Lake Baringo country. Jackson was to establish a station at Machakos, some 250 miles from the coast and on the frontier of Kikuyu country, to obtain treaties covering the region between Lake Baringo and Uganda and to succour Stanley's Emin Pasha Relief Expedition assumed to be returning by this way to the coast. Jackson was then to push on to Wadelai. He was forbidden to enter Uganda owing to the disturbed state of affairs there, and to avoid a repetition of the Hannington incident. German suspicions of any breach of the 'hinterland' agreement of July 1887 would also be allayed by such a diversionary tactic.

The main thrust into the interior was to be carried out by Lugard who was to clear a trade-route along the Sabaki River and protect it by stockaded stations, terminating at Dagoretti in the Kikuyu country, about 40 miles west of Machakos. A fifth caravan under Eric Smith was directed to find a practicable route to Lake Victoria for a railway from the coast.

As a result of these expeditions, Mackinnon informed a meeting of shareholders on 18 May 1892 that

> almost every mile of the country between Mombasa and the Lake
> is now well-known from frequent explorations of the Company's
> caravans.[5]

and as a result the Company had incurred expenses to the amount of £150,000, but 92 treaties had been obtained and approved by the Foreign Office.

Before leaving the subject of the British Emin Pasha Relief Expedition and the events leading up to Lugard's march to Uganda, it is of interest to advert to the early stages of the German Emin Pasha Relief Expedition, led by Carl Peters. Plans for a German Emin Pasha Relief Expedition to be led by von Wissmann had been mooted in Germany in early 1888. When Felkin heard of this projected German expedition, he wrote to Emin in June 1888, informing him of negotiations recently entered into with Mackinnon and the IBEAC, whereby Emin would remain in Equatoria as the employee of the IBEAC, and a copy of an agreement to this effect, along with letters from Sir Francis de Winton outlining details as to the IBEAC plan of action, were enclosed. When Mackinnon and associates had learned more about the proposed German relief expedition in August 1888, further steps were taken. During a pleasant cruise up to and about the island of Skye, in the autumn of 1888, Mackinnon, Leopold, Count d'Outremont, de Winton and George Mackenzie evolved their strategy. A letter was sent to Emin (five copies by different messengers) outlining a plan whereby he was to command a great 'Central African Province', and select his capital thereof; and a caravan route would be opened to it from Mombasa. He was warned of the German expedition which, under the guise of his relief, would seek to obtain treaties to the west of Lake Victoria and utilize his services to hold territory there. German newspapers in September 1888 were already proclaiming 'this expedition as likely to assist in consolidating German colonial enterprise in Africa'. In the face of this threat and in case Stanley could not get through, Mackinnon and associates had in abeyance another Emin Pasha relief expedition by way of Maasailand, which was to be led by Captain Swayne, RE. To head off the Germans in their presumed dash for Wadelai, Mackinnon and his Company also urged early delimitation of the British and German spheres by a line of delimitation to be drawn 'due westward from the southernmost point of Lake Victoria on the parallel of 2° South Latitude till it meets the eastern boundary of the Congo Free State as defined by the Berlin Convention'. Such a line would mean British encroachment on territory to the rear of the German sphere, and Salisbury would have none of it, in view of the 1887 'hinterland' understanding, which, he informed Mackinnon on 13 October 1888, it was assumed the Germans would also honour: they had propounded it! Salisbury was misled.

In February 1889 a German Emin Pasha Relief Expedition led by Carl Peters left Berlin for Zanzibar – making no bones as to its object – to reach Emin before Stanley and to enlist his services for Germany. Peters was refused permission by both the German and British governments to pass through their territory in his attempt to get to the interior. The German government pressed Prince Hohenlohe-Langenburg, President of the German East Africa Company, to withhold support from Peters. But there was much unofficial and semi-official sympathy for his enterprise. Minister of State, Hoffmann, in April 1889, in an address to the German Colonial Company, declared it worthy of government and public support; it was an important humanitarian, commercial and political enterprise, an opportunity to extend German control over a vast area in the heart of Africa.

With one hundred Somalis enlisted at Aden, it was Peters's plan to land at Lamu. But warned of British plans to intercept him, he proceeded to Bagamoyo. Here petty German officials threatened seizure of his ship and cargo and imprisonment of his party if he attempted to land, on grounds of its contravention of arms regulations. Peters seemed trapped. The British Admiral, Fremantle, patrolled the coast – watchful of any attempt to breach it. But, as Euan-Smith shrewdly guessed, Witu was the likely place for a thrust into the interior. Witu was a German protectorate, and on the basis of the 'hinterland' theory, territory behind it as far west as Uganda could be claimed by Germany. Peters eluded the blockade, disembarked at Kwyhu Bay on 15 June 1889, and was next heard of at Witu. On 27 July came news that he was on his way up the Tana River – into the interior.

German forcefulness and enterprise are exemplified to the full in Carl Peters. Here was Stanley, Emin, and Schweinfurth rolled into one: there was calculated ruthlessness, lack of scruple, an eye for the main chance and resourcefulness in the highest degree. Against Peters, and his energy and probing tactics, the Britisher, with his 'good form' and spirit of 'play the game', seemed peculiarly helpless. Only Stanley comes near Peters in character, and in paralleling the latter's motto in dealing with native peoples – 'Oderint dum metuant' – a motto to which Peters gave practical application on his way up the Tana and across the East African plateau. At the IBEAC port at Bokore the local chief was shot, food stores appropriated, treaty papers left by the Company were burned in public, its flag torn down and replaced by the German, and the whole place declared a German station. The Somalis who accompanied Peters on this expedition later retailed details of his methods. In the Kenya highlands where 'for seven days did we travel through this beauteous Kikuyu, whose flora already exhibits the forms of the temperate zone', and whose suitability for European settlement, Peters extolled, he found himself in the country of the Maasai, and was in his element as a trail-blazer who would brook no opposition. There is a mixture of contempt and admiration in his attitude towards the Maasai:

> Like Attila's Huns and other nomadic peoples they have developed in the highest degree a propensity for plunder and a thirst for blood. The continued flesh diet on which they live has physiologically increased their natural savageness ... They recognize only one kind of work, namely, war, and the protection of their herds ... Slaves from other tribes he altogether despises ...

the one thing which would make an impression on these wild sons of the steppe was a bullet from the repeater or the double-barrelled rifle, and then only when employed in emphatic relation to their own bodies.[6]

Stanley asserted that 'to get through the Masai in warlike fashion a man must have a force of at least one thousand Europeans at his back', but Peters, almost single-handed and dauntless with his 'double-barrelled rifle', shot down some 130 Maasai and cut off their heads which he hurled high in the air, and then sequestered their cattle, and burnt down their habitations:

What time the Advent bells were calling to church in Germany, the flames were crackling over the great kraal on all sides.[7]

Thus did Peters deal with the 'scourge of the steppes', and he claimed to have done what the IBEAC had failed to do – make a treaty with the Maasai. Peters left behind him an unenviable reputation for harshness and insensitivity, the more sullied because of the exultant glee with which he detailed his exploits. He left a lethal weapon to be deployed against 'exploitative imperialism' by its attackers in the later twentieth century. At the time the importance of Peters's expedition was that it had sparked off a race to Uganda.

6· Lugard and Uganda and German East Africa

The region to the north and west of Lake Victoria today known as Uganda, a region favoured by a reasonable rainfall, equable climate and able to support a considerable population, first received the impact of British penetration as the result of exploratory and missionary endeavour, rather than political impulse. The reputation of the Baganda as a people superior to their neighbours, with an avidity for religion, stems from the time of Speke's visit there in 1862. The advanced kingdom of Buganda, it would appear, was once part of an ancient polity, the empire of Kitara (meaning the country between the lakes) which embraced all of Uganda, including Bunyoro, Busoga and Bugwere, as well as Buganda, whose first ruler was Kintu, a legendary figure. The tombs of subsequent rulers of the kingdoms into which the empire of Kitara was divided date from the fifteenth century and are widely scattered, for the rulers were blessed with two tombs – one for their jawbone and personal effects, and the other for their bodily remains, the umbilical cord of all persons of high rank being carefully preserved as a relic of ancestry. These tombs, now shrines – large conical huts surrounded by a royal fence, the 'lubiri', with keepers and mnemenators (reciters) – have their place in local pride, and much care is taken of their preservation: they are the charters of the rulers of Uganda.

For the first Europeans arriving in Buganda it was an impressive prospect which greeted them: the broad sweep of road up Rubaga hill to the king's palace; the beautifully kept lanes between lofty fences of 'bisakati' (tiger) grass; and the elegant woven enclosures around the houses and gardens of the upper classes. Emin, who visited there in the 1870s, remarked that

one of the things a traveller notices when he enters Uganda is the cleanness of the people and of their dwellings, as well as the goodness of their roads and the improved cultivation. Their household utensils, jars, baskets, etc., are all beautifully made, and their bark cloth is fine, and made in considerable quantities.[1]

There was a remarkably well-organized system of government and social life from the Kabaka (king) and his ministers at the top, right down to the clans into which the Baganda were divided, each clan with its totem such as the 'waterbuck' clan and the 'grasshopper' clan, and all were taken most seriously. Thus did some Europeans after short residence in Buganda begin to read high notions into this novel world: they began to speak of earls, judges, Star Chamber, Keepers of the Palace and the Admiral of the King's fleet – all akin to a European state. And its people, especially the upper classes with their strain of Hima blood, exhibited an urbane charm which most Europeans found irresistible, and as has been noted, even the young, cocksure Speke succumbed to the allurements of a daughter of one of the Kabaka's sisters.

Under this urbane surface Baganda society was deeply flawed. There was vainglorious posturing, empty pride and conceit, and withal a cruel streak. The daily executions witnessed by Speke and other European visitors were ordered by Mtesa for trivial offences. Chaillé-Long on arrival in the kingdom of Buganda was accorded the signal honour of having 30 victims hauled off for execution to celebrate his visit:

M'Tese, suddenly rose from his seat, a slight but significant contraction of the eye had caused the disappearance of the 'marsalah', who quick to do their master's will, snatched from their turbans the plaited cord, and seizing their unresisting victims to the number of thirty, amid howls and fearful yells, crowned in blood the signal honour of the white man's visit to M'Tese.[2]

Even the great and intelligent Mtesa 'had this strange and bloody instinct common to African Kings' – he was a monster of the type of the famous King of Dahomey, wallowing in absolute power – here was absolute power corrupting absolutely. The Kabaka wielded the power of life and death over his followers, and they in turn made no show of protest, nay even went willingly, while weeping, to their execution. It was an enclosed society, entirely self-contained: nothing resembling an indigenous chart has come to light as existing among the Baganda and they apparently had no idea as to their place in the wider cosmogony of the world, until the coming of the Arabs about the mid-nineteenth century. Their world consisted of their own kingdom and that of the territory of their neighbours on which they preyed.

These neighbours, Busoga to the east, Koki and Ankole to the south-west and the powerful state of Bunyoro to the north-west, paid tribute to the ruler of Buganda, in varying amounts and at various intervals. This payment, however, did not secure them from further exactions and raiding by Baganda hordes. Busoga especially suffered from these raids. Suna, King of Buganda, had so raised the business of raiding into Busoga into a system, that he constructed 'Matumbi', undecked vessels, capable of carrying 40 to 50 men, to enter the creeks and inlets which indented the north-eastern shores of Lake Victoria around which Busoga bordered.

This then was the country to which the directors of the IBEAC sent Captain Frederick Lugard to bring its ruler into treaty relations with the Company. They could hardly have known the grave consequences that would flow from their decision. That all was not well in that remote inland region was apparent from the scraps of news filtering down to the coast. To understand the situation which confronted Lugard on arrival at Mwanga's court, it is necessary to trace the history of missionary enterprise in Uganda prior to this.

Speke, following his visit to Uganda in 1862, had urged missionaries to go there, and then came Stanley's direct appeal in 1875, which brought quick response from the Church Missionary Society. In 1877 three of its members, Lieutenant Shergold Smith, Revd C.T. Wilson and Alexander Mackay, arrived in Uganda, and in February 1879 they were joined by three more members of their society. But they were not to have the field to themselves. Pope Leo XIII, shortly after his election to the papal throne in February 1878, delegated the propagation of the faith in Central Africa to the White Fathers – a missionary order founded by Archbishop (later Cardinal) Lavigerie of Algeria, in 1874. An appeal from the CMS to Lavigerie to stay an advance on Uganda, the CMS being first in the field, came too late: a party of White Fathers was already on its way there. Father Lourdel and Brother Amans arrived in February 1879 and were joined by three more members in June of the same year. Thus the two Christian parties had taken up their respective headquarters on two hills adjacent to Mtesa's capital at Mengo, by 1879.

Christianity quickly took hold in Buganda. We read of Mackay, the 'modern Livingstone', as Stanley termed him, with his skilled carpentry at the turning lathe, interspersed with long hours with readers and at

Bible lessons; and the good Fathers of the Catholic Mission busy with religious instruction, their prayers and supervision of converts. How clever these converts were! Ashe, of the CMS mission, marvelled at the skill with which they supported the doctrine of their religion, that of transubstantiation, for example, being explained by the metaphor of eating a drum. But for Mtesa the novelty of this new form of religion and the long bouts of theological controversy into which he entered with gusto, and possibly with tongue in cheek, quickly wore off. Mtesa was no stranger to religion from the outside world, having been dallying with Islam for some years.[3] He quickly divined the long historical emnity between English and French, represented by the two branches of Christianity at his court – Roman Catholicism and Protestantism. The wary potentate assayed the roles the missions might play in any approaching duel with the Egyptians on his northern border: they were already at Mruli, some 160 miles from his capital. Emin Pasha, Governor of the Khedive's Equatorial Province, twice approached Mtesa for permission to advance through Uganda to Karagwe and the countries beyond for the purpose of making scientific observations, but Mtesa opposed this, for it might lead to a further movement south on the part of the Egyptians and further annexations. At first Mtesa felt the missionaries were accredited agents of HMG, and when in apparent response to his sending slaves to accompany the CMS missionaries, Felkin and Wilson, to the UK, there came in return presents and a letter from the British Foreign Secretary, he was confirmed in this view so much so that Kirk at Zanzibar felt it necessary to write informing him that the missionaries were only teachers of religion.

Disappointed to find that neither Christian party was able to supply him with the means of war, Mtesa became increasingly unfriendly and suspicious. He resented the weakening of the hold of ancient pagan gods on his people. By November 1882 he had become so hostile that the White Fathers withdrew to their station, Bukumbi, at the south of the lake. For a time only the useful handyman, Mackay of the CMS, remained in the field as a European Christian witness.

Mtesa died a pagan, on 10 October 1884, having never been converted to Christianity. His 18-year-old son, Mwanga, who succeeded him, was of lesser calibre than his father – he was capricious, lacking in courage and sapped by private vices reputedly acquired from the Arabs. He was soon in headlong collision with the missions, and there followed in the early summer of 1886 the cruel martyrdom of some 30 young Baganda youths, Protestant and Catholic, who, when faced with the awful question of life or death, chose the latter rather than forsake their Christian conviction. Their martyrdom only increased the number of 'learners' and interest in the mssions.

The early 1880s were years of high tension in Uganda. Joseph Thomson's arrival in Busoga from the east, in 1883, had reawakened the old tradition that danger would come from that direction. Mackay in September 1885

> could see well how much our deep troubles this last spring owed their origin to the rumour of Thomson's visit to Busoga ... In Buganda they look on the lake as a natural barrier preventing invasion from the south. When the Egyptians were north of Mruli, Mtesa was trembling. From the west they fear nothing ... the sore point is Busoga. From there they know the solid ground stretches off east all the way to the coast ... an open road.[4]

Mackay and Ashe guilelessly impressed on the apprehensive Mwanga that 'a great lord with large retinue' was approaching from the east. Thus Bishop Hannington, first Anglican Bishop of Eastern Equatorial Africa, after safe passage through Maasai country and trading on the good name that Joseph Thomson had left there, was murdered on the borders of Busoga by a chief, Lubwa, on Mwanga's orders. All members of the caravan were killed except a few useful tradesmen.

The mysterious comings and goings of other European travellers in East Africa in the mid- and later 1880s also caused tension in Uganda. Ashe speaks of the 'gradual encroachment of Egypt from the north with her powerful white pashas' as a constant source of alarm to the Baganda. Dr Junker, after joining Emin Pasha at Lado in January 1884, passed through Buganda in July 1886, on his way to the coast. And shortly after this, Major Casati, formerly in Gordon's employ, moved south to Kabarega's court, where his presence and that of a Zanzibar intriguer, Abdur-Rujman, were a constant irritant to Mwanga, already angered over Kabarega's failure to pay his customary present of salt.

In the same year the German explorer, Dr Fischer, approaching Uganda from the south, found the atmosphere so hostile that he withdrew to the coast. The rumoured approach of a white man (Henry Morton Stanley) from the Manyuema country to the west of Lake Albert seemed to Mwanga to complete the encirclement. By 1888 he was jittery, nervous, smarting in conscience over the murder of Bishop Hannington, and fearful of retribution. Bishop Parker had written to him, adjuring him to repent 'that you may escape God's judgement'. The virtuous Mackay, who denounced Mwanga's dereliction, was forced to leave Uganda in July 1887. By April 1888 only R.H. Walker and E. Gordon were left as English missionaries in Buganda. The trader Stokes, purveyor of news from the interior, informed the British consul-general, Euan-Smith, at Zanzibar in early 1888, that 'Mwanga really does not know where to turn for true advice'.

Arab influence was strong at Mwanga's court. His father Mtesa had aspired to ape the Arabs in dress – the white robe being worn by the Kabaka, prime minister and elders; and Mtesa had acquired a rudimentary knowledge of Arabic and possessed a copy of the Koran. There had been successful Muslim proselytization and the Arabs could flaunt attractions superior to those of Christianity. They were jealous of their monopoly of trade and had already thwarted an attempt by German merchants, Herder and Tuffin, to establish a trading agency at Tabora to the south of Lake Victoria. The Arabs in Buganda played on Mwanga's fear, telling him that Europeans had come 'to eat his country', and that the Germans were taking the Sultan of Zanzibar in their maw, and with the British were planning to divide the interior between them and build railways to Buganda and the lake.

In September 1888, Mwanga, by now thoroughly alarmed, appears to have made up his mind to rid his kingdom of all alien elements – Christian and Islamic alike. He devised a clumsy ruse of inveigling them into his boats at Entebbe with the intention of marooning them on an island in the lake or possibly to carry out their wholesale drowning, but it failed utterly. Mwanga's nerves gave way, and so also the support of his followers. Civil war followed with Mwanga fleeing to Magu at the south of Lake Victoria.[5] The Baganda, disregarding the old custom that the eldest son of the king must not succeed as Kabaka, now chose Mtesa's eldest son, Kiwewa, as Kabaka. He at first showed good sense and tact in filling the various offices of state, and fairly apportioned them among the religious parties. But he soon fell under the control of Muslim chiefs who had played a prominent part in placing him on the throne. Playing on Kiwewa's sense of insecurity, and warning him that the Christians would depose him, and, 'according to the custom of the white men, put a woman in his place', they brought about an attack on the Christians which resulted in the flight of all the missionaries to the south of the lake. At this stage, in their mutual plight, French and English missionaries drew together; 'the French missionaries assisting the English most nobly'. Would that this brotherly love had been sustained in the next few years!

The flight of the Christians left the Muslims with the field to themselves. Their attempt to circumcise Kiwewa by force led to his flight. His younger brother, Kalema, was now circumcised and proclaimed king, and then – following Baganda custom – he put to death all royal aspirants to the throne; in all 30 princesses and princes of the blood perished in the slaughter. But the Muslims in their excess of zeal overreached themselves; their attempts to circumcise by force, their violation of shrines of Baganda pagan gods – especially that of the war god 'Kibuka' at Mbale – raised violent opposition.

Meanwhile, in early December 1888, a penitent and bedraggled Mwanga, 'much changed from what once he was', appeared at the White Fathers' Mission at Bukumbi at the south of the lake, having been fleeced by the Arabs at Magu; 'he now begged for pardon for all that he did against our Christians' and again became the rallying point. With Stokes's help, and some good fortune in the way of arms seized from the Muslims, the Christians recaptured Mwanga's capital on 11 October 1889. The next few days were spent in dividing the offices of state among the victors.[6] Stresses previously present between the two Christian parties, but masked during the struggle with the Muslims, now appeared again despite a desperate attempt to maintain accord. The major chiefdoms were evenly divided between Protestant and Catholics, and below these there were alternating layers of lesser Catholic and Protestant chiefs – down to the lowest strata of sub-chiefs, all arranged as counterbalancing checks, and to avoid a direct chain of command through either Protestant or Catholic appointees. This artificially contrived counterbalancing of power between Catholic and Protestant appointees was a dangerous and difficult system to maintain, and there seems to have been a tacit understanding that a chief who changed his religion thereby forfeited his estates.

Even before this clumsy disposition of power had been worked out the trader Charles Stokes, ex-CMS lay missionary, who bore animus towards the Protestants because they did not give him sufficient ivory for his help in driving out the Muslims, remarked that

> Very strong and bitter religious feelings are held by both parties; they are more like the Orangemen and Ribbonmen of my own unfortunate country.[7]

But for the time being these feelings were held in check owing to the threat of the Muslim leader, Kalema, to the north, who had behind him the support of Kabarega. An expedition against Kalema in November 1889 failed, the pursuers becoming the pursued. Mwanga fled to an island refuge, Bulingugwe, in Lake Victoria, and his capital fell once more to the Muslims and their Bunyoro allies.

It was at this juncture that the IBEAC agent, Frederick Jackson, entering Kavirondo to the immediate east of Uganda, received letters from both Mwanga and Mackay appealing for help. Mwanga begged him

> to be good enough to put me on my throne, I will give you plenty of ivory, and you may trade in Buganda and all you like in the country under me.

and Mackay promised to do all possible to see the IBEAC 'the dominant power in all this region'.[8] These English missionaries had put too much spiritual energy into Uganda to see that territory forsaken, and they feared that its unsettled state would cause the IBEAC to abandon its plans to take over there. The Reverend R.P. Ashe, ruminating on the death in Africa of 12 English missionaries he had known, pleaded 'God grant that the suicidal policy of abandon adopted in the Sudan may not be followed in East Africa'.

Jackson, to whom these impassioned pleas were directed, resisted the temptation to go to Uganda, and wrote instead informing Mwanga that in return for his help, he would expect a treaty; but this brought from Mwanga a vague response, which promised nothing. Soon there were more urgent and desperate appeals, for Mwanga's fortunes in the interval had suffered a reverse. He would now accept the Company's flag, and he offered 'almost all the Company could wish'. But his reply came too late, for Jackson had left for the Suk country to the north-west of Mount Elgon. Before leaving, however, he had sent the flag which Mwanga had adverted to, indicating that its acceptance would bind him to the Company's terms. But again the goddess of chance intervened. In January 1890 a large store of arms fell to the Christians as ransom for release of a captured Muslim leader. Catholics and Protestants now united and, like the Christians of old, made an agreement on 3 February 1890 'not to kill each other'; joining forces they recaptured Mengo and harried the fleeing Muslims to the borders of Bunyoro.

At this moment the German explorer, Carl Peters, appears again on the scene. 'Having with sixteen Somalis, armed with rifles, marched from

Witu to Uganda, fighting all the way', Peters entered Kavirondo in January 1890 and came across the camp of the 'Jackson Emin Pasha Expedition', where he learned that Stanley, with Emin in tow, was on his way to the coast; that the Equatorial Province was abandoned; and that Mwanga had appealed to Jackson for help – but the latter had gone off hunting to the north of Mount Elgon, and anyway he was hesitant about entering Uganda. According to Peters's version, the headman of Jackson's expedition showed him the letters from Uganda which Peters opened because it was 'my simple duty to gain all the knowledge I could in any way acquire with regard to the lands that lay before me'. This opening of another's mail was later described by the British as dastardly, an unethical act; but Bishop Tucker made a similar decision in the same year, when travelling up-country he opened private down-mail from Uganda.[9]

The news of Emin's relief was a blow to Peters:

> what could have been the design of Providence in permitting us to advance so far, only to make it clear to us at last that our labours had been all in vain.[10]

But letters from Uganda in February 1890, asking him to aid the Christian parties and make Uganda a 'rampart against Mohammed-anism invading from the north', offered Peters the opportunity of working for the 'furtherance of the special interests of Germany', and he pressed on to Mwanga's court. Arrived there on 24 February 1890, he offered Mwanga a treaty under which his kingdom would be recognized as neutral territory (Cardinal Lavigerie about the same time was also pressing for this at the Brussels Conference) and in return Germany would receive trade concessions. The French priests supported Peters's treaty, but the English missionaries strenuously opposed it, for it would leave them isolated and vulnerable if the British Company were denied control of Uganda. They argued that Mwanga, having accepted the Company's flag, acknowledged the Company's rule. But Mwanga claimed that Jackson had given no help to him, and that if he were to seek protection of anyone, it would be 'the great emperor of the Germans', who had come to his aid.

The king and Catholic chiefs signed Peters's treaty on 3 March 1890, and the Protestant chiefs, after some hesitancy, signed the following day. With the treaty in hand, Peters did not tarry for he was anxious to report his treaty back home. He was impressed with Buganda, if not with its people, who were, he observed:

Proud even to passionate vindicativeness, brave and courageous –
even to cruelty, they have within themselves that instinctive feeling
of their superiority over others which is the natural and
indisputable condition of sovereignty.

He also noted the 'dangerous blessing afforded by the perennial banana,
the cause of general inclination to idleness'. But what a wealth of
richness the country possessed, and what a delightful climate! It was
with heavy heart that Peters learnt, on his way down to the coast, that
the Anglo-German Agreement of 1 July 1890 had rendered his work in
Uganda void:

> I learnt afterwards that, even before my expedition started,
> Uganda had been ceded to England, but no information of the
> cession had been communicated to us. A great German expedition
> had been allowed to march into these countries, without its having
> been thought necessary to vouchsafe any information whatever on
> that important transaction.[11]

Meanwhile Frederick Jackson had returned to Mumias on 4 March
1890, to find his mail tampered with, and Peters gone to Buganda. This
was grave news. But Jackson appears to have felt no sense of urgency, for
he delayed in Busoga and made a treaty with a local chief on behalf of the
IBEAC. It was not until 14 April that he arrived in Buganda, by which
time Peters had left for the coast.

Jackson's actions in Uganda are not entirely clear. The Catholic
missionaries averred that he and his colleague, Ernest Gedge, tried to
impose such severe terms on Mwanga that a revolution almost took
place. Bishop Tucker later admitted that these terms meant practically
handing over the country to the British Company – assigning to it all
taxes of the country and decreeing that only the Company's flag must be
flown. Mwanga adamantly opposed Jackson's terms, and despite

> all sorts of promises to induce us to go to his country, I regret to
> inform you that I was unable to do anything with him. He has
> absolutely no power but is ruled by the Roman Catholic priests and
> Catholic chiefs. Père Lourdel up to the time of his death opposed
> us in every kind of way and would not hear of the King signing the
> treaty.[12]

Thus Jackson left the country on 14 May, laying some blame for his failure to obtain a treaty on 'the indiscreet zeal of the Protestant missionary, Mr Gordon'. Jackson, however, like Peters, was impressed by Uganda: 'by far the most important country we have been in; and sooner than allow it to fall into the hands of rebels, as the entire Protestant party would have followed us and the Catholics could not hold the country by themselves', he decided to leave Mr Gedge there with some 30 men and 180 guns and ammunition

The genesis of the later troubles which so bedevilled the relations of the IBEAC in Uganda possibly lie in the activities of Gedge, who remained in charge at Mengo. In May and June, attempts were made by the Protestants, abetted by Gedge, to depose Mwanga and place his nephew on the throne; and in July and August alarms of war were sounded. An incident arose wherein a man was imprisoned for having stolen a bullock supposedly belonging to Gedge, who made no investigation but made an attack on the chief of the accused and his people. It ultimately turned out that the bullock never belonged to Gedge, and the charge of theft was false. The atmosphere became so unpleasant that in August 1890 Gedge left Buganda and withdrew to the south of the lake. The report he sent to his superior in Mombasa is that of a sour and disillusioned man – he condemned in sweeping, unmeasured and unqualified terms everything and everyone connected with Uganda.[13]

At the south of the lake Gedge met Emin Pasha. It was now that both learned of the Anglo-German Agreement of 1 July 1890. It was no great cause of satisfaction to either, for Gedge had been unable to obtain a treaty in Buganda, and despite the recent agreement a treaty with Mwanga was still necessary to bring his kingdom under control of the British Company. As for Emin, he had Peters's treaty in hand, but now, under the recent agreement it had no value, for Uganda was assigned to the British sphere.

Meanwhile at the coast, throughout the early summer of 1890, rumours continued to float concerning Uganda. Cardinal Lavigerie was supposed to have entered into agreement with the Germans to protect Catholic interests in Uganda; the Belgians were reported to be coming to Mwanga's help; the Unyanyembe Arabs led by Tippu Tib were about to recover Uganda for the Muslims; a purported letter (dismissed by Euan-Smith as 'likely concocted by an English Missionary') from Mwanga, invited the English to his kingdom. All these rumours were scotched with the arrival at the coast of Mgr Livinhac in July 1890, and of Jackson in September 1890. Livinhac made no secret that the French missionaries favoured a Franco-German pact; and Jackson confirmed that Mwanga 'would perform nothing' for the English. With Jackson there also arrived the two envoys representing the Protestant and Catholic parties in Uganda, who had come to the coast to find out for themselves the position of their country under the new dispensation of the Anglo-German Agreement. These envoys provided for Euan-Smith's delectation a powerful demonstration of the bitter relations existing in Uganda between the two Christian parties.

> Samuel Mwemba, the Protestant, and Victor Senezi, the Catholic
> – displayed, however, an actual intelligence that I have never met
> with among the ordinary natives of the coast, but the two seemed
> to hate each other with the whole force of the odium theologicum,
> and whatever was said to me by both as representing their joint
> opinion when they were together, was invariably discounted or
> denied by one or the other in a subsequent private interview, which
> I invariably sought for afterwards ... For this reason I soon came to
> learn that discussion or advice could not be of much value, and that
> whatever is to be the fate of Uganda it must be settled on the spot
> in Uganda with such ability and mental and material force as the
> representative of the Imperial British East Africa Company may at
> the critical time be able to bring to bear in support of any definite
> instructions which may be furnished in order to induce the King
> and country to accept the protection and influence of the
> Company.[14]

The envoys warned of pending civil war in Uganda. The return of the Company's flag by Mwanga was 'a strong and somewhat unusual mark of unfriendliness'. The envoys' wish to treat with foreign consuls in Zanzibar to ascertain the true status of Uganda was not at all to the liking of the British consular agent, nor their complaints of bad food and the housing provided by the IBEAC during their stay at the coast. It was with a sigh of relief that Euan-Smith and IBEAC officials hurried these difficult guests back to Uganda.

Everything now hung on Lugard who was on his way there. The need for an 'imposing and authoritative' military expedition which was to have been led by de Winton no longer existed, for Uganda was now in the British sphere. Lugard's task of obtaining a treaty from Mwanga would be eased by the recent death of Père Lourdel, which had 'cleared' the atmosphere of a very strong opponent to the English.

But Lugard faced another danger. The trader, Stokes, in German pay and wearing the uniform of a high-ranking German officer, was leading a caravan of 200 porters with a large supply of arms to Mwanga's capital. Mwanga, with these arms in hand, would be most difficult to deal with. Hence Lugard's resolve 'to march as fast as was in any way possible' to get to Uganda before Stokes. On his way to Uganda also was the Anglican Bishop, Alfred Tucker, on whom Euan-Smith pinned hope of reconciliation between the religious parties, and discovery of 'what it is that had to be done to remove the dissatisfaction'. It was Tucker's view that everything depended on Lugard's arrival in Uganda:

> a strong man with full authority should as quickly as possible, make his appearance at Uganda ... we ask freedom to worship God as we think best. This I fear we shall not get if Rome rules Uganda.[15]

In a long report of 24 December 1890, with an addendum dated 7 January 1891, Lugard recounts his journey to Uganda. It is a fine source of information on the topography and peoples of the country between Uganda and the coast. With a keen eye to its development, Lugard recommended a railway line from Mombasa to Malindi connecting the coast ports and acting as a check on the slave-trade and smuggling, and thence running inland by way of the Sabaki River route. He would also have a line of 12 to 14 heliograph stations between Mombasa and Uganda, flashing at a distance of 50 miles each: this would avoid the hazards of a telegraph line which could easily be cut by natives. He advocated the use of the camel and elephant to cut down the dependency on porters; but the elephant would have difficulty in foraging in the plateau area and there would probably be risks with the camel in a tropical terrain. The Sabaki route offered fodder, fuel and water, for some distance, hence Lugard's advocacy of it. Among incidents on his way inland were meeting a slave caravan almost immediately after crossing the Tsava River; making blood-brotherhood with a Kamba chief at Machakos; and opening a store here and placing it under a European, a Mr Brown. From Machakos he crossed a 'huge undulating plain, about 5,700 feet high' with no inhabitants to disturb the enormous herds of game. Fuel was scarce, 'and water not abundant'.

Lugard refused to pay hongo to the Kikuyu. They occupied a country 'wonderfully cultivated ... more so than any country we have yet passed through', and food was abundant, an ideal site for a station. Thus he made blood-brotherhood and a treaty with the Kikuyu chief, Wyaki, and then supervised the construction of a fort at Dagoretti (a few miles west of present-day Nairobi), a square stockade with 'sides 30 yards, with bastions at the diagonal corners, enfilading the four faces'.

Journeying through the region of the Great Rift Valley, Lugard passed many deserted Maasai kraals, but met no Maasai till Lake Naivasha was reached: the great rinderpest plague which swept the eastern side of Africa in the later 1880s had exacted a heavy toll from the Maasai herds. Passing on to the Mau escarpment, Lugard noted the singularly rich pasture here:

> grass is grazed down by game, the turfy grass is like the richest English pasture. The soil is good, and the streams contain deli-cious water, flowing among black volcanic (basaltic-looking) rocks. It is quite uninhabited, and could be made an admirable grazing ground for stock ... beyond the Elgeyo escarpment ... magnificent pasture might be admirably utilized for establishing cattle or sheep runs under European settlers.[16]

Thence descending into the more tropical region of Kavirondo he took over the men and loads left at Mumias by Jackson earlier in the year, and proceeded on to Wakoli's (Chief of Busoga, with whom Jackson had made a treaty), and here on 7 December, made blood-brotherhood with him and a treaty with a sub-chief Mbekirwao; both chiefs were most anxious to have these seals of the Company's authority. From Wakoli's, runners were sent off to Mwanga to announce Lugard's approach. The Nile was reached on 13 December, and seizing canoes he crossed over to the other side (he later learned that Mwanga had executed two persons for permitting this), and set foot on Buganda's soil 42 days after leaving Kikuyu. On 16 December a 'civil letter of welcome' from Mwanga was received, and by 18 December he was at Mengo, where, in an imperious manner, and ignoring the camp site assigned to him (it was a miserable site on which to camp, in a hollow), he chose instead,

> the top of a knoll about 800 yards from the King's hill, on which the King and most of the principal officers of State live. I got several messages from the King, saying it was a bad place, and he wished to give me a better, but I said I would look at the other next day; that my men were tired, and rain was imminent. I said I would

come to see the King next day. I afterwards found I could hardly have selected a better site.[17]

The next day he faced the etiquette 'so necessary in Uganda' and donned Court dress – 'a very old pair of hunting breeches and the jacket of a sleeping suit' and with a guard of Sudanese, he made his audience with Mwanga.

The King was by all accounts greatly scared at my high-handed procedure in crossing the Nile and marching so rapidly, without waiting for permission, or going through the usual etiquette. I had arrived from Qua Sundu in fifteen days, whereas it took Mr. Jackson thirty-five.[18]

Lugard arrived at a time of high tension in Buganda. There was internal dissension, the bloody affrays and wars with the Muslims, and then the action of Jackson and Gedge in trying to force terms on Mwanga; the religious cleavage had been further deepened by the French priests' support of Peters, and the Protestant missionaries' endeavours to secure the Company's rule in Uganda; and then the news of Lugard's approach;

a day or so before my arrival there had very nearly been a fight between the two parties, a scare having been set on foot that we had come to oust the Catholics from the country.[19]

Lugard was a taut, peppery, highly-strung individual, a stringy piece of biltong; a cleric *manqué*, of whom it might be said, as Daniel O'Connor said of the Englishman, he had all the qualities of a poker except its occasional warmth, or what the French statesman and historian, Guizot, described as characteristic of English foreign policy:

l'orgueil ambitieux, la préoccupation constante et passionée de soi-même, le besoin ardent et exclusif de se faire partout sa part et sa place, la plus grande place possible, n'importe aux dépens de quoi et de qui.[20]

Tough, reserved, and no doubt suffering from pain from the shattered arm he received in the affray with the Arabs on Nyasa (pieces of bone were still coming out years after the injury), he was singularly lacking in self-awareness, a trait peculiar to the Victorians.

He had no understanding of the French missionaries' point of view, and appears to have distrusted them from the first. They blocked his attempts to get a treaty from Mwanga, and for this he never quite forgave them, for he was in a hurry to obtain this treaty before Stokes with his arms arrived at Kampala; and also before the envoys who had been treating with foreign representatives at Zanzibar returned from the coast. In a letter to Euan-Smith, 8 January 1891, he states:

> I forward to you by the German mail a duplicate of the Treaty I have made with Mwanga. It has cost me infinite trouble. They are no longer in fear of the Mahommedans, and do not wish outside interference, as they did when Jackson and Peters were here. Moreover – they are a most clever and cunning people, and see the full point of every smallest detail. The priests too, are quick to put them up to everything, even could they not see it for themselves. I therefore had much trouble over the finance clause and over the registration of arms ... The King seems to try and exasperate me to the limit of my tether ... I scared him into signing (seeing that all the Chiefs had agreed to do so) and when he is not face to face with me tries to exasperate me in consequence.[21]

Mwanga signed the treaty under duress on 26 December 1890. It placed him in the category of an Indian prince under the British Raj. There was to be a British Resident – agent of the Company – at his court, who would enjoy a position of paramountcy similar to that of a British Resident at the court of an Indian prince. He would control the king's foreign policy and act as 'Arbitrator' with jurisdiction over all Europeans, who could only settle in Uganda with the Company's consent – a violation of Article VIII of the Anglo–German Agreement of 1 July 1890, whereby

> subjects of either Power will be at liberty to settle freely in their respective territories situated within the free trade zone.

The revenues of the country and customs and taxes (assessed by a committee under the Resident as ex-officio president) were to pay for the cost of occupation of Uganda by the Company. The stipulation in the treaty as to freedom of religion was in accord with the Anglo–German Agreement, but the provision that settlement of disputes between the Missions was to be left to the Resident, with right of appeal to the

Company in Britain, especially rankled with the French priests. Clauses providing for the suppression of the slave-trade and traffic in arms were in accord with the Brussels Act of 1890. An annex to the treaty rendering it invalid 'should another Whiteman, greater than this one, come up afterwards', showed that the Baganda had learned a lesson: they remembered Carl Peters's treaty-making and quick departure, so might not the same happen again with Lugard? More important was the mysterious codicil written in Luganda and attached to the treaty, which was to be the cause of so much religious bitterness and acrimony.[22] According to an appended note signed by Lugard and F.W. de Winton, the codicil was written 'by the Chiefs themselves in consultation, and read before the King'. An English translation of it by the Protestant missionary, the Reverend E.C. Gordon, reads as follows

> Now we Catholics want to read and to teach all people in your country as we please, and our former Agreement remain as we agreed, and this Agreement amongst ourselves is the same as your Agreement, also that our work be done as formerly, and respect among my people as formerly.

Lugard later claimed that the agreement referred to in the codicil was a 'mutual agreement' made between the Christian parties at the time they ousted the Muslims, and which, Lugard maintained, 'specially stipulated that if a man changes his religion he should forfeit his estates'.[23] But the only mutual agreement between the two parties of which there is trace is that made by the two parties on their return to Uganda, in the spring of 1890, which states:

> We Christians, instructed in the religion of Jesus Christ and of his Ten Commandments, promise and swear in the presence of the true God that we will not betray nor kill more of our friends who follow the Catholic religion: and even if we are stronger than they we will not kill them any more. He who acts contrary to these promises and kills his friends will be exposed on the Day of Judgement to all the rigours of Divine Justice.

The disputed interpretation of the codicil was to be a cause of infinite trouble, and was never settled satisfactorily.

Shortly after his arrival in Uganda, Lugard expressed his fear that the French priests would not come forth in an 'open and conciliatory spirit'.

The French priests did submit a statement of their grievances, but since it was in French, 'the Protestants could make nothing of them; and asked for a clear statement in English', and this, Lugard said, 'It is of course impossible for me to furnish.' Thus it would appear that the Catholics were not so irreconcilable as Lugard made out in his reports to the Company; and that the opportunity for peaceful discussion of Protestant and Catholic differences failed because no one on the English side understood the French language and, equally on the French side, no one sufficiently understood the English language to put the Catholic grievances into English. Lugard himself communicated with the French Fathers in schoolboy Latin learned at Rossall School.[24]

A difficult question also arose over the Ssese Islands in Lake Victoria which were the traditional seat of Baganda naval power with a fleet of war canoes based there, which were now in the control of the Catholics. Bishop Tucker in January 1891 urged that the English party should share in these islands, for the Roman Catholic chief who controlled them 'smothered' Mwanga's order to provide canoes to carry food and clothing to the Protestant Missions and as a result he, Bishop Tucker, was 'living on nothing but bananas and goat's flesh': 'Until Ssese is divided there will always be a burning and a very real grievance on the part of the Protestants.' A more burning issue was the eviction from estates of persons who changed their religion.

In February 1891, Lugard, feeling himself strengthened by the construction of a fort and the arrival of Captain Williams from the coast with additional forces, tackled this question.

> The main difficulty was regarding the estates which either party alleged to have been forcibly taken from them, and regarding the evictions of men of the opposite creed from estates under the authority of a big Chief who belonged to the rival party. I tried to form a Court of Arbitration, in which I would hear the circumstances from representatives of each side, and would act as Arbitrator. I found, however, that no one would agree that his Court should consist of less than some four on each side. This number led to violent and heated argument – either side telling a completely different story, both undoubtedly lying. In addition, the circumstances were so involved and intricate that I felt myself despairing of arriving at any solution.[25]

He thus handed over the question to Mwanga, as arbitrator, agreeing to support his decision. Lugard affirmed that Mwanga showed remarkable tact in his role of arbitrator. But when he issued his decision there was an uproar because it was considered to be unfair to the Protestants. A heated argument arose and Mwanga left in a passion. According to Lugard:

> disorder prevailed, for this was the signal for trouble. I remained, and sent for the King for a private interview with me alone. He returned, and I had a satisfactory interview with him. I pointed out that his country would be plunged in war, and he alone was the cause, because he would not do justice to the Protestants. He maintained that he did. I challenged him to prove it by dividing Ssese: he declined. I said all right, he must take the consequences. He then agreed to do so, and implored me to help him, and spoke in a most satisfactory way... Next morning, early, I found the whole country under arms for war.[26]

Lugard escaped by a hair's breadth at this crisis:

> the Catholics were very obstinate ... finally, the Sudanese, with fixed bayonets on the knee, and the Maxim ready for action, helped to persuade them, and the danger was averted within a shot.[27]

In March another difficult shamba (small estate) question arose. Lugard was again faced with the difficult question of reconciling forfeiture of estate on change of religion, with freedom of creed. He was faced with a dilemma. He had intimated from the first his intention of allowing absolute freedom of creed, but the Protestants insisted that if a man changed his religion he should forfeit his estate. This was stipulated, claimed the Protestants, in the mutual agreement made between the parties at the time they ousted the Muslims as it was necessary to maintain the politico-religious balance. Land and positions were party, not individual affairs, and the Protestants must be restrained by penalties from embracing the Roman Catholic faith. The Protestants implied that the mutual agreement was in writing but that the document had been lost. But the Baganda took great care of such documents. Lugard himself stated that the Baganda 'most fully understand the nature of the written contract, and consider nothing as absolutely final and binding unless put on paper', and Macdonald referred to the value they placed on a written document 'provided that it had been duly

Zanzibar Harbour
By South African Artist J. H. Pierneef (1886–1957)

ABOVE: Nairobi Station, 1902
BELOW: Native Labour Gang working on the Uganda Road, late 1890s

ABOVE: Carriers crossing an incline on the Uganda Railway
(Rogers Collection)

BELOW: Captain Lugard, F. de Winton and Grant at Kampala, Mengo,
January 11th 1891

signed by representative chiefs', and he 'could not find anything to warrant that the alleged agreement was ever made in writing'. The Protestants in talking of the alleged agreement used the term 'endagano' – a Kiganda word which could mean either a written or a verbal agreement – but they could give no time nor place when the purported agreement was made. The Catholics did admit that there was a custom among the Baganda of eviction on change of creed, but even when it would have been to their advantage to support it, they had protested against it. But such a formal agreement, even if it existed as a written document, could not be reconciled with the principle of religious freedom, as secured under the Company's charter and the treaty with Mwanga. Lugard himself had stated:

> I consider that by the terms of the Company's Charter, under which alone I administer this country, as well as by the terms of my Treaty with Mwanga, and in the whole spirit of British Colonial rule, absolute freedom of religion is granted all, Christian and Mahommedan alike.[30]

Lugard appears to have been misled by the Protestants into believing that the codicil referred to a signed agreement between the parties as to eviction from estates on change of creed, and he fell back on the Catholic claim that the 'mutual agreement' be honoured; but the mutual agreement to which the Catholics referred was an entirely different matter, and Lugard must have known this. But it must be repeated that, even if such an agreement as the Protestants claimed did exist Lugard had only accepted it 'provided no clause in it contradicted anything in our Treaty'. There appears to have been much tergiversation on Lugard's part!

The envoys arrived back from the coast on 31 March 1891 and confirmed that Uganda was in the British sphere. Lugard left next day on a campaign against the Muslims who were an immediate threat to the north of Kampala. According to Captain Williams, left in charge at Kampala:

> during the previous months practically nothing had been done as regards the burning questions which existed at the time. Two in particular, the division of Ssese, and the great question of turning out Chiefs and people who changed their religion, were left for me to decide or arrange.[31]

Williams dealt with the vexatious question of eviction by generally deciding two cases together and giving judgement – one to each side; Lugard also had 'paired off cases against each other'. This singular method of dealing with cases of law where rights of property were involved and which encroached on the undoubted prerogative of the king (according to custom he had the sole right to judge cases between his subjects) produced great dissatisfaction.

Meanwhile Lugard, campaigning to the north, caught up with and defeated the Muslims on 2 May 1891, and forced them back into Bunyoro. After sending the sick and weakly back to Kampala, and some preliminary reconnoitring to the west of Lake Victoria, he set out for Ankole and Ruwenzori in mid-June, with only 'Bartholomew's Political Map of Africa' in which 'the whole of these countries could be covered by a five-shilling piece'.

Lugard took with him 250 'fighting men' and 290 'armed porters', half the Europeans available and the only reliable Maxim gun. Williams was left with eight sound Sudanese, 40 porters and men whom Lugard sent back 'because they were useless'; and Lugard later drew further on Williams for additional men. Yet Lugard himself had claimed that 'a force of some 500 drilled men, at least, will be required to keep Uganda under control till the country is quieted'. Williams, in a singularly weak position, could do nothing else but follow a policy of conciliation and compromise. Lugard claimed that his journey to the west was

> to procure recruits for the Company's services from the Sudanese soldiers of Emin's late province, and forestall any attempt by Emin Pasha to secure these men; to check the arms trade from the German sphere into Unyoro and Uganda; to consolidate the Company's influence in Ankole and Toro to check the depredations of Kabarega's troops; and establish a base of operations against Unyoro in the future.[30]

But in the same report, he also states that it was his intention

> to proceed to Ankole in the endeavour to carry out my original instructions (vide telegram from Directors, dated about March 1890), and make a Treaty with Mtali, the independent King of that country and bring those territories under the Company's protection.[31]

His instructions from the IBEAC March 1890 (received at Kibwezi on 19 April) had adjured Lugard to

> Bear always in mind our great idea is to make treaties and secure supremacy for the Company in Uganda and also from the south of Victoria Nyanza to a point on Tanganyika where the 4° intersects it, so as to secure access to and free communication with Nyassa ... to secure if possible territorial rights in the way the German Government are working, and try to prevent anyone doing the same, or acting on behalf of others within the zone reserved for British influence.[32]

Control over western Uganda and territory between it and Lake Tanganyika, loomed large in IBEAC plans – part of the cherished dream of an all-British Cape-to-Cairo route which it was working for in conjunction with Cecil Rhodes. Stanley, during the course of the Emin Pasha Relief Expedition, had made treaties with chiefs in this region whereby they had ceded to him personally sovereign rights over their territory; and on 29 April 1890 he had transferred these treaties to the IBEAC. In an address at the Albert Hall in London on 5 May 1890, Stanley claimed that he had 'extended British possessions to the eastern end of the Congo Free State, having acquired many thousand square miles of territory', in return for his assistance to chiefs against their enemy, the Ware Sura (sharpshooters) of Kabarega. His most vital treaty was made on 23 July, with Uchunku, 'A sweet faced gentle-looking boy of about thirteen or fourteen years old, a true Mhuma with the Abyssinian features' – a member of the royal clan of Bahinda, and deputed by Ntare, ruler of Ankole, to make blood-brotherhood with Stanley. The validity of Stanley's treaty-making was soon questioned; for it encroached 20 to 30 miles beyond 1°S latitude into the hinterland of German territory and was thus a flagrant violation of the 'hinterland' understanding of July 1887; and it was questionable whether Stanley could transfer treaties made with him personally by African chiefs, to a third party, in this case the IBEAC.

With Stanley's treaty-making in doubt, Mackinnon at one stage contemplated using the CMS missionary, Mackay, to make good the IBEAC claim to the region. However, Mackay's death, in February 1890, intervened, and it was left to Lugard to make good the claim. There was special urgency for this in view of the Mackinnon/Leopold agreement of May 1890, and German infiltration into the British sphere. Langheld,

German officer at Bukoba, had penetrated deep into south-western Uganda under the guise of anti-slave-trade patrols; and Emin Pasha, to the west of Lake Victoria, was possibly heading for Wadelai with the intention of establishing a German corridor behind the British sphere, Lugard signed his treaty with Ntali of Ankole, on 1 July 1891, and thence marched to Lake Edward where he took over the nearby salt lake, 'a possession of more value than would be a gold mine', and constructed Fort George to check Manyuema raids across the Semliki River. He now learned that Emin Pasha was heading in a north-west direction, 'in search of Selim and his Soudanese or to get the hidden ivory from his old province'. By August 1891, Lugard was under the towering heights of Ruwenzori in a country with 'rich soil and miles on miles of banana groves'; where elephant abounded and the numerous forests contained excellent timber – 'acacia, tamarind and mteroanda' – the latter 'an excellent wood for gun stocks'. It was a land ideally suited for European settlement, with its general excellence only marred by the recent cattle plague which had destroyed 'perhaps millions of animals' throughout these regions.

In the kingdom of Toro, at the base of Ruwenzori, he installed Kasagama, the 'legitimate ruler' of Toro, whom he had brought back from Kampala (where the latter had sought refuge after his country had been overrun by Kabarega's forces), and made a treaty with him under which Kasagama recognized the Company's rule and in return received its protection. Fort Edward (Fort Portal) was established. Lugard then proceeded north-westward, impressing on the people *en route* that they were now under British rule and could live in peace. At Kavalli's, at the south-west corner of Lake Albert, he made treaties with the 'big chiefs', Kaboni and Mugyeni, and met the remnants of Emin's Sudanese forces under Selim Bey, still loyal to the Khedive. 'After some trouble and plain speaking' an agreement was made with Selim on 17 September, whereby he and his forces placed themselves under Lugard's orders.

> These Soudanese were, for the most part, clad in skins, but the higher ranks wore cloth manufactured by their people from cotton. Of this cotton they had large quantities, grown from seed brought down from the Soudan. They had artizans of all kinds, tools and appliances, and even distilled a spirit from the mtama grain, not unlike mild whisky.[33]

Lugard left Kavalli's on 5 October 1891 with a vast concourse: the

Sudanese, their families, slaves, women and children – in all 8200 persons – strung out for five miles on the march back to Kampala.

When clear of the borders of Toro, Lugard recommenced his siting of forts: Fort Edward, the most westerly, in a chain meant to link Ruwenzori with Lake Victoria; Fort Wavertree, the northernmost, garrisoned by four companies of Sudanese, despite their propensity for raiding and slaving. Then, after working his way slowly southwards, through the flat uninteresting country of southern Bunyoro, through swamps and marshes flooded by recent rains, he sited the forts of Lorne, Kivari, Ntara and Grant. By early December 1891 the chain was completed. It was with a sense of achievement that Lugard set out on his homeward journey to Kampala in December 1891.

He claimed impressive results for his trip to the west. He had frustrated the German expedition under Emin Pasha, brought into the Company's service the Sudanese forces – 'A fine body of men, ready armed and soldiers by profession' – and had gained for the Company 'all the country to the Congo border and along the Ruwenzori to Albert Lake to the north', including 'the greatest ivory preserve in the world' and a valuable salt lake. There was now a line of seven forts across southern Bunyoro and Toro which would contain the Muslims, and Kabarega – 'a man who had lost any claim to indulgence by his cruelties, a curse to his country'. Also Kasagama, the rightful King of Toro, had been reinstated. A feasible transport route had been opened up between Lakes Victoria and Albert. And, most laudable, Lugard's excursion to the west, over a period of nine months and covering 732 miles, had cost the Company nothing, for he had fed his men without expenditure, and had brought back salt and ivory (1300 lb) that more than covered the outlay for the expedition.

All this had an impressive ring. But by the time Lugard left Uganda, the so-called 'forts' had sunk back into bush, and the cost of transporting salt from the 'valuable salt mines' to Kampala barely covered its selling price – 12 to 13 rupees per load. And had not all this been bought at too dear a price? – for during Lugard's absence there had been a serious deterioration in the religious situation in Buganda.

Williams had attempted to act as arbitrator at the king's court in effecting the policy of eviction from estates, but the result was bitter disputes frequently ending in manslaughter, and Williams did not have the forces at his disposal to make his decisions respected. Both Christian parties accused him of partiality, and he was especially on bad terms with the Reverend R.H. Walker of the CMS, a 'harmless, well-intentioned, rather eccentric gentleman'. Unwisely, Williams tried to force the Company's flag on Mwanga in July 1891 and this nearly precipitated civil war; a rumour reaching Kampala that Lugard's expedition to the west had been destroyed did not help matters. At the end of seven months' strain Williams was worn out.

The evictions, cause of his greatest difficulty, were the result of a power struggle between the two Christian parties for possession of the great chieftainships and the power that went with them. Mwanga had disposed of these to the Christians for their assistance in driving out the Muslims: half to the Protestants and half to the Catholics, although, as Williams averred, the latter were substantially greater in number (two-fifths Protestant to three-fifths Catholic) – largely the result of the honour attached to the King's Party – the Catholic Party; for 'The King was nominally a Catholic and the Kabaka, even now when he has little power, was still a terrible name'. Also according to Williams, the Catholic priests were 'more numerous, more capable, and better organized' than the Protestant clergy. The Catholics wore a little medal round their necks, which, Williams thought, was 'a great thing to the negro mind'. Thus once the initial division of estates and offices had taken place after the war with the Muslims and the land was divided into two parts, more defections began to occur from the Protestant side than from the Catholic; and, according to Williams, 'there is the trouble'. In the face of increasing accession of strength to the Catholic side, the Protestants saw their position steadily eroded. They looked to the IBEAC and Lugard to right the balance in their favour.

Lugard apparently did not realize this serious state of affairs on his return from the west, and was perhaps overconfident with the addition of 100 Sudanese troops and forces, recently arrived from the coast, and those he had brought down from Lake Albert. He again angered Mwanga by trying to force on him the Company's flag; and then 'quietly sat down to answer his mail'. On 25 December 1891 instructions arrived from the IBEAC, dated 10 August 1891, ordering him to withdraw from Uganda, for the directors had decided

> to retire temporarily from Uganda, and restrict their operations for the present to the coast, with outposts at such places as Dagoretti, Machakos, and Taveta.[34]

This news would have an explosive effect on the situation in Uganda nor would it be allayed by further intelligence, on 7 January 1892, that evacuation was delayed for 12 months, owing to the CMS having come to the rescue by raising sufficient funds to administer Uganda until 31 December 1892. It was the Gordon episode all over again, and British prestige would suffer. Meanwhile events in Uganda were rapidly leading to civil war. A succession of gun thefts (with redress in the form of fresh thefts) brought matters to a crisis. On 20 January 1892 there took place what Lugard termed 'a cold-blooded murder of a Protestant in the streets of Mengo'. Mwanga dealt with the case immediately, and acquitted the accused on the ground that the Protestant had taken the law into his own hands and had violated Baganda customary law by forcing his way into the accused's enclosure. Lugard at once took the matter up and, despite Article XI of the treaty with Mwanga whereby the Company was to 'uphold the power of the King in his country', peremptorily demanded that the accused be executed. He reminded Mwanga

> that since the first day I had come to Mengo I had told him strongly that in every case of murder the murderers should be executed since one outrage was sufficient to plunge the country into war.[35]

This pressure on the king to reverse his decision brought him and his followers to an excitable pitch, coming as it did after trying to force the Company's flag on him and the Protestant attempt to wean him over from Catholicism. It was in this extremely delicate state of affairs that Lugard pleaded indisposition, and left the very important duty of deciding between war and peace to his hot-headed servant, Dualla, a Muslim. Lugard speaks highly of Dualla – a widely travelled man, whom the British Company considered using to negotiate a treaty with the Somalis, and a possible assistant to the British Resident in Uganda. Dualla, however, was a Somali, excitable, hot-tempered and arrogant; he was a thorough partisan, with but slight knowledge of Luganda. Lugard, however, was enamoured of him. How much wiser it would have been if he had employed one of the four Europeans on his staff for the task.

Lugard himself states – as regards the possibility of war – 'I saw on my return to Uganda that it was inevitable'; and he was under instructions 'to endeavour to be perfectly impartial', but in the last resort to 'consolidate the Protestant party' as the only real ally of the Company. His critics could say that Lugard apparently singled out the case of murder on 20 January (there had been other murders since Lugard came to Uganda and in no other case had he insisted that the murderer be executed) as a *casus belli*, and by injudicious pressure on Mwanga invited war.

On hearing that Mwanga had rejected Dualla's demand that he reverse his decision, Lugard warned the CMS the same evening of the imminence of war, 'and offered them an asylum in Kampala'; but he did not do the same for the Catholic Mission. The next day, 21 January, Lugard again pressed Mwanga to revoke his decision, but in vain. On 22 January Lugard received a letter from the king couched in uncompromising terms, along with a list of Catholic grievances. In response, Lugard reiterated his demand that Mwanga do justice, that is carry out the execution of the accused. On 23 January Lugard warned the Catholic Bishop of the danger of war. The same evening the latter also sent Lugard a list of Catholic grievances. The Catholics were now massing in great numbers at Mengo, and Lugard, seeing that they far outnumbered the Protestants who he claims 'had made no preparations whatever for war', issued the latter with 40 rifles and ammunition. In one report, Lugard states that this issue took place on the night of 23 January; in another report and in *The Rise of Our East African Empire*, he admits that it took place on the 22nd. Apart from the confusion as to date of issue of the firearms, the question arises why Lugard issued the arms secretly if, as he claims, he wanted it to be 'plainly known' to the Catholics that he intended to side with the Protestants.

The news of the secret issue of arms on 22 January, however, leaked out, and caused Mwanga to augment the supply of gunpowder at the palace on the night of the 23rd. On the morning of Sunday 24 January, a further and larger issue of guns was made by Lugard to the Protestants, so that in all they had now received 450 guns of which 150 were Sniders: – 'This I thought would about equalize the number of guns on either side'. By this action Lugard lost control over events. Further negotiations proved futile.

It is difficult to ascertain which side opened fire first. Ashe, of the CMS, said it was the Protestants. Lugard asserts that it was the Catholic side, and that he had forbidden the Protestants to fire until the last moment – thus a Protestant was the first to be shot! In the ensuing battle, in which the pyrotechnics were greater than the casualties, the Catholics were routed with the aid of the Maxim gun. The Catholic leader, Stanlislau Mugwanya, being nearly 'winged', fled with Mwanga to the lake. Rubaga, the Catholic Mission, was captured and looted, but the French Fathers were later found unharmed and taken under

Lugard's protection to the Fort.

After the fight at Mengo, Lugard, much sobered by the turn of events, adopted a conciliatory tone. He was now ready to restore Mwanga to his old position in return for the Company's flag being flown, and a British Resident to assist the king in trying criminal cases. The Catholics were offered what amounted to a complete pardon – restoration of their power and position as before the war. These concessions drew from the Catholics a haughty reply. They demanded that the Protestants 'hand over their arms and pay a fine'. In the face of this Catholic intransigence, Lugard was nonplussed. He held an empty capital, and 'If no Kabaka of the Royal Blood is installed in Mengo the result would be the break-up of the people here.' Thus he turned to Mgr Hirth to secure the return of Mwanga: without the Queen Bee there could be no rest in the hive. When he failed to obtain this he accused Hirth of preventing Mwanga from returning, although it was Mwanga's repugnance for his capital after the drubbing he had received there, which made him loath to return. On 30 January, in sheer exasperation it would seem, Lugard turned his Maxim on the Catholics huddled on the island of Bulingugwe, on the pretext that they had attacked Protestants on the mainland shore opposite (his purpose was really to stop Mwanga from collecting canoes there). In the face of this attack the Catholics fled to the Ssese Islands, and Buddu on the south-western side of the lake. The fear now arose in Lugard's mind that they might set up a separate kingdom. To add to the confused state of affairs, there was a reverse flight of 10,000 Protestants from Buddu into Kampala. The religious war seemed to have ignited the whole kingdom. Ashe of the CMS was so sick of the whole business that he could scarcely bring himself to write about it. His colleague, J. Roscoe, however, with a *schadenfreude* reminiscent of another age, spoke of 'the whole country in a blaze, with the Roman Catholic houses, which were fired by the Protestants – for three days and nights they were going'.

Disappointed over the failure of the Protestants at Kampala to go to the help of their co-religionists fleeing from Buddu, and soured over the turn of events and infighting among the Christians, Lugard reacted against the excess of zeal he had previously shown for the Protestant cause, and now even toyed with the idea of supporting the Muslims: 'I do not myself think that a Mahommedan King under the British would be so disastrous to the country as might be supposed.' And Dualla, sharp, clever Dualla, was at hand and might even be suitable as a 'Mahommedan Raj'. During the next few weeks Lugard was virtually isolated in Kampala – 'the whole country was against us and we were completely cut off from all communications'. There was growing uneasiness on Lugard's part as to the role he had played in recent events:

> I consider it absolutely essential that I should run home to England to meet the charges which the French Missions may put forward regarding this war, and which may be supported by the French Government.[36]

He wrote up his diary 'at enormous length' to meet any accusations the French missionaries might bring against him in England, and he asked the CMS missionaries 'to write some account of the revolution which has taken place in the country, in the last few days'. But the main need was to get Mwanga back to the capital before he left for England. Thus Lugard turned to the French missionaries who had continued to reside at the capital, and on 11 February 1892 he put before them proposals for a division of the country between the two Christian parties, in return for the restoration of Mwanga to the throne. The country would be equally divided, 'Mengo being between the two portions'. The Protestants, on hearing of this proposal, raised such an outcry that Lugard temporarily dropped it, but the French priests on 2 March raised it again with more exact details – 'division of country into two parts separated by a broad road from the capital to Toro, the Catholics having all the territory south of the road; and Mwanga would be restored and the Catholics would accept the English flag and English Protectorate.' Lugard, in reply, assured Father Achte:

> If I have guarantees that there will be no danger to the European Resident in the province of the Catholics ... I would not object to a division of the country on the conditions you name; but as I have before said, the return of the King is absolutely necessary ... And you, Father Achte, can trust the word of a British officer that when the King has returned I will do my utmost to effect a settlement satisfactory to both parties on the lines you indicate.[37]

Thus Mwanga, relying on Captain Lugard's word, and assured by the French Fathers that his life was not in danger, returned to his capital on 3 March 1892. Lugard reports:

> I brought him into Kampala, where his appearance was a very

marked contrast to what he had been before his flight. Haggard and thin, trembling with fatigue and fear, he could hardly either speak or walk, and was almost in a state of collapse, presenting a spectacle one could only pity. I escorted him inside, spoke a few words of welcome and gave him a small present, as is the Uganda custom the first time a guest enters. For once in his life I believe he was really grateful, saying that he had come expecting imprisonment, and was received as a welcome guest etc., that henceforth he was under the flag of the Queen utterly and entirely.[38]

Following Mwanga's return no time was lost in discussing the partition of the country. Lugard wished to give the Catholics

a portion, if not the whole of the Kaima's country, which extends from Buddu along the lake, close to the capital. In this I was most strenuously opposed by the Protestants, who adopted a tone almost of defiance, and the relations between us became extremely strained.[39]

Lugard thus reluctantly abandoned the idea of giving the Catholics all of Kamia's country, and in the face of much Protestant opposition, drew up a new partition whereby the Catholics would receive only part of Kamia's country – that part of it south of the Katonga River and known as Buganga; he also

secured for them the island of Lulambu, and I insisted in allowing them to retain the name and title of the Kimbugwe (in addition to the Pokino, Chief of Buddu) ... However, I met with the most obstinate resistance from the Protestant party, and this culminated at last in their writing me one of the most grossly insulting letters it is possible to conceive, and even hinting at *war*, though they held our rifles and ammunition, and had been saved from absolutely certain destruction and annihilation by us.[40]

This new division was incorporated in an agreement of 5 April 1892, which according to Lugard had the general support of the Catholic party, although as it turned out, only two Catholic chiefs had signed it, and these, Mgr Hirth claimed, were carefully selected as the two 'whose characters were the weakest, and who could not understand the

Kiswahili in which they were addressed' and they only signed under the pressure of 'a necessity from which it would have been useless for them to have tried to escape'.

By the agreement, the Catholic party, although the largest in the country, was given Buddu – described by Lugard as 'by far the richest province in Uganda' – although it actually comprised only about one-seventh of Buganda. Catholic missionary extension outside Buddu was subject to the permission of the Company's Resident (a distinct violation of the principle of religious liberty secured by the treaty with Mwanga, the Brussels Treaty, and Anglo-German Agreement of July 1890). No 'armed' Catholic was to leave Buddu, and the Company's writ was to run there. Although Lugard's long report of March–August 1892, states

> There is nothing in this agreement intended to be prejudicial to the interests of the Roman Catholic religion. It has been made at the express wish of the four leading Roman Catholic Chiefs lately, Kimbugwe, Sekibobo, Kago, and Tanliti. They prefer to have a separate portion of the country, to be reinstated in their former positions and they themselves have told me they prefer Buddu to the whole of Singo, Kitunga, etc.
>
> (Signed) F. D. Lugard,
> Captain Commanding.
> (And by Roman Catholic Chiefs.)[41]

and a copy of the agreement attached to Lugard's report, implies that four Catholic chiefs had signed it, the actual signed agreement gives the signatures of only two Catholic chiefs, and these Lugard admits did beg for 'an increase of territory', and later protested against the treaty as unfair, claiming that they had only signed under fear that war would recommence unless they did so.

The land settlement with the Catholics was paralleled by a 'broader settlement' with Mwanga, in a treaty of 11 April 1892, whereby he accepted Company suzerainty, its protection and flag, and agreed not to enter into treaty relations with nor grant concessions to any other power without the Company's consent. The Company's Resident was to sit in close watch on the king's actions, but was to uphold his power, honour and the display of his court. Freedom of religion and trade were guaranteed and Europeans in Uganda were to be subject to the Company in the matter of arms control and acquisition of land. Slave-trading and slave-raiding were prohibited. The cost of administering Buganda and its garrisoning was to be a direct charge on its revenues, not on the British Exchequer.

This agreement with Mwanga caused little ill-will. Not so that with the Catholics! Lugard was bitterly taxed for not carrying out his promise as regards the division of the country. He absolved himself, however, on the grounds that the Catholics had attacked the island of Kome – a Protestant stronghold – and in view of the 'startling news' that the Catholics were trafficking in arms (the Germans had recovered 60 breech-loaders from a looted caravan of the French Mission). But the attack on Kome had taken place nearly 20 days before Lugard's promise to the Catholics, and as for the trafficking in arms, Lugard himself, in issuing arms to the Protestants, had laid himself open to the same charge.

The deep anger of the Catholics in view of their conviction that Lugard had gone back on his word received support from Lugard's letter to Captain Williams, of 15 April 1892:

> Things are pretty awkward here. The Protestants have a come to loggerheads with me, and written me a most grossly insulting letter. I am afraid Ashe is at the bottom of all this; he told me, on my asking him point blank about it, that he had advised the Protestants to decline to do as I told them. I don't see any way out of this mess; they have insulted me, and decline to carry out my wishes ... I told them that I said all along that if the Roman Catholics accepted our terms quietly I wished to throw in some 'bonne bouche' at the end – either a bit more country, or an island, or a Chieftainship – what they liked. I said I was pledged to them in honour. Both you and I had spoken of a bit of Kamia's country to them. The Protestants were willing to give (as they even now say) *half* the country to bring back the King. But because they sent back the King, relying on our honour to take no advantage of them, these people wish to betray their trust.[42]

As regards the Muslims, the Protestants also 'wished to retain everything for themselves'. Thus Lugard, 'anxious to act justly to all, irrespective of creed', succeeded 'by some manoeuvring – offering them part of Unyoro, and so on, which they did not want, in getting them to accept the three small provinces of Kitunzi, Kasjuju and Katambala'. However, they refused to give up their king (Mbogo), and advanced on Kampala. Lugard with an armed force went forth and parleyed with them and they accepted Lugard's terms. On 1 June 1892, they added their signatures to the treaty between Mwanga and the Company.

Lugard's last days in Kampala were enlivened by Mwanga's caprices. Mwanga decided to change his capital from Mengo to a neighbouring hill, on the flimsy excuse that Mengo was unlucky, but more likely because it was too close to the fort. This was vetoed by Lugard. Mwanga then expressed a desire to become a Catholic, but the French priests would not have him, claiming that he had disgraced their religion. Nor were Mwanga's overtures to the Protestant Mission more successful, even though Mwanga was willing to support the Protestant cause. His religious oscillations could no longer be taken seriously.

In any case, Lugard's thoughts were now moving overseas – towards England. He was fortunate in that the arrival at Kampala, on 9 June 1892, of Captain J.R.L. Macdonald of the 'Imperial British East Africa Railway Survey'[42] provided him with the opportunity of returning to the coast with an armed escort, without 'taking a single rifle with me'. That relations between Macdonald and Lugard on their downward journey were not happy is evident from both their accounts. After his return to the coast, and when informed that Macdonald was instructed to report on the troubles in Uganda and his actions there, Lugard deposited a statement, entitled, 'The Case of Captain Macdonald, R.E.,' with the Foreign Office; to be opened only by himself, and if necessary, on Macdonald's return from Uganda.

This would suggest that Lugard was expecting an adverse report, and was ready to meet it with evidence of Macdonald's predisposition towards himself. Macdonald, on his part, stated that

> Captain Lugard asked me to conduct him and his caravan to the coast, as he was anxious to return as quickly as possible in order to represent the cause of Uganda at home. To this I agreed, but when, although we were in no sense under his order, he also asked me to detain an officer and 100 men to remain for duty in Uganda, I was obliged to refuse. However, I did the best I could. We handed over some rifles, a good deal of ammunition and what provisions and trade goods we were able to spare, to the Company's authorities. I also succeeded in getting a few Swahilis to volunteer to remain in Uganda, and thus allow some time-expired men to return to the coast.[43]

Lugard, although asking to travel under Macdonald's protection, resented being under the latter's orders, and

> He quarrelled with Macdonald to the end, for the engineer's last
> offences, in Lugard's eyes, were to interfere in Company
> administration at Kikuyu and to grudge Lugard a few rifles to
> defend his forced march to Mombasa to which, ahead of the rest,
> he now hurried.[44]

Macdonald provided 29 carriers for the transport of food for Lugard's
men (the figure would have been 50 but for heavy mortality among
Lugard's porters) and he left behind much needed Berthon boats for
fording rivers, and a number of his loads. According to Macdonald, at
one stage in eastern Busoga he had to overrule Lugard, for if he had had
his way, the survey expedition would have been involved in a full-scale
war over a supposedly murdered mail runner, who, however, later turned
up unharmed. It was a relief to them both when they parted company at
Kikuyu. No doubt, if Macdonald had known at the time that he would
be required to report on Lugard's actions in Uganda, he would have
refused to travel with him.

At Kikuyu, Macdonald heard of important mail he had missed, but
continued his journey coastwards, reaching Kibwezi on 7 September.
Here he met a large caravan bound for Uganda, with mail containing
orders directing him to return to Uganda and report on the 'true causes'
of the recent troubles there:

> On September 10th 1892, I turned my face up-country, and with
> forty porters and four Indians started my return journey to
> Uganda.[45]

Fresh orders caught up with him at Fort Smith – 'an *embarras de richesse*
– two contradictory ones'. One directed him to return to Uganda, the
other to the coast, and both were telegrams that arrived at Mombasa
within a few hours of each other. Macdonald acted on the more recent –
which recalled him to Mombasa, and 'with a glad heart continued my
way coastwards'. After marching 100 miles towards the coast he met
Bishop Tucker bound for Uganda, and from him received more recent
orders from Lord Rosebery, directing him to proceed to Uganda as
originally instructed. Macdonald again faced the weary return, up-
country:

I felt I was getting distinctly weary oscillating backwards and forwards between Kibwezi and Kikuyu. People at home had but a vague idea of the difficulties of communication in the interior of Africa, and could not have anticipated that the little delay in making up their minds meant for me an unnecessary walk of five hundred weary miles.[46]

Bishop Tucker was anxious to travel with Macdonald to Uganda but the latter felt it better that they remain apart

lest the Roman Catholic missionaries of Uganda should make capital out of such a combination. It seemed advisable that I should shun even the appearance of bias, that might have resulted from six weeks' travelling in company with their rivals of the Church Missionary Society.[47]

Meanwhile, Lugard arrived at the coast and learned that the man with whom he had been travelling, and with whom he had quarrelled, was on his way to Uganda to report on the troubles there in which he, Lugard, had been so directly concerned. Lugard's perturbation at this news is evident in his approach to Berkeley, the Company's Administrator at Mombasa, to intervene on his behalf. It was to no avail; the matter must be thrashed out. Lugard was later to claim that Eugene Wolfe, correspondent of the *Berliner Tageblatt*, sent to report on the troubles in Uganda, and who signed as witness of the evidence at Macdonald's inquiry, was a biased witness, and, throwing in a *non sequitur*, Lugard added that Wolfe, *en route* to the interior, had abandoned a sick porter. Bishop Tucker also abandoned a sick porter.

News of the troubles in Uganda first reached the outside world through the French priests who were able to get their story out by way of the lake route and through German territory. It was a strange tale which reached the French government: a religious war between Christian parties in the heart of Africa. On 8 April 1892, the French ambassador in London raised the matter with the British Foreign Office. That office was already aware that something was amiss in Uganda, for on 8 and 10 March 1892 Henry Labouchere, a leading radical MP, had raised questions in the House of Commons as to whether Lugard was a paid and active officer in the British Army, and what validity was accorded to treaties made by the IBEAC. (It was rumoured that the treaty made with Mwanga had been obtained under duress!) Should not an inquiry be held into the role of trading companies in Africa? These were pertinent questions to which no answers were readily forthcoming. During the recent debate on the Survey Vote for a Uganda Railway, some MPs demanded that Lugard's reports be laid on the table of the House. The reply of the IBEAC was not reassuring:

> I am instructed to inform you that my Directors have no direct objection to that course being adopted, provided the passages marked in red in the accompanying Reports are kept out. They treat solely of personal matters and negotiations which it is deemed undesirable to make public. The passages deleted in no way refer to the nature of the country, or bear upon the question of the railway.[47]

Until Lugard's reports were available there was only the French version to go by, and meanwhile the French government kept up its pressure, raising the question of compensation for damage done to French missionary property in Uganda. Had not the British government granted the IBEAC its charter and was not the latter thus responsible for its actions?

There was no way out but an inquiry into the matter, and on 24 June Lord Salisbury announced that Major Macdonald, then in East Africa in pursuance of the Railway Survey, would carry out this task. But it would be some months before Macdonald's report could be available, and in the meantime the French would not wait. Their pressure was unrelenting. They threatened to send an agent of their own to Uganda to make an investigation there. In the face of this new and dangerous turn of events

> the principle of making a Government liable for the acts of officials of a Chartered Company within a sphere of influence, was so vast and so novel, that I could not accept it without further reference to my colleagues ... I could not pronounce myself without the fortification of legal assistance.[48]

Rosebery sought out the learned opinion of the Lord Chancellor, Lord Herschell. The latter in careful and measured words pointed out that if the British government were to interpose to prevent such action by the French, this would be admission on their part of that responsibility with which the French had charged them. It was a neat legal twist and was not lost on Rosebery.

Lugard's arrival in England on 3 October 1892 added nothing to his reports, now in government hands, nor lessened the expectation with which Macdonald's report was awaited. Meanwhile, the Catholic cause in Uganda had been quietly taken up by the Duke of Norfolk, Earl Marshal and leading lay Catholic in the kingdom. Throughout 1892–93 Norfolk was assiduous in collecting evidence to refute Lugard's charges against the Catholics, and in pressing the Company and Rosebery for a 'full and open account of events there'. Although he failed to obtain this, Norfolk's persistent probing did much to keep the question on the boil. At last Macdonald's report, dated Kampala, 7 April 1893, was considered by a small Cabinet committee in June 1893. With its lengthy evidence and appendices it is a formidable volume to wade through. As to its impartiality? Gladstone questioned whether Macdonald was the right man for the inquiry – was he not a personal enemy of Lugard? Others, however, including Portal and missionaries both Catholic and Protestant, praised his 'clearness of judgement and impartiality'. The Reverend R.H. Walker of the CMS thought it would be a great blessing if Macdonald were appointed 'Governor of Uganda'. A note of deep commitment to the truth runs through Macdonald's report. He sedulously sought out all witnesses, and sought to put into perspective the vexatious 'mutual agreement' respecting eviction on change of religion. Macdonald could find no evidence that such an agreement existed. There was a custom to this effect, but no certainty as to its universal acceptance. Lugard had clutched at it as a way out of a dilemma into which he had been led by adroit Protestant advocates. And then he embarked on the crazy and dangerous expedition into western Uganda when he should have stayed at Kampala to sort out the problems there. On his return to Kampala he did not appear to have realized the tense situation that prevailed, and by his high-handed policy and injudicious action had precipitated civil war.

It was not difficult for Macdonald to show Lugard in an unfavourable light. The latter had improperly interfered in what was a matter of the king's prerogative, and, failing to get him to reverse his decision, had backed the Protestants in a war against the Catholics. By his issue of guns to the Protestants (Ashe of the CMS, candidly admitted that Lugard had 'served out 500 Sniders to the Protestants') and want of organization, he had lost control of the situation and precipitated the fight of 24 January. He had helped the Protestant Mission to bring its goods to safety but not the Catholics, when he knew that fighting was at hand. As to Lugard's accusations that the Roman Catholics had circulated reports of the Company's contemplated withdrawal from Uganda, it was in fact Lugard himself who first leaked out this news, despite his claim that 'he had not breathed a word of it to any living soul'. He had mentioned it to Williams and four members of the CMS. His statement, that the news of the Company's evacuation led the Catholics to adopt a defiant tone, was countered by Macdonald pointing out that, if the Catholics had meant to oust the Company, they had favourable opportunity to do so when Lugard was far away in western Uganda and Williams was left in a very weak state in Kampala. It was Macdonald's view that it was the 'plain policy' of the Protestants 'to force a crisis with the Catholics while they still could hope for the assistance of the Fort'.

Macdonald could find no evidence to substantiate Lugard's grave charge that Mgr Hirth was responsible for the king and Catholic party's refusal to make peace. Some of Lugard's charges against Mgr Hirth broke down on grounds of sheer chronological inaccuracy. It would have been physically impossible for Mgr Hirth to have been at the various places and at the times mentioned by Lugard. The charge that the Roman Catholics had constructed a fort at Rubaga – the French Mission headquarters in Kampala – was absurd; the so-called 'fort' was similar to other structures constructed by the Mission in East Africa and was 'harmless'. The charge that the Catholics had planned a war against the Protestants as early as mid-1891 was balderdash, and based on an extract from a letter written by one of the Fathers and published in a mission journal in Europe, and referred to a spiritual, not an armed crusade.

Lugard was to blame in refusing succour to the Roman Catholic Mission and in tactlessly allowing its property to be offered for sale to Protestant Baganda, even though, as he argued, this was the only way to recover it. The Catholic missionaries and Lugard were both prone to exaggeration, the former as regards their ill-treatment while prisoners at Kampala from 20 January to 2 March, and the latter in stating that he had treated them as 'honoured guests'. Following the battle at Mengo the Catholics placed themselves in the wrong in not accepting the fair and honourable terms offered by Lugard. As for the action against the Catholics after the Bulingugwe incident, this was justified on military grounds. In rounding out his report, Macdonald could see little positive result from this tragic war apart from its having abolished 'once and for all the dangerous and complicated system of land tenure and its attendant abuses'. But this had not been Lugard's goal in precipitating the war.

In a lengthy memorandum of 19 August 1893, Lugard replied to these charges. He claimed that Macdonald could not know the reasons which impelled him, Lugard, to act as he did, nor had he access to letters and correspondence between Lugard, the Missions, the chiefs and the king. And he protested strongly against a verdict so fatal to his character, which was based on a perusal of his reports which Macdonald had had leisure to collate and criticize from 'experience gained by events'. Lugard offered to place all his correspondence and his 'very full diaries' before the Cabinet Committee, even the printed proofs of his *The Rise of Our East African Empire*, then in the press, if they wanted a fuller account. He was especially bitter towards Macdonald for involving Herr Wolfe in the inquiry, for the latter had previously openly stated that the Protestants were to blame for the troubles in Uganda! He was a biased witness. Whether Lugard would have objected to Wolfe's association in the inquiry if the verdict had gone in Lugard's favour is another question. Respecting his journey to the west, this, Lugard claimed, was justified by the results obtained; and he had been impelled to undertake it because he was 'continually pressed by the Administrator to find some means of obtaining a return from the countries to cover expenses'. As to his leaving Williams in a weakened state in Kampala, Lugard considered that he had left him sufficient force. The accusation that he had interfered in the king's judicial function and in Kiganda law was irrelevant, it was rather a question of

> martial law; ... in the present disturbed state of the country it was necessary that an example should be made to check violence, which might at any moment precipitate war.[49]

As to leaving Dualla to conduct the very important negotiations, Lugard stated that his own head had been 'affected by the sun', and, anyway, Dualla was 'a most exceptional man', widely travelled – 'one of the most intelligent Orientals I have ever met'. Respecting the issue of arms, the most questionable of his actions, Lugard dealt with this in the briefest paragraph of his reply, merely stating that it did not take place until the Roman Catholics had beaten the war drums and turned out for war:

> It was necessary in order to save the weaker side from extermination, and prove to the hostile party that I meant to keep my word and support the Protestants.[50]

As to his treatment of the French Fathers after the attack on Mengo, he had offered them his own clothes and did not stop them going to Bulingugwe. He did regret his not going to see them but he could not speak French well, and felt he would be intruding; and 'circumstantial accounts I daily had of their hostile attitude' determined him not to fulfil his promises to give the Catholics more territory. In his own reports, however, Lugard claimed that it was Protestant opposition which caused him to break his word. Respecting his previous charge of a Catholic attack on Kome, he admitted that he might be wrong. As to his own military skill, Lugard waxed pompous:

> it is beyond the scope of the inquiry that Captain Macdonald should lay down an *ipse dixit* as to my conduct of the actual fighting. He is much my junior, and has hardly any war service, and that he should lay down a fiat as to whether various 'purely military measures' (undertaken by an officer senior to himself) were justified or not is contrary to the custom of the Service and I submit in no way indicated in his instructions.[51]

In a postscript to his reply to Macdonald's report, Lugard let himself go. He spoke of that false sentimentality which could make so much of the trouble between the Christian parties in Uganda, and yet overlook the disregard for human life shown 'in the dealings of many, if not most, of those who have been in Africa'. This passage was quickly picked up by the Lord Chancellor in his summing up, as irrelevant .

The Lord Chancellor, with Macdonald's report and Lugard's reply in hand, summed up his case in a brief memorandum, which, after the prolixity of Macdonald and Lugard, is a relief to turn to. It was the Lord Chancellor's view that the wise policy of Lugard, on his return from the west and finding affairs in Uganda in a critical state, was to allay excitement and danger, not aggravate them. Lugard had demanded that Mwanga reverse his decision – a high invasion of the latter's judicial prerogative – there had been other acts of lawless violence and Lugard had not thought such a strong measure necessary. Lugard stated that it was a case of martial law, but there was no state of war, thus no case for martial law. The unwise attempt to induce the king to fly the Company's flag had led to beating the war drums and a concentration of the Wafranzi (Catholic) party; and Lugard's claim that he issued arms to the Protestants because he could not allow them to be driven out of the country was ridiculous: his task was so to administer the country that no one would be driven out. Lugard in issuing arms to the Protestants had violated the Brussels Act. He had issued these arms to persons, who, in his words, were animated by the 'meanest and most rancorous jealousy and rivalry characterized by lying, theft and murder before the event'. It was the Lord Chancellor's view that Lugard had determined 'from the outset' to support the Protestants, and since he wished to leave for England at once

> he was willing or even anxious to precipitate a crisis and it may be to provoke hostilities rather than use every effort to prevent their breaking out.[52]

This was a serious charge, and Lugard was given opportunity to rebut it, but his explanations made little impression on the Cabinet committee. In a letter to his brother, Edward H. Lugard, he states that he found the Cabinet committee's questions 'distinctly hostile – apparently they have accepted Macdonald's views'. There was a touch of naivety in his parting shot: he offered to send the committee a copy of his book – the last word on the subject.

Meanwhile, the French impatiently waited for Macdonald's report to be 'weighed and considered' by the British government. But Rosebery could not make up his mind about it. The death of Portal in January 1894, shortly after returning from Uganda, had removed the key figure in the inquiry. And as regards the propriety of his involving Herr Wolfe in the inquiry, this would have to be referred back to Macdonald in Uganda. But with the Duke of Norfolk representing the Roman Catholic view with great energy, and the French government pressing vigorously for action, Rosebery, faced with the plethora of detail in Macdonald's report, the intricacies of the case and the 'ink-slinging' and 'oratorical efforts', felt that the British government was involved in 'something like a Chancery suit of the most ancient and persistent type', and 'I at any rate do not feel that we are much nearer the truth than when we first ordered Captain Macdonald to make his Report'. The inquiry might go on for months, 'perhaps some years'. But

> HMG ready as ever to show their real friendship for France, and their anxiety that no cause of complaint should arise in a territory which though not under their direct control, was at the time under a British Company, are willing as an act of comity, though not admitting any legal responsibility in the matter, to pay a certain sum towards the losses of the Roman Catholic Church in Uganda

during the outbreak.[53]

Rosebery would make such a settlement dependent on France taking action over the 'recent discreditable attacks by French officers on British Forces in West Africa and the return to Kampala by Mgr Hirth of Mwanga's nephews'. Negotiations over compensation to the French Mission were long-drawn-out and haggling. The British government was loath to admit responsibility for the Company's actions which payment of compensation would imply; the French on their part made the most of this bargaining counter. It was not until February 1898 that the matter was finally settled with the British government agreeing to pay £10,000 – one-tenth of the original sum asked by the French.

Macdonald's report was not made public until after the Second World War. Rosebery insisted on its confidential nature while negotiations were under way with France. If the reports were made public, then Lugard's reply would have to be made public, and so also the Lord Chancellor's summing up which showed Lugard's actions in a most unfavourable light, and this would strengthen the French case. Silence was the best policy, and Lugard, despite his desire for official vindication, was left to smart in private.

The question of Macdonald's report and Lugard's actions in Uganda was soon overshadowed by the greater question of the future of Uganda, which now faced the British government, in view of the IBEAC withdrawal from there on 31 March 1893. Sir Gerald Portal, Consul-General at Zanzibar, had been appointed Commissioner to inquire into the best means of dealing with Uganda after this withdrawal. Portal left Zanzibar for Uganda on 1 January 1893, and arrived at Kampala on 17 March 1893. His first impressions were most favourable: Uganda's physical features, its temperate climate and strategic position were impressive. According to Colonel Frank Rhodes, on Portal's staff, there was here a 'magnificent future market for European manufacturers'. The Baganda, according to Rhodes, were clamouring for shoes and stockings, opera glasses, etc and were daily developing 'fresh wants'. But Portal found the religious situation the most worrying. If the British withdrew, a war of extermination would follow. Yet if religious harmony could be maintained there was a wonderful field here for evangelization and the advancement of Christianity. The Baganda were a people of more intellect and civilization than any other in Central/East Africa. But there was a ring of hostility around their country. To the north lay Bunyoro, ever jealous of its southern neighbour, and there was danger that Kabarega might ally with the Mahdists against Buganda. Arabs based at Tabora in western Tanganyika and on the Upper Congo were foraying into the country to the south and west, eager to test the new and pitifully small administration in Uganda. The Manyuema were also a threat on its western boundary and required a watchful eye.

Portal, peppered with advice from Cecil Rhodes as to how to administer Uganda: 'not go wandering about the country to the mountains of the moon', found the internal situation there 'fraught with danger'.[54] Writing to his mother within a week of his arrival at Kampala, he commented 'this is a far more complicated, difficult, and disagreeable business than anyone anticipated'. Lugard's land settlement was most unsatisfactory. The Catholic party – 'by far the largest Christian party in Uganda' – was overcrowded and confined to Buddu – 'un septième ou un huitième de pays' – and was smouldering with resentment over their betrayal by Lugard. Even Ashe, of the CMS, admitted that the Protestants had received an overlarge share of the country. Mgr Hirth denounced the treaty of 5 April 1892 as not binding on the Catholic party. The Catholic chiefs who had signed it were dupes 'of insignificant position and with no authority'; they had regretted their act almost as soon as the deed was done. The Catholic party demanded restitution of their offices of state, chieftainships and privileges held before the battle of Mengo. They demanded re-partition of the country so as to give them at least as much as the Protestants. The latter, however, claimed that the Catholics contributed nothing in taxes or labour, and were illegally detaining the young princes (sons of Karema), even though Mwanga (now a Protestant) wished them to be returned to Kampala. Although Williams and Macdonald had attempted an equitable redistribution of territory and offices, they were balked by the Protestants who were prepared to defy their leader, Bishop Tucker, in the matter, and stated they would demand compensation from the IBEAC for any disturbance to Lugard's treaty. And, Portal noted,

> the Protestants are seriously uneasy, as they know that in the event of the withdrawal or non-interference of the troops at this fort, they would in all probability be thoroughly beaten and driven out of the country on the resumption of war by the Catholics.[55]

After a quiet appraisal of the situation, Portal soon saw that the existing state of affairs was highly dangerous and could not continue. The case appeared still clearer when he found that the Catholic demands for more territory were based upon promises made by responsible officers.

The Catholics had been led to expect a greater extent of territory than was comprised by Buddu alone, on the condition that they sent back the king to Kampala within a stated time. But when they returned the king they received only Buddu (with a Protestant nucleus within it), the islands of Luamba and Selima off its coast, and a small portion of Kaima – south of the Katonga River. Père Achte had appealed to Lugard as 'Le Représentant de Sa Majesté la Reine d'Angle-terre', and Lugard in reply did not disavow this appellation and spoke of the treaty as having been made 'in the name of the British'. Portal thus felt some moral obligation to carry out Lugard's unfulfilled pledge as regards the division of the country.

It was an achievement on his part to have brought Mgr Hirth and Bishop Tucker together on 7 April 1893, when all hope of an amicable settlement between the two religious parties seemed to have vanished. The agreement signed by the two bishops provided for a redistribution of territory and offices between the two parties. The Catholics were given several important offices which would admit them to a fair share in the Councils of State. They received an extension of territory nearly equal in area to the whole of Buddu which they then held, and comprising the province of Kaima, the island of Ssese and certain shambas which gave them a corridor leading from Buddu to the capital. There were to be two Katikiros (Prime Ministers) – one Catholic and one Protestant; two Majasi (Generals) – one Catholic and one Protestant; and two Gabunga (Chiefs of Canoes) – Catholic and Protestant. In return for these gains the Catholic bishop undertook to return the young princes (sons of Karema) to the capital, where they were to reside under the guardianship of the British Resident, thus removing the threat of one or other of them being proclaimed king by the Catholic party.

An understanding as to missionary extension outside Buganda to avoid religious strife was not easy to obtain. Mgr Hirth desired that northern and western Uganda be left to the Catholics. Bishop Tucker demurred. It turned out that both Missions aspired to missionary extension in western Uganda, especially in Toro. Portal, however, feared that since the people of Toro were in constant communication with the Baganda and were of a 'similarly excitable nature', fresh troubles would break out there. It was finally agreed that Bishop Tucker would refrain from sending missionaries into Toro 'for some months to come', and Protestant mission extension would take place in Busoga and towards the east. Catholic missions would work northwards or westwards into Bunyoro. This arrangement was of a temporary nature and subject to Vatican and CMS approval. The agreement as to redistribution of territory, offices and missionary extension was disappointing to the Catholics for they had hoped for greater concessions. Nevertheless, they accepted the dictum of their bishop in the matter as final. Not so the Protestants. They absolutely declined to abide by Bishop Tucker's advice, and threatened resistance even to the point of force. The cession of territory, titles of Rubuga, Katikiro and Majasi were the subject of endless dispute; Mgr Hirth could no longer guarantee the patience of his flock. Portal, on his part, showed endless tact and patience. He could have used force to carry out the need to fulfil the moral pledge made by Lugard, but he could give no guarantees for the future of Uganda owing to uncertainty as to the intentions of HMG as regards that territory. He sought spontaneous agreement with the two religious parties. This was obtained on 22 April 1893, whereby the agreement of 7 April 1893 was affirmed, with additional clauses concerning the king's sister (Rubuga); the young princes; the rules of precedence at court; and an article decreeing complete religious liberty which ended once and for all the pernicious custom of eviction from estates on change of creed.

Portal's mediatory work was completed by a meeting with Mwanga on 14 May 1893, and a treaty signed with him on 29 May 1893, under which the foreign relations of 'Uganda and its dependencies' were placed unreservedly in the hands of Her Majesty's Representative, who had also discretion to intervene in criminal cases between Mwanga's subjects if there was danger of miscarriage of justice. The assessment and collection of taxes and disposal of revenues of the country were subject to HMG's control. Mwanga bound himself to work for the abolition of the slave-trade and slavery.

With the religious question and relations with Mwanga settled and out of the way, Portal turned to other problems facing Buganda. Persistent Baganda raiding into Busoga was endangering European caravans passing through. Portal placed a force of 100 soldiers under an English officer in Busoga to repel these Baganda raids. Busoga chiefs were summoned to Entebbe (Port Alice), and a system worked out whereby they agreed to send Mwanga a payment of ivory and cattle twice yearly, in return for which Mwanga would end his raids.

In western Uganda, Portal reduced the garrison installed by Lugard at the salt lake – the latter's value had been much exaggerated. Bunyoro was the main problem, since its ruler, Kabarega, was unrelenting in his hostility towards Europeans. Bunyoro was rich in ivory, which was exchanged for powder and guns brought up from German territory through western Uganda, bypassing Buganda. With these arms Kabarega raided Toro and menaced Buganda's frontiers. The IBEAC, in a show of strength shortly before Portal's arrival, demanded from Kabarega payment of a large amount of ivory, on pain of immediate war. Kabarega challenged them to come and get it. Portal had no desire to make war on Kabarega and sought only to prevent his raiding Buganda, thus he ignored the challenge, even at the risk of seeming weak. To avoid conflict with Kabarega he arranged for the withdrawal of the Sudanese troops whom Lugard had quartered on Bunyoro's southern borders. Lugard had intended that these Sudanese should purchase their food with salt procured from the salt lakes, and should protect Kasagama against Kabarega. Instead they preyed on the surrounding country for food and booty, and left Kasagama to flee his kingdom in the face of attack from Kabarega. They flew the Egyptian flag and claimed Egyptian authority and protection when it served their purpose. There were stories of 'cruelty and rapine ... violation of women and circumcision of boys' by this off-scouring of Emin Pasha's rebellious troops and the slaves who accompanied them. They served little purpose, and a force of friendly Banyoro as a moving column under British officers, would have been more effective.

Throughout May 1893, Portal was busy cutting out lines for the military, laying down building sites and opening communications to the south of the lake. Meanwhile a host of administrative problems was laid at his door. His last duties in Uganda were attended with heavy heart. In the early morning of 27 May, his brother, Raymond, had died at Kampala after returning from Toro. The impersonal communication of this news to Rosebery gives no indication of Portal's inner suffering and stifled grief. During his last few days in Kampala he was sick with fever and exhausted in mind and body: he had been walking to and fro between Kampala and Entebbe, a distance of 22 miles, and following this up with a full day's work, presiding over meetings and endless litigation: 'Oh how these Baganda loved to talk!' After writing to his mother, Lady Charlotte Portal, in England, communicating to her the news of her son's death, he had immediately to turn to the arduous duties at hand. He never missed a day in writing up his diary, entering therein his views on Uganda and its people. He saw little to admire.

Behind the breath-taking beauty, the intense fertility and green verdure, the coolness of the evening air and the exhilarating mornings, the streams of running water and rich red soil, lay a dark and sinister shadow – the reverse side of the coin, so well described by Churchill 15 years later – as though an old-time wizard's curse had been laid over the land; a feeling of malignity, with the chill of the charnel house – the bones and skulls of the Kabaka's butchery – never far away; and that terrible Baganda smile – 'the grotesque, however terrible, is humorous in Africa'. Kampala had about it the reek of death. Thus Portal's move of his headquarters from Kampala to Entebbe 'a lovely place on the Lake', where there was also greater ease of communication with the outside world.

The Baganda were 'undoubtedly of a higher intellectual type than their neighbours ... most conservative in clinging to their traditional customs and forms of government'. And they had pride, but it was a 'pride synonymous with conceit'; and there was 'hopeless and unconquerable laziness'. They were 'almost universally untruthful ... they regard successful lying as a fine art'. They were 'narrowminded, fanatical, and innately cruel to a remarkable degree'. They would die for their creed 'but would also complacently witness wholesale massacre of every man, woman, or child who disagreed with their particular dogma'. And they had a predeliction for slaving: Portal (no enthusiast for the anti-slavery cause) was most dubious when 40 Protestant chiefs presented him with a paper stating they wished to follow 'coast custom' and free all their slaves, for this to him was 'too radical'; (and so also to Mgr Hirth) it was 'a pretext to avoid work on roads etc ... pleading as an excuse that they had no slaves'.

On 29 May 1893, Portal left Kampala for good. It speaks well of his reconciling efforts that he left no enemies behind him. In a letter to Mrg Hirth he expressed his thanks and goodwill for his co-operation in finding a fair settlement to Buganda's problems. The Epilogue, in the form of a valedictory, to his *The Mission to Uganda*, written with the haunting memory of his brother's death still in mind, expresses the hope that

> If some day on those eastern ranges a new race shall quicken into life, when peace and goodwill have supplanted internecine feuds in the child-heart of the savage, when the greed of the white has ceased to seek for profit in the damnation of the black man's body and soul, when the story of the slave-raider is only a sullen page in the past, then one would wish to dream maybe that, as they reap the harvests that are still unsown, men will speak with an almost

mythic reverence of the goodly man who came in the beginning
from the white Queen to give the country peace, and that the first
traditions of a land which has no memory yet, may gather round the
grave on Namirembe hill. (*The Mission to Uganda*, (Epilogue))[56]

Portal's work in Uganda and his recommendations as to the future
administration of that territory resulted, in 1894, in it becoming a
British protectorate. In the following year, 1895, the intervening
territory between Uganda and the Indian Ocean was also declared a
British protectorate. By the time these momentous decisions were
undertaken, the Germans, in their neighbouring territory to the south,
were busily involved in carving out a German East African colonial
empire, and it is to this subject that we shall now briefly turn.

Peters's expedition up the Tana, which might result in laying at the
feet of his Emperor a Central Equatorial Empire, received more acclaim
in Germany than in German East Africa. German officials on the spot
were too absorbed in the struggle to retain the coastline than to advance
on the interior, however much they might share in the dream of an
advance on a broad front, encompassing a vast area. The ultimate
fulfilment of this dream (so unlike that of British policy to the north) was
to require a heavy price: no wonder German graves are so widely
scattered in East Africa. Peters's eloquence and smooth tongue won over
his countrymen to a vision of a German East African Empire, even if its
attainment meant observance of the motif, 'subjugation of the barbarian'
at all costs. This was well expressed by Count Hatzfeldt, German
ambassador to London, in conversation with Euan-Smith in November
1889:

> N'est-ce pas invariablement le barbarisme qui se voit forcé de
> céder? Les Turcs comprennent ceci bien que c'est pour cela qu'ils
> sont toujours contre la civilisation. Ils se rendent compte qu'elle
> entraine leur ruine à sa suite[57]

and was given full effect in meeting the native uprisings which soon
clouded the first splendid prospect of the Germans in East Africa. In
pursuance of it they sought to subdue Mandara of Moshi, who, despite
agreements with Dr Jühlke and declaration of a German protectorate
over the Kilimanjaro region, played a double game: he entered into a
compact with the Maasai and, relying on their support, connived at the
slave trade and kept Kilimanjaro in a state of turmoil. So turbulent were

conditions there that in May 1889 the German East Africa Company was on the point of abandoning its station at Moshi. But Mandara could be played off against rival chiefs chafing under his pretensions to paramountcy. When von Wissmann in February 1890 appeared in the Moshi area with an armed force of 500 Zulus and Sudanese, Mandara was so impressed by this display of strength and German discipline that he joined them in an attack on his rival, Sina. The latter's submission had a salutary effect on other chiefs in the Kilimanjaro area, and they soon followed his example. Mandara in turn, acknowledged German authority.

His son, Meli, lacking his father's sagacity and ability, and encouraged by the defeat of Lieutenant Zelewski by the Wahehe, decided to try his chances with the Germans. He angered Carl Peters, Imperial Commissioner at Kilimanjaro, by 'dancing in scorn in front of the German fort'. Peters was out to crush 'this young fellow Meli', and cleverly drew into the affair the British by plying with spirits a weak-kneed IBEAC official; and so native spleen was turned against the British, and the CMS station at Moshi was forced to withdraw. Meli repulsed a German attack in June 1892 in which Lieutenant von Bülow was wounded, and the Germans were temporarily forced to withdraw from the Kilimanjaro area. But Meli's triumph was short-lived. In August 1893 the governor himself, Colonel von Schele, led the military against him, and after fighting off sniping attacks destroyed finally Meli's hang-out. Thus was ended the power of the Wachagga. Henceforth they gave little trouble to the Germans.

With the Kilimanjaro area under control, the Germans secured this, the most desirable part of their East African colony, by constructing a formidable bastion at Moshi, with a 'strong barbed barricade around it and ditches and ramparts revetted with stones and flanked by two small cavaliers at opposite salients', as a deterrent to the roaming Maasai and to safeguard the Pangani route. In the last of these punitive campaigns the German mailed fist was used with effect: 300 rebels were killed, including 21 chiefs, in the Kilimanjaro region, and Wachagga found colluding with the enemy were fined three rupees per head. The defence of Kilimanjaro was further secured in 1900 with the establishment of strong military stations at Arusha and Meru, and by a pact with the paramount chief Marealle. As a sign of the peace that had descended on the mountain area, a German scientific expedition, in 1900, carried out its learned studies there undisturbed.

News of German success on Kilimanjaro cowed the neighbouring restless Wasagara to the south, but farther inland, towards the great lakes, insurrections continued. German concern for the security of their caravan routes, the lifelines of the military, led them to launch campaigns against tribes in the vicinity of Ujiji and Mpwapwa in the summer of 1894. War was also made on the Maasai leader, Lenana, who was raiding near the German stations of Schirati and Ikoma. That the enemy were learning tactics from the Germans is evident in the stone fortresses that now began to appear. That at Mwanza, which was destroyed by the Germans in 1898, ended insurrection in the northern part of the German territory. To the south, however, a greater challenge was looming up, which centred on the plateau area around Iringa in the southern highlands where Mkwawa, paramount chief of the Wahehe, had arrogated great power to himself in grand fashion, and claimed tribute from far and wide. The Germans could not abide his claims. Unfortunately von Wissmann, the most able soldier, had departed from East Africa and Lieutenant von Zelewski, who was selected to teach the Wahehe a lesson, was a zealous but untried officer, and when he led an expedition against the Wahehe in August 1891 he neglected the most elementary precautions against ambush, and was the victim of a surprise attack in which he and most of his force perished. This was the most disastrous defeat to German arms in the 1890s and it left a burning desire for revenge among von Zelewski's colleagues, especially Lieutenant von Prince, detailed to guard his supply route. German power and repute were now at stake, but distractions elsewhere delayed retribution until 1894.

It came in that year in the form of a force led by the governor himself, Colonel von Schele who, with modern arms, well-planned commissariat and deployed scouts sent out well in advance, ensured that there should be no repetition of the von Zelewski disaster. Mkwawa on his part was prepared for the German assault, for his peace overtures to the Germans and offer to return the arms captured from von Zelewski had been spurned; he was thus awaiting 'the lightning' to come. By the end of October 1894, von Schele's formidable expedition had reached Mkwawa's stronghold on the Uhehe plateau. It was an impressive structure even by German standards. Its walls were bastioned and enfiladed like some medieval castle, and it had been constructed especially in anticipation of a German assault. When this commenced it stood up well to the pounding of German field guns, but was finally invested and taken, after falling to the age-old artful dodge of the scaling of its walls by the enemy. A great quantity of gunpowder and a vast herd of cattle (the loot of numerous Wahehe raids) sequestered in the fortress compounds, fell to the Germans. But Mkwawa escaped.

His wandering existence over the next few years and his continued attacks on Germans provided the spur for Lieutenant von Prince's crusade against him. The latter, now in command of the Iringa district, attempted to isolate Mkwawa from the support and supplies of his people. But Mkwawa still inspired great awe and loyalty among them, long after the substance of his power seemed to have gone: he was increasingly a legend among the Wahehe and adjacent peoples. And von Prince's first task was to consolidate German rule in the Iringa area. A station was established at Perende and a main fortress at the town of Iringa in 1896, and Mkwawa's kingdom was handed over to the rule of sub-chiefs. This done, there followed a war of attrition which gradually wore Mkwawa down. By keeping him steadily on the move and isolated from support and food, the Germans gradually sapped his strength and will. The end came in July 1898 near Pawaga, when a few hours before the Germans had caught up with him Mkwawa took his own life. The Germans decapitated the corpse and took the skull to Berlin and it was subsequently deposited at Bremen. It was returned to the Wahehe by the British governor in 1954. The war with the Wahehe left the Germans with a romantic respect for them: the 'Herrenvolk' of East Africa. With their chiefs' council disbanded and their warrior caste annihilated, the Wahehe remained henceforth constant and pacific under their new masters – even during the Maji Maji uprising of 1905–7, when fortunately for the Germans, the fort at Iringa was in their hands.

Defiance of the Germans elsewhere continued. The Yao, in the hinterland of Lindi and Mikindani, under their powerful chief, Matschemba, had made nominal submission to German rule in 1890 and 1895, but remained surly and contumacious. In June 1899, Lieutenant Wiest took the field against them. Matschemba was forced to flee into Portuguese territory, and the Germans followed up with the construction of a military post on the Ruvuma, their farthermost rampart on the south. Inland in the centre of their territory at Tabora the Wanyamwezi chief, Siki, had entrenched himself in a strong fortress whence he preyed on passing caravans, and boasted that he would rid the country of Europeans. A fruitless attack on Siki's fort by the Germans in June 1893 was followed up by a more successful one in January 1894, under Lieutenant von Prince. Siki, however, eluded capture by blowing up himself and family in the powder magazine. The Wagojo, inhabiting the region between Kilimatinde and Tabora, reputedly 'the greatest thieves and rogues in East Africa' for their preying on passing caravans, were next to receive chastisement at German hands. Following their intrigues with the Wahehe, von Prince, in early 1893, led a punitive expedition against them, and with the use of the terrifying effect of magnesium flares frightened them into desisting from their habits of depredation. A further defeat of Wagojo robber chiefs by von Reitzenstein, commander at Kilimatinde, put the seal to this. The Germans remained vigilant, however, and when, following the abandonment of their post at Ussandama there was a resurgence of Wagoja dacoity, they quickly reopened it in 1903.

In the farthermost north-west corner of their territory the Germans acquired the rich and populous area of Ruanda – a seductive and little known plateau world – by insinuating themselves in the wake of Belgian withdrawal when the latter were faced with widespread mutiny among their native troops. In early 1898, the Belgian post at Uvira on the north-western shore of Lake Tanganyika was occupied by mutinous troops, the Belgian commanding officer committed suicide and his successor fled into German territory. Belgian disaster was German opportunity. Under the pretext of retaliation for an attack on their post at Usumbura at the northern end of Lake Tanganyika, the Germans moved into Belgian territory and took over the kingdom of Ruanda, claiming that its ruler was desirous of German protection and that the Belgians had abdicated the territory; and was not the Rusizi River a natural boundary between the German and Belgian spheres? By the time the Belgians had retrieved their position, the Germans were firmly ensconced in posts on the Rusizi and Lake Kivu line. A brief show of confrontation by the Belgians soon collapsed, and they gave way. Only time brought Belgian redress. Ruanda was returned to Belgium as a mandated territory, under the League of Nations, after the First World War. The small kingdom of Urundi, a wedge of territory to the south of Ruanda, also fell into German hands when its king, Meuzi, submitted to Captain Bette in May 1899, and this was followed up by a further expedition against him in April 1903. The acquisition by the Germans of the strategic territory of Ruanda and Urundi, a populous and attractive region with a valuable source of labour between Lakes Albert and Tanganyika, raised in British minds the spectre of a German advance on the Upper Nile. The Germans at this time were probably aware that the final demarcation of the 30th meridian of eastern longitude would place them in a position to acquire the final coping-stone of a great East African empire.

German pride in their East African colony and the vigour with which native uprisings were suppressed, arose from a realization that it was the main jewel in the overseas possessions of the imperial crown. South-west Africa, at first thought to have the makings of a choice colony, had not proven so attractive as anticipated; and the Emperor himself, in 1891, had directed that all 'means available for colonial purposes should in the first instance be employed in East Africa'. But native uprisings placed a severe strain on German resources there, although suppressing them stimulated development – especially in communications. Telegraph lines were laid down, which connected Zanzibar and coastal ports and extended inland 200 miles to Mpwawa. By 1901 their extension to Ujiji was under way; the telephone was in general use for commercial and governmental purposes along the coast by the turn of the century. Harbours were improved, surveyed and buoyed, thus enabling quicker and easier handling of cargo. Following the Anglo-German Agreement of 1890 and the assigning of Zanzibar to the British sphere, Dar es Salaam became an important port. Its shoreline was tidied up and a plant erected for the washing and sorting of copal; fine new buildings – spacious and with a substantial air – appeared; and there soon arrived Lutheran and Benedictine missionaries with plans for schools, missions and hospitals. The wide and long avenues were graced with gold mohair, Cape Lilac and almond trees. Great attention was given by the Germans to hygiene – good drainage and cleanliness – the secret, so they claimed, of their low mortality rate. Unlike the squalid native quarters of Mombasa and other coast towns, those of 'Dar' and Tanga were the 'picture of tidiness and cleanliness'. When the learned Dr Koch gave a lecture to German officers at Dar es Salaam on 7 April 1891 on the insidious effects of malaria, he was listened to with attentive interest, and preventive measures, if not already taken, were quickly effected.

Dar es Salaam, the main centre and town, was a bustling place, with a population of 300 Europeans and 20,000 natives (including Indians and Arabs). Eight commercial companies, three hotels, three inns, the usual establishment of brewers, builders and butchers provided all the civilized amenities of a European town. There was a weekly newspaper and a well-equipped hospital. A continental touch was added in the fashionable practice of resorting to the hot sulphurous springs at Tanga – 'the water of which is said to contain the same healing properties as that of Aix la Chapelle'. The museum at Dar es Salaam established in 1899, with its 'plants and minerals' and its collection of 'lepidoptera and coleoptera' from East Africa signified the growing interest among scholarly-minded officials and army persons in the territory, and there were already rich holdings from East Africa in the ethnographical museum at Berlin to which that at Dar es Salaam had greatly contributed.[58] The development of the sisal industry in East Africa well illustrates this German bent for research. Dr Richard Hindorf, a 'tropicalist', introduced sisal bulbs from Florida to German East Africa in 1891. The results were most profitable; the dividends, however, accrued to the British rather than to the Germans. During and after the Second World War, when jute supplies from South-east Asia were cut off, the Tanganyika sisal industry prospered marvellously well.

Sir Arthur Hardinge, British Consul-General at Zanzibar, who visited Dar es Salaam in the mid-1890s has left his impression:

> This 'home of peace', to give it its English equivalent, was already a neatly laid out little city, with large, handsome official buildings, and a fine residence for the German Governor. A broad street known as 'Unter den Acazien', after the 'Unter den Linden' at Berlin, with a Kaiser Wilhelm's Denkmal or statue of the first Sovereign of reunited Germany at one end and a bust of the Iron Chancellor at the other, was perhaps rather too broad when exposed to the rays of a tropical sun, and it certainly contrasted in this respect with the narrow older streets of Zanzibar. In the evening, it was crowded with white uniformed German officers, civilian and military, for its European society was organized on strictly official lines, with separate mess-rooms for the 'Hohere' and 'Niedere Beamten', all of whom, as the tropical evenings grew cooler towards sunset, might be seen politely receiving and returning one another's salutes, from small tables laden with refreshing iced beverages from Hamburg.[59]

Tanga, second in importance after Dar es Salaam, was a well-laid-out town with 120 Europeans in residence; with hotels and shops and amenities such as ice and soda water; and a steam laundry which handled 6000 pieces a month for the German steamship line, not inferior to those at Dar es Salaam, and if the latter place had not already been chosen by the Sultans of Zanzibar as a 'haven of rest', it is probable that German headquarters might have centred at Tanga. Bagamoyo, on the coast, 50 miles north-west of Dar es Salaam, and former main point of entry to the interior, was now well in decline, but still an important dhow port and centre for the ivory trade, and although much overshadowed by the rise to prominence of Dar es Salaam and Tanga, the Germans had constructed a 'palace' – a governor's residence – there, so admirably and solidly built that it was still in official use under the British in the 1950s. Wilhemstahl, headquarters for Usambara district, interior from Tanga, was said to be pleasant and 'very German'. Along the southern reaches of the coast, life was much less 'Germanized', and for Europeans much more 'rough'. Kilwa and Lindi, main outlets for the grain districts behind them, were centres of trade for the Nyasa region. But even at Kilwa (Kilwa Kavinje) on the shores of a mangrove-belted, broad and shallow bay, with its air of seedy and somnolent decadence, there were by the end of the century three German and one Goanese firms and over 100 Indian shops. Kilwa Kisiwani, the *Quiloa* of the Portuguese, a low-lying and flat island of coral sand, about five miles in length, and with a deep, fine harbour landlocked on both sides, was a straggling town of a few hundred inhabitants. There was already talk of making it the terminus of a railway to Lake Nyasa – another Mombasa; but nothing came of it. Kilwa Kisiwani remained as the Germans found it, an empty ruin.

West of Kilwa, 150 miles inland, on the road to Lake Nyasa, was Mahenge, collecting centre for a developing rubber and grain export trade, from which military roads connected with 'Old Langenburg' and 'Wiedhafen' on Lake Nyasa and Iringa, headquarters of Uhehe and Usanga districts. To the north-west, in the centre of the territory, was Tabora main entrepôt, one which Carl Peters predicted would become the nodal point of a Cape-to-Cairo railway system. Although now much affected by the decline in the ivory and slave-trade it was still the home of the best porters in East Africa. There was a lively resident community there, of German, Dutch, Greek and Indian traders. Wheat, coffee, honey and hides from the surrounding districts were brought into Tabora. The large boma (fort) constructed by the Germans at Tabora signified the strategic importance they attached to the town; it was still in use as a government building in the later twentieth century. Ujiji and Bismarckburg (Kasanga) on the eastern and western shores of Lake Tanganyika were centres for German, Greek and Arab merchants trading in coffee and hides. Bismarckburg was the terminus for communications with Lake Nyasa, and a strong boma was constructed here in 1901 to secure German military control of the district. Usumbura, at the northern end of Lake Tanganyika, entry point to Urundi and Ruanda, was the site of a strong boma constructed in 1899. On the lake itself the steamship *Hedwig von Wissmann*, launched in midsummer 1900, and decked with a quick-firing Krupp gun, guarded the lake communications. At the southern end of Lake Victoria Mwanza was the trading centre for the rich cattle country of Usukuma and the Maasai plains to the eastward, and also departure point for lake communications with Uganda and for the north. Mwanza and Bukoba on the western side were the two main stations on the lake. Bukoba was the centre for the important coffee-growing industry which dated from Emin Pasha's time; flour milling was also a promising development.

Need for rapid and easy communications to deal with native uprisings had greatly speeded up road and rail-building in German East Africa. Surveys for a railway line from Tanga to Korogwe, and from Dar es Salaam to Bagamoyo, were under way by 1891/92. The Germans used the novel method of state lotteries to finance not only their anti-slave-trade campaign but also railway building and the placing of steamships on the inner lakes. The launching of a 50-ton steamer on Lake Nyasa by von Wissmann in 1891, was a master feat: by laying down a short length of railway line, 300 metres in length, and lifting this up as the sections of the dismantled steamship were pushed over it, and repeating the process, a thousand miles were traversed in a year.

So shaken were German officials by the uprisings in German East Africa in the first year of its administration that Julius von Soden, when offered the governorship in 1891, insisted on making a tour of inspection of the territory first, before accepting the post. Along with von Soden, two other appointments were made: that of Lieutenant Emil von Zelewski, Commander of the Imperial Protectorate Forces, who as already mentioned, met a tragic end; and Carl Peters, roving Commissioner, who disgraced the name of his government in his maladministration of the Kilimanjaro district. Von Soden from the start meant to curtail the military: his relations with von Wissmann were never smooth and it was a relief to them both when the latter left for Europe. The 'new men' who replaced him, however, were no less desirous of teaching the 'natives' lessons and sending military expeditions into the interior and placing armed steamers on the lakes to 'sweep' the shores with quick-firing guns. But von Soden saw this as provocative in the extreme, and destined to stir up otherwise well-disposed tribes. He had already seen what the severities of martial law had caused: the devastation of estates at the coast, the land untilled and depopulated, Arab landowners withdrawn to Zanzibar and Pemba, the old pattern of the caravan trade into the interior cracking, and with German hopes of controlling it and preventing its diversion to the Congo, Zambezi and Mombasa routes, of no avail. Von Soden's task was truly formidable.

He first sought to check the sale of firearms, and prevent 'raw' slave-trading, which was to be punished with the full rigour of the law and the penalty of death. District Commissioners were given full judicial powers over Africans, there was to be strict customs control and fair and efficient levying of duties at designated ports. But von Soden's tolerance of the institution of slavery (despite harsh laws against slave-trading) and his permitting a slave market to operate at Bagamoyo, brought severe British disapproval. He also found it difficult to work with Dr Kayser of the Foreign Office. Eugene Wolf, correspondent for the *Cologne Gazette*, ironically noted that the strain of working 'three administrations' – Governor, Company and Military – in German East Africa, was almost impossible. Von Soden's own alienation from Dr Kayser was too much for the former and he tendered his resignation in January 1895.

His successor, Hermann von Wissmann, also found the tripartite division of authority difficult to work with. More so, since the head of the military, Colonel von Trotha, had himself aspired to the governorship, and now found himself subordinated to a retired Major (von Wissmann) – a situation entirely repugnant to Prussian traditions. That von Wissmann, as governor, might be given higher brevet rank and authority over von Trotha, was unthinkable in prevailing Prussian military tradition.

Von Wissmann, possibly from earlier experience in East Africa, was imbued with a contemptuous disregard for the Arabs which he did not conceal. Although on good terms with the British consular agent at Zanzibar, he shocked the latter and left him with the impression that von Wissmann was less than a 'gentleman and Governor' in denouncing the Arabs as enemies of the human race and as 'stupid oxen'. In habits of work, lack of efficiency and personal hygiene, the Arabs were worlds apart from the Germans, and their attitude of 'Inshallah' (leave it to God!) was diametrically opposed to the stress and action of the German mind. Impatience of real or imagined Arab derelictions was an important factor in wearing down von Wissmann in the day-to-day administration of a territory where the Arab and Swahili way of life predominated. And this, compounded with difficulties in working with the divided aims of government and his own failing health, led to his retirement in 1896.

The appointment of Colonel Eduard von Liebert, as successor to von Wissmann as governor, marked the transition from the military to the era of commerce and trade. Although a military man himself, von

Liebert was out to keep down expenses, for the high cost of the recent military campaigns was still much in his mind. The suppression of native uprisings had opened up further areas to German settlement, and by 1896 coffee plantations of the German East Africa Company in the Handeni hills and Usumbura highlands were flourishing, and in the same region half a dozen German companies were experimenting with sisal and vanilla. Scientific-minded subcommittees of the *Deutsche Kolonialgesellschaft* were urging German settlement in East Africa, but the hit-and-miss method, the staking out of broad acres which characterized British colonization, as in Kenya, was to be avoided. German methodology and science could do better than this. At a time when Eliot, Commissioner for the East Africa Protectorate, had difficulty in obtaining a grant of £120 to encourage dairy farming, the Germans were instituting (in 1901) a full-fledged agricultural research centre at Amani in the 'Usumbura foothills, under the directorship of Dr Franz Stuhlmann. The use of steam tractors in German East Africa antedated that in British East Africa by some ten years. The practice of the German administration of pioneering plantations and then selling them as going concerns on the whole was successful. Five of the largest and best plantations in the Kilimanjaro region, in private hands by 1900, had been started as government concerns in 1897.

Only in obtaining an adequate labour supply were the Germans less successful than the British. As early as 1887 they had resorted to recruiting coolie labour from Singapore for the Usumbura region, and when Joseph Chamberlain, British Colonial Secretary, in 1886 refused permission for further recruitment from this source, on the grounds of German ill-treatment of this immigrant labour, resort was had to China and some hundreds of Chinese were imported for the Usumbura Coffee Plantation Company by the end of the century. To conserve the labour supply in their territory the Germans forbade recruitment of Wanyamwezi for service outside the country, and increasingly diverted the Wanyamwezi to work on government projects such as the Tanga railway line. On the whole, the Germans never successfully solved the problem of obtaining a sufficient supply of labour. They rebutted the charge that this arose from German brutality towards labourers, claiming it to be attributable to the scanty population in their territory and the disinclination of Africans to take up steady work.

Under a decree of 12 November 1897 regulating labour contracts, labourers were to have four holidays per month, and could not be discharged except for breach of contract. A hut tax introduced into

German East Africa in April 1898, varying from three to 12 rupees depending on rural or urban residence, and payable in cash (except for groundnuts, coconuts and sesame) had the effect of forcing natives to labour for wages. In the first year of its introduction, hut tax yielded nearly £20,000, and between April 1899 and April 1900 it brought in £31,856. Its collection in the Kilimanjaro region caused a riot, and the executions in reprisal for this led to von Liebert's recall in March 1901. Legal restrictions on shifting cultivation, maintained even during the severe drought and rinderpest plague of 1897-99, and laws against wasteful use of land, were all directed to the same end – to ensure a supply of labour for German plantations.

Control over land was also sought by the Germans. Under ordinances of September 1891 and November 1895 all land was declared Crown Land, excepting the Sultan of Zanzibar's estates at Dar es Salaam – bought out by the German government in 1897; the coastal strip; areas held by the German East Africa Company under the *Schutzbriefgebiet* of 1885; and land in active use. A decree of December 1896 set up Land Commissions and instituted Land Books for determining and registering land claims in each district. The Land Books were a veritable Domesday Book of their kind and collectively provide a valuable source of information on land use in the German territory. Land regulations were finally consolidated by an Ordinance of 1902, in the same year as the Crown Lands Ordinance in the British territory to the north. Land terms offered by the German government were particularly attractive to German settlers. Colonists with capital of £150 could ordinarily purchase estates of from 240 to 500 acres at ten pence an acre, although in more remote districts, such as Iringa, it was as low as four pence an acre. A lessee could convert leasehold to freehold by fulfilling easy conditions depending on the amount of leasehold land brought under cultivation. There were generous grants to retired servicemen in 1910: if they had served ten years they could purchase land at half-price. It was an attractive proposition, for a small pig farm in the Kilimanjaro area could produce £200 a year. Following the opening up of large tracts of land by the Usumbura railway and a trigonometrical survey of Usumbura and Kilimanjaro districts in 1900, 32 plantations – mostly sisal – were taken up in this region. The fine network of roads, well-bridged rivers and plans under way for light field railways in the Usumbura/Kilimanjaro region, were noted by Mr Percival, an English official sent there by the British East African administration to 'spy' on German development and gain some ideas. The lushness of the

Kilimanjaro area and the profitable nature of German farming so impressed Percival that he could not but rue that England had missed the opportunity to gain Kilimanjaro.

This choice area continued to attract settlers at such a rate that native rights to land were seriously affected, and although partially protected by German attempts to restrict alienation of land to Europeans, were not decisively dealt with until the British took over the territory. German plantation development elsewhere in their territory was not as intensive as in the Kilimanjaro area, except at Pangani where the Pangani Company had 5000 acres under sugar cultivation and had erected a sugar manufactory by 1899-1900.[60]

By the end of the nineteenth century the Germans had got the measure of their territory: its cartographical image was clear and now firmly fixed; its limitations and potentialities were now evident; there were here no vague corners of empire to police, no unwieldy troublesome frontiers to perplex and burden the official mind. Unlike the British territory to the north, where northern and north-western frontiers shaded into a vast undefined no man's land, the boundaries of German East Africa were clearly demarcated, and there were no troublesome neighbouring territories under European administration.

Having weathered the troubles of the 1890s, German East Africa seemed launched on a propitious course. The arrival of Count Adolf von Goetzen, who succeeded von Liebert as governor, in March 1901, marked a stage in its development comparable to that of the British East Africa Protectorate (Kenya) under Sir Charles Eliot, who was commissioner from December 1900, and in Uganda where Sir Harry Johnston had arrived in 1899 and introduced a new era. Like Eliot and Johnston, von Goetzen directed his energies to the task of developing the economy of his territory and seeking out new sources of revenue, rather than carrying out military forays. The collection of taxes was more important than costly military exploits in the interior. Von Goetzen remarked to Eliot in 1902, that things were looking up for German East Africa: this marked a new optimism. The Germans appeared to have served their apprenticeship in colony-making.

7· Demise of the IBEAC

The Uganda affair shook the IBEAC to its foundations, but it was but one of the many troubles which beset it at this time. The Company from its earliest stages had been subject to criticism from British officials for its failure to develop trade and to open up East Africa. Euan-Smith had urged the Company to take advantage of German troubles during the 1888/89 blockade of the coast and attract trade to the British sphere. At Tabora ivory was piling up; it had no outlet through the German sphere, and thousands of frasilahs of ivory would have found their way to Mombasa if the IBEAC had encouraged traders to bring it there. Euan-Smith lectured the Company on how it should organize its business. It should firmly establish its headquarters at Mombasa, set up a judicial court there, recruit Indian troops as the nucleus of a reliable military force, and it should establish a good vernacular school at Mombasa such as the Germans had done at Dar es Salaam. The Company should dig wells along its caravan routes in the interior and securely guard them. Predators, such as the Maasai, should be taught to respect the Company's power, and this would ensure safe passage through the Company's territory.

Throughout the late summer of 1889 Portal, acting Consul-General at Zanzibar, continued to list the Company's derelictions: its efforts to recruit forces from India and Egypt having been blocked by the Indian government and Evelyn Baring, it had sought to recruit from the Sultan's Guard, thus giving umbrage to the Sultan; it had failed to provide trained legal officers for its posts along the coast where litigation was rife between Asian, Arab and Swahili; it had poached on the Sultan's preserve by sending its steamer, *Juba*, to trade at the Benadir ports and thus enter into rivalry with the Sultan's steamer.

The Company, in the face of this criticism, recited a list of its achievements. Two steamers were employed along the coast and a stern-wheeler had been sent up the Tana; negotiations were under way for two steamers to be placed on Lake Victoria; material for 150 miles of telegraph line had been landed at Mombasa and was to be erected along the coast; 30 miles of light railway had been landed at Mombasa; at Mombasa the Company was building wharves; the Company had sent two large caravans and many small expeditions into the interior at a total cost of £20,000; it had established stations *en route* to Uganda. It had had to face the problem of implementing anti-slave-trade decrees, an eventuality never envisaged when it took up its charter. The General Act of the Brussels Conference in 1890 had authorized governments to delegate their responsibility in putting down the slave-trade to chartered companies. But the IBEAC claimed it had not the resources to undertake this, and that it received no government subsidies for the purpose. Even so its work for the abolition of the slave-trade was not inconsiderable: it had checked the slave-trade by opening up the country, and had secured the freedom of 4000 slaves over a two-year period, which compared most favourably with the 200 slaves annually liberated by the British anti-slave-trade patrol at sea. But to implement the major anti-slave-trade decree of 1 August 1890 was a different matter – it would shake the Company's control, for the Arabs believed that the decree emanated from the Company and vowed vengeance on it in return. Another major blow came with the government announcement in July 1891, that it would not underwrite the Company's proposed railway to the lake but would only support a survey vote. The Company was so disappointed over this that it gave notice, in August 1891, of its withdrawal from Uganda.

Thus, failure of the expected guarantee for a railway, rapid expansion and expense forced on it by the rivalry of German adventurers and the German Company who, unlike the IBEAC, had support of their government (as had also the Italian Company (operating north of the Juba), the South Africa Company, Portuguese and Belgian Companies), all left the IBEAC with no alternative but to withdraw from Uganda to the east, as far as Kikuyu.

Portal, in the face of this sad litany, remained unmoved. He suspected an ulterior motive behind the Company's dolorous tale. They were building up a case. The idea that their entire interests in East Africa might be bought out by the British government seems to have been in the minds of the directors by early 1892, and was a tantalizing bait. The conversion of Zanzibar into a free port on 1 February 1892 and the placing of the Sultan's dominions (including the coastal strip administered by the Company) in the free-trade zone laid down by the

Berlin Conference of 1884–85, prevented the Company (so it claimed) from collecting much needed revenue – the directors conveniently overlooked the fact that they had been well aware of the Sultan's intention of acceding to the free-trade zone principle from the first, and had assented to it. As the Sultan's 'vakeel', and administering authority in his name, in the coastal strip, the Company must now implement this principle. The reality of the loss they now suffered stung the directors into ranking this grievance high in their list of woes.

Thus, cramped by want of money, deriving scarcely any revenue from trade and faced with an ever-increasing administrative cost, it is little wonder that the idea of being bought out by government became an increasingly attractive proposition. This soon tended to impair the Company's sense of responsibility. Cheapness would come before efficiency at a time when the Company was building up its case for compensation. This would run as follows: the Company had been compelled by the 'exigencies of the situation in East Africa', by the national rivalry prevailing in the early part of 1890 and by national sentiment at home – in the press and in correspondence with government – to press forward and secure for Great Britain the regions of the interior. Salisbury, however, was unperturbed by this reasoning, and was apparently quite content to allow the Company to withdraw. He was counting on the railway to give Britain control over Uganda.

In August 1892 Salisbury's government gave way to Gladstone's last Cabinet. The new government had to decide promptly on the question of Uganda's future. The Company was unable to hold the country and, failing government intervention, Uganda would be lost. The new Foreign Secretary, Lord Rosebery, a Whig aristocrat and Liberal imperialist, did not doubt the wisdom of retaining Uganda. He had been influenced by a memorandum submitted in August 1892 by Major Wingate of the Egyptian Army, which had shown the adverse effect on Egypt which would follow a British withdrawal from Uganda, and had warned that the French might occupy Equatoria if Britain withdrew. On 20 September 1892 Rosebery circulated to the Cabinet a memorandum prepared by Sir Percy Anderson. According to Harcourt it was 'in the highest jingo tune, advocating the annexation of the whole country up the Albert Lake with a view to the "reconquest" of the Sudan via the Upper Nile'.

Thus the question of Uganda must be decided quickly in view of the imminent withdrawal of the Company. Within the Cabinet, however, 'Little Englanders' were opposed to any extension of British imperial commitments. The strongest exponents of this view were Gladstone, the Prime Minister, and Sir Wllliam Harcourt, Chancellor of the Exchequer. The latter was especially vehement in his denunciation of 'prancing proconsuls' such as Captain Lugard, who threatened 'all sorts of horrors' if Uganda were not occupied, and Bishop Tucker who 'swears he will remain at his post and die'. 'Every bogey is invoked to involve us in this horrible quagmire, which will be as bad as Khartoum.' Harcourt believed that the evacuation of Egypt was an honourable undertaking to which Britain was solemnly committed, and that to take over Uganda and seek control of the Nile Valley, was sheer folly. He instanced Gibbon's comments on the 'moderation of Augustus' and the first two centuries of the 'greatest and wisest Empire that ever existed', when the cardinal principle was the non-extension of empire; 'whenever it was departed from they came to grief'. Gladstone and Harcourt were determined to expose 'the true motives' of these jingoes for an 'equatorial Empire'. With such opposite views within its own ranks Cabinet unanimity was unlikely, and when it met on 30 September 1892 Harcourt quickly suggested that the Uganda issue should be shelved for three months: an agreeable alternative to the possible rupture and break-up of the Cabinet. On the other hand, the government announced that it was prepared to bear the cost of the continued occupation of Uganda by the Company until 31 March 1893. This offer was immediately accepted by the Company.

The three months' prolongation of the question was a godsend to Rosebery. Lugard arrived on 3 October and, immediately resigning from the Company, launched an intensive campaign for the retention of Uganda. Within a week of his arrival a long missive appeared in *The Times* – repeating old arguments – the geographical and strategical importance of Uganda, its commercial value and the great need to uphold British prestige. Lugard mixed freely with persons of consequence, Rosebery, Stanley and other 'pro-Ugandans'; and while on the 'oratorical warpath', did much to sway events. 'I think we have cause to anticipate that Uganda will not be abandoned by Government.' Delegations from the Church Missionary Society and the Anti-Slavery Society also pressed the government and were active in awakening public interest in the 'Uganda Question'. Of some 174 memorials and protests between October and December 1892, 101 were from religious bodies. They argued that the slave-trade would revive, and that renewed civil war and massacre of Christians would follow a withdrawal from Uganda. Cecil Rhodes, who happened to be in England in October 1892, also entered the campaign. Uganda was essential to his Cape-to-Cairo railway and telegraph plans. The Sudan, according to Rhodes, could be recovered from Uganda with some '2,000 Englishmen'. There were loafing about Piccadilly any number of younger sons, briefless barristers, impecunious clerks and the like, who would jump at the chance of 'exchanging a life of indigent monotony for gunpowder and glory'. Rhodes had offered to administer the Bechuanaland protectorate for £40,000 per annum. He now offered to administer Uganda as a province of the South Africa Company for a mere £24,000 a year whereas the British East Africa Company had asked £50,000. Rhodes's proposal, like that of Leopold's, to take over Uganda and Unyoro and administer them for Britain, was of too 'great novelty and singularity' for Queen Victoria to consider seriously. It would have meant handing over Uganda from one chartered company to another – to a one-man company under Rhodes – and it would mean cutting off Uganda from the coast, and all trade would thence pass southward over the lakes. Nevertheless, Rhodes's offer had a stirring effect. Harcourt admired his hard sense and knowledge of affairs – even Jingoism is tolerable when it is done on the cheap.

The campaign for the retention of Uganda had its effect. On 7 December 1892 it was announced that Portal would proceed to Uganda to report on 'the best means of dealing with the country, whether through Zanzibar or otherwise'. On 17 November 1892, Mackinnon, in an interview with Rosebery, argued that the Company should be recouped for its expenditure on Uganda, estimated at £200,000, and for 'Imperial purposes undertaken at the instigation of the late Government'. Mackinnon's threat that the Company if ill-treated might find it necessary to make over its treaties to some foreign power, brought the quick reply that 'Treaties could not be handed over like bank-notes': Rosebery declined 'even to discuss such a hypothesis'. Mackinnon then proceeded to claim that the late government had promised the Company rights of jurisdiction over its concession territory. But when Rosebery reached forward his hand to touch the bell to summon Sir Percy Anderson to testify on this matter, Mackinnon begged him not to do so. Finally, Mackinnon tentatively revealed that he was of the same view as Sir John Kirk that the Company should be bought out. Rosebery, with tongue in cheek, stated that he fancied that the Company would be disappointed if they expected to be bought out. Mackinnon then said that Kirk had put the amount at £450,000 to £500,000. Rosebery ventured that there was little prospect of the Company getting this, and that the matter was not entirely one between the British government and the Company, but also one between Zanzibar and the Company.

According to Rosebery, Sir William Mackinnon during this interview 'so lightly bounded from the position of a philanthropist to that of a financier that it was extremely difficult to appreciate what his real position was'. Mackinnon harped on the fact that he would be 70 on 31 of March – the day fixed for the Company's withdrawal from Uganda – and therefore on this talismanic day his work was done. He cared nothing for the loss of his money. But when Rosebery praised this philosophy, Mackinnon hastened to add that there was a shareholder who was not so easily satisfied – 'the proverbial concealed acting partner of financial firms'. And Mackinnon complained bitterly of one of the directors, Lord Brassey, who had written an injudicious letter to *The Times* undermining the Company's case for compensation, and, wretched man that he was, had only paid for 3000 of the 10,000 shares he had subscribed to, leaving Mackinnon saddled with the remainder at 'half-price'.

Mackinnon no doubt acquitted himself poorly at this interview. His arguments that government had forced the Company into commitments in the interior of East Africa were rejected outright by Sir Percy Anderson. There was ample written evidence in the Foreign Office to show that the initiative had come from the Company. It had been Sir William Mackinnon's ruling idea to join hands with Rhodes and so realize the project of a continuous British sphere from the Cape to the Nile. Mackinnon could not adduce any evidence to support the assertion that the Company were spurred into Uganda by the Foreign Office. When they, the Company, went there they had been reminded that under Articles 2 and 3 of their charter no territory would be recognized as under their administration until they could produce a treaty and obtain its requisite sanction from the Foreign Office.

The day following Mackinnon's interview with Rosebery the directors, their spirits now dampened by lowered prospects of a lucrative sell-out, saw an alternative vista opening up. The imperial guarantee financing the IBEAC occupation of Uganda to 31 March 1893 might be extended indefinitely. The Company thus offered to administer 'Uganda and the immediate territories for a payment of £50,000 a year for three years'. This proposition was rejected totally and completely by the Foreign Office: 'If the Company should remain for three years they would remain for ever at the cost of Her Majesty's government ... from all points of view it (the Company) is best to be rid of.'

By the end of 1892 the full story of the Company's maladministration, details of the Uganda episode and Lugard's role there, were coming in. Macdonald's railway survey report was now available and showed that the cost of the railway was far beyond the capacity of the Company. Portal, at Zanzibar, even before he was directed to proceed to Uganda, was most critical of the Company. In his view it should cease to be an administrative body, and should continue only as a trading corporation. Portal recommended that the whole mainland sphere along with Uganda should be made part of the Zanzibar protectorate, and administered by three commissioners: one for Uganda, one for the region between Uganda and the coast and one for Witu and up to the Juba; and they all should be subject to the British consul-general at Zanzibar.

Portal left Zanzibar for Uganda on 1 January 1893, and made record time, reaching the Nile on 12 March. His statement, made before leaving the coast with 400 porters and a planned timetable, that he expected to cross the Nile on 13 March 1893, was quickly picked up by the IBEAC. It pointed out that Portal's rapid march was only possible as the result of the good communications established by the Company.

Portal's adverse criticsim of the Company's administration was expressed in a series of letters to the Foreign Office while on his way inland to Uganda. His strictures were severe. During the five years 'they had been in East Africa they had done absolutely nothing to make roads, improve communication, or organize any sort of transport ... yet on these things hang the whole future of the country'. The Company published maps and made fine talk of their 'stations'; the latter, however, on examination were mere miserable habitations. The Sabaki stations had been abandoned and were in ruins; that at Tsava was 'a miserable little stockade, in charge of a Goanese half-breed boy'; the Nzoi station was 'a thatched hut 10 feet long, inhabited solely by a decrepit porter on the magnificent salary of 15 rupees per month'. At Kikuyu the European in charge looted and raided the surrounding country; and a Mr Leith in the Company's employ was guilty of 'all sorts of iniquities, including rape'. In Busoga he noted evidence of a punitive expedition conducted by officers of the IBEAC. Several villages had been burnt and a quantity of stock carried off. As he approached the Nile the hospitality and friendliness waned and suspicion increased. Portal learnt that this district had been visited the previous year by a hostile expedition of IBEAC troops under Captain Williams and, fortified by rapacious Baganda warriors, they had shaken off all control of the English officers on entering Busoga and embarked on an orgy of raiding.

Portal was convinced that there could be no progress in East Africa so long as the IBEAC, as at present constituted and retaining its charter and political power, remained on the scene. After five years' trial they had failed to fulfil any of the conditions of their charter, and Portal maintained they had forfeited the right to retain it. Portal also felt that the Company had exaggerated the potentiality of East Africa for European settlement. Hiw own view of East African attractions in this respect was very jaundiced. Apart from the stretch between Machakos and Kikuyu, the remainder was not worth occupying –

Since one day's march out of Kikuyu we have toiled and tramped for 170 miles over burnt, brown, arid plains and hills, absolutely desolate and uninhabited except by a few roving parties, of Masai whom we met with several thousand head of newly-looted cattle, near Lake Naivasha.[1]

Portal's impressions on entering Uganda after crossing the bleak Mau summit were more favourable, although he still did not see East Africa as an area for European settlement. Arriving in Kavirondo in eastern Uganda, he was impressed by its dense population, fertile country and abundance of food. It was in marked contrast to the country farther east, with fields of corn, potatoes and beans, which farther west were replaced by the 'extensive and well-kept plantations of bananas' of the Baganda. In Buganda he met a people 'more refined and intelligent than their neighbours': 'they clothe themselves, and make good broad roads and thoroughly understand bridging their swamps'. Iron was smelted and worked in roadside smithies, and here also food was plentiful. Uganda had high potential; it was the hub of a vast water system drawing trade from a wide region. Yet in developing it everything would hinge on transport to the coast.

During his stay in Uganda, from early March to end of May 1893, Portal was busily occupied with settlement of religious disputes, administrative details and the drawing up of his report on the future of Uganda. He had scarcely left Uganda when a rising of the Muslim party there threatened to bring about his recall. But the Sudanese remained loyal, and their seditious leader, Selim Bey, was deported to the coast, dying *en route* at Naivasha in August 1893. Portal, during his return to the coast, by way of Mount Kenya and the Tana River, did not see anything to make him change his mind about this portion of East Africa – all was 'desolate, rocky, thorn bush country', and the Tana River with its many rapids offered no easy access to the interior. The wonder is that Portal, with his low opinion of East Africa, recommended the retention of Uganda.

The Uganda issue meanwhile had become of very great importance in the development of British imperial policy, and it marked a split in the Liberal Party. When Parliament reassembled in February 1893, H. Labouchere, a leading radical Liberal MP and editor of the influential journal *Truth,* joined Harcourt, Morley and Gladstone in the anti-imperialist ranks, and during February and March they attacked both Rosebery and Lugard. The latter was defended in Parliament by Burdett-Coutts and Lord Ullswater, both with a vested interest in imperialism, as shareholders in the IBEAC. Debates in the House were replied to by Lugard in letters to *The Times,* and he personally met Harcourt and Labouchere but could not shake their views on the Uganda question. Lugard's book, *The Rise of Our East African Empire,* which appeared in November 1893, was timely, and was extensively reviewed. Miss Flora Shaw (Lugard's future wife), *The Times* reviewer, described it as 'the most important contribution that has yet been made to the history of East Africa with something of the grandeur of a modern epic'. It was an able book, subordinating polemical arguments to the grand theme of Britain's imperial responsibilities, and it cast Lugard in a role, no longer that of mere junior novice, but as qualified proconsul of empire. Lugard's entry into the society of the distinguished was now assured, and he met Lord Salisbury and Mr Balfour.

Portal arrived back in England on 27 November 1893, and visited Rosebery the same day, informing him that he was going to the country for two or three days to ponder over and finish his report. Rosebery, referring to the advance report which had arrived in August, stated: 'Hitherto I have not touched it with the tongs.' In the mean time the IBEAC requested that, if Portal's final report reflected prejudicially on the Company work, they might be given an opportunity to reply. Following Portal's arrival however, another long delay ensued, leaving the directors in a further state of anxiety. Gladstone's comment in the House of Commons on 27 December that he could not say when the subject would be in a sufficient state of 'ripeness' to be laid before the House did little to allay the perturbation of the directors. The government seemed to take secret satisfaction out of these delaying tactics, and the Company claimed that the Germans were taking advantage of them to attract trade to their sphere.

The directors of the IBEAC were increasingly apprehensive. Mr (later

Sir Rennell) Rodd, seconded from the Agency at Cairo, as acting consul in place of Portal, at Zanzibar, was most bitter over the exclusive privilege granted to the Company to establish a State Bank in Zanzibar, and its monopoly of issue of banknotes and so on for 50 years. The Company had never taken up the concession, although other banks were eager to come in under more advantageous terms for Zanzibar, and were prevented from doing so. The Company tried to sell this banknote concession, which had cost them nothing, to the Zanzibar government for £10,000. Rodd, angrily, accused the Company of 'doing' the Sultan. The Company even lost out on its silver coinage – prized later as collectors' pieces. During 1892 and 1893 the Company sought to free itself from commitments to the Sultan by buying up the rent due him, in the way the Germans had done, by three or four years' outright purchase at a radical discount. It also tried to get the Sultan to repurchase the coastal concession and financially assist the Company on the mainland: 'It makes us very savage out here, and Euan-Smith does not seem to have made any reservations of any kind, bad luck to him.'

Rodd reacted strongly against Foreign Office proposals to compensate the Company 'for retiring from a bargain which, though it was wholly of their own making, they had found unsuccessful'. In June 1893 the Company put forward a proposal to the Foreign Office that, although its expenditure in East Africa had been £500,000, it would be satisfied with £442,550 (£180,000 for the coastal concession and 10s.6d, in the pound for the total capital expended). Months went by without a reply and the Company was involved in a problem almost as worrying as that it had faced over Uganda in the previous year.

Under the Anglo-German Agreement of 1 July 1890 which had placed the northern boundary of the British sphere of influence at the Juba River, Germany had transferred her so-called protectorate of Witu to Britain. Before a British protectorate could be declared over the area, a party of Germans was massacred at Witu. Germany held Britain responsible for this and pressed her to seek redress for the killing of Germans. A punitive expedition, under Admiral Fremantle, which was sent to Witu forced its ruler, Fumo Bakari, to flee to nearby forests of Pumwani, from whence he waged a guerrilla war against his attackers. It was at this juncture that the IBEAC took over the administration of Witu. They faced a difficult situation: Fumo Bakari was on the run with a price of 10,000 rupees on his head, there was a sullen population and martial law was in effect in the area. After a brief and unfortunate experience with Bwana Sheh, a half-witted brother of Fumo Bakari, as

Sultan, the mantle fell on another brother, Fumo Omari, with whom the Company concluded a treaty. But even the annual subsidy paid to him by the Company would not lure Fumo Omari out of his forest stronghold to Witu, where he would be under Company surveillance. Fumo Omari remained in his lair and became a scourge to the surrounding district, poisoning the water-holes of his enemies and with his armed followers harassing the neighbourhood. In 1893 the Company was forced to call in government assistance against him. HMS *Philomel* was sent to Lamu, and light field guns breached Fumo's forest stockade, forcing his surrender. But no sooner had the British force withdrawn than he renewed his defiance. In addition to Fumo's contumacy, the Company was faced with a multitude of other woes: the recent and disastrous war in Uganda; Macdonald's censure of its activities in that territory; the Denhardt brothers' land claims at Witu; the accusation of humanitarians at home that the Company was dilatory in the anti-slavery cause, and then, most untoward of all, the strange aberration of the 'Freelanders' episode in the summer of 1893.

The Company, hoping to frighten government into action and a quick settlement of its claims, raised the spectre of the return of Muslim slavery at Witu in the wake of the Company's withdrawal from there (which it knew would bring strong protest from the Anti-Slavery society) and which it announced would take place at the end of July 1893, although it would still retain control at Kismayu. Following the Company's withdrawal, Rodd at Zanzibar despatched Generals Hatch and Mathew to dislodge Fumo Omari. His forest strongholds were invested with vigour and effect by field guns and rockets, and Fumo Omari was forced to flee. Rodd, who was present at this military engagement, now had opportunity to assess the worth of the district. It was of considerable fertility and, with adequate water supply, the marshy districts were suitable for rice-growing, and the flat terrain was adaptable to the use of broad-wheeled bullock carts and narrow-gauge trolley lines. Witu might become the central market town for the surrounding villages. The Church Missions in the area were more quick than was the Company to see the possibilities of the Witu district. The Neukirchen Mission Society had placed a naphtha screw-boat on the Tana River, the United Free Churches Mission established at Golbanti, near Ngao, in 1886, was in touch with nearby forest towns; and the newly arrived American Swedish Mission displayed great energy in establishing its station. IBEAC officials individually were not to blame for the Company's sloth. Bird-Thompson, an official in its employ, pensively remarked on 'the mess the Company has got itself into'.

Meanwhile in England, the Cabinet awaited Portal's final report. It already had those reports Portal had sent home in the spring of 1893, wherein he spoke of the good trade prospects in East Africa and of Uganda's strategic importance. The Christmas recess of 1893 intervened. Then, on 25 January 1894, came news of Portal's death from a virus infection contracted while he was in East Africa. Another delay ensued. It was not until April 1894 that Portal's final report, dated from Zanzibar 1 November 1893, was made public.

The Company, anticipating a hostile report from Portal in view of his previous outspoken comments about its activities in East Africa, prepared its case. It referred to Portal's misunderstanding and incomplete possession of the facts. But this was a difficult line to pursue in view of Portal's known integrity and uprightness, which were beyond dispute. Portal was universally respected. The Company then queried the authenticity of his report – suggesting that it might have been tampered with by someone in the Foreign Office during the interval between Portal's death and publication of the report. Portal had remained in Uganda until 30 May 1893, and an entry in the Portal Papers for 18 May reads 'finished final report'. This was the report, dated 24 May 1893, which was sent off immediately and received in London on 25 August 1893.[2] It is referred to by Anderson on 30 August and by Grey in the House of Commons on 4 September 1893. Portal specifically refers to it as a report which 'will be sufficient to assist your Lordship to form a judgment as to the value of the solution of this most difficult and complicated Uganda question which I shall have the honour to submit in a subsequent despach'. This subsequent despatch, Portal's final report, dated Zanzibar, 1 November 1893, was received in London on 6 December 1893, and it dealt with the overall question of the future of Uganda and the territory between it and the coast. This was the report ultimately made public by government. In it Portal called attention to Uganda's 'strategical position', which was

of great natural importance, dominating the northern and western shores of Lake Victoria, holding almost the only access to Lakes Albert and Albert Edward, and controlling the headwaters of the Nile ... the natural key to the whole of the Nile Valley and the richest parts of Central Africa.

Failure to hold it would result in the loss of 'the whole of that vast territory reserved by the Anglo–German Convention for the sphere of British influence' and it would most likely fall under foreign control which would then

> inevitably extend, not only over Uganda and its immediate dependencies, but would embrace all the neighbouring countries, the great lakes, the Nile Valley, and the natural highways of the interior.[3]

During the early months of 1894 the report was considered by Lord Rosebery and a committee under Sir Percy Anderson. Portal's arguments seemed unassailable. Britain was committed to the retention of Uganda on the grounds of philanthropy, strategy and honour (for the Company's treaties had left an impression with the people of Uganda that they were under British protection). A British withdrawal from Uganda would be followed by the entry of Islam from the north, or some other alien power, and the slave-trade would immediately revive. In the face of rivalry from France, Germany and the Congo State, Britain must maintain her position in East Africa. Portal considered whether Uganda might be administered through the Sultan of Zanzibar, who would act as Britain's 'tenant', but this would mean 'replacing the Cross by the Crescent', and would be difficult to justify in view of previous minimizing of the Sultan's claims to the mainland. Portal came round to the view that a small British staff responsible to the British agent in Zanzibar could administer Uganda (Buganda) through its native constitution. Portal's final recommendation that 'a declaration of a protectorate would probably be the simplest solution to Uganda' was adopted by Anderson's committee. A document to this effect was published on 11 April 1894, and government announced on 12 April its decision to declare a protectorate over Uganda. The question would be debated in Parliament on 1 June 1894.

There were able advocates for and against retention. Sir Charles Dilke denounced the unctuous prating about the 'true Briton' and his 'bona fides', and talk of honourable obligations under the Company treaties. Labouchere repeated his arguments against annexation. Chamberlain, for retention, made a powerful appeal to government to accept the obligations of empire. In the voting that followed, although 52 Liberals opposed the motion, Conservative and Union supporters carried the vote and government won a majority. Some of its most trenchant critics, including Harcourt, had been won over. On 18 June 1894 the proclamation of declaration of a protectorate over Uganda (i.e., Buganda) was officially made. Bunyoro, Toro, Ankole and Koki were later to be brought into protectorate relationship, by separate treaties.

Rosebery and the Liberal imperialists gained their victory in the opening months of Gladstone's last administration. The Prime Minister and his main supporter, John Morley, were averse to holding Egypt and Uganda, – and Waddington, French ambassador to London, hoping to capitalize on this, overreached himself in bypassing Rosebery and approaching Gladstone personally. It was a diplomatic mistake. Rosebery was adamant that Britain must stay in Egypt, and won the day. The French ambassador, now supremely discomfited, resigned.

The British decision to stay in Egypt was also a decision to stay in Uganda, for if Egypt was to be held, so also must the headwaters of the Nile and these lay in Uganda – 'The cradle of the Nile'. Milner's *England in Eypt*, published in 1892, with its warning of the danger of interference in Egypt's water supply, helped to swing the decision, and so too did the *Handbook to the Uganda Question* by E.L. Bentley (a former employee of the IBEAC) with its reminder that

> The relinquishment of Uganda to a civilized Power immediately imperils the safety of Egypt, as the diversion or blocking of the headwaters of the Nile could stop her water supply and starve her population.[4]

Portal had stressed the 'urgency of arriving at a settlement of the whole East African question'. He saw no future place in such a settlement for the IBEAC in its present form, with its charter and powers. The experiment of combining administration and trade in the same hands had proved a failure, but Portal recommended compensation for the IBEAC for 'such actual improvements as they have made within the territories of the Sultanante'. How to get rid of the Company – this was a question not without difficulty! The Company seemed to be making matters as awkward for the government as possible. It now claimed that its withdrawal from Uganda to Dagoretti in the Kenya highlands was only temporary, while awaiting the progress of the railway to Uganda; and following the declaration of a British protectorate over Uganda, the Company sent its agent, Mr Gilkinson, with secret instructions to plant the Company's flag in Kavirondo. According to the Foreign Office this was 'well outside the limits of the Company's sphere, as agreed on by their withdrawal from Uganda', and it sharply rebuked the Company: it was not open to it 'to re-establish the administration from which it voluntarily withdrew after formal notification and withdrawal'. The Company during 1894 levied duties – sometimes twice on the same item when it left Uganda, and again when it entered the coastal strip which the IBEAC administered in the Sultan's name. When Portal sent down to the coast 117 pieces of ivory on which duty had already been paid in Uganda, the Company collected another 3000 rupees duty on it at Mombasa, and deducted therefrom part of the rent it (the Company) owed the Sultan. The vexatious practice of the Company in levying porterage dues on the Mackinnon Road was irritating in that the Company failed to maintain its roads in good repair and keep water-holes open.

Meanwhile the Company, concentrating its dwindling resources at Kismayu, put on a good front. It stationed a small gunboat at Lamu; attempted to induce the Watora and Borani Galla along the lower Juba to come to the coast to trade; and transferred the sternwheeler, *Kenia,* from the Tana to the Juba River where it ascended as far as Bardera, 400 miles upstream. The Company, in an attempt to establish friendly relations with the Somali tribes (the Ogaden and Herti), paid them subsidies, but this merely awakened their avarice. Unfortunately too, for the Company, the enforcement of the payment of blood-money, the traditional form of compoundment for crimes of murder, paid to the family of the murdered man, now became the Company's responsibility, as the Sultan of Zanzibar's 'vakeel'. The Company was thus involved in endless family and tribal quarrels and native litigation, at a time when renewed arms trade kept the Somali heavily armed.

In the face of Somali unrest, the gunboat *Widgeon* was sent to Kismayu to protect Europeans there. Rodd, visiting Kismayu in February 1894, was most critical of the Company. The attempt to buy off the Somalis by subsidies was a failure, since the money could be better spent in garrisoning trading posts; the Company's steamer *Kenia* was now stranded upstream, and HMS *Blanche,* aided by Italian forces under Count Lovatelli, had to extricate the Company from its difficulties up the Juba. By the summer of 1894, the Company's writ ran no farther than the limits of the town of Kismayu. And then to add to the Company's woes there appeared that weird apparition, the 'Freelanders' (a socialist experiment), in the Company's territory in the summer of 1894; this was the last straw.[5] The arrival of the Freelanders raised the question whether the Company had the right to confer a valid land title on European settlers in this territory. It was the Foreign Office view that the Company did not have this right.

Hardinge, on the same day (31 May 1894) that he arrived in Zanzibar to take up the post of Political Agent and Consul-General, was instructed by Kimberley to inform the Sultan that HMG proposed to acquire the Company's concessions on the coast 'on behalf the Zanzibar government'. In June and July 1894, the Company informed government of its willingness to negotiate the surrender of its interests in East Africa. The rumour that government was seriously considering Portal's suggestion that a railway from the interior might well follow the Tana River route and terminate at Witu, outside the Company's territory, may have stirred the Company into action (the hint may have been intentionally dropped by the Foreign Office for the benefit of the IBEAC), for such an alignment of the railway would leave the Company stranded with a profitless coast, and it had always hoped to profit from the great expansion that would take place at Mombasa if a Uganda railway should start from there. The directors now intimated their willingness to negotiate for the Company's withdrawal from the coastal strip which it had leased in perpetuity from the Sultan, if generous compensation were paid by government for relinquishment of its charter and control over the interior. The Company implied that, owning the coastal strip, it could hold to ransom anyone or any attempt to occupy the interior, by strangling all communications and trade between there and the coast. Lord Kimberley replied that this threat was of 'unprecedented character' and required 'mature consideration'. When it became known in September 1894 that the compensation figure the directors had in mind for relinquishment of the coastal strip and their charter was £300,000, and that the Company intended to retain 'moderate' grants of land, its banking concession, and all assets in the form of private lands, buildings and stores, leaving it still a potentially obstructive force, Lord Kimberley replied that 'the demands of the East Africa Company are larger than we should be warranted in admitting'.

A Foreign Office counter-offer came on 14 November 1894: 'after careful investigation' it had been decided to recommend an offer of £150,000 to the Sultan for the surrender of his concession of the coastal strip. But as regards compensating the Company for its work in the interior, 'it would be a dangerous precedent to admit that a private Company is entitled to look forward in case of pecuniary loss to compensation for its shareholders from Imperial revenues'. However, government would make an exception because the Company were the pioneers through whose agency British influence was extended to the lake districts, and by their means the condition of the native inhabitants has been improved and the slave-trade has been suppressed in the territories administered by them. Moreover, the maintenance of posts at Machakos and Fort Smith, where a useful and effective control has been exercised by the agents of the Company, materially facilitates the work which has been undertaken by Her Majesty's government in Uganda.[6]

and thus it recommended a sum of £50,000 to the Company for relinquishment of its charter. In reply the directors, although they did not question the sum offered for surrender of the coastal concession, claimed that £50,000 was inadequate compensation for surrender of the charter, for, 'On the accounts worked out in this office', the Company had expended some £489,158 in its work in East Africa. In an interview with Lord Kimberley on 4 December 1894, the directors next put forth an ingenious scheme to 'wipe the slate clean', whereby government would contribute an additional £100,000 above its previous offer (£150,000 for the coastal strip and £50,000 for the charter) and the total of £300,000 compensation would then be invested in the Company's name, in 'Zanzibar bonds' with interest guaranteed by the British government. Kimberley rejected this scheme as 'sheer fantasy', and so also did he refuse to consider the Company's request for arbitration of their claims, for 'the Company had acted on its own initiative and naturally must take the consequences'. As to the threat that it would continue its operations if government's offer was unacceptable, Kimberley was 'too courteous to allow himself to say anything on this unpleasant topic'.

Hardinge was now informed by the Foreign Office that HMG would recommend repurchase of the Sultan's concessions for £150,000, plus an independent valuation of assets. Hardinge assumed that such repurchase would be 'on behalf of the Zanzibar government', and that the coastal strip would again come under the control of Zanzibar. This would please the Sultan – it would enhance his prestige and authority and would be most popular with the Arabs. Hardinge accordingly supported the repurchase by the Zanzibar government of the concessions for £150,000, and the private assets of the IBEAC for not more than £50,000. The entire 'nest-egg' of £200,000, belonging to the Zanzibar government could be used for this repurchase.[7]

In this final stage of the bargaining the British government, after 'chaffering like a furniture broker over the details of a valuation', informed the Company on 31 December 1894 that its private property within the concession territory would be repurchased at fair valuation to an amount not exceeding £50,000. The directors in response, fearing that the Sultan might select the best assets and at a valuation much less than £50,000, offered to sell the whole of the Company's assets in East Africa for £100,000. This Kimberley refused to consider, and he reiterated his previous offer. Kimberley played his last card on 21 February 1895. Government would set aside any 'valuation' of the Company's assets in the concession territory, instead would pay £50,000 outright for the surrender of all its assets in East Africa. The Company would thus receive £50,000 for its charter, £150,000 for the coastal concession and £50,000 for all its assets, a total of £250,000. Sir Percy Anderson seems to have known all along that this was the final figure that the Company, in its last desperate straits, would accept. Behind the outward imperturability of officialdom there was anxiety that the negotiations might break down before the latest anti-slave decree came into effect. The operation of this decree would be much eased if the Company was out of the way. It was a relief to the government when the directors announced on 23 February 1895 that they had recommended their shareholders to accept the offer, and that the Company was willing to terminate its administration by 31 March 1895. This willingness to terminate at such an early date was soon explained: a quarter rent for the coastal strip was due to the Sultan on 1 April 1895.

The transfer could not, however, be facilitated so quickly, for parliamentary sanction was required for compensation to the Company. Meanwhile, acceptance of the government offer by the Company's shareholders was confirmed at a special meeting on 11 April 1895. Compensation for the Company was also tied up with government's plans for the future of the mainland territory between Uganda and the coast. The original idea of the Foreign Office had been to extend the direct authority of the Sultan of Zanzibar over the entire territory as far as the boundaries of Uganda, or at least over the coastal strip from the Umba to the Juba, including Witu. Hardinge, under the impression that this was still the Foreign Office view, wrote a lengthy despatch in February 1895, explaining his plans for the future administration of the mainland when it came under the Sultan's authority. It would be divided into two protectorates – the Zanzibar Protectorate which would include the coastal strip, and the East Africa Protectorate which would take in the remainder of the region as far as Uganda and which would be under direct British administration. But Rosebery had now come round to the view of Sir Percy Anderson, head of the Africa Department at the Foreign Office, that it would be better to buy out the Sultan's rights in the mainland coastal strip for an annual payment of £17,000, and place the whole territory – from the Indian Ocean to Uganda – under direct British administration, with the British Agent and Consul-General at Zanzibar acting as 'Her Majesty's Commissioner for the East African Protectorate'.

On the 13 June 1895 Sir Edward Grey explained the situation to the House of Commons, and government's action in taking over direct administration of the mainland territory, including the coastal strip. The economy of Zanzibar might soon be adversely affected by the abolition of slavery and would not be able to bear any additional costs of administration, whereas by placing the coastal strip and mainland behind it under imperial control and the same English officers, economy and efficiency would be effected. As to buying out the IBEAC: it would receive a total of £250,000 of which £50,000 was to come from the imperial Treasury for surrender of the Company's charter and for the work it had done outside the coastal strip, and the remaining £200,000, which was to be paid by Zanzibar, was made up of £150,000 for the surrender of its lease over the coastal strip and £50,000 for its private assets. In the ensuing discussion in the House of Commons, the government was congratulated by Chamberlain on the tidiness and the 'simplification' with which it handled the matter, but Mr Labouchere, pernicious and persistent critic of imperial expansion, denounced the annexation and the making of Zanzibar responsible for payment for the surrender of a concession for which it had received 'absolutely nothing'.

It was notified in the *London Gazette* of 16 June 1895 that a British protectorate had been declared over the territory lying between Uganda and the coastal strip. Hardinge had heard the news on 14 June and also a reiteration of the reasons for the Foreign Office decision. Mombasa would become the terminus of a railway to Lake Victoria and would replace Zanzibar as the great port and mart of East Africa; if the coastal zone with Mombasa were placed under separate administration from the hinterland, there would arise complicated fiscal and administrative problems under a dual administration. Hardinge directed a flurry of telegrams (seven in all) to Kimberley, in a-last minute bid to get the scheme reconsidered, and persuade his superiors in London to adhere to their earlier proposal, which would conciliate the Sultan and Arabs, and was highly desirable in view of the pending measures for the abolition of slavery. Hardinge had so much assumed that the Company's concessions were to be repurchased on the Sultan's behalf, and that the coastal strip would again come under his authority, that he and Mathews had made plans to implement this, and it was to this end that he had supported the use of the 'nest-egg' of £200,000 received by the Sultan from the Germans, for the repurchase of the Cconcession and the Company's private assets. Now all this was set aside, and he was overruled (he later thought quite rightly) by his superiors, Rosebery and others, in London.

It was bitter pill for the Sultan as well as Hardinge and Mathews. So certain was Seyyid Hamid that he was about to regain his authority on the coast that he had plans under way for a state visit to the mainland to inaugurate the event. Both Hardinge and Mathews were left much disconsolate over these developments: they were deeply concerned lest they be thought to have betrayed the Sultan's interest and that he would no longer have confidence in the British. Kimberley's assurance that the Sultan would gain from the new arrangement, would have a better tenant than the IBEAC and a higher interest on his money, was little comfort. It ignored the blow to the Sultan's prestige, and the loss to Zanzibar of the £200,000 which could be used for local purposes; as for the paltry increase in interest – one-quarter of 1 per cent – it was scarce worth mentioning! Mathews was especially bitter that the £50,000 paid to the IBEAC for its private assets had come out of the Sultan's money, but these private assets were now the private property of the British government.

In the face of Foreign Office decision, reinforced by its warning to Hardinge that public opinion (namely the Anti-Slavery Society and its supporters) would not tolerate any reimposition of the Sultan's rule on the mainland, Hardinge bowed to the inevitable. In a final telegram of 23 June 1895 he acquiesced in the arrangement, but he could barely bring himself to break the bad news to the Sultan. On 25 June (the Sultan had been on the mainland during the preceding weeks, getting the feel of his old dominion again, in anticipation of taking it over), he informed him that, after 'exhaustive examination', the British government had decided that the coastal strip and the territory behind it had been so closely welded together during the preceding seven years' rule of the Company, that the administration of the two territories could not again be separated, and that there were doubts whether Zanzibar revenues could stand the extra strain which administration of the coast would impose. Therefore the British government would take it over and pay him an annual rent.[8]

Hardinge put on a brave front, telling the Sultan that he would receive rent for his coastline and interest for his money; the Sultan replied that he had previously received both interest and rent. As for the £200,000 which his predecessor had obtained from the Germans for the sale of his southern coastline to them, it was now to be used to buy out the Company's control over the other half, and he would end up with only the interest on the £200,000 and the annual rent for the coastal strip. It was a pretty story! The Sultan with the dignified fatalism of the East, and feeling himself 'like a little bird in the claws of a powerful eagle', submitted to the decision. Henceforth his faith in the sincerity and goodwill of the British government – the Raj – whom he had heard the Indians in Zanzibar extol, was severely shaken. From now on he increasingly turned towards Hilal bin Amur and other fanatical counsellors who were xenophobic and secretly hostile to the British. The annual revenue of £17,000 which he was to receive for his mainland territory would be spent as his English advisers, now in control of his finances, thought best. His monthly civil list was already inadequate for maintaining the limited oriental splendour to which he aspired. His only recourse was to have his civil list increased – thus his pathetic approach to Hardinge: 'My body is covered with sores; you can procure the ointment to heal them.' In this at least, Hardinge could help, and he obtained the Foreign Secretary's consent to raising the Sultan's civil list by an extra £3000 a year.

In retrospect, and from 'an exclusively Zanzibar point of view', Hardinge was in no doubt that the Sultan had lost out in the settlement which had followed on the withdrawal of the IBEAC from East Africa. It was generally felt that he had been the victim of sharp dealing on the part of the British government: Evelyn Waugh, during a visit to Zanzibar in the interwar years, needled British officials there as to the underhand way in which the Sultan had been treated in the settlement with the IBEAC.[9] However, seeing it all from the wider angle of imperial interests and the hope that the direct administration of the mainland by the British government, coupled with its opening up by a railway, would bring increased prosperity in which Zanzibar would share, this might be considered some compensation for 'the sacrifice she was called upon to make'. The episode, however, marked the end of Zanzibar's importance as the centre of the East African world, at least in British eyes. Henceforth British attention was chiefly dirtced to the mainland. As for the IBEAC, there was little to show for its brief and somewhat inglorious period of rule, apart from the re-employment in the new administration of 30 members of the Company's former staff.[10] The Company for all purposes had vanished into limbo. Its large map of British East Africa, specially constructed for its boardroom, found a place in Sir Clement Hill's room at the Foreign Office. The verdict on the Company's short history was harsh. In terms of the difficulties it had faced and the money expended it was probably too harsh.

8· Pax Britannica in Uganda

Sir Gerald Portal's work in Uganda had largely been confined to the Kingdom of Buganda, although in the parlance of the time that kingdom was synonymous with the wider amorphous area later embraced under the comprehensive term 'Uganda'. The task of extending Pax Britannica to this wider Uganda was left to Portal's immediate successors. Macdonald, who was in charge during the interval between Portal's departure at the end of May 1893 and the arrival of Colonel Colvile, as Commissioner, in November 1893, dealt with the withdrawal of the Sudanese as instructed by Portal, and this was completed by October 1893. The suggestion that these Sudanese might be employed in the construction of Cecil Rhodes's Cape-to-Cairo telegraph line was set aside as impractical; instead they were settled at Entebbe, under British eyes, and retained as a military force. Their removal from the borders of Bunyoro was greeted with relief by the peoples on whom they had of late battened, but fellow Muslims in Buganda saw their establishment at Entebbe as an accession of Muslim strength in Buganda, and quickly signalled this by asking for more territory and by refusing to carry out road work. Macdonald nipped this proto-rebellion in the bud, disarmed the Sudanese and sent their ringleader, Selim Bey, down to the coast.

It was left to Colonel Colvile, to deal with the legacy of the religious wars which continued to harass the Uganda administration and to complicate the extension of Pax Britannica. The Catholics claimed that Portal's promises, in spirit and in fact, had not been honoured. Portal was now dead. The Catholics were bitter. The Protestant Katikiro, strong in the feeling of his own ascendancy and with something of conceit and arrogance in his manner, was always accompanied by a large crowd of retainers. The Catholic Katikiro appeared from time to time to complain or accuse the Protestants of religious persecution. The jealousy of the two Katikiros often resulted in violent quarrelling in 'barazas' (meetings) before the king, each blindly followed by the chiefs of his party.

Religious strains were transmitted beyond Buganda by lay teachers and missionaries. This was especially true of Toro, where Kasagama, a Protestant partisan, was warned that his bias might lead to his removal from office. A distinct improvement was discerned in his behaviour following the departure of Mr Fisher of the CMS. British officials in Uganda pointed out that Catholic missionaries interfered less with the administration than Protestant missionaries.[1] Colvile, at loggerheads with the CMS over the supposed severity of sentences he had passed on CMS adherents, stated that no such complaints ever came from the Roman Catholic fathers, chiefly because of their acceptance of the extinction of their political power, 'an acceptance which seems to be beyond the capabilities of their Protestant brethren'. Continued charges of religious discrimination evoked a memorandum in August 1894 from the Duke of Norfolk who had staunchly supported the Catholic cause during the religious wars of 1892. At that time he had requested Lord Salisbury to appoint a Catholic Resident for Buganda, but this was refused.[2] Norfolk now raised the matter again and requested that some Catholics be appointed to the Uganda administration, and that judicial power be vested, not in the Resident, but in an officer appointed for this purpose – 'as in Matabeleland'.[3] The Foreign Office, in reply, could not undertake to employ a proportion of Catholic officers – for this was tantamount to applying a religious test to condition of employment; as for judicial power, the Commissioner must have paramount authority.[4] It is of interest that in the following year Norfolk's suggestion, so peremptorily dismissed when first put forth, was taken up, and Lieutenant Dugmore 'specially selected as being a Catholic' was appointed to the position of Second Class Assistant in the Uganda administration.[5]

Religious tension was eased somewhat by the arrival of the Mill Hill Mission (Bishop Hanlon and four Catholic priests) in October 1894. They took up a position on a hill (Nsambya) on the outskirts of Kampala, and a promising start was made by this Mission. Its establishment was largely the result of initiative taken by Mr W.H. Bishop, a prominent Catholic industrialist, and a director of the IBEAC. Deeply grieved over the old dichotomy of French-Catholic versus English-Protestant antagonism so firmly entrenched in Ganda thinking, and the cause of religious wars and accruing bitterness, Bishop felt that this might be broken down by the entry of an 'English' Catholic Mission on the scene. The arrival of the Mill Hill Mission drew from Bishop Tucker the remark that it signalled 'a second act of wanton aggression' (the first being that of the arrival of the White Fathers in Uganda in 1879). But the British administration welcomed it, and received with satisfaction the news that the Mission intended to work in eastern Uganda. For although this would cut across the informal agreement of Mgr Hirth and Bishop Tucker which had assigned this area to Protestant missionary activity, it would be all to the good, for 'intermingling will cause ill-feeling to subside'. A further breaking down of religious enmity came with Mwanga's flight in July 1897 when many chiefs in Buddu were outlawed for contumacy. No religious distinction was made in making new appointments, although Buddu was primarily a Catholic district. In future, vacancies would be filled from an outside district 'in such manner as will bring about as early as possible the termination of the existing isolation of creeds'. The acerbity and outward hostility between the two Christian parties was thus gradually tempered even though the old latent suspicion remained.

Colvile pursued this settlement of the religious question against a background of increasing challenge from Kabarega, the 'old pagan ruler' of Bunyoro. Kabarega had driven Kasagama from his kingdom and had invaded Busoga. He refused to pay the customary tribute of salt to Buganda, and flaunted thousands of Baganda slaves (mostly women) at his capital – the 'only remaining slave-trade centre in Central Africa'. Kabarega had legitimate grievances of his own: he had been sorely tried by the Sudanese quartered by Lugard on his southern borders; Kasagama of Toro was far from an exemplary ruler (as the British were soon to discover), and was a persistent gadfly to Kabarega; and as for the Baganda – traditional enemies of Bunyoro, and in decline on the eve of British arrival – they clung to the British coat-tails and vaunted their new-found strength in the eyes of the Banyoro.

In the face of British and Belgian encroachment, Kabarega stood out defiantly, the last independent native ruler in this part of Africa. When rumours spread that he was planning to link up with the Dervishes, Colvile decided to cut the claws of this turbulent ruler. Macdonald had already planned hostilities against him, and Colvile now took up these plans, at one stage even contemplating using the Arab leader, Tippu Tib, in an attack on Kabarega. This novel idea was set aside and instead Colvile, using Baganda forces, pushed Kabarega back out of the southern portion of his kingdom, occupied the salt mines at Kibiro and cut off his supply of arms from across the Kagera River. An effective cordon across southern Bunyoro was laid down by military posts and patrols from Kibiro and Hoima to the River Kafu. By June 1894 the first phase of the campaign was over. It was at this stage that Hardinge, Commissioner at Zanzibar, instructed Colvile to seek amity with Kabarega. Hardinge saw events in Uganda against a much wider canvas than did Colvile. In the spring of 1894 there were rumours of an imminent Dervish attack on the Congo Free State and Bunyoro. Kitchener, with great authority, urged the British to 'use the negroes of the Upper Nile to protect Uganda and drive back the Dervishes'. Hardinge was also much concerned over troubles in Jubaland and Somaliland where the threat of the Mad Mullah and a jihad against the European would soon become omnipresent. Thus Hardinge saw the Dervishes, not Kabarega, as the great danger.

But for Colvile, it was Kabarega, lurking on the northern fringes of Buganda, who must be eradicated. A surprise attack by Captain Thruston on 11 November 1894, at Machudi near the Somerset Nile, resulted in Kabarega's cattle and personal property being captured; Thruston claimed that 'had it been a clear night I should probably have taken him alive'. However, in the attack a prize almost equal to that of Kabarega himself fell to the British. The

> brass spear and sceptre, the insignia of his office, which have been consecrated by special witchcraft, and which he and his people hold in great veneration ... the loss of these articles is to Kabarega as the loss of his kingdom, and he will go so far as to make his submission in the hope of regaining them.[6]

Kabarega did not make his submission, and following the invaliding home of Colvile at the end of 1894, and the arrival of Berkeley as Commissioner in June 1895, the campaign was renewed. Colonel Ternan and Major Cunningham, heading a large force of 20,000 Baganda, 'rash and injudicious without being especially brave', and with food supplies strained to the limit, penetrated the Lango country north of Kioga, and tightened the cordon across southern Bunyoro by a patrol of the Nile as far north as Dufile. This campaign brought in much booty and many prisoners – including 450 Baganda women captives and thousands of head of cattle. Mwenda, headquarters of Arab gun-runners who supplied Kabarega, was taken. The main prize, however, was the capture of the Queen Mother and her son, who were taken to Kampala. In the face of this collapse of his fortunes, Kabarega withdrew north to Fatiko, from where he continued to make warlike noises.

With Kabarega out of the way, the British administration could turn to extending its authority to outlying parts of Uganda – a task made difficult with a skeleton staff, denuded by home leave being granted to officers every two years this with travelling time added: this meant that about one-third of the staff was absent from the country at any one time. With this attenuated administration however, Busoga, in eastern Uganda, was brought under control and an exemplary officer, Mr W. Grant, placed in charge. In the Mau district, also in eastern Uganda, Mr F. Jackson effectively checked Maasai resistance and stopped attacks on caravans. In Kavirondo district, between Lake Victoria and Mount Elgon, Mr C.W. Hobley, an ardent anthropologist and geologist, brought his district under strict purview. In western Uganda Kasagama of Toro, like Mwanga of Buganda, chafed under strict British control and resented having to pay a tax of 1500 lb of ivory annually to the British. He was brought into Kampala, like a naughty boy, for a lesson in good manners and for instruction in the need to contribute to the protectorate's finances. Kasagama and chiefs might resent British tutelage but they were dependent on British protection against Bunyoro and Buganda.

The area least affected by British administration was Ankole in south-western Uganda – the remotest parts of which, in the Mufumbiro region especially, are unsurpassed elsewhere in Africa in the nobility of their natural features and magnificent topography. Lugard had passed through Ankole in 1891 and had made blood-brotherhood and treaty with its ruler (the Omugabe) Ntare. No administrative post was set up however, and in 1893 a German party under Major Langheld made a leisurely exploratory journey through Ankole, causing Ntare to appeal for British protection under Lugard's treaty. To strengthen Ntare's confidence in British protection Major G.G. Cunningham made a new treaty with him on 29 August 1894, whereby Ntare placed himself entirely in British hands with control over his foreign policy, and gave to the British free access to his kingdom. Ntare died in 1895. In 1896 the Uganda Protectorate was extended to embrace Ankole. Despite this apparent strengthening of British control in Ankole the Ba-Ruanda raided there unchecked in 1896. It was not until Mr, R.J.D. McAllister established an administrative headquarters at Mbarara, in December 1898, and the ending of the disputed succession following Ntare's death by the accession of Kahaya in 1902, that Ankole can be truly said to have been brought under British authority.

The extension of Pax Britannica throughout Uganda was complicated by boundary-making. The assigning of geometric boundaries to a country where topographical features were imperfectly known was a questionable procedure; it was not known for example until 1896 that the Ituri and Semliki were two rivers, not one. The surveyor and boundary-maker pinned down the geographical reality behind the cartographical work of European map-makers who had never set foot in Africa. Natural boundaries, such as the Umba, Semliki and Kagera Rivers, would have eased the task of suppressing the slave-trade and the constant counter-raiding for woman and cattle that went on across boundaries. A change-over to natural frontiers was the answer, but it would open such a Pandora's Box that no administrator dare suggest it.

East African boundaries in the interior have their origin in the convention between the International Association of the Congo and Germany of 8 November 1884, and the Berlin Conference of 1884-85, whereby the geographical limits of the Congo Basin were defined as embracing 'all the regions watered by the Congo and its affluents, including Lake Tanganyika, with its eastern tributaries'. More precision as to its eastern limits came with the formation of the Independent State of the Congo on 1 August 1885, whereby the 30th meridian was described as part of its eastern boundary line. The Uganda Protectorate's western boundary was thus tacitly laid down before the protectorate came into being. The Mackinnon treaty of 24 May 1890 would have reverted to the more natural frontier line of the Semliki River and Congo/Nile watershed to the immediate west of Lake Albert. In the long run, when the line of the 30th meridian was shown to have been incorrectly positioned on maps, this was the boundary partially resorted to.

To Uganda's south there were no great natural divisions to indicate a territorial frontier, and the Anglo-German Agreement of 1 July 1890 defined the boundary as the 1st parallel of south latitude, deflected so as to include Mufumbiro in the British sphere. There was a strong case for the inclusion of Mufumbiro in the British sphere in that it was an Englishman, Speke, who was the first European to sight Mufumbiro, and Stanley's treaties of 1889 were interpreted as covering the region. A corrected line of the 30th meridian was to show that their inclusion had been at the expense of the Congo State, and so also with Ruwenzori and much of Toro – on their western sides they both fell well into the Congo. As to the Congo/Nile watershed, it was ultimately shown to be sufficiently west of Lake Albert to leave a narrow strip between it and the lake in British hands, thus cutting Leopold off from access to the Nile. It was his persistent drive to regain this access which made the Nile problem particularly acute for Uganda.

The Upper Nile, the vast amorphous region to the north of Uganda, *res nullius*, as the French termed it, was little known to the outside world. European travellers and officials in Gordon's employ had largely kept to the riverain routes, and even Emin Pasha, with long and extensive experience in the region, had supplied little information about it apart from zoological and botanical data and observations as to the suitability of Mount Agarde as a European sanatorium.

British interest, focused on the Upper Nile by Gordon's death, continued to be attracted there, first by Mahdist victories and the Khalifa's regime, and then, when a British occupation of Egypt took place, by concern over control of the waters of the Upper Nile. Egypt's increasing population and development of an elaborate irrigation works dependent on a regular supply of water meant that the annual inundation of the great flood plain would no longer suffice for her needs. The White Nile, rather than the Blue Nile and Atbara, was the great regulator of a steady supply of water for Egypt and it was essential that this source be not tampered with. This concern was highlighted by the very low Nile of 1888. About the same time international attention was attracted to the Upper Nile by the death of King John of Abyssinia in 1889, by Italy's Treaty of Ucciali with his successor, Menelik; and by the latter's circular of 10 April 1891, claiming all territory to the west – as far as the right bank of the Nile 'the ancient frontiers of Abyssinia'. Then came the dramatic push to Wadelai in October 1892 by Leopold's daring agent, van Kherckhoven.

These events made this vital part of Africa the focus of two powers especially, France and Britain. German interest in the Upper Nile had receded following the abortive Carl Peters's Emin Pasha Relief Expedition and the Anglo–German Agreement of 1890; and Italian aspirations had been removed by the Anglo–Italian treaty of 15 April 1891, which acknowledged British paramountcy in the Nile Valley. There remained only Britain and France, with Leopold a close contender. When Salisbury protested against the latter's action in sending the Kherckhoven expedition to Wadelai, Leopold countered by adducing the Mackinnon treaty in support of his action, and was backed in this by Lugard on the ground that the Upper Nile had been abandoned when Egypt withdrew from the Sudan and was open to the first power to take it from the Mahdists. This was also the French view. An able West African administrator, Liotard, had already in 1890 declared his intention of creating a 'French region with a door opening on the Nile', and the grand concept of a great block of French territory across Africa, from the upper Ubanghi to Jibuti, was already emerging in the minds of many Frenchmen. The Kherckhoven expedition and Leopold's designs threatened its fulfilment. To remove this threat the French entered into an agreement with Leopold for a line of demarcation to follow the course of the Chinka River and the 7th parallel of north latitude, to the north of which the French would have a free hand, and to the south of which Leopold would be free to extend as far north as Lado, but the French Chamber under pressure from the colonial group failed to ratify this agreement. Leopold, however, adhered to it, and further discussion in 1893–94 failed to shake him from his stand. The French and British faced a stubborn and skilled negotiator.

All this came at a time when French interest in the Upper Nile was intensifying. Apart from the desirability of acquiring a large waterway, command of a vital river and linking up their West and East African possessions, much French interest, official and unofficial, had been stirred by the writings in 1893 on Nile hydrography by the persuasive and well-connected French engineer, M. Victor Prompt. He showed that scientific pressure on the waters of the Upper Nile, especially the White Nile, at the right point could bring Egypt to her knees; and with the recent British occupation of Egypt still smarting in French minds, this was potent news. There was also much French interest in the project for a railway from Jibuti to Harrar and the Nile, for which the Swiss engineer, Alfred Ilg, Menelik's confidential adviser, had obtained a concession which he was soon to hand over to the French, in 1896. There was no doubt as to the real and increasing interest of the French in the Upper Nile. It led to the Anglo–Italian treaty of 5 May 1895 for delimitation of the frontiers of British and Italian Somaliland, and acknowledged Harrar as pre-empted territory for Italy. In West Africa Britain also sought to check French expansion in the Lake Chad area by treaty with Germany in November 1893, which recognized the western frontier of the German Cameroons as extending to Lake Chad. Germany then did the unforgivable in British eyes, when soon after, by a Franco-German Protocol of 4 February 1894, she gave France leave to expand to the north as far as Lake Chad and to the east 'as far as they chose to go'. This perfidy not only opened the door to the Nile to the French but blocked British aspirations in the Lake Chad region. For Anderson this was sheer treachery, and it brought boundless scorn from Rennell Rodd.[7] The latter blamed Germany for the atrocity stories and alleged infamies regarding rubber collecting in Leopold's Congo: Germany aspired to ultimate control there. As to France, with her right of pre-emption to the Congo, Germany was less concerned; France would be defeated in the next great round of arms.

The French or Belgian advance on the Nile caused Colonel Colvile in Uganda to send Major Owen north to make a 'dash on Wadelai' in the autumn of 1893. Owen found Wadelai abandoned by the Dervishes; he made a treaty with the paramount chief there, placed a steel boat on Lake Albert and strengthened the posts at Hoima and Kibiro. Also, in the autumn of 1893, Sir Rennell Rodd had been sent off to Brussels to prepare the way for the agreement signed with Leopold on 12 May 1894, whereby Britain recognized the Congo State's eastern boundary and gave Leopold the lease of a vast area between the Nile-Congo watershed and the Nile, and extending north as far as 10°N latitude. That portion of the lease east of the 30th meridian would expire on Leopold's death, but the remainder – west of the 30th meridian, would continue under Congo State control. Leopold also got a strip of territory, 25 km, wide, stretching from the Nile/Congo watershed to the western shore of Lake Albert and including the port of Mahagi: thus was the Congo State assured of access to the Nile system.

In return for these generous concessions, Britain received minimal gains, apart from obtaining the Belgians as a buffer against the Dervishes, for she obtained only a lease from the Congo State of a strip of territory 25 km wide, 'extending from the most northerly port on Lake Tanganyika to the most southerly point of Lake Albert Edward'. Thus was reaffirmed the Mackinnon treaty in securing an 'all-red route' through East Central Africa.

The 1894 agreement with its Article 3 was denounced in England by Harcourt, the 'Little Englander'; and France, having recently failed in her negotiations with the Congo State and much exercised over the Anglo–Italian Agreement of 5 May 1894, refused to recognize it. The Germans also protested, on the grounds that Article 3 violated the Anglo-German Agreement of July 1890, whereby the western boundary of German East Africa was to march 'coterminous' with the Congo Free State. German and French pressure forced Britain and Leopold to remove the offending Article, by the Declaration of 22 June 1894. Leopold further squared himself with France by an agreement of 14 August 1894, which confined his lease on the Upper Nile to an area (the 'Lado Enclave'), east of the 30th meridian, and south of latitude 5°30'N.

Despite this truncation of his lease, Leopold came out of the affair much better than Britain. The latter was left practically empty-handed. She might have repudiated her agreement with Leopold on the grounds that its terms had not been fulfilled (the Intelligence Division at the Foreign Office urged this). She could have done so without any great loss to herself, for she was already secured of untrammelled communication through German territory under the Anglo-German Agreement of 1890, and of free navigation on Lake Tanganyika under the Berlin Act of 1885. But Britain, from late 1894 to early 1896, was faced with increasing French challenge on the Upper Nile, and she had no wish to provoke Leopold. The appointment in September 1894 of M. Liotard, an ardent advocate of French expansion on the Upper Nile, as Commissioner of Upper Ubanghi, was followed in February 1895, by pronouncements from de Brazza and M. François Deloncle in the French Chamber affirming the legitimacy of such expansion, and at the same time challenging the right of Britain to stay in Egypt. Then came news of French expeditions advancing on the Nile both from the east and west. It was this latter which evoked from Sir Edward Grey, British Under-Secretary for Foreign Affairs, in March 1895, his oft-quoted warning

> Egyptian and British spheres together do cover the whole of the Nile waterway....any advance into the Nile Valley by France would be viewed as an 'unfriendly act'.[8]

Despite this warning, French official approval was given in November 1895 for the Marchand Mission's advance on the Nile. Britain at the time was under sharp warning from President Cleveland that the USA exercised a Monroe Doctrine surveillance in the Venezuela/British Guiana boundary dispute, and there was soon an added strain on British nerves over the Kruger Telegram incident of January 1896. Salisbury was thus in no mood to treat with the restless pushing Leopold when, having sent in Baron Dhanis to occupy the Lado Enclave, in August 1895, he now raised the novel suggestion that he be granted a lease of the whole of the Sudan north of Khartoum. In the face of this untoward request, Salisbury feared lest he be betrayed 'into some disrespectful commentary'.[9]

The French threat to the Upper Nile had already caused the London Chamber of Commerce, on 10 April 1895, to pass a resolution urging Britain to take immediate action to construct the Mombasa railway, 'to assure control of the Nile Valley from Uganda to Fashoda'. Added to the pressure of events was the renewed activity of the Dervishes in early 1896; a reported pact between Menelik and the Dervishes was soon given substance in their joint plan of attack on Kassala, and then came the fateful defeat of the Italians at Adowa in March 1896. In the same month the French refused to countenance the use of Egyptian funds for the expedition under Kitchener, which was to lead to the fall of Dongola in September 1896. In this keyed-up state of affairs, the Russians, although latecomers to Africa, also made trouble by pressing for a conference on international control of the Suez Canal, and by making the most of her supposed religious affinity with Coptic Christian Abyssinia, Russia supported the French in Abyssinia possibly with a view to obtaining port facilities there; French and Russian officers trained Abyssinian artillerymen; and the Russian Red Cross Mission at Addis Ababa was a centre from which political and military officers could extend Russian influence in Abyssinia. A report in January 1896 of an agreement between Menelik and the Khalifa for a simultaneous attack on the Italians, followed two months later by the resounding defeat of the latter at Adowa, rounded out this catena of events.

The Italian defeat at Adowa in March 1896 led to an undignified rush by the leading powers enter into negotiations with the new-found African hero, Menelik. France was the first to do so. M. Lagarde, Governor of Jibuti, headed a mission to Menelik in early March 1897 and obtained renewal of the French–Abyssinian treaty of friendship of 1843; arranged for delimitation of the French Somaliland frontier with Abyssinia, and smoothed negotiations with Menelik by handsome presents in money and arms. Menelik in return, with Ruritanian touch, conferred on Lagarde the title of Duke of Entotto (the ancient capital of Shoa); and Alfred Ilg, Menelik's adviser and favourable to the French, was now made Counsellor of State. There is no doubt at this time that the French were Menelik's favoured darlings. There was no end to their perfidy in British eyes. Lagarde carried on sly negotiations with the Khalifa, seeking his support against the British, and he backed Menelik against the Italians.

A British approach to Menelik followed shortly after that of the French. Sir Rennell Rodd's mission to Abyssinia in 1897 resulted in a treaty with Menelik on 14 May 1897, whereby the latter was to refrain from sending arms to the Dervishes and would grant Britain equality of economic privileges in his kingdom. The British failed to weaken the French position at Menelik's court; the French were already getting his co-operation in a joint advance on the Nile. Captain Marchand had left

France in May 1896 with a last-minute directive from the Foreign Minister, Hanotaux: 'Go to Fashoda.' To match up with Marchand, three expeditions were directed Nilewards from Abyssinia, and another in the autumn of 1897-98 reached the country north of Lake Rudolf. It was this concentrated advance towards the Upper Nile, from both west and east, which confirmed Salisbury in the need for a British force from Uganda to reach there first. Hence Macdonald's expedition.

Macdonald's formal instructions were to

> explore the districts adjacent to the Italian sphere – in which the Juba is believed to rise ... to determine the exact line of demarcation between the British and Italian spheres in East Africa as laid down by the Protocol signed 24th March 1891 ... to establish British influence with the natives in such a manner as effectively to secure the territory against other powers.[10]

His real object was to 'secure a continuous territory between the Uganda Protectorate and the 10th degree of North Latitude, the recognized southern limit of the Egyptian dominions' so as to forestall a French advance on the Upper Nile. Sir Rennell Rodd, in an interview with Salisbury on his return from Abyssinia in early summer 1897, found the latter preoccupied, not with Abyssinian encroachment in Somaliland – for Salisbury was never much concerned with 'light lands in Africa' – but with the French advance on the Nile;

> he listened with great attention to my report, sitting huddled up at his table with a rug on his knees ... the only comment I could elicit from the reserve of the Foreign Secretary, when I explained the imminent danger of Marchand's arrival on the Nile before we had reached Khartoum, was 'Well, let us hope he won't get there'.[11]

Macdonald estimated his arrival at Fashoda as at 1 January 1899. He set aside his original plan for an advance inland from Berbera, which would have excited French suspicions and antagonized the Abyssinians, and instead he proceeded inland from Mombasa. With the added boost of the first few miles of the newly commenced Uganda Railway, he was well on his way there by late July 1897. He was to collect 300 Sudanese troops, to be provided by Colonel Ternan of Uganda at a pre-arranged rendezvous near the Eldama Ravine. The Sudanese as promised duly arrived, but they were in restive mood. They had seen constant fighting in Bunyoro, Nandi and Buddu under a constant change of officers. They now faced the prospect of a long weary march under Macdonald, a well-known disciplinarian, to an unknown goal. Their pay was low, less than Swahili porters, and usually in arrears. Yet this alone would not account for their insurrection. They were never accustomed to luxury, having lived with Emin Pasha under most precarious conditions and without ordinary comforts. They delighted in excursions which offered excitement and booty. They were natural soldiers revelling in military life. Their real grievance was that Macdonald would allow them only one follower per man, and they were accustomed to having large numbers of females in constant attendance. Ternan, however, later claimed that the mutiny was an attempt by the Sudanese officers to take advantage of unsettled conditions in Buganda and set up a Muslim state there, and that they were encouraged in this course by a rumour circulating among Muslims in Buganda that a passage in the Koran indicated the cessation of European rule in the current year.

Within a week of their rendezvous with Macdonald the Sudanese demanded release from the expedition. When this was refused they bolted and turned, and with Macdonald and Jackson following after them, headed for Uganda by way of Mumias. They created havoc *en route*. In the Nandi country they burnt alive 100 natives in a grass hut in revenge for the murder of three of their comrades, and they threatened to scorch and sear their way through to Buganda. To this threat was now added the news that Mwanga had escaped from the Germans, had declared himself a follower of the Prophet and was collecting forces in Buddu. This presented the danger that the Sudanese garrison in Buddu would join the mutineers, and to prevent this Macdonald hurried hence. He defeated Mwanga's forces, disarmed the Sudanese in Buddu and sent them back to Kampala. The crucial stage was yet to come: the mutineers attacked Luba's, a fort commanding the main crossing of the Napoleon Gulf between Busoga and Buganda, on 9 January 1898, and its three European occupants, Captain Thruston, Pilkington of the CMS and Lieutenant Norman Macdonald (brother of Major Macdonald), were killed. The mutineers escaped and headed for Kampala, having made overtures in advance to fellow Muslims there and offering to place Mbogo on the throne. In the face of this threat Kampala took on the aspect of a beleaguered town. Quick resolves had to be taken. All persons suspected of disloyalty were disarmed and troops concentrated at Kampala fort, telephone communication between Port Alice (Entebbe) and Kampala was set up; and powder and shot ordered from the

Germans at the south of the lake. Macdonald's troops and Mbogo's loyalty saved the day. In this moment of high tension the mutineers, when only 15 miles east of Kampala, suddenly wheeled north, having decided to join up with the Sudanese troops in southern Bunyoro and Toro. Macdonald set out with all speed to intercept them. Lieutenant Scott with newly arrived Indian troops was sent ahead to disarm the Sudanese in southern Bunyoro. The latter fortunately remained loyal. The mutineers were finally overtaken to the immediate north of Lake Kioga, and were brought to ground in a fierce attack on 24 February 1898. They were forced to give way and to withdraw to the north. They would have suffered total defeat but for the fact that Captain Harrison was hampered in the use of his Maxim owing to the large number of women in attendance on the enemy.

The Sudanese continued to be rounded up over the next three years, but with more Indian forces expected in the spring, Uganda was safe from immediate danger.

The mutiny had been a costly affair – raising the estimates for 1898/99 by £98,437. On the credit side, the Buganda had proven their loyalty, and attention had been drawn to the parlous state of military defences in British East Africa. The Intelligence Division of the Army had been pressing for reform of the military ever since Mbaruk's rebellion in 1895-96. A complete review of the kind of troops best suited to East Africa was now instituted.

As to Macdonald's expedition, it had received a devastating blow from the mutiny, and it is surprising that Macdonald returned to the work so violently interrupted. His men had suffered ill-health; stores and escort were much reduced; and his Swahili porters' term of enlistment was drawing to an end. There was also the possibility that an expedition under Mr H.S.H. Cavendish, now in the Rudolf region and with a well-equipped caravan, might complete the task assigned to Macdonald. The Intelligence Division of the Army urged this. The Foreign Office was much concerned that Marchand's expedition approaching from the west, and the Bonvalot mission under command of the dashing Marquis de Bonchamps approaching from the east (it was reported to have reached the Didessa River, main tributary of the White Nile), would beat the British to the Nile. A dash by a well-organized British force was essential to prevent 'effective occupation' of the Upper Nile by the French.

When Berkeley, Commissioner, arrived back in Uganda from leave in April 1898 (Colonel Ternan had been acting-Commissioner in his absence), he carried instructions for Macdonald to complete his mission.

Berkeley desired to share in the credit which would accrue 'from the successful junction with Anglo-Egyptian forces in the north'. In consultation with Macdonald plans were made for a combined movement, with Uganda troops, steam launch and canoes working up the Nile and Macdonald moving overland through Karamoja, the two forces then joining up at Lado and making a final push on to Fashoda. Berkeley soon had a change of mind. He could not spare supplies and forces for a combined operation owing to renewed fighting with Kabarega and the recall of forces under Captain Harrison to the coast; also part of the steam launch was missing. Berkeley thus urged Macdonald to give up the idea of an advance on Fashoda. It was best, he claimed, if Macdonald handed over his Swahili porters and stores to the Uganda administration. Even in the face of such discouragement Macdonald refused to turn back. He suddenly announced on 29 May 1898 that he would advance through Karamoja to the Nile basin ... 'it would almost appear that I made enemies by declining to accept local views'. He had received news of the probable date of the fall of Omdurman, and now informed Salisbury that he hoped to reach Lado by October 1898. Unknown to Macdonald, soon after his departure for the north, Berkeley dispatched an expedition under Major Martyr, down the Nile: 'Nile Reconnaissance' as it was called, was to establish stations at Wadelai and Dufile and 'obtain closer touch with the Nile to our North'. Martyr was allocated the steam launch which should have gone to Macdonald, the missing part having apparently turned up.

From base camp at Save, just north of Mount Elgon, Macdonald sent Captain Austin to the Rudolf region to carry out reconnaissance there as far as 6°N latitude. Meanwhile Macdonald, with some 100 Sudanese, pushed north-west towards Lado, arriving at Tarangole on 22 October 1898, where he ascertained that the Nile to the north of Lado was blocked by sudd. Since his supplies were running out and he dared not make further demands on his Swahili porters and troops, he retraced his steps to Save, making treaties with the Bari chiefs *en route*. Austin, however, reached Lake Rudolf and extended British treaty country as far north as 6°N latitude.

It was only on his return to Save in November that Macdonald learned of the expedition sent north by Berkeley. There is anger and bitterness expressed in his letter to the Foreign Office:

Had this Uganda expedition been in co-operation with me, I could have easily communicated with it and by securing fresh trade goods, and sound men in place of our sick, would have undoubtedly been able to accomplish more. But the movements of the expeditionary force, the orders for which were issued by the Commissioner of Uganda on the 7th July 1898, and which must have been contemplated on an even earlier date, were not communicated to me until 7th October, when it was too late to be of assistance to me.[12]

Martyr got as far north as 6°N latitude, ascertained the whereabouts of the Dervishes, established forts at Affudu (near present-day Nimule), Limogi and Fort Berkeley and made treaties with Madi and Shuli chiefs. He confirmed that the Belgians had moved into the leased territory under the 1894 agreement, and that the British had thereby obtained a buffer against the Dervishes. In forts at Rejaf, Lado, Kero and Bedden (opposite Fort Berkeley), the Belgians had garrisons totalling 2000 armed men; they had launched a large paddle steamer on the Nile, so large that it had difficulty navigating the river's 'sinuosities'. The waning of imperial rivalry between Britain and the Congo Free State was evident in the friendly relations between Belgian and British officers in their respective forts on opposite sides of the Nile near the Bedden rapids. The mountain and upland region to the immediate east of Obbo were already being used as sanatoria by them both.

These three expeditions, Macdonald's, Austin's and Martyr's, especially the former two, put the geography of northern Uganda in order. Martyr traversed country already well known, but Macdonald and Austin surveyed hitherto unknown country. Their work stood firm until a topographical survey was made in the twentieth century. As a result of Macdonald's efforts, Johnston, when he arrived in 1899, was able to extend the Uganda Protectorate's boundaries over territory already well surveyed by Macdonald. Something at least had been retrieved from his ill-fated expedition.

By March 1899 Macdonald was back at Mombasa, and soon on his way to England. Meanwhile diplomacy had rendered the situation in the Nile Basin free from immediate danger and no more costly adventures would be undertaken there. The disputes between France and England over the Upper Nile were terminated by a Declaration, signed in London on 21 March 1899, by Lord Salisbury and M. Cambon, which delimited the respective spheres of influence of the two powers in the disputed area. The whole drainage system of the Nile was reserved to England and Egypt, with France having a free hand in the rest of northern Africa, west of the Nile Valley not yet occupied by Europeans. This massive partition of half a continent by two European powers did not excite the enthusiasm of the rest. Germany, however, was soothed by promise of observance of the 'Open Door' policy on the Upper Nile; and although Italy protested meekly, she followed Germany. Russia had no interest in that quarter. The Declaration may thus be said to have been recognized by the world in general. But not by Leopold.

He continued to press his claims to the Bahr el Ghazal now that the French were discomfitted and had withdrawn from it. British authorities in Uganda were also eager to seize it. Kitchener opposed such a move, and so did Salisbury. When Johnston, Special Commissioner in Uganda, planned an expedition into the Bahr el Ghazal in the spring of 1900, it was vetoed by the Foreign Office in no uncertain terms.

British authorities in Uganda had their hands full with local problems without taking on a grandiose plan for an advance to the north. Berkeley, who had succeeded Colvile as Commissioner in April 1897, was much absorbed in the day-to-day details of administration which were gradually being worked out. The commissioner's headquarters at Entebbe, about 25 miles from Kampala, was the hub from which British authority radiated. George Wilson, ex-IBEAC official in charge of the Kampala station, exercised a strong personal influence over the king, chiefs and population as a whole. Under his tutelage, and with his love of 'shauri' (discussion and harangue), orderly legislation and debate emerged from weekly 'barazas' (meetings) over which he presided in paladin-like fashion, and which were attended by a host of curious onlookers. Native legislation and statutes, the result of much talking and careful deliberation, were recorded in English and Luganda. Native law and British law were gradually welded into an amalgam suited to the needs of the country. A host of questions had to be attended to: the abolition of the practice of taking women as captives in times of war; the right of a husband to beat his wife; introduction of sanitary regulations; rules for attendance of chiefs at the capital during a portion of the year; performance of provincial duties by sub-chiefs; registration of native marriages; ratification of native administrative acts by the king and his council – an endless array, many of which posed knotty problems, especially over land tenure, came before the courts. The commissioner, in his exalted state, might deal with matters of high or low concern, ranging from intervention with the Kabaka, on his inflicting the death penalty; to Manyuema slave-raiding into western Uganda; the question of language allowances for officers; and the ordering of gold signet rings for chiefs who had assisted in the recent campaign against Bunyoro – and a ring for Mwanga – 'a little larger than the others and with "M" and a crown engraved on it'. While these minutiae of state were being shaped into a body of administrative practice there was constant cognizance of the old danger lurking on Uganda's northern frontiers, for Kabarega was now stirring again. After taking up his position at Fatiko, on being pushed out of southern Bunyoro, he had carried out a blood purge among his followers, in which 300 persons perished. He opened up direct communication with the Dervishes, and throughout late 1896 and early 1897 continued to raid into his old kingdom to the south over which the British, in his absence, had declared a protectorate in June 1896.[13] And soon, compounded with the re-emerging troubles with Kabarega, was that posed by Mwanga, who now raised his head. Mwanga had been convicted in December 1896 of smuggling ivory into the German sphere – 'in a moment of aberration under evil advice', so he claimed. He was fined, and close surveillance placed over his finances. This he founded exceedingly irksome, and he was soon conspiring with Gabriel, his Mujasi (head of his police) and with Manyuema raiders in western Uganda, to join him in common cause against the European. It was also rumoured that he planned a Catholic kingdom in Buddu, and, more portentous – for it would throw Buganda into confusion – he contemplated another change in his religion. Colvile, forewarned of this, stationed troops in Buddu. Mwanga then fled to Ankole, taking refuge with a colony of bhang (hemp) smokers. He was now declared an outlaw, and his infant son, Daudi Chwa, proclaimed his successor, under a regency. Successful military engagements against his supporters forced Mwanga to flee still further south, into German territory where he continued to intrigue. The Germans, embarrassed by this unwelcome guest, placed him in restrictive residence at Mwanza at the south of the lake.

In late December 1898 Mwanga escaped from the Germans, and with some 500 Muslim Baganda fled north to Bunyoro where he threw in his lot with Kabarega and the remnant of Sudanese mutineers (some 250 in number) who had taken refuge there. The combined rebel forces eluded a pincer movement led by Captain Fowler and Lieutenant Coles, and escaped into the Bugoma forest. In December 1898 Major Price caught up with them, meted out severe punishment, and dispersed the remainder. They later regrouped and rallied under the old stalwart, Kabarega, now in savage mood, for he had lost his kingdom, and one of his sons, Tosiya, had been placed on his throne by the British in early

1898. He was ready for a final challenge of arms with the British. In this final engagement, however, Lieutenant Evatt forced Kabarega and Mwanga, with their gaggle of mutineers and Muslim Baganda, back into Lango country where they suffered heavy loss of prestige when several thousand of their women deserted them. The Bukedi also, formerly Kabarega's allies, now began to withdraw and silently slip away to their homes, no longer willing to suffer for his waning cause. The final denouement was soon at hand. In a surprise manoeuvre, on 9 April 1899, Evatt captured both Mwanga and Kabarega in the south Lango country. It is a measure of their mutual disrelish for 'Ingleza' rule that these two potentates, whose kingdoms so long had been at enmity with each other, now found themselves bedfellows, prisoners of the British and deported to the Seychelles. On his way to exile in the Seychelles, Mwanga completed his religious oscillations by conversion to Lutheranism at Kismayu. He died in the Seychelles in 1903. Kabarega was allowed to return to East Africa in 1923, but died at Jinja on the way to Bunyoro. His line was not extinguished, for he left 250 children.

As to the remnant of the mutineers, some 103 in number, isolated in the Lango country north of Lake Kioga and joined by bands of renegade Lango, they continued to be a source of annoyance to the Uganda administration. They organized themselves into a military company under their own 'Sergeants and Sergeant-Major'. This small republic of fugitives maintained a remarkable discipline. Guards and routine duties were performed rigorously. There was intense loyalty to their leaders whose orders were obeyed with strict fidelity. Increasing hostility of the Lango instilled a sense of cohesion among the mutineers which might have been otherwise lacking, and the habits of former military service under the British remained strong with them. Their station was a collection of huts and houses spread over a considerable area, on an admirable site near the junction of the Oloin and Toshi Rivers. Many of the houses were rectangular and built in the European fashion, the whole being surrounded by a light palisade. An entry post on a high platform with a commanding view of the surrounding country and a tall flagstaff erected in imitation of an official station, produced an atmosphere reminiscent of an Indian frontier station or a desert fortress in Nubia. The mutineers and their Lango allies were exceedingly well-armed, being supplied with rifles not only from Kabarega but from raids on caravans. In Emin Pasha's time the Lango had cut up a column of 200 Sudanese in the Umiro country, destroying it to a man. Remington rifles belonging to this ill-fated body were met 'everywhere' well into the

twentieth century. Offers of lenient terms of surrender to the mutineers
brought in a mere handful of repentants.

In early 1901 a full-scale campaign was launched against them by
Major Delmé-Radcliffe. The operations against the mutineers took
nearly four months. Heavy rains, swamps and grass up to nine feet in
height impeded progress at every step. The mutineers took refuge in
waterlogged regions, but their pursuers were remorseless. Captain Petrie
entered a papyrus swamp, up to his neck in foul-smelling mud and water
at every step, to drive out the mutineers, and was recommended for the
Victoria Cross. The first weakening of the enemy came in October 1901
when a number of Lango chiefs were persuaded to come over to the
British side, and entered into a ceremony to remove blood-brotherhood
rites made with the mutineers:

> Dr Bagshawe, with due formalities, injected a dose of apomorphine
> into the cicatrix of the incision made in the 'blood-brotherhood'
> rites. This made the patient violently sick in about five minutes. A
> few nauseous draughts afterwards completed the operation, and
> the subject's satisfaction in the breaking of the spell.[14]

Whether these mysterious rites were worth the fighting power thus
gained was doubtful. The Lango could rarely be trusted for they had
many relatives and friends on both sides, but by the end of December
1901 the campaign was over; only five mutineers of the original band
remained at large. Pax Britannica extended to the Sudanese borders.

Amidst the distraction of the Upper Nile question and the mutiny of
the Sudanese troops, the demarcation of Uganda's boundaries and
extension of administration had continued. That a delimitation of the
30th meridian would show its true position to be much farther east than
assumed was suspected by both Belgian and British authorities, although
both were covertly satisfied that the other side was unaware of the error.
Leopold hoped to get the slopes of Ruwenzori, salt ponds at Katwe and
Fort Henry by a corrected line, and the British hoped to get Leopold to
commit himself to the Semliki as a more satisfactory boundary line,
before the error in the 30th meridian's position was discovered. Its
correct position was determined at Khartoum in May 1900, and then
confirmed by the German–Belgian commission at work in the Kivu
area, in the same year. In the interval both Germans and Belgians were
intruding themselves into the Mufumbiro region, and it was in this
period also that Johnston's proposal for an expedition into the Bahr el

Ghazal was vetoed by Salisbury, for it would have given umbrage to Leopold when Britain was seeking his agreement on the Semliki line. Leopold, 'second to none at a hard bargain', would accept a Semliki boundary in return for fulfilment of his May 1894 treaty – that is including his receiving the southern Bahr el Ghazal and West Nile District and the Mahagi Strip. He wanted full-blown redemption on Britain's part, now that France was out of the picture. There followed offers, counter-offers, and at one stage the threat of military conflict, before Leopold relinquished his claims, retaining only the Lado Enclave and lease of the Mahagi Strip.

No adjustments were made to Uganda's southern boundary with the German sphere, defined as the latitude 1°S but which crossed the Kagera River near its mouth, and then, 60 miles to the west, met it again. This resulted in a considerable tract of land, traditionally part of Buganda and Ankole, being included in the German sphere. The Baganda here continued to look to their chiefs in the British sphere, and Baganda rebels found it a congenial place to flee to, being among their own people but under the umbrella of German protection. British officials in Uganda emphasized the Kagera line as the natural frontier for southern Uganda, as it would 'greatly assist in solidifying the Waganda', in checking an illicit trade in slaves, arms and powder and in halting German encroachment into British territory. They urged that Britain exchange this tract for a line bisecting Kilimanjaro, or, alternatively, might not the Germans agree to a Kagera line in exchange for Mufumbiro? This was not to be, for nothing would induce the Germans to part with their great prize, Kilimanjaro. Its inclusion in the German sphere by the 1890 Agreement has been attributed to the Kaiser's infatuation with the mountain. It was rather the fact that Dr Fischer, a German, had been there before the British, and also German treaty rights had priority on grounds of effective occupation. As for the Mufumbiro region, the Germans were already infiltrating there. A German map of 1895 shows a portion of Koki and Ankole as being in German territory,[15] and German officials in April 1900 were in temporary possession of Kabale, well within British territory. Elsewhere the Germans were not too concerned whether they encroached on British territory; their discovery of a gold reef on the eastern side of Lake Victoria and in their territory led them to seek its continuance northwards into the British sphere. The British likewise transgressed the German boundary. Captain Whitehouse, on the eve of his survey of the northern (British) half of Lake Victoria in 1901, landed at Shirati in

German territory and gave the chief there a medal and assured him that he was under British protection. That relations between the Germans and British throughout these incursions on each other's territory remained amicable indicates the minor concern they caused on either side. The Germans, in friendly manner, invited Captain Whitehouse to extend his survey of Lake Victoria to their half of the lake, and soon an Anglo-German boundary commission was at work, from December 1902 to early 1904, demarcating and marking with cairns the boundary between the lake and the Congo State. By January 1906 the stretch from Lake Victoria to the Indian Ocean had also been surveyed by an Anglo-German commission. On the Uganda-Congo side, drawing on the fine work of the Duke of Abruzzi's expedition in Ruwenzori, a demarcation was completed by April 1908. Finally, at Brussels, on 14 May 1910, an Anglo-Belgian delegation agreed on a boundary line for the Mfumbiro region, and for the transfer to Belgium of the western side of Lake Albert where the Mahagi Strip had long ceased to have meaning. The position of the 30th meridian, as finally fixed at this Brussels meeting, showed it to have been originally placed 25 miles west of its true position. It had been a grave error. As late as 1960 Toro in western Uganda was pressing claims to territory in the Congo on the basis of the mistaken position of the 30th meridian in the 1890s.

Uganda's north-eastern boundary with Ethiopia, placed by the Intelligence Division in 1890 at 8°N latitude, was reduced by the Anglo-Ethiopian agreement of 1901 to 4½°N latitude, and this was confirmed by treaty with Ethiopia on 15 May 1902, with a concession, never taken up, for right of way through Ethiopia for a railway to connect the Sudan with Uganda. An agreement between Ethiopia, the East African Protectorate and Uganda in 1906 rounded out their mutual frontiers. Macdonald had some lively ideas as to the alignment of a railway to tap the resources of the Upper Nile from a point which he termed a 'commercial boundary', from where it would be equally cheap to ship goods either to Alexandria or Mombasa, and which would cross the Nile at about 4°N latitude (near present-day Nimule). A railway would be constructed to here from Port Florence on Lake Victoria, or alternatively from Naivasha, skirting the western flanks of Ethiopia and Lake Rudolf and thus linking Mombasa with the Nile. Macdonald saw such a railway ultimately being extended on to Khartoum. He was years ahead of his time in ideas of railway lines in East Africa.

His views comported well with those of Cromer and Kitchener, who held that Uganda was merely an extension southwards of Egypt's old

Equatorial Province, and that the Cape-to-Cairo vision was now possible of fulfilment, following Kitchener's reconquest of the Sudan. Cromer could see 'no pressing necessity' for a definition of a Uganda-Sudan boundary – they were all one territory! He urged Uganda to look to the north, to the Nile and Khartoum, for its communications. There was an excellent steamship service on the Nile, and mails from Uganda could reach London in 25 days. Lieutenant-Colonel Martyr, in charge of Nile District, had established a regular postal service with native runners armed with Sniders, wearing 'a blue cotton uniform' and on a salary of ten rupees per month, delivering the mails with 'surprising celerity'. With the advent of the Uganda Railway at Lake Victoria at the end of 1901, the refreshing and novel idea of Macdonald's 'commercial boundary' and railway alignment according with it, quickly faded away. It might have given an entirely new twist to the development of East-Central Africa.

The decline of the importance of the Upper Nile was now a reality. Winston Churchill in his journey up the Nile in 1907 observed that Wadelai was a pathetic collection of deserted billets – the Belgians had pulled out. The theatre a few years previous of international rivalry and of legendary figures – Baker, Gordon, Emin Pasha and Stanley – all was now quiet there. The allure of the Upper Nile was a thing of the past. With Leopold's death on 17 December 1909, the lease of the Lado Enclave expired and it reverted to British rule, and was formally transferred to the Sudan on 16 June 1910. At the same time the boundary along the Nile/Congo watershed west of Lake Albert was replaced by the Semliki River and the median line of Lake Albert, with Mahagi Port left to the Belgians. In 1914 a demarcation of the Uganda-Sudan frontier resulted in the southern portion of the Lado Enclave being incorporated in Uganda to become the West Nile District, while the area to the east of the Nile, from Nimule northwards, including Gondokoro and Nimule districts, passed to the Sudan. Agreement was also reached on the frontier eastwards to Abyssinia at the northern end of Lake Rudolf. In September 1926 Uganda ceded to the Sudan an area in the vicinity of Tereteinia to reunite tribal groups such as the Latuka, severed by the 1914 boundary. Also transferred to the Sudan was the healthy mountainous region of south-west Lautuka with its rich food supplies and accessibility to the Nile, making it easier to implement sleeping sickness regulations. This arrangement placed the Madi tribe on both sides of the Nile near Dufile entirely in Uganda.

Uganda's eastern boundary resulted from two major cessions to

Kenya. The transfer was made in 1902 of her Eastern Province (extending eastwards to Lakes Naivasha and Baringo and including much of the western highlands of Kenya, Laikipia, Uasin Gishu, Nandi and Kavirondo) to the East African Protectorate. Rudolf Province, sparsely populated by nomadic pastoral tribes, and also part of Uganda, but more readily accessible from Kenya, was formally transferred to the latter territory by Order in Council in 1926 which also defined the whole interterritorial boundary from a point on parallel of 1°S latitude to the Sudan boundary near Mount Zulia, thus establishing the Uganda–Kenya frontier as it is today. For convenience of tribal control in 1931, the 'Karasuk' area of Kenya west of the Turkwell River was transferred for administrative purposes to Uganda, although continuing to be legally Kenya territory.

9· East Africa under HMG

Sir Gerald Portal during his mission to Uganda turned his mind to the broad divisions into which East Africa should be demarcated for administrative purposes following the anticipated withdrawal of the IBEAC. He proposed that the boundary of Uganda to the east should extend as far as Kavirondo, and that Uganda should be under one commissioner. The territory between Uganda and the coast should be administered directly through the British Consular Agent at Zanzibar, aided by an establishment of British officers and native soldiery. Portal estimated that the whole British sphere in East Africa could thus be administered for as little as £50,000, much less than that asked by the IBEAC for administering Uganda alone. Portal's early death prevented him from playing an important role in shaping British East Africa's future administration.

The real work was done by the Committee on the Administration of East Africa set up by the Foreign Office in April 1895, and very much under the directing hand of Sir Percy Anderson, aided by Colonel Colvile, who had had direct experience in Uganda. The Committee recommended that the whole of the Mau plateau and Naivasha area as far east at Dagoretti (near present-day Nairobi) to where the IBEAC had withdrawn, should be included in Uganda. There would be a commissioner for Uganda, and another (the Consular Agent at Zanzibar acting in this capacity) for the territory between Uganda and the coast. The Sultan's coastal strip would be made over to HMG at an annual rent of £11,000; and the £200,000 invested in British Consols on the Zanzibar government's behalf should be used to buy out the IBEAC lease of the coastal strip.

Within the broad divisions laid down by the Committee, further divisions would be necessary. In Uganda, apart from the newly created extension to the eastwards, these could be based on the historic kingdoms. As for the vast territory between Uganda and the Indian

Ocean and stretching from the Umba to the Juba, transferred to HMG in a ceremony at Mombasa on 1 July 1895, no such historic kingdoms existed there, and the administrative divisions here derived very much from the previous pattern of administration of the IBEAC and the historic claims of the Sultan of Zanzibar, with Hardinge himself adding his own notions. It was a grand opportunity presented to Hardinge: he was free to divide and administer a vast region as he best saw fit, and he had at hand a small cadre of experienced officials taken over from the IBEAC. In dealing with the explored and known part of the East Africa Protectorate[1] Hardinge acted as though it were a smaller India. He created four provinces. Seyyldie, Tanaland, Jubaland and Ukamba, each under a sub-Commissioner; each province in turn, was divided into districts, under a District Officer and Assistant. The remainer of the protectorate, extending north from the Lorian Swamp to Lake Rudolf and Ethiopia, was left a no man's land: a large portion of this later became known as the Northern Frontier District of Kenya.

The first of the provinces, Seyyidie (King's land), included the coastal strip (the last remnant of the Sultan's ancient claims on the mainland), where the Sultan's flag would fly alongside the Union Jack. In addition to the coastal strip, it included the immediate hinterland and the waterless desert extending inland some 50 to 100 miles, which gave the province a natural boundary on its western side. Seyyidie was inhabited mainly by agricultural Bantu tribes, with political and social institutions of a very primitive character. Its people, especially near the coast, were Muslim in religion and had adopted the Muslim practice of interment of their dead, instead of leaving them to be devoured by hyenas. There was a large Arab and Swahili population in the coastal strip and in Mombasa and Malindi, and this factor provided a basis for the division of Seyyidie into the three districts of Malindi, Mombasa and Vanga, each with its own headquarters, in addition to the provincial capital at Mombasa.[2] Seyyidie Province was the home of the Nyika group of Bantu peoples. The entire group traced their origin to the legendary city of Shaingwaya, believed to have been near Somalia. The Giriama, the largest of the group, occupied a portion of the Nyika, some 20 miles inland and between Mombasa and the Sabaki River, numbering about 70,000 persons. Originally settled near the mouth of the Sabaki River they had been forced by pressure from Maasai raids and the loss of great herds of cattle to move southwards to the more fertile Kilifi District where at the time of British arrival they had settled down, cultivating cotton, cashew nuts, some tropical fruits, cassava, rice, millet, sorghum and eleusine.

Associated with the Giriama were smaller subtribes, the Ribe, Rabai, Kauma, Jibana and Kambe. With the cessation of Maasai raids and their own rapid increase in numbers, the Giriama, by the mid-1890s, were daring to push northwards across the Sabaki River, their former frontier on that side.

In the polity of the Giriama and allied tribes great emphasis was laid on a system of elders, instead of hereditary or military rulers. These Elders (Kambi), a sacred association numbering some 5000 persons, were ranked in ascending degrees of importance, passage through which was by initiatory rites and the giving of gifts. An inner circle of Elders at the top included three supreme Elders (the interpreters of the ancient tribal mysteries and customs), and the 'Fisi' or 'Hyenas' (six senior Elders of the six clans into which the Giriama were divided, along with a few other sages or wizards) who administered the sacred Hyena oath to suspected criminals. The dread power of the 'Fisi' arose from their ability to invoke sudden death (usually by secret murder) for those guilty of perjury, scepticism, or violation of the consecrated fields of the sacred Hyena (the living shrine of the dead ancestors of their race) which were closely guarded by the 'Fisi'. The Elders were themselves exempt from military service, but summoned on the sacred drum the young men of fighting age to war. Allied to the Giriama and with similar institutions were the smaller communities of the Duruma and Digo, the region to the immediate south of the Giriama, who were later arrivals than the latter. The Duruma, unlike other people of the Nyika group, remained possessors of large herds of cattle, despite threat from Maasai raiders.

To the north of the Giriama, and somewhat mingled with them, were the Wasania – a dwarf-like people, occupying the wooded western part of the Malindi District. Entirely naked, and with habitations of the most primitive kind – often the hollow trunks of trees – the Wasania were probably the survivors of an earlier race. They displayed considerable acumen and lively wits in maintaining their position in the midst of more powerful neighbours with whom they had established a symbiotic relationship. They accepted passively their role as slaves to the Galla, and gave the chiefs of the latter one tusk of every elephant killed. Although living chiefly on small game which they killed with their poisoned arrows, they also managed to bring down elephant by hamstringing them with their knives. The Wasania were purveyors of a particulary kind of virulent and deadly poison to other tribes, especially the Giriama, receiving in return trade goods from the coast.

To the immediate north of Seyyidie was the province of Tana, or

Tanaland, named after the river whose valley it largely comprised, extending inland from the Indian Ocean to the foothills of Mount Kenya and to the Lorian Swamp. It was about three times the size of Seyyidie and consisted of three districts: Lamu District – taking in the archipelago of the same name and Witu protectorate; Port Dunford District – based on the small harbour of the same name (it was later transferred to the neighbouring Jubaland Province); Tana District – the largest of the three – comprising most of the Tana River Valley.

Lamu, chief port and capital of the province, was sited on an island of the same name, and along with Siyu, Faza and Pate formed a miniature archipelago a few miles off the mainland, and was formerly administrative centre of the IBEAC (Captain Rogers, formerly in IBEAC employ, continued on as sub-Commissioner under the new administration). Lamu was the scene of the bizarre attempt by the Freelanders to found an international socialist colony in 1894. Lamu was a town of considerable antiquity. Its mixed population included a few hundred Arabs and many Bajun, the latter a coast people of Bantu type with an admixture of Arab blood who were found all along the coast from Mombasa to Kismayu, and who lived almost entirely as fishermen and agriculturists, and who were also actively engaged in the mangrove pole (boriti) industry. At Lamu the fair skins and features of some of the Swahili population was warrant for their claim to Persian descent; and it was here, so it was averred, that the purest Swahili on the coast was spoken. With its white buildings and Islamic architecture, Lamu was impressive from a distance, but closer scrutiny revealed, as in the case of most East African towns, the usual aspects of semi-decay and disrepair.

The largest tribe in the Tana Province were the Pokomo, the furthest north of the Nyika group, a large unwarlike Bantu tribe of agriculturists and fishermen, who inhabited the banks of the lower Tana River and whose flood waters they utilized to irrigate their food crops of rice, cassava and maize, As non-Muslims they supplemented this diet with fish and meat. Dug-out canoes from hollowed tree trunks served as the chief means of transport, and during flood-time the life of the Pokomo took on a decidely aquatic character. The British found the country of the Pokomo easy to administer – most parts of it could be visited by boat when the flood waters inundated the outer reaches of the Tana River.

Also in Tanaland Province were the Galla, part of that great nation whose origins lay in southern Ethiopia and western Somaliland, two branches of which, the Boran and Orma, under pressure from the Somalis had pushed southwards into what was now the East African

Protectorate. The Boran occupied the more remote part, between Lake Rudolf and the Juba River, with concentrations at Marsabit, Garba Tulla and Moyale, and with a permanent water supply at the Uaso Nyiro River. The Orma, the most southerly penetration of Hamites into the protectorate, lived in the bare and thinly populated steppes of the upper reaches of the Tana and on the uncultivated plains to the east and west of it, unaffected by its fertilizing waters and headstreams. They also extended into and mingled with the Bantu Pokomo in the Tana River District, where there was permanent water supply for their cattle. A tall, handsome, warlike nomadic pastoral people, the Galla bore a considerable resemblance in physical appearance, institutions and way of life to the Wahima of south-western Uganda. Cattle was their principal form of wealth, and the breed evolved by the Boran and Orma were of an exceptional hardiness.

Their political organization was patriarchal, a loose monarchical type of government by hereditary rulers (termed kings by Europeans), of whom Afalata of Boran was believed to be the greatest. The Galla were distinctive in that they assigned a higher place to their women than was usual among African tribes, and they tended to monogamy. Although largely Islamicized, there was widespread adherence to a pre-Islamic tradition of a supreme being, the 'Waka', and of a sacred book in which was enshrined the holy tablets of their faith; but unfortunately this book had been devoured by a cow – hence the engrossed interest with which the Galla examined the entrails of their slaughtered cattle, hoping to retrieve the long-lost volume. A good deal of mystery and romance was attached to this remote people. Information about them, prior to European exploration in the 1890s, derived mainly from native reports and accounts by Mr Wakefield, a missionary who had travelled on the upper Juba in the later 1860s, and also from the ill-fated expedition of Baron von der Decken in 1867 (the remains of his steamer were still visible on the Juba in the mid-twentieth century). At the coast it still was rumoured that the Galla were Christians. Hardinge stated:

> the more I learn of the Boran and Rendile Gallas, the more I am convinced that they are the people spoken of by Krapf in 1849 as the still surviving Christian remnants at the Equator of whom I hear in Shoa and it is a curious fact that every Somali girl from the interior whose mother or grandmother was a Boran woman captured by the Somalis, wears as an ornament a round white shell or stone, having a black leather cross upon it.[3]

Great trade opportunities lay in contacting the Galla country, with its varied products: ivory, coffee berries, nitrate of soda, ponies, cattle, donkeys, goats, glue, barley, indiarubber and hides. The kingdom of Boran was reputedly rich in ivory, gold and horses, a land where the houses of the wealthy were surrounded by ivory stockades; and at one place, Jan Jan, white, red and dark green stones, much desired for decorative purposes and as a valuable trade commodity, were obtainable. At Konso on the Juba, a colony of weavers produced a cotton cloth which was exported to great distances. The trade-routes to the Boran country passed through the region of the Somali, who had intruded themselves between the Galla and the sea, isolating them from European contact. The IBEAC had failed to tap the rich reserves of the Galla trade, and to break the monopoly of the Somali over it.

Jubaland, the most northerly province in Hardinge's administrative structuring, stretched from Tanaland in the south to the Juba River in the north; it extended inland less than half the distance of Tanaland, and was much more desert-like in character than the former. It was divided into two districts – Kismayu District and the Juba River District. Its coast was of dreary and forbidding aspect, and its interior unproductive and barren. In its desert character and in its peoples, Jubaland more rightly belonged to the Horn of Africa. Apart from the fertile well-watered valley of the Juba, and the brief flush of green that appeared on the inland plateau during the short rainy season when the tall grass sprang up, and as quickly died down, all was dry bare plain and isolated clumps of mimosa and thorn bush scrub, with a few plants yielding fragrant resin and balsam. Water was obtainable at only a few water-holes visited by wandering pastoral nomads. Its few towns were unimposing and confined to a coastal strip notorious for the difficulty it presented for the harbouring of ships during the south-west monsoon.

Kismayu, on the coastline some 200 miles north of Lamu, and sited on a sandy plain facing the sea, just south of the mouth of the Juba River, was the only place north of Manda Bay where vessels could shelter at all seasons of the year. It was a town of about 250 houses and a few mosques – some well-constructed and of stone. It had a population of about 1200 persons of mixed race, including a few Indian trading families. Immediately to the north and on the outskirts of the town was a large Somali village of grass huts, and nearby was the settlement of the Swedish Christian Mission with large stone houses and surrounding native huts. There was a substantial import of rice; and fresh mutton and lamb were always available at Kismayu; and when, in the late 1890s, a fresh water supply was laid on by the pipeline from the Juba River, a few miles away, life for the few Europeans there became tolerable. The town was the centre of an exotic trade in ambergris, orchella seed, ostrich feathers, shark fins, incense, ivory and hides. It was the main outlet for Somali middlemen who held a monopoly of the trade between the interior and the coast, a trade which they jealously guarded.

The peoples of Jubaland Province were predominantly Hamitic and of a nomadic pastoral type, but there were two exceptions. At the coast and extending inland for some 20 to 30 miles were the Waboni, the survivors of the earliest inhabitants, holding a helot position in relation to other tribes much like that of the Wandorobo in regard to the Maasai. Europeans who first met them described them as similar to Australian aborigines, with their 'curved nostrils like those of a horse' and their custom of marriage by combat, using knives, however, instead of clubs. They were an aquatic people, their lives revolving around the coming and going of the rains and the swelling and receding of Lake Hardinge, a great sheet of water which appeared during the rainy season, and which they traversed in their canoes, and from which they obtained their principal diet, fish. Their ritual of shooting arrows into the sky to make rain come down, their tiny huts resembling oversized acorns and their flight on the slightest approach of danger like so many wild birds, was bound to make the Waboni an object of interest to Hardinge, always fascinated by the unusual. Despite their reputation for using poisoned arrows, the Waboni presented no great obstacle to European control.

The Wagosha inhabited a hundred-mile stretch of the lower Juba and cleverly utilized its periodical flooding to irrigate the land on either side for a distance of up to three or four miles in depth. This agricultural productivity, and the nearby forests rich in timber and rubber, made Gosha truly the 'Dongola Province' of the Juba – the East African Nile. The Wagosha numbered from 40,000 to 50,000 persons, mostly runaway slaves who had fled their Arab, Somali and Galla masters, and whose numbers were continually augmented by newcomers. The Somali and Galla tolerated this defection of their slaves on condition that the Wagosha regularly handed over to them large quantities of ivory. The Wagosha possessed no regular government, each village or group of villages being administered by its own local headman, who maintained his authority by persuasion or fear. The most important of these 'runaway' slave chiefs with whom the British came into contact was Nasib Pondo, 'a crafty old greybeard', who wore the Arab 'Joho' and turban, and aspired to a reputation as a powerful magician. The

Wagosha, although nominally Muslim, Swahili-speaking and surrounded by pastoralists, differed from the latter in that they drank native beer, were sedentary in habit and good cultivators. They were timorous and wary and lived in considerable dread of the Somali, but were protected by the tsetse fly which infected Goshaland and by the fringe of forest surrounding it which deterred the Somali with their cattle from entering the district. The Wagosha, like the Waboni, presented no great obstacle to European control, and were accounted as usually friendly, the IBEAC having made treaties with them.

In striking contrast to these Bantu cultivators were the pastoral 'Somali' (probably from *zu mal,* Arabic for 'possessors of wealth'), that great branch of the Hamitic race which occupied the Horn of Africa as far down as the Juba and even extended into the British sphere. They lived in the steep country and on the undulating sandy plains lying behind the tsetse-ridden coast, constantly moving from water-hole to water-hole, ever seeking new grazing ground for their herds of cattle, on which they lived almost entirely. The two principal Somali tribes with whom the British had to deal were the Ogaden and Herti, both of whom claimed descent from Durod bin Ismail, an Arab, who several centuries previously came over from Arabia and married a woman of Dir. In Somali tradition this ancient migration was still fresh in mind, reflected in the southward movement of the race which was still in progress in the nineteenth century. The Herti remained near the coast, the Ogaden farther inland. About the mid-nineteenth century the Herti moved southward by land and sea, and settled near Kismayu at Yonte on the right bank of the Juba, where they became known as the 'coast' or 'Mijjertein' Somali. The Ogaden split into two divisions one of which remained in the Webi Shibeli River area while the other, numbering some 5000 warriors, crossed the Juba and settled near the Afmadu wells about 100 miles north-west of Kismayu. This latter branch of the Ogaden constituted a nuisance for the British. Under an assertive chief, Murgan bin Yusuf, they made a show of sovereignty over the territory from the Afmadu wells to Kismayu. They lived in wretched huts, had few possessions, but put on a great show of dignity and bearing, with their white robes and deference to the higher principles of Islam; but there was also cupidity, and the subsidies provided them by the IBEAC merely awakened their avarice and increased their insolence. Like the Galla in their love of cattle, the Somali were rendered more fanatical and treacherous by their zeal for Islam without knowledge of its more detailed injunctions as to piety and peace.

The polity of the Somali was in striking contrast to that of the Bantu tribes farther south, their sheikhs and chieftains holding their position by strength of their following and social and religious position. The Somalis were most impressive to European travellers who visited their country. They were dedicated Muslims, a fine, handsome and manly race, and although long converted to Islam, they accorded their women a much higher place than was usual among Muslims and did not require them to live in purdah. The shapely heads and white beards of the older sheikhs which gave them a distinctively patriarchal air, 'their clear eyes and quick intelligent gaze ... the outcome of a healthy life unaffected by the use of stimulants', made them impressive figures for British officers acquainted only with the more primitive tribes further down the coast. There was, however, another side to the Somali. Their intelligence was only equalled by their uncurbed insolence. Burton had remarked 'They have all the levity and instability of the Negro character ... light-minded as the Abyssinians', and (quoting Gobat) they were 'constant in nothing but inconstancy – soft, merry, and affectionate souls, they pass without any apparent transition into a state of fury'. There was no doubt as to the capability of the Somalis as fighters; they were extremely cunning in warfare, and capable of extraordinary feats of physical endurance. They carried small round shields of giraffe hide and fought in pairs with stabbing spears and knife, one man seizing his adversary while the other stabbed him. They had tactical preference for ambushes, and close fighting in thick bush country. In the Somali, according to Hardinge, 'a great recruiting field lies at our hand virtually untapped',

> The race, in my opinion, has no equal in this part of Africa, either in intelligence or courage. They have come down from the north like a conquering host, driving the Gallas and Bajunes before them. They have till recently succeeded in keeping Europeans entirely out of their country: they are not afraid of Maxim guns, cannon or other firearms.[4]

The King's African Rifles were later to find their best soldiers among the Somali.

The Somali were great travellers. Normally the limit of their penetration southwards was the Tana River, but in April 1901 they raided in great strength down into the Maasai country south of Mount Kenya, and established a strong settlement at Biscaya, inland from Port Durnford. Well-worn tracks throughout their country testified to their nomadic habits. Their huts were of the slenderest kind, being merely sticks placed in circular form in the ground, drawn together at the top, and covered with thick, well-made mats of aloe fibre, resembling the yurts of Turcoman tribes of Central Asia. When travelling, they carried their mats, together with skins, milk and ghee vessels, and small children on magnificent well-trained trek oxen, led by a string through their noses. Captain Osborne's expedition of 1901 captured several of these oxen and found them to be remarkably docile and well-trained, able to carry large loads when led by people familiar with them. The Somali, with their combination of austere nomadic patoral habits, their volatile nature as fighters and their religious zeal, were a people who must be taken into consideration. Both under British rule in East Africa and later under an independent Kenya, it could not be forgotten that there was a formidable race on the north-eastern frontiers.

Hardinge's boundary arrangements received radical alteration in April 1902, when Teita District was transferred to Seyyidie Province (with whom its trade connections and communications were most closely allied), and the territory north of the Thika River including Mount Kenya was constituted as a new province – Kenya. More important was the transfer of Uganda's large Eastern Province to the East Africa Protectorate and its division into two new provinces, Kisumu and Naivasha (the latter 'comparatively empty', with cool climate and of high agricultural potential, became an attractive area for European settlement).

The province of Ukamba, the largest in Hardinge's arrangement, bordered Seyyidie on the west and comprised the territory of hills and plains to the east of present-day Nairobi. It was largely occupied by Bantu tribes: the Wakamba, the Wakikuyu and Wateita – mainly agriculturists and resembling the Wanyika in their lack of a supreme chief or king, and in common possession of tribal lands. Each settlement had its own headman and elders, whose authority rested partly on age and experience and partly on personal qualities. The Wakamba, warriors and hunters and skilled in the use of the longbow and deadly poisons, were to provide the Kenya government with a fertile recruiting ground for its army and police forces in the twentieth century, especially during the Mau Mau Emergency. Ukamba Province, divided into four districts – Teita (including later a sub-district, Taveta), Uli, Kitui and Kenya Districts – had its capital at Machakos. Later Nairobi, owing to its healthier climate and half-way position between the coast and lake, was chosen for this purpose.

To the immediate west of the Wakamba were the large tribe of Bantu agriculturists, the Kikuyu, whose tribal lands occupied the fertile triangle bounded by Nairobi on the south, the Aberdares on the north-west and Mount Kenya on the north-east, an area largely covered by Kenya District. Small offshoots of the Kikuyu, the Embu and Meru, occupying the southern and eastern slopes of Mount Kenya respectively, were also intensive cultivators, although the Meru living in the dry plains to the immediate south-east of Mount Kenya were cattle keepers, more like the Wakamba. A lesser and shy people, the elusive Wandorobo, lived in the Fort Hall area, and were hunters and gatherers of honey, but were surrogate to the Kikuyu. The Kikuyu were rich in tribal legend, steeped in the mystic beliefs, ritual and witchcraft of their ancestors who originally came from Mount Kenya (Kiringwayo). They were a purposive and industrious people, but when the first white settlers arrived they found them much unsettled owing to raiding and warfare with the Maasai, and with their land decimated by smallpox and famine.

Hardinge estimated the total population of Ukamba Province at about 700,000 souls, largely Bantu agriculturists, but there was also the important pastoral and predatory element of the Nilo-Hamitic Maasai, consisting possibly of no more than 25,000 persons and on the decline, who occupied the grassy steppes to the west and south of the Kikuyu and in the Rift Valley, stretching down into German East Africa where a few of them had turned to agriculture. Living only on meat, milk and blood, and grazing their flocks and herds at will over a vast territory, they had devised an effective military organization which had inspired fear among other East African tribes and kept coastal peoples from penetrating inland.

The Maasai military organization of youths, or *Laioni,* were trained from childhood in boy regiments under a so-called *Legonan,* a youth of their own age. There was a system of age grades with military service compulsory for youths from 17 to 30, and this provided a standing army of young warriors, the *moran,* not unlike the Zulu impis. The rigorous physical training, exclusive devotion to military duties, the restraint placed on regular marriage before a certain age was attained and, in general, the severe martial discipline pervading the entire society from infancy to extreme old age, had built up a unique fighting machine. Rites of passage for the *moran* included 'bloodying' their spears by killing a lion. Lean and tough, inured to incredible hardships, a young warrior could walk 60 miles without food or water, and tackle a lion with only a spear. The fierce sanguinary battles among the young 'cadets' for the possession of the immature girls, known as 'dittos, who cooked their food and performed other menial duties, were surpassed in ferocity by the fights for captured cattle which signalized a return of the warriors from a successful raid; for each warrior wished to offer as many cattle as possible to his father, and thus achieve a step towards his own marriage, and a release from the exhilarating but strenuous life of military service.

Up to about 1880, the Maasai were still to be feared, frightening off Arab slavers, levying tribute on all who dared pass through their country, and even harrying the cultivated coast regions. Gradually internal dissension, and the great onslaught of smallpox and rinderpest took their toll from man and beast alike, and when Joseph Thomson passed through their country in 1883 the Maasai had already passed the peak of their power. The advent of the Pax Britannica was to hasten further this decline and curtail the wild, free existence of these sons of the steppes.

Their system of raiding their Bantu neighbours to replenish their stock, and to sharpen the fighting instincts of their warriors, was to leave them particularly vulnerable when this raiding and despoliation was no longer permitted under British rule, and at a time when the smallpox epidemic and cattle plague forced them to raid ever farther afield. Their enemies took advantage of this opportunity to turn on the hornets who had stung them so unmercifully in the past. The unguarded kraals were now plundered and the womenfolk and children carried off as slaves. Famine and disease compounded to wreak a fearful toll. Hardinge tells of how, with doubtful success, he endeavoured to explain to an old Maasai chief that the old days had gone forever.

The leading figure among the Maasai was the *Laibon* – a great medicine man, military leader, priest and diviner, combined in one. At the time of the arrival of the British, the *Laibon* was Lenana, a 'tall dignified and courteous chief', son of Mbatian, the previous *Laibon*. Lenana was soon won over to the British side when they refrained from exacting retribution from him for the murder by the Maasai of an English trader named Dick. Dick had fought off a Maasai attack on a large Swahili caravan in which 400 men were killed, and had gone down fighting. The Maasai so admired his bravery that they honoured his grave by heaping a stone cairn on it. Lenana was so impressed by British fairness in the matter that 'from that moment he became a firm friend to the English and a confident believer in their justice'. Another son of Mbatian was Sendeyo, who refused to acknowledge Lenana's authority, and there followed a bitter fratricidal war, with Sendeyo crossing into German territory, and Lenana and followers remaining on the British side of the frontier.

Akin to the Maasai were the complex of Nilo-Hamitic pastoral peoples, occupying much of what is today north-western Kenya, and straddling the western rim of the Great Rift Valley. They comprised the Nandi, Kipsigis, Elgeyo, Pokot (Suk), Samburu and Turkana. Their wealth consisted in cattle, and they constantly sought to augment the numbers of these and to seek new grazing ground for them. This led to raids and counter-raids, in which women and children were as often the prize of war as were cattle. These raids, usually at night, provided a fierce and sanguinary training for the young *moran*. The social system of the Nilo-Hamites varied in its closeness to that of the Maasai, from the Suk with scarcely any age-sets, to the Samburu of the Leroghi Plateau and Maralal district, whose young men were true *moran*, and like the Maasai, after the brief flowering of youth with its fighting and womanizing, quickly sank into the drunken stupor of old age, finally taking their place among the Elders. The Nandi, probably the best known of these Nilo-Hamites, were formerly a warrior race, but after a brief flurry of resistance to British rule, settled down to cultivate the land, although still remaining cattle keepers.

In the eastern part of Uganda, later included in Kenya, were the Nilotic Luo, who had come down from the north in a series of migrations, and were still struggling for a foothold on the shores of Lake Victoria. They were renowned warriors, fighting in a tight-knit phalanx, protected by a wall of huge shields and long spears: even the dauntless Maasai esteemed the Luo as fighters. Still farther to the west, in what was then Uganda's Eastern Province, but what was later to become part of the East African Protectorate, were the Abaluhya, a large group of Bantu-speaking peoples (formerly including the Kisii of South Nyanza), inhabiting the high ground to the immediate east of Lake Victoria and extending north to Mount Elgon, and west of the Nandi escarpment. This wedge of Bantu-speaking peoples perhaps reflected the earliest known Bantu intrusion in East Africa. The Abaluhya, harassed by night-raiding Nandi on the east, and day-fighting Luo on the west, were forced onto higher ground, where they had taken up their abode at the time the British entered their territory.

The ruins of their fortified villages, on the slopes of Elgon and the Kano plains near Kisumu, still gave evidence of their former power and wide-ranging domain.

This then was the vast panorama of land and peoples which fell to the British government when it took over control from the IBEAC, but the new administration had scarcely entered into its stewardship before it was faced by a formidable uprising headed by the Mazrui chieftains of Seyyidie Province.

The Mazrui uprising of 1895–96, which followed a dispute over the succession to the chieftainship of Takaungu, lasted for some ten months, and overlapped the transfer of administration from the IBEAC to the British government. It taxed the new administration to its limits, and so threatened the incipient Uganda Railway that reinforcements had to be called in from India. It belied British claims as to their peaceful occupation of East Africa, a contrast it was averred to the Germans and their Bushiri revolt.

The Mazrui connection with East Africa goes back to 1670, when Seif bin Sultan of Oman took Mombasa from the Portuguese and left a Mazrui, of the Ghafiri clan in Oman, in charge. Subsequently, when Mombasa was in Arab hands (it was lost and recaptured three times from the Portuguese before it was finally taken in 1730), a Mazrui was in control. They thus came to regard the governorship of Mombasa as rightfully theirs, and the natives of Mombasa and surrounding district looked upon them as their natural leaders. The rulers of Oman had unwittingly spawned rivals to their claim to sovereignty over this part of the East African coast.

When in 1837 Sultan Said of Oman, in the face of continued Mazrui contumely, took Mombasa (and promptly sent off Chief Rashid bin Salim and 20 followers who had surrendered under promise of pardon to die in the dungeons of Bundar Abbas), the unity of the Mazrui state was broken. It split into two divisions. A senior branch under Mbaruk bin Rashid (ie son of Rashid who had died at Bundar Abbas) based itself on Gazi, some 30 miles south of Mombasa, and claimed sovereignty over the coast from the Umba River northwards to within a few miles of Mombasa, and inland over the Digo and Guruma tribes, who were made tributary and treated as slaves. A junior branch, based at Takaungu, about 30 miles north of Mombasa, claimed suzerainty from there over the coast as far north as Malindi.

Mbaruk was a troublesome element almost from the settling of the Mazrui branch at Gazi. He warred on the junior branch at Takaungu, and found himself ranged against Sultan Said who had sided with the Mazrui of Takaungu. On Said's death in 1856 his successor, Majid, made peace with Mbaruk and confirmed him as Wali of Gazi, and gave him a subsidy. But this high and over-mighty subject was not so easily curbed, and in 1870 broke out in rebellion. A force had to be sent against him, and his subsidy was stopped. Majid's death in 1870 brought peace. His successor, Barghash, had no wish to pursue the quarrel with Mbaruk and restored his subsidy. In 1880 Mbaruk angered over the imprisonment of a relative by Barghash and the failure of Wanga to send him the usual present of a wife, plundered and burnt the town. A force under General Mathews was sent against him, and he fled to his inland stronghold of Mweli, 15 miles from the coast, where he held out for three weeks and then fled northwards to Mombasa, which place he looted along with other coast towns. It was not until 1882 that he was forced to surrender and made his submission at Zanzibar, following which he returned to Gazi, but without the subsidy. An uneasy peace followed, and then, at a most awkward juncture, on the arrival of the Anglo-German boundary delimitation commission, he again reared his head.

The Germans had early divined the enmity between the Mazrui and the sultanate at Zanzibar, and they sought to exploit it for their own ends. They averred that Mbaruk was no rebel, but the legitimate representative of an honourable dynasty, one with far older and juster claims to sovereignty over Mombasa and surrounding territory than the Albusaidi sultanate at Zanzibar. The latter were but usurpers and alien intruders. This was powerful talk, and music to Mbaruk's ears. In mid-January 1886 Dr Lucas of the German Kolonization Society proceeded to Gazi, and impressed on Mbaruk the extent of German strength in East Africa – witness the German fleet in East African waters – and offered German protection and an end to the badgering of British anti-slavery campaigners. The Gazi chieftain could not resist such blandishments. Despite the warnings of a British officer, Lieutenant E. Smith, he signed a treaty of alliance with the Germans and hoisted their flag at Gazi. Kirk at Zanzibar soon got wind of this, and sent a force against Mbaruk. The German flag was hauled down and Mbaruk was driven into the bush – just in time, for the delimitation commission had now appeared on the scene.

Kirk departed from East Africa in 1886 and his successor, Euan-Smith, was less ardent in upholding the Sultan's claims on the mainland; he sought good relations with Mbaruk. He admired the latter's 'clean model town' at Kakoban, and the way he kept his followers in order. Mbaruk on his part remained distrustful of the British, and refused to meet Euan-Smith when he visited Gazi in the autumn of 1890.

The IBEAC, when it took over the administration of the coast in 1888, faced a truculent Mbaruk and to moderate his hostility reinstated his subsidy – 1000 rupees a month – on the understanding that he would furnish the Company with troops when required. On two occasions Mbaruk bailed the Company out of trouble, helping to quell an incipient revolt at Mombasa and putting down a serious disturbance at Wanga but the relationship between the IBEAC and Mbaruk remained uneasy. Mbaruk was quick to discern the weakness of the Company: its limited financial and military resources; its abortive attempt to impose a hut tax in Giriama; the abandonment of Uganda and Witu; and the marking of time on the coast while waiting to be bought out by the British government. More serious estrangement arose over the Company's failure to prevent Christian Missions from harbouring runaway slaves from Arab masters and from proseletyzing among the Muslims at Mombasa and neighbourhood. When the coast was under the direct rule of the Sultan the Missions were constrained in their attempts to convert Muslims, but with IBEAC in control they entered 'with unholy zeal' into a campaign against Islam, holding forth against the followers of the Prophet and denouncing them, even in the public market-place at Mombasa. They partitioned Mombasa into 'districts' (each under a lady 'district visitor' as in an English parish), and worked with great zeal. The Company, aware of the influence wielded at home in England by the Missions, and having also on its board of directors a number of mission sympathizers, was reluctant to check their zeal. The IBEAC also, through no fault of its own, incurred unpopularity with the Arabs, in having to enforce anti-slavery legislation, an obligation imposed on it under its charter.

Mbaruk maintained that the Company had promised him increased wealth and power – even control over the entire country between Wanga and Kilifi; and when this was not fulfilled he was embittered, nursed revenge and was contemptuous of the Company. He habitually disregarded its orders. At Wanga, where one of his sons was governor, and the Company's Resident was an empty figure-head, Mbaruk spread it about that the Resident was under his authority.

Meanwhile the junior house of the Mazrui, based on Takaungu under Salim bin Hamis, remained loyal to the Company and the Sultan. Its chieftain, Salim bin Hamis, never accepted a subsidy but made his annual visit to Zanzibar and received his present in money which sustained his dignity and maintained his fighting force of 1200 slaves. When infirmity descended on him his eldest nephew and heir apparent and also by name Mbaruk bin Rashid but younger than Mbaruk of Gazi, became his representative. On Salim bin Hamis's death in February

1895, the Company's agent, Kenneth Macdougall, District Officer at Malindi, appointed Salim's son, Rashid bin Salim, as his successor as being the safer man and more loyal to the British, and passed over the young Mbaruk of Takaungu with the better claim, and also the latter's brother, Aziz. Both were thought to be turbulent and ill-disposed towards Europeans. In 'baraza' with Elders and Arabs, MacDougall got their recognition for the Company's choice, and obtained from young Mbaruk and Aziz a nominal promise of obedience. To conciliate Mbaruk Rashid bin Salim made over to him his own late father's personal slaves, and these Mbaruk promptly armed and marched away to Gonjoro, and then refused to recognize Rashid bin Salim as Wali of Takaungu, and proclaimed his brother Aziz as such. He then proceeded to enlist the support of his older namesake, Mbaruk of Gazi, in the overthrow of his cousin and the Company. In the face of this, J.R.W. Piggott (the Company's agent at Mombasa) appealed for help in June 1895, and a force of 310 bluejackets and 200 Zanzibaris, backed up by three British warships, was sent to Gonjoro. The Takaungu rebels then retreated to Sokoke from which they were dislodged, and, looting Tanganiko, they fled for refuge to Mbaruk of Gazi. The British government, which had just taken over the administration from the IBEAC on 3 July 1895, then formally declared the Mazrui chiefs as rebels.

The transfer of the administration on the whole signified little change for the inhabitants of Seyyidie. The demise of the IBEAC had long been talked about, and much anticipated. There was expectation that it would be followed by the restoration of Arab rule: 'God has had mercy on us, and has heard our prayers.' Instead, the Arabs found themselves again under non-Muslim rule – British officials only accountable to the imperial government. It is most likely that Mbaruk of Gazi, if he had realized that he would have to deal with the British government, rather than a trading Company, would have refrained from giving succour to the rebels. He possibly expected that, as on previous occasions, he would be called in to restore order, and then could dictate his own terms, even to placing his own nominee in the chieftainship of Takaungu, and uniting the whole coast under Mazrui rule. However, events overtook him, and prestige and honour, rather than his real interests, prevented him from backing down. He dallied over surrendering the rebels, and when Hardinge and Mathews met him, a 'dignified long-bearded Arab sheikh', at Likoni on Kilindi Creek, just across from Mombasa, he still offered to put down the rebellion. This declined, he promised the surrender of the rebels. Meanwhile, Aziz, like Pope Julius of old, swore that he would not shave until he had attained his goal, and would then shave his beard in the chief mosque at Takaungu. He failed in his objective, and found refuge with Mbaruk of Gazi. The latter could now have effected the surrender of the main leaders of the rebellion, and this he promised if Hardinge would meet him in person at Gazi. However, when Hardinge arrived at Gazi on 24 July 1895, backed up by Admiral Rawson with a force of 300 bluejackets, 85 Sudanese and the warships *Barossa, Blonde,* and *Phoebe,* riding at anchor off Gazi, and with the *St George* at Mombasa, the rebels fled to Mweli. Wanga was looted and burnt, and Wasin threatened. Mbaruk had gone over completely to the side of the rebels.

Hardinge still hoped to avoid outright war: he restrained Rawson from shelling Gazi, sent Mbaruk a copy of the Koran, and gave him a fortnight in which to submit. Mbaruk's reply was evasive. He pleaded loyalty, but would not submit so long as British forces occupied Gazi; and he threatened that if any move were made on Mweli he would retreat inland, to Teita. Such tergiversations were now beyond bearing, and a force of 220 bluejackets, 84 Marines and 110 native troops moved on Mweli, which, after four days march and fighting off rebels, was stormed and taken; its commander, Mbaruk's brother, was killed, and the remainder of the rebel leaders sent flying. It was unfortunate that the pursuit was not now followed up.

The arrival of Indian troops was awaited, and four precious months went by during which the rebels regrouped and gained accessions from disaffected elements, the most important of which, in October 1895, was that of Hamis bin Kombo, the Swahili Chief of Mtwapa, to the immediate north of Mombasa. Of ancient lineage, representing the old native reigning family that pre-dated Portuguese and Arab conquests, he was conspicuous for his fanaticism and hostility to the British and the anti-slavery cause. His accession brought the war to the outskirts of Mombasa, threatening the newly erected Kilindini Railway station, and the mission stations of Freretown and Rabai which overlooked Mombasa harbour on its north. British forces were thus locked up at Mombasa which could well be used elsewhere.

Mbaruk had rallied after his defeat at Mweli and throughout the autumn of 1895 had waged guerrilla war from the German frontier right up to Malindi, and threatened the Mackinnon Road, looting a most valuable load of cloth from a camel caravan of Smith, Mackenzie and Company. Hardinge, like an old trooper, entered the field despite illness and depression over the death of a dear friend, 'the brave Captain Lawrence' in the campaign, in October 1895. The arrival of an Indian contingent under Captain W. Barratt and Lieutenant F.E. Scott, at Mombasa on 30 December 1895, relieved pressure on Mombasa and the nearby missions. But the opening bid of the Indian troops was not auspicious; they were misled through the treachery of guides to dried-up wells, and were without water for a prolonged period under a tropical sun before finding their way back to the coast. An attack on Malindi was repulsed but much of the town was burned and at Wanga and Shimba the rebels had slipped away. The British were now alarmed lest the powerful Giriama tribe might go over to the enemy, for a band of young Giriama had attacked a British force under Captain Wake, and it was thought that Mbaruk was retreating westwards into Giriama with the hope of bringing the influential Giriama chief, Ngonio, on his side. Hardinge, now recovered in health, sought to prevent this. He was diverted by a mutiny of Kiriboto Arab mercenaries taken over from the IBEAC, who refused to go into action, it being the Fast of Ramadan. Thus Hardinge foot-slogged through Giriama accompanied by an Indian and Baluchi guard and he persuaded runaway settlements on the Sabaki River to desist from joining the rebels; and finally, on 31 March 1896, in a meeting with the Giriama Elders at Tandia, he obtained from the latter a promise on the solemn 'Oath of the Hyena' that they would help in driving the Arab rebels out of their land.

This was a gain for the British side, and came within a week of the disembarkation of the 24th Beluchistan Regiment at Mombasa. Lord Salisbury, worried that the rebel movement might impede progress of the Uganda Railway, had asked for additional forces from India. The newly arrived regiment was immediately directed against Mbaruk's forces operating north and south of Mombasa. The strategy evolved for the regiment was to occupy food centres in the Nyika and gain control of the hinterland. With a line of posts along the Uganda Road to the north, another along the Umba River to the south, the waterless desert to westward and the Wateita waiting to give them a hot reception if they advanced in that direction, the flying columns based on advanced depots at Mkono and Mweli would be operating on an enclosed area. The rebels would be pushed south-west into Duruma country – towards German territory, where von Wissmann, the governor, had agreed to disarm them, if and when they appeared there.

The short sharp campaign which followed on this strategy was arduous in the extreme. The Commander of the 24th Beluchistan

Regiment, Lieutenant-Colonel Pearson, in reporting to the Adjutant-General in India, averred that the obstacles met with in East Africa were far more formidable than any met with in campaigning in India. There was the impenetrable wilderness of thorn bush in the Nyika, the blistering force of the sun, the stifling heat – never a cool breeze to kiss the brow. The never-ending flatness of the country made signalling difficult. The scarcity of water and being constantly misled by the natives in this respect made it a constant nightmare for the 1500 loin-clad porters toiling along the few pathways which threaded this wilderness, with 60 lb loads of rations (rice and dried fish for themselves, and dhal and ghee for the Indian troops) on their heads, cooking pots slung over their shoulders and with a constant eye out for snipers, while all the time food and ammunition supplies were deteriorating. In these conditions the advantage lay with the enemy, who knew the terrain perfectly, the sources of precious water and potential strongholds of defence. It was only by keeping the enemy constantly on the move, by bewildering him with fictitious reports of widespread British presence and the effective use of the Maxim when brought to close quarters, that his confidence was sapped and his will finally broken. The British, too, had an advantage in having control of the coastline and sea-ways, which enabled them to move supplies and forces to vital points for an advance inland.

Operations went remarkably smoothly. The northern and southern lines were taken up, Shimba and Mkongo fully stocked with supplies and a containing pressure was kept on Mbaruk. As the lines shortened he moved southward, his trail being well marked by abandoned kerosene tins – some still full of gunpowder – which traced him to the Umba River. Then, with scarcely two weeks gone since the 24th Beluchistan Regiment entered the campaign, came news on 11 April 1896 that the rebels had crossed into German territory; and then a little later, news that von Wissmann did not intend to hand them over to the British. Hardinge meanwhile, on 12 April 1896 in a despatch to Salisbury, had outlined his plans for dealing with the rebels. There would be a general pardon for the rank and file, but the chiefs must unconditionally surrender and wait for clemency, for theirs was the more grievous offence. Mbaruk had usurped the Sultan's authority and was guilty of high treason; young Mbaruk and Eyoub bin Mbaruk must be interned as political prisoners. There were others, Asiz, Hamis bin Kombo, his son Mahomed and Mwenyi Jaka (who had deserted while acting as a guide to Mweli), who were not only rebels but guilty of acts of wanton barbarity, even murder, and should be executed or kept in rigorous confinement.

Hardinge was reluctant to press hard on the 'noble Mazrui clan which once made an alliance with the Representatives of British Power', and he would treat it with every consideration and indulgence: 'A civilized Arab society cannot be treated as if it were Uganda'. Mbaruk of Gazi's estates would be kept in trust, and one of his sons might be made Wali of Gazi or Wanga. Hardinge, who had said, 'My own heart was and remained for long afterwards in the Mohammedan East', had great sympathy for Islam and the Arabs: he did not press for the extradition of Mbaruk of Gazi, for it would have been embarrassing to deal harshly with him. He saw a place in the future administration of the protectorate for Arabs of 'good family', to act as Kaimakam, Wakil, or Moawin, and to help in judicial and administrative work. He spoke of the 'impolicy of England, a great Mahommedan Empire', in making an enemy of the powerful Arab race and in supporting aggressive missionary propaganda against Islam. British officials should disassociate themselves from missionary societies, be strictly neutral and show scrupulous respect for mosques and ministers of this 'noble religion'. As for the 'extremely anodyne and innocuous system of slavery' existing on the coast, it had no connection whatever with the slave-trade and it would die, as it was rapidly doing, a natural death.

Meanwhile the refugees, some 3000 in number (including camp followers) now in German territory, and over whose future Hardinge pondered, were encamped near Moa, about five miles south of the Anglo-German frontier. Here on 17 April 1896, Mbaruk and 1100 followers surrendered. It was a bedraggled fighting force that was asked to lay down its arms. They had only 600 rifles between them and of these 18 were ancient breech-loaders; many were armed with bows and spears. Despite the weak state of his fighting force Mbaruk was far from cowed, and proposed to the Germans that they jointly attack the British. The Germans would have none of this, and von Wissmann and Hardinge met at Jasin, on the German side, on 21 April 1896. The surrender was complete and complete disarmament was achieved at Moa on 24 April 1896. Von Wissman intended to settle the refugees near Tanga, but in deference to British wishes, that they be kept as far away from British territory as possible, the main body were brought down to Dar es Salaam. The remainder at Tanga found employment on plantations and in road-making, others returning to the British sphere. By September 1896 von Wissmann could report that he anticipated no further trouble from the rebels. The Germans throughout the affair had been most co-operative with the British, and Lord Salisbury conveyed the 'cordial thanks' of HMG to von Wissmann. The British authorities in Cape Colony, in turn, gave valuable help to the Germans faced with the Herrero rebellion in German South West Africa.

The amnesty granted by Hardinge excluded from pardon 11 chiefs including Mbaruk of Gazi, young Mbaruk, Aziz and Hamis bin Kombo. All others concerned in the rebellion, excepting those guilty of murder and serious crimes, were free to return home. Mbaruk of Gazi had committed high treason; he had assumed the title of Emir ul Mumenin (Commander of the Faithful), implying sovereign authority: for him there could be no pardon. However, in view of former services rendered by him and his former friendly relations with the British, his lands would be held in trust, and divided on his death, in accordance with Muslim law, among his heirs who had taken no part in the rising. Three Mombasa sheikhs, and the Cadi of Takaungu, whom Hardinge had recently banished to Maasailand for complicity in the rebel attack on Takaungu, were allowed to return to their homes at the coast but were restricted from visiting Mecca or Muscat, in case they might intrigue.

This magnanimity in dealing with the vanquished was explained by Hardinge on the grounds that he had no wish 'to weaken or depress the Arab and Swahili aristocracy ... the natural rulers of the land'. He wrote to Mbaruk of Gazi, almost apologetically, expressing regret that he had been forced to wage war on him. In reply, Mbaruk, pious Muslim that he was, ascribed the strife and troubles of the late war, to the immutable decrees of God. Hardinge, later, reflecting on the Arab rebellion, wondered if it might have been avoided by appointing Mbaruk of Gazi as a kind of Governor-General of Seyyidie, but was of the conclusion that this would have made the task of implementing anti-slavery legislation extremely difficult. It was best that Arab power be broken.

To do so had cost the British Exchequer £20,297, and this in the first year of the new protectorate, when £12,750 had to be paid to the Sultan of Zanzibar as rent for the coastal strip. With expenditure of £58,357 for the new administration, the cost totalled £91,404, which, less revenue of £32,670, left a charge of £58,734 to be covered by 'grant in aid' from the British government.

Seyyidie Province recovered quickly from the rebellion, although the people of the Nyika were slow to believe that Mbaruk's power had really been broken. He had recovered so often from previous defeats that the Giriama prophesied trouble for the Germans in giving harbourage to him: he was a dangerous man. The Arab sheikhs of Seyyidie desired co-operation with the new British regime, and were willing to assist in its administration, even bringing in disarmed fighting slaves of the outlawed Hamis bin Kombo. The Shimba Hills were now opened up and became an important coffee-growing centre. Indian traders who had gone over to German territory for safety, and through pique at not being compensated for losses suffered in the rebellion, at first refused to return, but seeing stability and profits revive on the British side decided to come back. Armed opposition to the British administration was over in Seyyidie, but military operations were soon to recommence in another quarter of the protectorate.

The British were drawn into military operations in Jubaland Province on behalf of the Galla, a people who inhabited the vast no man's land between the Tana and Juba Rivers. The renewed sufferings of the Galla in the 1890s, at the hands of their traditional tormentors, the Somali and Ethiopians, evoked the sympathy and support of the British. The origins of the Galla are obscured by legends and by an unrecorded past. It would appear that they were part of an early Hamitic invastion of the Horn of Africa from Arabia in the seventh century. Over the following centuries they expanded down into what is now Somalia, and into south-west Ethiopia. The Somali people who followed in the wake of the Galla, and a little later in time, also came from Arabia, and settled on the southern side of the Gulf of Aden. By the eleventh century they had moved southwards into the Horn proper. Coincident with the movement of Galla and Somali southwards was the thrust northwards of the Zenghi, a black people who moved up the East African coast as far north as the Tana River area, where their descendants are found today among the Pokomo. The retreat of the Galla southwards was curtailed by the Zenghi moving northwards, and at about the same time Somali pressure from the north prevented any movement of the Galla in that direction. They were driven into the savannah country south-east of the Ethiopian plateau where they intermarried with the indigenous people. They subsequently infiltrated Ethiopia, and by the fifteenth century had become a powerful and conquering race, capable of putting 300,000 mounted spearmen into the field. Their martial qualities and horsemanship ensured their ascendancy over the Semiticized Cushites of central Ethiopia. They invaded the basin of the Shibeli River in the sixteenth century, annexed part of Shoa and penetrated as far east as Malindi, on the Indian Ocean. By now a nation of numerous tribes, the Galla occupied an enormous area, from the southern tip of Tigrai and from the Nile tributaries on the west, to Harrar on the east, and to the

Tana River on the south. Although increasingly acculturated to the Semitic Hamites and in some instances embracing Christianity, they retained their separateness and elements of indigenous social institution.

The Galla might have subdued the whole of Christian Ethiopia but for the entry of the Portuguese there, and the placing of firearms in the hands of the Shoans. At about the same time the Galla were afflicted by smallpox and sorely weakened. The invasion of Ethiopia by the Muslim leader, Ahmed Gran of Adel, with Somali assistance, brought Ethiopia to the point of collapse, and it was only saved by the defeat of Ahmed Gran by the Portuguese in 1542. This victory closed the gateway to Somali expansion on the west and diverted them southwards, in turn forcing the Galla and Zenghi before them – down almost as far as the Tana River. Domination of Somali over Galla, of Muslim over pagan, and the continuous pressure of Somali movement southwards and their policy of 'shegata' - making blood-brothers of a potential enemy while infiltrating his territory – demoralized the Galla. By the late nineteenth century they had lost their ascendancy over their Cushite neighbours, the tables were now turned against them and there was vengeance for centuries of Galla aggression. There was widespread enslavement of the Galla by the Ethiopians, and the Somalis joined in to drive them south of the Juba River. The knell of the Galla as a great nation was sounded. Their retreat into Jubaland Province with the Somali close on their heels came at about the time British administration was introduced into that part of East Africa. The woes of the Galla soon became a major British concern.

This concern was much enhanced by tales brought back by European explorers who journeyed through the Galla country in the 1890s, such as Captain Swayne who reached Ime on the Shibeli River, and Prince Raspoli and Captain Bottego who explored the Galan, a main tributary of the Juba. Especially important for information on the Galla were the reports of Dr Donaldson Smith, an American, who made an extensive journey from Berbera into the interior as far as Lake Rudolf, and thence returned in October 1895, by way of Marsabit and the Guaso Nyiro, skirting the Kenya highlands, and down to the Tana River on the east. Donaldson Smith detailed the sufferings of the Galla: the horrors of the slave-trade, slaughter of their warriors, the castration of their youths, the capture of their women .... They loved to tell of their former glory. Now the Abyssinians are master? The latter wore the 'gruesome trophies' of their forays, much as a Scotsman would sport his sporran.

With Menelik's accession in 1889, the Abyssinians had embarked on imperial expansion, moving steadily southwards, raiding and enslaving the Galla, taking all before them and leaving behind strongly fortified posts from which to collect tribute. Their victory over the Italians at Adowa (March 1896) had set the Abyssinians aglow with pride and puffed with vainglory. They now raided with impunity into British Jubaland and established stations in the rich coffee and grain-producing country of the Abyssinian foothills adjoining that of the Boran Galla, and penetrated the lower reaches of the Juba. Meanwhile, the Somali were pressing down from the north-east. The Galla, caught between these two moving jaws, Ethiopian and Somali, suffered grievously. That matters were going badly for them was evident in their continuous appeals for British help. When in 1896 the Abyssinians raided down from the Sidamo plateau into the eastern part of the Boran Galla country and looted their way across to the Juba, Mr A.C. Jenner, sub-Commissioner of Jubaland Province, made an extensive journey into the interior to check on these depredations. He brought back tales of near annihilation of the Galla, and of the wholesale looting of their cattle by the Abyssinians. Confirmation of this state of affairs also came from Messrs Cavendish and Andrews who journeyed down from Berbera to the Boran country and Lake Rudolf, and thence to Mombasa in 1897. They themselves had a narrow brush with a large Abyssinian force under Ras Makunna, Commandant of Harrar, raiding far from home. Cavendish found the Boran Galla 'exceedingly anxious to obtain English proection against the Abyssinian raids'. Grim indeed was the tale he told:

> The Abyssinians castrate all the men they catch and put a bullet through their wrist. They also occasionally mutilate women, by cutting off a breast.[5]

Instances of mutilation were in evidence at nearly every Boran village, and Cavendish was asked why such things were permitted under the British flag. Lord Delamere and Dr Atkinson, who travelled down to the Rendille country from Abyssinia in 1898-99, reported that the Abyssinians had established permanent posts within the British sphere, and were levying heavy tribute on the Galla. They were even penetrating into the bush-clothed escarpment verging on the *golbo*, the waterless camel country where only hardy nomads survive, now part of the Northern Frontier District of Kenya. These Abyssinian raids caused Delamere and Atkinson to detour far to the west, through Rendille country.

It was only prolonged drought and famine which halted these Abyssinian raids southwards. And it was well for the Galla, for the British could have done little to stay an Abyssinian advance in their direction. The British at the time were also faced with renewed challenge from the Ogaden Somali in Jubaland Province. Reports were coming in that they were again 'spitting, an insolent gesture as the infidel passed' them in the streets of Kismayu, and that they were making derisive remarks as to the weakness of British authority. In response to this challenge the British fort at Turki Hills was rebuilt, and a stockaded post established at Yonte, 18 miles up the Juba. Kismayu was placed under close police surveillance and Somalis were forbidden to enter the town. A punitive force sent against the Ogaden Somali main encampment at the Afmadu wells in early 1896 brought their submission, and this, followed by the death of their leader, Murgan Yusuf, in the same year, gained a temporary peace. The new leader, Ahmed bin Murgan, however, was not to be trusted.

In early 1897 came a new flare-up, a succession of outrages on caravans and police posts, and the Ogaden again raised the old question of 'blood-money'. They also resented the check on their slaving activities and restrictions on their young warriors indulging in their traditional practice of 'washing their spears'. The resentment welled up into open warfare against the British. The latter, absorbed with affairs in Uganda and suppression of the Sudanese mutiny there, at first were not in a position to deploy adequate forces against the Ogaden. It was not until April 1898 that Indian forces, 460 men of the 4th Bombay Rifles and 27th Bombay Infantry (Baluchis) were hurried from Uganda over the newly completed stretch of the Uganda Railway, to reinforce the local force of the East African Rifles at Kismayu. A miniature arena of war soon developed in the 40-mile stretch between Lake Wama and Afmadu. Lake Wama, a brackish lake whose waters were normally undrinkable, became a focus of Ogaden attention during the dry season when water was unobtainable anywhere else. The Ogaden resorted to it until about the beginning of July when the rainy season commenced, and they would then return to the sweet water wells of Afmadu and to the good grazing there for their herds.

It was British strategy to exploit Ogaden dependence on a water supply for their herds in prosecuting the war against them. A column despatched to Lake Wama in early April failed to make contact with the Ogaden before the latter retired with their cattle to the north of the lake. In anticipation that they would return to the lake, Hardinge, who arrived

at Kismayu in early May 1898, decided to establish a strong post at the
lake, to keep watch against the return of the Ogaden, and also as a base
for an advance on Afmadu to the north-west. This advance would
commence at the beginning of the rainy season in July.

The Ogaden appear to have surmised what was afoot. On 30 May they
directed an attack in an unexpected direction – to the east against Yonte,
midway between Lake Wamu and Kismayu. Although repulsed in the
attack on Yonte, a month later they inflicted heavy losses on Indian
troops surprised on the march near Lake Wama. This resulted in the
British bringing in more outside forces. The four Indian companies of
the Uganda Rifles were brought from Mombasa to free the local troops
at Kismayu for action in the interior and to strengthen posts on Lake
Wama.

When war broke out with the Ogaden Somali, the British fortunately
had the support of the rival Herti Somali clan who gave valuable
assistance, acting as desert scouts and police. The Italians also came to
the aid of the British, providing oxen and camels for transport.
Missionaries on the outskirts of Kismayu were brought into the town.
Kismayu took on a siege atmosphere with the large numbers of British
forces marshalled there throughout the summer of 1898. Containing
pressure was maintained on the nomadic Somali in the interior by
seizure of their cattle and depriving them of water-holes. The
revictualling of lonely police posts up the Juba, and the carrying out of
sorties from the base at Yonte into the sand-dune and bush-covered
country, was a wearying task for the British. In August 1898 a series of
successes came their way. A column of Indian troops under Captain Fry,
4th Bombay Rifles, brought pride to their regiment when they crossed
over Lake Wama and surprised an Ogaden encampment and captured a
large number of cattle. A few days later this success was repeated when
another expedition under Major Quentin carried out an operation near
Lake Wama and captured many cattle of the enemy. These losses in the
way of cattle was perhaps the most serious blow that could be struck at
the Ogaden Somali.

The appearance at this stage of the Abyssinians to the north was, in a
sense, a blessing for the British. The Ogaden, fearful of the Abyssinians
massing in their rear, and faced with increasing British tactical successes,
began to treat for peace. They were given a stipulated time in which to
pay a fine and restore captured arms. When they failed to comply, a force
of 400 men under Major Evatt marched to Kerkumes, to the immediate
south of Lake Wama, and then on to Soyah and Lake Wama. The

Ogaden sultan made his submission in September 1898. The Ogaden were treated leniently, apart from a fine of 500 cattle as blood-money for the murder of non-combatants. Evatt, in an excess of enthusiasm for extending British authority and in carrying out his sweeps against the Ogaden, continued on to the north to Heleshid on the upper Juba, which he meant to hold as the headquarters of a British expeditionary force in this region. Hardinge appears to have gone along with Evatt in this extension of British authority in the interior, on the upper Juba, for after visiting Lake Wama he had decided against making it the main site for permanent station: its water was undrinkable for much of the year, and the Ogaden only resorted there during the dry season. Instead he supported the establishment of a station of Indian troops at Yonte, with lesser posts at Kerkumes to the south of Lake Wama; at Mabangu Kizungu, on the Juba, at the extreme north of the Gosha region; and with a detachment of police at Songoro M'fula, also on the Juba and to the south of the Gosha region. Heleshid, over 200 miles up the Juba, as the farthest extension of British authority in that direction, was meant to impress both Ogaden and Somali with the long arm of British military power. The operations against the Ogaden and the establishment of British posts over such a wide area in the Jubaland Province had brought for the British more respect from its inhabitants, and by August 1900 Jenner reported that relations with them were more cordial than at any time hitherto.[6]

The enthusiasm of officials in East Africa for the expansion of British authority into the farther reaches of the Jubaland area was not shared by the Foreign Office. By 1898 the British government was looking upon any extension of British responsibilities on the upper Juba as egregious folly. The area was remote and unsettled. Hardinge at Zanzibar was not even certain whether the westernmost portion of it lay in the East Africa or Uganda protectorate. The lesson of Macdonald's frustrated expedition and the Sudanese mutiny in Uganda was still fresh in mind. To the Foreign Office in London, Galla difficulties and Abyssinian encroachment seemed very remote and of lesser concern than the need to contract responsibilities. A forward policy was not the order of the day. Already in February 1898 Cavendish, although he had incurred great expense in fitting out a second expedition and was backed by the Royal Geographical Society and the British Museum, was refused permission by the Foreign Office to lead it into the region of the upper Juba, on the grounds that its heavy armament (twelve-pounders and Maxims) might stir up the natives there. Permission was also refused

J.B. Stanford and David W. Carnegie to enter the upper Juba region, and likewise Dr Donaldson Smith, whose previous work in the region was still fresh in mind and highly regarded.

This policy of retrenchment was not to the liking of either Hardinge or sub-Commissioner Jenner, who both felt that British control on the Juba must be made effective, and 'not merely confined like that of the Sultan of Zanzibar to a small strip in the vicinity of Kismayu'. They argued for better steamship communication on the Juba, and the 'dotting of police posts about'. The British should make their presence known in the interior, claimed Jenner, and in pursuance of this, in the spring of 1899 he ascended the Juba as far as Lugh. He found the reputed Abyssinian menace to be a real threat. Bands of Abyssinian spearmen and riflemen were much about, both on foot and mounted; and it was only the recall of their commander, Waldreh Gabra, to partake in a military campaign at home, which halted Abyssinian advance eastward and down to the Shibeli itself. Jenner's report on the upper Juba exploded the myth of its extraordinary richness and fertility. The long-standing stories of riches in ivory and precious stones in the country of the Boran, to which Hardinge himself had subscribed, were shown to be false. Jenner found only starkness and poverty.

His trip up the Juba in the Spring of 1899 marks the end of British expansion in that direction. Salisbury gave warning about the same time that

This advance towards the northeast (from the East Africa Protectorate) must be put off until there is less severe pressure in other parts of the Empire[7]

and Sir Clement Hill of the Foreign Office, who visited Kismayu in December 1899, reaffirmed Salisbury's view. There must be concentration of strength at the mouth of the Juba, but no more ventures inland. This new policy of contraction of responsibilities was reflected in the 'Outlying Districts Regulations' of January 1900. Only authorized persons were permitted to enter the northern areas of the protectorate, and they must put down as security a deposit of £100. Violations of these Regulations were to be severely punished. Herein lies the origin of the special treatment accorded the north-eastern part of the protectorate (later Kenya Colony) in the twentieth century.

There was added reason for curtailment of British expansion in the upper Juba region. In the summer of 1900 a new and grave threat to

European control in the Horn of Africa appeared with the rise of Sayyid Mohammed ibn Abdullah Hassan (termed 'the Mad Mullah' by the British), who was born about 1864, near Kirrit in the southern part of what was later to become British Somaliland. On a pilgrimage to Mecca in 1894 he came under the influence of and joined the reforming Sufi order, the Salihiya, and on his return 1895, with the added prestige of one who had made the Haj, he launched a jihad against the infidel. The subsequent misery, turbulence and cruelty which followed in the wake of his eventful career has been attributed to a degree of insanity arising from an unskilled trepanning operation performed on him while still a youth, whereby a bone was removed from the top of his head. If such tale be true, the supposed mental derangement did not affect the Mullah's skill as a desert fighter nor his stature as a messianic leader exercising great influence over his followers. By 1899 his passionate outbursts against the infidel and his truculent and rebellious attitude brought him into sharp conflict with British authority based at Berbera. In August 1899 the Mullah established himself at Burao, about 100 miles inland from Berbera, with a force of 1500 men. Proclaiming himself the Mahdi, and denouncing as unbelievers all who refused to join him, he arrogantly challenged the British Consul-General at Berbera to a duel of war. The Mullah was accordingly declared a rebel.

By early 1900 he had raised wide support, even from the Ogaden Somali hundreds of miles to the south, and was receiving arms from French adventurers, through Jibuti. The Mullah's arrogance and the cruelties inflicted by his followers raised opposition among many Somali tribes, but his ever-increasing strength in arms and fighting men secured him undoubted influence and prestige. It was at this stage that it was rumoured that the Mullah might even advance southward into greater Somaliland as far as the Benadir coast.

Jenner, a great admirer of the Somalis - 'I have never met natives of Africa who show higher qualities' - was one of the first casualties in the long campaign against the Mad Mullah. In November 1900, Jenner made a tour 100 miles inland from Kismayu to confirm news of the Mullah's rumoured approach. He disregarded the usual precautions of a zeriba and armed guards for his camp, and also he was in an area much unsettled by a serious quarrel over grazing rights between the Herti and Ogaden Somali. Jenner was killed in a night attack on his camp. This was the signal for an unleashing of tribal fanaticism, and by the end of November 1900 thousands of tribesmen, excited by the Mullah's victories in the north, were in revolt in southern Somaliland. Large forces were again marshalled by the British. A punitive expedition was launched against the Ogaden believed responsible for Jenner's death. Land forces were supported by naval craft which at night played their searchlights on the Somali coast and fired their guns into the scrub bush beyond the coastline. The Italians came in to support the British with a camel corps. The Afmadu wells were occupied. A flying column under Colonel Ternan penetrated the waterless interior to Samasa, 57 miles from Afmadu, but failed to advance any farther. This was interpreted by the Somali as a defeat for the British. The latter for all their flurry and initial action had gained little. Meanwhile the 'Mad Mullah' to the north posed a menacing challenge. It was evident that a tide of anti-European feeling was sweeping through the length and breadth of the Horn, from the banks of the Juba right up the illimitable reaches of the Haud and as far as the Gulf of Aden. British officials, come over from the old IBEAC, and with previous disappointment in administering the Juba region still fresh in mind, were dire in their prophecies. The Juba, they claimed, should be abandoned: it was only 'a bore and an excrescence on the Swahili and Uganda protectorates'.

Sir Charles Eliot who took over in late 1900 as Commissioner of the East Africa Protectorate, like Hardinge was reluctant to withdraw the British military presence from the upper Juba. He believed that patrols were necessary to keep the Somali in check:

> if they do not see any signs of our activity for a few months they will conclude that the British Government is dead ... they have short memories and their processes of thought are incredibly childish.[8]

But by April 1901 Eliot was of different view and downright pessimistic: the threat of the 'Mad Mullah' to the north, the continued troubles in Jubaland, where military operations had cost over £25,000 by February 1901, had brought disillusionment.

> I very much doubt whether this Province is worth the money which is spent upon it ... It would be better to leave the deserts alone for the present and devote our attention to those parts which are both accessible and profitable ... we must let the Somalis quarrel among themselves ... in the event of our wishing to open up relations with the Boran country, we could probably do so quite as well from Kenia and Ukamba as from Jubaland.[9]

Eliot's thoughts were turning more and more from the stark wastes of Jubaland to the Kenya highlands 'with their cool and invigorating climate, fertile soil and wide pastures', the only place in East Africa suitable for European settlement. He was

> penetrated with the conviction that it is useless to spend lives and money on subduing barbarous inhabitants of barren deserts, and that most primitive expeditions are a mistake. But it is absolutely necessary to protect the borders of the quasi-civilised areas, otherwise those will contract and the general movement of the Protectorate will be retrogressive.[10]

Thus he favoured retrenchment in the Juba area. The Afmadu wells should be abandoned. Only Gobwen and Yonte, on the Juba, some 22 miles from Kismayu, should be retained as posts on the river, and along with a steam launch would suffice to keep watch on its lower reaches.

The prolonged troubles in Jubaland highlighted the need for reorganization of the East African armed forces. Continued dependency on Indian troops was unwise; they might suddenly be recalled 'in the event of war with a European power'. The Germans had fallen back more and more on native troops and were even recruiting the Manyuema, reputed cannibals though they were. Considerable study of the potentiality of various tribes for the role of troops was given by British officials, and it resulted in one conclusion only, namely that the Sudanese were still by far the best native African soldiery. Eliot had favoured using the Maasai, whose purported martial qualities were a strong recommendation, but it was soon found that their diet of meat and milk made them awkward recruits to feed. Their fighting qualities were excellent, but they lacked the necessary self-discipline for a trained military force. The Baganda, in far-off Uganda, were also considered as a potential military force, for they were quick and intelligent; but they were too dependent on their native food, and there was also doubt as to their reliability if employed outside their own country. Thus all in all the Sudanese, despite their recent mutiny in Uganda (the Intelligence Division blamed this on failure to heed their grievances) were still by far the best military material available. They could be supplemented by a camel corps, and if commanded by British non-commissioned officers (abstainers if possible) and Arabic-speaking commissioned officers, would be an admirable force. Eliot also favoured an amalgamation of the armed forces in East Africa similar to that which had taken place in West

Africa in 1898. The Uganda Railway, completed to Lake Victoria at the end of 1901, gave quick assess to all parts of East Africa, and a General Military Reserve, based at a central point, say Kikuyu in the Kenya highlands, could easily be drawn on. Colonel Mannings's suggestion for a volunteer corps of Punjabis, recruited from the railway workers, did not appeal to Eliot, for he had a poor opinion of the Indians in East Africa. Eliot preferred African troops.

Thus it was that the King's African Rifles came into being in January 1902. Made up of infantry, camel corps and military, and a Somaliland battalion, its formation was timely. It received its major baptism in the campaign against the 'Mad Mullah', against whom the British were now deploying increasing forces. A rare opportunity to finish off the Mullah at an early stage in his career was lost in October 1900. The Mullah had crossed over the frontier line into Ethiopia, and apparently unaware of British forces so close at hand, was resting in camp, with all his herds out grazing. Major Plunkett, when on the point of seizing the Mullah, received an order from the Consul-General at Berbera, forbidding any invasion of the frontier line. Such an opportunity was not to occur again![11]

The constant accession to his ranks of well-armed tribesmen from the Mijjertein, plus the fact that he was an extremely agile foe, who knew the terrain and every available water-hole, made the Mullah a worthy opponent. He could always withdraw into the desert when pursued; his fighting men were schooled in hardship, and, like the Wahabis of old, were fanatically devout and loyal to their leader, ascetic in habit and 'sworn to throw up all wordly advantages'. British forces were also hampered by instructions not to be drawn into pursuit, and that operations should 'so far as possible be of a defensive nature'. The Mullah raided constantly and dispossessed tribesmen along with their families and tens of thousands of head of stock, came over to the British, who at one stage had some 12,000 camels under their protection. By November 1902 the Foreign Office was beginning to realize that this was no mere frontier skirmish, but a full-scale war against a capable enemy. Operations were now placed under the command of Brigadier-General Manning, and a build-up of supplies and forces commenced at Berbera, which took on the appearance of a great tented city. In December 1902 control was taken over by the War Office. In late December of the same year forces were landed at Obbia. By 2 January 1903 the opening scene was set. Supplies were landed and troops encamped at Obbia, ready for the next advance. None dreamed at this stage that the drama would not end until 1920.

10· Transport and Communications

The opening up of the interior of East Africa and establishment of a reliable system of transport with the hinterland dominated all other considerations. Until this cogent problem was settled the declaration of a British protectorate over Uganda meant little or nothing. The old laborious, time-consuming foot-slogging and porterage of goods on human heads would no longer suffice for the needs of an inland administration.

It was a problem which had exercised the minds of nearly all European explorers from the earliest years of the nineteenth century. Burton in 1860 drew attention to it and urged the laying down of a tramroad from the coast to the interior lakes. Schweinfurth, in 1874, after deprecating reliance on human porterage – much of their load was made up of food to be consumed on the journey inland – and pondering on the possibility of using elephant transport, came round to the view that a hand-truck 'something like that used by the Chinese, running upon a single large wheel, which the framework, that contains the goods, spans like a bridge', and propelled by two men (one in front and one behind), would be the most successful form of transport. The explorer, Cameron, came outright and advocated a railway to the interior: he saw no future in either animal or human porterage:

> I would recommend the acquirement of a port – Mombasah for instance – from the Sultan of Zanzibar by treaty or purchase, and thence to run a light line of railway to the Tanganyika via Unyanyembe, with branches to the Victorian Nyanza, and to the southward through Ugogo. Such a line might be constructed for about £1000 a mile. ... Such a railway advancing into the country would at once begin to make a return, for the present ivory trade to Zanzibar should be sufficient to pay working expenses and leave a margin for profit, without making any allowance for the increase trade.[1]

Plans for a railway to the interior formed part of the proposed Mackinnon concession of 1877; and the firm of Boustead and Ridley in putting forth plans in 1879 for opening up the interior gave detailed figures as to the cost of constructing a railway. The missionaries, Felkin and Wilson, in 1882, and Consul Holmwood in his support for the British East Africa Association in 1884–85, sketched a hypothetical railway line linking up East Africa and the Upper Nile, thereby bringing Zanzibar into communication with Khartoum. The Emin Pasha Relief Committee, backed by Rhodes/Mackinnon negotiations, got no farther than declaring its intention to build a railway 'at some future date'.

All these plans for a railway into the interior assumed its starting-point from the East African coast, and when the IBEAC, with its charter in hand in 1888 selected Mombasa as its headquarters, it based its plans for a railway (to be theirs in 'perpetuity') on the assumption that Mombasa would be its terminus at the coast. Throughout 1889 little was done by the Company in the matter of railway building: it was too concerned over German rivalry, the blockade of the coast, and rumours of a pending Anglo-German agreement, to define their spheres of influence. By March 1890 the sole sign of railway activity on the part of the Company was some 30 miles of rails dumped on the wharf at Mombasa.

The Anglo-German Agreement of 1 July 1890, followed by the Brussels Conference of 2 July 1890, in listing the building of railways into the interior as one of the best means of achieving the ending of the slave-trade in the interior, gave added impetus to IBEAC plans for railway building, and on 26 August 1890 there took place an official inauguration of a railway from Mombasa to Taveta (it was merely a tramway, later to be relaid on Mombasa Island). This auspicious beginning was followed up by an expedition under Captain A.F. Eric Smith to examine a practicable route for a railway from Mombasa to Lake Victoria and the best site for launching a steamer on Lake Victoria.

Smith, with four employees of the IBEAC – S.S. Bagge, Dr J.S. Macpherson, J. Martin and A.H. Neumann – and Baganda envoys (returning to Buganda after having been brought down by Jackson in the previous September), left Mombasa on December 1890, and by January 1891 were at Dagoretti (Kikuyu) where the expedition separated. Martin, Bagge, Macpherson and the Baganda envoys proceeded to Kampala where they arrived on 31 March 1891. Smith and Neumann struck west from Lake Naivasha – through Sotik and Lumbwa – to Kavirondo; and then, in search of a steamer port on Lake Victoria, continued west to Luba's and Mumias in Busoga, where they arrived at the end of April 1891. On the return journey from Busoga, Smith, accompanied by Martin whom Lugard had sent back to the coast for more ammunition, examined the Eldama Ravine route while Neumann reappraised the Lumbwa–Sotik route to Naivasha, in the course of which he was attacked by natives who inflicted heavy losses on him, prior to his rejoining Smith near Kedong.

Arrived back at Mombasa on 16 July 1891, Smith wrote up his reports. He animadverted on all aspects of East Africa generally, and the IBEAC in particular. This disillusionment and sharp criticism may have been the result of the dejected state in which Smith wrote up his reports: in his own words 'since my return I have had fever nearly every day and am a wreck now, and writing under the more or less intoxicating influence of quinine'. According to Smith, the Company's attempts at station building after some two years, had left no result whatever. The peoples of East Africa were 'treacherous dogs', and those of Sotik were 'true savages, and very naked, drunk and friendly'. In Busoga, that 'land of bananas and plenty', the chief accomplishment of its people was thieving. The 'palmy' days of the Maasai were now apparently past and they were left a decadent and crapulous people.

As to the feasibility of a railway from Mombasa to the Lake, Smith listed obstacles to its building: lack of water between the coast nd Machakos; the very unbroken ground between Machakos and Nzoi, the rugged Kikuyu country; the sharp gradients, steep hills and valleys of the Mau escarpment; and as for a site for launching a steamer on Lake Victoria he had completely failed to find any suitable spot. It was his view that 'throughout the whole of the country I do not see where any profit can accrue to any railway which may be constructed'. East Africa was 'unprepossessing country': 'I really don't see how – barring the discovery of gold – any good is to come out of it'. If however, despite his discouraging remarks, the Company still insisted on building the railway, Smith recommended that it run inland somewhat south of its present line, as far as the meridian of Naivasha, and thence north to Naivasha, from where it would proceed to the Mau, ascending that escarpment at the point where it is ascended by the railway today.

In the same month that Smith left for the interior, Mackinnon requested a government subsidy to assist in building the railway. He instanced a Belgian subsidy of £400,000 to build a railway in the Congo Free State, and argued that an East African railway would be a 'great nation measure'. The FO in acknowledging these arguments added some of its own: it claimed that the railway, apart from the economic benefits accruing from it, and the opening up of the country, would be a practical step towards ending the slave-trade and this in turn would save £100,000 annually on the anti-slave-trade patrol. The alternative to a railway to hold the interior was a series of military stations and flying columns and this would cost at least £25,000 annually. The Foreign Office also added that since the railway would pass through a sterile area over a great part of its distance, and would have no lateral feeders, it would depend on the dense population surrounding the lake districts for revenue, and to tap this revenue widely would mean placing steamers on those lakes, an operation which could only be done expeditiously after the railway was built. Salisbury, for the Foreign Office, would support an annual subsidy of £25,000 for 25 years and a 2 per cent guarantee on paid-up capital of £1,250,000. The Company demurred: it asked for a 3 per cent guarantee and an annual grant of £35–40,000 for 25 years. It also favoured a gauge of 24 inches, as against a metre gauge.

Meanwhile the two eminent engineers, Sir John Fowler and Sir Guiford Molesworth, consulted by the IBEAC in the matter, submitted their report in July 1891. They placed the cost of the railway at 50 per cent higher than either the Company's or the Foreign Office estimate. The Treasury too placed it on the higher side, and requested that before any financial support from government could be considered, a 'reliable official survey' was necessary. In Parliament, government backing for a survey was opposed by the Liberals, with Gladstone rejecting any argument that the British government was under obligation under the Brussels Act to support a railway. He claimed that a railway would bring bloodshed and confiscation of land from the natives, and instanced dangers from the Maasai as recorded by various travellers. Despite these gloomy warnings, government agreed to support a survey vote of £20,000, with the IBEAC agreeing to pay anything in excess of this amount up to a sum of £5000.

With Stanley's warning to Joseph Thomson in mind, that to penetrate the Maasai country 'Take a thousand men, or make your will', and provided by the IBEAC with a powerful escort of Indian troops and hundreds of porters, and some 60 donkeys, and tube wells for finding water, Captain J.R.L. Macdonald, the leader, speedily organized his expedition. His second in command was Captain Pringle who had served under him on the north-western frontier in India. Also in the party were employees of the IBEAC – Lieutenant P.G. Twining, H.H.L. Austin, F.G. Foaker and F.J. Jackson – making in all seven Europeans, 41

Indians, 411 Swahilis and some 60 donkeys. They set out from Mombasa in two parties on 21 and 24 December 1891, less than four months after Macdonald had received his original orders at Bombay to report to London.

The official report of Macdonald's expedition describes the daily route traversed with the aid of compass, aneroid barometer and pedometer, and the position of each camp checked by latitude and azimuth or distance observations. Small mention is made of incidents such as the death by drowning of an interpreter in the Nzoi River; the fatalities from smallpox and dysentery; desertions, deaths from bee stings, attacks by red ants and hyenas; camp wash-outs and rain storms (these details are in Pringle's diary rather than official reports). In the face of these exacting tolls, however, the expedition made steady progress. By January 1892 the Teita route had been surveyed, and by March the expedition was at Kikuyu. Here it separated, one party under Pringle proceeding to Ugowe Bay, and the other, under Macdonald, taking a more northerly route to Mumias where the two parties joined up on 18 May 1892. The danger of attack from hostile tribes had not materialized. At one stage the survey party had been surrounded by a large band of Sotik who fortunately did not attack.

Leaving half the caravan at Mumias to survey harbour facilities on the lake, Macdonald and Pringle pressed on to Uganda, arriving at Kampala on 9 June 1892. Their stay was brief. By 16 June, accompanied by Lugard, they were on their way back to the coast. On the return journey alternative routes for a railway were surveyed, but this resulted in little or no variation from the up-country route surveyed. At Kibwezi, where they arrived on 4 September 1892, Macdonald received orders directing him back to Uganda to report on the causes of the religious wars that had taken place there earlier in the year. Captain Pringle, left in charge of the expedition, proceeded to the coast, where he arrived at Mombasa on 23 September 1892, and on him devolved the task of drafting the survey report. The expedition's arrival was heralded by a statement from Cecil Rhodes that he was prepared to extend his telegraph line from Salisbury north to Uganda without any contribution from the British government, so certain was Rhodes that the Survey Report would swing government opinion in favour of a railway. It would need this heartening encouragement to help it on its way when it was submitted to Parliament in June 1893. For the Liberals under Gladstone were now back in office (since August 1892), and the Treasury had recently signalled that money would not easily be forthcoming for an East African railway: it had just turned down the proposed railway from Berbera to Hargeisha in British Somaliland, as uneconomical. Macdonald's report would have to carry much conviction to win over government and Treasury approval.

The report was pragmatic and clear in its recommendations for the construction of the railway. The estimated length of the railway line was 657 miles, the total cost – £2,240,000 – an average of £3409 for a railway gauge of 3′6″ – also included the rolling-stock and placing a light draught steamboat on Lake Victoria. No insuperable physical obstacles were anticipated in constructing the line. There would be no tunnels and such gradients, curves, embankments and bridges as would be necessary were all reasonable. Cheap wood fuel was available along most of the line, and the actual clearing of the right of way would immediately provide large supplies of wood fuel at no extra cost. To construct the railway, Macdonald looked to India for a labour force: he saw little prospect of Africans coming forth in sufficient numbers for this purpose. Anticipating that the Treasury would demur at the cost of the line, Macdonald had proposed a line for light traffic only. To make it suitable for heavier traffic would involve an addition at sum of £445,000.

As for the exaggerated notion that the railway would deliver a 'crushing blow' at the slave-trade, Macdonald was cautious. The railway would not traverse the routes normally used by slave caravans – those from the far interior usually followed a course further south and passed through German territory to Bagamoyo, while slaves from the Kikuyu country were usually taken to the coast by a northerly route, or southwards to join up with the slave-trade passing through German territory. Nevertheless the railway would give more flexibility to an anti-slavery campaign and by providing swift and easy communication across the dreaded Nyika, where for 200 miles food supplies and water were virtually unobtainable, would make it highly suspicious for any caravan which chose to run this formidable gauntlet in preference to using the railway services.

Even with anticipated earnings of £62,000 a year there would still be a deficit of £71,840 per annum, assuming 3 per cent interest a year on estimated capital outlay. Macdonald anticipated, however, that the railway would develop a profitable trade in products which would more than double the estimated annual earnings.

The Liberals who had strongly opposed the survey vote and the building of a railway were, however, brought round to declaring a protectorate over Uganda, in view of the great weight attached to Sir Gerald Portal's views. He had made it clear that Britain had incurred heavy responsibilities in Uganda which forbade any abandonment of that territory, and he recommended the establishment of a protectorate over it. He then went on to emphasize the need for a railway to hold Uganda. On his way back to coast from Uganda, after his mission there, he had diverted from his line of march to examine the possibility of the Tana River route as a line for a such a railway. Portal emphasized insistently 'the all important and over-shadowing question of transport and communications'.

His voice – even from the dead – carried much weight with the Liberal government which had sent him to Uganda, and in the debates in June 1894 on Uganda's future, government came out in favour of declaration of a protectorate over that territory, but it would not go so far as to meet the cost of a railway there. Instead a Director of Transport was appointed to superintend communications with Uganda: this meant continued reliance on the primitive method of human and animal porterage.

Fortunately this would be on an ever shrinking scale, for the great enterprise of the railway could not be shelved for ever. It would revive again. In the interval, however, dependence for transport would still be on the old methods. The IBEAC had established a mail service but this was highly undependable and had no clearly defined route into the interior, mails more often went inland by way of the German sphere. Mackinnon's Road from Mombasa to Kibwezi by way of Duruma, the Taru desert and Tsavo, a distance of 200 miles, was adequate for wheeled traffic but to the west of this was a mere footpath to Uganda, by way of stations – Kikuyu, Eldama Ravine and Mumias.

In 1895, following the withdrawal of the IBEAC, Captain Sclater of the Royal Engineers commenced the opening up of a rude cart road from Kibwezi to the lake, connecting Kikuyu and Eldama Ravine stations with those at Navaisha and in the Nandi country which had been established for the protection of caravans. With a small party of assistants brought from Nyasaland, a small construction force of 100 Indians and 150 Swahilis and a few Italians picked up in Mombasa, Sclater forged ahead. He had the advantage of the 200 miles of the Mackinnon Road as far as Kibwezi, but from here on he had to make his own road up over the Kapiti plains and across the head-waters of the Athi River. Sclater's road skirted what is now the northern environs of Nairobi and then continued on by way of Kabete and Fort Smith (Kikuyu) to the west. By September 1896 Sclater was at the Nandi station, and by June 1897 was able to report:

The Uganda Road is now completed and open for wheeled traffic
from the head of the railway to the lake at Port Victoria.[2]

This laconic and quietly confident statement was overoptimistic, for the
road was no more than a track in places, and a journey over it was a
punishment which few could endure. From the coast, inland for some
200 miles, the going was easy – bridges had been constructed over the
Voi River and other watercourses, the road had a good surface and was
passable for wheeled transport over the Kapiti plains and through the
Rift Valley. Up over the Kikuyu, Mau and Nandi plateaux, it was but a
narrow track tunnelling through dense forests, cleared only to a width
sufficient for the passage of a single vehicle. The foliage of large trees
meeting overhead shut out the sunlight and air; and the track beneath
partook more of the character of a ditch formed for the collection of
forest drainage than of a highway for wheeled traffic. For the greater part
of the year the surface of the forest road between the Eldama Ravine and
Kakamega was a slough of mud, tangled roots and stumps of trees, and
from Mumias to Port Victoria there were some 40 miles of swamp where
the track was almost impassable.

An improvement came in early 1899 when the lake objective was
moved from Port Victoria to Kisumu on Ugowe Bay, thus avoiding the
swampy stretch and shortening the road by over 45 miles. The problem
of surmounting the escarpments on either side of the Rift Valley and the
Nandi escarpment – the latter an abrupt declivity of 2000 feet – was
solved by placing a service of porters at their base and summits, and
maintaining a shuttle service between them. From Kisumu transport
was relatively easy across the lake to Port Alice (present-day Entebbe) by
means of a steam launch, a steel boat hired from the CMS and by native
dhows.

Practically all forms of transport, ranging from steam tractors to
camels, were experimented with during the period 1894-1902. Steam
tractors, although they at first impressed with their capacity for heavy
traction over sharp gradients and rough surfaces, and their use in tsetse
fly country near the coast soon revealed weaknesses. As a result of
broken draw-bars, too few engineers and mechanics and the constant
worry over the water supply, as well as the fact that in hauling its water
supply and winding itself out of inclines and water-holes it often
traversed 30 miles to cover six, the steam tractor was pronounced a
complete failure by the Director of Transport in July 1898.

The experiment with camels was even more disappointing and short-lived. In Jubaland and northern parts of the East Africa Protectorate, in Boran and the Rudolf area, thousands of camels were in use. Macdonald recommended them for transport purposes in East Africa. They could carry the equivalent of four or five porter-loads, and were fairly cheap to purchase; at Berbera they cost £6 with another £3 added by the time they arrived at Mombasa. The IBEAC and Smith, Mackenzie and Company obtained a few camels from India but these died from pneumonia and want of a suitable diet within a short time of arrival. Italian contractors imported nearly 200 from Somaliland for use in the interior but by the time Kikuyu was reached only 40 were alive; the remainder had slithered and cut themselves to death in the mud and rocks of the upland escarpments.

It was perilous to use bullock or other animal transport in the tsetse-infested tract between the coast and Kibwezi, but in the upland country to the west there was less hazard. A few horses were imported into the coast region in 1896 by the 24th Beluchistan Regiment, but all died within two months of arrival. They appeared to thrive in the upland interior, but not until they could be rapidly transported across the tsetse fly belt by railway was it possible to get them inland. Mules were imported from Cyprus in 1898, but the tsetse fly also finished most of them off shortly after arrival; only a few survived the journey inland. Donkeys were more successful; they were tough and seemed to suffer less from the effects of climate and were fairly easily fed, but were obtainable only in limited numbers, and were too light for heavy draught work.

The heavy ox-wagon of the South African veldt, capable of carrying up to two tons, was too unwieldy and required a very large team of oxen they did not give such good results as the light Indian carts drawn by two bullocks, or the light two-wheeled 'Maltese carts' hauled by mules. Good drivers were hard to come by. Sikhs employed as bullock-drivers would not touch rhino or wildebeest meat and 'missed their rum'. Cape boys were unsatisfactory as mule drivers 'being prone to drink and trouble with women'.

In the end, epidemics of pleuropneumonia which wiped out oxen, 'South African' horse sickness which carried off most of the mules, broken axles and drunken drivers, wore down the transport system to the stage where it was farmed out to contractors. This short-lived experiment ended in court action for non-fulfilment of contracts and subcontracting to irresponsible agents. The only arrangement which seemed to be successful was that of Smith, Mackenzie and Company which in early 1895 let out their contract to the German East Africa Company which transported goods to Uganda through the German sphere.

In the end, the old familiar method of human porterage was resorted to, but here too was unceasing anxiety and much hard work. The organization and management of a caravan of porters was no simple matter. Provision of adequate stocks of rice, beans and maize was essential. Game could be obtained in some stretches, as in the Kapiti plains and Rift Valley; and it was a thankful blessing, for it improved the humour and physical condition of the men. Government stations when established were a great boon, for here reprovisioning and recuperation of the porters was possible.

Careful assemblage of trade goods for the various tribes was necessary. Such goods were essential to purchase food for the porters, and also as hongo (tribute) to ease passage of the caravan through alien territory. Unless one was experienced, or made careful enquiry at the coast, in assembling trade goods, miscalculation might have grave results. Taste varied from tribe to tribe. The Maasai showed little interest in beads, but had a great passion for iron wire from which they fashioned their distinctive lion spears. Iodine, in small amounts, whether for its dye or medicinal quality it is difficult to say, represented to the Maasai something equal in price to a cow – their dearest possession. The Wakamba were more prosaic in their tastes: cloth and beads, of most kinds, were acceptable. With some tribes the fashion in beads was constantly changing; some preferred small red or pink beads while others refused anything but blue or yellow, and by next season the position might be reversed. Cloth was always a useful commodity, but here too certain kinds were more desirable than others.

The recruiting of porters posed particular problems. The Germans restricted recruiting of the Wanyamwezi, the traditional porters, thus the recruiting of porters in the British sphere was usually at the coast or among the Wakamba. The Wakikuyu were available for local purposes but they appeared to suffer from the extreme change in food and climate when at the coast. Inland, the Baganda were averse to acting as porters. The Nilotic and Nilo-Hamitic peoples, including the Maasai, were reluctant to hoist loads of 60 to 70 lb on top of their heads: it would disarrange their elaborate system of hairdressing. The Maasai had all they wanted 'in the way of food, drink, women and the chase', so why take on this arduous employment?

A strong porter could carry as much as 70 lb on his head, although goods were usually made up in 50-lb loads. The average progress of a caravan was about eight or 12 miles a day. The special runners in the mail service, however, who carried 25 to 30 loads of mail a month up-country, often Maasai, would cover two to three times this distance. The mail pouch weighing about 25 lb was usually strapped to the back, so that it did not hinder free running. As railhead advanced, the work of the runners gradually decreased.

The average wage of a porter by the mid-1890s was about ten shillings per month, with an additional four shillings provided in the form of a posho (maize flour) ration. Porters on engagement were given a liberal advance of wages − too liberal in fact, for this custom of an advance, sanctioned by long usage, more often resulted in a drunken debauch on the eve of departure, and left a gaggle of muddle-headed porters struggling to hoist their loads at the outset of the long journey into the interior. The first few marches were the most arduous, a few miles a day only being traversed until the men were travel-hardened. The apportioning of water and rations was a calculated careful art based on much experience. In dangerous neighbourhoods, as among the notably treacherous Wakikuyu around Fort Smith, the keeping of caravans on the march and rounding up stragglers was a demanding task, and there was also the erection of necessary bomas and thorn fences at night, and the stationing of sentries − this usually fell to the Swahilis, Somalis and Indians. There was constant thieving to guard against. Amicable relations had to be maintained with the natives of various districts through which a caravan passed. The abuses of one caravan would be paid for by subsequent caravans. The giving of presents, so frequent in the 1870s and 1880s, was waning by the 1890s. No longer was it the practice to give every petty chief a valuable present; this only created precedents and the next oncoming caravan met escalated demands. The principle became accepted that presents would be given only for food or other assistance.

The larger the caravan the more economical it was to operate, but its organization was a task of some magnitude: it meant immense detail in the apportioning of loads and other duties. With almost mathematical precision and percentages, contingent losses from sickness and desertion must be reckoned: desertions were usually assumed to run at 7 per cent of the total number of carriers and this must be allowed for.

The main and overriding worry was the need to sustain the good health of the porters. Fever, ulcerations, sores, diarrhoea and, most persistently, constipation − from the almost exclusive diet of grain, beans, and posho (maize flour) – all wrought their toll. The dreaded smallpox was a haunting worry. Porters from the coast were ill-equipped to withstand the cold of the highlands where pneumonia was the killer. At high altitudes of 8000 feet and over it was wise to wait until the heavy morning mist had been dispersed by the sun before setting out. The stretch through the highlands was a severe trial for carriers. The bitter wet cold at night, forced marches, hail storms which, though rare, could be dangerous. In their waywardness, porters would part with their few possessions, such as crude cooking pots and blankets, in return for some trifle which caught their fancy, or the service of a female.

Colonel Berkeley of Uganda, and Sir Lloyd Mathews at Zanzibar, were the first to draw attention to the need to ameliorate the lot of porters on the Uganda road, and to improve conditions under which they laboured. Mathews described the pathetic life of wretched porters struggling over the escarpment in pouring rain and sleet, 'coughing their lives away' and existing on their little flour allowance, without shelter, warmth, or adequate clothing, and 'all after a long day's march carrying loads of up to 80 lbs on their heads'. Portal also recommended a system of registration, inspection and control of native-led caravans.

It was largely as a result of Berkeley's and Mathews's efforts that 'Regulations on the Treatment of Porters' were promulgated in November 1895, under which registration of porters was made obligatory; flogging was to be done with 'a light stick' only and was not to exceed 30 strokes; blankets and medicine were to be provided. Continued pressure from Mathews and Colonel Ternan of Uganda brought supplementary regulations in June 1899, whereby provision of adequate food supplies, construction of shelters *en route* and limitation on weight of loads was effected. The lot of the porter was now at last made more endurable; he would soon, however, be a figure of the past. The railway was approaching the lake.

The project for a railway to the lake, although turned down by the Liberal government in June 1894, was too strong and vital a concept to be shelved for long. It had re-emerged within the year, in the face of railway building plans in Africa by other European powers. France was contemplating a 2000-mile trans-Saharan railway, and Germany the construction of a central line in German East Africa with well-planned feeders. The Germans were much ahead of the British in railway building in East Africa, although subsequently losing the lead. The idea of a coast railway between Dar es Salaam and Bagamoyo was dropped in 1891 for a railway to the fertile Kilimanjaro area; but fear that the British might tap the Kilimanjaro region by rail before the Germans hastened the latter along with their plans. By the end of August 1894 the first section of a railway from Tanga to Korogwe at the foot of the Usambara Hills was opened. A novel suggestion for a joint British–German railway from Tanga and Mombasa and branching out at a short distance from the coast, to the Kavirondo Gulf and Speke Gulf, on Lake Victoria, never got farther than on paper: negotiations between a Mr Cawston, an English financier, and the German government, whereby two million pounds capital was to be raised in England and Germany, broke down in November 1894 because the Germans thought the railway would unduly favour British interests. German plans for a great central railway from Dar es Salaam to Tabora, with branches to Lake Tanganyika and Lake Victoria, and connecting with Tanga, Korogwe and Bagamoyo, brought strong reaction from British financiers, resulting in a delegation to Lord Kimberley from 68 chambers of commerce in Britain, and a warning that 'if the Germans forestall us it will be a blow for our prestige and commerce and if they get to the Lake first we will have to use their line' An announcement on 11 February 1895 in the *National Zeitung* that the German central railway would be backed by the imperial government, and was designed to attract commerce from the Congo and Uganda Protectorate, provided added incentive to the building of a Mombasa–Lake Victoria Railway. The Congo Free State was building a railway to connect the Upper and Lower Congo, with a loan of £600,000 interest free from the Belgian government. Italian plans for railway building in the Horn of Africa were countered by Menelik, who granted Alfred Ilg, a Swiss engineer, a concession for a railway from Jibuti to the White Nile by way of Harrar, Entotto and Kaffa, in March 1894. Ilg in turn transferred this concession to the French, much to the chagrin of the British. Fears of French railway building and advance on the Upper Nile stirred the London Chamber of Commerce on 10 April 1895 into calling on HMG 'to assure control of the Nile Valley from Uganda to Fashoda', and to construct the 'Mombasa Railway'. The ignominious defeat of the Italians at Adowa in March 1896, was a standing lesson on the importance of a strong communication link with the interior if an inland territory was to be held. The lesson was not lost on Lord Kitchener in his plans for reconquest of the Sudan, nor was it lost on the Liberal government in Britain. Lord Salisbury and the Opposition pointed out the danger of leaving the field to Britain's rivals. Little could be expected from the failing IBEAC which could not even pay its annual rent, let alone finance the building of a railway. The directors of the IBEAC were in the last throes of negotiations with HMG to buy them out. Old familiar arguments that the railway would strike a blow at the nefarious slave-trade could no longer work their former magic; it was the realistic threat of foreign economic competition, rivalry for control of the Upper Nile and the need to tap Uganda's much eulogized riches, which stirred government into appointing a commission of inquiry under Sir Percy Anderson to report on the feasibility of building a railway at a cheaper rate than that envisaged by Macdonald. The commission was charged to treat the question as a matter of urgency.

It presented its report in April 1895. Its findings supported Macdonald's survey report in all essentials but reduced the estimated cost of the railway from £2,240,000 to £1,755,000 (which with interest would rise to £1,865,000 and ultimately to £4,000,000) partly by recommending a three-foot gauge and other economies. The railway was estimated to bring in revenue of £60,000 a year, and would save government £33,500 a year in transport costs. The Commission recommended that government provide the capital and build the railway itself, and work it with its own officials: this would ensure harmonious relations between railway authorities and protectorate administrations and make it easier to obtain rolling-stock and other materials from India. Rounding out their report, the commissioners urged that to prevent the 'thriving trade of Uganda' being thrown into the hands of the German railway if the latter reached the interior first, the British railway should be constructed 'as speedily as possible'.

It was a cogent report, and on 27 May 1895 Rosebery reported to the Queen that in the face of it, the Cabinet had decided that the construction of the Uganda Railway should be undertaken at once. It instanced the effect of the Jibuti Railway in snapping up trade which formerly went to Berbera in British Somaliland, as warning of what would happen if the Germans got their railway to the lake before the British. When, on the 13 June 1895, Sir Edward Grey announced the government's intention of constructing the railway, German response was that 'whichever railway arrives first will obtain a practical monopoly of the hinterland trade'. Although German railway construction was subsequently to lag behind that of the British, in its initial stages it had stirred the British into taking the firm decision to build the railway to Lake Victoria. So well developed was the system of human and animal porterage in the German territory that it seemed to take the impetus out of railway building. The central line, Dar es Salaam to Tabora, was not commenced until 1905, and did not reach Lake Tanganyika until just before the First World War.

The British government's decision to build the railway itself seemed wise, for it could do so at a more economic figure than if contracted out, and it would avoid the worries of double supervision, guarantees as to quality, subcontracting and the inevitable maximizing of company profits, all of which would add to the real cost of the railway In the interval between the appointment of the Anderson Commission and the government decision to build the railway itself, private bids at a very low figure had come in, but they asked for too much in the way of subsidies or were of such singular character as could not be countenanced: one for example, asked that for 'every English mile of railway laid' it should receive in return the freehold of 6400 acres of land; and another proposed

> an elevated single rail system with symmetrical girders and reversible rails at a height of at least 3'3" from the ground, to escape the destructive power of the silaceous dust.[3]

There was also concern that private constructors might lack 'necessary delicacy' in treating with natives (the experience with the IBEAC was still in mind).

Salisbury, now returned to office in June 1895, and resolved that the line be constructed by government, upon Indian methods and with Indian labour, appointed the Uganda Railway Committee in September 1895, to preside over the enterprise. Its chairman was Sir Percy Anderson of the Foreign Office, who held the post until his death in July 1896, when he was succeeded by the Hon. (later Sir) Francis Bertie. On the latter's resignation in January 1903 Sir John Kirk became chairman and continued as such until the dissolution of the Committee in September 1903. The Committee's choice of Chief Engineer fell upon Mr George Whitehouse, who brought to this venture wide experience in many parts of the world, and who held his appointment until 1904.

The impress of Lord Salisbury's thinking is shown in the more substantial railway line constructed: with metre gauge and heavier rail – 'steel throughout the whole length' – and sleepers of the 'steel pea-pod pattern', except in places where 'sodium salts' might be found, and where creosoted pine or 'pingadu' sleepers from Burma would be used. Metre gauge was in use on nearly half of India's railways, and its use in East Africa would facilitate securing rolling-stock from India. The Egyptian–Sudan Railway was also using the metre gauge south of Luxor, and there was the possibility that some day the East African railway might link up with it.

The railway was generously endowed by the imperial government with a belt of land, a mile wide, on either side of the line, from the limit of the Sultan's ten-mile wide coastal strip, to Lake Victoria. Income derived from this land, either through rent or sale, would reduce the capital cost of the construction of the railway. A proclamation acquiring this zone, approximately 700,000 acres in area, most of which was believed to be unoccupied, was issued in May 1897.

From the outset government stressed the importance of speed in completing the railway – even to the point of intimating that HMG might supply additional funds, if necessary to achieve this. When at one stage it appeared that the government of India was unwilling to supply the necessary labour, China was considered as a possible source. Inquiries as to the possibility of obtaining Africans as labourers showed no large numbers available. The railway would largely be driven through districts sparsely populated. The first section of the line ran through the largely uninhabited Nyika and the sparsely settled, rising plateau country of the Wakamba beyond it. Even the famine of 1898-99 drove only a few of the Wakamba to work on the railway and they would not work continuously and systematically: the fear of the slave-driver was still fresh in mind, and the habit of working for wages had not yet caught on. To have brought labourers down from Uganda (if it had been possible to recruit them there) would have been a lengthy and difficult task. The traditional recruiting grounds for labour in East Africa were the Wanyamwezi, who were accustomed to working for wages as porters and carriers and to long periods of absence away from home, but the Germans prohibited recruitment of labour from their territory. Attempts to recruit native labourers at various points along the railway met with little success. Even during the work on the last section of the railway, that terminating at Port Florence, and nearest to Uganda, it was difficult to persuade the Baganda to work on the line, owing to their still persistent dread of the turbulent Nandi and the Maasai. The largest number of African labourers ever employed at one time on the railway was 2600, and on the whole never averaged more than 2000.

The British government was virtually forced to turn to India as the source of labour for constructing the railway. Considered opinion always came round to the view that this was the right course. India was the natural and nearest recruiting ground for labour. Since so much in the way of on Indian experience, material and expertise was drawn on in building the railway, it seemed right that recourse should be had to Indian labour. Transportation from India to East Africa was direct and rapid; the transition, culturally and climatically, from India to East Africa, was much easier for Indians than to many other parts of the world.

The India Office gave its approval in October 1895 to the recruitment of Indian labour after amending the Indian Emigration Act and scheduling East Africa as a country to which such emigration was permitted and thus making recruitment possible. There quickly followed the appointment of a special recruiting agent in India with a large recruiting staff, and the establishment of detention camps with medical staff for screening recruits before they left India.

Rules for recruitment were rigorous and detailed: coolies were to be engaged for three-year contracts, with right of return passage to the locality in India from which they were recruited within six months of expiry of contract, and this right could not be forfeited. They were also to have liberty to remain in East Africa if they chose to do so; the nature of their employment on the railway must be specified in the agreement; wages were to be in cash and not less than 15 rupees per month, and free rations were to be included; pay was to commence not later than the date of embarkation. The engagement could be terminated by the Chief Engineer at a month's notice.

Recruiting depots at Bombay, Karachi and Lahore, were soon sending a stream of recruits by chartered steamer to Mombasa. A few shiploads of Indian labourers destined for Durban in South Africa were diverted to East Africa to work on the railway. The Crown Agents encouraged recruitment of Indian labourers on the grounds that they might settle down on expiry of their contracts, and form a valuable and industrious community in East Africa.

There was only a semblance of screening and medical checking of recruits, and many were probably physically unfit; but the charge that the majority of Indians employed on the Uganda Railway were of poor moral and physical type from the slums of Bombay is unsustainable. At least 50 per cent of the recruits were from the fighting races of northern India. W. H. Manning, Commandant of the Armed Forces in British Central Africa, had such high regard for their fighting ability that he recommended them as a nucleus for a reserve battalion to defend the Uganda Railway in case of mutiny among the regular African troops.

Rates of pay, 3 annas or 4½ d. per day (1 anna = 1½ d.), for these workers on the railway, were attractive in Indian terms and drew all the labour required. By January 1896 the first batch of 1000 labourers had arrived; and in the next five years over 32,000 Indian labourers were transported to East Africa to work on the railway; and by 1900, when recruitment ceased, the number of coolies employed on construction of the railway had reached 19,742. The flow of labour was comparatively smooth, apart from an interruption in 1897 by an outbreak of the plague in India. In September of that year recruitment was recommenced, only to be halted in the following month. In January 1898 the British Indian Steamship Navigation Company's ship *Bundara* was refused permission to land coolies at Mombasa, on the grounds that the vessel was infested with plague. When the British Consul, Sir Arthur Hardinge, refused permission for a quarantine station to be set up on the mainland, the steamship company stood to lose £50,000 on the transaction, and warned that complete cessation of coolie labour from India might result from the affair. A compromise was arrived at with the infected coolies being sent to Faza Island near Lamu for quarantine. Recruitment then recommenced.

The problem of transporting thousands of Indian labourers across the Indian Ocean, the establishment of work camps, commissariat arrangements, policing of cantonments, dealing with the human flotsam which gravitated to the camps – soldiers, broken-down medical officers, prostitutes and pimps – was a task of great magnitude, and imposed unforeseen costs on the railway. Also the great polyglot of Indians, employed in a vast array of positions in the construction of the railway – jemadars, surveyors, medical orderlies, artisans, accountants, clerks, fitters, firemen, masons, line-layers, pointsmen and thousands of unskilled 'jungle-slashers' – posed a great social problem. Eliot considered that the railway coolies were the most criminal and litigious class in the protectorate. Their camps, squalid and vice-ridden, had a disturbing effect on the surrounding African populations, as among the Nandi whose women were enticed away by the railway workers. Jackson describes the railway camps in Kavirondo:

There were two in particular I knew well, as they were more or less standing camps, between Lumbwa Station and the tunnel, and there was another near Fort Ternan. I passed them on foot, and that was enough: I never had the courage to walk through one. Apart from the squalor, they were crowded with prostitutes, small boys and other accessories to the bestial vices so commonly practised by Orientals ... there were rumours of the Lumbwa becoming restive on account of so many of their women being inveigled away from their homes and harboured in these sinks of iniquity.[4]

The Chief Engineer and advance party arrived at Mombasa on 11 December 1895, to find no accommodation available for them until the arrival of corrugated iron and wooden houses from England. Prior to the arrival of a steam barge and iron freight boats and construction of a temporary pier, facilities for unloading cargo were woefully inadequate and primitive. In the mean time cargoes, if not lightened, were thrown into the water to be collected at low tide.

The first task of the advance party was to secure a more detailed survey of the line than that provided by the preliminary reconnaissance of Macdonald and Pringle: theirs was a useful general plan only. A survey party set out from the mainland opposite Mombasa, in January 1896, and surveyed the line to Mazeras and across the Taru desert; another party, commencing from Kibwezi at Mile 190, in August 1896, worked backwards until it met the first party. In October 1896 a third survey party laid out the line between the Athi plains and the Rift Valley. Rapid survey work was impossible through the thick thorn bush country of the first two 200 miles of the route, but beyond Kibwezi the country became more open, and the marking out of the line was completed as far as the Kikuyu hills west of Nairobi, by October 1898 – a distance of 360 miles from the coast, and 140 miles ahead of the construction gangs.

In the mean time the Chief Engineer, Whitehouse, had marched over the anticipated route by September 1898, up to Port Victoria on Lake Victoria, and sailed along the shores of that lake to Ugowe Bay (present-day Kavirondo Gulf). Its outline was seen to differ widely from that shown on current maps – these were largely based on Stanley's erroneous conjectures. From the inlet at the head of the Gulf, which he named Port Florence, Whitehouse examined the country at the summit of the Mau escarpment, and with the information thus obtained the final marking out of the line could proceed from the Rift Valley to Ugowe Bay, the last peg being driven at Port Florence in April 1900. The verification of a more direct and practicable route between the Rift and Ugowe Bay was much as indicated by Sir G. Molesworth in 1891, and was a material saving in distance over the alignment originally projected by Macdonald. Molesworth's tentative suggestions had proved remarkably correct.

While this more accurate survey of the route of the railway was being determined, there had been much activity at its terminus at Mombasa.

At first it was proposed that the terminus should be on the mainland – immediately opposite Mombasa Island. This plan was soon set aside when it was found that the shoreline rose too suddenly and too steeply to provide sufficient flat expanse for a large railway terminus with its many go-downs, freight sheds and all the wharfage facilities for a great port. The starting-point of the railway was fixed at Kilindini on the south side of Mombasa Island where excellent deep water facilities existed for the landing of goods and boat passengers. The old port on the north side of the island was too open to the ocean and wholly inadequate for large vessels and offered little protection from heavy seas or naval bombardment in the event of war. Molesworth, in his report, waxed eloquently on Kilindini's advantages:

> there is an excellent harbour and completely land-locked, with a capacious and well protected anchorage ... the port possesses great facilities for development, and sites for wharehouses and wharves capable of almost indefinite expansion.[5]

A tramway was laid down to connect the Old Port to Kilindini and this shifted the emphasis of attention to the new harbour site. The purchase of land on the island for a railway depot and buildings proved a tortuous business, for the land speculators had already moved in and there was much inexperience in this matter of land requisition on the part of the few protectorate officials – mostly ex-IBEAC officials. The resulting lawsuits with town developers provided a tempestuous, though brief episode.

Siting the terminus of the railway out on Mombasa Island meant stepping back as it were, to get a flying start to surmount the sharp acclivity of the mainland coast. It also involved the construction of a bridge – the 'Salisbury viaduct' – over the channel between the island and the mainland, leaving an opening through which dhows could pass. With this bridge built, and the first consignment of the permanent way having already been landed at Mombasa in June 1896, construction of the railway could commence. The railway line arched around the southern side of the island and headed northwards over the viaduct. The 12-mile ascent to Mazeras station, a climb of some 500 feet, was through a stretch of luxuriant tropical vegetation. The receding panoramic views of the inlets of the Indian Ocean and Mombasa harbour provided the tourist with an exhilarating start into the interior.

This attractive 'send-off' was short-lived. From Mazeras onwards, after crossing a 400-foot trestle bridge over a ravine, the line was driven through the Taru desert – flat, dense thorn bush country, without any relief. The task of driving the railway line through this forbidding 200-mile stretch – from Mazeras to Makindu – proved to be the most trying of the whole traverse to the lake. The thick bush, flat country and absence of any natural relief permitting an open view of the general lie of the land, rendered survey and alignment work exceedingly difficult, and also the construction of the right of way. An official report records that

The earthwork here is a mere nothing compared with the clearing of the dense thorny jungle and the grubbing up of the stumps. Further added to this, the jungle will not burn readily, and more clearing is necessary than would otherwise be required to allow the jungle, when felled, to be drawn clear of the track.[6]

By July 1897 railhead was 69 miles from Mombasa, but the Uganda mutiny quickened progress. At the end of 1897 Whitehouse hurried back from leave, with direct instructions from Salisbury to speed up construction so as to reach Kikuyu by Christmas 1898. There was now so much concentration on pushing on with the Uganda Railway that Sir Rennell Rodd, in London in the summer of 1897 urging construction of a light railway from Berbera into the interior of Somaliland, failed to evoke any interest for his project from either Parliament or the Treasury. The absence of water added much to the trials of the labour force, but soon, to overshadow all, a new and terrible fear descended on them.

Tsavo provided a dramatic point in the railway's progress inland. Not only was a formidable task faced here in laying the Tsavo bridge, but a bizarre and terrible episode in which man-eating lions terrorized the labour force – killing 29 of their number – brought the whole operation to a standstill. Railhead had scarcely reached Tsavo, 133 miles from the coast, towards the end of 1897, when all work was halted for three weeks by an invasion of prides of lions, who at night dared to enter the light of the camp circles to prey on the sleeping occupants. The frightful and paralysing effect of these attacks was such that it culminated, in December 1897, in the panic-stricken men demanding to be sent back to Mombasa, and hundreds of them stopped the first passing train by throwing themselves on the track in front of the engine. The men tossed their possessions onto the train and fled from the dread spot. Indian coolies came to regard as useless any attempt to shoot the lions, believing them to be the angry spirits of former African chiefs who had adopted the form of lions in an attempt to stop the construction of the railway:

> for the next three weeks practically nothing was done but build 'lion-proof' huts for those workmen who had sufficient courage to remain. It was a strange and amusing sight to see these shelters perched on the top of water-tanks, roofs and girders – anywhere for safety – while some even went so far as to dig pits inside their tents, into which they descended at night, covering the top over with heavy logs of wood.[7]

Eventually, in December 1897, the reign of terror ended when the lions were killed by an engineer officer, Lieutenant-Colonel J.H. Patterson, DSO, and the coolies were able to continue their work unhindered.

The rate of progress in 1897 was much slower than anticipated. Macdonald's military force and accompanying caravan were taken across the Taru desert on the newly laid line as far as Mile 65 – giving him a head start on his long march to Uganda; but soon the railway had to assist in ferrying troops and supplies when the Uganda mutiny broke out, and although this was an important factor in saving the administration in Uganda from the mutineers, it was a serious disruption of the main work of railway building. There was also the lion episode already described, and the epidemic of plague. An engineers' strike in the United Kingdom resulted in a serious disruption of vital supplies of locomotives. The labour force was depleted by malarial fever, and the nefarious jigger made its appearance to try nerves and flesh. In June 1897 10 per cent of the entire work-force was in hospital. The tsetse fly wreaked havoc among the transport animals, destroying 50 out of 150 transport mules and 450 out of the 550 bullocks imported from India. This most serious drawback was only overcome when steam tractors were introduced beyond railhead. A drought followed the exceptionally heavy rainfall of April and May 1897. Despite these interruptions, the first section of the railroad was opened to Mile 100 for goods traffic in December 1897, and for passengers by 1 February 1898. Only at Voi, an engine-changing station at Mile 100, near the fertile Teita hills and the first principal point reached by the railway, had there been some relief from the dust, heat and lack of water. Shops and rest-houses were established here, and Voi was to be the later connecting point for a branch line to the Kilimanjaro region.

The annual report to Parliament in July 1898, on the progress of the railway up to March 1898, showed that 263 miles of the line had been surveyed, and that rails had reached Tsavo River, at Mile 139, 1500 feet above sea -level, and on the verge of the Ukamba country. Here there was a pure water supply, the only one since leaving Mombasa; other water-holes were so impregnated with lime and salts as to be injurious even to the boilers of locomotives. The more rapid progress of the railway in 1898 was largely the result of improvement in transport ahead of the line. The introduction of two powerful traction engines in May 1898 enabled large numbers of men to work up to 20 miles beyond railhead – one traction engine ran more than 260 miles in 22 days. They had winders by which they could haul themselves up steep slopes and take up loads in sections. Experience had also taught that Woolwich carts (drawn by mules or bullocks) were all right if burdened with no more than a 500-lb load, but that even lighter carts, weighing only 300 lb, were the best.

The scarcity of water continued to be a problem until Kibwezi, at Mile 195; from here on conditions changed for the better. By September 1898 the rails had reached Makindu, at Mile 207, with an altitude of 3000 feet and sufficiently advantageous climate, for European employees of the railway to make it their permanent headquarters. Makindu marked the change from the hot, dry, tsetse-ridden country to the superior environment of the rising interior plateau. The malarial belt was now well behind the workers. The Nyika country, that accursed land of thorny scrub, heat and stinking water-holes, which had tried the patience, courage and perseverance of the railway builders to the full, was now past. It was a relief when the first railway engine rolled smoothly over this stretch of the line.

The slow rate of progress had caused considerable criticism and had resulted in a commission of inquiry under the chairmanship of Sir Guilford Molesworth. The resulting report in March 1899 stressed the difficulties which the engineers had faced, but also the value of the railway even in its unfinished state – witness the role it played in getting troops and supplies to Uganda, and also in bringing them down when they were needed during the recent fighting at Kismayu, obviating the dispatch of a regiment from India. Indian traders were already taking up sites at points along the railway; and as Africans through whose territory the railway passed showed much interest in acquiring English trade goods and in selling their own products to obtain them, the traffic in ivory on the railway was already considerable.

The extent of the line laid within the first 12 months of construction was only 98 miles, but in the next six months it was already 70 miles and the pace of work was increasing. At the end of 1898 rails had reached Mile 246 and in country now more open and park-like, with water available at regular intervals. The task of sustaining the large work camp of 5000 workers and their followers was now eased. In early December 1898 Sultan Hamoud of Zanzibar travelled over the line as far as that point now marked by the railway station 'Sultan Hamoud' – through country which he and his predecessors had claimed as their domain without ever setting foot in it.

At about Mile 280 and at an altitude of 5000 feet, the upper waters of the Athi River were reached, and here, on the Kapiti plains, displayed like a fragment out of the Pleistocene Age, was a great array of magnificent game animals. There was now an increasing sharpness in the air, an the exhilarating freshness in the mornings and the evenings were cool; work under these conditions proceeded more rapidly. The rails reached Nairobi at Mile 326, and an altitude of 5575 feet, on 28 May 1899. The intervening strip between Kapiti plains station and Nairobi was not constructed without incident. There had been a recurrence of the lion terror in March 1899 (to be repeated in June 1900). It was while the Makindu-Nairobi section was under way that Mr Ryall, Assistant Superintendent of the Railway Police was taken by a lion: Ryall and two other men arranged to sit up for a lion that had been prowling about Kima station (Mile 255). It fell to Ryall's turn to watch while the other two slept. He must have fallen asleep, for the other occupants of the carriage were awakened by the lion treading on one of them. The carriage opened by a sliding door at the end, and it is supposed that the jar of the lion springing on to the carriage platform caused the door to slide to. The lion was therefore in a compartment 8x7 feet with three men, and it escaped through a small window, taking Ryall with it. This sad occurrence led to a reward being offered for the capture or death of the man-eater (it was subsequently killed) and for a number of years a reward of Rs 200 was given for every lion killed within the mile zone of the railway. This unusual item of expenditure appeared in railway accounts up to 1902. The stony Athi River proved to be a most difficult river to bridge. The temporary bridge constructed in the spring of 1899 was washed out in the early part of 1900, and rebuilt nine times in the next five months. The prolonged droughts of the late 1890s were followed by heavy rains in 1900–01, causing numerous wash-outs and casualties between Makindu and Nairobi.

At Nairobi there was much work in constructing workshops, locomotive and carriage sheds, sawmills, stores and buildings, workmen's dwellings for thousands of men, staff quarters and permanent homes for Europeans in both the railway and protectorate administration. By the end of the century there had grown up around it all a great city of tents, for the pace of building could not keep up with demand.

At Nairobi the flat open plains terminate, the country commences to rise and the line of hilly, wooded country and open grasslands is most clearly defined. The railway was now carried through the steeply ascending and intensely cultivated Kikuyu district, where the heath and upland aspect near Limuru is more reminiscent of the Scottish highlands than central Africa. At the summit of the Kikuyu escarpment, Mile 359, a rise of 2300 feet is attained in about 30 miles. There is then a most sudden and rapid descent to the escarpment edge overlooking the Rift Valley to the west, where a scene suddenly unfolds before the eye which is almost overpowering in its grandeur and dramatic sweep to distant landscapes. This sudden confrontation with the Great Rift Valley, with Mount Longonot looming up in the distance, is still an unforgettable experience for those who travel that way to Uganda.

The descent into the Rift Valley posed an awesome engineering task. The survey party had surmounted it by a rope lift. The rail-laying party, with its massive supplies of equipment, steam tractors, draught animals and thousands of workmen with their accompanying piles of goods, had to devise a more ingenious method to achieve this descent of more than 1500 feet with inclines of 50 per cent and more. The solution devised was an arrangement whereby a steel rope lift and pulley controlled loaded wagons secured on to carriers; these running up and down sets of rails bedded against the valley slopes. A double line was constructed so that the weight of a loaded wagon descending, would haul up an empty wagon on the second set of rails. In the steeper central portions it was necessary to have carriers with one set of wheels higher than the other, but with a horizontal top. The wagons were then run on to the railway carriers, secured in place, and then lowered or raised from the top to the bottom of the 1500-foot declivity at a speed controlled by brakes on the drum, round which passed the 1¼-inch steel hawser which linked together the ascending and descending loads. The inclines were expensive (they cost £31,356) and took time to complete, but they enabled the rail-laying party to get on with their job of laying the rails along the valley floor. If they had waited until a permanent line was constructed down the Rift wall it would have meant an insupportable delay, for the permanent line was not opened until 4 November 1901, by which date the 'inclines' had been in operation since 3 May 1900. It enabled railhead to advance to Mile 545, 170 miles beyond the point where it would have halted if it had had to wait until the permanent right of way down the valley wall was completed.

The construction of the permanent line was no less an ingenious feat than the 'inclines'. It was achieved by cutting out a road bed in the side of the valley wall and carrying this down in gently descending fashion to an outlying spur far below, and running it along this spur until it levelled out on the valley floor. It involved the construction of numerous viaducts varying in height from 38 to 85 feet, and in length from 117 to 776 feet, across ravines and rock cuttings. The permanent line so constructed, although more circuitous and less dramatic, was also certainly less spine-chilling than the 'inclines'.

In the Rift Valley floor where the altitude drops down from 7400 feet at the escarpment top to barely 6000 feet, the going was fairly easy and the railway was driven in a straight line in a north-westerly direction to Naivasha at Mile 390, and Nakuru at Mile 447 – both sited in the Rift Valley plains and destined to become centres for the European settler community. Naivasha was the first administrative station on the railway in the Uganda Protectorate, but owing to the greater importance of Nakuru as an engine-changing station, where houses for divisional officers were built, it was made the customs station for goods entering the Uganda Protectorate, until this office was done away with when the change in the boundary of the two protectorates took place in 1902.

The ascent of the western side of the Rift Valley up over the densely wooded summit of Mau escarpment, the watershed for streams flowing into Lake Baringo on the north-eastern side and for those flowing into Lake Victoria to the south-west, took the railway to its highest point – an altitude of 8321 feet – and a distance of 500 miles from its starting-point at Mombasa. Here also, on the Mau escarpment, were formidable engineering problems: they involved spanning nine ravines with viaducts and with numerous cuttings in a distance of 73 miles, and at a cost of £135,000. The task was undertaken by an American firm with much success. Much of this was unforeseen expense, and by March 1900 the railway had already cost three million pounds, and the Committee were asking for another two millions. Lord Salisbury adamantly held out for more money in the face of Liberal criticism, his supporters stressing the civilizing and economic value of the railway.

The descent from the high point of the Mau escarpment to Lake Victoria was held up by heavy rains and trouble with the Nandi and

Lumbwa tribes, both highly nervous over the presence of some 6000 workmen in the vicinity of Fort Ternan. Following this there was a straightforward and easy run to the lake, through dense undergrowth, thick woods thinning out into grass country, scattered thorn trees and the open flat plains below the Nandi escarpment; and finally a quick run to the lake. This last section, although comparatively flat, posed considerable difficulties for line-laying owing to its swampy nature.

A prolonged dry spell at the end of 1901 fortunately enabled this last section of the line to be pushed through without delay to its terminus at Port Florence. On 20 December 1901 the first train reached the lake, a distance of 584 miles from Mombasa. Port Florence, at the head of a shallow bay on the north-east corner of Kavirondo Gulf, at an altitude of 3726 feet, had little to commend it as a lake port and inland terminus of the Uganda Railway. It was the receptacle for pent-up sewage, its sluggish waters impounding all the lake debris washed into that corner of the Gulf. It had a hot humid climate and was unhealthy for Europeans. Anchorage was inadequate for large boats unless there was constant dredging. The choice of Port Florence was unfortunate. An original proposal to run the railway line through the high Nandi country north of Kavirondo Gulf and terminating at Port Victoria would not only have given a much superior port, but would have avoided the swampy section to the immediate east of the Kavirondo Gulf. This proposal was turned down owing to the additional expense that such a prolongation of the railway – another 80 miles – would have entailed. In relation to the total length of the railway, to cavil at this additional expense seems short-sighted economy. Once the decision was made and the line built, the fact of Port Florence had to be accepted, as there was neither money nor enthusiasm to lift the matter to a new level of assessment. It would be another 30 years or more before the line was carried to a new terminus – Kampala in Uganda.

With its existence as the terminus secured, Port Florence soon partook of the character of an active lake port, with its extensive ship building yards, pier and wharf and usually one or two steamers anchored alongside and with pennants flying, giving the whole a maritime aspect. Such aspects were soon to be found at other lake ports – Entebbe, Port Bell and Jinja. The completion of the railway link with the lake was further rounded out by the placing of steamships on the lake – ultimately a flotilla of five. The launching of the first of these, the *William Mackinnon*, in June 1900, had a strange saga behind it. The *William Mackinnon*, 62 tons, in a dismantled state (made up in 3000 loads) had been sent into the interior from Mombasa in 1895. Its subsequent progress was snail-like, and after reaching Kibwezi in 1897 the work was abandoned until 1899, when the Uganda Railway took over the task of its transport to the lake. Six years after the first load was picked up by a porter at Mombasa, the last load was deposited on the lake shore. The steamer was launched in June 1900 and was in full operation on the lake by 1901, only just before the railway itself arrived there. It would have been more practical to have waited and sent the dismantled steamship up by rail. The many delays in its transport into the interior had been caused by the Uganda mutiny, loads going astray, the drain of porters for military requirements, attacks by the Nandi and, finally, its assemblage at the lake being in the hands of a drunken lot of engineers. The saga of the *William Mackinnon* could scarce have been in the mind of Joseph Chamberlain when, speaking at Nairobi, in December 1902, he declared his own and British pride in the great achievement of the Uganda Railway.

That the railway was completed within the allotted time, despite rain, wash-outs, failure of supplies (a ship carrying railway material had run aground on a reef at the entrance to Mombasa harbour), plague which slowed up and even threatened cessation of the labour supply from India, marauding lions and constant harassment by a Treasury with an ever-watchful eye on expenditure, is a tribute to the heroism and dedication of the many unnamed workers. This is a story on its own.

A great imperial enterprise had been completed. The greatest inland lake in Africa had been tapped by a railway from the Indian Ocean, and there was now a thin but tenuous line of communication with the interior, connecting, like a central cord and its adjacent ganglion, the scattered posts along the Uganda road, with the railway termini at the Indian Ocean and an inland lake. It engendered a feeling of security hitherto lacking in remote up-country areas. There was now easy access for troops into the interior, and an alternative route for the movement of forces into the Sudan.

In the first year of its running the railway faced a series of challenges: the Nandi revolt, the carrying away of bridges and portions of the line by flood, the breaking down of railway posts, giraffe entangled in telegraph lines and monkeys swinging on these lines and twisting them into an inextricable tangle. There was also the constant pilfering of railway property, especially in the Nandi and Mau area where natives displayed great ingenuity in stealing telegraph wire – highly prized as decorative coils for their women – and where large railway spikes were found to make effective cudgels for breaking the head of an enemy. Much construction still had to be done at various points along the line – over the escarpments and with the huge viaducts over ravines; wash-outs were bound to find any weakness in bridges and embankments.

The question of fuel, anticipated as a problem for the railway, was fortunately solved as already mentioned by the ample supplies of wood along most of the route, even in the Taru desert where scrubby growth was adequate for wood-burning engines, and along those portions of the line where wood was scarce, coal was available at the low price of 32 shillings per ton – thanks to British coaling stations on the way to India, especially that at Aden.

Divided supervision in running the railway and in its administration proved to be a problem and a source of contention between the Uganda Railway Committee directly responsible to the Foreign Office and Treasury in London, and the protectorate administration in East Africa. The local railway administration was jealously administered separately from the protectorate administration – much to the chagrin of the latter. It was a situation in a sense similar to that which had existed between the Foreign Office, IBEAC and local administration. The same personal problems arose – acrimony, charges of wastefulness, duplication of services and personal rivalries.

The railway had been driven through hitherto unknown country, and, as it turned out, the most attractive areas – climate and soil-wise – were bypassed. The railway would perhaps have served the territory better if it had gone farther north, through Machakos and by way of Mount Kenya, and across to Lake Victoria by way of the Mau plateau and Nandi escarpment, thus interlinking the best and most habitable portions of the country, from a European point of view. This, however, would have meant added expense, and prolonged the construction of the railway at a time when there was much haste to complete it.

The full cost of the railway began to bear in by the time of its completion, but a full tallying up would not come for another 25 years. At an early stage it was realized that government's promise to build the railway more economically than private enterprise could not be fulfilled. The early estimates of cost of construction – Macdonald's and the Anderson Committee's – in the range of two million pounds, were wide of the mark; the figure had risen to £4,000,000 by the time the railway had been completed, and by 1902 it was £5,244,000. Yet its cost, almost £10,000 for every mile of rail, greater than that of railways in Lagos and the Gold Coast, was however less than similar lines for the Congo, Cape,

Natal, Mashonaland and Beira. When payments toward it finally ceased on 15 November 1925, the total amount of loan, interest and sinking fund (all paid by the British taxpayer) amounted to nearly £8,000,000. The expectation that these sums might be recouped by the British Treasury, from increased land values accruing in the railway zone, never materialized.

Before any portion of the railway was opened to the public, traffic on it had already commenced for government purposes. The Uganda mutiny had caused large movements of troops and supplies along the portion of the line already completed; and administrative needs in Uganda and the East Africa Protectorate resulted in large quantities of goods and many passengers being conveyed over the line. It was reckoned that by the end of 1901 over 6551 tons of stores (largely for Indian traders who supplied the wants of the men employed in construction), and 57,556 passengers, had been carried by the railway at a total charge of £58,436. Under the old caravan method (at a cost of £180 per ton to the lake) the figure would have been £566,536 – a saving thus gained of over half a million pounds sterling. After the rails reached the lake and lake steamers began tapping its commercial basin, freight and passengers carried by the railway rapidly increased. Even so, the railway ran at an annual loss of between £45–60,000 up to 1905; thenceforth it was gradually reduced until by 1907 it was producing a small surplus. Not, however, from the massive piles of ivory in the interior, as Holmwood had so optimistically predicted, nor from land sales along the railway as the Treasury had anticipated. The surplus came from the more prosaic pursuits of European husbandry: potatoes and dairy products from the Kenya highlands, mvuli timber and cotton from Uganda, and government mail and stores; and the increasing quantity of goods for Indian merchants in the interior. With rates on the railway kept at a reasonable level – they were lower than those on South African railways – the old caravan trade and foot-slogging porters soon became a thing of the past, except in remote outlying areas.

The impulse given by the railway to the general life and economy of British East Africa is revealed in the General Report for Uganda for the year ending March 1904, which shows that trade in that territory increased by 86 per cent over the previous year, that imports nearly doubled and exports went up by 64 per cent. When feeder lines – rail and road – were under way, commerce was attracted from as far away as the Congo Free State; and those parts of German East Africa adjacent to the nearest points on the Uganda Railway and circumjacent to Lake

Victoria. The opening of a road from Voi to Taveta in 1898 attracted the products of the Kilimanjaro area to British territory. Two steamships circumnavigating Lake Victoria drew commerce from an ever-widening economic basin

But much more was expected of the railway than this impact on trade and communications in East Africa. It would dovetail in with Cecil Rhodes's vision of a Cape-to-Cairo railway and a telegraph line linking the two ends of the continent. The Rosebery treaty of 1894 with the Congo State, which had provided for a right of way for Rhodes's line along the western shore of Lake Tanganyika, had not been ratified as we have seen, owing to opposition from Germany and France. Rhodes however continued to seek an alternative arrangement. His railway line reached Bulawayo in November 1897, and his telegraph line was at Blantyre by early 1898. He was anxious to secure an extension through Uganda to the Sudan. Kitchener had wired from Khartoum: 'I have founded a post to the south of Fashoda; when are you coming up?' Kitchener, in projecting a railway from Halfa to Abu Hamad for the reconquest of the Sudan, was so fired by Rhodes's enthusiasm for a Cape-to-Cairo scheme, that he insisted on the South African standard gauge. Following the reconquest of the Sudan, Rhodes, in the spring of 1899, made a grand tour to rally support for his scheme. Kitchener and Cromer in Egypt were warmly enthusiastic; but as to his interview with Leopold, Rhodes spoke of him afterwards with loathing: 'it will be very difficult ever to get him to any practical conclusion unless he has by far the best of the bargain'.

With the Kaiser, whom he visited in March 1899, Rhodes found himself on the best of terms. He had come expecting a hostile Germany. His projected railway would cut across the German East African central railway, and would divert trade to the British sphere. Although Rhodes was associated in German eyes with the 'Jamieson Raid' and 'perfidious Albion', the German government had taken pains to harness public opinion in his favour: Rhodes came to Germany *persona grata* if not *persona gratissima* and his relations with the Emperor were most amicable. He had only to mention the magical word 'Mesopotamia' to win his case. It had been the Emperor's dream for many years 'that English goods should be carried to India on German rails'. Rhodes developed the grand concept of a German railway to Bushire on the Persian Gulf whence English ships would convey goods to Bombay; the reopening of the canals, dating from the time of Nebuchadnezzar; and construction of a bridge over the Bosphorus, thus placing German interests on Russia's southern flank and preventing a thrust by Russia to the Persian Gulf. So eloquently did Rhodes play on the Emperor's fancy that he expressed regret that Mr Rhodes was not his chief minister, for with such a man His Majesty 'could have done great things'. Germany and England had much in common. France represented 'the decadent Latin races'. Anglo–German relations in the spring of 1899 were more friendly than they had been for months. Feeling among Germans that their country had got the worst of the Zanzibar/Heligoland bargain no longer existed and British prestige was high. The recent victory at Omdurman, and subsequent withdrawal of Major Marchand from Fashoda, no doubt contributed to this change, but Rhodes's visit was in the nature of a personal diplomatic triumph.

An agreement between Rhodes and the Kaiser, signed at the end of 1899, provided for the extension of Rhodes's telegraph line through German East Africa. In return Rhodes would help in obtaining for Germany a renewal of landing rights in Ireland for the German trans-Atlantic Emden–Waterville cable. The German government would have the right to take over Rhodes's telegraph line after 40 years. Rhodes was to have his railway up to the German frontier by 1904; the Emperor would supply him with material and labour and an escort through German territory. Rhodes promised that any railway from South Africa to the west coast would run through German South West Africa. Within a week of these fruitful conversations, Rhodes was arranging for telegraph poles and material to be sent to Mombasa. By the spring of 1900 his telegraph line was at Kasanga on Lake Tanganyika; by February 1901 it had reached Ujiji. But within little over a year Rhodes himself was dead. His railway from the south never got remotely near German East Africa.

It was a bold, if not noble concept: a great central African railway line running up the full length of the spine of Africa, and linking together great feeder lines in South Africa, Rhodesia, German East Africa, Uganda and the Sudan into one grand system of communications. Such a line, drawing on the central lakes, would have caused a vast reorientation and development of lines of trade, and realignment of political and social forces in the continent. The Berlin–Baghdad railway became a reality; Rhodes's dream remained unfulfilled. The traveller was destined to wait in vain to enter the 'Cairo Express' at its Cape Town terminus!

Churchill, when he journeyed through East Africa and up the Nile in 1907, grasped Rhodes's vision. He envisaged 'The Victoria and Albert

Railway' which would 'traverse the country between the great lakes, and join together these two noble reservoirs with all their respective river connections', giving control of a whole vast system of interconnecting Central African lakes and rivers. Then, by means of a railway line of 150 miles connecting Jinja with Kakindu on the Victoria Nile, and Mruli with a point on the Nile below Murchison Falls, and another stretch of 110 miles of railway from Nimule to Gonkokoro, there would thus be married 'two gigantic systems of steam communication' – in all perhaps 20,000 miles. By the time this juncture had been achieved, Rhodes's Cape-to-Cairo railway would have reached Lake Tanganyika, leaving only the short gap between the northern point of that lake and Uganda to be encompassed, to give 'a transcontinental line, if not wholly of railroad, at least of steam traffic and of comfortable and speedy travel'.

Churchill's concept of a comprehensive system of steam communication received partial recognition in that a survey for the extension of a railway from Jinja towards Lake Albert was undertaken within the year, and resulted in the commencement of the 'Busoga Railway' in 1910, which was opened on 1 January 1912. This 61-mile railway starting from Jinja (and bypassing the Ripon Falls), connected Lake Victoria with Namasagali, the first navigable point on the Victoria Nile, and gave access to the great cotton-growing areas around Lakes Kioga and Kwania. A seven-mile railway linking Kampala with Port Bell on Lake Victoria was also commenced in 1910. The labour force employed in the construction of the 'Busoga Railway' was made up entirely of natives from Busoga, which gave the lie to those who had earlier claimed that Africans would not work for day wages. With the construction of the 'Busoga Railway' – a very short stretch – railway-building momentum stopped. Nevertheless the grand concept could not wither away, it would revive and gain substance many years later, in the 1960s, with the extension of a railway from Soroti to Gulu and across the Nile at Pakwach, to Arua in the West Nile District. It was also to be seen in a much larger and vital project – the Tan-Zam railway linking Dar es Salaam to Lusaka in Zambia (built by 25,000 Chinese, and a showpiece of China's foreign aid to Africa). Even so, Rhodes's dream remains unfulfilled. Vital gaps remain to be linked: that between Shallal in southern Egypt and Wadi Halfa in northern Sudan, and between Wau in the southern Sudan and Arua in northern Uganda.

Paralleling the development of railway connections with the interior of East Africa was the extension of steamship communication along the East African coast. Already by the early 1890s, that coast, so long untrammelled by European sea traffic, was well served by European steamship lines. What this meant to Europeans long isolated from home and familiar scenes is expressed in the words of the missionary, W. Salter Price, in 1890:

> Fourteen years ago an English steamer entering Mombasa harbour was a rare sight, which put us all in a flutter of excitement – now it is a matter of daily occurrence, and sometimes as many as six or eight fine vessels are seen at one time riding at anchor on its quiet waters.[8]

The British India Steam Navigation Company, the French 'Messageries-Maritimes', the Portuguese 'Mala Reales' and the German East Africa line were represented at East African ports. It frequently happened that steamships of these various lines arrived and departed from Zanzibar 'within a few days of each other'. By early 1897 the German African Steamship line, previously running from Aden to Zanzibar, and government-subsidized, extended its sailings to Dar es Salaam, Tanga and Mombasa, and connected with a German steamship service between Beira and Hamburg, by way of the Cape. In 1897 the Austrian Lloyd line introduced an East African service to connect with their sailings to India.

British and German authorities ran a local steamship service along their respective coastlines. The Germans showed the flag with a regular three-weekly service between Tanga and Mikindani; and the IBEAC, in emulation, directed its steamer, the *Juba*, to convey troops, officials and stores along the coast. The Sultan, not to be outdone, directed his tramp steamer to visit Benadir ports, in what proved to be a desultory timetable. Following the demise of the IBEAC and the taking over of the Benadir ports by the Italians, there was an interval in which no British service contacted that coast until Hardinge introduced a monthly service between Zanzibar, Pemba and coast ports up to Kismayu, whence the Italians subsidized its extension to the Benadir.

The Boer War stepped up the development of steamship communication with the East African coast. The Germans strove to obtain a monopoly of sea trade from Natal northwards, and constructed a floating dry dock at Dar es Salaam in 1900. Although the structure sank in 1902, it was refloated at great cost of time and energy, and within a year was catering for the German steamship line. To compete with German 'sales' aggression, and to take advantage of the prospects offered by the 'vast tracts of fertile lands opened up by the Uganda Railway' in British East Africa, the Union Castle line in mid-1901, and the British India Steam Navigation Company in May 1902, extended their services from the Cape northwards, with their steamers calling fortnightly, at points from Durban to Mombasa – the latter now the greatest port between Beira and Aden.

In September 1903 the Uganda Railway Committee was dissolved, and control of the railway was handed over to the government of the East African Protectorate. The tidying up of the work of construction was completed by September 1904. By this time the slave-trade was a thing of the past, and the arguments around which the case for the construction of the railway had originally revolved were forgotten. Sir Edward Grigg, Governor of Kenya, in 1924, with perspicacity had pointed out that without the railway there could have been no history of Kenya as a British settled area. And Sir Harry Johnston, Special Commissioner to Uganda during the years of the railway's completion, saw it as 'one of the mightiest factors yet introduced into Central Africa for transformation of a land of complete barbarism to one at any rate attaining to the civilization of settled India'.

11· The Indians in East Africa

Indian contact with East Africa is of ancient origin. The same monsoon which brought the trader from Arabia also brought the trader from India. The prosperous Indian trade referred to in the *Periplus* is affirmed by Strabo and Pliny and by Chinese sources of the ninth and tenth centuries. Iron-working which was introduced into East Africa in these early centuries may have come by way of India rather than from Bantu sources to the west, as generally assumed. The great trading kingdoms of Chola in south-east India, Sri Vijaya of Sumatra, Gujarat based on Cambay, and Bahmani of the Deccan, from the ninth to the fourteenth centuries, brought the East African coast into their trading orbit, and were probably responsible for the introduction of Maldive cowries (used as currency) and 'trade-wind' beads into East Africa, and for a reverse trade in East African slaves to India and China. Marco Polo in his *Travels* refers to ships from Malabar visiting Madagascar and Zanzibar, and that the north-east monsoon enabled the journey to be done in as little as 20 days. This trading prosperity on the East African coast was at its height when the Portuguese made their appearance in the Indian Ocean at the end of the fifteenth century: Duarte Barbosa noted that Mombasa was a town 'of great trade' and with a good harbour where many ships 'both of those that sail for Sofala and those come from Cambay in India' were anchored.[1]

Throughout the Portuguese period Indian traders held their own on the East African coast, with rich Indian Muslims continuing to make the pilgrimage to Mecca and the link with India being maintained by Indian families in East Africa. Colonies of Indian traders appeared at Aden, and at Muscat where they were numbering 1200 by the eighteenth century. While the Portuguese empire in the Indian Ocean waned and disappeared, the strength of the Indian trading community appeared to increase. When Captain Smee visited Zanzibar in 1811 the Hindu traders there held 'the best part of its trade' in their hands, although subjected to outrageous exactions at the hands of the Sultan's vakil, the rapacious eunuch Yakut. Hindus were of inferior status in the eyes of Muslim Arabs who treated them as easy prey. At Mombasa where Captain Owen visited in the 1820s Indian traders were 'helpless and unprotected', fleeced by the Arabs, but showing remarkable resilience and recuperation in the face of these difficulties. Burton speaks of the 'fat and wealthy Banian traders' at Berbera who were treated by the Somalis as their 'milch cows' – 'the African cheats by measuring the bad cotton cloth, and the Indian by falsely weighing the other valuable articles he receives in return'.

When Sultan Said moved his court from Muscat to Zanzibar in the 1830s many Indians followed him there and Said found them valuable stewards of his financial affairs. The key post of Customs Master was usually held by a Hindu, who farmed out customs on the mainland to his Indian agents. It was a lucrative contract netting its holder in the first years over 70,000 Maria Theresa dollars (£14,000) and rising to about 500,000 dollars by 1890. The Hindu Customs Master (the post was held by the firm of Jairam Sewji for most of the nineteenth century) and his colleagues were the 'real ruling power at Zanzibar', and Ladha Damjim, a 'venerable old Hindu with a shrewd and intelligent face' and of 'upright conduct' was confidential adviser to Sultan Barghash.

A commercial treaty with Said by the British in 1839, followed by the establishment of a British consulate at Zanzibar in 1841, brought greater security and trading advantages to Indians in East Africa, their numbers in the 1840s being about 3000 in Zanzibar and Pemba and about an equal number on the mainland, where Burton found about 100 at Mombasa and similar numbers at other points such as Kilwa along the coast – giving a total of about 6000 Indians in East Africa by the mid-nineteenth century.

Under the presence of the British consul there was alleviation from the harassment and unauthorized exactions that the Indians had endured under the Sultan's Liwali (governor), Khadi (judge) and Jemadar (military officer). When Barghash attempted to come down harshly on Indian traders for illicit dealing in cloves in 1870 the British consul successfully intervened on their behalf. The ending of the East India Company's trading monopoly, with the Royal Navy taking over the Indian Navy's duties at the mid-century, gave inducement to Indian trade with East Africa; and under the protection of the British consul there, the Indian trader found new confidence. Burton and Speke visiting the mainland in early 1857 observed that

Nothing could exceed the mingled pride and yearning pleasure these exotic Indians seemed to derive having us as their guests. Being Indian officers, they looked upon us as their guardians and did everything they could to show they felt it so. Our conversing in their own language, and talking freely of their native land, must, as indeed they said it did, have felt to them as if after a long banishment they were suddenly thrown amongst their old and long-lost friends.[2]

To Grant the obsequiousness of the Indians (they rose and salaamed him on every occasion) was embarrassing 'to a painful degree'.

Indian traders were reluctant to move inland away from the greater security they now enjoyed on the coast. Burton, at Rufiji in 1859, learned of a Hindu trader despoiled of all his goods only a few miles inland; and Frere, journeying southwards from Mombasa in 1873, noted the Indian trader clinging to coastal points:

> The Banians generally keep to the ports, or within a short journey of the coast or navigable parts of large rivers. The trade with the far interior is almost exclusively in the hands of Arab half-castes, and Swahili.[3]

In 1882 Indian merchants at Mombasa complained of robberies they suffered, and in 1883 they petitioned the British consul for protection against them. Not all Indian traders were timid. Musa Mzuri, a Muslim of the Ismaili Khoja sect from Surat whom Burton met in September 1859, had been trading at Tabora since 1825, and was now doyen of inland traders. Elsewhere, however, Indians were entrenched at the coast in the Sultan's domains; Frere marvelled at their 'silent occupation' from Mozambique up to Cape Guardafui. Over two millions sterling of Indian capital was invested at Zanzibar where one firm alone had £430,000 outstanding in loans and mortgages. The wholesale and retail trade in European and American goods and the financing of the caravan trade in the interior was in their hands. Indian merchants backed Arab traders even to precarious limits, knowing always that the latter must ultimately return to the coast, and into the hands of his creditor. The Indian on the Mrima (coast), facing extortion, heavy duties, haggling, quarrelling, competition and the monotonous round of coast fever, had little compensation in return apart from his profits on trade. The local 'Jumbe' extracted ground rent from him, the Jemadar levied an arbitrary percentage on his profits; and the custom house extracted 20 frasilahs of copal on every 100 frasilahs shipped, and charged him storage and freight. The risks in financing Arab traders were great: an Indian merchant, Trikindas of Pangani, lost over £20,000 in bad debts. No wonder the Indian merchant covered himself by demanding and getting high interest on the loans and goods he advanced to the Arab trader in the interior.

The role of the Indians in the slave-trade of East Africa is not easy to assess for it was of a discreet nature and usually indirect, although now and then flagrant cases of Indian involvement came to light, as when a slave dhow captured by Captain Blomfield in 1870 was found to be Indian-owned. The Indians never took a strong moral stand against the slave-trade as did the European. Hindu usage and Muslim practice recognized it as legal, and Indians separated from their wives in India frequently took African concubines or employed slave labour. Indians received slaves in satisfaction of debt and mortgage transactions, farmed these slaves out, and renounced their British protected status when it served their interest as slave-holders. Elton found the Indians at Kilwa to be active entrepreneurs in the slave-trade, in league with Lalji, the Custom's Master and advancing goods to slave-traders at enormous interest, and selling the slaves brought in under their orders and on high commission.

The great Slave Trade Act of 1807 and the Abolition Decree of 1833, had not touched British India, and it was not until 1843 that slavery was ended there, but even this latter decree did not affect slave-holding by subjects of Indian protected states, of whom there were about 4000 – chiefly from Kutch – in East Africa. General P. Rigby, appointed British Consul at Zanzibar in 1858, deemed this to be a scandal which he set about to eradicate. By an Act of 1861, fortunately approved retroactively by the British government, he forbade Indians (he made no distinction between 'protected' and British 'subject') from holding slaves, subject to heavy fines and with no compensation for Indian owners of slaves – had not these been held illegally? Rigby spurned compromise when a delegation of wealthy Indians sought modification of the decree. He imprisoned one of their members for purchasing a Galla girl, and placed another, owner of 400 slaves, in chains for failing to heed the decree.

Rigby's actions caused a glut of slaves in the Zanzibar market and many were promptly re-enslaved by the Arabs. Rigby's successors, Pelly and Playfair, by making a distinction between British 'protected' and British 'subjects' permitted renewed slave-holding not only by those of the first class, but the second as well, for the latter, by placing themselves under the Sultan's protection, could evade British jurisdiction. It was not until the treaty of 5 June 1873 that slave-holding by Indians was finally ended. To implement this treaty as it affected Indians, Kirk, British Consul, and Captains Elton and Wharton proceeded to the mainland in late 1873 and issued in all 2000 freedom papers to slaves formerly held by Indians. Kirk visited the coast north of Mombasa, and Elton to the south of it. Two hundred slaves held by Indians at Mombasa and 300 at Kilwa were freed, and similar numbers at lesser points along the coast. Finally in 1875 action taken against slave-owning Indians in Pemba freed 213 slaves there.

In the Portuguese sphere to the south Indians continued to hold slaves. Lieutenant O'Neil, British consular agent there, reported that they were financing the slave-trade at Angoche. And within the Sultan's dominions they evaded the 1873 decree by keeping slaves in the names of Arab and Swahili wives until the anti-slavery decree of 1 August 1890 ended this practice. Indians were among those culprits resorting to the use of the French flag for protection for slave-running. One Indian, a British subject, used the ruse of his wife being a native of the French island of Nossi Bé to obtain this flag for his slave ship. Thus did the Anti-Slavery Society in 1892 maintain that effective steps against the slave-trade meant action not only against the Arabs, but the rich 'Hindis' of Zanzibar

> who advance thousands to the Arabs to carry on their work – and here, you would perhaps strike a more vital part of this horrid system than you imagine, and bring to account subjects of our Queen who disgrace our name.[4]

Euan-Smith in 1890 stated that

> Among the whole body of Arabs there will probably be found none more anxious for a return to the whole system of trade in its former channels – with the concomitant horrors of slavery and the slave trade, the ivory trade, and all that it involved, than the British Indian merchants enjoying the protection of Her Majesty's Government.[5]

With the collapse of the Arab commercial community following the abolition of slavery, their plantations in Pemba and Zanzibar fell into the hands of their Indian creditors. In Pemba, in the 1890s, Hardinge remarked as regards a Banian, known as 'Buddu', that

> he pretended to me that he never took more than 20% per annum of interest: an examination into some of his transactions proved that he rarely obtained less than 60% and in one of them was charging 150%.

> These Indian usurers are the middlemen through whom the Arabs sell their cloves sometimes receiving from them in return instead of money comparatively worthless merchandise which the Indians have bought for the local market and could not sell. They form a mutually self-supporting ring, one Hindi or Banian who had a business at Chaki-Chaki, acting as agent for others who lived in other towns, and who, in their turn act as his men of business there, and thus constitute a combination against which the Arab planters, improvident and hopelessly unbusiness-like, find it impossible to struggle. Their places of business are to be found not only in the two or three larger towns, but throughout the country districts, where many of them I am assured, combine with the keeping of a shop and the advance of loans on interest, the sale of cheap and poisonous spirits to the natives, and the purchase of stolen cloves, and other plantation products at reduced prices.[6]

Arabs had foolishly incurred new loans at very high interest on the expectation of compensation for loss of their slaves and were soon helpless in the hands of Indian money-lenders, paying from 75 to 150 per cent compound interest on these loans. Their estates were so heavily encumbered that neither could the owner sell, nor the mortagee afford to foreclose. Indeed it was more to the advantage of the latter to draw his interest by keeping the nominal Arab owner as sort of unpaid manager, forcing him to buy provisions from his creditor. Under these conditions many plantations fell into a neglected state. Erstwhile slaves fared no better than their former Arab masters for they were now informed by Indian employers that since they were no longer supporting their former Arab masters they could manage on reduced wages.

The construction of the Uganda Railway gave a whole new twist to the Indian connection with East Africa. Some 32,000 Indians were recruited to work on the railroad in the period 1896-1901, and of these about 7000 remained in East Africa. This large influx of Indians in such a short time gave a pronounced Indian colouring to the East African scene. It brought, according to Johnston, a two-mile wide swath of British India from Mombasa to Lake Victoria. British Indian administrative practice now took hold in East Africa, along with Indian law, police, postal and currency rules, transport and communication systems, adding to an already deep dependency on the India militia for East African defence. Zanzibar Sultans for long had relied on Baluchi mercenaries to garrison their coast towns, and the IBEAC recruited a contingent of 300 Punjabis for police duty. Following declaration of a British protectorate in 1895, this Punjabi force was designated the East Africa Rifles, augmented by some 300 Swahili and Sudanese, but continued resort was made to Indian troops: the 24th Bombay Infantry deployed against the Mazrui in 1896, the 27th Bombay Infantry against the Sudanese mutineers in Uganda, 1897-8, and the 4th Bombay Infantry against the Mad Mullah of Somaliland. In 1902 forces serving in Central-East Africa were amalgamated in one corps – the King's African Rifles, – and dependency on this continued until the First World war, when large-scale Indian forces played a vital part in holding East Africa against the Germans. No wonder visitors to East Africa were surprised to find themselves in an outpost of British India.

Followed the completion of the railway in 1901 some 2000 Indians were employed in its running. The middle ranks of the administration and posts as waiters and chefs were usually staffed by Goans. The subordinate clerical ranks and accountancy posts were largely filled by Parsees, while police, survey and railway maintenance departments were manned by Punjabis. Many of the 7000 ex-indentured Indians who remained in East Africa entered into shopkeeping, and their small 'dukas' at main centres and along points of the railway line became part of the East African social scene, providing small oases of civilization in the interior. There was also a large flow of voluntary immigration from India to East Africa in the two decades from the mid-1890s onwards, of over a thousand persons annually. The cheapness of ocean transport from India to East Africa and the familiar society which they entered on arriving there was doubly appealing to Indians. Truly, East Africa was India's 'North America'! Even in far-off Uganda the Indian population rose from a mere handful at the beginning of the century to 2000 by 1911, and in the East Africa Protectorate it was about 11,000; in Zanzibar at this date the Indian population had risen from 4000 at the end of the century to about 10,000 by 1911.

Plans for settling Indian agriculturists in East Africa were toyed with by a number of British officials. Such settlements, they argued, would bring relief to the miserable poor of India, provide a stimulating example of industry to the African, promote the economic development of British East Africa and hasten the day when it would no longer be dependent on subsidies from the mother country. The IBEAC in 1891 had directed Mr W.W.A. Fitzgerald, an agricultural expert, to study the feasibility of settling Indian cultivators at the coast. Fitzgerald made a survey of the coast north of Mombasa with this in mind and in his report strongly recommended such settlement, but the IBEAC was soon in its last throes and nothing more was heard of the plan. More concrete and interesting was the suggestion in 1895 by George Mackenzie (formerly in the Company's employ) that the deep valleys in the immediate hinterland of Mombasa be dammed so as to provide a permanent water supply for irrigation and intensive cultivation by Indian agriculturists. Mackenzie got no official support for this scheme, but a few years later, in 1901, when he brought forth another plan for settling time-expired coolies and Punjabi agriculturists in 'three or four blocks of village communities on suitable country along the line of the railway ... What you want is a few decoy ducks, giving them liberal terms on which they can fatten', he was supported by Johnston – it was preferable to granting land to mere 'concession hunters'. To Eliot, however, Whitehouse, Chief Engineer on the railway, expressed doubts whether Punjabi cultivators would emigrate to East Africa – it would most likely be the inferior type from Bombay, Oudh districts and Madras who would come, and also the Indian familiar only with the irrigation system of India was unlikely to fare well in East Africa, apart possibly from the Tsavo River area. For the ex-coolie labourer on the railway, no less than for the Punjabi cultivator, the prospect of tilling unbroken ground in East Africa with the heat heavy on his shoulders, midst a local African population whom he considered beneath him, was not a tempting offer; it might also prejudice his chance of return to India – the dream of every Indian, for they were essentially 'birds of passage'. With the example of the 'passenger' Indian (who paid his own way to East Africa) before him, the ex-railway coolie preferred to go outright into business.

Apart from some interest evinced by Sikhs and Punjabi Muslims in the King's African Rifles in a plan of General Manning, Inspector-General, for setting aside plots of land for them in certain areas unsuitable for white settlement, which would be inalienable from the family of the original holder and with the occupier liable to military service under a retaining fee of three rupees per month, nothing came of plans for Indian settlement in East Africa. The Indian militiamen in East Africa were not attracted to settling in primitive territory – *terra incognita* – away from regiment and friends and home in India, and thus when approached in the matter were wary. They requested what appeared to be exceedingly generous terms: free passages for themselves and family from the Punjab; free grants of ten acres of land for each family and no taxes payable for the first three years; a pair of oxen and a milch cow and 100 rupees for purchase of seeds and implements; free food supplies till the first crop was harvested; and a settlement officer, known and trusted by the Punjabis, to supervise such settlements.

Likely areas for siting them were the Kisumu district; along the banks of the Juba and Tana Rivers in their lower reaches; and the Shimba Hills range just inland and south of Mombasa. In all these areas there was fertile soil and water supply for irrigation similar to that in India. The Shimba Hills area was especially attractive and was recommended by a party of Indian officers who visited there. It was thought that a settlement of up to 250 Indian families might be located there, with other settlements established as far down as the German frontier. These settlements of Punjabi and Sikh cultivators would act as a military reserve on call in emergency and subject to one month's annual training in the reserve; this would allow the Indian military contingent to be dispensed with – a saving of £20,000 yearly. The settlements would produce cotton, foodstuffs and other commercial products for export. The design and conception of all this seemed admirable, at least on paper.

Enthusiasm soon waned, followed by more sober reflections. There was now fear that Indian settlements might face attack from natives – Kikuyu, Maasai, Galla, Lumbwa or Nandi. The Nandi especially in the Uganda Protectorate's Eastern Province, were particularly troublesome: their forays threatened the existence of the Uganda Railway. There was also opposition from the British Treasury as to the cost of underwriting Indian settlements in East Africa with proceeds from land sales within the railway zone: such proceeds, the Treasury argued, should go towards the cost of building the railway. The settlement of the Indian as an agriculturist never caught on apart from a few exceptions. A small party of 30 Indian families farmed 600 acres near Kisumu – growing rice, cotton and sugar-cane; a small group of Indians at Kibwezi, 200 miles inland from Mombasa, were employed on sisal estates; a few Indians cultivated vegetable gardens near Nairobi; and a party of Khojas from Kutch ploughed land near Lamu with oxen. This comprised the sum total of Indian agricultural cultivation in British East Africa, and even in these enterprises Indians were soon drained off into the more lucrative 'duka' trade. There was a brief revival of the idea of Indian agricultural settlements in 1906 and a settlement officer was sent to the Punjab, but Indians there were unwilling to emigrate except in village communities and under conditions too expensive to meet. An attempt by the British East Africa Corporation in 1907 to settle Indian coolies on sisal estates also came to nothing. With the arrival of European settlers and affirmation of a 'White Highlands' policy, interest in settling Indian agriculturists quickly waned. The view of Eliot and other officials that the highlands were not congenial to Indians – 'The coolness of the highlands is not appreciated by them' – was not scotched till 1920 when the Indian government challenged that if the issue was one of climate it should be left to climate to decide. But this is anticipating the 'Indian Question' of the future.

Meanwhile, debarred from the White Highlands and with plans for agricultural settlement set aside, Indians turned to commerce as the area where their money-making proclivities could best flourish. Churchill, journeying up to Uganda in 1907, already saw the brown man as the rival of the European, for the Indian, subsisting on a few shillings a month and with his industry and thrift, sharp business aptitude and economic superiority, would always outflank the European in commerce.

Expansion of Indian traders into the interior had come with the Anglo-German Agreement of 1890, and was hastened by the building of the Uganda Railway. The Indian duka, that welcome and familiar institution began to appear wherever European influence and administration made the way safe inland, and this was true of both the German and British spheres. Count Hatzfeldt commented in December 1895 on the Indians 'who themselves travel about the "Hinterland" to dispose of their merchandise and bring back the products of the country in exchange'. In Uganda 'Indian traders advanced their posts from Kampala to Toro, and all the posts at which European or native soldiers were established in the Nile Province, besides opening bazaars at all the stations in the eastern half of the protectorate'.

Some Europeans deprecated the Indian as a raffish and unattractive specimen of humanity, a parasite rather than producer, one who had played a nefarious part in the slave-trade; as late as 1890 there were convictions of Indians for slave-dealing. Hardinge was repelled by their rapacity and avidity for money:

They bear, in fact, except that they enjoy British protection, and can therefore assume a very independent attitude towards the Government authorities, a striking resemblance, in their character and dealings with the population, to the Jews of Roumania and southern and western Russia.[7]

During the famine of 1898 Indian traders raised the price of rice and imported grains by 50 per cent. They did an illicit trade in German 'eau de Cologne' (a cheap spirit disguised as perfume) and when the British attempted to halt this trade they closed their shops as a body, thereby punishing a whole neighbourhood with no other recourse to trade goods. Frederick Jackson, reporting for Taveta District in 1902, claimed that Indian shopkeepers paid Wateita porters in cloth which was 'little better than a swindle ... I have informed these Indians that this practice must cease, and that they must pay the men in cash'. Marius Fortie, trader in German East Africa before the First World War, refers to scores of Hindus arrested by the Germans and lectured on the need for commercial honesty in dealings with Africans for 'they had been found cheating the natives and giving short measure in cloth'.

Sharp practice on the part of the Indian trader caused the European to refer disparagingly to his coolie origin, but all were not such. There were prominent Indians such as Allidina Visram and A. M. Jeevanjee, with long and honourable connections with East Africa pre-dating the building of the railway. A.M. Jeevanjee, and his brother T.M. Jeevanjee, arrived in East Africa in 1890. An illiterate bullock-driver, he seized the opportunity of supplying the Uganda Railway with stores and established steamship connections with Bombay, Mauritius and Jeddah – carrying pilgrims to Mecca. He also founded the newspaper *African Standard* at Mombasa in 1901 from which emerged the *East African Standard* at Nairobi two years later. Allidina Visram and Haji Sewjie were merchant princes at large in the extent of their business ramifications and multitude of persons in their employ. By the turn of the century Visram and associates had taken most of the trade in Uganda from Arab and Swahili traders, and were registering porters in Bunyoro for service in the Congo, and Visram's agent at Hoima was sending 1500 loads of freight by the Nile water system to the north, thus providing revenue for government boats.

These more prominent Indian merchants were imbued with a philanthropic outlook, and generously bestowed large sums of money on civic enterprise and did much unpublicized charitable work in their own communities. With the Muslims it was a point of honour and religion to give alms, and the more unostentatious the act, the more meritable. Criticism of the small duka owner also overlooked the beneficent role he played in stimulating trade and introducing a money coinage into the interior. Tax-collecting in cash rather than in kind was aided by the Indian trader's purchase of the African's beeswax, hides, semsem oil and crocodile skins in return for cash. For the District Commissioner and his wife living in remote up-country areas the presence of the Indian duka with its civilized amenities made life bearable. The District Commissioner welcomed, nay invited, the Indian trader to settle in his district:

He is in East Africa what the Greek or the Syrian is in the Sudan. He hands you in the remotest regions the products of Manchester or Cawnpore. On Government Stations he is prepared to offer you the amenities of life, such as tinned peaches, cigarettes, boots, breeches, petrol or Mobiloil. Farther afield he sits on his haunches at the cross-roads under a sheet of corrugated iron, the vendor of native requirements. I remember once, when I thought that I was quite at the back of beyond finding an Indian ready to sell me some Sunlight Soap.[8]

Already by 1903, an Indian carpenter at Fort Portal on the eastern slopes of Ruwenzori, was making furniture with the well-known marking 'PWD' (Public Works Department).[9]

12· Sir Harry Johnston and Uganda

In the spring of 1899 Ternan, Wilson and Berkeley, the three principal British officers in Uganda, were all in bad health and Berkeley had been ordered to leave the country on doctor's orders. The British Treasury was concerned over expenditure incurred since 1894 and greatly increased by the recent mutiny. Revenue from the ivory trade proved illusory. The cowrie shell, an outmoded currency, the supply of which was uncontrollable, was a brake on economic expansion. The territory remained dependent on a British subsidy which, from 1894 to 1898, ranged between £49,000 to £95,000 a year. The British Treasury pressed strongly for native taxation to relieve this burden on Britain. There was no foreseeable paying commodity, and everything hinged on transport. There were positive aspects however: the Baganda were eager and quick to learn, and had apt teachers in the Christian Missions, whose work extended in ever widening circles outside Kampala. More detailed knowledge of outlying districts was coming in: reports on the Lake Baringo district from Major Gorges; on south-west Ankole from Lieutenant Mundy; and on the Nile district from Major Delmé-Radcliffe, all of which spoke in the most favourable terms of prospects for development in these areas. And there was the ever approaching Uganda Railway. The Uganda Protectorate was on the eve of a great thrust forward.

It was time to shift from military to civil rule; time to place the administration on a permanent and satisfactory footing, and for this a commissioner with ability and enthusiasm was required. In July 1899, Sir Harry Johnston, with extensive experience in the British Central Africa protectorate and other parts of Africa, was appointed Special Commissioner for Uganda at a salary of £2800 – 'equal to that of a Major-General commanding a first class district in India'. Johnston was informed that Uganda was in a 'plastic state', and ready for development. The railway would soon reach the lake and open up the country.

He was to raise revenue as he saw fit, reorganize the military, and bear in the mind the possibility that the two protectorates of East Africa and Uganda might eventually be merged into one. He received the usual injunction to work for the abolition of slavery.

Following a 'brilliant reception' in Kampala on his arrival on 20 December 1899, Johnston immediately commenced negotiations with the regents and chiefs, which culminated in the Buganda Agreement (originally termed the Uganda Agreement) of 10 March 1900.[1] The way in which relations with the Baganda were settled would determine the British position in Uganda as a whole, for Buganda was the most central and important of the inter-lacustrine states. Buganda had remained loyal to the British in the recent Uganda mutiny, and British gratitude would be shown by settling the affairs of the kingdom in a way satisfactory to its ruling class. In these negotiations Johnston relied heavily on the assistance of F.C. Jackson, acting sub-Commissioner in Buganda, and on missionaries, especially Tucker and Walker of the CMS, who had already requested Johnston, before his arrival in Uganda, to confirm the 'Protestant Church in Uganda' in all its sites and shambas. The Protestant missionaries were much more vocal than the French Catholic Fathers in these negotiations, for the latter were aliens in a British protectorate and much subdued. The Mill Hill Mission was too recently arrived to play an effective part. During the long drawn-out negotiations with regents, chiefs and missionaries, Johnston despaired at times of reaching a settlement. The Baganda were wily and tenacious bargainers, and Johnston was often tactless in his comments as to their empty pride, vanity and lazy nature. Several times he threatened to call off the negotiations, to place an embargo on all land, to cancel the appointments of chiefs, or hand the whole kingdom over to the mercies of the Egyptian Sudan or to the Germans. The latter, he noted, would gladly administer a harsh discipline.

The missionaries and Jackson helped to mollify and explain. Bishop Tucker warned against pressing the Baganda too far, and hinted that open rebellion might ensue; on the other hand, he reminded the chiefs that their land, excepting traditional burying land – 'Butaka' land – was held at the whim of their king, and would be more secure under a British settlement. Land was all important to the Baganda chiefs, the main symbol of their power, and source of income. Tucker's warning had its effect, but before the land problem could be settled Johnston had to assess what this would mean in the light of accessions of territory which he was ready to concede to Buganda. In return for the transference from the Kingdom of Uganda to Her Majesty the Queen of all rights of suzerainty, taxation, etc., over the adjoining districts of Toro, Busoga or Unyoro.[2]

Johnston secured for Buganda additions of territory from other districts. He claimed that he merely 'recognized existing facts', but it is difficult to escape the conclusion that the rights of less important districts were sacrificed and used as bargaining counters to win Baganda assent to the Agreement. The district of Kabula, part of Ankole, was added to Buganda on the grounds that

in order to suppress brigandage this Kabula district has been for some time past in the possession of Uganda soldiers under a Uganda chief.[3]

Bavuma and adjacent islets in Lake Victoria (promised by Macdonald to be separate from Buganda), 'for various reasons' (Johnston does not list them), were attached to Buganda rather than to the adjoining province of Busoga. Perhaps the most daring and questionable decision was the inclusion within Buganda's boundaries of territory south of the Kafu and Ukusi Rivers taken from Bunyoro during the war of 1894. The British were seemingly unaware that the royal tombs of Bunyoro lay within these so-called 'lost counties'.

With the boundaries of the kingdom thus inflated, Johnston turned to his land settlement. He had met Ternan on his way up to Uganda, and Ternan's suggestions for a land settlement in Buganda, along with Johnston's ideas derived from his settlement with the Makololo in Nyasaland, provided the basis for the land negotiations in Uganda. Working on the basis of a Buganda comprising some 19,600 square miles and divided into 20 counties (sazas), Johnston worked out a bipartite division whereby the British government would take over direct control of 10,560 square miles – to be held in trust. Of this, 50 square miles were already taken up by government stations, 1500 square miles assigned as forest land and the remainder was mostly swamp and the waste land. Mwanga had granted old Kampala to Lugard in 1891, Entebbe in Buganda and Lubwa's territory in Busoga, to Colvile in 1894. The firm of Smith Mackenzie had received leased sites at Kampala, Mumias and Port Victoria in Kavirondo in 1895-96. The remainder of the kingdom was shared out among the Kabaka, the royal household, twenty leading chiefs, and the Missions.[4] A great block of 8000 square miles was divided among 1000 minor chiefs, each of whom received approximately 8 square miles. The Roman Catholic Missions, in relation to the number of their adherents, received proportionately less than the Protestants; on the other hand the Mill Hill Fathers who had been in Uganda for only four years seem to have been generously treated. The most imposing feature of the settlement was the apportionment of the entire land of a kingdom which had never been surveyed, and whose topography and exact area was imperfectly known. The details were set out by Johnston, writing to Salisbury in April 1900. The Kabaka received 350 square miles, the Katikiro 20 square miles, the Chief Justice 15 square miles and the Treasurer 10 square miles. They were to receive fixed salaries as follows: Kabaka, £650; the three chief ministers, £300 each (when acting as Regents − £400 each); Mbogo £250; the Namasole (Queen Mother), £50; the 20 county chiefs, £200 each; the two Catholic princes (nephews of Mwanga), 8 square miles each and £50 annually until 18 years of age. The CMS received 40 square miles, the Catholic White Fathers 35 square miles and the Mill Hill Fathers 17 square miles. Of the 20 counties, 8 were placed under Catholic chiefs and 11 under Protestant chiefs, the Muslims receiving only one district 'corresponding to the small degree to which Islam is now represented among the Baganda'. The rigidity of the appointments on religious lines was more apparent than real. 'At any time for good and sufficient reasons, the Commissioner may call upon the native government to remove a Chief from any particular district and replace him by another Chief who may be of different faith.'

The Baganda retained under the agreement their traditional central government: Kabaka, and Lukiko consisting of three native ministers Katikiro (Prime Minister), Chief Justice, Teasurer, 20 county chiefs, and 66 other members nominated by the Kabaka.[5] By August 1902, out of the total 89 members of the Lukiko, 69 were chiefs who had received 8 square miles or more of territory. Of the 89 members 49 were Protestant, 35 Roman Catholic and 5 Muslim. The Lukiko's legislative and judicial decisions were subject to ratification by Her Majesty's representative. The Kabaka was granted the title of 'Highness', but was placed under the tutelage of the British government in the matter of making appointments to the Lukiko. The right to inflict the death penalty, and power to conscript his people for military service, were dependent on the assent of the British representative.

The question of raising and control of revenue loomed large in the Agreement. It had already been considered by Johnston before his arrival in Uganda, for he had consulted 'most of the tribes, and chiefs on my road through the eastern part of the protectorate to Kampala'. Under the Agreement there was instituted a hut tax, and gun tax of 3 rupees each per annum, with numerous exemptions for the royal household and chiefs – even the Queen Mother was granted free gun licences. Great importance was attached to the efficient collection of revenue, and if the conditions for this were not fulfilled Her Majesty's Government might consider the Agreement abrogated. Likewise the Agreement would be considered abrogated if the Kabaka, chiefs or people of Uganda pursued at any time a policy disloyal to the British protectorate. Only the English version of the Agreement was binding on both parties – an indication that the study of the Luganda language and its nuances was not so well advanced at this stage; and there was also perhaps a desire to avoid a disputed interpretation, as in the case of the notorious Treaty of Ucialli which had brought so much trouble on the heads of the Italians in Ethiopia.[6] The excessive number of witnesses (27 persons) arose from the desire of the Katikiro that all the leading men of the country, especially the chiefs of the counties or districts, should witness the Agreement 'they would then not be able at a future date to plead ignorance of its provisions and its binding nature on the Kabaka, Chiefs, and people of the Country'.

The finer details of the Agreement, especially in regard to land, were only worked out later. The implementation of the land proposals resulted in the violation of 'Bataka' land, evictions and uprooting of homes and families – 'until everyone was sorted out and settled down in his place'. The phrase in the Agreement – 'one thousand chiefs and private landowners' was confusing, for it could mean 1000 chiefs and additional landowners to any number – by 1902 it had risen to nearly 4000. Similar naivety was seen in confusing square miles with miles square.

There were definite immediate gains from the Agreement. The Bakopi (peasants) were in a better position than previously. They were now free to purchase or rent land from estate owners, or could become tenants on Crown Land with access to Crown forests; and this freedom of choice had a salutary effect in deterring native landowners from exploiting their tenants. On his way up-country in October 1899, Johnston had spoken of the possibility of land being sold outright to 'Europeans, Indians or Negro settlers', but it would be limited to 100 acres freehold. He was averse to a 'broad acre' policy for European settlers. 'Johnston's land settlement restricted the possibility of white settlement in Buganda.[7] The more fertile and salubrious districts were quickly taken up by the chiefs. Crown Land, for the most part, was confined to poorer country, swamps and tracts in outlying parts of the kingdom, largely ridden by tsetse fly. When, on completion of the 'mailo' survey in the twentieth century, it was revealed that Buganda's land area was some 2290 square miles less than originally estimated, Crown Land was reduced by this extent to make up the deficiency.

Johnston was pleased with his Agreement. It involved, he claimed, 'no special grant supplementary to the sanctioned estimates', and he felt that he had extracted all he could from the Baganda; for example, his game laws, prohibiting the killing of elephant in other parts of Uganda, allowed the killing of male elephants in Buganda, for the Agreement had restricted so many privileges of the Baganda that he 'dare not prevent killing elephants altogether'.

Before he could learn Salisbury's reaction to his Agreement, Johnston had left for Fort Portal at the foot of Ruwenzori in western Uganda. The Toro Agreement with Kasagama, ruler (Mukama) of Toro and chiefs of Toro was signed on 26 June, 1900.[8] This was no replica of the Buganda Agreement, for, as Johnston said, 'Toro is ours because we have placed and maintained the present king on the throne'; and it was not so much an agreement as an imposed settlement. Six administrative divisions were defined, excluding 'Bwamba', that portion of Toro bordering on the Congo Free State which was to be administered by the protectorate power until a boundary agreement was arrived at with the Congo Free State. The right to nominate successors to the chiefs was reserved to the British government, and if the Agreement was infringed the British government could annul it, or deport the Mukama and chiefs.

The salt lakes and revenues accruing from them were declared to be the property of Her Majesty's Government; the elephant was to be strictly protected; a hut and gun tax instituted, with wide exemptions for the Mukama and chiefs. Since Britain had placed and maintained Kasagama on the throne, there was no need to provide subsidies for him and his chiefs as in the case of Buganda; but they were to receive 10 per cent of taxes collected, and were granted estates ranging from 50 square miles for the Kasgama, down to 10 square miles for lesser chiefs. The remainder of the kingdom was declared Crown Land. The Toro Agreement put the seal on the work initiated by Lugard in 1891.

Johnston agreed with Colonel Ternan that Bunyoro was 'conquered country', and that no treaty could be made with its ruler and chiefs until their loyalty was assured. No formal agreement was made with Bunyoro until 1933.

Following the signing of the Toro Agreement Johnston went south to Lake Edward and then retraced his steps northward, crossing the Semliki into the Congo Free State and meeting the Belgian officer in charge at Fort Beni. He was impressed by the good substantial buildings of the Belgians at Fort Beni: 'I am afraid there is nothing so good to show in the Uganda Protectorate in the way of well-built European houses or barracks for native troops and workers'. It was during this journey to the west that Johnston, in his own words, 'escorted to the Congo Free State to be repatriated', a group of nine pygmies whom he had taken from a German traveller at Entebbe. The German had captured 19 pygmies in the Congo to take to the Paris Exhibition of 1900 and had managed to get to Entebbe with them before the Belgian authorities, highly incensed over his action, caused the British to apprehend him. This quixotic act accomplished, Johnston visited Ankole in August 1900, and had a glimpse of Mount Mufumbiro, 'the Kitchen' or 'Cooking pot', in the farthest corner of south-west Uganda. He appointed a chief, Kahaya, as paramount chief of Ankole, but informed the Banyankole they would not be ready for an agreement similar to that made with Buganda for at least another two years. Kahaya and chiefs, impatient at such deferment, resolved not to wait this long, and when they visited Kampala in April 1901 they appealed to Jackson for an agreement similar to that he had made with Toro. Jackson had already stated that this was not practical

> until they had improved in their methods of administration and grasped what would actually be required from them. They were I fear a little hurt at being told that Ankole was so backward.[9]

On 7 August 1901, after Johnston had left Uganda, Wilson, sub-Commissioner of the Western Province, concerned over gun and slave-running into Ankole from German territory and apprehensive over German activity in Ankole where they were making overtures to the Banyankole, felt it urgent to bind the Banyankole to Britain, and in full baraza at Mbarara, his chief, Frederick Jackson, Acting-Commissioner, signed an agreement with them. Ten administrative divisions were outlined, and that portion bordering on the Congo Free State was left as a separate administrative area under a European official. Estates of up to 10 square miles and more were granted to the leading chiefs, and hut and gun taxes instituted with exemptions for the chiefs, who were to receive

ten per cent of the taxes collected. The killing of elephants was prohibited. The Ankole Agreement in its particulars was more akin to that
made with Toro, rather than the Buganda Agreement. Johnston, the
progenitor of the two latter agreements, had no say, however, in the
making of the Ankole Agreement.

After leaving Ankole in August 1900 he had journeyed back to Fort
Portal, where he learned that the Foreign Office had given grudging
approval to his Buganda Agreement; it would request no changes in this
Agreement lest it would shake the confidence of its native signatories.
The hand of Sir Clement Hill, Head of the Africa Department at the
Foreign Office, could be seen in minor criticisms, such as that Johnston
should have imposed a gradowated hut tax, and that a land survey
should have been carried out before a division of the kingdom was made.
In reply to the first criticism, Johnston pointed out that a gradowated
hut tax would have led to missionary societies claiming the lowest rate
for their converts – as a means of winning adherents to their ranks; and
as to the second, a proposed land survey had been turned down by the
Foreign Office in 1898, and Johnston had been saddled with a military
surveyor, 'the proud Captain Pirrie', who would not deign to carry out
civilian work. Hill's reminder as to the need for tact and judgement in
collecting taxes was gratuitous. Hill appears to have had an almost
instinctive dislike for Johnston. He had opposed his appointment, for
Johnston had unorthodoxly short-circuited the Foreign Office
kindergarten in getting his post. Hill disliked Johnston's fussiness over
native names and African nomenclature in general, and his absorption in
ethnology. Both men in their own way were conceited, and this made for
mutual repulsion.

By early October 1900 Johnston was back at Entebbe. He had barely
time to arrange for Jackson to lead an expedition to eastern Uganda
against the Nandi and secure transport through their country, before Sir
Clement Hill himself appeared on the East African scene. The latter's
first criticism was of the punitive expedition launched against the
Nandi. Temporary peace should be made with them, and greater energy
directed towards the completion of the railway, so essential in case of
resurgence of trouble on the Upper Nile or a repetition of the Uganda
mutiny. At a meeting at Entebbe with the military, civilian and
missionary bodies, convened in Johnston's presence, Hill asked for an
account of Johnston's work. Bishop Tucker, not too overcome in the
presence of high officialdom to speak out, as was his opposite number
the Catholic bishop, stood up and gave a straightforward summary of all

Johnston had done and the difficulties he had faced in achieving results. Bishop Tucker's speech made an impression, and for the rest of his visit Hill was 'amiability embodied'.

Following Hill's visitation Johnston resumed his peregrinations, first to the Ssese Islands at the end of the year, to assess timber and india-rubber resources, and then to the eastern part of the protectorate. During the next three months he visited Nandi, Elgon and Bukedi as far as the Turkana country, while making his base at the Eladama Ravine station. He speeded up the launching of the steamship *William Mackinnon* on Lake Victoria, by getting rid of the drunkards in charge who had wasted a year doing nothing.

Johnston, on taking up his appointment, had been instructed by the Foreign Office to bear in mind that Uganda might eventually be merged with the East Africa Protectorate. He pondered much over this, and also the siting of a joint capital for such a merger. The concept of an unbroken sphere of British influence, an entity unfettered by intervening boundaries, from the coast inland to the farthest borders of Uganda, was not new. It was present during the negotiations between Britain and Germany in the 1880s for demarcation of their spheres of influence in East Africa, and also when the IBEAC took over the administration of the British sphere and directed its operations to the whole. The idea of a railway when first mooted was one of a line which would link together all of British East Africa into one domain.

The first step towards a division of the British sphere into two administrative regions came in 1893, when the IBEAC withdrew eastwards to Kikuyu and the British government took over the territory it vacated. The IBEAC however continued to administer the region between Kikuyu and the coast, until 1 July 1895, when it too passed to the control of the Foreign Office and was separately administered from Uganda. The division was confirmed in the report on the administration of the East African territories in 1894, which placed the boundary line between the two protectorates as a line to the immediate west of Kikuyu.

Such a brittle and artificial conception of two protectorates could not overcome the underlying unity of interests which knit them together, and the idea of federation persisted, as in the introduction of Indian law into Uganda in 1899 (it was already in effect in the East Africa Protectorate), and the view was expressed that it was 'desirable to combine the administration of the two Protectorates'. In various Orders in Council, 1897, 1899, 1900 and 1902, for appointment to the Judiciary, the creation of a Court of Appeal, and application of Indian Acts, it was thought necessary to avoid diversity of forms and procedure, and, in the words of the Law Officers of the Crown, 'to assimilate as closely as possible the legislation of the two Protectorates'. In March 1900, Johnston urged the establishment of a High Court to act as Court of Appeal when the 'fusion between Uganda and the East Africa Protectorate takes place'. And in the autumn of 1900, while in the eastern part of the protectorate, he dwelt much on the matter of federation. Romanticizing, and drawing on Indian parallels in the matter, Johnston reported to Salisbury that Mombasa would be the 'Bombay', and Entebbe the 'Calcutta'. The joint capital – the 'Simla' of East Africa – would be well up on the Mau plateau near Mile 475, where the railway began its descent into the Nyanda Valley, equidistant between Mombasa and the farthest points of Uganda and 'in easy communication by railway with the Indian Ocean and by railway and steamer with all parts of the Victoria Nyanza'. Here would reside the High Commissioner for East Africa, with three commissioners under him – at Zanzibar, Mombasa and Entebbe, respectively. Johnston would have preferred the Eldama Ravine station as the central capital – it had 'suggested itself to Administrator after Administrator, traveller after traveller, as the capital of a United East Africa', but it had an indifferent water supply, and was 20 miles from the railway. Johnston's flight of fancy stirred little interest in the Foreign Office, no more than the similar fine imagery of Sir Arthur Hardinge, Commissioner at Zanzibar, who, also under the overshadowing influence of India, and adept in drawing parallels from there, could write thus:

In Northern and Western Ukamba, in Masailand, and on the woody hills of Kikuyu, with the massive mountain system culminating in the peaks of Kenya on the north, and the Masai steppes spreading southwards to Kilimanjaro, the weary European, exhausted by the heat of the coast belt, and even more so of Zanzibar, breathes again, like a tired Anglo-Indian who has left the sultry plains of Bengal and Oudh for the fresh, invigorating atmosphere of Simla; for the punkah is no longer a necessity in Ukamba, and the nights are always cool and often cold.[10]

Salisbury thought such grand talk of a 'Simla' for British East Africa was premature and should wait the fusion of the two protectorates. A survey in 1901, of the site at Mile 475 (present-day Londiani) revealed its unsuitability, and a site at Njoro was selected instead. But by November

1901 the idea of a federal East Africa had been dropped in favour of a transfer of the Eastern Province of Uganda to the East Africa Protectorate.[11]

Throughout discussions on postal, telegraph and customs matters in 1900, and during the dispute over apportionment of customs revenue between the two territories, the idea of a future federation was tacitly assumed. It had been decided in 1896 that customs revenue for the two protectorates should be jointly collected. The arrangement never worked well. Goods ostensibly bound for Uganda did not always arrive there. Much of Uganda's imports still came by way of German territory. There was irritation in the Uganda administration over delay in paying to Uganda her portion of customs revenue collected at the coast, and much annoyance over the East Africa Protectorate charging £100 for stationery used in correspondence, and 25 rupees per porter, when the normal charge was 10 rupees. Worst of all, in Uganda eyes, was a charge on the import of horses to Uganda when no such animals existed there. Hence the peremptory tone of Johnston's instructions to his superior, Sir Arthur Hardinge, 'transfer to our bankers all sums due to the Uganda Protectorate'. Hardinge's flattering offer to leave the designing of new joint stamps for the common postal service to Johnston's 'well-known artistic taste' mollified the latter. In October 1900, it was agreed that

> In the future and until the two Protectorates obtain that natural fusion which will be the settlement of all their difficulties, it is better as we are both agreed, that their relations should be on a strictly cash basis.[12]

At a conference in Mombasa in November 1900 it was agreed that 10 per cent (Johnston pressed for 40 per cent) of customs collected at the coast should go to Uganda, a percentage calculated on the basis of imports by rail to Uganda as recorded at Naivasha. In March 1901 a united postal service for Uganda and the East Africa was established. There seemed further indication of coming federation in Sir Clement Hill's remark to Colonel Hayes Sadler, prior to the latter taking up his appointment as Commissioner of Uganda on 1 April 1902, that the amalgamation of the two territories 'was not a remote possibility'. That Hill could make this remark at a time when arrangements were already under way for the transfer of Uganda's Eastern Province to the East Africa Protectorate, a transfer which would underline the separateness of the two territories, strikes a note of unreality.

Johnston, after a brief return to Entebbe in 1900 for Christmas, journeyed back to the eastern part of the protectorate. His last few weeks in Uganda were spent in the company of a kindred soul, C.W. Hobley, in exploring Mount Elgon. Pleasant days were passed in collecting botanical specimens and studying Bantu speech forms. It was during his Elgon excursion, in April 1901, that Johnston met the Muganda Chief, Semei Kakungulu (also known as Kakungura), who claimed that Johnston during this visit promised him the title of 'Kabaka' (king) of Bukedi.[13]

Kakungulu was the apotheosis of that type of Baganda agent used by the British in administering outlying portions of the protectorate as they extended their control outside Buganda. This involved the extension of Baganda administrative practices and political organization: counties (sazas), sub-counties (gombolas), and parishes (mirukas), into occupied parts of Bunyoro, and eastern parts of Toro. There were soon complaints that Baganda agents were lording it over the Banyoro and Batoro in these regions. They were the most hated type of agent, foreign tax-collectors, and herein lies the source of much of that hearty dislike with which the Baganda were regarded outside their own territory. The severest criticism of the use of surrogate Baganda as agents for the British administration came from the eastern part of the protectorate, where Kakungulu was administering Bukedi. In reward for his valuable services during the Sudanese mutiny, and operations leading to the capture of Kabarega and Mwanga in 1899, Kakungulu was placed in charge of the little-known Bukedi country in the immediate vicinity of Lake Kyase, to the west of Mount Elgon. He held the title of 'Omusaza' (county chief), and was given a grant of 20 square miles of land near Mbale. Kakungulu also claimed that Johnston, when visiting the district in April 1901, expressed himself so pleased with Kakungulu's work, that while standing on the slopes of Mount Elgon and waving his arms to the west and north he said: 'I will ask that you may be made King of all this country'. Johnston made the important proviso that this largesse did not include the Mount Elgon area, which he wished to be kept for white settlement. Henceforth Kakungulu assumed he was king, and dug his own tomb '30-40 feet deep, and 15 or 20 feet in length and breadth'. He soon became a veritable thorn in the side of the British administration. Although he checked the raiding of the Bukedi people and established his authority over them, his methods of doing so were vicious in the extreme: he and his followers paid themselves handsomely in cattle taken from the suppressed, and the latter were forced to pay hut and gun tax while Kakungulu and followers went scot-free. The Baganda flocked to join Kakungulu, to share in these spoils and estates, in such numbers that the regents in Buganda appealed to Kakungulu to halt the exodus. Increasing complaints of Kakungulu's nefarious exactions were now coming in, and an inquisitor, Mr W.R. Walker, in late 1901, was delegated to report on the state of affairs in Bukedi. The result was a 'complete revelation'. The people of Bukedi were practically destitute, many being reduced to feeding on rats. There were no cattle, sheep or goats in the country except those belonging to Kakungulu and his followers. Kakungulu had extended his rule far beyond his original 'saza': he was truly a 'Kabaka' in the making. The investigation however resulted in his being ordered to reduce his territorial claims and clean up his methods of administration. Those Baganda who had moved into Bukedi to share in the spoils were ordered home, subject to loss of estates in Buganda. In the face of acceptance of this fiat, or being deposed, Kakungulu resigned his post and retired to an estate at Mbale. Despite the obliquity cast on much of his work, not all was bad: he had done good work in making roads, centralizing administration, introducing trade and accustoming natives to appeal to a central authority instead of settling disputes by force.

By mid-May 1901, his dealings with Kakungulu finished, Johnston withdrew to the Eldama Ravine station. Here, during his last few days in Uganda, he could review the success of his tax schemes for the previous year. He noted with quiet satisfaction that total revenue was over £66,000, with hut and gun tax bringing in £34,000 made up in the form of cash and negotiable goods, including 'young elephants, zebras and other wild animals'. Hut tax, in the form of labour, resulted in the clearing of the forest at Entebbe, construction of a port there and the building a road from Mengo to Lake Albert. There was much evasion of payment of hut tax by overcrowding in huts; missionaries reported as many as 20 persons living in a single hut, and claimed that gross immorality resulted. However, Johnston had done well, at least on paper, and the Foreign Office and Treasury had recently commented favourably on the reduced grant-in-aid for the current year – £172,000, as compared to £204,712 for the previous year, and this despite the large item of £19,435 for a telegraph line included in the current year. With this note of success ringing in his ears Johnston quitted Uganda. He returned to the coast by the newly completed railway line, boarded a steamer at Zanzibar on 27 May 1901, and was back in England by early June. His final report on Uganda was written up by the close of September 1901, and his official connection with that territory severed on 1 October 1901.

Uganda was not to experience the same tempo as set by Johnston until the governorship of Sir Andrew Cohen in the 1950s. Many of Johnston's proposals for developing the natural resources of the country were imaginative, if not always practical, for example his advocacy of using elephants for transport purposes; and developing

> this very important source of wealth in the Protectorate ... captured elephants might be trained and tamed and used to carry loads and perform other useful services, there is no saying what valuable results might not come from it in the use of trained elephants for internal communication in these African jungles.[14]

Johnston converted the Foreign Office to the idea, and £5,000 was included in the 1902-03 estimates for the capture and training of elephants. Plans were drawn up for two elephant farms, at Fort Portal and Entebbe. Negotiations to obtain trained male elephants and mahouts from Bengal and Malaya produced a shock. It would cost £200 or more to deliver an elephant to Uganda. Johnston's successors felt they had been saddled with an impractical and costly scheme. They could see little use for trained elephants apart from hauling timber, and Uganda timber could not compete with Mau timber easily available along the railway. Jackson was so critical of the scheme that the £5000 was removed from the estimates, and plans for training elephants quickly dropped. Johnston's concern, however, for elephant conservation, and his suggestions for this, received ultimate recognition in the setting up a large elephant reserve in Bunyoro.

Johnston, in his wide-ranging and varied interests, was comparable to Colbert, Louis XIV's improving minister, in the New World. He sent off to Kew Gardens in England samples of rubber, seeds and geological specimens for analysis. He prophesied a great future for coffee as a paying crop in Uganda, but made a strange miscalculation in thinking that cotton had little future in the country's economy. He envisaged the development of the Nile's electrical potential, and suggested the reservation of a mile-wide strip on either side of the Nile, from its exit at Napoleon Gulf to Ripon Falls, utilizing the electrical potential at Affuddu and 'turning the Murchison Falls to account electrically'.

Johnston was alert to the new and exotic, and exhorted his officers in the remote corners of the protectorate to report to him and send in unusual specimens of flora and fauna. Especially dear to his heart was

Captain Delmé-Radcliffe in the remote Nile District, who sent him a pair of skulls of 'rare wild dogs', and, strange to tell, reported on a fish 'which chirrups like a bird'. Uganda was not to see Johnston's like again.

At the time of Johnston's leaving Uganda the protectorate had attained its greatest extent territorially. It consisted of six provinces, and on its eastern side ran almost to the outskirts of present-day Nairobi. Yet even before Johnston had severed his connection with Uganda, steps were already under way which would reduce the size of that territory by well over a third. The original conception of a boundary line between Uganda and the East Africa Protectorate following the withdrawal of the IBEAC was one which would divide the highland area between them. During the Foreign Office deliberations of 1894 on the administration of East Africa, when Lugard's advice carried much weight, consensus of opinion was that the boundary should run north from the German sphere to Lake Rudolf, and along the edge of the Laikipia Kikuyu escarpments, thus bringing Uganda's eastern boundary so far east as to include Lakes Naivasha and Baringo. This suggested demarcation received support from the Committee on the Administration of East Africa, under Sir Percy Anderson, in April 1895, and was given effect when the British government took over from the Company as of 1 July 1895. The result was the division of British East Africa into two spheres, one from the coast up to and including the eastern portion of the highlands, and the other taking in the western portion of the highlands and what is present-day Uganda. The Maasai, a tribe whose unique mode of life had aroused a great deal of interest among European officials, especially Sir Arthur Hardinge and Major Macdonald, were thus placed, as it was thought, under one administration.

In the early part of 1900 the boundary question came up again. Macdonald's expedition of 1897–98 had revealed the need for further definition of Uganda's eastern boundary northward to Lake Rudolf. At the same time, the wanderings of the Maasai were upsetting Hardinge's calculations, for the Maasai, although they had long had their abode near Naivasha, had recently, under their leader, Lenana, moved their headquarters to the east of Mount Kinangop, from where they ranged westwards up to the Laikipia escarpment. Hardinge was now of the view that the boundary should be readjusted to place the Maasai wholly within the East Africa Protectorate. Johnston favoured the boundary agreed on in 1894 on the grounds that it gave Uganda a choice highland area soon to be opened up by the railway, it would bring increased revenue and importance to the Uganda administration and place

Uganda in a more equal position with the East Africa Protectorate which controlled the ports of entry at the coast and the customs revenue that went with them.

By October 1900 Johnston was, however, complaining of the difficulty of administering the 'unwieldy Mau district' from Entebbe, and suggested that a separate administration be set up for it. Johnston's suggestion came at the time of Sir Clement Hill's visit to East Africa, and when the railway was approaching the lake. Hill did not favour Johnston's idea of a separate administration for the Mau district nor did he feel optimistic about the early prospect of federation. Hill, perhaps influenced by Macdonald's plan for railway extension northward from Londiani to link up with the Sudan, rather than with Buganda (which would have communication with the Uganda Railway by way of the lake), thought that the railway system should be under one administration. The boundary between the two protectorates according to Hill should run from a point on the north eastern shore of Kavirondo Bay, northwards, and to the immediate east of the Nandi escarpment.

Eliot, however, pointed out that the boundary suggested by Hill would divide the Wakavirondo, and suggested a boundary placed even farther west, on the principle that 'the whole of a tribe should be under one administration'. All districts inhabited by Wakavirondo should be transferred to the East Africa Protectorate, leaving to Uganda those populations 'more akin to the Baganda'. According to Eliot the highland area with its potentialities for European settlement should be under one administration, and Johnston, already retired to England and writing up his Special Report on Uganda, spoke of it being 'admirably suited for a 'white man's country'.

The decision to transfer came in November 1901, following an exchange of views between Eliot and the Foreign Office, an exchange in which the Uganda administration played little part (Johnston had already departed and the new commissioner had not arrived). It was agreed that the transfer should be brought about as soon as the railway arrived at the lake. In a communication of 28 January 1902 Hill informed Sadler as to the reasons for the transfer: it was basically 'to place under the East Africa Administration those tribes which are connected with the Maasai and Wakavirondo, as well as all the country traversed by the Railway'.

Prior to the official announcement of the transfer, the determination of the new boundary in the Mount Elgon area was left to Hobley and Jackson. Hobley favoured a line running to the immediate west of the mountain, leaving the fertile south-west slopes to Uganda, and tribal connections with the Wakavirondo in this area unaffected. Jackson wanted a boundary to the east of the Elgon, thus leaving the whole great elevated mass within Uganda as a sanatorium. Jackson, supported by Eliot, argued that the tribal connection in this area with the Wakavirondo was not a close one: he also maintained that Uganda authorities through their agent, Kakungulu, were administering this area and were experienced in dealing with its native peoples.[15] Jackson's view prevailed and the boundary was ultimately drawn to the immediate east of Elgon. The boundary to the north of Elgon was left somewhat flexible, the relationship and alliances of tribes there being practically unknown. There was a growing realization that tribal interests should not be disregarded in boundary-making.

By an Order dated 5 March 1902, delivered by telegram of 6 March 1902, Lansdowne gave his instructions for 'placing the Eastern Province of Uganda with the East Africa Protectorate' as from 1 April 1902: 'I have given the name of the 'Lakes Province' to the new province, and as soon as you are in a position to suggest a definite description of its western boundary, will take any steps which may seem requisite to further regularize the position', and further, on 19 March 1902, Lansdowne directed that the boundary of the new province should be settled as soon as sufficient information was obtained, and 'it would seem desirable if practicable, that when it is fixed, Mt Elgon should remain in the Uganda Protectorate'.

Within ten days of Eliot receiving official instructions for the transfer he had made proposals, which Lansdowne accepted, for the division of the large unwieldy 'Lakes Province' into two lesser one – Kisumu and Navaisha. Kisumu, with its large African population, its lower altitudes, and circumjacency to the unhealthy Kavirondo Gulf area, was a contrast to the highlands and sparsely populated country of Navaisha. Eliot had already, in March 1902, marked out the latter for European settlement.

With this division made, there remained but the tidying up of the boundary between the two protectorates. A small commission, comprising C.W. Hobley for the East Africa Protectorate, and William Grant for Uganda, was able to complete its recommendations by 25 June 1902. The commissioners had kept in mind the need for a boundary which would take into account tribal divisions, and they recommended a line that would run along the Sio River, from its mouth at Berkeley Bay on Lake Victoria, up to its confluence with the Sango River, and along the latter to the source of the Malawa River; thence northwards along the eastern flanks of Mount Elgon, to the River Suam, and following that river north-eastwards to its confluence with the River Turkwell; thence along the latter to where it debouches into Lake Rudolf, on the western side of that lake.

As a result of the transfer the long-standing problem of the pestiferous Nandi was now the East Africa Protectorate's concern. And the inclusion of the Eastern Province and its hut tax system into the protectorate, led directly to the general application of that tax throughout the latter. The transfer also meant that seniority and promotion accrued to officials in Uganda, while, in the other protectorate, more government posts were made available in an attractive, healthy and upland area.

The transfer of Uganda's Eastern Province to her eastern neighbour meant that Sir James Hayes Sadler, Johnston's successor, appointed Commissioner in December 1901, took over a much reduced protectorate – one with five, not six provinces as previously. Uganda was now more of a physical entity, embraced between the lakes and encompassing the ancient basin of Lake Victoria. Its peoples were largely of Bantu and Nilotic stock. The kingdom of Buganda, now more centrally placed and with the capital town, central administration, main military installations and missionary headquarters within its boundaries, was by far the predominant part of the protectorate. Uganda was 'African' territory, with little scope for European settlement.

Johnston, by Government Notice of 9 April 1900, had placed severe restrictions on non-natives acquiring land. In Churchill's words:

> Uganda is a native State ... It finds its counterparts among the great native States of India, where Imperial authority is exercised in the name and often through the agency of a native prince and his own officers.[16]

Within the limitations of what an 'African' territory implied, Johnston had laid a good base on which to build. Hill, in his instructions to Sadler on the latter taking up his appointment, made little mention of Johnston's achievements. He spoke of the recent reorganisation of the military without mentioning that this had been Johnston's work. He referred to the civil administration which Sadler would find waiting him, and to the roads now connecting the outlying areas; wheeled traffic could now pass between Entebbe and Butiaba on Lake Albert. Sadler travelled over this road in 1902, being the first Commissioner of Uganda to visit the Nile district as far north as Wadelai. The Nile district, although not quite attaining what Johnston termed the 'silver age of Emin', was rapidly recovering from the desolation wrought by the Dervishes. The cutting of the 'sudd' on the Nile by Major Malcolm Peake, 'one of the most creditable actions which white civilization had produced in Africa', had much eased navigation between Uganda and Khartoum', and was of 'the greatest benefit to the starved and miserable natives of the Nile bank and the isolated and sickly Europeans who upheld the Uganda administration'. The railway had reduced the journey between Kampala and the coast from three months' travelling to three days. One result of this greater ease of communication with Uganda was

> a plague of explorers, sportsmen and amateur collectors, they invariably end by living like parasites on one official or another.[17]

Potatoes from the highlands of the East Africa protectorate were now available in Uganda, and tinned goods and bottled beer were no longer luxuries. Kampala and Entebbe were settled communities. Kampala presented an appearance which was a far cry from the lone British presence on 'the hillock which was contemptuously given to Captain Lugard by Mwanga'. Now there were 'German stores at which most articles needful to the European settler can be purchased, besides the well-provided Indian bazaar'. These signs of European civilization had spread even to outlying posts, so much so that Churchill, travelling through there in 1907, could speak of Masindi, in Bunyoro, thus:

> There are real houses, standing on high stone platforms with deep verandas and wire gauze windows. The roads are laid out in bold geometry of broad red lines. There are avenues of planted trees, delicious banks of flowers, a prepared breakfast, *cold*, not cool, drinks, a telegraph office, and a file of *The Times*. What more could an explorer desire or the Fates accord?[18]

Entebbe was 'admirably laid out and planned into residential, trading and native quarters with almost academic completion ... and the Hindu quarters were north of the European and separated from it by a clearing of a mile in length'. There was a hospital with two English nurses in residence by the spring of 1902. At a branch of the National Bank of India the Katikiro had recently opened an account for 500 rupees, 'prior to leaving to attend the coronation ceremonies in London'. By the end of the year most of the chiefs in Buganda were banking salaries paid to them by the administration. Tax collection was becoming a routine business. All this had come to pass during Johnston's term of office.

Sadler enjoyed a quiet lull after the busy and tempestuous pace of his predecessor. His instructions referred to federation as only a remote possibility, the question was not to be pressed. Although the transfer of Uganda's Eastern Province to the East Africa Protectorate meant a loss in revenue of £11,545, it also meant a saving of £24,000 annually to the Uganda Protectorate, and the estimates for the financial year, 1902–3, showed expenditure down by £55,000, and a reduction in grant-in-aid of £42,000. The territory now had a definite stamp of its own, and as such was launched into the twentieth century. Eliot visiting Uganda in 1902, referred to

the enormous difference between the Kingdom of Uganda and East Africa. To cross the lake is like visiting another continent. The country is cultivated and thickly populated. There are good roads, fences and houses, all constructed by the natives. The people are all clothed, and it is a reproach not to be able to read and write. Christianity is the fashion, and the whole place consequently a paradise for missionaries of all sects.[19]

13· White Man's Country

Lord Delamere, having journeyed down from the torrid wastes of Somaliland, and finally, emerging on the Laikipia plateau in early 1898, after climbing out of the low hot basin of Baringo, was deeply stirred by the glorious panorama spread out before him; open wind-swept downs from the green foothills of Mount Kenya in the east, to the cedar-forested slopes of the Aberdares in the south-west. His aristocratic English soul could not refrain from exclaiming that here was the most wonderful sheep country in the world. From that moment, we are told, East Africa claimed Delamere as her own.[1] Delamere had already made four journeys to Somaliland in the previous six years; and on his fourth he seems to have made up his mind to settle in East Africa.

He was not the first European to succumb to the attractions of the East African highlands. Joseph Thomson, in 1884, on entering the region, declared that a more charming prospect could not to be found in all Africa

> probably not even in Abyssinia ... Though lying at a general elevation of 6000 feet, it is not mountainous, but extends out in billowy, swelling reaches, and is characterized by everything that makes a pleasing landscape. Here are dense patches of flowering shrubs; there noble forests. Now you traverse a park-like country enlivened by groups of game; anon, great herds of cattle, or flocks of sheep and goats are seen wandering kneedeep in the splendid pasture. There is little in the aspect of the country to suggest the popular idea of the Tropics. The eye rests upon coniferous trees, forming pine-like woods, and you can gather springs of heath, sweet-scented clover, anemone, and other familiar forms ... The country is a very network of babbling brooks and streams.[2]

And Carl Peters, four years later, added his encomium. The region was beyond all question, the pearl of the English possessions, with the exception of Uganda. It is unfortunate that this cool and fruitful land lies so far distant from the coast; otherwise it would most certainly be suited for colonization by European agriculturists.

There was fulsome praise from other travellers: Frederick Jackson, passing through on his way to Uganda in 1889, spoke of the ideal climate and ample rainfall of the highlands, a land where English vegetables grew luxuriantly and where there was excellent grazing. Even those two grumblers, Captain Eric Smith and Sir Gerald Portal, who had disagreeable things to say about much of East Africa, excepted Kikuyu land from their animadversions. Smith conceded that 'almost anything could grow' in Kikuyuland; and even for Portal, the region between Machakos and Kikuyu was 'eminently suitable for Europeans', and with 'complete immunity – at least for the present – from telegrams or interviews, circulars or companies, dinner parties or duns'. What a varied crew of observers passed their verdicts, and all favourable: Bishop Tucker, and newspaper correspondents, Ernest Gedge of *The Times* and Herr Wolfe of *Tageblatt,* affirmed the fertility of Kikuyu. Herr Wolfe stated that

> There is everything that can be desired ready to hand – plenty of water, fuel, a rich and fertile soil, a tractable population, a healthy climate, and cheap means of sustenance for settlers. The tobacco of the country, which I am smoking, tastes very nearly as good as the favourite Transvaal tobacco. The potatoes are large, sweet, and mealy, and the peas which I have are better than those we have at home.[3]

Cardinal Lavigerie, for the White Fathers, probably retailing the accounts of his missionaries in the field, stated that, as regards the highlands of East-Central Africa, 'The nature of the soil, the heat of the sun, and the abundance of water contribute to make this country one of the richest and most beautiful in the world.'

Lugard, following his careful traverse of the interior, 1890-92, extolled its possibilities for European settlement and future place in the empire:

> the time is not far distant when the teeming population of Europe will turn to the fertile highlands of Africa to seek new fields for

expansion. It is possible, therefore, that British Central and British East Africa may be the embryo empires of an epoch already dawning, empires which, in the zenith of their growth and development, may rival those mighty dependencies which are now the pride of the Anglo-Saxon race.[4]

Kikuyuland ranked high in Lugard's esteem, a country with rich soil, well watered by numerous streams and with abundant rainfall:

> The climate is cold and bracing; slight frosts occur at night. The hills are clothed with springy turf, or covered with bracken – the flora is largely that of Europe. The district between Kikuyu and Mount Kenya is especially healthy and fertile.[5]

C.W. Hobley, geologist to the IBEAC, who journeyed from the upper Tana to Ukambani and Mount Kenya in November 1891, discovered that the rich upland area of Kikuyu also extended to the south-west of Mount Kenya, where there was fine open rolling parkland, thinly wooded, covered with green turf, and excellent pasturage.

> The spot recommended for European colonization lies between the Kitui mountains and a range to the east of them. Here is a wide valley some eight miles broad and about forty miles long, with a stream running down the centre, with water-pools in places. The soil is alluvium of unlimited depth, except at the edge of the valley.[6]

Kikuyuland already possessed valuable timber, and could produce temperate fruits, tea, cotton and jute, and a tree 'which the Somals called kath, – an evergreen shrub with a leaf like the arbutus, an excellent substitute for tea', single shrubs being valued in Aden at $1000 each, the leaf being highly desired as a drug, inducing a mild degree of intoxication. This was that 'kath', so widely used in the Yemen as an intoxicant, and which provided a highly lucrative export for the highlands of Ethiopia: might not East Africa capture some of this market?

Equally attractive as Kikuyu, in the eyes of some observers, were the plateaux on the western side of the Rift Valley, the Mau escarpment and the 'Laikipia' (between Baringo and Mount Kenya). Joseph Thomson placed the attractions here on a level with those of Kikuyuland. Laikipia with its rich carpet of grass, offered 'the very finest of pasturage'. Prior to the transfer of Uganda's 'Eastern Province' to the East Africa Protectorate in April 1902, Johnston had declared:

> In the Eastern part of the Uganda Protectorate there is a tract of country almost without parallel in tropical Africa: a region of perhaps 12,000 square miles, admirably well watered, with a fertile soil, cool and perfectly healthy climate, covered with noble forests, and, to a very great extent, uninhabitated by any native race. This area lies at an altitude not less than 6000 feet, and not more than 10,000 feet. It is as healthy for European settlers as the United Kingdom, British Columbia, or temperate South Africa ... I am able to say decidedly that here we have a territory (now that the Uganda Railway is built) admirably suited for a white man's country.[7]

And Lugard wrote

> Of the still higher plateau of Mau I have myself spoken enthusiastically ... This area is uninhabited, and of great extent; it consequently offers unlimited *room* for the location of agricultural settlements or stock-rearing farms. Here, if anywhere in Central Africa, in my opinion, would be the site upon which to attempt the experiment of European settlements. The soil is extremely rich, and is covered with an excellent and luxuriant pasture throughout the year, with which is mixed white clover and trefoil. The country is intersected by small streams, the rainfall is abundant, patches of forest supply bamboos and timber for building and fuel. Game roams over the acres of undulating grass, and the climate is cold and bracing ... Here also I would suggest the experiment of a model farm like those established in South Africa by Mr. Rhodes.[8]

The central position of the Mau, half-way between the coast and Uganda, would be the ideal site for a transport depot and for experiments in taming elephant and zebra, in harnessing the buffalo and other animals for draught purposes. Here also could be inaugurated the growing of coffee, tea, indigo, fibre, tobacco, wheat, cotton and, in Lugard's words, 'a hundred other tropical and sub-tropical products'.

With its rolling savannahs of rich pasture, the district was ideal for ranching, sheep-farming and cattle runs. The South African ostrich, whose plumes were more valuable than the indigenous species, could be farmed. Sheep's wool and Angora's hair would form articles of export. The treeless portions of the Mau could be afforested with *Eucalyptus globulus*, a most useful tree, providing excellent timber and a source of fuel. Captain Pringle described the pasture on the Mau as the finest kind, 'perennial, mixed with clover'; the climate was 'salubrious and equable', and with a 'fine rainfall'; the fatness of the flocks and herds on the Mau were proverbial. Captain Eric Smith also stated that the Mau offered the finest pasturage he had seen in the interior; and Francis de Winton, with long experience of ranching and stock-raising in North America, claimed that it presented the finest natural pasturage he had ever seen, 'anywhere'.

Amidst this sonorous rhetoric there was only one dissenting voice, that of Portal. Writing from the 'Top of the Mau Mountains, 8,600 feet', in February 1893, and greatly disappointed with the dismally and bitterly cold Mau Mountains ... 'either rock or else heavy red clay burnt as hard as brick and very heavy, sticky and almost impassable to caravans during the rains of June and July', he declared that those who eulogized East Africa 'were looking through rose-coloured glasses'.[9] As for the Maasai, they were an 'unmitigated curse to the country ... to keep up with the terror of their name they commit excess terror'.

At the time of the arrival of the first Europeans in the early 1890s, there were two agricultural belts, thickly populated by the natives, between the coast and Uganda: They were the Kikuyu country – from Mount Kenya down to the Maasai plains – and the Kavirondo country – round the eastern shore of Lake Victoria. In the first of these regions European settlement first commenced around IBEAC posts at Machakos and Dagoretti. The latter post was sited near Ngongo Bagas, a well-known staging and camping site for Swahili caravans from the coast. Charles New and Thomas Wakefield in the 1860s had referred to it as 'Ngongo Pagazi' (possibly from 'pagazis' – a meeting-place for porters). Thomson, in 1883, described it as the 'eye' or spring of the Bagas – one of the headstreams of the Athi River. It was situated on the confines of Maasailand, within easy reach of the rich food-producing Kikuyu country, and Lugard, on his way up-country in 1890, built a station here. He camped first on a knoll 'in the very heart of the villages and fields of the Kikuyu', but, soon aware that this would lead to friction (Teleki had clashed with the Kikuyu here two years previously), and directed by local Kikuyu chiefs, Wyaki and Miroo, he selected 'a charming site' – 'Dagoretti', on the edge of the cultivated portion of

Kikuyu, about five miles from Ngongo Bagas. At the same time Lugard complemented Jackson's treaty with Kamiri of the previous year, by making a treaty with Wyaki in October 1890. Jackson and Gedge had camped at Kikuyu and made blood-brotherhood and a treaty with 'Kamiri of Kikuyu' on 11 August 1889. Lugard departed for Uganda on 1 November 1890, leaving George Wilson in charge of the post. Despite Lugard's claim that Wilson 'succeeded admirably', the latter twice evacuated the fort in the face of Kikuyu hostility – possibly the result of looting activities by porters of the coast caravans, camped at the site. When Lugard returned from Uganda, in August 1892, he found Dagoretti abandoned. Wilson had left IBEAC employ to work for the Scottish East African Industrial Mission at Kibwezi. A new fort, Fort Smith, was erected at the end of 1891, by Captain Eric Smith and W. J. Purkiss, not on the site of Dagoretti, but at Lugard's original choice of site, within the southern limits of Kikuyuland.[10]

The new station (now under the command of Captain R.H. Nelson, assisted by Purkiss) remained the centre of strained relations with the Kikuyu. Purkiss narrowly escaped assassination, and one of his headmen was killed. This trouble it would appear arose over the acquiring by the IBEAC of 345 acres surrounding Fort Smith, which was opposed by the Kikuyu chief, Wyaki, who repelled all friendly advances, and was thus replaced by a more amenable Kikuyu chief, Karurui.

Captain Macdonald arrived at this critical time on his way down from Uganda in October 1892, and was called in to help against the Kikuyu. He arrested Wyaki and escorted him down to Kibwezi, where he died at the Scottish Mission Hospital. The Kikuyu remained threatening, alarmed at the increasing number of Europeans passing through their territory. When Macdonald arrived at Fort Smith in October 1892, Captain Eric Smith, James Martin (caravan leader) and Herr Wolfe were there. From 6 to 13 November 1892, Bishop Tucker with a large party under G.C. Leith (caravan leader), remained at Fort Smith; and Ernest Gedge, *The Times* correspondent, stopped over there from 17 to 24 December 1892. On 26 December, Nelson died, leaving Purkiss in command. On 30 January 1893, Portal's mission arrived to find Fort Smith 'practically in a state of siege'. There was a temporary reprieve during Portal's fortnight's stay, but the fort was invested by the Kikuyu soon after his departure, and was only saved by Ainsworth coming to the rescue from Machakos. In mid-1893, Purkiss, now an invalid, was replaced by F.G. Hall.

Hall was successful in asserting control over the surrounding tribesmen, aided by the fragmented nature of Kikuyu society. Even Maasai aggression had failed to induce cohesion among the Kikuyu, or produce a leading chief. The Kikuyu clustered on the many ridges into which their country was divided, separated from their neighbours and warring with each other. Hall played on these divisions, supporting one faction against another, and when it suited his purpose even encouraged their raiding. He gained co-operation from the Kikuyu chief, Kinanjui, his 'Fidus Achates', and brought the broken remnants of the Matatapatu and Kapite Maasai, about 1000 in all, with their leader Lenana, under the protection of the Fort, when they were sorely worsted by the southern Maasai from Kilimanjaro. He gave them asylum, and inspirited them by permitting them to join in raiding with their former enemy, the Kikuyu. A strange turn of events had come to pass under Hall's ameliorizing influence.

With frequent caravans now passing through Fort Smith, and transport with Uganda on an organized basis, the Kikuyu gradually accepted the European presence. Within the year following Hall's move there, Fort Smith had its first European settler in Dr H.A. Boedeker. It was natural that the first European settlers would gather round the Company's posts at Fort Smith and Machakos. Provisions were obtainable here and produce could be sold, and there was security against native attack. Unwittingly, however, they laid the basis of the profound problem which was to bedevil British rule in Kenya in later years: European settler and Kikuyu were vying for the same land.

The earliest accounts of Europeans who travelled through Kikuyuland, indicated that it was intensively cultivated. Thomson attested to this, and observed that 'at Ngongo we had reached the southern boundary of the country of the Kikuyu'. Ten years later, Hall, in charge of 'Kikuyu station' (Fort Smith), still placed Ngongo Bagas as the southern boundary of Kikuyu,

> a narrow strip of country about 100 miles in length and 15 to 18 miles in width, bounded on the north by the snow-clad Mount Kenya and on the south by the ridge named Ngongo Bagas, east by the Athie (or Kapotie) plains and west by the Kikuyu escarpment ... at one time entirely covered with forest but now only a narrow belt encircling the whole ... With the exception of small patches of excellent grass which are preserved for grazing purposes and a few small swamps every available piece of ground is under cultivation and the district might well be described as one vast garden."

Lugard affirmed that the cultivation of the Kikuyu was 'prodigiously extensive, indeed the whole country may be said to be under tillage'.

The Kikuyu, originally from the lower Tana River area and who had worked their way up to Mount Kenya, subsequently taking over the forested area south-west of that mountain as far as Ngongo Bagas, were agriculturists and cultivators rather than roving warring nomads. They sought protection in the forests against the Maasai and Kamba, and here they cleared their plots, built their beehive-shaped wattle and daub huts, kept sheep and goats and grew maize. Their shifting cultivation had a destructive effect on the forest, and when the first Europeans arrived in the early 1890s large areas in its centre were denuded, and the Kikuyu were venturing forth and wearing away at its circumference. By the mid-1890s the forest belt had been pushed back several miles from the boundary recorded by Thomson in 1884. The Kikuyu were still relying on this forest belt for protection, but indicative of the decline of their traditional enemy, they permitted a settlement of the Maasai in their midst. Thomson had already noted:

> Curiously enough, however, though they are eternally at war to the knife with each other, there is a compact between them not to molest the womenfolk of either party. Hence the curious spectacle is exhibited of Maasai women wending their way with impunity to a Kikuyu village, while their relatives are probably engaged in a deadly fight close at hand. In the same way the Wa-kikuyu women frequently carry grain to the Maasai kraals to exchange for hides.[12]

The Maasai, although inferior in numbers to the Kikuyu, much eclipsed the latter in the interest their culture and habits awakened in the minds of Europeans. They exhibited certain similarities to the Zulu, in overall fighting stamina and power, in their history and dress and customs, and in their being trained and inured to warfare and not allowed to marry until they attained the status and donned the toga of full-fledged warriors. They were essentially roving pastoralists, and had very little art or industry in their culture. Their diet was mainly milk and meat and occasionally blood. They traversed great tracts of country, often during the night, to surprise the enemy. Their shields were of hide and similar in shape and size to the Zulu shield, and their war costume sported rings of colobus monkey skin tied to their legs below the knee. They plastered themselves with grease and red ochre, and were often armed with knobkerries or clubs, as well as their famous spears.

In origin they derived from an early mixture of Nilote and Hamite – their height and slenderness, and limbs and features, yielded strong evidence of Semitic strain. Their cradleland probably lay in the region between the White Nile and Lake Rudolf.

The life of the Maasai revolved round warfare and cattle: they deemed that all the cattle in the world had been bestowed on them at the beginning of creation. They ranged from the Uasin Gishu and Laikipia plateaux in the north down to Kilimanjaro in the south as far west as the Loita Plains and east to the Teita Hills; their raids sometimes took them down to the environs of Mombasa. The movement of Maasai stock from north to south was channelled through a vast cattle run in the Rift Valley between Lakes Naivasha and Nakuru. In their vast, amoeboid-shaped, domain in East Africa, the Maasai pursued a unique and rarified way of life. Although with a reputation for unrestrained savagery, they abstained from preying on the fauna around them, except perhaps for the lion, and it is to this abstention that present-day East Africa owes them much thanks for the great spectacle of wild life which still presents itself to the eye in Kenya and parts of Tanzania. There were two main sections to the Maasai – the Maasai proper, and the so-called Kwavi or 'agricultural Maasai', the latter being located chiefly at Lake Natron and south of Mount Meru in German territory, and on the plateaux east and west of Lake Baringo. The Maasai proper were in turn subdivided into the Kaputiei division – mainly on the Kapite plains; the Laikipia branch; and the En-aiposha, which was the largest and centred in the Rift Valley in the rich grazing grounds around Naivasha, and had two main subdivisions, the Loita and Purko. These, in turn, were under leaders, *laibons,* whose powers were primarily ritualistic and prophetic, and were most dramatically exhibited among the En-aiposha who ranged from Naivasha down into German territory. A succession of wars had so prevailed between these different divisions in the latter years of the nineteenth century, especially between the Uasin Gishu and Laikipia clans of the northern branch, as to depopulate the Laikipia at the time Delamere made his appearance there in early 1898. This strife within the Maasai was most dramatically exhibited in the conflict between the two branches of the En-aiposha, with supremacy gradually settling with the Purko under the powerful *laibon,* Mbatian. By 1884, although never acknowledged as such, he exercised paramount authority as chief *laibon* over most of the En-aiposha. His death in 1890 left a disputed succession, followed by a fratricidal war between his two sons, Lenana and Sendeyo. The latter, supported by the Loita section, based his followers in German territory, and grazed his cattle intermittently on both sides of the border, often raiding into British territory against his brother, Lenana, who remained in the British sphere. Lenana, harried also by neighbouring Kikuyu, sought refuge with about 1000 followers at Fort Smith in 1894, and here in 1895 there also gathered remnants of the Kaputei and Matapatu clans, making in all some 5000 Maasai refugees under the protection of Fort Smith. In March 1896 they were established at Ngongo Bagas, under British surveillance to prevent their quarrelling with the Kikuyu. At Ngongo Bagas the Maasai set up a huge kraal, 3400 yards long by 1000 yards wide, and all 'one mass of filth'. The *moran* would not work, and the women carried on prostitution, with much opportunity for this in the constant coming and going of caravans near their site. Added to this source of income was the sale of firewood to passing caravans. A main grouping of the Purko section of the Maasai remained concentrated near Lake Naivasha.

Internecine warfare which weakened their ranks, along with an outbreak of smallpox in the mid-1880s, and the wiping out of their cattle by pleuropneumonia and rinderpest, wellnigh encompassed the ruin of the Maasai. Jackson, Lugard, Peters and Captain Smith all recorded this decline. Smith met only a few Maasai kraals between Machakos and Dagoretti, and where traditionally the Maasai had pushed their grazing rights into the embayments of wooded foothills from whence they launched their lightning-like raids on Kamba and Kikuyu, there was now a remarkable change. The Maasai encamped outside the forest of south-west Kikuyu, on the grass plains between the River Kedong and Ngongo Bagas, were in a state of puerile decrepitude:

> their cattle seem to be decimated by disease just as much here as on the over-fed and over-stocked pastures of Naivasha ... the whole of the west shore of this lake is hardly approachable for the number of dead beasts ... indeed their palmy days appear to be of the past ... when owners of great herds of cattle and sheep, they were insolent and quarrelsome – now that their only possessions, cattle, are dead and dying, they are amenable enough.[13]

The substance of the Maasai had gone; the tide had turned against the 'scourge of the steppes'. Their name might still strike terror in the hearts of their neighbours, and they could still rouse themselves to former fury, as when, in the Mbé country south-east of Mount Kenya, Commander Dundas in 1893, witnessed a scene following a Maasai raid on the Kamba:

On our return through the Mbé country, a most harrowing sight
presented itself: what only a few days before were prosperous
villages, standing amid fields of grain, were now smoking ruins;
bodies of old men, women and children, half-burnt lay in all
directions; here and there might be seen a few solitary individuals,
sitting with their head buried in their hands, hardly noticing the
passing caravan, and apparently in the lowest depths of misery and
despair. On questioning several of these unhappy beings, I was
informed that the Maasai had unexpectedly arrived one morning
at dawn, spearing and burning all before them and carrying off
some 250 women, and large herds of cattle. Only a few of the
unfortunate people had escaped by flying to the mountains.[14]

However, by the mid-1890s, the Kamba and Kikuyu were retaliating
with spear and knobkerrie, giving the Maasai a taste of the punishment
they had formerly meted out. It was this weakened state of the Maasai
which enabled Hall to exercise control over them. He allowed them at
times some limited raidings, as a fillip to their morale, and as a check on
Kikuyu pretensions. He absolved them from the death of the trader,
Andrew Dick, in 1895, an unexpected act of magnanimity which seems
genuinely to have impressed the Maasai. In Maasai weakness lay
European opportunity, and Crauford, acting Commissioner at
Mombasa, recommended encouragement of their inter-feuding to the
point of their own self-destruction. Captains Smith and Sclater and John
Ainsworth had small regret for Maasai decline.

In nearly every instance the Maasai is the aggressor, their hand is
as a rule against every man ... they are the Ishmaelites of East
Africa ... drones to whom the great degradation was for a warrior
to till the soil, and apparently the women, while they live with the
Elmoran, will not work either.[15]

In the face of this decline, the Kikuyu ventured forth from their forest
retreats and commenced cultivation on its fringes, but they too were
soon struck down by smallpox and famine. Such were their losses, that
Dr Boedeker, in the Fort Smith area in 1896, estimated that 70 per cent
of the Kikuyu were wiped out within the year. The limit of their advance
is marked by the present railway line, between points Athi River and
Limuru, scarcely reaching the outskirts of present-day Nairobi. In
southern Kiambu, they were concentrated in great numbers and carried

on intensive cultivation, and here the Kikuyu suffered grievously from disease and famine, as was testified by early Europeans passing through this district.[16] The railway line near Limuru was said to be 'a mass of corpses'. The effect of this onslaught on the Kikuyu was still evident in the numerous human skulls lying about in southern Kiambu in the early twentieth century. Any advance that the Kikuyu might make as the Maasai were weakened or were restrained by the white men, was soon followed by a hasty withdrawal in the face of disease, famine and Maasai resurgence. In 1896 the Kikuyu temporarily occupied the present site of Nairobi township, but beat a speedy retreat in the face of Maasai advance and reoccupation. These middle years of the 1890s were a turbulent time for both Kikuyu and Maasai in this area, and of this we have few recollections, apart from those of travellers passing through on the way to Uganda:

> If a traveller came along just after a Maasai raid he found the country deserted which perhaps 9 or 12 months later would be under resumed cultivation.[17]

It was in this state of mutual enfeeblement, of Maasai and Kikuyu, that the first European settlers arrived. They found immense areas of unoccupied land, buffer states between hostile tribes, or inferior land – the result of overgrazing and overcultivation, and land from which the Maasai had recently driven its occupants. Although the IBEAC evinced interest in encouraging European settlement, the Company was too much absorbed in securing its position in Uganda and with its financial problems, and had too short a life-span to give sufficient attention to European settlement. In July 1893 the Foreign Office had approached the Company in the matter of 100 to 500 Boer families from Natal who wished to take up land in East Africa, and were ready to send out an advance guard to seek a suitable area in which to settle. The scheme had the backing of the Governor of Natal, and the blessing of Cecil Rhodes, who considered the Boers 'a remarkable people ... the best settlers you can have as they require little or no assistance'. The IBEAC by this date, however, was too deeply involved in plans for its withdrawal from East Africa, and it failed to follow up the project. A rare opportunity was thus lost, of gaining a large group of hardy settlers who would have given the territory a much needed boost at an early stage in its development.

There was only a trickle of settlers in the next few years: 19 Europeans at Machakos by the spring of 1896, including Mr and Mrs J. Watt and their five children (Watt had taken up residence at Machakos in early 1894, and combined fruit-farming with missionary work). In 1894 Dr H.A. Boedeker had obtained his building plot at Fort Smith, and shortly after acquired 66½ acres at that place, paying the Kikuyu chief, Wangeni, six goats and six cows. In 1896 he obtained further acreage from Kinanjui, for '5 cows, 3 bales of Amerikani, four 60 lb. loads of beads, and 4 loads of brass wire'. Boedeker claimed that he was offered the land free when the Kikuyu found out that he was a doctor, but Hall stepped in and would permit only regular purchase.

In the autumn of 1896 David Wallace, Surgeon, previously in practice in Bow, London, accompanied by a farm assistant and blacksmith, and Mr and Mrs J. McQueen, joined Boedeker at Fort Smith. McQueen was later credited with having built the first European house in Nairobi, in 1898. On 1 December 1896 the first European child, Francis George Kikuyu Wallace, was born at Kikuyu station (Fort Smith). Up-country travellers noted with surprise fresh-faced European children and signs of a familiar civilization at remote posts, midst the Kikuyu and Kamba. The trading firm of Smith, Mackenzie and Company acquired the site of its store at Fort Smith in 1892, under original title-deed recorded at Mombasa, for a purchase price of a bale of cotton cloth, five oxen and a quantity of beads. It also obtained, after the IBEAC had introduced land regulations in July 1894, a lease of 1200 acres at Ukambasi (between Machakos and Kikuyu), and then an additional 10,000 acres there, in May 1897. In the same year, the Company formed the 'Kikuyu Coffee Syndicate' (in partnership with Major G.E. Smith, Captain Sclater and Mr G.W. Lewis) to develop the 143 acre 'Mirimbi Coffee Plantation', near Nairobi; the latter acreage was acquired for four head of cattle.[18] Sixty acres were acquired from Kinanjui by Mr J.R. Watcham at Fort Smith in 1899. Watcham was still farming the site in 1932. A 90-acre site, 'Verbi's Mount', in the Teita ills, was acquired by the Church Missionary Society, in the same year, and in 1898 the flamboyant John Boyes, self-styled 'King of the Kikuyu', asserted that at a 'peace-meeting of warring Kikuyu tribes', he was given the Mountain (Kenya) and later 'sealed the gift with a present of sheep to the Wanderobo' (the original occupiers, pre-dating the Kikuyu). A site at Muthaiga was acquired by Mr Sandbach Baker in 1901, and the Kiambu mission site was acquired by Father Bernard in the same year. Dr A.E. Atkinson had taken up land five miles from Nairobi, and was upgrading his stock with an imported Berkshire boar, and a Shorthorn bull, a present from Lord Delamere's estate, Vale Royal. J. and W. Patterson were growing tobacco and coffee at Dagoretti, as also were W. Macallister at Ngong and G. Caine at Limuru; this about rounded out the list, In all, possibly a dozen European settlers were cultivating land on the edge of Kikuyu by the turn of the century.

Land transactions between European and native were peaceful during these few first years. The African had no idea of the concept of land ownership in the European sense, although willing to dispose of 'occupation' rights. Lugard in 1891 wrote that personal acquisition of land 'was unknown among the savage tribes of Africa, where tenure is merely tribal'. Ainsworth acknowledged that

> the Kikuyu had no ideas on the subject of buying and selling land, all they understood was the receiving compensation for any disturbance, and like all other tribes in the country they were only concerned in land individually occupied.[10]

Buying and selling, in the African mind, pertained to something tangible and transportable: personal belongings, wife, beast, or produce. In Kikuyu society the concept of rights of occupation over land held collectively by the important social group, the *mbari*, an extended family or lineage connection (what might be termed a clan, tracing common descent from a known male ancestor), recognized a distinct form of usufruct over a defined portion of land – the *githaka*, with each individual enjoying use of a particular portion of it, and the produce from it. There were hundreds of these small clans, each with its *githaka*, occupying a ridge or two, and loosely ruled by a council of elders, of whom the senior was a petty chief of limited authority which rested mainly on his personality. There was no hereditary chieftainship, no paramount chiefs, no internal system of taxation, nor rudimentary civil service. Here was the ideal polity extolled by philosophers of old. Persons from outside the *mbari* might be allowed to cultivate portions of the *githaka*, in return for gifts to the elders. These outside tenants were termed *ahoi*, and it is most likely that the first Europeans who settled among the Kikuyu were thought of by the latter as such *ahoi*, temporary tenants.

Absolute ownership of land was unknown among the Kikuyu. One had the right to clear and occupy it for the purpose of cultivation. There was, however, no right to 'own land'. Thus the plaintive cry of the Kikuyu in a memorandum submitted to a Parliamentary Commission of 1924, that

When the Whitemen first came, we did not understand that we
were to be deprived of any of our land, nor that they had come to
stay.[20]

The British administration at the time seemed unaware that any such
system of native land occupation as the *githaka* existed, and condoned
purchase of land from native occupiers, in the European sense of
freehold.

The IBEAC in its lifetime made 97 treaties with native chiefs in East
Africa; they involved no loss of rights over land in tribal occupation, nor,
indeed, was there specific mention in them as to disposition of land.
During its short existence, the Company discouraged land speculators.
Ainsworth, in evidence before the Carter Commission in the early 1930s,
and seemingly forgetting Eiyeki's opposition to acquisition of land at
Fort Smith, asserted that the land upon which Dagoretti and Fort Smith
stations were built had been acquired by the Company in fair and
peaceful purchase from native occupants. In April 1891 Sir Francis de
Winton, the Company's administrator, forbade 'all dealings in land
between Europeans of whatever nationality and natives', unless recorded
with the Company. The 'Freeland' episode, to which reference has
already been made, hurried the Company into publishing land
regulations on 4 July 1894. Under these provision was made for various
types of leases: small 'country lots' for 21 years and at no fixed rent;
grazing leases of up to 20,000 acres at $\frac{1}{2}d$. per acre per annum; and
agricultural land up to 2000 acres at $\frac{1}{2}d$. per acre for the first five years
but increasing thereafter. In both cases leases were for 21 years.
Homesteads of 100 acres could be had at rent of $2d$. per acre for the first
five years, with occupation compulsory, and thence, if $2\frac{1}{2}d$. per acre had
been spent on permanent improvements, fee simple would be granted.

The Company's land rules had scarcely been introduced before the
Company itself was negotiating its withdrawal from East Africa. The
announcement on 13 June 1895 that HMG was taking over the
administration of the region between the coast and Uganda was
accompanied by a pronouncement that government intended to build a
railway to the lake. The latter announcement made an early decision on
land policy vital. In March 1896 government gave notice that land
regulations were being considered, and in the mean time the land rules
of the IBEAC would remain in force. On 27 May 1896 notice was given
that the Land Acquisition Act (1894) of India would be brought into
force for land required for the railway; and on 12 June 1897 Hardinge

published rates of compensation for such; a similar announcement was made in Uganda on 23 June 1897. The value of such land would be calculated by the Collector, with little difficulty it would seem with the native peoples, either in acquiring land for the railway, or for government roads.

In the interval between the demise of the IBEAC and the introduction of new land regulations by HMG, private land transactions took place, some of which have already been referred to. The price paid for 100 acres in these transactions, 'seventy goats or their equivalent in cloth, wire and beads', was less than the current market value of a wife or concubine: however, in the native mind only the rights of occupation had been sold. The European purchasers, and F.G. Hall who registered these transactions – such as Boedeker's purchase from Wangeni – were under the impression that freehold had been acquired. News of these early private dealings in land between Europeans and natives brought sharp instructions from London that such were not permitted: all land transactions must be arranged through HM's Commissioner or his representative. It would seem that at the time of these early transactions in land, the Africans believed that Europeans were merely temporary occupiers who would ultimately move on, like the Swahili caravans which came and went, and the Company and its agents – now vanished from the scene. The idea that land itself was an article of commerce, of value in barter transactions, quickly caught on: one Kikuyu at Fort Smith put in a claim for all the land between there and Nairobi, a claim, however, which received no recognition from the administration. The drafting of land laws was meanwhile proceeding. The 'homestead system' of Canada was considered, but rejected as 'wholly out of place in East Africa'. The idea of 21-year leases was taken from Gambia. A suggestion by the Crown Agents for the appointment of a Land Commission similar to that set up in Bechuanaland was unfortunately not taken up. It would have revealed the deep complexity of the land question, the gulf between European and African thinking in the matter; time only would reveal this. The Foreign Office, too, was inexperienced in dealing with problems of landholding in a raw and primitive country. However, a few basic principles began to emerge. There would be no direct land dealing between native and would-be settler; 'appropriation of land must be under direct control of the Administration which was to guard the interests of the natives'; a distinction was made between 'unoccupied' and 'occupied' land; the Crown would have rights of disposal of 'occupation' rights.

As these deliberations proceeded Hardinge was increasingly restive, and pressed for early publication of land rules: 'We ought to have some rules, the simpler the better, which we invoke in reply to applications'. Hardinge's thinking in terms of land for Europeans was much more generous than, for example, that of Hall who was imbued with a protective instinct towards the Africans. Hardinge would grant leases for 999 years, or in perpetuity, and in the case of agricultural land would require that only one-quarter of such land be planted within the first five years. These leases would be acquired on payment, in advance, of 20 years' rent, calculated at the low figure of 1 pice (one farthing) per acre per year; this would mean the grant of unoccupied land (Hardinge placed no limit on its size) for a term of 999 years for the cash down payment of 5d. an acre. This was indeed generous! Hardinge, however, argued that only a generous land policy would attract good settlers to East Africa at a time when the great open spaces of Canada and Australia were available to them. East Africa was a primitive and largely uninhabited area with large tracts of good agricultural land, and this invited a 'broad acres' policy. Restraint in the granting of land would retard European settlement. Hardinge's views however were not incorporated in the somewhat hasty land policy drawn up by the Foreign Office and published as land regulations on 17 January 1897.

These land regulations set aside Hardinge's suggestion of 999 years' leases. Instead the Commissioner was empowered to grant leases, under certificate of occupancy only and with no limit on size, for a term not exceeding 21 years, but renewable for a further 21 years if certain conditions of occupancy and improvement were fulfilled. At least one-quarter of the land must be planted within the first five years, in 'coffee, cocoa, cotton, indigo, rubber', or other plants approved by the commissioner; there were also conditions as to rent, residence, cultivation and other pertinent matters. Certificate of occupancy would not be granted in respect of any land which was lawfully held by a native or non-native under a documentary title which Her Majesty's Commissioner was prepared to recognize. Government reaffirmed that under native law and custom only the right of occupancy could be sold.

In March 1897 private land dealings between natives and non-natives were again denounced, and government issued notices on 26 April and 31 August 1897 which warned of 'certain evil disposed persons' who had been acquiring land from natives at inadequate prices, and laying claims to waste lands in the coastal strip. Such claims must be submitted immediately to the administrative officer in charge of the district concerned.

The land regulations of January 1897 brought only a trickle of enquiries from would-be settlers. Hardinge continued to press for more liberal terms. His persuasive prose was not without effect. In October 1897 government announced that new land regulations were being drafted. They were promulgated on 29 December 1897, and under them the period of leases was extended from 21 to 99 years, and the commissioner was empowered to determine any special additional conditions under which certificate of occupancy might be granted to a European settler. Alienation of land that would be injurious to native interests was prohibited. Clause 7 of the regulations, however, left to the Commissioner the interpretation as to whether such alienation was injurious or not.

> A certificate will not be granted in respect of any land which at the time of the commencement of these regulations is cultivated or regularly used by any native or native tribe, but may be granted if the Commissioner, after such inquiry as he may think fit, is satisfied that such land is no longer so cultivated or regularly used, and that the grant of a certificate would not be prejudicial to native interests.

Under the regulations of December 1897, the interpretation was that freehold remained the property of the commonwealth, of which government, as the protecting power, was the guardian. Hardinge specifically referred to this in late December 1899:

> when a native parts with any land we must not treat the matter as a sale of freehold rights, but more as a sale of occupier's rights, freehold rights remaining the property of the commonwealth.[21]

It was an easy transition from this concept to the next, namely, that the protectorate government, as guardian of the commonwealth, could declare what, was 'occupied' and what was 'unoccupied' land:

> the Collector would always be within his rights to call upon any native occupier to either cultivate land which has been allowed to run out of cultivation beyond reasonable time for such land to remain fallow, or to have the same declared Crown Lands.[22]

This shifting emphasis as to where ultimate control of land lay did not mean however, at least not yet, that land-grabbing by Europeans on a large scale would be tolerated. Ainsworth, in July 1899, stated: 'One thing we desire to avoid is Europeans and Indians taking up land, and the purchasing of land, and holding the same as speculation.' Smith, Mackenzie and Company's application for 50,000 acres was turned down because the Company could give no assurance that it could cultivate more than 500 acres.

The extension of leases to 99 years under the Land Regulations of December 1897 did not have the anticipated result. Settlers sought either a perpetual lease or freehold tenure. If a lease, they wanted the right to sell it after five years. They wanted to establish a patrimony. Landholding on a temporal basis, even if for 99 years, had little appeal for them. Something more was needed to make the land rules attractive. By the summer of 1899 the railway had reached Nairobi and would soon be creeping through the Rift Valley, where land applications were expected. They were not forthcoming. The Foreign Office at the end of 1899 turned again to the question of a land policy for East Africa, and consulted the Law Officers in the matter.

Their opinion, given in February 1900, was that HMG might declare waste or unoccupied lands to be Crown Lands and could make grants of these to individuals, in fee simple (freehold) or for any term. This decision of the Law Officers gave the go-ahead for a clear-cut land policy. In Uganda (including the Eastern Province) it was given effect under a Government Notice of 9 April 1900, whereby HMG acquired the sole right of disposal over waste and uncultivated land in that protectorate, and non-natives were forbidden to acquire land without consent of HMG's representative. By Notice of 10 May 1900 government appropriated a one-mile-wide zone on either side of the railway line, 110 miles of which ran through Uganda territory at this date. The drafting of land rules for the East Africa Protectorate under this new interpretation was a long drawn-out process. It was not until August 1901 that the East Africa (Lands) Order-In-Council was promulgated. Under it Crown Lands were defined as

all public lands within the East Africa Protectorate which for the time being are subject to the control of Her Majesty by virtue of any Treaty, Convention, or Agreement, or of His Majesty's Protectorate, and all lands which have been or may hereafter be acquired by His Majesty under 'The Lands Acquisition Act, 1894'.

The defining of public land was left to the commissioner, who was also empowered to sell or lease Crown Land 'on such terms and conditions as he may think fit, subject to any directions of the Secretary of State'.

The introduction of this legislation had not kept pace with the advance of the railway to the lake. Railhead was at Lake Nakuru by October 1900. As yet there was no great rush to take up land. Sir Clement Hill, on his way to Uganda in October 1900, and writing from Lake Nakuru, noted that 'the ordinary Britain may be proud of his countrymen's work on the Uganda Railway'; however, he made no mention of European settlers. Nor was there any movement of European settlers to the country lying between Nairobi and Mount Kenya. This attractive region, the former goal of the Freelanders in 1894, had been favourably commented on by early travellers: Chanler, Mackinder and Dr Kolb. Portal had recommended the establishment of a post in this district. And Sir Charles Eliot, who succeeded Hardinge as commissioner in October 1900, wished to direct settlement here – away from the railway line:

> It is desirable to open up the country at some distance from the railway, which otherwise is likely to become a sort of iron Nile, concentrating cultivation and civilization on its banks, and leaving the rest of the country a desert.[23]

Thus Fort Hall, in the southern foothills of Mt Kenya, was established in 1901 and connected with the railway by a cart road. This was expected to give security for settlers in this region. It had a dependable rainfall and labour was available. Plans for stock-raising in this district were quickly under way; Hardinge had already arranged to import bulls from India for breeding purposes. All that was awaited was a set of attractive land rules. Until these appeared at the end of 1902 few white settlers established themselves in the Fort Hall area. They were also deterred by the depredations of Kikuyu marauders. It was not until punitive operations against the Kikuyu were undertaken in the period 1902–4 that white settlement in the Fort Hall and Nyeri districts took place.

A famine in the Machakos area in 1899-1900 retarded white settlement there. Ainsworth was too busy setting up famine camps and supplying food to stricken natives to attend to European settlement. Some would-be settlers were already tiring of waiting for new land rules, finding the present terms singularly unattractive. Arthur Newmann dropped his application for ten square miles in the Naivasha area for a large stock-breeding ranch including domestication of zebra and elephant, when he found he could only get leasehold, despite Jackson's offer of it rent free for the first five years and a penny an acre for the remainder of the lease period.[24] A party of South African settlers who wished to take up land in the Naivasha area for ostrich farming quickly lost interest when informed that leasehold only was available.

Sir Charles Eliot, on taking over from Hardinge as commissioner in October 1900, gave a powerful impulse to white settlement. In writing to Lansdowne in April 1902, pressing the cause of white settlement, he stated:

> The highlands – that is Machakos and the Athi Plains, the neighbourhood of Nairobi, Kikuyu, the Rift Valley, the Mau and Nandi Escarpments – I believe to be one of the healthiest districts for Europeans in the world, equal to the English climate at its best, and far superior to it on an average.[25]

Eliot thought the best way of making the Uganda Railway pay would be by developing the highland area with its rich agricultural potential. The natives had left it undeveloped, and under the theory of 'beneficial occupation' – that land should in the long run go to the man who can turn it to the greatest productivity – as against what Eliot termed the 'blank, amorphous barbarism' of the natives, white settlement should be fostered.

In his writings and depatches, Eliot stressed the suitability of the highlands for European settlement, and claimed that the encouragement of the latter was the main priority of the British administration. The native races had failed abysmally to improve their environment. Writers such as W.M. Ross, who could refer to the Maasai as 'little more than cattle-lifters', and likened them to those 'of the Highlands of Scotland in earlier years', were indulging in romantic sentiment and excessive tolerance. For Eliot, Maasaidom was a 'bloody, beastly system founded on raiding and immorality … We are not destroying any old or interesting system, but simply introducing order into blank, uninteresting, brutal barbarism … the Maasai and many other tribes must go under. It is a prospect which I view with equanimity … white interests must be paramount.'

For Eliot an attractive land policy was vital and urgent if settlers were to be gained. By April 1902 the vast area of upland country suitable for European settlement, and formerly comprised in Uganda's 'Eastern

Province', was now part of the East Africa Protectorate, and it was believed it would attract enquiries for land from England and South Africa. However, Eliot affirmed that only a policy of granting freehold land, as in New Zealand, Australia and Canada, would bring them in. In the spring of 1902, under the authority of the August 1901 Orders in Council, Eliot and officials, especially Ainsworth, set out to produce the ideal land ordinance. In their deliberations they were fortified by the report of Mr R.N. Lyne, Director of Agriculture, Zanzibar, an advocate of European settlement and large holdings, who gave a most generous estimate as to the area of land suitable for such. After much cogitation, and drawing on bits and pieces from land laws elsewhere, Canadian land laws, and even a ruling in Cyprus regarding the raising of goats, a hybrid draft began to emerge. Even before it finally appeared as the Crown Lands Ordinance of 1902, a signal of the generous terms in the offering was indicated in a Land Notice of 1 August 1902, whereby it was announced that agricultural and pastoral land of average quality, in blocks of up to 1000 acres, might be acquired freehold for 2 rupees (2s. 8d.) per acre, or on lease of 99 years at 15 rupees (£1) per 100 acres, per annum. Zebra and ostrich farming land was leased at lower rates according to locality. Land within the one-mile-wide railway zone might be leased and so also land near coast towns and on Mombasa Island.

The Land Notice was quickly followed up by the Crown Lands Ordinance of 1902, which was approved by Lansdowne on 20 August 1902, and promulgated in East Africa on 23 August 1902. The Ordinance repeated the 1901 Order in Council's definition as to Crown Land: it must be unoccupied for 12 months before declaring it as such, but the commissioner was given wide and discretionary powers in making rules for leasing and granting it, but not to sell or lease any land in occupation by natives. Occupation was not defined, but left to the interpretation of the local government. Land containing areas under native occupation could be leased, but such areas were deemed excluded from the lease. This protection however terminated when such occupation ceased, the area then passing to the lessee. Disputes over such occupied land were to be dealt with by the Collector of the District, with appeal to the sub-Commissioner of the Province.

Eliot was now on leave, and Frederick Jackson, acting Commissioner, turned his mind to the matter of a homestead system for settlers, which would supplement the Land Rules of 1 August, for the latter were designed for settlers with some capital. The rules which Jackson, who was no enthusiast for European settlement, introduced for homesteads on 1 November 1902, were so stringent in their clauses as to development and protection of native and forest rights, that they drew vigorous protests from intending settlers. The latter distrusted officials because they saw them as having no real stake in the country: they were employed by the Foreign (or Colonial) Office, and might be transferred elsewhere at any time. Settlers, on the other hand, had gone out to Kenya for good and had developed the land, and considered it their own 'for once and for all'.

Eliot, on his return from leave, lost no time in dismissing Jackson's rules (although retaining those of 1 August 1902), and, despite a cautionary reminder from Lansdowne as to the need for care in making excessive land grants, introduced 'Rules for the Purchase of land under the Crown Lands Ordinance of 1902', dated 21 December 1902, and promulgated on 1 January 1903.

These land rules provided for the purchase of agricultural land, freehold, up to 1000 acres (above this Foreign Office approval was required) at the rate of RS 2 (2s.8d.) per acre. The railway zone was breached, except for

> One hundred feet on either side of the Uganda Railway line and such area round any station as may be marked off by the Railway authorities.[26]

The rules provided for purchase of homesteads of 160 acres at 2 annas (2d.) per acre, with purchase money payable at end of three years, or spread over 16 years from time of purchase, and there was right of pre-emption during the first three years of a further 480 acres (not 320 as Jackson had stipulated), provided certain conditions as to cultivation and occupancy had been fulfilled as regards the original purchase. Under the rules of the Notice of 1 August 1902, which still prevailed, leases were not to exceed 99 years, with no specification as to maximum area, and grazing land could be rented for as low as 12 rupees (16s.) per 100 acres, if suitable only for zebra or ostrich farming. Leases could not be reassigned without consent of the commissioner.

The new land rules were introduced at the time Joseph Chamberlain, Colonial Secretary, visited the protectorate, travelling up the Uganda Railway as far as Fort Ternan, in December 1902. Like Eliot, Chamberlain favoured doing 'all in our power to draw settlers and to render the country attractive and inviting'. Its future lay in wheat and wool, and he would have 'grain and other agricultural products grown at every Railway and Government station', to show passing travellers what the country could produce. He would sell to first comers plots of land in the zone adjoining the railway. Mr R.B. Buckley, of the Indian Irrigation Department, visiting the protectorate at the time, also favoured European settlement, and recommended the establishment of model agricultural farms (as the Germans had done in the neighbouring territory), testing of different crops, irrigation and trial borings for water.

These were cogent views in support of Eliot. In April 1903 he could report that the quadrangle between Nairobi, Kiambu, Kikuyu and Limuru, in the vicinity of the railway, was completely surveyed, and taken up by some 100 Europeans. In the same month a Survey and Land Office was opened at Nairobi. The time was ripe according to Eliot to disperse settlers over a wider stretch of territory. Under a Notice of 14 May 1903, following up his suggestion to Lansdowne of 5 January 1903, Eliot offered free grants of unoccupied land up to 640 acres, outside the railway zone, between Miles 14 to 274 (Mazeras to Machakos Road), and between Miles 473 and 534 (Elburgon and Fort Ternan). In these free grant areas, 640 acres would be let for experiments in grazing, at nominal rent for the first ten years. It was this offer of free land which especially appealed to Lord Delamere as the bait which would attract settlers to East Africa. Writing to a friend, J.P. Jackson, on 23 June 1903, Delamere stated

> These 640 acre plots are free but there are survey fees amounting to £1 a hundred acres or thereabouts. I have been to New Zealand and Australia and I never saw as good land to be bought for one-tenth or one-twentieth of the sum. New Zealanders here now say that the same class of land in New Zealand would be worth £10 an acre.
>
> P.S. If any Cheshire or Lancashire man brings me a letter from you I will see he gets a good 640 acres free.[27]

Under Notice of 15 July 1903 Eliot allowed more generous leases of pastoral land, up to 10,000 acres (in Eliot's view 'a holding of moderate size'), at $\frac{1}{2}d.$ per acre, and if conditions for leasing were fulfilled, 'nothing shall prevent the lessee of one area taking up a second area, nor prevent the Commissioner granting larger areas on special conditions'.

With permission from Lansdowne, on 27 May 1903, to offer up to one-quarter of the land in the railway zone for sale, Eliot issued a Notice of 27 July 1903, whereby plots of land of up to 160 acres could be sold within 100 feet of the central line and within one mile of any railway station, with the purchaser having the option of a 99 years' lease on an additional 480 acres adjoining the original plot. The price varied from 1s. 4d. per acre, for land between Miles 16 to 276, and Miles 475 to 536, and 8s. per acre for the coveted stretch between Nairobi and Kikuyu. In August 1903 Eliot pressed for more discretion in selling land: 1000 acres was too low a figure – 'three or four persons' with a few thousand pounds had applied for 2000 to 5000 acres of agricultural land, and when it was not forthcoming went on their way. Eliot went on to say

> The British settler – least the variety which turns up here – has two marked peculiarities or prejudices – Firstly, he wants freeholds and not leases; it is no use trying to persuade him that a 99 years' lease is practically a freehold – he talks about his great-grandchildren and goes away. Secondly, he dislikes official formalities and delays ... and a good salesman should humour his customers.[28]

Eliot proposed that the limit for sale of agricultural land be raised to 5000 acres, and for grazing land up to 32,000 acres (50 square miles) to meet the enormous land appetite of colonists – 'particularly South Africans, who mostly ask for 40,000 acres', for there was ample land to meet this hunger:

> I calculate that we have something like 4,000,000 acre of grazing ground, excluding the Athi Plains, Rift Valley, Settima, and all the districts where settlement is at present contemplated.[29]

That a more generous land policy was producing the desired effect was reflected in Lord Delamere's letter to J.P. Jackson, in England, on 2 September 1903.

> All the men worth their salt at present in the country are writing home to their relations and friends to join them. There are four settlers within short distance of Nairobi who have lately got out their brothers ... A man called Sandbach Baker who was formerly a Manchester cotton merchant and went broke gambling on cotton is one of the dairy farmers ... Coffee promises a certain high

return ... It grows *extraordinarily* well ... and for good clean coffee there is an unlimited market in London. Grazing land, which is said by New Zealanders and others to be first class, can be hired on a 99 years' lease (which will almost certainly be convertible some day into freehold) up to 10,000 acres at a ha'penny an acre per annum ... A South African who has much experience was here the other day and said he wouldn't take 20 acres in South Africa for one here.[30]

Jackson awakened much interest among the people of Cheshire and Lancashire as to settlement in East Africa. The visit to South Africa in August 1903 of Mr A. Marsden, Collector of Customs at Mombasa, for the purpose of stirring up interest there in settlement in East Africa, elicited many enquiries. Before the year was out South Africans were coming to East Africa; and the Afrikaners, such as Loijis, Erasmus, Botha, Joubert, Meyer, Prinsloo and Klopper, whom Theodore Roosevelt met, and much admired, when he visited East Africa in 1908, were inspired to come there, either directly or indirectly by Marsden's visit. For Roosevelt, these Afrikaners had the three prime requisites of any race: 'they worked hard, they could fight hard at need, and they had plenty of children.'

With such powerful advocates as Delamere and Marsden, the free 640-acre plots were soon taken up. A suggestion made at the time, that a tax be levied on land transfers as in Northern Rhodesia, was set aside. It would have dampened much needed enthusiasm for land settlement in East Africa. A number of persons who acquired large holdings there from 1903 onwards had already visited the territory prior to this, for the sake of adventure or on a 'sporting tour'. Lord Delamere's expedition, which had come down from Somaliland in 1898, acquired £14,000 worth of ivory, and its medical officer (Dr Atkinson) remained behind, and had been 'steadily shooting elephants ever since'. Delamere's breath-taking view of the Laikipia plateau, on emerging from the Baringo depression in early 1898, came at a time when it was virtually unoccupied, because of the near annihilation of the Maasai, owing to their interfeuding, and the wiping out of their cattle by rinderpest. Delamere's return to the coast, by way of Kikuyu and Wakamba country, led him through rich and fertile country, but his heart remained with Laikipia, and he was back there in early 1900 reassessing it. When he finally returned to East Africa, in early 1903, his first application was for land on Laikipia. When this was refused on the grounds of the remoteness of Laikipia from the railway and administrative centres, he applied for 100,000 acres between the Aberdares and Naivasha. This also was turned down, for it might cause hardship to the Maasai. Delamere finally settled for 100,000 acres, on a 99 years' lease, on the western side of the Rift Valley, between Njoro and the Molo River. His 'Equator Ranch', on the lower slopes of the Mau escarpment, backing on to its deep forests which rise to over 10,000 feet, and looking out over wide game-dotted plains to the Aberdares to the east, was a choice site. There is a note of quiet satisfaction in Delameres's account of its acquisition:

> I have got my 100,000 acres of land but not at the place originally intended, but I think at a better, though a little further from the coast. I have been unable to get freehold but have got a 99 years' lease at $\frac{1}{2}d$. an acre per annum.[31]

Was it mere coincidence that this was the site eulogized by Eliot, in writing to Lansdowne, in April 1902

> Njoro, where the first low slopes of the Mau Escarpment begin to rise from the plain. This district is one of the most favoured in East Africa. In its general features it may be roughly compared to the country round Nairobi and the eastern slopes of the Kikuyu Hills, but is in every respect superior. The climate is more bracing, water more plentiful, and the soil richer and deeper. As in many other parts of this Protectorate, the scenery is strikingly English: the green knolls and woods would be an ornament to any park in the United Kingdom.[32]

A Scottish shepherd and pure-bred stock were brought out from the United Kingdom. However, stock-raising proved a disappointment, and Delamere turned to wheat. Soon he was back to stock-raising. Many trials and keen losses were experienced, before the solution to successful farming in East Africa was found. Meanwhile, the mantle of leader of the settlers had descended on Delamere: he became President of the 'Farmers and Planters Association', with 23 members and formed in January 1903. Theodore Roosevelt, who spent the first ten days of December 1909 at Njoro, on the edge of the Mau escarpment, with Lord Delamere, remarked on the 'beautiful farming country', and that Lord Delamere was a practical and successful farmer. Delamere's home and library were expressive of civilized living.

Lord Delamere set a pattern soon followed by others. His brothers-in-law, Galbraith and Berkeley Cole, sons of the Earl of Enniskillen, Captain Grogan and Lord Cranworth, were drawn to East Africa either as a result of passing through on a shooting trip, or being persuaded to take up land by friends already settled there. The establishment in February 1903 of a new station, Nyeri, in the Kenya Province, at the foot of Nyeri Hill, a well-known landmark some 20 miles north-east of Mount Kinangop, opened up a district well supplied with water and ideal for growing vegetables. The strong military position of the station ensured protection for settlers, who now began to move into this area. The casual manner in which land could be acquired in the protectorate at this time is evident in the statement of Captain Cowie before the Carter Commission many years later. Cowie, then on leave from the army, stated that he

> liked the country so much that I interested myself in the land straight away ... I selected 10,000 acres – two farms of 5,000 acres each ... I paid my survey fees and went away.[33]

Cowie returned two years later to take up his land. Major Grogan, who had trekked up to East Africa from the Cape in the late 1890s and had gone on to Cairo, later returned to settle in Ukamba Province. He stated before the Carter Commission in 1932 that

> About 1906 or 1907, I came down to this part with my wife to shoot. Wandered for a month – no natives anywhere. The Kapiti Plains were acquired by me in exchange for some land that the Government wanted to extend Kaimosi Reserve between the Marasurua and Sageri Rivers. I gave back 10,000 acres that I had there and took up this land on the Kapiti plains in exchange. I have known Africa since 1896.[34]

For these gentlemen the East African highlands were singularly inviting, not only for their physical and climate attractions but also for the abundant labour there. Labour was available at a wage as low as 2d. per day, with the worker providing his own food. Here one could live midst broad acres, in a climate and setting as near ideal as could be imagined. Winston Churchill, journeying through East Africa in 1907, confessed that he too, felt the appeal:

> For the first time in my life, I have learned what the sensations of land-hunger is like ... the desire to peg out one of these fair and wide estates, with all the rewards they offer to industry and inventiveness in the open air ... thousands of fertile acres, with mountains and river and shady trees, acquired for little or nothing.[35]

Here could be reproduced a way of life fast vanishing in England.

> This country is different from other countries, like Australia and Canada, where every man does his own work. Out here everyone depends upon the African for manual work. The European supervises only.[36]

All was not rosy, however, for the first white settlers in the East African highlands. The rinderpest peril, which had wiped out native stock in the 1890s, did much to dissuade settlers against going into stock-raising. Their first attempts, especially those with smaller holdings near Kikuyu and Machakos, were with agriculture, such as dairy farming (Eliot budgeted £120 to encourage it); market gardening – Eliot claimed to have seen brussel sprouts six feet tall, growing near Machakos; and fruit-growing. Mr C.E. Smith, who came out in 1897 and acquired 2000 acres, went into fruit-growing, and by 1908 was producing apples, peaches and plums at Machakos, finding a ready market for these in Nairobi.

The great potential of the highlands for producing the finest quality coffee, in areas between 4500 and 6000 feet in altitude, was not generally realized, although coffee-growing was introduced at St Austin's Mission near Nairobi, in 1900. The possibilities of tea-growing in the Kericho district were only realized at a later date, and similarly the silk industry, starting with the mulberry tree imported from Japan in 1903 and with silk worm eggs from France, made feeble steps. Market gardening, especially potato-growing, was the most promising venture in the first years. Along the whole East African coast from Aden in the north to Durban in the south, there were few areas comparable to the East African highlands for producing such a profitable crop. Mr R.N. Lyne, in his memorandum on the agricultural prospects of the highlands, strongly advocated the growing of potatoes, two crops of which could be obtained in a year. Hitherto, potatoes were usually imported from Portugal, and were unpalatable on arrival; now they were obtainable from the Machakos and Dagoretti districts. Potatoes had become the main export by the turn of the century, finding a ready market in South Africa. Between January 1902 and March 1903 over 600 tons of potatoes were exported there, and in November 1904 five full train-loads of potatoes were carried to the coast for shipment to Johannesburg. Delamere saw potatoes as the ideal crop for the small farmer in East Africa:

> for an agricultural farmer with a small capital, the staple product is potatoes. They grow extremely well here for several years without manure. The crop varies between two to ten tons to the acre. Through freights from Nairobi to the South African ports run to three pounds a ton. Prices there vary from £8.10.0 to £13.10.0 a ton.[37]

Some of the smaller and best-run farms, with emphasis on market gardening or dairy products, were near Nairobi which offered a market for their products. Ngongo Dairy was started by Mr J.T. Oulton in 1902 and consisted of a farm of 2500 acres near Dagoretti. Homestead Farm, of 1000 acres near Nairobi, was owned by Mr Sandbach Baker, who had come out from Cheshire in 1901 on the advice of Eliot, and had gone into the production of dairy products. By 1908 Homestead Farm was one of the 'show places' of British East Africa. Not all farms near Nairobi were on the small scale. Mr H. H. Heatley took over 20,000 acres 14 miles from Nairobi (between the Rewero and Kamiti Rivers) in 1904. This ranch with its fine dairy so impressed Theodore Roosevelt, when he visited there in 1909, and that also of Northrup (later Sir) McMillan's 'Juju Farm', on the edge of the Athi plains, at the junction of the Nairobi and Rewero Rivers, with its fine library and drawing-room and the cool, shaded verandah, that he could not but express confidence in the wide and elevating prospects awaiting them.

The Eastern Province of Uganda, which was transferred to the East Africa Protectorate on 1 April 1902, contained the Nandi and Mau plateaux in its new and small province of Kisumu, and these were the subject of warm praise from both Johnston and Lugard, as eminently suitable for European settlement; however, although now opened up by the Uganda Railway, they did not first attract the eye of white settlers. In the whole of the Lumbwa district, in the best land immediately south of the railway, there were only 16 European farms by 1908. Naivasha Province, part of the former Eastern Province of Uganda, was more attractive to Europeans interested in stock-raising on the grand scale. It comprised the Rift Valley, between the Mau and Elgeyo escarpments on the west, and the highlands of Kipaperi and Settima and Guaso Nyiro on the east, traditional country of the Maasai. By the turn of the century, the Maasai could no longer roam at will. Eliot saw no place for them in the Rift Valley, in their old nomadic state.[38] Within the year negotiations were under way to place the northern Maasai in a reserve on Laikipia; the southern Maasai would stay south of a line drawn from Suswa to Ngong, along the Mbagathi River. A area of five square miles near Naivasha would be reserved for the Maasai circumcision ceremonies, held every eight years. There would be a connecting road between the two parts. Lenana soon settled down near Nairobi, and the northern Maasai congregated near Nyeri station; their turbulent past would soon be only a memory. The Maasai, although accustomed to an almost exclusive diet of meat, milk and blood, were reported to be resorting to government stations to purchase wheat, flour, rice and sugar.

The southern part of Naivasha Province, richly endowed with good soil and rainfall, was ideal for cereal growing and stock-breeding. The pastoral Maasai, despite their recent troubles with rinderpest, had given a lead to the importance of stock-raising in this area. Land nearest the railway was first taken up by Europeans. The two main points of white settlement were Naivasha and Nakuru. North and west of these points, and in the outer parts of the Rift Valley, land was leased principally for grazing. Mr R.B. Wills, who came from India in 1901, concentrated on rearing ostriches and Angora goats at two ranches, Willisdale and Crescent, in the Rift Valley, and seems to have made a satisfactory living despite the belief that the East African ostrich, being of a coarser and larger variety than that in South Africa, was less valuable, and that the Angora goat could not compete with the local variety of African goat. The largest acreages acquired by Europeans tended to be in Naivasha Province. Robert Chamberlain, who arrived from South Africa in 1903, took up a farm of 32,000 acres on the Enderit River, at Elmenteita, and the Honourable G.L.E. Cole, Delamere's brother-in-law, on arriving in East Africa in 1903 took up land on Laikipia. When it was incorporated into a native reserve, he acquired a farm of 25,000 acres on the slopes of Eburru Mountain, near Lake Elmenteita, with another 11,000 acres in Mount Kenya district. His brother, R.B. Cole, prior to arriving from India in 1905 acquired 8000 acres at Njoro, and another 15,000 near Mount Kenya. Mr G. Doering acquired 25,000 acres between Gilgil and Naivasha; and Dr A.E. Atkinson, who arrived in 1900 and started a sawmill near Nairobi, went into partnership with his brother, E.C. Atkinson, in acquiring 20,000 acres near Molo and 10,000 acres near Londiani, and operating the Equatorial Saw Mills near Molo. Lord Hindlip in 1904 took up 27,000 acres in Naivasha, and his partner, W.J.P. Faucus, owned in aggregate over 14,000 acres at widely scattered points, from Mazeras to Londiani. Mr A. Gray and Dr Penny in 1904 acquired 10,000 acres some ten miles from Molo, at an altitude of 8000 feet; four years later they had a prize herd of 280 cattle and 1200 sheep running on their estate. Lord Delamere by 1908 held a lease of 100,000 acres at Camp Njoro, managed by an Australian, Mr J.R. Wood; he also owned Soysambu Estate of 45,000 acres at Lake Elmenteita. By the outbreak of the First World War, the way in which these estates had grown in size, were connected up with others, or divided through family settlements and mortgages, was reminiscent of the old British West Indies Sugar plantations in the early nineteenth century. The process of augmentation, purchases, leases and applications is well set out in returns of Annual Reports for the protectorate, later Colony of Kenya.

Heavy losses and much strain and heartbreak were sustained before success and affluence came, despite what the listed acreages might seem to indicate in the way of wealth and easy living. The trials and disappointments of Lord Delamere in the way of stock-raising and grain-growing have been well chronicled. It was difficult in the first years to persuade the Maasai to co-operate in burning and burying the carcasses of infected beasts, and to move their flocks away from white settler districts; the Wakamba were much more co-operative in this respect. Mr Feltham, at Kui, in a few weeks lost 118 of his prize herd of 330 cattle, built up at great cost and with much care. It was a shrewd move on the part of the administration to impose hut tax in the neighbourhood of white settlements: this quickly persuaded offending herdsmen to decamp with their contaminated flocks. Disappointments and experiments came in quick succession before the desired strains of grain and livestock were obtained. Government might help with advice and the establishment of a livestock experimental farm at Naivasha, but only pragmatic doggedness on the part of the individual settler brought success in the end. There was no escape from dependence on hard physical labour. Fortunately for the white settler this was available in the African population. It might be of an unreliable and erratic nature, but the wage paid for it was pitifully low.

Eliot, academic though he was, did his best to help the settlers. He encouraged experiments in training zebra, along the lines of that pursued by Baron Bronsart in German East Africa; and sent observers there to report on the success of German experiments. A zebra ranch was started on the Morendat River near Naivasha station, under the auspices of R.J. Stordy, Veterinary Officer. By early 1903 over 90 head of zebra were stalled and handled for breaking-in. Many of the zebra, however, died from the effects of internal parasites, and others proved impossible to domesticate. An ostrich farm was started near Naivasha and on the Athi, but, as with the zebra-training schemes, never caught on. It was not in novel ventures such as these that settlers could hope for success, rather in traditional pursuits of stock-raising and grain-growing. The concept of large-scale ranching developed by such persons as Lord Delamere, Lord Cranworth, ex-Indian Army officers, and settlers from South Africa – English 'gentlemen' who thought in terms of at least 10,000 acres – belied Eliot's hopes that 'immigrants of the farmer class with a capital of from £300 to £500 might safely settle in East Africa'. The 'broad acre' complex had set in.

Not all European settlers were affluent. Mr E.G. Holmes, owner of 'Bona Vista' farm of 640 acres, started in 1902 with capital of £50. Two years later he had 50 acres under cultivation, and owned a prize herd of cattle and 100 pigs – 'Berkshire pure-breds'. Mr A. Paice and Mr S. Herd, who settled in Nyeri district in the early twentieth century, faced strenuous conditions and isolation, and with little capital to back them up. Paice, on arrival, worked on a farm for £4 per month, and borrowed £400, the necessary proof of means, before being allocated a farm of 3083 acres. The protectorate however was glorious country in which to live, and with an ideal climate; the exhilarating prospect of attaining the 'lifestyle' of aristocratic neighbours was a spur to high endeavour and determination to overcome all obstacles.

Nairobi, the urban and main centre of this developing white settler community, had few natural advantages to justify its existence. Its origins go back to April 1897 when Mr G. Whitehouse, Chief Engineer of the Uganda Railway, chose it as the headquarters station for the Mombasa–Kikuyu section of the railway because of its wide, flat expanse, suited for railway yards, sidings and shops, and because of the available water supply from Nairobi stream. At the time of the arrival of the IBEAC, there was no thought of a major town springing up at Nairobi. The Company, however, by siting its station first at Dagoretti, and then later at Fort Smith, gave the place much importance, and so also the large concentration of Maasai at nearby Ngongo Bagas, over which the administration kept a watchful eye. In July 1899 the railway headquarters for the whole line was moved from Mombasa to Nairobi, thus ensuring the latter's permanency and development. Its population grew rapidly. Hardinge in December 1899 commented on the large Indian and Goanese community there, and that many Europeans made it their centre. Natives in increasing numbers gravitated to Nairobi, seeking employment as domestic servants, town employees and railway workers. Many also found openings at the turn of the century with the numerous shooting safaris based on Nairobi, when rich Englishmen and Americans were out to 'try their luck' at big game hunting. The most notable of these was ex-President Theodore Roosevelt of the United States. Natives hired for these shooting safaris were well paid, and in intervals between employment laid up at Nairobi, living in comparative ease while waiting for the next safari. One such village of 'safari' porters was that at the site of what was later Lady McMillan's estate, 'Chiromo'; and between here and Nairobi were several others, but they had to be moved out as the town grew. On the ever-widening outskirts of this sprawling frontier town were the huts of Sudanese and Maasai women, who sold firewood, distilled vile vitriolic liquor and carried on prostitution, thus causing the local burghers to speak gravely of the need to raise the 'moral tone' of this aspect of the growing young city.

The transference of the railway headquarters to Nairobi was completed by early 1900. It was now the 'Crewe' of East Africa. In March 1900 the township was surveyed. The population was over 7000 and it was reported that the one-storeyed prison was inadequate. Municipal regulations were introduced and the drainage of the Nairobi marsh was commenced. There was a good deal of resiting of residences on a ridge on the south side of Nairobi because of the mortality among Europeans. A few fine residences, the homes of senior railway and administrative officials, began to appear, a welcome contrast to galvanized roofs and mud-brick dwellings. In 1900 new barracks were built for the East African Rifles. Nairobi began to take on the atmosphere reminiscent of an administrative centre of a large district in British India. There were references to bazaars, cantonments and 'police lines'; talk of sanatoriums, nursing homes and 'cool weather retreats' – the Mau especially was recommended for recuperation from blackwater fever.

Despite Eliot's deprecation of the choice of Nairobi as the site for the railway headquarters and main up-country town (as late as 1901 he was still pointing out the superior advantages of Machakos), it continued to grow. Eliot, in April 1902, referred to it as a collection of tin huts; set without any regard to sanitation on a plain which is periodically flooded – the doctors have unanimously recommended that the town of Nairobi should be moved bodily to the hills, and nothing left on the plain but the railway station.[39]

However, seven years later, Theodore Roosevelt commented:

Nairobi is a very attractive town, and most interesting with its large native quarter and its Indian colony. One of the streets consists of little except Indian shops and bazaars. Outside the business portion, the town is spread over much territory, the houses standing isolated, each by itself, and each usually bowered in trees, with vines shading the verandas, and pretty flower-gardens round about.

Much of Eliot's animus directed towards Nairobi at the time arose from his strong feelings against Indians there; they were blamed for the outbreak of the 'true and typical bubonic plague' in early 1902. This plague appears to have been a continuation of that which closed the port of Bombay in 1896, and seriously disrupted recruitment of Indian labour for the Uganda Railway. In the autumn of 1899 it had appeared in the Indian bazaar at Nairobi and Patterson, the British officer in charge, had promptly burned the bazaar to the ground. Its outbreak in 1902 caused numerous deaths and a scare, not only in Nairobi, but as far afield as German East Africa, where quarantine stations were set up on the Taveta–Moshi road to prevent it spreading borderwise. The plague was finally tracked down to the Indian bazaar in Nairobi, where it had been introduced from India in rice bags infected by rats. In an attempt to eradicate the plague, there was a temporary clean-up of the more undesirable features of Nairobi. Infected buildings were torn or burnt down, and all the Maasai kraals and Somali and Swahili villages were shifted out a quarter of a mile onto new ground. Mass inoculations and greater attention to sanitation were signs that a lesson had been learned. Despite early disappointments as to its development, and Eliot's animadversions on its choice as main headquarters, there was no going back. In 1907 the administrative headquarters for the territory was transferred from Mombasa to Nairobi, adding to its importance; it was already the headquarters for the railway and the 3rd Battalion of the King's African Rifles. There were now European shops and a well-built Indian bazaar, and along the banks of the Nairobi stream were numerous market gardens from which the local market was supplied daily with European vegetables. The East Africa Horticultural Society was founded at Nairobi in 1901. With its cricket fields and sports grounds, and a race-course, Nairobi evinced confidence in its future as the main centre of the protectorate.

By the beginning of 1902 there were only some 200 Europeans in Kenya, so slow had been the first movement of settlers. Up to 31 March 1904 land had been allotted to 130 Europeans, and by 1907 Land Office records show that 165 holdings had been disposed of to Europeans. Yet from this small community there was already heard the premature cry, 'no taxation without representation', and in it was also discernible the signs of the strains and tempers characteristic of the settlers of the White Highlands in the 1920s and 1930s. On 4 January 1902 there was held at Mr T.A. Wood's hotel in Nairobi the first meeting of a European Committee of 35 persons out of which grew the 'Colonists' Association'. The avowed purpose of the Committee was to encourage European settlement and to recommend that freehold tenure be granted to leasehold land, after rent had been paid for a period of 30 years, and the members asked for a relaxation of the stringent regulations on leasing land in the railway zone. They were hostile to the increasing Indian element in the protectorate. A resolution was passed, declaring

that further immigration of Asiatics into the country is entirely detrimental to the European settlers in particular and the native inhabitants generally.[40]

It urged government to establish model farms as the Germans had done in German East Africa. Settlers could then come and see for themselves what could be done in the way of farming in the highlands. Finally, a society was formed as a result of the meeting, 'to promote European immigration into East Africa', and the 'Emigrants' Information Office' in London was requested to draw up a pamphlet on East Africa for intending settlers. Eliot supported the settlers in these attempts to associate and to consolidate their position in defence of their own interests, in the same way as might be expected of English country gentry. That this was a life-style to which they aspired and to which they would tenaciously adhere in the future, they now signalled. They were to reproduce it with remarkable fidelity in the next few decades.

The new world that was shaping up around Nairobi was not the only scene of European development. At the other end of the railway, at the ocean terminus of Mombasa, much activity was in progress, and the shift of the railway headquarters from there to Nairobi, in 1900, had no appreciable effect on slowing down Mombasa's development, nor also the removal of the administrative headquarters of the protectorate to Nairobi in 1907. Mombasa was already the greatest ocean port between Beira and Aden. It had drained off trade and shipping from Zanzibar, and that the commissioner was more continuously in residence at Mombasa than Zanzibar was reflected in the increasing number of dispatches written by Hardinge from Mombasa. In March 1898 he reported to Salisbury, 'My duties on the mainland have prevented my being much in Zanzibar during the last six months.' The other towns and harbours on the coast north of Mombasa, Malindi, Lamu and Kismayu, were mere dhow ports; Mombasa topped them all. The effect of the commencement of the railway was immediately reflected in the tripling of the volume of imports passing through Mombasa in the period of July 1895 to May 1896, at which latter date the population of the town stood at over 25,000. Many Indians were already established there when the railway commenced, but their numbers now greatly increased and were augmented over the next decade. By 1896 four European (three English and one German) trading firms had branch agencies at Mombasa. To cope with the influx of population, Indians, Africans and Europeans (mainly Greeks and Italians employed in construction work), and to deal with the petty disorders attendant on a large seaport, a European Inspector of Police was appointed. That symbol of gregarious Europeans in the tropics, 'the Club' – the Mombasa Club – was founded in August 1896 and by the following year had moved from temporary premises in the main street to an excellent site on the sea front. In 1903 the Club proudly announced that its membership had so increased from the original 60 that a new reading room had been added, and the billiard room enlarged so as to contain three tables. By 1907 the Mombasa Club had 560 members, not all generally resident at the coast. It was at the Mombasa Club that ex-President Roosevelt was dined in 'splendid fashion' in 1909, with the Chamber of Commerce (founded in 1903) entering into the occasion with great aplomb. The establishment of a Public Works Department (with its ubiquitous stamp PWD) under Mr S.C.E. Bay, marked an important step, and when the Survey and Lands Office was separated from it in April 1904 the PWD became a full-fledged department on its own. Liquor regulations, streets and roads regulations, water reservoirs and town amenities – all the tokens of municipal status – now appeared, and with them a great rise in the cost of living at Mombasa. There was much land speculation, consequent on the choice of Mombasa Island as the terminus of the Uganda Railway. Hardinge singled out Messrs Charlesworth, Pilling and Company especially, for charging 'exorbitant sums' for land they had acquired in expectation of rising prices.

The establishment of regular steamship communication overseas, and a fortnightly steamer service between the coast ports and Zanzibar along with the commencement of the railway, brought much development at Mombasa. And when to this was added the enormous increase of imports (mostly from India; a Crown Agents' appointee at Bombay dealt solely with the business) of railway material and large quantities of food supplies for the railway construction gangs, the result was that by 1900 the port was handling over 4000 tons of cargo per month. The old dhow harbour on the northern side of island was entirely inadequate for this surge of imports. Its entrance passage was too small, and its immediate shoreline was crowded with squalid shanties, 'midst which cargo had to be lifted up a 30 foot cliff'. 'There was scarcely room to breathe', in the words of one European official. There were neither docks nor quays. By the autumn of 1900 there were complaints that the streets of Mombasa were blocked with freight, exposed to the weather, dumped incontinently about, and guarded by a motley collection of askaris. In the face of these conditions improved port facilities were sought elsewhere on the island. The IBEAC, in its earlier years and when in more expansionist mood, had made a survey of Mombasa Island with a view to finding an alternative and better harbour site than the old dhow port. They had selected Kilindini (place of deep water), on the south-west side of the island, as ideal for harbour development. Indeed, Kilindini had no rival on the whole East Africa coast in the facilities it offered as a deep water harbour, and the IBEAC was in the process of transferring its installations there when the administration of the protectorate passed out of its hands into those of the British government in 1895.

Sir George Molesworth, speaking for the Uganda Railway Administration, in his Report of 1899, and with strong support from the Chief Customs Master at Mombasa, expressed deep concern over the inadequate port facilities at Mombasa: the old dhow port was 'absolutely unfitted to be the main port of British East Africa'. At Kilindini however there was 'an excellent harbour completely land-locked with a spacious and well-protected anchorage', and the transfer to there should be made as soon as possible. 'Unless something is soon done, the present port arrangements must lead to deadlock.' The old port should be reserved exclusively for dhows.

When, in 1900, an oil company established its depot at Kilindini, and the merchant community petitioned that the customs office be sited there, developments quickly followed. A new harbour site, with customs houses, piers, mooring buoys and an iron lighthouse – with 25-mile beam (in 1898 several vessels, one carrying railway material, had run on to the reef at the harbour entrance) – all appeared within the year. In August 1900 Hardinge remarked that Mombasa was 'becoming a city'. When in October of the same year the statue of the late Sir William Mackinnon was unveiled, the ceremony was attended by local government officials and Sir Clement Hill, Permanent Under-Secretary for African Affairs at the Foreign Office, who was on his way to Uganda.

Optimism for the future of East Africa was reflected in various speculative schemes put forth for its economic development at the turn of the century. They ranged from that of Mr Rule, for a monopoly over pearl fishing rights in Zanzibar waters, to that of Messrs Palmer and Gray for a monopoly of all timber cutting along the Uganda Railway. Both were turned down, for they contravened Article V of the Berlin Act of 1884/85, which forbade 'monopoly or favour of any kind in matters of trade'. In its keen desire to develop new sources of revenue, the administration unwisely gave approval to a number of firms for the stripping of bark (from which a dye was extracted) from the mangrove forests of Tanaland Province, despite warning from the Director of Kew Gardens that such stripping would be injurious to these forests. More practical was the concession granted at Witu for a plantation of 20,000 acres for the production of indiarubber. Expectations of mineral wealth proved illusory. In May 1902 the Consolidated Finance Corporation, with experience in mining in Western Australia, planned to launch a large-scale expedition to explore mineral resources in the 'hinterland' behind Mombasa, where, according to tradition, there were coal and gold deposits; a fuller investigation resulted in the Corporation dropping this project. Among the schemes to develop the protectorate none surpassed those of Messrs Anderson and Hall, of Mombasa, in their grandiose nature and novel suggestion. The only flaw in the plans of these two gentlemen was that they assumed government financial backing. Their plans included the establishment of a direct line of steamers between England and Mombasa; building a railway from Freretown to Malindi; municipal schemes for Mombasa – installation of electric and water supply and sanitary arrangements; and a bank with right of note issue (government was especially chary of this, in view of the failure of the IBEAC plans for banking rights in Zanzibar). Lesser plans of Anderson and Hall included irrigation of the Taru desert; development of salt works; market gardening; clearing of forest land and investigating the mineral wealth of East Africa. Eliot was of the view that these were

> most excellent schemes, and I doubt nothing but Messrs. Anderson and Hall's power to make them pay, unless they find gold or precious stones.[41]

And there was much need to make such schemes pay, for both the Foreign Office and Treasury were concerned over the high cost of administering the East Africa Protectorate and Uganda. Subsidies from the imperial exchequer for the two protectorates for the year ending 31 March 1899 amounted to £256,000. Much of this arose from the cost of suppressing the recent mutiny in Uganda. The expenditure alone for the East Africa Protectorate for the relief expedition to Uganda amounted to £11,275, and the former protectorate had also to meet the heavy cost of the Jubaland expedition against the Ogaden Somali. This military activity and its concurrent expenditure adversely affected the export trade and revenue from it. The Jubaland expedition had caused a diminution in export trade at Kismayu of £13,400.

In September 1900, on the eve of his visit to East Africa, Sir Clement Hill had appealed for suggestions as to how a productive trade might be developed in the two territories, and Salisbury reminded Eliot that Britain was subsidizing the East Africa Protectorate to the tune of £90,000–100,000 a year. He should stay clear of ventures which cost money, and rather think of ways of developing revenue:

> At this juncture owing to the expenses of war in South Africa and those arising from the condition of affairs in China, it was not the best moment to select to ask HMG to sanction expenditure for the East Africa and Uganda Protectorates beyond the bare necessities for the Administration.[42]

Eliot was determined to make the country pay, and like Johnston in Uganda he urged the founding of Departments of Agriculture, Mines and Forests, and instituting a geological survey, for apart from Lake Magadi's soda resources little was known about the mineral resources of the protectorate. He wanted the native population to contribute more to the protectorate's revenue, beyond that of mere barter trade. Revenue-producing crops such as indiarubber, ivory, grain, cattle, hides, timber, cowrie shells, copra, semsem oil and bark, should be encouraged, for this would stimulate the import trade. The latter was largely made up of rice, unbleached cotton cloth, kerosene oil, iron wire (made into small iron chains for the Giriama), blue ukuta beads and thick blankets for the Kikuyu, and it was largely in the hands of the small Indian trader, and could be tapped for import duties. How to tap the barter trade of the Africans directly was a much more difficult matter: they were usually too comfortable to sell their ivory or collect indiarubber, beyond the mere needs of subsistence. The answer was a hut tax, payable in cash, which would stir them into unwonted economic activity, and make them realize that 'taxation is a natural part of European Government'. The pending transfer of the Eastern Province of Uganda to the East Africa protectorate raised the anomaly of hut tax being levied in one part of the protectorate but not in the other. Thus hut tax was introduced generally throughout the protectorate in January 1902. It produced only 4880 rupees in the period January to March 1902; a poor beginning, it is true, but the idea had been introduced and hut tax was soon an accepted fact of life. Among the Kikuyu its introduction brought to the fore African personages who might be designated as 'chiefs'; in consultation with the Collector or District Commissioner they were responsible for the collection of hut tax. In Kikuyuland, each elder was master of his own village, but a district of villages was under a 'chief'. One such chief, entrusted by the British with responsibilities for collection of hut tax, was Karuri, whose district ran from Fort Hall west to Tusu. This was indirect rule in the making!

This was all very pleasing to Lansdowne, who in the interval had the benefit of the views of Sir Clement Hill, now returned from East Africa. To Lansdowne, the East Africa Protectorate was but one territory in a vast and newly acquired British Empire in Africa. There was shortage of administrators and military in running it. Thus he outlined for Eliot the broad lines of policy of HMG in regard to the development of Foreign Office protectorates. Officials were to spread their influence 'gradually over the natives, and to teach them by degrees the advantages of civilization by attracting them to European centres'; there should be no pushing on of outposts unless there was fair prospect of commerce, or if such posts were well received by the inhabitants:

It is not the wish of HMG to force their way amongst tribes who are hostile, and though it is unfortunately unavoidable at times to make a display of strength, action likely to provoke such a contingency should be, if possible, avoided.[43]

The message was clear. No new commitments were to be taken. Peace and good order were paramount and although there was need to 'impress the natives with the strength and mobility of our force', no great increase in that force was admissible; that which existed must consist of the best material and be made the most of.

In the face of such exhortations as to need for economy, Eliot, with some diffidence, requested that £2000 be allocated for the building of a residence of the Commissioner at Nairobi, even though

Visitors of consideration are already frequent and are likely to become more so. When the German Governor came here I had to turn out my staff into tents to find him a bed and his staff had to sleep in railway carriages.[44]

He would hold down the cost of administration wherever possible. African chiefs would be encouraged to supply native labour for the building of roads. Direct or indirect pecuniary encouragement would be given to the various missionary bodies, to undertake 'the education of a class of youths who would become serviceable to the Protectorate as clerks or interpreters'. To assist in the administration of the coastal strip with its large Arab and Swahili population a number of young Arabs would be sent off to Egypt to be educated in English and Arabic. Eliot could not refrain from impressing on Lansdowne the need for more European officials – at least 15 Collectors and 25 Assistant Collectors were required. At present there were only half that number in the protectorate. It was not wise to leave a European officer isolated on his own, up-country: there should be at least two to a post. A solitary life could lead to 'most distressing and even fatal results'. Officers should be encouraged by bonuses to learn languages, such as Kikuyu and Maasai. More doctors were needed: in May 1899 there were only 12 doctors in the whole East Africa Protectorate. A proper land survey was needed, since land rules had now been published. There was need for accommodation at Nairobi as a hot-weather retreat for heads of departments at Mombasa: 'prolonged residence there in the hot season is apt to create an excited and irritable frame of mind, which is not good for dealing with public business'. These were the cares of office.

For the aspirant settler, however, there was a new and exciting spirit in the whole challenge of East Africa. To the north of Nairobi, Fort Hall and Nyeri stations had opened up most attractive country, and were important trade centres with Indian bazaars, native markets and a small colony of coast traders. European settlers eagerly moved into this area. Churchill saw these European settlers in this exotic East African environment at a time when they were 'all struggling, all fretful, nervous, high-strung, many disappointed, some despairing, some smashed'. Capricious fortune exacted a high price in this new colony. Theodore Roosevelt, visiting there within a year of Churchill's journey through the territory, saw it in a more favourable light than Churchill. The British were embarked on a most laudable enterprise. Roosevelt had been much impressed with the young Englishmen whom he had met on board ship on his way out to East Africa: they were going out 'to take command of black native levies in out-of-the-way regions' and they 'might have walked out of the pages of Kipling'. Roosevelt would give every encouragement to white settlement in the highlands of British East Africa:

> Not only do I firmly believe in the future of East Africa for settlement as a white man's country, but I feel that it is an ideal playground alike for sportsmen and for travellers who wish to live in health and comfort, and yet to see what is beautiful and unusual.[45]

The *Handbook for East Africa* of 1903 had already struck a similar note. It declared that settlers would be attracted to East Africa not only by the agricultural and economic possibilities, but by the picturesque grandeur of the scenery and the unrivalled opportunity offered for sport. There was no country, the *Handbook* claimed, that could afford such quantities of game of every variety as East Africa and that too within easy distance of the railway, so that the farmer's toil might without difficulty be varied by a day's shooting under the most pleasant conditions. As an exordium, would-be settlers were assured that they need have no fear about living in this hitherto reputed savage country: 'Peace now reigns in both East Africa and Uganda.' Scientists were developing natural resources of the country, prospectors were searching for gold and precious stones, planters and settlers were cultivating the rich soil of the highlands, and the civilizing effect of missionary enterprise was making itself felt among the natives:

It is to be hoped that by careful management and proper supervision the Protectorates will before long become self-supporting and form an important colony of the British Empire.[46]

Finally,

East Africa is a land where the settler may make a home, where children can thrive and where periodical visits to Europe become a luxury and not a necessity as in most tropical climes. The day is not far distant when the country will be covered with snug homesteads, each surrounded by its substantial stables and cattle sheds, orchards and gardens, while the country as far as the eye can see will be a rippling expanse of golden grain or snowy cotton, blending into the forest clad slopes of the Mau and Kikuyu and backed by the magnificent peaks of Kenya and Kilimanjaro.[47]

The 'sunbeam period'[48] had begun.

Epilogue

The incursion of British power and its impress on the way of life of the East African peoples brought for them a profound and unprecedented experience. It wrought a greater change in their world and circumstance than had occurred in preceding millennia. The responsibility for these territories would rest with the British whose conscience had been moulded by the imperial ethic of their time. A foreign rule with its different set of values was enforced on the East African peoples. They were subjected to a system of formal relations, completely alien and not of their own making. This would apply, not only *vis-à-vis* their new rulers, the British, but also as regards neighbouring tribes, for tribal relations were also regulated by the British. No longer would the age-old confrontation of warring tribes be tolerated. Weaker tribes formerly riven by fear of sudden attack and annihilation from fiercer and stronger rivals breathed a gentler air. The cessation of the slave-trade brought a new dignity and a feeling of freedom and security hitherto unknown. The influence of Christian missions increased, not only against tribal paganisim, but also in the fields of education and medicine. A new dimension enclosed the East African scene. In this new state of affairs there could be no retrocession. Only advance.

Adjustment to the new conditions was attained more easily by those East African tribes showing the greatest flexibility, aptitude for change and eagerness to enter into a way of life infinitely different from any previously experienced. This accommodation was made most successfully by the Baganda and other sedentary tribes; and, perhaps, least of all by remote pastoralists such as the Karamojong of north-eastern Uganda, and the Maasai and Samburu of Kenya.

British rule in East Africa by the beginning of the twentieth century was faced with no unsolved riddles; no questions of magnitude remained to be dealt with. Native peoples were remarkably quiescent; those who had been punished were now subdued, rendered harmless. There might be minor flare-ups: raiding for women and goats east of the Athi River; skirmishes with the Meru and Embu in the neighbourhood of Mt Kenya; and rapacious native agents of Baganda sub-imperialism might damn the good name of the British in Bukedi. These were small worries, and they could be corrected by the appropriate measures. For the most part the ordering work of the British went on quietly, steadily and, they would claim, beneficently.

British East Africa was surrounded on all sides (with the possible exception of Ethiopia) by territory controlled by friendly European powers or at least by powers with whom there were established relations. Unlike India, there was no dangerous frontier, no 'Forward' policy, no constant watchfulness to be maintained on its borders. No warrior peoples lurked on outer fringes, and there were no outposts of empire to man. A Pax Britannica truly reigned.

The East Africa Protectorate and Uganda were fortunate in the men who headed their administrations at this high noon of empire. Eliot and Johnston, in their own way, were men of high calibre, original thinkers and clever calculating administrators. 'Cockalorum' Johnston, with his taste for natural history, varied and rich interests in ethnology and botany, was probably the richer amalgam. His achievements in Uganda attest to his mental and physical energy. Eliot, the man of intellect, cool, detached, shrewd, assaying, was apparently far-seeing, but he could only see his territory as one in which its native peoples would play a lesser and subordinate role to the white settler community. In this respect, Eliot, in the context of his time, was not exceptional. He tended to underestimate the capabilities of the Kikuyu; alert, industrious, purposeful agriculturists, who occupied the vantage point of the highlands.

Within the few years encompassed by the administrations of Johnston and Eliot, the peoples of East Africa encountered a striking change in their material circumstances. This was especially true in the matter of communications. The three months' journey on foot up from the coast to Uganda was merely a subject of reverie. A ready market existed for articles of commerce – hides, crocodile skins, semsem, maize – products previously unsaleable. Wearing of clothes had become fashionable; there was a desire for utensils, luxury articles – soap, and parasols; and, *mirabile dictu*, bicycles appeared on primitive pathways. British East Africa was caught up in the outside world. There could be no going back.

Notes

Preface
1. Foreign Office Confidential Print (henceforward FOCP) 7405/97, Johnston to Salisbury, 9 Apr. 1900 (enclosure: Delmé-Radcliffe's report).
2. E.B. Cromer (Earl of), *Ancient and Modern Imperialism* (London, 1910), p 75.
3. Quoted by V. Buxton, in Preface to A.B. Lloyd, *Uganda to Khartoum*, (London, 1911), p 9.
4. T. Rooosevelt, *African Game Trails* (New York, 1910), pp 4–5.
5. Sir James, Robertson, *Transition in Africa: From Direct Rule to Independence* (London, 1974).
6. Cromer, *Ancient and Modern Imperialism*, p 124.
7. R.C. Bridges, 'Europeans and East Africans in the age of exploration', *The Geographical Journal*, vol 139, Pt 2, June 1973, p228; *Journal of Royal Society of Arts* (1877).
8. G. Cecil, *Life of Salisbury* (London, 1922–32), iv, p310; R. Robinson and J. Gallagher, *Africa and the Victorians* (London, 1961), p 17.
9. Lovat Fraser, *India under Curzon and After* (London, 1911), p213.
10. M. Perham, *Lugard: The Years of Adventure; Lugard: The Years of Authority* (London, 1956 and 1960).

Chapter 1
1. R. Hakluyt, *The Tudor Venturers*, ed. R. Hampden (London, 1970), p 140.
2. J.H. van Linschoten, *Linschoten's Voyage*, Hakluyt Society (1885).
3. W.A. Spray, *Surveying and Charting the Indian Ocean: The British Contribution 1750-1838* (London, PhD 1966) pp 228–9.
4. Abbé Rochon, *A Voyage to Madagascar and the East Indies*, transl. from the French (London, 1792), pp xxxiv–xliv.
5 E.V. Axelson, *The Portuguese in South-East Africa 1600–1700* (Johannesburg, 1960), Appendix.
6. Thos. Cavendish, *Voyage Round the World* (London, 1589), i, 293.
7. G.S.P. Freeman-Grenville, *The East African Coast: Select Documents* (London, 1962), pp 152–3; R. Hakluyt, *Principal Navigations*, Hakluyt Society, vol vi (1904), pp 392–5.
8. *The Voyages of Sir James Lancaster ... to the East Indies*, ed. Sir Clements Markham, Hakluyt Society (1877).

9. V.A. Smith, *The Oxford History of India* (London, 1958), p 367.
10. Court Minutes of the East India Company, 14 Nov. 1657.
11. F.D. Arnold-Forster, (Rear-Admiral), *The Madagascar Pirates* (New York, 1957), pp 72–8, 138–9).
12. *The Journal of John Jourdain, 1608–17*, Hakluyt Society, 2nd Series, No 16 (1905).
13. R.B. Serjeant, *The Portuguese off the South Arabian Coast* (London, 1963), pp128,150.
14. C.R. Low, *History of the Indian Navy (1613–1863)* (London, 1877), ii, 114.
15. W.S.N. Nicholls, *The Swahili Coast* (London, 1971), pp 75, 198–201.
16. A. Bissell, *A Voyage from England to the Red Sea 1798–99* (London,1806).
17. H. Salt, *A Voyage to Abyssinia and Travels into the Interior ... and East Coast of Africa* (London, 1814).
18. T. Smee (Captain), *Voyage to the Eastern Shores of Africa* (London, 1811).
19. *Transactions of Bombay Geographical Society*, i (1844).
20. C.U. Aitchison, *A Collection of Treaties, Engagements and Sanads Relating to India and Neighbouring Countries* (Delhi, 1933).
21. Sir John Milner Gray, *History of Zanzibar from Middle Ages to 1856* (London, 1962), p 232.
22. S.M. Edwardes, *Rise of Bombay* (London, 1902), p 163.
23. D.R. Banaji, *Slavery in British India* (Bombay, 1933), pp 73–5.
24. India Office Records: Bombay Political and Secret Consultations, v.32 (1812), 388–90.
25. Aitchison, *Collection of Treaties*, X, 128.
26. Admiralty Records (PRO), i, 2188: Farquhar's letters (June–July, 1822).
27. Zanzibar Archives: Hamerton to Bombay government, 1 Feb. 1843.
28. Sessional Papers XVIIIs Nourse to Admiralty, 5 Jan. 1823.
29. W. Owen, *Narrative of Voyage to explore the Eastern Shores of Africa*, 2 vols (London, 1833), i, 366.
30. Owen, *Report to Admiralty*, i, iii, 24 (Adm.i, 2269).
31. Owen, *Narrative*, i, 71–2.
32. Owen, *Narrative*, i, 192.
33. Owen, *Narrative*, i, 193.
34. Owen, *Narrative*, i, 318.
35. Owen, *Narrative*, i, 359.
36. Owen, *Narrative*, i, 342.
37. Owen, *Narrative*, i, 364–5.
38. Owen, *Narrative*, i, 405–6.
39. Owen, *Narrative* i, 412–14.
40. Owen, *Narrative*, i, 434.
41. Owen, *Narrative*, ii, 155.
42. Owen, *Narrative*, ii, 13–14.
43. Owen, *Narrative*, ii, 377.
44. Owen, *Narrative*, ii, 13-14.

Chapter 2

1. A. Bissell, *Voyage from England to the Red Sea 1789–99* (London, 1806).
2. Zanzibar Archives: Hamerton to Bombay government, 5 Sept. 1844.

3. N.R. Bennett and G.E. Brooks, *New England Merchants in Africa* (Boston, 1965), p 400; N. Isaacs, *Travels and Adventures in Eastern Africa*, 2 vols (London, 1836); E. Roberts, *Embassy to the Eastern Courts of Cochin China, Siam and Muscat, 1832–4* (New York, 1837); S.W. Ruschenberger, *Voyage Round the World*, 2 vols (Philadelphia, 1838).
4. Zanzibar Archives: Hamerton to FO, 31 July 1844.
5. Zanzibar Archives Hart's Report, p 277.
6. Zanzibar Archives: British Agent, Muscat, to Bombay gov't, 9 June 1840.
7. Zanzibar Archives: Hamerton to FO, 24 July 1849.
8. Zanzibar Archives: Hamerton to Malet (Bombay government), 15 Feb. 1850.
9. R.H. Croften, *A Pageant of the Spice Islands* (London, 1936), pp 86–113.
10. FO 54/1, Peacock to Stuart Mackenzie, 27 Aug. 1834.

Chapter 3
1. RGS Archives; Banks Papers Nos 706-7. Proceedings, 1810, 35 (quoted in R.C. Bridges, 'Speke and the Royal Geographical Society', *Uganda Journal*, Vol 19, p 24).
2. Lady J. Listowel, *The Other Livingstone* (London, 1973).
3. Listowel, *The Other Livingstone*.
4. W. G. Blaikie, *Personal Life of David Livingstone* (London, 1880), p 279.
5. Sir Samuel Baker, *Explorations of the Nile Tributaries of Abyssinia* (London, 1868), p 734.
6. G. Schweinfurth, *The Heart of Africa* (London, 1878), p 29.
7. RGS Letter Book, Smyth *et al.* to Galloway, 11 March 1850.
8. *J.RGS*, xxix (1859), 5. According to Speke his addiction to African exploration originated during his years as a subaltern in India, when he conceived the idea of collecting fauna for his father's 'growing museum'.
9. J.H. Speke, *Journal of Discovery of the Source of the Nile* (London, 1863), p 247.
10. C. New, *Life, Wanderings, and Labours in East Africa* (London, 1873), pp 378–81.
11. H.M. Stanley, *In Darkest Africa* (London, 1878), i, pp 27–8.
12. Stanley, *Darkest Africa*, i, p 396.
13. Stanley, *Darkest Africa*, ii, p429.
14. R. Burton, *Lake Regions of Central Africa* (London, 1860), i, p323.
15. R. Coupland, R; *Exploitation of East Africa 1856–1890* (Oxford, 1938), p 132.
16. A. Shorter, 'Nyungu-ya-Mawe and the Empire of the "Ruga Rugas"', *Journal of African History*, 9 (1968), pp 235–59.
17. J. Thomson, *To the Central African Lakes and Back* (London, 1881), i, p 267.
18. Owen, *Narrative*, i, pp 71–2.
19. R. Burton, *Lake Regions*, ii, pp289, 337; Winston Churchill, *The River War* (London, 1899), p 25; Sir Bartle Frere, *East Africa as a Field of Missionary Labours* (London, 1874), p 70.
20. Sir Philip Mitchell, *The Agrarian Problem in Kenya* (Nairobi, 1947).
21. G. Schweinfurth, *The Heart of Africa* (London, 1874) i, p 186.

Chapter 4
1. Private papers of Robert, Third Marquess of Salisbury, S.P.21 (Misc. 1878-80), Salisbury to Temple, 2 Sept. 1878.
2. *The Story of the House of O'Swald, 1831–1931* (Hamburg, 1931), pp 18–20.
3. Bismark to von Roon (Minister of War and Marine), 9 Jan. 1868, *Reichs Colonial amt* (Deutsches Zentralarchiv, Potsdam).
4. Lord Edmond Fitzmaurice, *The Life of Granville George Leveson Gower*, 2 vols (London, 1905), ii, 337. For the European scramble in Africa as a whole, see R. Oliver and G.N. Sanderson (eds), *The Cambridge History of Africa 6: from 1870 to 1905* (Cambridge, 1985).
5. Earl of Cromer, *Modern Egypt*, 2 vols (London, 1908), i, 216–17, 392.
6. FO 83/1711, Granville to Malet, 25 May 1885.
7. FO 83/1711, Granville to Malet, 25 May 1885.
8. FOCP 5156/143, Malet to Granville, 4 June 1885.
9. FO 84/1746, Memorandum by Anderson, 18 July 1885.
10. FO 84/1748, Memorandum by Anderson, 22 July 1885.
11. FOCP 5157/252, Text of German notification, 16 Aug. 1885.
12. Sir George Arthur, *The Life of Lord Kitchener*, 3 vols (London, 1920), i, 142.
13. FOCP 5466/64, Buchanan to Mackinnon, 24 Mar. 1886.
14. FOCP 5271/161, Kitchener to Kirk, 14 Feb. 1886.
15. J. Martineau, *Life of Sir Bartle Frere* (London, 1895), ii, 98.
16. FOCP 5271/155, Kitchener's Memorandum, 10 Feb. 1886.
17. A. Hodges, *Lord Kitchener* (London, 1937), pp 87–8.
18. Hodges, *Lord Kitchener*, pp 87–8.
19. FOCP 5271/168, Minute by Lister, 20 Mar. 1886.
20. Arthur, *Life of Kitchener*, i, 147.
21. *Cologne Gazette*, 22 Oct. 1886.
22. FOCP 6550/315, Strachey to Salisbury (enclosure), 25 Mar. 1887.
23. *North German Gazette*, 27 Jan. 1889.
24. *North German Gazette*, 27 Jan. 1889.
25 *East African Standard*, 28 Sep. 1962.
26. FOCP 5673/239, Colonel Euan-Smith to Salisbury, 1 June 1888.
27. Stanley, *In Darkest Africa*, i, 62.
28. Africa No. 11 (1888), 985: Salisbury to Malet, 2 July 1887; E. Hertslet, *Map of Africa by Treaty* (London, 1896), ii, 615–27.
29. Hertslet, *Map of Africa*, i, 345ff.
30. FOCP 6051/189, IBEAC Memorandum, 12 Mar. 1890.
31. M. de Kiewiet, *The History of the IBEAC 1876-1895* (London PhD, thesis, 1955), pp 141–59.
32. FOCP 7018/109, Hardinge to Salisbury, 13 Aug. 1897.
33. FOCP 6124/38, Memorandum by Anderson, 12 Jan. 1891.

Chapter 5
1. *Die Tagebücher von Dr. Emin Pascha*, edited by Franz Stuhlmann (Berlin, 1927), iv, 440ff.
2. Stanley, *In Darkest Africa*, i, 410.
3. Stanley, *In Darkest Africa*, ii, 265.
4. Lugard Papers: Mackenzie to Lugard, 12 and 22 Mar. 1890.

5. P.L. McDermott, *British East Africa or IBEAC* (London, 1895), p 394.
6. C. Peters, *New Light on Dark Africa* (London, 1891), pp 221–5.
7. Peters, idem,

Chapter 6
1. A. J. Mounteney-Jephson, *Emin Pasha and the Rebellion at the Equator* (New York, 1891), p 302.
2. C. Chaillé-Long, *Central Africa: Naked Truths of Naked People* (London, 1876), p106.
3. A. Oded, *The Muslim Factor in Buganda (1850–84)* (Tel-Aviv, 1974), Ch. iii.
4. FOCP 5271/10, Incl. 3, Extract from letter by Mackay, 29 Sept. 1885.
5. D.A. Low, *Buganda in Modern History* (London, 1971), pp 29–32.
6. FOCP 6051/147, Revd. E. Gordon to Euan-Smith, 25 Oct.1889.
7. FOCP 6051/337, Stokes to Euan-Smith, 6 Oct. 1889.
8. FOCP 6051/299, IBEAC to Euan-Smith, 26 Apr. 1890.
9. FOCP 6123/227, Bishop Tucker to Euan-Smith, 14 Sept. 1890.
10. Peters, *New Light on Dark Africa*, p 360.
11. Peters, *New Light on Dark Africa*, p 363.
12. FOCP 6105/285, Jackson to Euan-Smith, 9 June 1890.
13. Zanzibar Archives: Gedge to IBEAC, 20 Aug. 1890.
14. FOCP 6123/116, Euan-Smith to Salisbury, 27 Sept. 1890.
15. FOCP 6123/227, Bishop Tucker to Euan-Smith, 14 Sep. 1890. For Lugard's activities in Uganda, see J.A. Rowe, *Lugard in Kampala* (Kampala, 1969).
16. Lugard's *Report,* 7 Jan. 1891, pp 96–7.
17. Lugard's *Report,* p 99.
18. Lugard's *Report,* p 99.
19. Lugard's *Report,* p 99.
20. F.P.G. Guizot, *Mémoires* (Paris, 1858–61), vii, 309.
21. FOCP 6127/115, Lugard to Euan-Smith, 8 Jan. 1891.
22. FOCP 6127/33, Treaty between Mwanga and the IBEAC, 26 Dec. 1890.
23. C-6555, *Africa No 4 (1892)*, Incl. 11, Lugard to IBEAC, 24 Dec. 1892.
24. See Lugard's letter to Père Achte of 9 Mar. 1892 (FOCP 6454/346, Appendix IX, 65.
25. C-6555. *Africa No 4 (1892)*, Incls. 2 and 3, Lugard to IBEAC, 13 Aug. 1891.
26. *Africa No 4,* Lugard to IBEAC, 13 Aug. 1891.
27. *Africa No 4,* Lugard to IBEAC, 13 Aug. 1891.
28. *Africa No 2 (1893)*, Lugard's Report, No 4, Mar.–Aug. 1892.
29. Macdonald's Report, Evidence, No 14, Statement by Captain Williams, 12 Jan. 1893.
30. C-6555, *Africa No 4 (1892)*, Lugard's Report, No 3, pp 117–18.
31. *Africa No 4,* Lugard's Report, No 3, p114.
32. FO 84/1984, Mackenzie to Lugard, 12 and 22 Mar. 1890.
33. C-6848, *Africa No 2 (1893)*, Lugard's Report, 11 Jan. 1892.
34. FOCP 6261/138, IBEAC to Lugard, 10 Aug. 1891.
35. C-6848, *Africa No 2 (1893)*, Lugard's Report, 4 Feb. 1892.
36. *Africa No 2,* Lugard's Report, addition to, 3 Mar. 1892; R. Oliver, *The African Experience* (London, 1991), pp179–180.

37. C-7109, *Africa No 8 (1893)*, No 15, Lugard to Père Achte, 6 Mar. 1892.
38. C-6848, *Africa No 2 (1893)*, No 4, Mar.–Aug. 1892.
39. C-6848, *Africa No 2 (1893)*, No 4, Mar.–Aug. 1892.
40. C-7109, *Africa No 8 (1893)*, Incl. 4 in No 15, 28 Dec. 1892.
41. FOCP 6454/348, Incl. 6, Lugard to Williams, 15 Apr. 1892.
42. For papers respecting the proposed railway from Mombasa to Lake Victoria see *Africa No 2 (1892)* and *Africa No 4 (1892)*.
43. J.R.L. Macdonald, *Soldiering and Surveying in British East Africa, 1891-1894* (London, 1897), p 96.
44. M. Perham, *Lugard: The Years of Adventure* (London, 1956), p 325.
45. Macdonald, *Soldiering and Surveying*, p 96.
46. Macdonald, *Soldiering and Surveying*, p 128.
47. Macdonald, *Soldiering and Surveying*.
48. C-6555, *Africa No 4 (1892)*, No 2, IBEAC to FO, 9 Mar. 1892.
49. C-6847, *Africa No 1 (1893)*, No 31, Rosebery to Dufferin, 21 Oct. 1892.
50. Macdonald's Report, Lugard's Memorandum no, 19 Aug. 1893.
51. Macdonald's Report, Lugards Memo, 19 Aug. 1893.
52. Macdonald's Report, Lugards Memo, 19 Aug. 1893.
53. FOCP 6538/4, Memorandum by the Lord Chancellor, Jan.–Mar. 1894.
54. FOCP 5638/116, Memorandum by Lord Rosebery, 12. Feb. 1894.
55. FOCP 6538/123, Rhodes to Portal, 8 Dec. 1892.
56. FOCP 6454/348, Portal to Rosebery, 8 Apr. 1893.
57. (Sir) G. Portal, *The British Mission to Uganda* (London, 1894), Epilogue.
58. FOCP 6025/227, Euan-Smith to Salisbury, 3 Nov. 1889.
59. *Tanganyika Standard* (Dar es Salaam), 12 June 1954.
60. Sir Arthur H. Hardinge, *A Diplomatist in the East* (London, 1928), p 103.
61. FOCP 7690/50, Eliot to Lansdowne, 5 Jan. 1901.

Chapter 7

1. FOCP 6454/279, Portal to Rosebery, 2 Feb. 1893.
2. *Africa No 2 (1894)*, Nos 1 and 2.
3. *Africa No 2 (1894)*, No 9.
4. E.L. Bentley, *Handbook to the Uganda Question* (London, 1892), p 8.
5. R.W. Beachey, 'A socialist experiment in East Africa', *Makerere Journal* (1962).
6. C-7646, *Africa No 4 (1895)*, No 1, Anderson to IBEAC, 14 Nov. 1894.
7. For details of the buying out of the IBEAC and repurchase of the coastal strip see FO 107/25, Hardinge to Kimberley, 14 Dec. 1894; FO 107/6, Roseberry to Rodd, 9 Feb. 1893; C-7646, *Africa No 4 (1895)*.
8. FO 107/36, Hardinge to Kimberley, 25 June 1895.
9. E. Waugh, *A Tourist in Africa* (London, 1960).
10. FO 107/36, Hardinge to Salisbury, 6 July 1895.

Chapter 8

1. J.R.P. Postlethwaite, *I Look Back* (London, 1947).
2. FOCP 6127/149, Cardinal Manning to Salisbury, 3 June 1892.
3. FOCP 6617/277, Norfolk to FO, 27 Aug. 1894.
4. FOCP 6617/332, FO to Norfolk, 7 Sept. 1894.

5. FOCP 6805/87, Salisbury to Berkeley, 29 Oct. 1895; FOCP 6805/117, FO to Dugmore, 12 Nov. 1895.
6. C-7924, *Africa No 1 (1896)*, Report on Military Operations against Kabarega.
7. FO 64/1331, Minute by Anderson on Malet to Rosebery, Nos 28–9, 13 Mar. 1894; Sir J. Rennell Rodd, *Social and Diplomatic Memories* (London, 1922), i, 347.
8. *Hansard*, series iv, xxxii, 388–406.
9. *The Letters of Queen Victoria* (ed. G.E. Buckle) (New York, 1930–2), iii, 24–5.
10. FO 2/144, Salisbury to Macdonald, 9 June 1897.
11. Rodd, *Social and Diplomatic Memories*, ii, 187–8.
12. FOCP 7400/157, Macdonald to Salisbury, 13 Dec. 1898.
13. FO 3/6861, FO to Colonial Office, 30 June and 15 July 1896.
14. FOCP 7946/59, Delmé-Radcliffe to Colvile, 10 Oct. 1901.
15. Dietrich Reimer, *Karte von Deutsch ost Afrika* (Berlin, 1895).

Chapter 9
1. The term 'East Africa Protectorate' was formally applied under notice in the *London Gazette* of 1 Sept. 1896.
2. See R. Turton, *The Northern Frontier District of Kenya* (PhD thesis, University of London, 1971).
3. FOCP 6805/53, Hardinge to Salisbury, 17 Sept. 1895.
4. FOCP 6805/53, Hardinge to Salisbury, 17 Sept. 1895; see also FOCP 7159/22, Hardinge's memo of 12 Sept. 1895.
5. FOCP 7032/151, Report by Cavendish to Intelligence Division, War Office, 10 Dec. 1897.
6. Zanzibar Archives: Jenner's Report, 31 Aug. 1900.
7. FOCP 7402/144, Salisbury to Hardinge, 15 Feb. 1899.
8. FOCP 7823/77, Eliot to Lansdowne, 29 Apr. 1901.
9. FOCP 7823/77, Eliot to Landsdowne, 29 Apr. 1901.
10. FO 2/450, Eliot to Lansdowne, 1 Oct. 1901.
11. H. Moyse-Bartlett, *The King's African Rifles* (1956), p 32.

Chapter 10
1. V.L. Cameron, *Across Africa* (London, 1877), ii, 332.
2. FO 2/114, Sclater to FO, 7 June 1897.
3. FOCP 6617/36, Pauling to Kimberley, 8 Apr 1895.
4. Sir Frederick Jackson, *Early Days in East Africa* (London, 1930), pp 325–6; 'See also letter from Frank Hall to Lt-Col E. Hall, 15 Aug. 1899 (Hall Papers, Rhodes House, Oxford).
5. *Africa No 5 (1899)*.
6. F. Holderness Gale and S. Playne, *'East Africa (British)'* (London, 1908–9), pp 195ff.
7. J.H. Patterson, *The Man Eaters of Tsavo* (London, 1907), pp 72–3.
8. W.S. Price, *My Third Campaign in East Africa* (London, 1890), ii.

Chapter 11

1. *The Book of Duarte Barbosa,* Hakluyt Society (1918–21), i, 19–21.
2. Speke, *What Led to the Discovery of the Source of the Nile* (Edinburgh, 1864), pp 198, 229.
3. FO 84/139, Frere to Granville, 7 May 1873.
4. FOCP 6339/94, Anti-Slavery Society to Salisbury, 16 Feb. 1892.
5. FOCP 6093/310, Euan-Smith to Salisbury, 24 Feb. 1890.
6. FOCP 6951/130, Hardinge to Salisbury, 10 Jan. 1896.
7. FOCP 6951/130, Hardinge to Salisbury, 10 Jan. 1896.
8. H.G. Greshford Jones, *Uganda in Transformation* (London, 1926), p 212.
9. Entebbe Archives: Unyoro and Western Province Correspondence, 1 Oct. 1903.

Chapter 12

1. The Agreement is reproduced in full in Appendix C, in M.S. Kiwaruka, *A History of Buganda* (London, 1971). For a detailed study of the negotiations leading to the Agreement see D.A. Low and R.C. Pratt, *Buganda and British Overrule* (London, 1960), and D. Apter, *The Political Kingdom of Uganda* (Princeton, 1961).
2. FOCP 7405/95, Johnston to Salisbury, 6 Apr. 1900.
3. FOCP 7405/95, Johnston to Salisbury, 6 Apr. 1900.
4. FOCP 7405/95, Johnston to Salisbury, 6 Apr. 1900.
5. Entebbe Archives: A8/2, Wilson to Sadler, 21 Aug. 1902.
6. FOCP 7405/50, Johnston to Salisbury, 12 Mar. 1900.
7. FOCP 7403/82, Johnston to Salisbury, 13 Oct. 1899.
8. For a scholarly account of the history of Toro, see K. Ingham, *The Kingdom of Toro* (London, 1975).
9. FOCP 7868/78 Jackson to Lansdowne, 31 Jan. 1901.
10. A. (Sir) Hardinge, *Diplomatist in the East* (London, 1928), p 148.
11. FO 2/297, Minute by Hill, on Johnston to Salisbury, 18 Nov. 1900.
12. FOCP 7689/83, Johnston to Hardinge, 12 Oct. 1900.
13. For a detailed study of Kakungulu see M. Twaddle, *Kakungulu and the Creation of Uganda 1868-1928* (London, 1993). See also Entebbe Archives, A5/8, Ternan to Evatt, 13 Oct. 1899; In correspondence, Busoga, 13 Nov. 1903.
14. FOCP 7690/127, Cunningham (quoting Johnston) to Lansdowne, 15. Jan 1901.
15. FOCP 7946/123, Eliot to Lansdowne, 25 Jan. 1902.
16. W. C. Churchill, *My African Journey* (London, 1908), p 82.
17. FOCP 7690/148, Johnston to Lansdowne, 24 Jan. 1901.
18. Churchill, *My Africa Journey,* p100.
19. FOCP 7953/91, Eliot to Landsdowne, 9 Apr. 1902.

Chapter 13

1. E. Huxley, *White Man's Country,* 2 vols (London, 1935), i, 53.
2. J. Thomson, *Through Masai Land* (London, 1887), p 237.
3. *The Times,* 9 Feb. 1893.
4. F.D. Lugard, *Rise of Our East African Empire* (London, 1893), i, Intro. p viii.

5. Lugard, *Rise of Our East African Empire*, i, p 418.
6. C-6555 *Africa No 4, 1892*, No 2, Incl. 5, Report by Hobley.
7. Cd 671 (1901), Report by HM Special Commissioner on the Protectorate of Uganda, p 9.
8. Lugard, *Rise of Our East African Empire*, i, pp 419–20.
9. FO 2/60, No 28, Portal to Rosebery, 24 May 1893.
10. FOCP 6261/200, Incl. Smith to de Winton, 10 Aug. 1891; Report of Kenya Land Commission, hereafter referred to as *Carter Commission*, Cmd 4556 (1934), i, 494.
11. FOCP 6557/175, Report by F.G. Hall, 19 Mar. 1894.
12. Thomson, *Through Masai Land*, pp 177–8.
13. FOCP 6261/200, Incl. 2, Smith to de Winton, 10 Aug. 1891.
14. *Scottish Geographical Magazine* (March, 1893), quoted in Lugard, *Rise of Our East Africa Empire*, i, 89.
15. FOCP 6403/321, Ainsworth to Pigott, 30 Dec. 1892.
16. R.A. Bullock, *Ndeiya, Kikuyu Frontier, the Kenya Land Problem in Microcosm* (University of Waterloo, Ontario, 1975).
17. *Carter Commission*, iii, H.D. Hill's evidence.
18. *The History of Smith, Mackenzie and Company* (London, 1938), pp 30–7.
19. Carter Commission, i, 496.
20. Lady Evelyn Murray Cobbold, *Kenya, The Land of Illusion* (London, 1935), pp32–3. For a history of Kenya from the perspective of the later twentieth century, see W.R. Ochieng (ed.), *A Modern History of Kenya 1895–1980* (Nairobi, 1989), and B. Berman and J. Lonsdale, *Unhappy Valley* (London, 1992), Books 1 and 2.
21. FOCP 7404/17, Hardinge to Salisbury, 28 Dec. 1899.
22. FOCP 7404/17, Hardinge to Salisbury, 28 Dec. 1899.
23. FOCP 7823/165, Eliot to Lansdowne, 13 Mar. 1902.
24. FOCP 7867/10, Jackson to Lansdowne, 12 Sept. 1901.
25. FOCP 7953/90, Eliot to Lansdowne, 9 Apr. 1902.
26. *Official Gazette*, 1 Nov. 1902; *Official Gazette*, 1 Jan. 1903; FOCP 8098/106, Eliot to Lansdowne, 5 Jan. 1903.
27. Huxley, *White Man's Country*, i, 108.
28. FOCP 8192/168, Eliot to FO, 10 Aug. 1903.
29. FOCP 8192/168, Eliot to FO, 10 Aug. 1903.
30. Huxley, *White Man's Country*, i, 109.
31. Huxley, *White Man's Country*, i, 103.
32. FOCP 7953/91. Eliot to Lansdowne, 9 Apr. 1902.
33. *Carter Commission*, i, 1880.
34. *Carter Commission*, ii, 1895.
35. Churchill, *My African Journey*, pp 38–9.
36. *Carter Commission*, iii, 2887.
37. Huxley, *White Man's Country*, i, 108.
38. Cd 2099 (1904), 'Memorandum on Native Rights in the Naivasha Province', C. Eliot, 7 Sept. 1903.
39. FOCP 7953/91, Eliot to Lansdowne, 9 Apr. 1902.
40. FOCP 7946/82, Eliot to Lansdowne, 21 Jan. 1902.
41. FOCP 7953/37, Eliot to Lansdowne, 24 Mar. 1902.

42. FOCP 7689/22, Salisbury to Eliot, 27 Oct. 1900
43. FOCP 7867/51, Lansdowne to Eliot, 19 Jul. 1902.
44. FOCP 8040/259, Eliot to Lansdowne, 19 Nov. 1902.
45. T. Roosevelt, *African Game Trails. An Account of the African Wanderings of an American Hunter Naturalist* (New York, 1910), pp 4–5.
46. *Handbook for East Africa, Uganda and Zanzibar* (1903, 1905 ed.),π p 15.
47. *Handbook for East Africa* (1903,1905), p 45.
48. The term is from Huxley, *White Man's Country,* ii, 236.

INDEX

Wakoli, 203
Walker, R.H., 195, 213, 226
Walker, W.R., 388
Wallace, David, 408
Wallace, Francis George Kikuyu, 408
Waller, George, 115
Wangeni, Chief, 408
Wanika people, 102
Ward, Mr, 48
Watcham, J.R., 408
Waters, R.P., 47, 49
Watt, Mr and Mrs J., 407
Waugh, Evelyn, 270
Weis, Lieutenant, 127
Wharton, Mr, 368
White Fathers, 192, 193, 196, 274, 379
White, Captain, 9, 10
Whitehouse, George, 293, 343, 347, 349, 371, 428
Wiest, Lieutenant, 240
William IV, 49
Williams, Captain, 10, 207, 209, 210, 213, 214, 221, 227, 228, 232, 256
Wills, R.B., 426
Wilson, George, 180, 193, 288, 330, 376, 382, 401
Wilson, C.T., 192
Wingate, Major, 252
de Winton, Sir Francis, 179, 180, 186, 187, 201, 206, 400, 410,

von Wissmann, Hermann, 141, 144, 145, 146, 174, 177, 178, 185, 186, 238, 239, 245, 246, 314, 315, 316, 317
Witu, 118, 156, 161, 182, 188, 260, 265, 267, 311, 434; cession of, 183, 184, 259; German interests in, 130, 151, 152
Wolfe, Eugene, 224, 228, 230, 246, 397, 401
Wood, J.R., 427
Wood, T.A., 431
Wyaki, Chief, 203, 401

Yakut, Sultan's vakil, 365

Zanzibar, 4, 5, 9, 10, 14, 15, 21, 22, 23, 26, 32, 33, 36, 38-64, 69, 80, 85, 98, 105, 108, 111, 118, 122, 126, 130, 134, 136, 138, 139, 152, 154, 166, 174, 175, 176, 182, 245, 255, 259, 266, 268, 270, 310, 329, 330, 364, 366, 370, 432; as centre of firearms trade, 55; as centre of slave trade, 16, 17, 18, 59, 61, 62, 88; British coaling-station at, 137; British interest in, 242; conversion to free port, 251; decline of, 270; establishment of British consulate, 365; fertility of, 45; German interest in, 128; under protection of Italy, 155
zebra ranching, 428
von Zelewski, Emil, 143, 238, 239, 245